023329

WITHDRAWN
★   FROM   ★
STOCK

INTRODUCTION TO
OPERATING SYSTEMS

WILLIAM A. SHAY

University of Wisconsin-Green Bay

HarperCollinsCollegePublishers

Sponsoring Editor: John Lenchek
Project Editor: Ann-Marie Buesing
Art Director: Julie Anderson
Cover Design: Kay D. Fulton
Cover Photo: DPI/Uniphoto, Inc., New York
Photo Researcher: Judy Ladendorf
Production Administrator: Brian Branstetter
Compositor: Precision Graphics
Printer and Binder: R.R. Donnelley & Sons Company
Cover Printer: The Lehigh Press, Inc.

For permission to use copyrighted material, grateful acknowledgment is made to the following copyright holder.

Figure 1.14 D.R. Cheriton, et al. *Computer* 24, No. 2, Feb. 1991, pp. 33-48, © 1991 IEEE.

Figure 3.28 L.J. Kenah, Ruth E. Goldenberg, and Simon F. Bate. *Version 4.4 VAX/VMS Internals and Data Structures*. New York: Digital Press, 1988.

Figure 5.67 *UNIX Programmer's Manual*. Seventh ed., Vol. 2. Bell Telephone Laboratories, Inc., Holt, Rinehart, and Winston, 1983.

Introduction to Operating Systems
Copyright © 1993 by HarperCollins College Publishers.

All rights reserved. Printed in the United States of America. No part of this book may be used or reproduced in any manner whatsoever without written permission, except in the case of brief quotations embodied in critical articles and reviews. For information address HarperCollins College Publishers, 10 East 53rd Street, New York, NY 10022.

Library of Congress Cataloging-in-Publication Data

Shay, William A.
    An introduction to operating systems / William A. Shay
       p.   cm.
    Includes index.
    ISBN 0-673-38122-6
    1. Operating systems (Computers)   I. Title.
QA76.76.063S5525   1992
005.4'3--dc20   92-594
                           CIP

96 97 98 99 9 8 7 6 5 4

Contents

Preface

Purpose of the Book

Many operating systems texts fall into one of two categories. Books in one category focus primarily on principles and concepts. They often put a heavy emphasis on and provide a very formal treatment of operating system design principles. However, they give little or no attention to specific operating systems. Books in the second category are designed principally around one operating system such as UNIX, MVS, Macintosh, VMS, OS/2, or MS-DOS. They also discuss principles and concepts, but all of the illustrative examples come from the chosen system.

We feel that principles and concepts are important and that they are a necessary part of education. But principles and concepts alone are not sufficient. Most professionals do not spend their days reciting formal theory to their supervisors. They must instead put their knowledge to the ultimate test of evaluating specific systems and solving given problems. Consequently, we believe an important part of education is to supplement theory with a wide range of examples taken from a variety of systems. This shows the future professional that there are different ways to implement the theory they learn.

There are two major goals of this text. One is to provide a firm foundation in the principles and concepts of operating systems design and discuss major issues. The other is to show how several operating systems have implemented them. We believe very strongly that a book can effectively combine theory and application and provide a balanced view of the field. This book describes <u>what</u> an operating system does, <u>how</u> it may do it, and <u>why</u> there are different approaches. The what, how, and why are essential to education. It is sometimes said (in jest, we hope) that those who know "what" work for those who know "how." Those who know "how" work for those who know "why." Those who know "why" work for those who know nothing. This text was designed with the first three groups in mind.

One unique feature of this text is that it has two types of case studies. The first type gives an overview of a particular operating system and how it has implemented some of the important topics covered in this text. This allows the reader to apply what he or she has learned and understand the different ways operating systems deal with a topic. Chapter 8 is devoted entirely to four popular operating systems: MS-DOS, UNIX, VMS, and MVS. The second type of case study provides a discussion of how an operating system deals with one specific topic. Because these case studies deal with just one aspect of an operating system they are treated in more detail than is otherwise typical. Chapters 2 through 6 all finish with such a case study.

Another unique feature of this text is the inclusion of an operating systems simulation project in the appendix. The project has been developed over a period of several years and has been used successfully in an operating systems course at the University of Wisconsin-Green Bay. The appendix contains software that simulates typical and random events that occur as a typical program runs. Events include I/O requests, I/O finishes, aborts, new programs, synchronization primitives, and normal finishes. The project is to design and write an operating system that responds to the events. It assumes that multiple programs compete for memory and the CPU. The project operating system must accept program code, manage memory, schedule, block, and wake up programs as necessitated by the occurrence of events.

The simulator contains parameters that affect the frequency of event occurrences. This allows it to simulate heavy or light I/O activity. It also allows programs to run uninterrupted for short or long periods of time. The simulator is written in Pascal and does not depend on hardware specific details. This gives the student the experience of writing a simple operating system without having to learn a lot of hardware specific details.

≡≡≡≡≡ Benefit to the Reader

Most students will not likely be asked to design operating systems of the future. The vast numbers of graduating seniors simply go on to do other things. So why study operating systems? Many students will have to interact with computer systems of one type or another. Many will be asked to develop or design application software. Others will be asked to evaluate software that fits stated needs. Still others will go on to graduate school.

In all cases the computer is an indispensable tool. The computer professional will encounter many different systems. He or she must learn them quickly. There is no way a single book will prepare anyone to solve the inevitable problems that will be encountered along the way. But a book can prepare a student so that the additional work and reading becomes less intimidating. Indeed, a firm knowledge in operating systems concepts can provide the student with enough knowledge to acquire yet more knowledge about a particular system. It is, in fact, the ultimate in bootstrapping.

Book Outline

Chapter 1 is an introduction and raises fundamental questions. What is an operating system? What does it do? Why is it needed? What types exist? Why is its study important? Chapter 1 provides a motivation and justification for succeeding chapters. It also introduces the current topic of operating system research, distributed systems. Specifically, it defines what a distributed system is, what the many problems facing researchers are, and gives numerous references for further study.

Chapter 2 deals with memory management. One of the first things computer science students learn is that programs consist of machine code and that it must reside somewhere for the programs to run. They also understand very early that there are many programs competing for memory and a chance to run. As such, memory management seems a logical place to begin. Simpler concepts of fixed and variable partitions are presented first. More complex issues of dynamic address translation, paging, segmentation, and protection appear later. The intent of the chapter is, in part, to present the technical details of these topics. However, the intent is also to illustrate the problems associated with simpler approaches, and to provide rationale for more complex ones. Indeed, without understanding the reasons that lead to a certain design, one cannot know why it exists. The chapter finishes with a discussion of memory management in an Apple Macintosh computer.

Chapter 3 discusses I/O programming. The ability to do I/O is another topic students learn early in the computer science curriculum as they read and write to terminals, printers, and data files. This chapter introduces the reader to disk and tape drives. More important, it covers the operating system's role in transferring data between disk and tape drives and memory. Topics include device drivers, controllers, programmed and interrupt driven I/O, direct memory access, channels, buffering, and multiplexing. The chapter concludes with a discussion of I/O under the VMS operating system.

Chapter 4 discusses scheduling. We place this chapter after the one on I/O because I/O programming is an important consideration in scheduling. This chapter presents design objectives such as maximizing throughput, maintaining consistency, responsiveness, and efficiency. Attention is given to the types of programs and the expectations of the program's users. Chapter 4 discusses different strategies and indicates their advantages and disadvantages.

It emphasizes that no single strategy is best all the time and that the achievement of one objective often comes at the expense of another. This chapter's case study is scheduling under IBM's MVS operating system.

Chapter 5 presents concurrency, a difficult but extremely important issue in operating system design. It starts by defining concurrency and giving several examples that illustrate the power of concurrent processing. But concurrency is deceptive. It is an easy concept to describe, but difficult to understand completely. One of the reasons for this is that events no longer occur in strict sequence. They may occur simultaneously or in random order. Removing sequentiality adds a new dimension to the problem-solving process that is difficult to master. Consequently, several classic concurrency problems and their solutions are presented to help introduce the student to the problems caused by concurrency. These solutions involve concurrency constructs such as semaphores, monitors, and concurrent languages. The chapter also deals with deadlock, a serious side effect of concurrency. It examines the conditions under which deadlock can occur and ways of dealing with it and detecting it. Finally, UNIX pipelines are described at the end of the chapter.

Chapter 6 discusses auxiliary storage management, the allocation of disk space and the scheduling of multiple disk accesses. It also describes directory and file structures. Last, security issues are described, including backups, passwording, access modes, and encryption. MS-DOS disk management is the case study.

Chapter 7 provides a discussion on performance measurement. We want to point out that although empirical observations play an important role in design, so does mathematical modeling and simulation. In order to determine how an operating system will perform, a model of it may first be created. Equations can then be generated that predict how it will perform. They can estimate statistics such as the average number of waiting programs and their average wait times. The chapter introduces methods used in queuing theory and is aimed at those receptive to mathematical concepts and complex formulas. Chapter 7 can be omitted without affecting continuity of the text.

The last chapter, Chapter 8, contains case studies of four popular operating systems: MS-DOS, UNIX, VMS, and MVS. Reasons for the choices are pragmatic. They are four well-known systems within distinct classifications: MVS for large computers; MS-DOS for small computers; and UNIX and VMS for midsize computers.

Questions and exercises are provided at the end of each chapter. We have distinguished questions and exercises. Exercises generally require shorter, concise answers. Questions usually require essay answers. They are intended to promote discussion and are most effective when given to a group of three or four students.

══ **Acknowledgments**

This book lists a single individual as author. That is misleading as there are several people who made significant contributions. I am grateful for the comments and many suggestions from the following individuals:

- Samuel T. Chanson, *University of British Columbia*
- Charles Frank, *Northern Kentucky University*
- H. George Friedman, Jr., *University of Illinois, Urbana-Champaign*
- T.F. Higginbotham, *Southeastern Louisiana University*
- James H. Hu, *Southeastern Louisiana University*
- Daniel C. Marinescu, *Purdue University*
- Charles M. Shub, *University of Colorado at Colorado Springs*
- Virgil Wallentine, *Kansas State University*

I am especially indebted to Dr. Lance Leventhal, Slawson Communications, Inc. His thorough technical reviews and honest evaluations brought the manuscript a long way from its first revision.

Special thanks go to those among the staff at HarperCollins whose assistance and contributions have been very important: John Lenchek, Sandy Cubelic, Brian Branstetter, Julie Anderson, and Ann Buesing.

I am also grateful to my family who had to do without me during the many evenings and weekends I needed to get this book finished.

Last, one would like to think that with reviewers and revisions, all errors have been eliminated. I have never seen an error free text and, unfortunately, I doubt that will change here. However, I accept all responsibility for any errors. Any error detection or correction algorithms may be sent to William Shay, Department of Information and Computing Science, University of Wisconsin-Green Bay, Green Bay, WI 54311-7001 or through email at shayw@uwgb.edu or shayw@uwgb.bitnet.

William Shay

1

Introduction

1.1 What Is an Operating System?

Recent years have seen tremendous changes in computers. They have become cheaper, and at the same time, more powerful. There is a wide range from small, inexpensive computers to very large and powerful ones. Perhaps nothing has enhanced the public perception of them more than the personal computer. They are used by individuals for many things such as word processing, spreadsheets, filing systems, and entertainment. At the other end of the spectrum are the large computers that have access to vast amounts of information and can perform millions of computations per second. They are used in satellite imagery, weather forecasting, defense systems, and flight simulations.

Regardless of size, cost, and capabilities, all computers have several things in common. First, they consist of hardware that can perform computations, make decisions, and store information. Second, the instructions needed to perform these tasks are unintelligible to most users. There have been many examples where a personal computer sits unused in a corner of someone's living room collecting dust because the purchaser did not know how to use it or found it too difficult to learn how.

Definition

This brings us to the third common component, the operating system. What is it? Primarily, an operating system is a program that allows people to use a computer's hardware (CPUs, memory, and secondary storage). In fact, a well written one makes it not only easy to use, but fun too.

Users do not give instructions to the computer. Instead, they give them to the operating system. The operating system then directs the hardware to perform desired tasks. The important thing is that an operating system is not part of the computer. It is a program that must be either purchased separately or included with the purchase of a computer.

Functions

The next question is, "What does an operating system do?" This is a difficult question and the answer can fill a book. To begin, consider an analogy. Imagine that you had the only available calculator (say, in the Tibetan mountains or on a desert island) and many impatient people wanted to use it. You would probably feel like the anxious person in Figure 1.1. How can you give everyone what they need? Who should use the calculator first? What do you do if someone keeps it too long? What do you do when someone insists their calculations are secret and no one must look? What do you do if they want to store their results somewhere? Good luck!

Figure 1.1 Many impatient people wanting to use your calculator

But this comical situation is like the real tasks that an operating system often faces. That is, there are resources than many people want to use. Without something to perform the previously listed tasks, there would be conflicts and mass confusion. Thus, operating systems actually do many things. Among them are:

- Allow programs to store and retrieve information.
- Insulate programs from hardware specific details.
- Control the flow of data among the components of a computer.
- Allow programs to run without interference from other programs.
- Allow independent programs to periodically cooperate and share information.
- Respond to user's errors or requests.
- Enforce a schedule among programs requesting resources.

In general, we can say that an operating system should make as many users as happy as possible. Of course, happiness depends on the user's expectations. Even the U.S. Declaration of Independence insists only that people are entitled to "the pursuit of happiness," not to its achievement. For example, even the most optimistic user cannot expect a personal computer to analyze, in five minutes, all federal tax returns submitted during the past five years.

≡≡≡
Brief History

Operating systems is a dynamic field. Many of today's sophisticated systems have almost no resemblance to the early ones. But how have they changed? Let us look at a brief history.

The first electronic computer (the ENIAC) had no operating system. It was much like today's cheap hand calculator. (Although we grant that it was much larger). They both had to be operated manually. The calculator requires you to push buttons before it does anything. The buttons you push determine what calculations it does. The ENIAC required engineers to connect wires and set switches and relays before it would work. However, once the engineers did their work, the computer would perform calculations automatically. If users wanted different calculations, they had to rewire the computer.

At first, this was not a serious problem. After all, requests for computer generated results were few and far between. But the situation soon changed. During the 1950s, simple operating systems were developed that allowed programs to be submitted (usually on punched cards) in sequence and stored. When one program finished, the operating system allowed the next one to enter and begin running. All the computer's resources were devoted to just one program at a time.

This was satisfactory for a while since applications were still relatively few. But as the needs grew, longer lines formed. Programs at the end of a long line had to wait a long time. This was especially problematic when the program at the end of the line was short and the one in front of it was long.

The next stage in development (early 1960s) was to store several programs in memory simultaneously. They would then share a computer's resources. In other words, rather than executing in sequence, the programs would take turns. Each would run for a while and then the operating system would turn the CPU over to another. This allowed the short ones to get in faster, and since it shared resources, to finish faster. This also allowed terminals to be developed and used effectively. A user could log on from a terminal and access resources almost immediately.

However, new problems developed. People found more applications for the computer. Increased applications required more computing power. Migrations to a larger computer meant a change to a new operating system. As a result, people had to be retrained to use a new system and programs often had to be rewritten.

In the mid–1960s, IBM introduced an operating system that could run on any of several computers, from smaller, inexpensive ones to more powerful and expensive ones. The ability of one operating system to run on several computers was one of the most significant steps in their evolution. Larger computers could now be bought and used without major retraining efforts and rewriting of all the programs.

People continued to find new applications. In some cases, they were discovered and developed so quickly that it made more sense to have two or more computers. Thus, instead of replacing old ones, new computers often ran alongside them. Instead of taking turns with computer resources, users could now operate them simultaneously. Operating systems became more sophisticated because there was more hardware to use.

During this period, the type of program that people ran also changed significantly. The original computers were used primarily for making calculations. But many businesses began to see the computer as a tool for managing information. Since information often had to be accessible to many users, the need to establish communication between separate computers began to evolve. Operating systems no longer were for self–contained systems. They had to interface with complex data communication networks.

Today, some of the most significant issues in computer science deal with communications among computer systems. The ability to communicate safely and effectively among incompatible computer systems will challenge researchers in the years ahead.

Figure 1.2 summarizes the major advances in the development of operating systems.

Figure 1.2 Evolution of operating systems

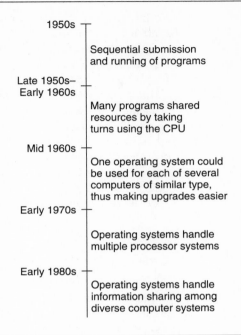

1950s ┬
　　　Sequential submission
　　　and running of programs

Late 1950s– ┴
Early 1960s
　　　Many programs shared
　　　resources by taking
　　　turns using the CPU

Mid 1960s ┼
　　　One operating system could
　　　be used for each of several
　　　computers of similar type,
　　　thus making upgrades easier

Early 1970s ┼
　　　Operating systems handle
　　　multiple processor systems

Early 1980s ┼
　　　Operating systems handle
　　　information sharing among
　　　diverse computer systems

Relevance

The last question we pose is, "What does this have to do with me as a user?" As stated previously, operating systems make the computer's hardware usable. That is precisely why they are so important to any user. They define what many perceive as a computer's personality. For example, operating systems that produce short terse messages are less likely to be used than those that provide organized, clear, and informative statements. This also means the computers those systems run on are less likely to be used.

While the user interface is extremely important, there is more. An operating system defines what the user can do and how efficiently he or she can do it. It defines what hardware can be connected to a computer. It also defines what programs the computer can run. The last reason is especially important because that is why people use computers in the first place. There are many examples of programs that will run under one operating system but not another. More aggravating, there are many examples of programs that run under an old version of an operating system, but not a new one, and vice versa.

Both casual users and professional programmers are more likely to know more about an operating system than the computers themselves.

≡ 1.2 Types of Operating Systems

We have stated that there are many different types of computers. Not surprisingly, it follows that there are many different types of operating systems. Some simple ones dedicate all the computer's resources to one application at a time. Some allow a user to run multiple applications simultaneously. Still more complex ones serve the needs of many users simultaneously.

But an operating system must consider more than just the number of applications or users. In some cases, it is sufficient to respond to applications in sequence. That is, there is no need for quick responses. On the other hand, some operating systems try to ensure a prompt response to a user's needs. In still other cases, a system must respond within a fixed amount of time to avoid disasters. It all depends on the users' needs, their expectations, and the applications that run.

Let us now describe some different environments.

≡ Single–Tasking

The simplest environment is where one user runs one application at a time. This is typical of how many PCs are used. Such systems are called *single–tasking* (Figure 1.3). As the name implies, the operating system allows one program (task) to run at a time.

Figure 1.3 Single–tasking system

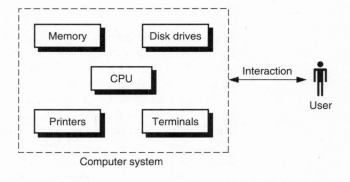

Computer system

This type of operating system has a few major responsibilities: *I/O processing*, *disk management*, and *memory management*. For example, the operating system must

- Read and interpret keyboard entries.
- Send data to a disk, printer, or other output device.
- Maintain lists of files on a disk and keep track of available disk space.
- Keep programs, compilers, editors, and other system programs in separate memory locations.

A key point is that single-tasking operating systems handle many of the low-level details so the user never sees them. It also provides basic functions for the user and programmer.

Single-tasking systems have some disadvantages. For example, suppose you are compiling a long program and your supervisor calls and reminds you that she needs last month's progress report in an hour. You must stop the compilation and start the word processor to create it. As far as the operating system is concerned, only one activity or task can be in progress at a time. It would certainly be more convenient if you could write the report while the program compilation continued. The single-tasking nature of many PC operating systems is a limiting feature now that people commonly depend on PCs for many different functions.

Multitasking (Single–User)

Multitasking systems (Figure 1.4) represent an advance from the single–tasking system. Many still allow only a single user, but he or she can have several activities proceeding at the same time.

Figure 1.4 Multitasking system

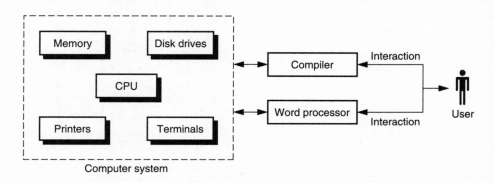

Consider another example. Suppose you start printing a long document such as this book. A single–tasking system will not allow you to do other work during the many hours the printing requires. A multitasking system lets you do other things, such as editing a file, while the print job is running. As you interact with the editor, we say the print job runs in the *background*.

For all intents and purposes, the editor and print job are working at the same time. In reality, the operating system recognizes two entities; the editor and the print job. It allows them to alternate use of the CPU and other resources. They take turns so quickly, you never notice the interruptions. Of course, printing takes longer than it would if you took an extended coffee break and did nothing else. But the multitasking ability lets you schedule your activities better.

Since a user has several activities in progress at the same time, operating system functions such as memory management become more complex. Multiple tasks means more software must reside in memory. The operating system must ensure that programs do not interfere with each other. It also must perform scheduling. Several programs want to use the CPU, and the operating system must decide which one gets it, and for how long. The system must also detect when a particular program is waiting for something, such as an editor waiting for you to press a key.

Multiuser Systems

Multiuser systems, also called *multiprogramming* systems, (Figure 1.5) are more complex than single–user systems. Not only must the operating system keep track of all the users, it must also prevent them from interfering with each other or prying into each other's personal (or at least computing) lives and work.

Figure 1.5 Multiuser system

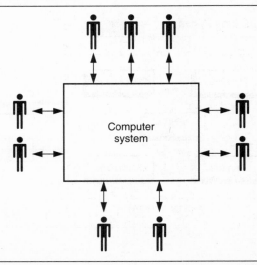

For example, consider the computing applications for a large company. Many applications, including the payroll, run on a single mainframe. Payroll software has access to personnel records which contain, among other things, salary rates. It also produces pay checks.

Now suppose that a payroll and an inventory program are both running (Figure 1.6). Consider what happens if the inventory program tries to access memory occupied by the payroll program. The person in control of the inventory program has access to payroll information. This usually constitutes a violation of privileged information. Worse yet, what if the access is an update? The inventory manager might provide himself or herself with a 50% salary increase. An operating system must prevent this kind of activity. Even "harmless" actions like putting a list of everyone's salary on the company bulletin board can cause a lot of trouble.

Figure 1.6 Unauthorized access of main memory

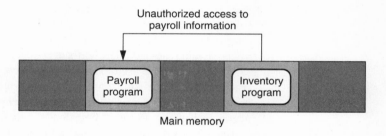

On the other hand, sometimes programs must share data. For example, suppose a company stores last year's sales figures in a database. One program might fetch them and give them to a statistical program for analysis. In this case, one program should have access to the data generated by another.

Scheduling also becomes more important in a multiuser computer. With a single user computer, the operating system has to satisfy only one user's needs. In a multiuser computer, it must satisfy the needs of many. This can be difficult or impossible. Since many programs must share the computer's resources, the operating system must decide who gets what, and when. Often, it will assign a priority to each program. But how does it decide what priority to give? Each user believes his or her program should have the highest priority and all others a lower priority. How does the operating system resolve this conflict? How does it determine which programs truly deserve high priority?

There are several kinds of multiuser computers, depending on the types of programs they handle. The programs' types often dictates how the operating system responds to them. Let's consider several types.

Interactive Programs

An *interactive program* is one that a user activates from a terminal. Generally, the user enters a brief command. The operating system interprets it and takes action. It then instructs the user to enter another command by displaying a *prompt character* or message. The user enters another command, and the process continues. The user works with the operating system in a conversational or interactive mode.

Interactive users expect quick responses. For example, if you enter a command to list your files, a delay of more than a few seconds is annoying. The operating system must therefore favor interactive users. It should respond to their needs quickly to avoid slowing them down.

Batch Programs

Batch programs dominated computing from the 1950s to the early 1970s. Commands to compile or run programs, or to access data files, were coded on punched cards. They were then put in a card reader from which the operating system could read and interpret them sequentially.

Cards are seldom used today, but the batch mode still exists. A user can store commands in a file and submit it to an operating system batch queue. The user can then log off and do something else. The commands, however, remain in the queue. Eventually, the system responds to them.

Batch users differ from interactive users in that they do not expect immediate responses. The fact that they submit the file to the queue and then do something else is proof. The operating system depends on this in its scheduling. It knows that a small delay in responding to a batch program will go unnoticed. As a result, batch programs sometimes have lower priority than interactive ones.

Real Time Programs

Real time programming imposes time constraints on responses. It is used when prompt responses are essential. Interactive users prefer quick responses, but real–time users demand them.

Examples include software that must respond to external events. One familiar example is the air traffic control system at an airport. Complex software must maintain the location, altitude, speed, and direction of all aircraft within a certain distance. If a new aircraft enters the region, the system must respond. Any delay is more than just inconvenient; it may be disastrous.

Other real time examples are robots, vehicle controllers, monitoring of laboratory experiments, nuclear reactors, chemical plants, and control of equipment in manufacturing plants. In all these cases, delay in response can cause the underlying system to malfunction. The commands to turn a missile must come at exactly the proper times, not later when it has already destroyed the wrong target. Alarms must sound immediately when a nuclear reactor begins to overheat, not after the surrounding area ceases to exist.

Virtual Machines

In general, multiuser systems allow users to share access to a computer's resources. Since an operating system defines what resources exist, the users generally see the same ones. There is another type of system, a *virtual machine monitor*, that allows each user a unique view of his or her computing environment. The monitor allows multiple operating systems to exist simultaneously. Each user can then specify which one he or she wants to use. This gives each user the illusion of having one's own distinct computer (virtual machine). To the user, the virtual machine is real.

Perhaps the most widely recognized example is IBM's VM/370 operating system. It lets each user believe he or she has a personal IBM System 370 (or similar architecture) computer. In reality, a high level *control program* manages each operating system.

The ability to run multiple operating systems has advantages. New operating systems or new versions may be tested while normal applications run simultaneously. If one fails, the virtual machine fails. But since it is only an illusion, the real computer keeps running; the other programs are unaffected.

Fit to Environment

Operating systems are written for many different computers and environments. This, of course, makes their study more difficult. We find that principles that work well in one place may not work in another. For example, an operating system for a batch–oriented environment may sacrifice quick response for efficiency. This would be inappropriate in an interactive environment and disastrous in a real time one.

On the other hand, ensuring a quick response requires additional complexity. This, of course, is appropriate for interactive and real time systems. But the additional complexity may reduce the number of programs that run in a batch environment.

≡≡≡≡ **1.3 Operating System Concepts**

Although operating systems vary according to the environment for which each is designed, they still share many common features. Let us now concentrate on some of them.

≡≡
Layered Design

Many operating systems implement the interface between user and computer as a series of steps or *layers*. This is an implementation of the familiar "top down" approach to software design. The top layer defines the functions and the bottom one contains the lowest level details to carry them out. The layers in between correspond to stages of refinement. Figure 1.7 shows the primary ones for several operating systems.

Figure 1.7 Operating system layers

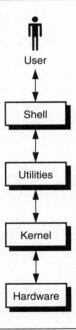

The figure shows the user communicating with the top layer. It consists of operating system routines designed to respond to a user's commands. We call this the *shell* or *command interpreter*. This is the part of an operating system that the user is most familiar with.

But the shell does not actually carry out the user's commands. The reason is that many commands, even though they appear simple, are actually very complicated. For example, a simple command asking the operating system to print the contents of a file requires it to do many things, such as:

- Determine if the file exists.
- Determine if the user has legal access to it.
- Determine the file's structure.
- Find it.
- Read the file.
- Determine where its contents should be printed.
- Write it to the output device.

The utilities layer in Figure 1.7 contains many routines that do these things. Note that even though the figure shows the utilities as a single layer, they may actually be organized in many layers. This is highly dependent on the operating system.

The last layer is the *kernel* or *nucleus*. You can think of it as the "heart" of the operating system. It contains the most frequently needed and critical routines. When a user makes a request, the utilities do most of the checking and preparation necessary for carrying it out. But, the last step in finally giving the user what he or she needs is often done by the kernel.

≡≡≡
Processes

Figure 1–7 shows the interface between a user and the hardware. But this is still a simplified view. There are often many users and many hardware components. Frequently, there are conflicts when users enter commands. In fact, one user may have several independent programs running simultaneously which may make conflicting requests. To complicate matters even further, some languages allow one program to specify the execution of several simultaneous activities. Each of these may make conflicting requests. Thus, to state that the operating system responds directly to the user is not only a simplification, it is sometimes wrong.

To study an operating system, we must consider how it responds to all the independent activities that may exist. We call such an activity a *process* (or task). It represents any independent entity that runs and competes for resources. Figure 1.8 shows the relationships among a user, program, and a process. The number of programs per user and processes per program vary. But, in general, it is important to distinguish among them. The operating system is not concerned about the user, or even the program (at least directly). Its primary responsibility is to the processes that run and compete for resources.

Figure 1.8 Relationships among user, program, and process

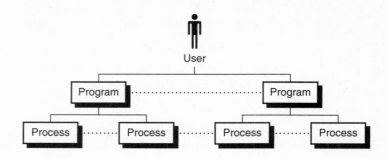

Resources

We may now state that an operating system must respond to the needs of a process. But what are these needs? Primarily, processes request resources. Figure 1.9 shows some of the ones a process uses.

Figure 1.9 Operating system managing processes and resources

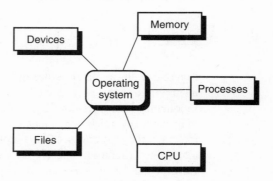

Memory. A process requires memory in which to store its instructions and data. Therefore, an operating system must make sure it gets a sufficient amount. But memory is a finite resource. The operating system should not let a process have so much that others cannot run. Also, privacy and security demand that a process not be able to access another's memory arbitrarily. The operating system must not only allocate but control access to this resource.

CPU. The CPU is another resource that each process needs to execute its instructions. Since there are usually more processes than CPUs, the operating system must control its use; but it must do so fairly. Important processes should get CPUs quickly and less important processes should not use it to the exclusion of others.

Devices. Devices include printers, tape drives, and disk drives. As with the CPU, there are usually more processes than devices. What happens if several processes want to write to the same printer or same drive? The operating system must track who has access to what. It must also control the flow of data as processes read and write to the devices.

Files. The operating system is expected to locate a particular file quickly. It is also expected to locate a particular record in it. Since devices often contain many thousands of files, and a file may contain many thousands of records, this is a complex task.

Concurrency

One of the most difficult problems in managing resources occurs because many processes exist simultaneously. We say the processes are *concurrent*. Requests by concurrent process often results in conflicts. How does an operating system handle them? It varies, depending on the situation.

For example, concurrent process often access the same file. The operating system should ensure that one process will not change data that another is using. Can you imagine an airline reservation system allowing two people to reserve the same seat on the same flight, or an air traffic control system allowing two planes to enter the same air space?

Another example is where one process generates data that another will use. The operating system must ensure that the second one does not attempt to use it before the first one generates it. This is important in I/O processing where several different processes participate in the data transfer.

In both examples, the operating system must regulate the order in which processes access data. We call this *synchronization* and it is an important concept in the study of concurrent processes.

Design Criteria

Managing resources and performing its functions are obviously important criteria for operating system design. But, they are not the only ones. For example, ease of use is another criterion, especially important when the users are not computer or programming professionals. Frequently users are accountants, engineers, salespeople, architects, writers, doctors, lawyers, etc. These professionals often do not have time to learn complex systems. It is more important that they be able to use the computer efficiently. This, of course, is best achieved if it is easy to use.

Consistency. Consistency is another important design criterion. Professionals often plan their daily activities around getting information from a computer. They must have a reasonable estimate of how much time it will take. This is difficult if the computer takes five minutes to produce monthly sales figures for a product one day, and two hours to produce them the next. Granted, the number of processes using the computer will affect the response. However, if the number of processes remains nearly constant, so should the response time.

Flexibility. Perhaps one of the most difficult criteria is flexibility. This can mean many things. An operating system should be written so that a new version does not prohibit running old applications. No one wants to rewrite software whenever a new version of an operating system is installed.

An operating system should also allow for adding new peripherals easily such as new disk drives or printers. Frequently, first time users have modest computing needs. But as they gain experience, they find new ways of using the computer. As applications increase, so does the need for faster and higher capacity drives and higher quality printers.

Portability. Portability is another issue. This means the operating system runs on several types of computers. In many cases, the computers must have similar architecture. Portability gives the user more flexibility. He or she can move applications from one computer to another without having to learn a new system. UNIX is an example of an operating system than runs on very different architectures.

≡≡≡
Tradeoffs

All these design criteria are important; unfortunately, it is usually impossible to achieve them all. Frequently one criterion must be sacrificed in favor of another. Designers must thoroughly understand the environment in which the operating system runs. This way, they can determine which criteria are most important to the user.

For example, some operating systems place a heavy emphasis on the user interface. They provide elaborate instructions to the user and provide many ways to recover from making incorrect entries. Because additional code is required to do this, such systems are often bigger and run more slowly. But in a market consisting of noncomputing professionals, it is a sensible tradeoff.

Another tradeoff is maintainability versus efficiency. Programmers often use sophisticated logic to do certain things faster or with less memory. Unfortunately, the logic is usually more difficult to understand, and consequently, to modify.

Classic examples are sort routines. For example, a bubblesort is conceptually simple and easy to code and modify. However, it is notoriously slow for large data sets. Other routines such as a heapsort or a quicksort are much more efficient, but require additional knowledge of hierarchical data structures or recursion. This makes them more difficult to understand and modify. As with any software, designers must balance the savings of efficient programs and the savings of easily modifiable ones.

══════ 1.4 Example Operating Systems

Which design criteria are most important depends strongly on the computer and the environment. Let us now describe popular operating systems and the computers on which they run.

══ Macintosh

One of the most popular personal computers is the Apple Macintosh. Models include the Macintosh Plus, Macintosh SE/30, and Macintosh II family. The series is perhaps best known for its operating system that revolutionized user interfaces. Before it, most systems required users to type commands. One had to memorize commands or repeatedly search for them in a manual. The commands were often cryptic and difficult to learn.

The Macintosh associates special symbols (icons) with each program, file, and disk. It then uses sophisticated graphics to display them. The user can enter commands by manipulating the icons with a mouse. For example, a user can copy a file to a disk by moving its icon to the disk's icon. Also, a user can delete a file by moving its icon to a "trash can" image. He or she need not memorize commands. Users can also select functions from pulldown menus. This is done by using the mouse to select headings displayed at the top of the screen, and additional functions appearing below each heading.

MS–DOS

In the early 1980s, IBM entered the personal computer market with its PC. Its operating system, developed by Microsoft Corporation, was MS–DOS (or PC–DOS). Since then, many PC clones have become available.

IBM's strategy was to make its PC popular in the business community. It succeeded as MS–DOS is the world's most popular operating system with millions of copies in use. Thousands of applications such as word processors, spreadsheets, accounting packages, databases, and communications managers run under it. It is a single–user, single–tasking system, although there are provisions for limited multitasking on the AT (see reference [19] at the end of this chapter).

OS/2

The emergence of more powerful PCs (including IBM's PS/2 series) created the need for a more powerful operating system than MS–DOS. Also, users began to depend on their PCs for more complex tasks. Microsoft developed OS/2, an operating system for computers based on advanced processors such as the 80286, 80386, and 80486.

Many OS/2 commands resemble ones in MS–DOS. This allows users to switch easily from one to the other. OS/2 also contains many powerful features lacking in MS–DOS. For example, it allows multitasking, and can handle up to 16 megabytes of memory. Another significant feature is the graphical interface called the Presentation Manager, similar to that of Apple Macintosh. It provides a powerful but friendly user environment.

OS/360 Family

IBM has also produced the most popular mainframe family, the System/360 and its successors such as the System/370, 4800, 308x, and 309x models. The concept of a family of compatible computers varying in capabilities and price was unique. Used in batch environments, early System/360 models ran the OS/360 operating system. The operating system later evolved into two versions, OS/MFT and OS/MVT.

Popular OS/360 successors today are MVS (Multiple Virtual Storage) and VM (Virtual Machine). As previously noted, VM implements the virtual machine concept. MVS represents many years of operating system design and evolution. It is a powerful system that can support thousands of concurrent tasks.

The language used to communicate with OS/360 (Job Control Language or JCL) is complex. Users often attend classes or training sessions to become familiar with it. In fact, entire textbooks such as references [26–27] cover it.

UNIX

Of course, IBM is not the only developer of operating systems. Another of today's most popular systems is UNIX. Developed in the 1970s at Bell Laboratories by Ken Thompson and Dennis Ritchie [34], it is noted for its portability. Unlike most operating systems, it can run on many different types of computers. This is possible, in part, because much of UNIX is written in the high level language C. It has both multiuser and multitasking capabilities. It is a popular operating system in universities, and in research, systems development, computer aided design, and networking applications.

Many different versions of UNIX exist. Among the most popular ones are AT&T's UNIX System V; the University of California, Berkeley's 4.3 BSD (Berkeley Software Distribution) system; and the Open Software Foundation's OSF/1. UNIX runs on computers such as the UNISYS 1100 series, DEC VAX, IBM 370, and personal computers and workstations based on the Motorola 68000 family, Intel 8086 family, Sun Microsystems' SPARC, and other microprocessors.

VMS

VMS is the primary operating system for the Digital Equipment Corporation (DEC) VAX family of computers. The VAX/VMS system provides powerful multiuser and multitasking abilities. It is used in batch, interactive, and real–time environments.

The VMS operating system works very closely with the VAX hardware. In fact, some operating system functions are actually designed into the hardware. For example, the VAX architecture supports instructions that allow a process to run with a higher priority. Also, initiating I/O requires instructions that appear to do nothing more than manipulate data within memory.

1.5 Distributed Systems

So where are we in introducing operating systems? We have briefly described their development, some concepts, and typical examples. The next question is, "What are some major current topics in operating systems research?"

A major current research area is *distributed systems*. In the early days of computing, mainframes provided all the business computing power. When a business' needs grew beyond its computer's capabilities, it had to buy a new mainframe. This was costly and often required considerable personnel retraining. Today, personal computers and workstations provide more power at lower cost than old mainframes. They can also be connected to a network. When needs grow beyond their combined abilities, more PCs or other hardware can be added. This, of course, means that neither hardware nor software is maintained at a central location; rather, they are *distributed*.

Architectures

Connecting PCs and other hardware is not the only way to distribute resources. It can also be done by defining new computer architectures. The traditional von Neumann architecture with one CPU and one primary memory is still common, but is being challenged by many architectures designed to exploit parallelism. Most fall into one of three categories [48]:

SISD. *S*ingle *I*nstruction stream, *S*ingle *D*ata stream. This is the traditional von Neumann machine that fetches and executes one instruction at a time. It also fetches data one element at a time. There are several types of SISD machines. For example, some do not fetch the next instruction until they finish executing the current one. By contrast, a *pipelined* machine [49] fetches the next (and sometimes more) instructions before completing the current one. The result is that multiple instructions are in the CPU at different stages in their analysis or execution. Such pipelined CPUs are more complex, but can do several things simultaneously. The result is more throughput per unit of time and better overall performance.

SIMD. *S*ingle *I*nstruction stream, *M*ultiple *D*ata stream. There are different types of machines in this category. For example, in a *vector machine* (e.g., Cray–1 [50] and Cyber 205 [51]), an instruction specifies vectors (one–dimensional arrays) as operands. One instruction could add corresponding components in two vectors. Compare this to the traditional architecture that requires a loop to add each component in sequence. Another type (e.g., Connection Machine [52–54]), consists of many processing elements designed to execute identical instructions in parallel. The Connection Machine may have up to 65,536 elements and they can exchange data through hardware connections. A front–end processor (a DEC VAX or Symbolics 3600 series computer) provides instructions and data to a sequencer. A sequencer is a device that interprets instructions and converts them to a form used by the many processing units.

MIMD. *M*ultiple *I*nstruction stream, *M*ultiple *D*ata stream. MIMD machines (e.g., Cm* and BBN Butterfly[52]) have multiple CPUs that work independently. That is, each works on separate instruction streams asynchronously. Such architectures can execute multiple processes at the same time. This is especially useful when a program is very compute intensive and the number of instructions is too large for sequential execution in a reasonable time. Different instruction sequences can be assigned to each processor for parallel execution. Typical applications are weather forecasting, plasma flow, geological analysis, and simulations.

There are many ways to connect resources. One is to use a common bus (Figure 1.10). Any two devices communicate over it. Its advantage is its simplicity, but there is a drawback. If a device wants to communicate when the bus is busy, it must wait. When there is a lot of traffic, this degrades performance.

Figure 1.10 Common bus communications network

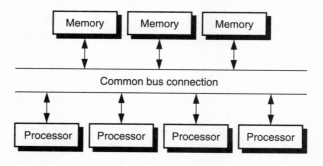

Other approaches involve complex communication networks that allow several devices to transmit at once. Some examples include crossbar switches, hypercubes, and multistage networks. The interested reader can consult reference [55] for more details.

The most difficult issues occur when processors can work independently. This implies no centralized control, and protocols must allow processors to share information in an orderly way. For example, some distributed systems are *tightly coupled*. Many processors can access common (shared) memory and share information in it. They may be connected by a common bus or by another connection scheme referenced earlier.

Figure 1.11 General communications network

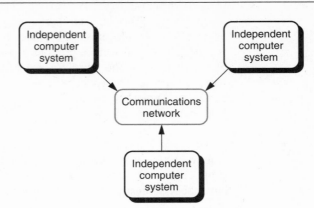

Other systems are *loosely coupled*. They consist of independent computers, each with its own operating system. Each works separately but can communicate when necessary, usually via messages. For example, multiple workstations connected to a file server and a printer define one type of loosely coupled system.

Communication among devices may be very difficult. Computers with different architectures understand different languages, store data in different formats, and communicate at different rates.

Consider an analogy in which representatives from several countries meet to discuss trade agreements. They do not just all begin speaking at once. First, there is a language problem. Each speaks a different language, so translators are needed. But, even if they all spoke the same language, they must still observe a *protocol*. It defines the rules and the manner in which they begin and proceed with discussions. If all involved do not agree to a protocol, the discussions become chaotic. People speak out of turn or simultaneously. An orderly discussion occurs only if the participants follow rules.

Similarly, if computers are to communicate, protocols must be defined and used. Otherwise, effective communications are impossible. In part, this is where a distributed system enters the picture. What is it? It provides basic networked functions, much as an ordinary operating system provides basic functions on a single computer.

It is far beyond the scope of this book to discuss distributed systems in detail. There are many books and articles on the subject. We will, however, briefly introduce some major issues and list references for further reading.

Cache Coherency

Each processor in a tightly coupled system usually has its own *cache memory*. It is a very fast (and expensive) memory in which a small subset of instructions and data reside. By accessing the cache instead of main memory, processors can work faster and, in architectures like that in Figure 1.10, there is less bus activity.

Problems can occur when processors have common elements in their caches. For example, suppose two processors access X from shared memory (Figure 1.12a). Consequently, each processor's cache has a copy of X in it. Now suppose one processor changes X to Y and stores it in shared memory (Figure 1.12b). The other processor's cache has incorrect data. We refer to this as the *cache coherency problem*.

How do we solve it? One way is to simply inform the other processors that their cache copies are invalid when shared memory changes. For example, one approach (*snoopy protocol*) requires each cache to monitor all bus activities. If the cache detects a change to something it has a copy of, it can invalidate the copy. The next reference is then rerouted to shared memory.

Figure 1.12a Caches before change to shared memory

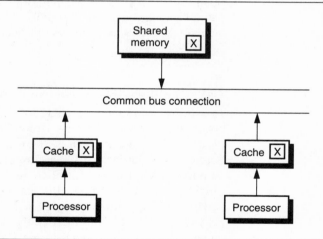

Figure 1.12b Caches after change to shared memory

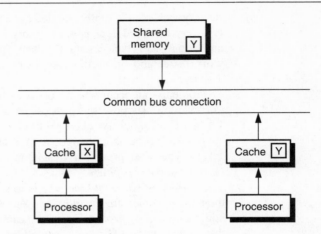

If all devices communicate via a common bus, "snooping" is simple and the protocol works. However, for more complex architectures, snooping is often impractical as it would require the cache to snoop on many different connection paths. Consequently, other protocols are necessary. They are more complex and we refer the reader to references [39, 56, and 57].

Remote Procedure Calls: Clients and Servers

In a loosely coupled system, processes execute independently but may communicate when necessary. How? One common approach is defined by a *client-server* model. A *client* is a system user or process that requires a *service*. Services vary but include file access, printing, communication links, database activities, and process control. A *server* is the hardware and software that provides the service. In general, client and server run on different computers.

How do they communicate? One common mechanism is the *remote procedure call* (RPC). Superficially, it resembles a conventional call in a language such as Pascal, but there are differences. For example:

- The caller (client) and the procedure it calls (server) often run on different computers.
- A client must pass all parameters by value rather than by reference. The reason is that passing a parameter by reference amounts to passing its address. But if the server runs on a separate computer, it cannot access the client's memory.

- Servers often run with a higher or "privileged" priority. In other words, they can access system resources that a client cannot. This is often required due to the nature of the service the server provides.

- Suspension and resumption mechanisms are necessary for timely execution of services. A service should not be provided before the client is ready, and the client often must be suspended until the service is completed.

RPCs are commonly implemented using *send* and *receive* communications primitives. The *send* primitive specifies a destination and a list of items to transmit. The client provides the list, but the destination information is usually determined by the system. How this is done depends on the network over which the processes communicate. Ideally, a client should be able to specify which service is needed and depend on the system to make the connection. Hiding precise locations from the client makes these primitives especially useful in distributed systems.

The *receive* primitive specifies a source and a list of items to receive. A server will not provide a service until after it executes a *receive*. When a client executes a *send*, the list of items is sent, and it waits for the service to be completed. When a receiver executes a *receive*, it receives the list of transmitted items. If they have not yet been sent, it waits.

Figure 1.13 shows an example client and server. After the client executes *send*, it enters a wait state. It will remain there until the server responds and provides the service. After the server executes a *receive*, it performs its task, sends a message back to the client, and continues. When the client receives the message, it also continues.

Problems can occur when processes run on different computers, such as:

- Messages may be lost or garbled due to transmission interference.

- The server or client could abort between its *send* and *receive* primitives.

- What if a server executes a *receive* but there is no client asking for a service? More generally, how does a server know when to execute a *receive*?

Figure 1.13 Client and server processes

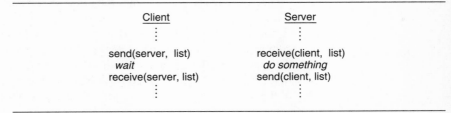

Usually a timer mechanism prevents either process from waiting forever. Also, conditional statements allow a server to execute a variety of *receive* primitives or to do other things if no calls are pending. Problems become even more complex when clients make many calls to different servers and servers receive many calls from different clients. Further discussions of these and other RPC issues appear in references 2, 61, and 62. We also develop this further in Section 5.9 where the Ada language is discussed.

Fault Tolerance

Another important issue in distributed systems is *fault tolerance*, the ability of the system to respond to hardware or software failures and maintain reasonable service. For example, suppose a hardware component in a distributed system fails. What happens to the rest of the system? If the component is one of many workstations in a local area network, probably just one user is affected. If a file server fails, many users are inconvenienced. If the failed component blocks the flow of coolant to a nuclear power plant or disorients the nation's air defense system, there may be no more users.

Fault tolerance must be designed into any system where people cannot intervene quickly enough to avoid serious problems. Examples include communication systems, nuclear power plants, unmanned space probes, air traffic control, defense systems, and factory automation.

Understanding fault tolerance is difficult. Understanding how a system works correctly is difficult enough. Understanding the many ways in which it can fail is a real challenge. What components can fail and how? What can cause failures? Do they affect other components? Is there a chain reaction and, if so, what happens?

Designing fault tolerant systems invariably means including redundant components (hardware or software) capable of taking over if a failure occurs. Obviously, they increase the system's cost and complexity. Also many design questions arise. How many extra components are needed? Which ones should be duplicated? What types of failures can we tolerate? Which ones cause disaster? Should we provide backup components even if a failure is highly improbable?

There are many issues in the study of fault tolerance such as [58, 76]:

Error detection. It is not as easy as you might think. Waiting until the component fails to provide a service is usually too late. The failure should be detected immediately, not when it causes a disaster. In this case, detection is trivial but is of little use. It conveys images of an inspector digging himself out of the rubble of a power plant saying, "I think we have a problem."

Sometimes self-checking logic is built into a component to test it periodically. The component is given inputs, and its outputs are compared with expected results. If a mismatch occurs, a fault is likely. Error detecting and correcting codes may also be used to protect against problems in a communications network. Extra bits are calculated from the data and added to a transmission. When the data is received, the bits are recalculated and compared with the ones in the transmission. Again, a mismatch implies a problem.

Fault containment. It means preventing errors from spreading. In distributed systems many components depend on the results of others. A simple example is the client-server relationship. If a client calls a server that produces incorrect information, the client will also fail. Of course, if the client is a server for another client, a chain reaction of failures may begin. Can the client provide its service despite the failure of a server? Understanding the system and client-server relationships is essential.

System repair. One way to repair a system is simply to replace the failed component. In some architectures, the component may be replaceable, meaning that it may be removed physically and replaced. In other architectures, a replaceable unit might have several components such as processors, controllers, or memory. Thus, one component cannot be replaced without replacing others. Grouping components thus becomes a design issue.

Another way to repair the system is to avoid the failed component by redistributing the workload. In some systems, processes and essential information are duplicated. Thus, in the event of a failure, another processor may handle the duplicate.

Recovery. Damage may occur in the time between detection and repair. If so, a recovery period may be necessary. Typically, this requires the system to be rolled back to a state (recovery point) prior to the error. Appropriate recovery points are built into the design and are established regularly as the system operates. This may be done by saving pertinent information. Using frequent recovery points minimizes the amount of damage but increases overhead. Overhead decreases with fewer recovery points, but more will be lost when recovery is needed.

We have just touched the tip of the iceberg and if you would like to read more on fault tolerance, references 58, 59, and 60 describe it in more detail.

≡
Scalability

A distributed system, like any other, has finite resources which exist for users to do work. What happens when the number of users increases? The system should be able to adapt to increasing demands on its resources. This may be difficult since resources are finite and can easily become saturated under heavy loads. It is important to be able to distribute loads as evenly as possible. We certainly want to avoid situations where many processors are saturated with requests while others have nothing to do.

Of course, even the best system cannot meet continuously increasing demands. There will invariably be a point where new resources must be added. But how this is done is critical. Can a new resource be added without redesigning the entire system? What impact will a new resource have on communications traffic? After all, more resources means more traffic. Will new resources require more work by schedulers and further burden existing processors? A truly scalable system should adjust to increasing needs and allow easy addition of new resources.

≡
Distributed File Systems

An integral part of any computer is its file system. The file system defines the data structures and software that maintains files for all system users. It also provides protection and coordinates access to shared files. On a conventional system, the structures and software are centralized.

By contrast, a distributed file system has servers, clients, and storage devices all in different locations. For example, consider a corporate office in New York with a research and development (R & D) site in Denver and a sales office in San Francisco. The executives in New York want access to all employee records and a spreadsheet for analysis purposes. R & D employee records are stored in a computer in Denver, the salespersons' records are in a computer in San Francisco, and the spreadsheet is in the computer center on the 18th floor.

The executives do not want to worry about what is where. Ideally, they want to access records and software as though they were stored physically in their offices. In other words, to the executives, the records should be easily accessible even though they are in different locations and possibly on different types of computers.

There are many key issues in distributed file systems, such as:

Transparency. This means any user can access any part of the system. Furthermore, the user should not have to know where the files are. Conversely, the user can make requests from anyplace within the system.

Storage. Who decides what files are stored where? What criteria are used to make this decision?

Consistency. Access to files should be independent of location. Even if the executives' offices move from New York to Ponca City, Oklahoma, they should still be able to access the files the same way. The files should be unaware that Ponca City has fewer cultural attractions (you may have to substitute rodeo for opera) but far less crime and lower rents.

Security. Distributing data and providing access via communications links require strict security measures. Providing many access paths to data makes it harder to watch them all for illegal access. Furthermore, one fallout of making authorized access easy is to make guarding against unauthorized access difficult.

Access control. Do we want to allow multiple users to access a common record? If not, how can we prevent it? If so, what happens if one of them changes it? How will it affect the other users?

Naming. What seems like a trivial issue is actually very important. A user assigns meaningful names to a file, but the system must translate them to physical locations. In a conventional centralized system, the physical location usually consists of a device identifier and a location on the device. In a distributed system, the physical address must also indicate where the device is located.

There are three approaches to naming [78]. One uses a combination of a host name and local names. The host name locates the site, and the local name locates the device in the site. A second approach allows remote files to appear attached to a user's local computer or workstation. This is done by combining a remote directory with a local one when the user logs into the system. This gives a view of a single, albeit larger, directory and is the approach used by Sun's Network File System (NFS). The third approach requires a single naming mechanism for all files in the system. All users see the same set of names which, in some cases, are provided in UNIX-like directories.

There are several examples of distributed file systems [78]. The Locus system is upward compatible with UNIX. It provides a single hierarchical directory to its users, making the files' locations transparent. It is designed for the true distributed system in which locations and resource types are completely transparent.

The Sun NFS is designed for file access across local area networks. Using the client-server model, users mount remote file systems so they appear as a single directory. NFS is a popular file system, running on well over 100,000 computers.

The Andrew file system, developed at Carnegie–Mellon University, divides its file space into two parts, a local space and a shared space. The local space is unique to each workstation, whereas the shared space is on file servers which may be anywhere. This allows users to share common software and still maintain the privacy of some files.

Security

Defining secure network file systems is a challenging task. Strict security is difficult even when everything is centralized. The situation is much worse when things are scattered.

With the advent of more distributed systems, security has become a more important and more visible issue. Easy access to computers and networks has created a new generation of intruder programs called *viruses*, *worms*, and *Trojan horses*. They are inserted into a system without authorization. Sometimes they replicate, spreading from one computer to another via a network. They destroy files or make small, unauthorized changes to them. The latter are especially dangerous since, if they are not detected quickly, the files are rendered useless and all backups are infected.

Files and computer systems must be protected from intruders. Too often, users do nothing to protect their data. Defining passwords and locking files help create secure systems. Still, clever hackers can often overcome them. Options such as encrypting data make a file's data incomprehensible to the intruder. Sources of all accesses can also be tracked. Ideally, systems should provide easy access to those who are authorized, while keeping out those who are not. This is difficult to do on a large scale.

We will discuss security further in Chapter 6. Also, references [41, 42, 61, and 63–69] cover the issues in detail.

Performance

Another important concern is the analysis of how well a distributed system works. Performing functions accurately is one thing; doing them efficiently is quite another. We expect overhead. But how much is acceptable? How can we measure performance? Perhaps more important, how can we predict it? We should be able to estimate how well a system will perform before implementing it.

One approach is to use mathematical models. By making some assumptions, we can develop equations to calculate several useful quantities. For example, how many processes run per unit of time? How long does one typically wait? What is the average number waiting? A fascinating fact is that we can find approximate answers without writing any code.

Another way to measure performance is to use *simulations*. A simulation is a computerized model designed to behave like a real system. The model can be run and measurements taken to see how it performs under any conditions. Simulations are particularly important in analyzing real–time systems, since these systems are useless if their responses do not meet the stated criteria. Few people will use a system that responds slowly and often loses transmissions due to overloading.

For example, reference [57] describes the use of simulations to analyze cache coherence strategies and trace the efficiency of various parallel algorithms. Reference [70] discusses fault simulation to study system responses to failures. Reference [71] discusses the Time Warp Operating System for the Caltech Mark III Hypercube Multiprocessor. In it, the authors construct simulations to measure the system's performance.

Example Distributed Systems

Amoeba. Amoeba is a distributed system created as a research project at the Vrije University of Amsterdam [61, 74, 75]. A major goal is to make Amoeba appear as a centralized system, thus hiding the multiprocessor arrangement. Users log on to the system using a diskless workstation such as the Sun–3, VAXstation, or an X-Terminal. Afterwards, Amoeba decides what hardware services the user needs. For example, if a user wants to run a program, Amoeba decides where to run it. The user is unaware of what computer he or she is actually using.

An important component of Amoeba is its processor pool. It is a group of processors that Amoeba assigns dynamically to activities. For example, if an application requires compilations of several source code files, Amoeba can allocate one processor for each compilation and they can be done in parallel. After the compilations, Amoeba returns the processors to the pool. Amoeba also allows the number of processors to change. This allows new ones to be added, creating a more powerful system. It also allows Amoeba to adapt if some processors fail. It reduces the number of processors in the pool and continues running, albeit at a reduced performance level.

Amoeba depends heavily on the client–server model described earlier and provides a wide assortment of servers. This leaves the kernel to do communication, scheduling, and memory management, with the bulk of the remaining tasks handled by users and servers.

Amoeba's file system is unusual. Rather than storing a file using disk blocks or sectors, the server stores it contiguously on a disk. Conventional systems use disk sectors to maximize what a disk can hold; contiguous storage can cause unused disk fragments, thus wasting space. On the other hand, contiguous storage allows a process called a *bullet server* to read files much faster. Since a higher capacity drive often does not cost much more than a lower capacity one, Amoeba's designers decided to emphasize access speed and deal with less efficient use of disk space by using larger disks. We should note that a bullet server never rewrites any files. It cannot change an existing file.

Amoeba processes contains many parts (*threads*) that can run in parallel on many processors. Often the threads must communicate and synchronize their activities to ensure orderly execution of a task. (Chapter 5 discusses synchronization and communication primitives.) Consequently, research efforts have gone into the design of parallel solutions to classic problems such as the traveling salesman problem [75].

Athena. Another distributed system is Athena, developed at MIT and sponsored by Digital Equipment Corporation and IBM [73]. Its design was driven in part by the desire to have students learn just one system for all their educational computing needs. Currently, it has 1,000 workstations that students use 24 hours per day. It also has file servers, Postscript printers, about 90 gigabytes of disk storage, and multimedia work stations that support full motion color video.

Athena workstations have local hard disks, and any user can use any station. Private files appear to be in a central location, although they may actually be stored on any of several file servers. Files are attached to the workstation's file hierarchy before being used. In contrast to private files, those that would normally reside on multiple workstations are housed centrally. This, of course, minimizes redundancy and traffic.

In Amoeba, user tasks are assigned to processors dynamically. By contrast, Athena activities default to the local workstation. Of course, network services are available to the user and appear to be local, making the organization transparent.

Mach. The Mach operating system was developed at Carnegie–Mellon University [61, 72]. It allows access to many processors and allows communication between them. It can emulate UNIX and run on DEC VAX,

IBM RP3, and Sun 3 systems. It supports both loosely and tightly coupled systems and is actually the kernel of a distributed system upon which programming interfaces can be built. It is the basis of the Open Software Foundation (OSF)'s version of UNIX.

Mach processes consist of multiple threads that may run on different processors simultaneously. One feature of Mach is dynamic load balancing. That is, scheduling of threads is designed to keep all processors busy and to maximize performance. To do this, the Mach kernel has a local run queue (priority queue) for each processor. A thread bound to a processor is in its local queue. Mach also has a global queue in which threads not bound to a processor reside. When a processor needs to run a thread, it checks its local queue. If the local queue is empty, the processor checks the global queue. If that is empty, the processor idles.

Another Mach feature is *gang scheduling*. It is used for applications containing many threads which must run in parallel to achieve reasonable performance. The gang scheduling mechanism defines a *processor set* (collection of processors). Instead of binding a single thread to a processor, the threads from an application are bound to a processor set. Threads can run on any processor in the set. Conversely, a processor can run only threads assigned to its set. Scheduling within a set is similar to that described previously, using a global–run queue for processors in a set.

Plan 9. Researchers at Bell Laboratories are developing an ambitious distributed system called *Plan 9* [77]. Ultimately their goal is to provide a distributed computing environment for approximately 30,000 people. The system would have thousands of CPUs and file servers located in main departments throughout the company. Three major components of Plan 9 are CPU servers, file servers, and terminals. Plan 9 also allows for workers to readily access computer facilities from their homes and take full advantage of powerful home and portable computers.

File servers provide system–wide access to the files. The file server is a dual processor computer with 64 MB of memory, a 600 MB disk, and a 300 GB optical disk. It connects to other computers and terminals using a high–speed communications link. It provides different file systems to clients, depending on the application.

The terminals (locally designed machines called Gnots) are diskless workstations. Each has a 68020 processor, 4 or 8 MB of memory, graphics capability, keyboard, mouse, and windowing capability. Each has no disk storage as the file server provides what is needed.

There are several CPU servers. One, for example, is a multiprocessor with 128 MB of memory and no disk storage. Again, the file server provides what is needed. Its functions include compilation, text processing, and various applications. It can communicate with the file server using a high speed communication link.

V System. The V system, designed at Stanford University, is designed to connect workstations [80]. It has a relatively small kernel, a copy of which runs at each network node. However, nodes cooperate in ways that make the distributed organization transparent to a process. An important part of the V design is fast communication implemented using a client–server mechanism.

Processes in V may be grouped and identified by a number. For example, file servers can be grouped, as can the processes associated with a program. Processes in a group may be at the same network node, or they may be distributed. Conversely, a process may belong to several groups.

Grouping processes allows an operation called *multicasting*. It is the ability to send a message to an entire group of processes. V uses multicasting in several ways such as in scheduling. For example, it schedules using a priority system. That is, the processors should always run the highest priority processes. When there is just one processor, this is not difficult. However, many of them increase the complexity of priority scheduling. V associates each process with a processor, and scheduling is done locally for each processor. Of course, the highest priority process associated with one processor may have a lower priority than that associated with another. To keep high priority processes from excessive waiting, a kernel routine periodically does load balancing. That is, it uses its multicasting ability to reassociate (migrate) processes to other processors. Of course, multicasting raises major new security and privacy issues.

V has also been used in research to explore the feasibility of connecting many workstations and writing compute intensive programs that use the multiprocessor arrangement for parallel execution [80]. Some classic problems such as the traveling salesman problem and matrix operations were programmed using a model that defines subtasks and assigns them to processors. In cases where intermediate results must be shared or distributed to other processors, V multicasts them.

Sprite. The Sprite system was developed at the University of California at Berkeley. It is part of another project (SPUR) to design and construct high performance workstations [78, 81]. The network interface and the file system are similar to those provided by UNIX version 4.3 BSD. Sprite provides the same file hierarchy to each workstation, thus providing complete transparency of a file's location.

One important aspect of the Sprite design is file caching. This is motivated by the large amounts of memory commonly available, used as cache, and the increasing number of diskless workstations. When a client requests a file from a server, the most recently accessed blocks are stored in both the client's and the server's cache. Caching reduces the number of disk accesses and increases speed and performance. It also reduces the amount of traffic in the network and provides better scalability.

One problem occurs when several clients request a common file from a server. Because of caching, several copies of the file exist. If one client decides to change the file, the others' copies become invalid. However, Sprite ensures that a client's file access will always return current and valid data.

To do this, Sprite assigns version numbers to files. When a client opens a file, Sprite provides the client with the file's current version number. Now suppose the client closes the file and subsequently opens it again. Because of caching, file information may still be in the client's cache. Upon reopening, the version number returned is compared with that of any remaining cache copies. If they differ, the cache copies represent an old version and are replaced.

Sprite can also enable and disable file caching. If a client opens a file with the intention of writing to it, Sprite disables caching for it. That is, Sprite informs all other clients that have opened the same file that they can no longer use their cache copies. All subsequent file references must be routed back to the server until Sprite enables caching.

Paradigm. Our last example, Paradigm, or *Para*llel *Dist*ributed *G*lobal *M*emory [79], differs from the others in an important way. It is a multiprocessor architecture with a shared memory designed to execute parallel algorithms. One goal of Paradigm is to show the viability of a shared memory multiprocessor with hundreds of processors. Of course, a significant problem with so many processors is the large amount of traffic between them and memory. Paradigm addresses this problem by using a complex structure with local common buses, multilevel caches, and a switching network.

Several processors, each with its own private cache, are connected via a bus and mounted on a board or multiple processor module (MPM) (Figure 1.14). The bus also connects an on–board cache (backup to the local caches) and a network interface. Several MPMs are grouped together via a group bus and share an interbus cache (backup to the on–board cache). The MPM groups and a memory module are finally connected via a memory bus to form a Paradigm node. This and other nodes are connected to a switching network.

Paradigm runs the V distributed operating system. Its ability to group processes and its multicast mechanism allow the management of processes within network nodes. The Paradigm model has been tested by implementing an algorithm that solves very large systems of equations. The compute intensive nature of the problem is ideal for an architecture allowing many computations to be done in parallel.

Figure 1.14 Paradigm node architecture

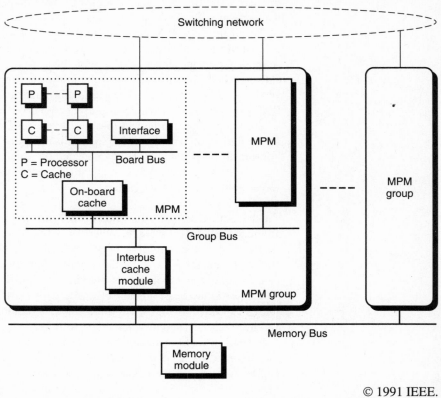

© 1991 IEEE.

Additional References

Where can you learn more about operating systems and distributed systems? We have cited many references for distributed systems topics. In addition, References [1–14] discuss standard operating systems principles. References [5 and 14] each include a detailed case study of a single operating system along with its source code. References [6 and 7] provide several case studies. Other references cover one operating system such as MS-DOS [15–21], OS/2 [22–25], UNIX [28–33], Macintosh [35–37], and VAX/VMS [38–40].

Exercises

1. Categorize each of the following operating systems as single–tasking, multitasking (single-user), or multiuser.
   - MS–DOS
   - VMS
   - VM
   - OS/2
   - Macintosh
   - UNIX
   - MVS

2. Consider the following applications. Would each be best categorized as batch, interactive, or real time?
   - word processing
   - program that prints monthly checking and savings account summaries
   - language compiler used by university students
   - airline reservation system
   - aircraft navigational system
   - hotel reservation system
   - software that monitors fission in a nuclear power plant
   - program that computes weekly averages for members of a bowling league
   - architects CAD (Computer Assisted Design) system for creating drawings
   - library checkout system
   - telephone switching system
   - building security system

3. Which of the following are part of an operating system's responsibilities?
   - Send program output to a line printer.
   - Translate a high–level language into machine code.
   - Check spelling in a word processing file.
   - Store a spreadsheet program in memory.
   - Locate a database file.
   - Check user keyboard entries for typographical errors.
   - Determine how long a program may run.
   - Locate a memory cell during an instruction's execution.
   - Prohibit access to an employee's personnel file.
   - Organize and list all computer games stored on a disk.

4. Which of the following are reasonable operating system design criteria?
   - Should perform its functions efficiently.
   - Should be well documented.
   - Should run on every type of computer.

- Should be easy to modify.
- Should run on all computers of a particular type (e.g., all personal computers).
- Should be usable by those without extensive knowledge of the hardware.
- Should be usable only by an individual who has a thorough understanding of the computer and its resources.
- Should be compact so that all its code will fit in memory.
- Should protect data from unauthorized access.
- Should work with different hardware configurations.

Questions

1. Why is it important for an operating system to distinguish users, programs, and processes?
2. What things can an operating system do to make the computer appear "friendly" to the user?
3. "User friendly" is a term made popular during the 1980s. However, operating systems existed much earlier than that. Why wasn't the term popular before then?
4. One program may spawn multiple processes. Give an example of a problem that may be solved by doing several computations independently.
5. Refer to one of the references at the end of Chapter 1 and list alternative ways of organizing processors and memory.
6. Describe another cache coherency scheme from one of the references [39, 56, 57].
7. Give an example of an application where designing fault tolerance is probably not worth the cost if the probability of a failure is near zero. Give several examples where fault tolerance is essential no matter how small the probability of failure.

References

1. Barron, D. W. *Computer Operating Systems for Micros, Minis, and Mainframes*. 2nd ed. New York: Chapman & Hall, 1984.
2. Bic, L. and A. C. Shaw. *The Logical Design of Operating Systems*. 2nd ed. Englewood Cliffs, NJ: Prentice–Hall, 1988.
3. Brinch Hansen, P. *Operating Systems Principles*. Englewood Cliffs, NJ: Prentice–Hall, 1973.
4. Calingaert, P. *Operating System Elements: A User Perspective*. Englewood Cliffs, NJ: Prentice–Hall, 1982.
5. Comer, D. *Operating System Design: The XINU Approach*. Englewood Cliffs, NJ: Prentice–Hall,1984.
6. Davis, W. S. *Operating Systems: A Systematic View*. 3rd ed. Reading, MA: Addison–Wesley, 1987.
7. Deitel, H. M. *An Introduction to Operating Systems*. 2nd ed. Reading, MA: Addison–Wesley, 1990.
8. Finkel, R. A. *An Operating Systems Vade Mecum*. 2nd ed. Englewood Cliffs, NJ: Prentice–Hall, 1988.

9. Lane, M. G. and J. D. Mooney. *A Practical Approach to Operating Systems.* Boston, MA: PWS-Kent, 1988.
10. Madnick, S. E. and J. J. Donovan. *Operating Systems.* New York: McGraw–Hill, 1974.
11. Milenkovic, M. *Operating Systems: Concepts and Design.* New York: McGraw–Hill, 1987.
12. Silberschatz, A. et al. *Operating Systems Concepts.* 3rd ed. Reading, MA: Addison–Wesley, 1991.
13. Pinkert, J. R. and L. L. Wear. *Operating Systems: Concepts, Policies, and Mechanisms.* Englewood Cliffs, NJ: Prentice–Hall, 1989.
14. Tanenbaum, A. S. *Operating Systems: Design and Implementation.* Englewood Cliffs, NJ: Prentice–Hall, 1987.
15. Angermeyer, J. et al. *The Waite Group's MS–DOS Developer's Guide.* 2nd ed. Indianapolis, IN: Sams, 1989.
16. Duncan, R. *Advanced MS-DOS Programming.* 2nd ed. Redmond, WA: Microsoft Press, 1988.
17. Norton, P. and R. Wilton. *Programmer's Guide to the IBM PC and PS/2.* Redmond, WA: Microsoft Press, 1988.
18. O'Day, K. *Understanding MS-DOS.* Indianapolis, IN: Sams, 1988.
19. Simrin, S. *The Waite Group's MS-DOS Bible.* 2nd ed. Indianapolis, IN: Sams, 1988.
20. Wolverton, V. *Running MS-DOS.* 3rd ed. Redmond, WA: Microsoft Press, 1988.
21. *The MS-DOS Encyclopedia.* Redmond, WA: Microsoft Press, 1987.
22. Duncan, R. *Advanced OS/2 Programming.* Redmond, WA: Microsoft Press, 1989.
23. Krantz, J. I., A. M. Mizell, and R. L. Williams. *OS/2 Features, Functions, and Applications.* New York: Wiley, 1988.
24. Letwin, G.. *Inside OS/2.* Redmond, WA: Microsoft Press, 1988.
25. Schmitt, D. A. *The OS/2 Programming Environment.* Englewood Cliffs, NJ: Prentice–Hall, 1989.
26. Brown, G. D. *System 370 Job Control Language.* 2nd ed. New York: Wiley, 1987.
27. Janossy, J. G. *Practical MVS JCL for Today's Programmers.* New York: Wiley, 1987.
28. Bach, M. J. *The Design of the UNIX Operating System.* Englewood Cliffs, NJ: Prentice–Hall, 1986.
29. Bourne, S. R. *The UNIX System V Environment.* Reading, MA: Addison–Wesley, 1987.
30. Kernighan, B. W. and R. Pike. *The UNIX Programming Environment.* Englewood Cliffs, NJ: Prentice–Hall, 1984.
31. Poole, P. C. and N. Poole. *Using UNIX by Example.* Reading, MA: Addison–Wesley, 1986.
32. Rochkind, M. J. *Advanced UNIX Programming.* Englewood Cliffs, NJ: Prentice–Hall, 1985.
33. Sobell, M. G, *A Practical Guide to the UNIX System.* 2nd ed, Menlo Park, CA: Benjamin/Cummings, 1989.
34. Ritchie, D.M. and K. Thompson. "The UNIX Time–Sharing System." *Communications of the ACM* 7 (July 1974):365–375.
35. Chernicoff, C. *Macintosh Revealed Volume 1: Unlocking the Toolbox.* Hasbrouck Heights, NJ: Hayden, 1985.

36. ___. *Macintosh Revealed Volume 2: Programming with the Toolbox*. Hasbrouck Heights, NJ: Hayden, 1985.

37. ___. *Macintosh Revealed Volume 3: Mastering the Toolbox*. Indianapolis, IN: Hayden, 1989.

38. Kenah, J. K. et al. *Version 4.4 VAX/VMS Internals and Data Structures*. New York: Digital Press, 1988.

39. Levy, H. M. and R. H. Eckhouse, Jr. *Computer Programming and Architecture: The VAX*. 2nd ed. New York: Digital Press, 1988.

40. *VAX Architecture Reference Manual*. edited by T. E. Leonard. New York: Digital Press, 1987.

41. Stoll, C. "Stalking the Wily Hacker." *Communications of the ACM* 31 (May 1988): 484–497.

42. Special section on the Internet Worm. *Communications of the ACM* 32 (June 1989): 677–710.

43. Black, U. D. *Data Networks: Concepts, Theory, and Practice*. Englewood Cliffs, NJ: Prentice–Hall, 1989.

44. Held, G. *Data Communications Networking Devices*. 2nd ed. New York: Wiley, 1989.

45. Housley, T. *Data Communications & Teleprocessing Systems*. 2nd ed. Englewood Cliffs, NJ: Prentice–Hall, 1987.

46. Stallings, W. *Data and Computer Communications*. 2nd ed. New York: Macmillan, 1988.

47. Tanenbaum, A. S. *Computer Networks*. 2nd ed. Englewood Cliffs, NJ: Prentice–Hall, 1988.

48. Flynn, M.J. "Some Computer Organizations and Their Effectiveness." *IEEE Transactions on Computers* C-21 (Sept. 1972):948–960.

49. Tanenbaum, A. S. *Structured Computer Organization*. 3rd ed. Englewood Cliffs, NJ: Prentice–Hall, 1990.

50. Norrie, C. "Supercomputers for Super Problems: An Architectural Introduction." *Computer* 17 (March 1984):62–75.

51. Kozdrowicki, E.W. and D. J. Theis. "Second Generation of Vector Supercomputers." *Computer* 13 (Nov. 1980):71–83.

52. Shiva, S. G. *Computer Design & Architecture*. 2nd ed. New York, NY: HarperCollins, 1991.

53. Hillis, W. D. *The Connection Machine*. Cambridge, MA: M.I.T Press, 1985.

54. Hillis, W. D. "The Connection Machine." *Scientific American* 256 (June 1987): 108–115.

55. Skillicorn, D. B. "A Taxonomy for Computer Architectures." *Computer* 21 (November 1988):46–57.

56. Stenstrom, P. "A Survey of Cache Coherence Schemes for Multiprocessors." *Computer* 23 (June 1990):12–25.

57. Chaiken, D., C. Fields, K. Kurihara, and A. Agarwal "Directory–Based Cache Coherence in Large–Scale Multiprocessors." *Computer* 23 (June 1990):49–59.

58. Nelson, V. P. "Fault–Tolerant Computing: Fundamental Concepts." *Computer* 23 (July 1990):19–25.

59. Siewiorek, D. P. "Fault Tolerance in Commercial Computers." *Computer* 23 (July 1990):26–38.

60. Ancona, M. et al. "A System Architecture for Fault Tolerance in Concurrent Software." *Computer* 23 (October 1990):23–32.
61. Coulouris, G. F. and J. Dollimore. *Distributed Systems: Concepts and Design*. Reading, MA.: Addison–Wesley, 1988.
62. Kochan, S. G. and P. Wood. *UNIX Networking*. Indianapolis, IN: Hayden, 1989.
63. Satyanarayanan, M. "Scalable, Secure, and Highly Available Distributed File Access." *Computer* 23 (May 1990):9–22.
64. McLean, J. "The Specification and Modeling of Computer Security." *Computer* 23 (January 1990):9–16.
65. Cooper, J.A. *Computer Security Technology*. Lexington, MA: D.C. Heath, 1984.
66. Gasser, M. *Building a Secure Computer System*. New York: Van Nostrand Reinhold, 1988.
67. Cronin, D.J. *Microcomputer Data Security: Issues and Strategies for Business*. Englewood Cliffs, NJ: Prentice–Hall, 1986.
68. Lobel, J. *Foiling the System Breakers: Computer Security and Access Control*. New York: McGraw–Hill, 1986.
69. Moultin, R.T. *Computer Security Handbook: Strategies and Techniques for Preventing Data Loss or Theft*. Englewood Cliffs, NJ: Prentice–Hall, 1986.
70. Markas, T., M. Royals, and N. Kanopoulos. "On Distributed Fault Simulation." *Computer* 23 (January 1990):40–54.
71. Jefferson, D. et al. "Distributed Simulation and the Time Warp Operating System." *Operating Systems Review* 21 (November 1987):77–93.
72. Black, D. "Scheduling Support for Concurrency and Parallelism in the Mach Operating System." *Computer* 23 (May 1990):35–43.
73. Champine, G., D. Geer, and W. Ruh. "Project Athena as a Distributed Computer System." *Computer* 23 (September 1990):40–51.
74. Mullender, S., et al. "Amoeba: A Distributed Operating System for the 1990s." *Computer* 23 (May 1990):44–53.
75. Tanenbaum, A. S. et al. "Experiences with the Amoeba Distributed Operating System." *Communications of the ACM* 12 (December 1990):46–63.
76. Cristian, F. "Understanding Fault-Tolerant Distributed Systems." *Communications of the ACM* 2 (February 1991):56–77.
77. Pike, R., et al. "Designing Plan 9." *Dr. Dobb's Journal*. #172 (January 1991): 49–60.
78. Levy, E. and A. Silberschatz. "Distributed File Systems: Concepts and Examples." *Computing Surveys* 22 (December 1990):321–374.
79. Cheriton, D., H. Goosen, and P. Boyle. "Paradigm: A Highly Scalable Shared–Memory Multicomputer Architecture." *Computer* 24 (February 1991):33–46.
80. Cheriton, D. "The V Distributed System." *Communications of the ACM* 3 (March 1988):314–333.
81. Ousterhout, J. "The Sprite Network Operating System." *Computer* 21 (February 1988):23–36.

2

Memory Management

2.1 What Is Memory?

Not long ago people programmed computers by setting switches and relays and connecting wires. The very first computers were just that—"computers." Their basic function was to compute; that is, they could add, subtract, multiply, and divide. People literally had to "hard wire" them to run a program. An engineer had to reset switches and reconnect wires. The notion that the computer could "remember" a program was a dream. Now, the alternative is a nightmare beyond any reasonable person's imagination.

Most readers of this book have written many programs. You probably stored them where you could easily find them, such as on a floppy disk. Maybe you use a mainframe where you can compile or edit programs you wrote earlier. In either case the computer "remembers" the program. Like people, it has a memory.

Long and Short Term Memory

There are two types of memory, long term and short term. Long term memory (*secondary storage*) remembers information for long periods, such as days, weeks, or months. The most common storage devices are magnetic disks and tapes. We will not distinguish here between floppy disks and hard disks, or between cassettes and reel-to-reel tapes. Functionally, they are identical; the differences are in speed and storage capacity.

Information is stored magnetically on a tape or disk. The surface retains its contents for a long time. (Of course, you had better not leave your disks in a hot car trunk.) Disks and tapes are also easy to transport and relatively inexpensive.

This type of storage medium is relatively cheap. Unfortunately, retrieving information from it is a relatively slow operation.

Short term memory costs more than long term memory. Sometimes we use the terms RAM (Random Access Memory) or *primary memory* for short term memory. Retention in short term memory depends on a constant power supply. Loss of power or even fluctuations in the supply can cause a loss of information. As a result, we cannot use short term memory for permanent storage. It is too dangerous, expensive, and unpredictable. On the other hand, we can access information in short term memory much faster than in long term memory. A RAM access typically takes one-thousandth as long as a disk access.

Units of Memory

The smallest unit of memory is a *bit*. It is like a device with two stable states, such as a light bulb (see Figure 2.1) that can be either "on" or "off." Symbolically, we can refer to the light bulb being on as "1" and off as "0."

Figure 2.1 Electric device with two states

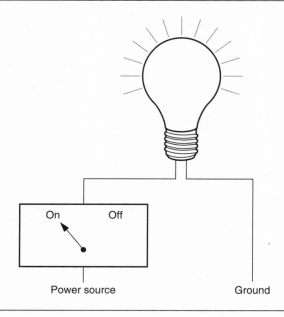

Current memories consist of semiconductor devices, not light bulbs (despite the movies where computers have flashing lights and huge voltages). However, since the physics of semiconductor theory is outside the scope of this book, we will simply assume that memory consists of bits regardless of the technology.

One bit may represent just two distinct states. However, we can combine bits to represent more. For example, two bits can represent four possible states. They are:

00
01
10
11

Thus, each combination represents one of four distinct pieces of information. Three bits can represent eight possible combinations. (Can you list the combinations?)

We may combine bits into groups called *bytes*. We then combine bytes into *words* and words into *pages*. The number of bits in a byte or the number of bytes in a word varies by machine, and we will not specify it further.

However, recall that a program is really a collection of machine language instructions. Furthermore, each instruction consists of a specific number of bits. In this chapter, we are not concerned with variable length instructions and assume that instructions have equal length.

System Components

Figure 2.2 shows the basic components of a computer. The arrows between blocks indicate data paths. The Central Processing Unit (CPU) executes arithmetic and logical operations. It controls the access of data and instructions from memory. For an introduction to computer organization and CPU architecture, you should consult a text such as reference 1 or 2 at the end of this chapter.

Figure 2.2 Typical computer system

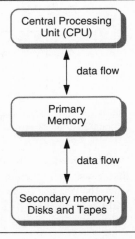

The CPU continually performs *fetch-analyze-execute* cycles. That is, it locates and transfers (fetches) a machine language instruction from memory, and stores it in a CPU register. The CPU then analyzes the instruction. If the instruction is valid, then it is executed. The CPU repeats these steps until the process finishes.

But where do the instructions and data reside when the process is not running? Program code usually resides on disk or tape (secondary memory in Figure 2.2). But the code for an active process must be in RAM, because the program requires frequent accesses to its own instructions and data.

Thus, we must transfer the instructions and data from secondary memory to primary memory. The CPU can then quickly fetch the machine instructions for analysis and execution. In short, the entire process executes much faster.

To the user, memory exists so his or her program and data have a place to reside. However, to an operating system designer, memory exists to give many processes a place to reside. In addition, other software such as editors, compilers, assemblers, linkers, system library routines, and debuggers all must reside in memory when they execute. But memory is a finite resource that is in demand by a potentially large number of processes. Something or someone must manage it. This is one of the operating system's responsibilities.

You might ask, "What must the operating system do in order to manage memory?" Typical issues in memory management are:

- Where can we put a new process without annihilating another that is currently in memory?

- How can we prevent a running process from altering another's data?

- What happens if a process needs to execute, but there is no room in memory?

- Should we allow a process to occupy large sections of memory at the expense of keeping others out of memory?

- What happens if a process requires more memory than the system has?

- How can two or more processes access common memory without interfering with each other?

- Suppose that memory is full, but a process not in memory must run. What must we remove from memory?

- How can we determine if the current management scheme is efficient?

An operating system must protect processes from accidental or malicious destruction by other processes. Furthermore, it should guarantee that legitimate processes have rightful access to memory. To put it simply, we want to satisfy all users all the time. While this goal is admirable, it is very difficult (in fact, usually impossible) to achieve. (What if 100 people all want their long programs to run to completion within the next 10 seconds?)

At best, there will always be some unhappy users of a system. At worst, there is the potential for unauthorized access to information and the criminal use or destruction of it.

In this chapter, we examine issues and methods of memory management. Section 2.2 discusses memory management in single-user systems because the problems are simpler that those in multiuser systems. However, memory management in single–user systems is not trivial to implement. The case study in the last section shows an example where the implementation is not trivial.

In Sections 2.3 and 2.4 we consider systems that store multiple processes in memory. We examine problems in these systems, and potential solutions such as variable and fixed partitions. However, these solutions can also cause additional problems such as fragmentation or unusable sections of memory.

In Sections 2.5 through 2.7 we examine ways of dividing a process' code into several pieces called pages. However, the pages are often stored in noncontiguous areas of memory. We shall see that this causes problems with referencing data and instructions. Remember, as programmers we see a program or procedure as a set of consecutive commands. What happens if the system stores them in noncontiguous areas of memory? How can the commands be fetched in sequence if they are not stored in memory consecutively?

Next, in Sections 2.8 and 2.9 we generalize further by allowing a process to be only partially in memory. Now we must answer questions such as, "How can we execute a process when some of its instructions are not even in memory?" "How do we decide what resides in memory and what does not?" "Does the process run slower?" "If so, then how much slower?" "What do we gain by storing part of the process elsewhere?"

The chapter concludes with an examination of the internal memory management of an Apple Macintosh computer in Section 2.10. We will see that even a single-user system may experience certain problems that can affect the user in unexpected ways.

═══════ ## 2.2 Single-User Systems

A single-user system has only one person who makes requests to the operating system or initiates application programs. However, there may be several processes running concurrently; that is, the system may be *multitasking*. (To review the discussion of the terms "programs," "processes," and "tasks" see Chapter 1.)

Concurrency is a key issue in operating systems, and will be discussed in detail in Chapter 5. This section considers only single-user, single-tasking systems. We assume that a single application program resides in memory.

Many personal computers fall in this category. At first glance you might think that memory management would be simple. Certainly single-user systems are simpler than multiuser systems, but they should not be underestimated.

Although there may be only one application program in memory, other things must also reside there. Typical examples are language compilers, text editors, assemblers, debuggers, and parts of the operating system itself. We certainly do not want a process to destroy their code or data.

Resident and Transient Programs

Many operating systems such as the popular MS-DOS consist of *resident (internal) programs* and *transient (external) programs*. MS-DOS resident programs include the user interface, such as the one that responds to keyboard commands. They also include utilities that allow users to copy, delete, display, list, and rename disk files. The transient programs include less frequently used routines, such as ones that copy or format disks. Resident programs reside in memory whenever the computer is operating. Transient programs reside there only when needed. In fact, the system may swap a transient program in and out of memory many times.

Figure 2.3 shows a memory map for a single user, single tasking system. There are separate areas for resident and transient programs. The resident program area's contents do not change. The transient program area's contents may change frequently as the user enters different commands.

Figure 2.3 Memory allocation in a single–user, single–tasking system

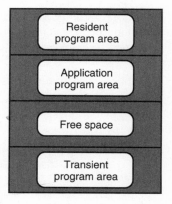

The application program area in between the resident and transient program areas contains a user's process. Depending on the sizes of the various areas, there may be some free memory space. As a process expands, it may use the free space. Memory management is necessary to keep the process separate from the resident and transient programs.

Let us define memory management at this point. It must do the following:

1. Keep resident programs, transient programs, and processes in separate areas.
2. Make sure a process only references memory within its area.

In general, memory management involves much more, but we will add functions as we progress.

Protection

The overall design specifies where operating system components reside. During a system boot, resident programs are loaded into a prescribed area. The operating system reserves memory locations for a process and transient programs. Thus, the separation of a process from the resident and transient programs is not a difficult task.

One way to enforce valid memory references is through special CPU registers, often called *boundary registers*. They contain the low and high address (boundary) values allocated to the process.

For example, suppose a process resides between locations 2000 and 6000, inclusive. Figure 2.4 shows the boundary registers. The high one (Hi–Loc) contains 6000, and the low one (Low–Loc) contains 2000. The operating system defines the boundary registers when it stores the process in memory.

Figure 2.4 Boundary registers in a single-user, single-tasking system

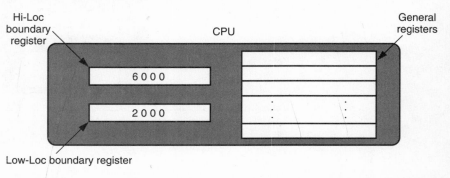

Hi-Loc boundary register

CPU

General registers

6 0 0 0

2 0 0 0

Low-Loc boundary register

As the process executes, the CPU examines the effective memory references of each instruction. This is done during the instruction analysis. Values greater than the contents of *Hi-Loc* or less than the contents of *Low-Loc* are illegal. They cause a trap that transfers control to a special handling routine.

It is better to store boundary values in CPU registers, rather that in memory. This reduces the time needed to execute each instruction. To see why, suppose the CPU had to fetch the boundary values from memory whenever it executed an instruction. Each instruction would then require an extra memory reference. But that involves a significant part of the instruction execution time. Extra memory references thus make processes run much slower. If the values are in the registers, the CPU can make the comparisons much faster.

We should add that not all computers restrict memory references to a process' area. On some personal computers, a picture of a bomb may suddenly appear on the screen, or the computer may simply stop responding to keyboard entries. This painful experience is a *system crash*. It may occur if a process accidentally (or otherwise) stores data in memory locations that contain essential operating system code. The operating system is damaged, and can no longer respond to commands.

≡≡≡≡≡ 2.3 Fixed Partitions

Originally, even the largest computers were single-user systems. At the time, this presented no problems because few computing applications existed. But professionals in many fields began to discover new applications, resulting in a heavy burden on computers. They simply could not handle the growing number of requests quickly. Frequently, a short process would wait a long time because a large process was controlling the computer. Lines of users would form as they wanted their programs run. A system was needed that could handle more requests at the same time.

A *multiprogrammed system* has many processes resident in memory simultaneously. Users simply submit them to the computer, and it accepts and schedules them according to some predefined criterion. For example, many systems execute multiple processes through a round robin technique; in other words, the processes simply take turns using the CPU. The operating system usually lets each process use it without interruption for a fixed period. If the process has not finished or given up control of the CPU because of a supervisory call or an error, the operating system temporarily halts it. It then gives the CPU to another waiting process. (Chapter 4 will cover scheduling in detail.) This allows many users to share the facilities.

But, sharing is not unique to multiuser systems. Some single-user systems provide *multitasking*. That is, they let a user have more than one activity in progress at the same time. For example, a personal computer user may be running a time consuming process such as sorting a large database, recalculating a big spreadsheet, or checking the spelling in a long document. Rather than just wait for the process to end, the user may prefer to do other work. For example, while the long process is running in the background, the user may use a word processor to write angry letters to newspapers, politicians, or bill collectors. The word processor and the long process must share the computer's resources. Operating system designers must ensure that the two activities do not conflict.

Some languages even let you construct a program in which you can define concurrent activities. As it runs, it may spawn new processes that then compete for system resources. (Concurrency is an important topic and Chapter 5 describes it in detail.) For now, however, the major concern is that multiple processes may reside in memory simultaneously. Please note that multiprogramming does not usually mean that multiple processes are running simultaneously. Rather, they take turns running if there is just one CPU.

A logical question to ask is, "How many processes can reside in memory at one time?" If they can all reside there, the operating system can switch control from one to another much more rapidly. This is because the system does not have to look for them in secondary memory. As we shall see in Chapter 6, disk accesses are relatively slow.

To envision just how quickly processes take turns, think of many people working at terminals connected to a mainframe. Everyone is either typing or getting output from the computer. But in a single CPU environment, only one process is actually executing at a time. Each one controls the CPU briefly, but the switching time is so short that the users all think they have exclusive use of the computer.

If multiple processes reside in memory simultaneously, the issues of management and protection are more complex. Not only must the system protect itself from the users, but it must also protect the users from each other. Allowing one process to arbitrarily change another is dangerous and unacceptable.

One simple approach to memory management in multiprogrammed systems involves dividing memory into fixed size regions called *partitions*. The operating system must have a table of entries indicating which partitions are available, called the *partition table*.

Fixed partitions have sizes that are defined at system generation time and stay the same unless the system is rebooted. However, there are two options: the partitions may all be the same size, or they may vary. Either way, once the sizes are determined, they do not change.

Equal–Sized Partitions

To illustrate the first option, suppose a system has 500K words of memory. Suppose further that the operating system needs 70K words for resident programs and another 30K for transient programs. Then 400K of memory remains for user processes. To store five processes simultaneously, the partitions must be 80K words each. Figure 2.5 shows the divided memory. The first partition starts at location 70K, the second one starts at 150K, and so on.

Figure 2.5 Fixed, equal–sized partitions

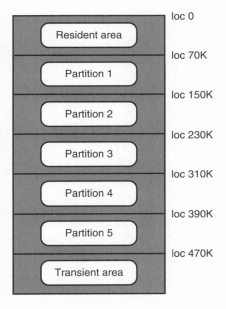

When someone starts a process, the operating system examines the partition table. If an entry indicates an empty partition, the loader stores the process' code in it. The operating system changes the partition's table entry to show that it is occupied. When a process finishes, the operating system changes the partition's entry back to indicate free status. The loader may then store a new process there.

Let's take this example a bit further. Suppose that three processes (A, B, and C) enter the system. Suppose process A enters partition 2, process B enters partition 3, and process C enters partition 5. Figure 2.6 shows the resulting arrangement of memory, and Table 2.1 is the partition table.

Figure 2.6 Fixed, equal–sized partitions containing processes A, B, and C

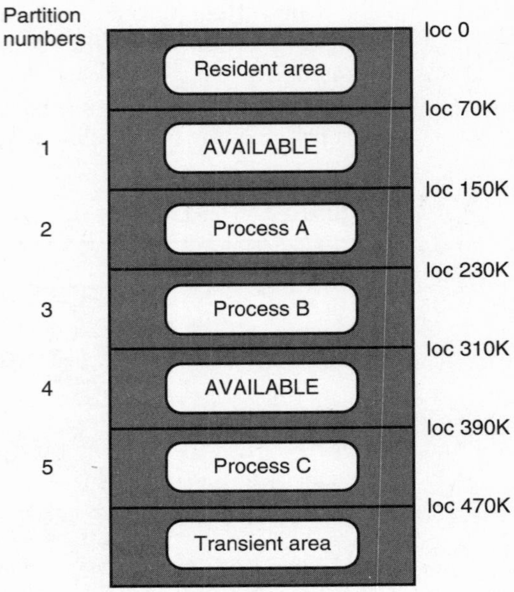

Table 2.1 Partition table for fixed–sized partitions

Partition number	Free/ occupied	Starting Location	Size	Process ID
1	free	70K	80K	—
2	occupied	150K	80K	A
3	occupied	230K	80K	B
4	free	310K	80K	—
5	occupied	390K	80K	C

Now suppose process D enters the system. The operating system scans Table 2.1. The second column indicates whether partitions are available (1 and 4 are free). As a result, the loader may store process D in memory beginning at location 70K or at 310K.

Suppose the operating system chooses partition 4. Figure 2.7 shows the updated view of memory.

Figure 2.7 Fixed, equal–sized partitions containing processes A through D

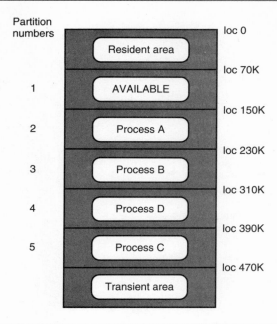

But what happens if processes try to enter faster than others leave? Specifically, what happens if a process tries to enter the system when all partitions are occupied? If there are more processes than partitions, one solution is to store the additional processes in a queue, as shown in Figure 2.8. If a process finishes, freeing a partition, the loader can then fill it with the process at the front of the queue. A single queue is only one way of handling waiting processes. Other approaches include priority queues and multiple queues.

Figure 2.8 Single queue of new processes waiting for an available partition

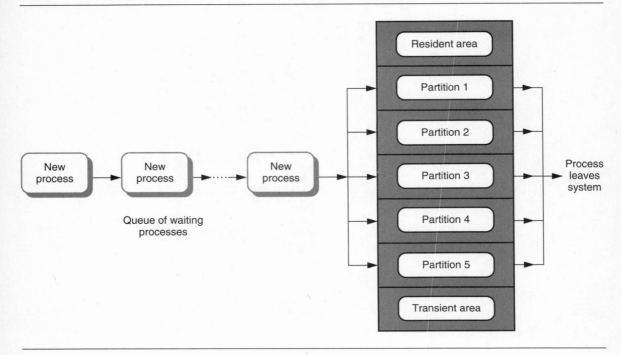

Fixed–sized partitions have one major advantage over single–tasking systems. A long process does not delay others as much. A process that requires a lot of CPU time would occupy just one partition. Like any other process in memory it will compete for the CPU. Depending on the scheduling approach the operating system will let it use the CPU only part of the time. As a result, shorter processes still can get into memory, do their work, and exit. However, total throughput may decrease because of the extra operating system intervention.

Unfortunately, fixed partitions utilize memory inefficiently. The partition size is part of the operating system design. As such, it may not match the memory needs of the existing processes. In the above example, each partition was 80K in size. In an environment where all processes require about that much memory, the design works well. But this is not realistic. What happens when many processes require much less memory? Suppose process A requires only 30K. Figure 2.9 shows how this affects partition 2 from Figure 2.7.

Figure 2.9 Fragmented 80K partition

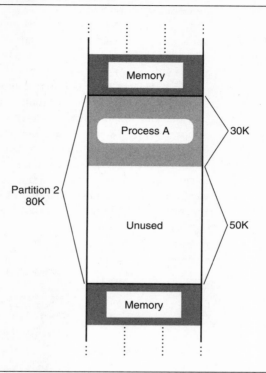

Even though process A requires only 30K of memory, the system assigns it an entire 80K partition. As you can see, the extra 50K is wasted. No other process can use it because the operating system allocates memory by partition.

We refer to the problem of wasted memory as *fragmentation*. It is insignificant if the partition size closely matches the memory requirements of the processes. However, fragmentation becomes substantial if there are many small processes. A lot of memory is simply unused, and the entire computer is underutilized. Furthermore, if a process needs more than a partition's worth of memory, the problem is even more severe. The partition is too small, and the process simply cannot run on the system.

Variable–Sized Fixed Partitions

How can we solve these problems? Let us return to the design of the operating system. We want a memory management scheme that will allow multiple processes. The flaw in our design was that the partition size did not match the processes' requirements.

In practice, assuming that all processes will require 80K of memory is unrealistic. For example, most student programs are very small. Of course, they may seem quite long in light of the unrealistic amount of time instructors give you to write them!

Most systems have both small processes and large ones, and usually they coexist peacefully. This is a simple and perhaps obvious observation. However, the inability to predict the size of a process leads to significant problems. Suppose we know in advance that many small processes will enter a system. Suppose we also know that there will be an occasional large process (perhaps around 160K). Instead of creating five equal–sized partitions, could we instead have a variety of sizes? For example, partitions 1 and 2 might consist of 40K each. Partitions 3 and 4 might be 80K each, and partition 5 would contain the remaining 160K. Figure 2.10 shows the arrangement.

Figure 2.10 Fixed, different–sized partitions

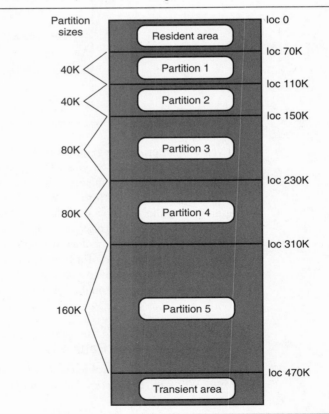

Suppose, as before, that processes A, B, and C are in partitions 2, 3, and 5, respectively. Table 2.2 is the partition table.

Table 2.2 Partition table for different sized partitions

Partition number	Free/ occupied	Starting Location	Size	Process ID
1	free	70K	40K	—
2	occupied	110K	40K	A
3	occupied	150K	80K	B
4	free	230K	80K	—
5	occupied	310K	160K	C

As before, process A requires 30K of memory. Figure 2.11 shows the fragmented partition. As you can see, the fragmentation now is only 10K instead of 50K. The operating system's view of memory is a closer match to the processes' actual requirements. We have reduced the problem of fragmentation, but it did not go away.

Figure 2.11 Fragmented 40K partition

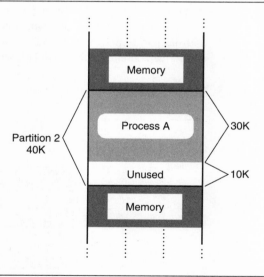

These examples only illustrate the concepts of fixed partitioned memory. In practice, the size and number of partitions depend on the operating system design.

Memory Protection in Fixed Partitions

Memory protection does not differ much from the description in Section 2.2. With fixed partitions, the operating system's view of memory is more complex than in a single–tasking system. However, the individual process' view of memory stays the same. In other words, the system should allow a process to access anything within its partition, but nothing outside. As before, we may use two special registers, *Hi-Loc* and *Low-Loc* to bound valid memory references. One difference, however, is that the system must now change *Hi-Loc* and *Low-Loc* whenever it gives control of the CPU to a new process. This was not necessary when there was only one process and partition.

The system will usually keep the value of *Low-Loc* in a *Process Control Block* (PCB). This is a table of information the system maintains on each process. It usually contains attributes such as priority, execution time limits or printed page limits, maximum allowable disk space, and memory allocation data. It contains everything the operating system must know about a process. We will discuss process control blocks in Chapter 4.

When the system gives control of the CPU to a process, it finds the value of *Low-Loc* in the process control block. It can then add the partition size and place the sum in *Hi-Loc*. For example, suppose the system is about to give process A control of the CPU. Since the system initially put process A in partition 2, it stored the starting location 110K in its process control block. The system can now retrieve that value and place it in register *Low-Loc*. It can then add the partition size (40K) and store the sum (150K) in *Hi-Loc*. Figure 2.12 shows the contents of the boundary registers.

Figure 2.12 Contents of boundary registers when process from partition 2 is running

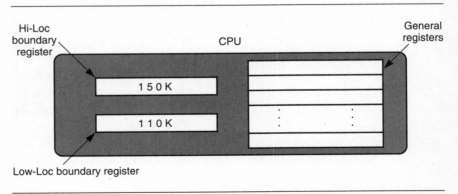

Whether the partitions are all the same size or variable, the two options of fixed memory partitions have one thing in common. Once the operating system's view of memory is defined, it does not change. If the processes' memory requirements change little over time, the design can work well. However, if the number and size of processes change a lot, fixed partitions provide an inflexible view of memory.

≡≡≡ 2.4 Variable Partitions

Memory management through fixed partitions of unequal size helps reduce fragmentation. It creates a view of memory that more closely meets the requirements of running processes. The system can assign a process with modest memory requirements to a small partition. Similarly, it can assign a process with large requirements to a large partition. But have we really solved the problem?

If our objective is to minimize fragmentation, then it certainly makes more sense to store a 30K process in a 40K partition rather than in an 80K partition. But there is still 10K of wasted memory. Perhaps the system can find a process whose requirements match the partition size more closely. But what if no such process exists? Regardless of partition sizes, we can always create examples of processes whose memory requirements are not close matches.

The flaw here is that the operating system designer must try to predict the size of processes to find the best partition size. If the processes never change, then we can make such predictions with some accuracy. But what about environments where processes change as new applications arise? Sometimes processes must be modified to satisfy new regulations or company policies. The point is that a process' requirements usually change frequently. We are seldom able to predict the number and size of processes over long periods of time.

Furthermore, revising the operating system to correct a disparity between the fixed size partitions and process requirements is not practical. We could not tolerate the required changes in the *Job Control Language* (language used to communicate with the operating system) or interruptions in the daily runs of processes. What we need is a view of memory that can vary to meet the needs of the current mix of processes. A good system conforms to a user's needs, not vice versa.

Perhaps the solution lies in *variable partitions*. Here we do not predefine the partitions. Instead, the operating system defines them dynamically based on the needs of current processes. The operating system creates a partition whose size matches the process' memory needs exactly. When the process finishes, the system then releases the memory.

For example, suppose that Table 2.3 shows the memory requirements of processes entering the system. Suppose also they enter in the order shown.

Table 2.3 Memory requirements of entering processes

Process–ID	Memory Requirement
A	30K
B	10K
C	140K
D	40K
E	20K
F	130K

The operating system creates a partition for each process. Figure 2.13 shows the arrangement of memory. In this case, each partition matches the process' requirements exactly. As a result, there is no fragmentation.

The table needed for memory management becomes more complex. It no longer has a fixed number of entries. Instead, it varies with the number of partitions. Furthermore, the table must also contain the location of any free space. With fixed partitions, all free space existed in available partitions. With variable partitions, it must be explicitly specified. Table 2.4 shows the partition table corresponding to the arrangement in Figure 2.13.

Figure 2.13 Variable–partitioned memory with 6 allocated partitions

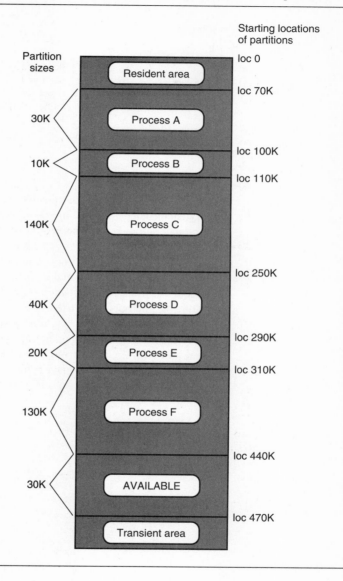

Table 2.4 Partition table for variable-partitioned memory

Entry	Process ID	Free/Occupied	Starting Location	Size
1	A	occupied	70K	30K
2	B	occupied	100K	10K
3	C	occupied	110K	140K
4	D	occupied	250K	40K
5	E	occupied	290K	20K
6	F	occupied	310K	130K
7	—	free	440K	30K

Fragmentation

On the surface, this approach appears ideal. The operating system's view of memory is consistent with the processes' requirements and in Figure 2.13, there is no fragmentation. Furthermore, since there is no predefined partition size, we need not worry about a process being too large. The system can handle large processes, as long as they do not require more memory than it has. Processes with needs that exceed the available memory are discussed later in this chapter.

But let's see what happens when some processes finish and leave the system. Naturally, the memory they used is now available. But the way in which the system keeps track of it may cause problems. For example, suppose that processes D and E finish. The operating system can change the third columns of entries 4 and 5 in Table 2.4 from "occupied" to "'free." Figure 2.14 shows the new view of memory. What is wrong with the view in Figure 2.14? Think carefully! Look at the picture before you continue reading.

Figure 2.14 Variable–partitioned memory with 4 allocated partitions

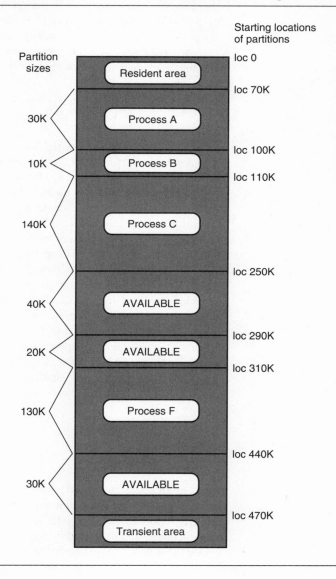

What happens if a new process that needs 50K of memory enters the system? What the system should do is clear. It should put the new process in the locations between 250K and 310K. But given the current view of memory, it cannot do this. Remember, its view depends on the information in its tables. If the third column of the fourth and fifth entries in Table 2–4 are simply marked as free, the operating system will not see a 60K available partition. It will see a 40K partition and a 20K partition. Neither one is large enough for the new process. As a result, it will wait in a queue until a larger partition becomes free. Again we find that available memory may not be used. Clearly, this is inefficient management and another form of fragmentation.

Coalescing

What can we do? We could write routines that scan the partition table, looking for adjacent free partitions. If we find some, we can combine them by replacing their entries with a single entry. The new partition's size is the sum of the old ones. Figure 2.15 shows how memory looks if we do this.

The operating system can then put the new process in free memory beginning at location 250K. (Can you draw the diagram of the operating system's view of memory afterward?)

We use the term *coalescing* to describe the combination of adjacent partitions of free memory. Coalescing requires a more complex operating system. It may appear to be simple to find adjacent partitions, but it is somewhat involved in practice. Remember, pictures tend to simplify matters. But the partition table contains the needed information. Algorithms must be designed to search through the tables and look for adjacent free partitions.

Without coalescing, the operating system will see many small free memory partitions. In an extreme case, all of memory may be available, but, if the system sees it as many very small partitions, a new process may still not fit, despite the fact that there are no other resident processes. This is the ultimate in memory waste.

Compaction

But is coalescing sufficient? Suppose the memory view of Figure 2.15 is current. What happens if a new process that requires 70K of memory wants to run? The operating system will search the partition table, looking for a free partition large enough to hold it. As the figure shows, there is no such partition.

Does this make sense? Even though no single partition is larger than 60K, there is 90K of available memory. The problem may become worse. If process A finishes, another 30K of memory becomes free. Now a total of 120K of memory is available. Still, the process that requires only 70K cannot fit into any available partition. Once again we face the problem of inefficient memory management.

Figure 2.15 Variable–partitioned memory with coalesced partitions

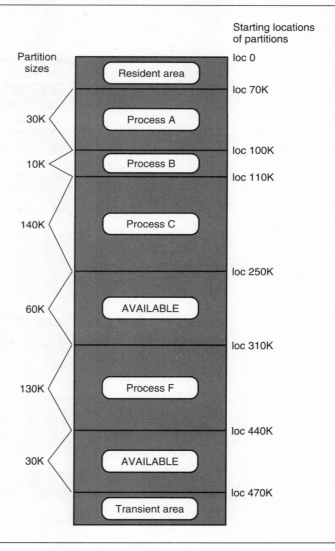

What can we do? In this case, searching through the partition table and coalescing partitions is not enough. Memory itself has been fragmented into small unusable (with respect to the 70K process) pieces called *holes*.

Since the holes are separated physically, one alternative is to rearrange the processes in memory to make free partitions adjacent. For example, if process A finishes, the view of memory from Figure 2.15 changes to that in Figure 2.16.

Figure 2.16 Variable–partitioned memory before compaction

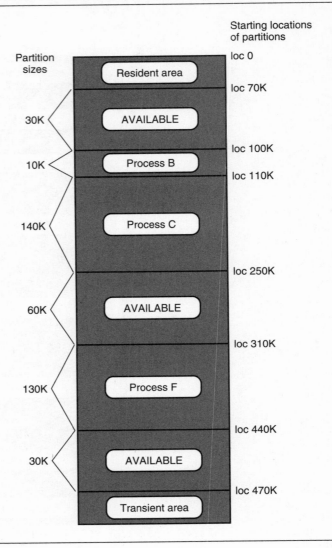

We would need system routines to relocate all processes to contiguous areas starting at the lower end of user memory. Thus, in this case the system would move process B from locations 100K through 110K to locations 70K through 80K. It would move process C to locations 80K through 220K. Finally, it would move process F to locations 220K through 350K.

The relocation of processes to make all occupied partitions contiguous is called *compaction*. Figure 2.17 shows memory after the system compacts the view of Figure 2.16.

Figure 2.17 Variable partitioned memory after compaction

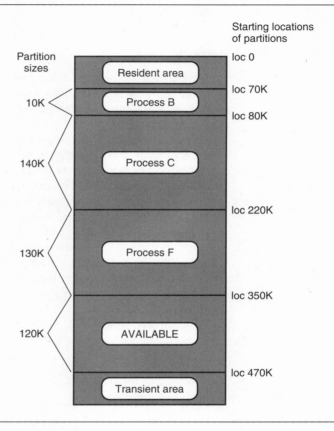

On paper, compaction appears to be an elegant solution. However, it can be costly. This is because moving processes around in memory has a price. The references each instruction makes depend on the process' location in memory. If the process moves, the references are incorrect.

There are basically two answers to this problem. One is accept the cost and relocate processes physically to new areas. This may involve changing the memory references in the instructions or altering a *base register* that contains the process' starting address. Several textbooks deal with relocation during linkage editing. The interested reader should consult references such as [3,4].

The other answer is to design a system in which the process' memory referencing instructions are independent of its location in memory. In such systems, an instruction's memory reference is altered during analysis to correspond to the actual location. At first, this may seem peculiar, but it is common. *Dynamic address translation* is discussed in detail in the next few sections.

2.5 Virtual Memory

The partitioning of memory in the previous section seemed to cause as many problems as it solved. Analysis shows that the difficulties have one main source: the attempt to keep free memory in a contiguous block to maximize its use.

Perhaps this is the wrong approach. Instead of rearranging the memory to match a process' needs, perhaps we should ask how a process might use arbitrary free memory. Can we create a process so its needs are compatible with an arbitrary configuration? For example, suppose that free memory exists in noncontiguous areas. Can we view a process as distinct sections of code and then place sections in noncontiguous areas?

Indeed, we can. In fact, it is often done in multiuser systems. The idea is to divide a process' code and data into distinct sections called *pages*. Correspondingly, we divide memory into units called *frames*. A frame is a contiguous section of memory the same size as a page. To store a process in memory, we simply store its pages in available frames. Note that frames need not be contiguous.

Let's consider an example. Suppose an operating system manages memory with twenty frames. Suppose also that the following processes exist with the listed memory requirements.

Process ID	Number of Pages
A	3
B	4
C	1
D	4
E	1
F	6

If the system stores the processes in memory in order of process ID, Figure 2.18 shows the arrangement.

Figure 2.18 Memory allocation for processes A through F

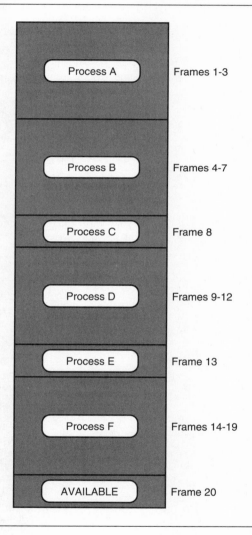

Now suppose the following sequence of events occurs:

- Process C finishes.
- Process E finishes.
- A new process (G) requiring three memory frames starts.

Figure 2.19 shows the memory allocation after processes C and E leave the system.

Figure 2.19 Memory allocation for processes A, B, D, and F

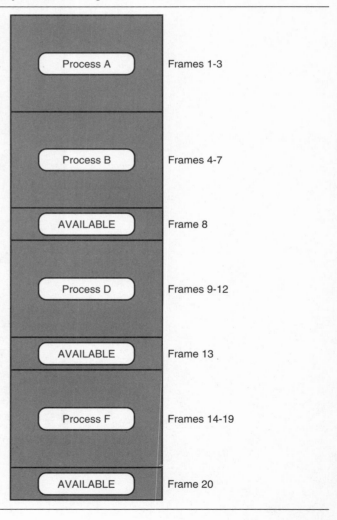

If the operating system used variable partitions to manage memory, it could not put process G in memory. Since there are three unused frames, this certainly is not sensible. However, by dividing process G's code into 3 pages the system can then store each page in an available frame. Figure 2.20 shows the result.

Figure 2.20 Memory allocation for processes A, B, D, F, and G

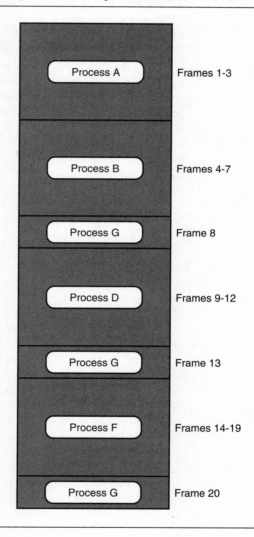

But wait! Before we start dividing processes into pieces and scattering them about memory, we must consider the consequences. You are certainly correct if you think dividing a process into pages raises new questions.

For example, how do we enforce memory protection? With partitions, CPU registers contained the bounds of valid memory references. But this works only because a process' code resides in contiguous locations. We have now removed the requirement.

How does the process even execute? We know the CPU reads instructions from consecutive locations. If they no longer lie in such locations, how does the CPU find them? For example, suppose process G is running. What does the CPU do after executing the last instruction in frame 13? Does it start executing instructions from process F in frame 14? We certainly hope not.

Also, how does the more complex view of a process affect the user or programmer? Programmers are accustomed to believing their programs lie in contiguous memory locations. If a process' pages are scattered through free memory, is its utility reduced? For example, how could a programmer use a debugger without knowing where his or her code actually lies? What if an array is split over two or more pages? How do we preserve the programmer's view that an array occupies contiguous locations?

Consider yet another problem. In a dynamic, time–sharing environment, there is no way to predict what memory frames will be available at a given point in time. Yet, when a process enters memory, it must be prepared to run. Part of the preparation is to adjust memory references to be consistent with where the process will eventually reside.

In short, we are saying a process cannot be prepared to run until we know what memory is available for it. Yet, at the same time, the system should not allocate memory to it until it is ready to run. How can we resolve the apparent conflict? The next section answers these questions. For now, we differentiate the user's view of memory from the operating system's view.

Despite the fact that a process is stored in noncontiguous memory, the user is unaware of the arrangement. In fact, the user still believes it resides in contiguous memory. The user's view is called *virtual memory*. More specifically, virtual memory refers to the locations (*virtual addresses*) the CPU uses to fetch the process' instructions and to the ones the instructions reference. They are the locations created by the assemblers or compilers and linkers. Virtual memory is where the process appears to be.

By contrast, *real memory* refers to the locations in which the process actually resides. The two usually are not the same. For convenience, the operating system lets the user believe the process resides in specific contiguous locations. Since the system does the dividing, the user need never know what happened. The hardware and software completely fool the user into believing the virtual memory configuration actually exists (Figure 2.21).

Figure 2.21 Virtual and real memory views

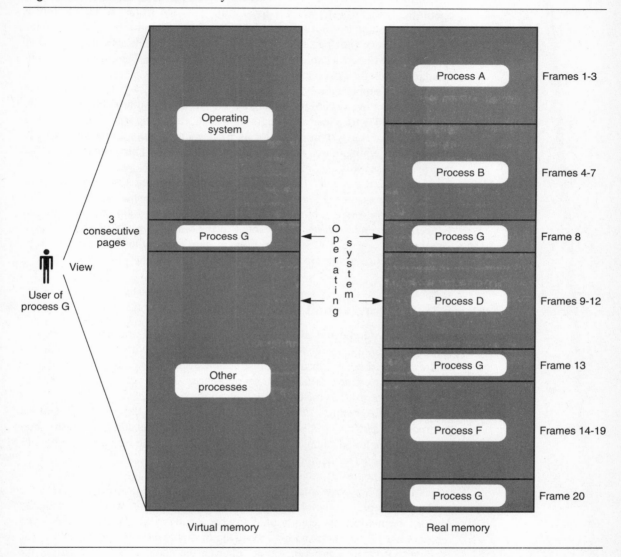

Obviously we must answer some questions. The next few sections describe the mechanisms that convert a virtual address into a real one. However, let's pose one more question first. How big should a frame and a page be?

Consider the extreme case where each frame is just one byte. Since the operating system must track the availability of each frame, it has to store a tremendous amount of information. For example, if there were eight megabytes of user memory (not particularly large by today's standards), the operating system would need a table with eight million entries. This is large by any standards, even the government's (well, maybe not).

However, suppose the system divides memory into 1024–byte frames. In this case, the operating system must maintain the status of just 8000 frames, and the table has 8000 entries instead of eight million. Clearly, this is a big savings. The tradeoff is that the system may allocate more memory than a process needs. A process that requires three and one-half frames will get four instead. Thus, the approach causes waste.

In general, if we make the frames larger, the operating system tracks fewer of them, (We assume a fixed total amount of memory.) and requires a smaller table. However, there is more waste. Allocating a whole frame when a fraction is needed generates waste proportional to the frame size. On the other hand, smaller frames reduce waste. The problem here is that the table must be very large. In practice, frame sizes often range between 512 and 4096 bytes.

≡ 2.6 Address Translation: Virtual to Real Memory

One way to handle the discrepancy between the real and virtual views of memory is through a *page table*. We use it to translate a virtual address to a real address. This is done during the instruction cycle. Remember, a compiler or linkage editor creates virtual memory references. The process' instructions and data appear to reside at the corresponding addresses.

The term *dynamic address translation* describes the conversion of an instruction's address field during its execution. Doing this during the instruction cycle has a major advantage. We can create code that will execute, regardless of where it is placed in memory.

This is a powerful advantage for software writers. They need not worry about loading a process into specific locations to execute properly. In effect, the process becomes independent of the memory locations in which it eventually resides. Remember, we cannot predict what locations will be available when a process is ready to run. Another advantage of this approach is that it allows the system to relocate a process without altering the code. This is often a normal consequence of scheduling.

Let's now discuss the page table and the mechanics of dynamic address translation. First recall the typical format of a machine language instruction. Figure 2.22 shows an example using direct addressing.

Figure 2.22 Machine language instruction format for direct addressing

The memory address has two components, a page number and a relative position on the page (or offset). For example, suppose that the memory address is 32 bits long, and that frames are 512 bytes long. (This also means that process pages are 512 bytes long.) Figure 2.23 shows the memory address.

Figure 2.23 Memory address using 32 bits

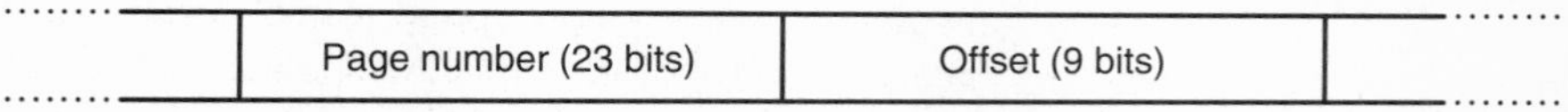

Page number (23 bits)	Offset (9 bits)

The 9–bit offset can have 2^9 (512) values, one for each byte on a page. Thus, a reference to "memory location 1030" (Figure 2.24) means the byte at offset 6 on page 2. (We number pages and offsets starting at zero.)

Figure 2.24 Representation of memory reference 1030

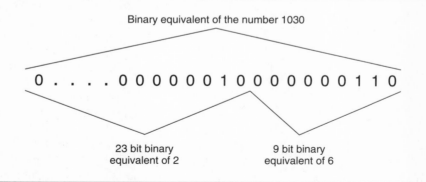

To see how the page and offset are determined, write 1030 as a 32–bit integer. The twenty-three high–order bits (0...010) are the page number. The nine low–order bits (000000110) are the offset. However, the page is "virtual"

page 2, not frame 2. During the instruction cycle, the CPU replaces the virtual page number with the frame number. The instruction then references the frame.

All memory referencing instructions in a process contain virtual addresses. The instruction cycle will replace every one with a corresponding real address before the instruction is executed. But how does the conversion occur? Where is the real address stored so that the CPU can do the translation quickly?

The answer is system dependent. However, one technique is to make the page table part of the CPU architecture. The Xerox Sigma series of computers did this. We first use it as a model to describe the basic idea, and discuss other implementations later.

To create a page table, define a series of CPU registers. Each table entry corresponds to one register. Typically, there is one entry for each virtual page. Each entry contains the frame corresponding to a particular virtual page of a running process. Remember a process has a virtual memory space determined by its memory references. When the system stores the process in memory, it uses whatever frames are available. At this point, the memory references in the instructions do not correspond to real locations. However, before the process receives control of the CPU, the operating system loads real frame numbers into its page table entries. Then, during the instruction cycle, the CPU analyzes each memory reference. The page number refers to a page table entry. The entry, in turn, contains the frame number. The instruction then references the frame.

With this setup, the system can relocate a process easily. All it must do is redefine the page table entries. This idea is similar to indirect addressing except that it does not require an extra memory reference. In this implementation of dynamic address translation, the extra reference is to a CPU register. This makes the translation quick and efficient.

Let us illustrate the method with an example. Suppose that a user creates a process that runs in virtual pages 80 through 84. In other words, all its references are to pages numbered 80 through 84. Now suppose that when the process gains control of the CPU, it resides in frames 91, 99, 104, 123, and 128. Figure 2.25 shows the user's virtual view of memory, the real view, and the contents of the page table.

Before the process receives control of the CPU, the operating system loads the frame numbers into page table entries 80 through 84. Now, as far as the process is concerned, the instructions and data are still on pages 80 through 84.

Now suppose the first instruction is at offset 0 on page 80. When the process begins execution, the program counter will contain that address. During the instruction fetch, the value 80 will be in the high–order address bits. But, 80 actually refers to an entry in the page table. The CPU uses the value in that entry to determine the frame to be accessed. In this case, it fetches the first instruction from offset 0 on page 91 (the contents of the 80th entry).

Figure 2.25 Virtual memory, real memory, and page table

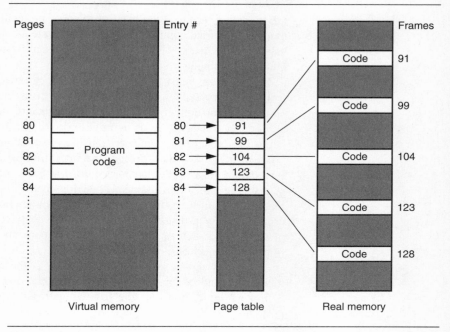

Next, the instruction is decoded and executed. Suppose that it references the address given by offset 73 on page 84. Again, this is a virtual address. The CPU will replace 84 with the value in entry 84 of the page table. This is the frame to be referenced. Here the instruction actually references offset 73 on page 128.

If the process did not branch, the next instruction is obtained from offset 1 on page 80. Through dynamic address translation, the CPU really fetches it from offset 1 on frame 91. The instruction is analyzed and every subsequent memory reference is routed through the page table. Note that code that appears to reside consecutively on pages 80 and 81 is actually stored on pages 91 and 99. Thus, dynamic address translation changes what appears to be consecutive references.

Of course not all systems implement page tables exactly this way. However, the use of a page table for relocation is common, and our discussion illustrates the logic used to convert virtual addresses to real addresses. We will discuss other implementations in the next two sections.

2.7 Memory Protection In Paged Systems

Let us now return to the subject of memory protection. The same forces (large numbers of varied applications) that complicate memory management have also made protection a key issue. It is especially significant in time sharing and other multiuser computer systems.

Such systems must protect users from each other and sensitive information from unauthorized "snoopers." Computer crime and computer viruses have become major concerns. Designers must insure that a running process has access only to what it needs in order to do its job. An attempt to access storage beyond its predefined boundaries must be thwarted immediately.

Designers must also protect the operating system from user processes. Imagine the disaster that could occur if a process arbitrarily altered scheduling or resource allocation routines. A devious person or disgruntled ex–employee might redesign the operating system to give unauthorized preference to certain users. Worse yet, that person might provide ready access to private, privileged, or secure data such as payroll information, personnel or medical records, sales figures or projections, or defense plans.

What may not be so obvious, however, is the need to protect users from themselves. Indeed, programmers are often their own worst enemies.

For example, consider the following fragment of an assembly language program:

```
X      RESERVE   1
          .
          .
          .
       STORE     R4, Z
Z      ADD       R4, X
          .
          .
```

Perhaps in the haste of typing, the programmer inadvertently entered **STORE R4**, **Z** instead of **STORE R4**, **X**. After all, the X and Z keys are close together on the keyboard.

Consider what happens when the process runs. Suppose that it reaches the instruction **STORE R4**, **Z**. When the CPU executes the instruction, it stores the contents of R4 in location Z. This, of course, destroys the previous contents of Z. In other words, the instruction **ADD R4**, **X** is no longer there, but the programmer is unaware of its unfortunate demise. The programmer believes it to be there, and it still appears in the most recent source listing.

When the CPU looks for the next instruction, it accesses location Z. Of course, Z does not contain the instruction **ADD R4**, **X**. Instead, it contains whatever data the previous instruction stored there.

When the CPU analyzes the instruction, it will, if the user is lucky, detect some abnormality in the code. If this happens, the process aborts. If the user is not lucky, the instruction will do something unexpected. In such cases, the error may not show until much later. Eventually, the user will no doubt try to find it with the aid of a source listing, although unfortunately, the listing does not reflect actual contents of Z. The programmer has literally destroyed part of his or her own program.

This example illustrates what programming errors can do. You may also imagine a program loop designed to clear consecutive memory locations. Suppose a logic error in the terminating condition caused the loop to continue indefinitely. The area to be cleared could expand forever. Eventually, it might include the program itself. The result is a "Chesire Cat" program that erases everything in its path until it finally erases itself and disappears. It does not even leave a grin behind. You could call it a self–infecting virus.

Most memory protection schemes allow different levels of protection for each page. That is, each page can be protected to different degrees. Table 2.5 contains a typical scheme with four levels. Level 3 may, at first, seem a bit impractical. It's like a motion picture that gets a censorship rating of XX — No one admitted. But, as we will see, level 3 is useful.

Unrestricted access means precisely that. An instruction can read, change, or execute (if possible) any word on the page.

Table 2.5 Access codes for virtual pages

Protection Level	Type of Protection
0 (binary 00)	unrestricted access
1 (binary 01)	can access but cannot alter
2 (binary 10)	can access but cannot alter or execute from
3 (binary 11)	all access prohibited

Level 1 restricts change. Suppose an instruction has referenced a word on a page with protection level 1. The instruction may read the word, and the CPU may even execute its contents. However, any attempt to alter its contents will cause a protection violation that makes the process abort.

Frequently, systems store instructions on pages with level 1 protection. Thus, the self–modifying code described previously would cause an abort. Tracking down a protection violation is usually far easier than debugging a self–modifying process.

Protection level 2 prevents the execution of instructions from a page. Finally, level 3 prevents any access at all. The operating system and other processes usually reside on pages protected at the highest level. Thus, if a running process attempts to access anything outside its allotted area, an exception occurs and access is denied.

But how do we implement protection for noncontiguous frames? One technique involves a 2–bit extension to each page table register discussed in Section 2.6. The extension indicates the protection level for the virtual page.

Consider the example described at the end of Section 2.6. That is, a process occupying 5 pages resides in virtual memory beginning at page 80. The process actually occupies frames 91, 99, 104, 123, and 128. Suppose further that pages 104, 123, and 128 contain instructions and pages 91 and 99 contain modifiable data.

Figure 2.26 shows the page table with the 2–bit extension to each entry. Suppose an instruction references a memory location. The CPU will check the extension field of the location's page table entry. It can then determine whether a protection violation has occurred. If one has, it causes a trap and the process aborts.

Figure 2.26 Page table and protection registers

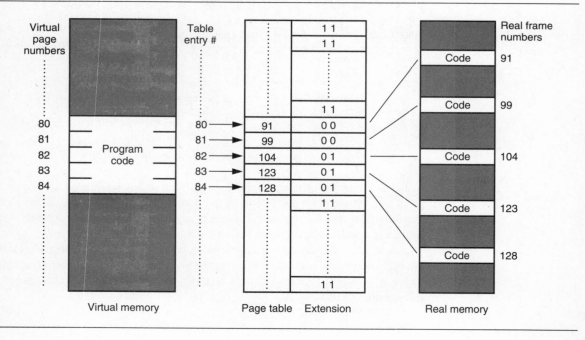

In the current example, the process will abort if it references a virtual page numbered below 80 or above 84. This is as it should be. These pages belong to other processes. The process has unlimited access to anything on virtual pages 80 and 81. This is correct since these pages contain modifiable data. Lastly, it cannot alter anything on virtual pages 82, 83, or 84. However, it could access instructions on these pages. Again, this is appropriate since the pages contain code.

2.8 Segmentation and Paging

The use of pages, page tables, and virtual storage all help reduce fragmentation. That is, they reduce the amount of extra memory allocated to a process. But is that enough? For example, does a process that requires 70K of memory really need it all the time?

The principles of structured design lead to modular software. Some modules may be alternatives that exist, because the programmer does not know the exact data (as opposed to the type of data) in advance. Thus, designers usually build decision making capabilities into a process that lets it access modules depending on the characteristics of current data.

For example, suppose that a university bookstore uses an inventory management program to track its books. Typical transactions are:

- Change the number of books in stock.
- Add entries to the database.
- Delete entries from the database.
- Produce a monthly sales report.

An individual transaction will require the code for one activity. Must all the code be in memory?

Suppose the bookstore ordered a large shipment of new texts, and it had to add many entries to the database. Should the code that deletes, modifies, or produces reports also be in memory?

Suppose Figure 2.27 shows the structure diagram for the program. Assume that the modules represented by the squares on the second level are independent of each other; that is, the transactions are separate. As the process runs, must we store all its code in memory? Why not store only what it currently needs? If this is possible, the process will occupy less memory. More memory is therefore free for other processes. The result should be more efficient memory use. However, this policy raises new questions. How can the system determine in advance which modules it should store in memory? What happens if a new transaction requires a module that is not currently in memory?

Figure 2.27 Structure chart for inventory problem

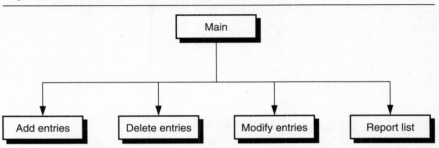

We have already seen that a user's view of a process need not be consistent with its real location. A virtual page may lie in any frame. Suppose a given page does not contain any current code or data. In this case, there is no reason to keep it in memory. Potentially, one could argue that the process might need it later. But, if that is the case, the system can load it into memory when needed.

Consider also large processes. Software such as operating systems or sophisticated data management systems often requires more memory than a computer has. In this case, we have no choice. The whole process cannot be stored in memory.

Until now it was assumed the entire process was in memory as it ran. In the remainder of this and the next few sections, we describe management techniques that allow a system to store only part of a process' code in memory. We call this *segmentation*.

In a segmented system, a process consists of *segments*. Now, the segments are not arbitrary parts of a process. The code in a segment shares common attributes. For example, all the instructions in a process may be put in one segment, while the data may be put in another. This allows the instructions to be protected at one level, and the data at another. Another example might even place instructions in distinct segments. One segment might contain instructions that no other process can access. The other would contain instructions that are shared by other processes. In any case, segments provide a way to view a process logically rather than as a collection of physically distinct parts.

When a process is ready to run, the system allocates blocks of memory to it. There is usually one block for each resident segment. However, there may be fewer blocks than segments. (Figure 2.28) The system will store only the segments the process needs in memory. As the process runs, the system will also remove segments it no longer needs.

Initially, the system stores in memory the segment containing the starting point of the process. The starting point is determined by a compiler or assembler together with a linker. It is usually in the load module and is available to the system when the process is ready to run.

Figure 2.28 Virtual view of memory

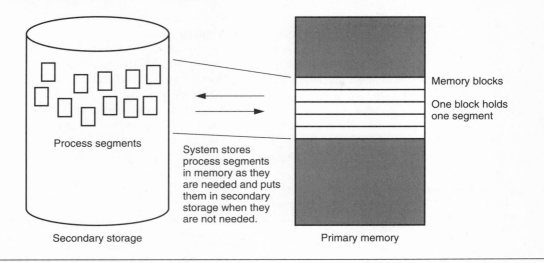

Process segments

System stores
process segments
in memory as they
are needed and puts
them in secondary
storage when they
are not needed.

Memory blocks

One block holds
one segment

Secondary storage

Primary memory

When a process begins running, the CPU analyzes each memory reference. If a reference is to a segment already in memory, execution proceeds as usual. But if it refers to a segment not in memory, a *segment fault* occurs. The process is interrupted, and the operating system must bring the needed segment into memory. Only afterward can the CPU execute the instruction. This continues until the process finishes.

As you might guess, many questions arise. For example:

- How does the system detect a segment fault?
- What happens if a new segment is needed but the process has used all its allocated space?
- How can the system handle segments that the process needs initially but not later?
- How does the generation of segment faults affect response times?

≡≡
Segment Faults

The system can detect segment faults through a modification of the dynamic address translation method described in Section 2.6. There we presented a virtual to real address translation based on a page table. The virtual address contained a page number and an offset. The page number actually determined a page table entry. The CPU then determined the real memory reference by accessing the specified table entry.

We also assumed that the process' virtual space was the same size as its real space. Consequently, there was one page table entry for each virtual page and, hence, memory frame. The page table itself consisted of CPU registers. This allowed very fast access to real frame numbers.

In segmentation, we do not assume that the virtual space is the same size as the process' real space. In many cases, the real space is much smaller. Its size is often the maximum number of blocks the system will allocate to a process. This value is usually determined by system designers.

In segmentation, address translation works much the same as in paging. A virtual address contains a segment number (instead of a virtual page number) and an offset. The segment number actually refers to an entry in a *segment table* stored in memory. Figure 2.29 shows a typical segment table entry.

Figure 2.29 Segment table entry

f : residence bit	Disk location of segment if f = 0	Real memory location of segment if f = 1	Segment size	Access codes

f = 1 means segment is in memory
f = 0 means segment is not in memory

The first field of an entry indicates whether the segment is in memory or in secondary storage. If it is not currently in memory (say f = 0), the second field indicates its disk location. If it is in memory (say f = 1), the third field indicates the real address of its memory block. The segments are not all the same; the fourth field specifies size. This is necessary so the system will know how much memory to allocate to the segment. The fifth (and last) field contains access codes which control the types of accesses that an instruction may make to a segment. The actual values are system–dependent. The key point is that the system can use the codes to limit accesses in a way similar to that described in the previous section.

Now when the CPU executes an instruction, it examines the virtual address. It uses the segment number to locate an entry in the segment table. It then looks at the first field. If the segment is in memory, it gets the real memory location from the third field. If the segment is not in memory, a trap occurs and the process issues an I/O request for it. The second field specifies its disk location.

Now let's think about the consequences of storing a segment table in memory. Suppose the CPU refers to the table during the execution of every machine language instruction. This effectively doubles the number of memory references for each instruction, and for the process as a whole. There is one memory reference to locate a table entry, and a second to execute the instruction. Furthermore, a memory reference accounts for a large part of an instruction's execution time. So doubling the number of references increases execution time and hence process response time significantly.

To avoid this "double dipping" into memory, some systems have a few *associative registers* in the CPU. Figure 2.30 shows the components of such registers. If the first field contains a segment number, the segment is in real memory, and the second field specifies where.

Figure 2.30 Associative registers entry

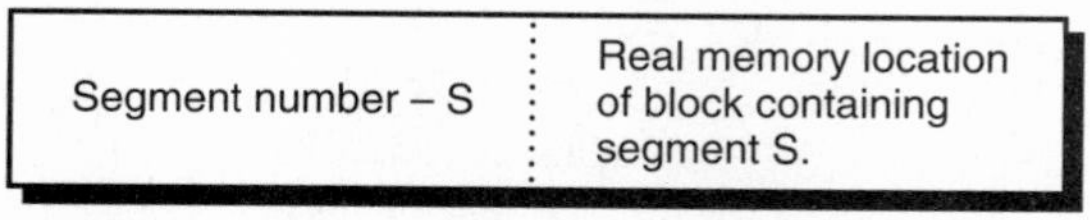

Segment number – S	Real memory location of block containing segment S.

During instruction analysis, the CPU simultaneously compares the contents of each associative register with the segment number in the address. If a match occurs, the processor determines the corresponding block address. It then uses the offset to determine the relative position in the block and makes the reference.

The simultaneous comparison of the contents of each register with a segment number is part of the instruction cycle. In practice, associative registers suited for simultaneous searches are expensive. The number of such registers is thus generally small. However, we shall see later that a small number of associative registers does not significantly affect response time of a well–structured process.

If no match occurs in the associative registers, the CPU must look in the segment table in memory. At this point, the segment number determines a table entry, and the logic proceeds as described previously. Afterward, however, the segment number and corresponding block address are placed in an associative register. Thus, future references to that segment are handled through the registers.

For example, suppose we have a system with four associative registers for address translation. This number is smaller than typical practice, but it simplifies the example. Suppose further that a process containing eight segments enters the system. Let's assume that the virtual addresses refer to segments 0 through 7. Suppose initially that only segments 4 and 7 are in memory. Figure 2.31 shows the associative registers and their contents.

Figure 2.31 Contents of associative registers and real memory

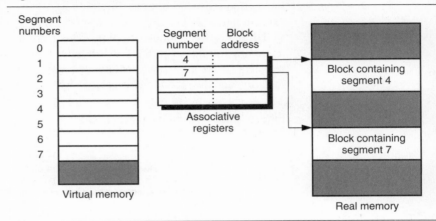

Figure 2.32 shows the segment table. We do not show the segment size or access code fields since they have no bearing here.

Suppose the CPU is about to analyze an instruction that references segment 4. During the analysis, it searches all four associative registers simultaneously. It must search all four since there is no way to know which register may have the segment number. In this case, it finds segment 4 in the first associative register, and obtains the real block address. It then adds the offset from the virtual address and makes the memory reference.

On the other hand, suppose that the instruction references segment 5. In this case, a search of the associative registers produces no match. Therefore the CPU must examine the segment table.

Figure 2.32 Segment table contents

Segment number	Flag	Disk location	Block memory location	
0	0	disk address	—	Block containing segment 4
1	0	disk address	—	
2	0	disk address	—	
3	0	disk address	—	
4	1	—	————	Block containing segment 7
5	0	disk address	—	
6	0	disk address	—	
7	1	—	—	

Real memory

Segment tables are usually found in predetermined locations, perhaps accessed through a special register. It is sometimes called a *Segment Table Origin Register* (STOR). Suppose the table reveals that segment 5 is not in memory. At this point, a segment fault occurs and process execution is interrupted.

Entry 5 contains the disk address of the actual segment. The segment is then read from disk, and the system stores it in an available memory block. The system also stores the segment number and block address in the associative registers and the process continues to run.

In this example, Figure 2.33 shows the location in memory of the new segment and the new values in the associative registers. Future references to segment 5 will be translated to the real block address via the associative registers.

Figure 2.33 Associative registers and real memory after segment 5 is in memory

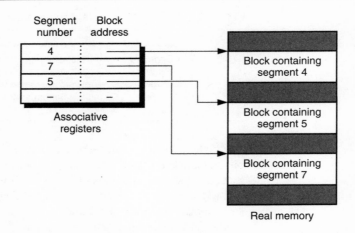

Segmentation with Paging

Segmentation offers many advantages in memory management, since the system may store only needed segments in memory. The option of variable sized segments is also useful since a process can vary in size depending on what it is doing. We can create small segments for simple parts of a process, and larger segments for the more complex parts.

But segment sizes depend on the process. Since memory blocks are a hardware resource, their sizes are system–dependent. How can we match block sizes with segment sizes? Do we not run into the same problems we had in trying to match partition sizes to process sizes in Section 2.3? By fixing the block sizes we are predicting how large the process segments are.

Sections 2.5 through 2.7 described the division of memory into fixed size frames. The system could closely match a process' memory needs simply by varying the number of allocated frames. This is more difficult to do with variable sized blocks, unless we dynamically define a block to be a specified number of frames. By doing this, we can preserve a process' view that virtual memory is segmented. Yet, we can preserve the system's view that real memory consists of fixed size frames.

To accomplish this, we must redefine what the virtual space of a process looks like. Previously, we said that a virtual memory address consisted of a segment number and an offset. Let's expand the example so that each segment is a fixed number of pages. Thus, to specify a memory location, we must specify its segment number, relative page number (in a segment), and offset (within a page). Figure 2.34 shows how to put this information in a virtual address.

Figure 2.34 Virtual address for segmentation with paging

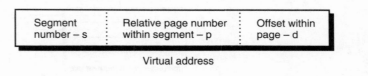

Virtual address

The high–order bits of the address contain the segment number. The low–order bits contain the offset. The bits in between specify the relative page number. Since each segment consists of a fixed number of pages, the system can allocate a block of memory that consists of a fixed number of frames. Thus, the system still allocates memory on a frame basis.

But how do we translate a virtual address into a real address? Actually, the method is similar to what we have already described. As with pure segmentation, we can use associative registers to specify addresses of allocated memory. The difference is that an associative register contains three items: segment number, relative page number within the segment, and frame number containing the virtual segment's page.

To preserve the ability to allocate memory by frame, we do not require that all pages in a segment be in memory. Some may be in secondary storage. The associative registers will specify pages that are in memory. When the CPU analyzes a virtual address, it simultaneously searches the associative registers to look for the specified segment and page numbers. If it finds them, it substitutes the real frame number and makes the memory reference.

But what if the processor does not find the segment and page numbers in an associative register? As before, it must reference a segment table in memory. The difference is that here, the segment table does not specify the location of a segment as it did with pure segmentation. Instead, each entry specifies the location of a page table.

Each entry in the page table may contain the following:

- Residence bit indicating whether the page is in memory or in secondary storage.
- Disk location of the page if it is in secondary storage.
- Frame number if the page is in memory.
- Protection bits

These are basically the same items in the segment table entry of Figure 2.29. The difference is that we have pages, not segments. Thus, if the CPU does not find a particular segment's page in the associative registers, it accesses the segment table. It examines the entry corresponding to the segment and finds the location of a page table. It then looks at the page table. The page number determines the table entry. If the residence bit indicates the page is in memory, the CPU uses the frame number to determine the real memory location. Otherwise, the system must begin an I/O to read the page into memory. This is called a *page fault*.

Let's illustrate the method with an example. Suppose there is a process with segments 0, 1, and 2. Suppose also that each segment consists of pages as shown:

Segment 0	Segment 1	Segment 2
page 0	page 0	page 0
page 1	page 1	page 1
page 2		page 2
page 3		page 3

Suppose also that the following pages are in the indicated frames. All other pages are in secondary storage.

Segment and page number	Frame number
segment 0, page 2	frame 49
segment 0, page 3	frame 73
segment 1, page 0	frame 86
segment 1, page 1	frame 35
segment 2, page 0	frame 61

Figure 2.35 shows the segment table, page tables, associative registers, and real memory.

Figure 2.35 Segment table with associated page tables for dach segment

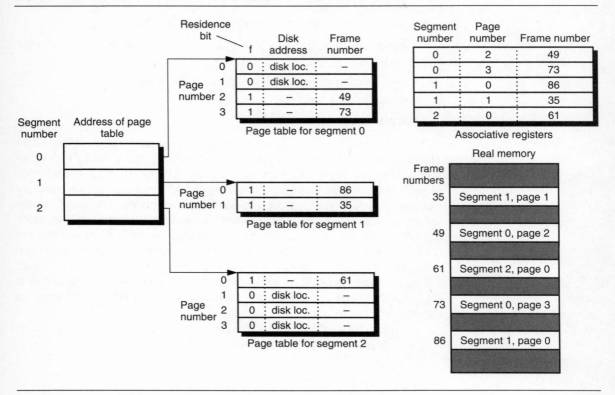

Suppose that the CPU analyzes the virtual address given by segment 2, page 0, and offset 35. It simultaneously searches all associative registers. In this case, it finds segment 2 and page 0 in a register. The register also contains the frame number 61. Thus, the real memory reference is to offset 35 in frame 61.

Now suppose the CPU analyzes a virtual address given by segment 2, page 1, and offset 41. A search of all associative registers does not find a match. Therefore, the processor looks at the segment table. Since the virtual address contains segment 2, the processor looks at entry 2 in the segment table. This entry contains the location of the corresponding page table. Thus, the CPU must make another memory reference, this time to the page table for segment 2. Since the virtual address contains page 1, the CPU looks at entry 1 in the page table. The residence bit in entry 1 indicates that the desired page is not in memory. The entry also contains the disk location of the page, and the system must then read it. Once the system reads the page and stores it in a frame, it places the segment number, page number, and frame number in an associative register. Finally, it refers to offset 41 in whatever frame the system stored the page.

Frame Size

In segmented systems, we vary the size of the allocated blocks by varying the number of frames. But what about the frame size? We have said that all frames are the same size, but what should it be? Is there a best choice?

Ideally, frames should not be too large. In an extreme case, the result is memory management very similar to the fixed partitioned management of Section 2.3. The frame becomes so large that the entire process may fit in it. In this case, the frame is actually a partition.

In general, large frames cause more fragmentation. If frames are 5K in size, unused memory will be anywhere between 0 and 5K. If the frames are 1K, unused memory will be between 0 and 1K. From this, one might easily conclude that smaller frames mean less unused memory space. But this is wrong because having smaller frames means we have more of them. Having more frames, in turn, means the operating system needs a larger table (frame table) to maintain the status of each frame. Larger tables require more memory. The result is less space for the user. Indeed, if the frame is too small, the frame table might need more than the total amount of memory available.

Having small frames also generally means more transfers between memory and secondary storage. As Chapters 3 and 6 will show, the time needed to transfer data depends more on the number of requests than the amount of data. For example, we can generally read 5K of data nearly as fast as we can read 1K, if both require only one read. But, five separate reads of 1K each will take much longer than one read of 5K. We want to avoid excessive numbers of I/O transfers.

One can describe mathematically the expected amount of unused space due to fragmentation and frame tables in terms of frame size and the size of a frame table entry. This is useful if our only concern is to minimize unused space. Then calculus provides a way to estimate optimal frame size.

For example, suppose we make the following definitions:

f = frame size
t = size of frame table entry
n = total memory
m = expected number of processes

Suppose, on the average, for each process the fragmentation due to nonuse of a full frame is about half a frame, or $0.5*f$. Multiplying this by the expected number of processes gives $0.5*f*m$ for the average fragmentation for all processes.

Suppose that the frame table's size is equal to the product of the number of frames and the size of a frame table entry. The number of frames is the total memory divided by the frame size. Therefore, the number of frames is **n/f**, and the table size is $t*n/f$.

Thus, the total unused space is $0.5*f*m + t*n/f$

The problem with minimizing this expression, as any calculus student knows, is that when **f** increases, the $0.5*f*m$ term dominates, and the unused space is large. On the other hand, when **f** is small, the $t*n/f$ term dominates, and the unused space gets large again. We can minimize the unused space by finding the value of **f** at which the first derivative is 0. In other words, find **f** for which

$$\frac{d}{df}(0.5*f*m + t*n/f) = 0$$

Taking the derivative and solving for **f**, we get

$$0.5*m - t*n/f^2 = 0$$

or

$$f = \sqrt{2t*n/m}$$

What does this formula mean? For example, consider a system with two million bytes of memory and twenty resident processes on the average. Also assume that each frame table entry consists of four bytes.

In this case, we have

$$\begin{aligned} t &= 4 \text{ bytes} \\ n &= 2*10^6 \text{ bytes} \\ m &= 20 \text{ processes} \end{aligned}$$

Thus, we can minimize unused space by choosing a frame size

$$f = \sqrt{2*4*2*10^6/20}$$

$$\cong 894 \text{ bytes}$$

Again, let us emphasize that if the only concern is to minimize unused space, the above formula dictates frame size. However, there are other factors such as the amount of time spent on I/O requests, behavior patterns of processes, size of virtual addresses, shareability of memory, and cost of memory. The model becomes much more complex, and the best size becomes an elusive quantity. The value often depends on specific hardware and application software. Some texts and research papers address the quantitative analysis of frame size in more detail. The interested reader may refer to references [5-8] at the end of the chapter.

2.9 Page Replacement Strategies

The previous section described how to translate a segment and page number to a frame number. We saw what happens when a process references a page that is not in memory. Most systems allocate a fixed amount of memory to each process. What happens if page faults cause the process' memory requirements to exceed its allocation? What does the system do?

For example, suppose a process is limited to no more than ten pages in memory. If it generates a page fault, the system must get a new page from secondary storage and store it in memory. But what if there are already ten pages in memory? Storing the additional page puts the process' allocated memory over its limit.

The operating system has two choices: increase the limit, or remove a page currently in memory. The first choice is usually not practical. We cannot set a precedent by allowing even the most deserving process to exceed its page limit. Otherwise, what is the point of having limits? Thus, we resort to the second choice. The operating system must remove a page currently in memory. This will free a frame, and the system can store the new page there. So now we come to another question: Which page should the system remove?

Optimal Replacement

If we could examine a process' future activity, the answer would be simple. Our first choice would be to remove a page the process no longer needs. If there is no such page, our second choice would be to remove the page that the process will not need for the longest time. This is called the *optimal replacement policy*. The idea is to minimize the number of page faults. If we remove a page that the process will soon reference, another page fault will occur quickly. The operating system will intervene again, and this will slow down the process.

The optimal replacement policy tries to keep seldom used pages out of memory. This leaves room for frequently used pages. If they are in memory, there will be fewer page faults. The operating system will cause fewer interruptions, and the process will finish more quickly.

Unfortunately, the operating system has no crystal ball to determine which page a process will access next. Future activity usually depends on a process' internal logic and its data. Since the operating system knows nothing about either, we need other ways to decide which page to replace. We will examine some other page replacement strategies, and outline arguments in favor of and against them.

Random Replacement

Probably the easiest replacement strategy to implement is a random choice. In other words, if a page must be removed from memory, choose one at random. The system does not have to analyze the process' referencing patterns. Nor does it need to try to predict the process' future behavior; it just picks any page.

A word of caution is in order here. Although a random choice seems simple, truly random choices are often not. They may involve a complex random number generator. In practice, a policy of picking a page for no performance–related reason (i.e., a "don't care" replacement), may be more sensible than a truly random choice.

Regardless, there are several arguments against a random or "don't care" choice. They do not even try to guess which pages the process really needs. For example, what if the strategy replaces the page containing the process' next instruction? Then another page fault occurs almost immediately. Surely a replacement strategy should at least avoid such an obviously bad choice.

Earlier, we implied that a system cannot predict a process' future activity. On the other hand, it can often determine which pages are likely to be referenced. Process logic is generally sequential, especially if the processes are well–organized. In other words, suppose a process executes an instruction from a given location. Then it is likely to execute the instruction in the next location also.

Similarly, if a process accesses one array element, it is likely to access others. There are exceptions, but modern programming methodologies encourage tightly–organized code and data. All you must ask yourself is, "How often do my programs reference arrays sequentially?" or "How often do my programs contain loops that execute commands sequentially?" Thus, an operating system may use recent page references to predict which ones will likely be referenced again. Such predictions are the basis of several page replacement strategies.

FIFO Replacement Strategy

The FIFO (First In First Out) strategy works as follows: Replace the page that has been in memory the longest. The rationale is that a new page probably is in memory because of a recent page fault. If the page contained a necessary instruction, then there are probably other instructions that the process needs. If that page contained some necessary data, then there is probably other data that the process needs.

Pages that have been in memory for a long time were probably referenced very early. Newer pages will probably be referenced again soon. They are therefore logical choices to remain in memory.

The system can implement this strategy by maintaining a queue. Its entries correspond to pages in memory. Whenever the system stores a new page in memory, it also stores a corresponding entry at the rear of the queue. If the system must replace a page, it takes the one represented by the entry at the front of the queue. The system also deletes the entry. There is more overhead than for a "don't care" replacement, but the method at least tries to predict which pages the process will access next.

Although a FIFO strategy is appealing, it can make bad choices. Sometimes an old page may still be active. Maybe it contains code or data used throughout the process' life. For example, a main program in Pascal or C often coordinates calls to modules or procedures. Thus, the system will immediately store the pages containing the main program's code in memory when it begins. If it exceeds its memory limit, these pages will be replaced. Of course, once the logic returns to the main program, those pages must be brought back in. Similar problems occur when a process uses shared procedures such as compilers or text editors. Their pages may be used repeatedly. If one of them is replaced, a page fault will soon occur.

Belady's Anomaly. There is a peculiar phenomenon, called *Belady's Anomaly* (see reference 9), that can occur under a FIFO strategy. Certainly, the number of faults that occur depend in part on how many pages a process has in memory. For example, suppose the system allocates a certain number of frames to a process, and the process runs to completion. Next, suppose the system allocates more frames, and again the process runs to completion. Which run generates more page faults?

You probably guessed that more frames make for fewer page faults. This certainly seems reasonable, but it is not always true. A process may actually generate more page faults in a larger virtual space.

For example, suppose a process consists of five pages (1–5). Figure 2.36 shows page requests that it might generate. The figure also shows the pages in memory after the execution of each instruction. One case is for three frames and the other is for four.

Figure 2.36 Belady's anomaly

Instruction number	Page requested	Pages in memory (3 frames)			Pages in memory (4 frames)			
1	Page 1	–	–	1	–	–	–	1
2	Page 2	–	1	2	–	–	1	2
3	Page 3	1	2	3	–	1	2	3
4	Page 4	2	3	4	1	2	3	4
5	Page 1	3	4	1	No change			
6	Page 2	4	1	2	No change			
7	Page 5	1	2	5	2	3	4	5
8	Page 1	No change			3	4	5	1
9	Page 2	No change			4	5	1	2
10	Page 3	2	5	3	5	1	2	3
11	Page 4	5	3	4	1	2	3	4
12	Page 5	No change			2	3	4	5

With three frames allocated, a page fault occurs for every instruction, except for those numbered 8, 9, and 12. The total is nine faults. However, for four frames, a page fault occurs for every instruction except for those numbered 5 and 6. Thus, the total is ten faults. There are more faults with four frames than with three frames.

Now, we do not suggest that this is always true. It certainly depends on the sequence of references. The key point is that what seems obvious, and what is actually true, are not always the same. One must be very careful about making claims.

Least Frequently Used (LFU)

Previous arguments suggest that the length of time a page is in memory is not always a good indicator of how soon the process will need it again. A page may be in memory a long time because it contains code the process needed initially but not since. On the other hand, it may contain code or data required throughout the process' run. In the latter case, replacing the page would be a mistake. But how can we tell the difference? Perhaps one way is to consider how often a page is referenced.

This is the motivation behind the next replacement strategy—*Least Frequently Used*. Here, the system counts how many times a particular page is referenced. When it must replace a page, it chooses the one that has been referenced the least.

For example, suppose a process references pages as shown:

page numbers 1, 2, 3, 1, 3, 1, 3, 1, 3, 4....

If the system allows only three frames, it must replace a page when the process references page 4. In the FIFO scheme, the system replaces page 1, since it has been in memory the longest. But in the LFU scheme, it replaces page 2. This is because the process has referenced page 2 only once. It has referenced pages 1 and 3 four times each.

This strategy requires more overhead than FIFO. With FIFO, the system added an entry to a queue only when it stored a new page in memory. The LFU strategy requires a counter for each page. Furthermore, whenever an instruction references memory, the associated page counter must be incremented.

There is also a flaw in the LFU strategy. With FIFO, the system considers only how long a page has been in memory. It does not consider the number of references. With LFU, the reverse is true. The system considers only the number of references to a page; it does not consider how long it has been in memory.

The problem is that new pages have usually been referenced the least simply because they have not been in memory very long. Thus each page fault is likely to replace the newest page (a Last In, First Out or LIFO strategy). After all, the process has not had a chance to reference that page very often. This runs counter to the idea that new pages are the most likely to be referenced again.

Imagine, for example, what happens if a process is at its memory limit and starts working on a new page of code and a new page of data at the same time. Under LFU, it will be constantly swapping these two pages in and out of memory.

As another example, consider the Pascal procedure in Figure 2.37. Suppose the rows of array **A** reside on distinct pages, and that none of them is in memory before the procedure is called. Suppose also that before it is called, it is one page short of its memory limit. Consider what happens when this procedure is called and the system replaces pages on an LFU basis.

When the procedure references page P_1, a page fault occurs. Remember, none of the array is in memory yet. The system then stores page P_1 in memory. The maximum number of pages is now in memory. The procedure continues by referencing page P_2. Another page fault occurs. This time the system must replace a page. But the procedure has referenced page P_1 only once, so the system replaces it with page P_2. When the procedure cycles through the loop and references page P_1 again, another page fault occurs. Remember, the system replaced page P_1 when it stored P_2 in memory. So now the system must get page P_1 again and replace another page. Guess which page that is! If you guessed page P_2, you are catching on. So, when the procedure subsequently references page P_2, a page fault occurs again.

Figure 2.37 Logic to initialize an array for which each row resides on a distinct page

```
Procedure Initialize(Var A : some array type);

Var
  i : Integer;

Begin
  For i := 1 to n do
    Begin
      A[1,i] := i;          {statement-1 : references page P₁}
      A[2,i] := i;          {statement-2 : references page P₂}
    End;
End;
```

You can probably see what is happening. Every time the procedure executes a statement, a page fault occurs. The system just keeps swapping pages P_1 and P_2 between memory and secondary storage. This should not happen. As the procedure executes, the system should keep both pages in memory. It should replace some other page when the second page fault occurs, but LFU does not do this. Once again, a good idea has turned sour.

Least Recently Used (LRU)

The LFU and FIFO strategies represent two extremes in the criteria for page replacement. FIFO does not recognize frequently used pages. LFU does not recognize frequently used pages that have become inactive. Indeed, for the program in Figure 2.37, LFU does not replace a page that was frequently referenced in the past, but has become inactive since entering the loop. Just the opposite should be true: we would like to know if a page becomes inactive.

LRU looks at whether a page has been referenced recently. More accurately, it replaces the page that has not been referenced for the longest time. The rationale is to keep pages with recent references in memory. Remember, such pages are likely to be referenced again soon. LRU does not care how long a page has been in memory, or how often it has been referenced.

LRU is a good strategy, but it is relatively expensive to implement. The system could store the time of the most recent reference for each page. Such logic could be built into the analysis of each instruction, assuming there is hardware to support storage of the time values. We would not want to store them in memory as this would require extra references. Furthermore, when the system must replace a page, it must find the minimum of all time values.

Another implementation is to maintain a list of pages starting with the most recently referenced and ending with the least recently referenced. The system would always replace the page at the end of the list. But maintaining the list is costly.

Yet another solution is to associate a capacitor (see reference [8]) with each page. When a page is referenced, a charge is applied to the capacitor. But the charge decays. As a result, its magnitude can be converted into a length of time since the last charge, or last page reference. When the system replaces a page, it looks for the capacitor with the smallest charge.

None of these implementations is cheap. But that is not a big problem since there is another strategy that is almost as good as those above and can be implemented more efficiently.

══

Not Used Recently (NUR)

The *Not Used Recently* scheme separates pages into four groups. Two bits labeled **R** (referenced) and **M** (modified, sometimes called a *dirty bit*) define a group as follows:

Group	**R** bit	**M** bit	Meaning
1	0	0	Pages in this group have not been referenced or modified recently.
2	0	1	Pages in this group have not been referenced recently, but it have been modified.
3	1	0	Pages in this group have been referenced recently, but have not been modified.
4	1	1	Pages in this group have been referenced recently and has been modified.

Whenever a process references a page, the **R** bit is set to 1. Whenever it modifies a page, the **M** bit is set to 1. However, the system will periodically clear the **R** bits. How often this occurs is an operating system parameter. Thus, the word "recently" in the description refers to the time since the last reset. Note that the system never resets the **M** bits. We never want to forget that a page has been changed. (Why?)

If the system must replace a page, it first looks for one from group 1. However, there may be no pages in that group. It must then look for a page from group 2. If there are no pages from group 2, it looks for a page from group 3, and, if necessary, from group 4.

If a page was once heavily referenced but has since become inactive, then eventually the clearing of its **R** bit will put it in group 1 or 2. This makes it a likely choice for replacement. Pages in groups 3 and 4 have been referenced since the last clearing. If the time between clearings is not too long, then these pages have been referenced recently. This is a good indication that they are still active, and as a result, they are not as likely to be replaced.

We distinguish between groups 1 and 2 (and also between 3 and 4) on the basis of page modification. If a process changed something on a page, then its modify bit is set to 1. If the **R** bits are equal, we prefer to replace an unmodified page, because all we must do is store a new page in the frame. However, if we replace a modified page, we must first write it into secondary storage, otherwise, the changes are lost. Thus, there is more work involved in replacing a modified page.

As you might expect, the NUR strategy can make bad choices. For a short time after the system clears the **R** bits, active and inactive pages are indistinguishable. Therefore, if a page fault occurs shortly after the system clears the **R** bits, it could in theory replace an active page. However, since normal activity quickly sets the **R** bits of active pages, indistinguishability is short lived, and is not a major problem.

≡≡≡≡≡ 2.10 Process Behavior Under Paging

We have stated before that we want to minimize page faults. Again, the reason is the time and overhead required to obtain a page from secondary storage. I/O devices operate much slower than a CPU. Thus, every page fault causes significant increases in process execution time. Is there anything a programmer can do to avoid, or at least reduce such delays?

A good strategy for page replacement tries to select pages that are unlikely to be referenced again soon. Some strategies described in the last section were based on one fundamental principle. "Recent reference patterns are a good indicator of future patterns." However, this is not a natural law of computing. Rather, it is an empirical observation of process behavior. Thus, the way in which you design software can affect its validity.

For example, consider the following code written in a high level language

```
For I := 1 to 100 do
  For J := 1 to 100 do
      WriteIn(A[I,J,]);
```

This code prints each value in a two dimensional array. Consider also the following code.

```
For J := 1 to 100
   For I := 1 to 100
      WriteIn(A[I,J]);
```

What is the difference? One prints a row at a time, and the other prints a column at a time. In an introductory class, the instructor will usually describe an array as a random access data structure. In other words, your program can reference any position in an array as quickly as any other. Therefore, there should be no difference in the execution times of these sections of code. Unfortunately, this may be far from true.

Memory is organized linearly. That is, it consists of locations numbered from 0 to some value. Therefore, compilers must convert two–dimensional arrays into a linear data model. Two–dimensional arrays are usually stored in *row major order*. The elements of each row are stored consecutively, and the rows are stored in consecutive areas.

Suppose the process containing either section of code resides in a virtual space of eleven pages, and that each page has a capacity of 500 array elements, or five rows (Figure 2.38). Suppose also that one page contains the code to write array elements, and the other ten pages hold the elements.

Suppose we execute the first section of code that prints a row at a time. A page fault occurs when the process references the first element of rows 1, 6, 11, 16, 21,...,91, and 96. Once the system stores a page in memory, the process can access all five rows on it without further page faults. Thus, the code causes a total of twenty page faults.

Figure 2.38 Pages containing rows of an array

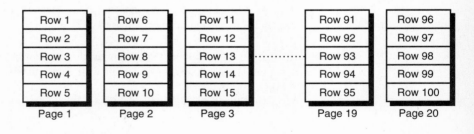

Row 1	Row 6	Row 11		Row 91	Row 96
Row 2	Row 7	Row 12		Row 92	Row 97
Row 3	Row 8	Row 13	·········	Row 93	Row 98
Row 4	Row 9	Row 14		Row 94	Row 99
Row 5	Row 10	Row 15		Row 95	Row 100
Page 1	Page 2	Page 3		Page 19	Page 20

Now consider the other section of code. The inner loop alone refers to the first element in each row. Therefore, for the reasons just outlined, it will cause twenty page faults, and it has only printed the first column.

What happens when the process executes the inner loop the second time? This depends on which pages are in memory when the process finishes the first pass through the loop. As the process executed the inner loop the first time, the first ten page faults cause no replacements. (Initially, the only thing in memory is the code to write the array.) However, each of the next ten page faults will require replacements.

Suppose that the system uses a FIFO replacement strategy. Then the system replaces page 1 when the eleventh page fault occurs. Similarly, it replaces page 2 when the twelfth fault occurs. After the twentieth fault, the system has replaced pages 1 through 10, and pages 11 through 20 are in memory. In other words, only rows 51 through 100 of the array are in memory.

Now consider what happens when the process executes the inner loop the second time. The reference to the second element of row 1 causes a page fault. The same is true for each reference to the second element of rows 6, 11, 16, 21...46. These ten faults bring rows 1 through 50 (pages 1 through 10) back into memory. Unfortunately, the system has replaced pages 11 through 20. Therefore, each reference to the second element of rows 51, 56, 61...96 causes another page fault. Thus, the second execution of the inner loop causes twenty more page faults, and it only prints the second column.

We can repeat this analysis for each pass through the loop. The bottom line is that twenty page faults occur during the printing of each column. The total is 2000 (20 faults x 100 columns) page faults! Ouch!

What can the programmer do? Careful organization of data and planned accesses to it can make a big difference in process efficiency. Similarly, modular design can help. Excessive use of GO TO's or branches can cause references to code not in memory. Again, more page faults than necessary may occur. Through modularization, we can create segments that combine modules frequently used together. We can then store these segments in just a few frames. This helps to reduce the number of page faults.

Principles of Locality. Attention to modularization and organization lead to two phenomena that often occur in well–constructed software: *spatial locality* and *temporal locality*.

Spatial locality means that a process that references a memory location will usually also reference nearby locations. This is especially true when we process data sets sequentially. It is also true because the sequential logic of a process causes the execution of instructions in consecutive memory locations.

Temporal locality means that a process that references a location will likely reference it again relatively soon. This is due to frequent use of loops that execute a set of instructions repetitively.

Through research, Denning (see reference [10]) has developed the *working set theory of program behavior*. Well–organized software tends to make memory references in localized patterns. Once a process references a page, it will probably reference it often. Furthermore, the process will probably reference many other locations on the page. Because of this, the number of pages needed by a process during a short time is likely to be small. We refer to those pages as the *working set*.

We can define the working set as the collection of pages needed for process execution over a period of time. If it is in memory, no page faults will occur, at least for a while. If a page fault does occur, the working set is probably changing. This is a normal consequence of a process' behavior as it performs different activities.

Ideally, a page fault means that the process needs a new page, and at the same time there is some other page it no longer needs. The system can then replace the one it no longer needs. Unfortunately, although they can serve as models, ideal processes almost never occur. However, carefully organized software and data can approximate an ideal process fairly well.

As a process runs, new pages are added to its working set and unneeded pages are removed, so the working set gradually changes. But the number of pages needed during any period of time should remain relatively constant (see Figure 2.39).

Figure 2.39 Change in a process' working set time

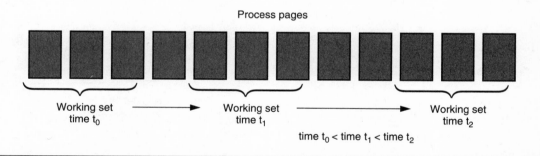

In the working set model, the number of allocated frames should equal the number of pages in the working set. If there are fewer frames, many memory references will cause page faults. Thus, the system spends more time shuffling pages in and out of memory than it does executing the process. We call this excessive swapping *thrashing* (see reference [11]). In an extreme case, the system does too much I/O. It spends a lot of time working without accomplishing much. One may compare it to an organization of paper shufflers.

This is analogous to working on a research project, and using a library which places a limit on the number of books you can check out. If the limit is smaller than the number of books you need, you spend a lot of time taking books back just so you can check out more.

On the other hand, if there are more frames than pages in the working set, then there are pages in memory that do not need to be there. In other words, the process is occupying space it really does not need, and another process could use the space. In extreme cases, the number of processes that can reside in memory simultaneously decreases significantly. As a result, scheduling overhead increases significantly, and productivity suffers.

Figure 2.40 (see references[5, 12]) illustrates the relationship between the number of frames allocated to a process and the average number of page faults per reference. Here we have a process whose database and logic were carefully designed. As the graph shows, if the number of allocated frames is small, then little of the process is in memory. The probability of referencing something not in memory is high; therefore, the average number of page faults is high.

Figure 2.40 Page fault rate for a well–organized process

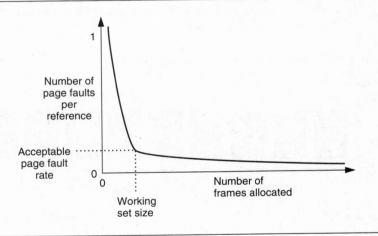

However, as the number of frames increases, the average number of faults decreases. When the number of frames is equal to the theoretical working set size, the number of page faults is at an acceptable level. More frames will further decrease the page fault rate. However, the decrease is insignificant.

Figure 2.41 Page fault for a poorly–designed process

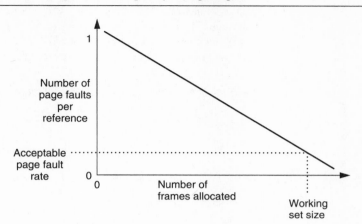

Contrast Figure 2.40 with Figure 2.41. Figure 2.41 shows the same relationship between the average number of page faults and the number of allocated frames. But this graph refers to a poorly designed process. As you can see, the number of page faults still decreases as the number of allocated frames increases. However, when the number of frames is small, the decrease is much more gradual. A much larger working set is necessary to obtain the same acceptable page fault rate. Therefore, a poorly–designed process requires much more space to operate at the same level of efficiency as a well–organized process.

2.11 Working Set Size

The working set approach to memory management is an important concept. Over a short period of time, there is no need to store all of a process' pages in memory. However, having only a few there raises other questions. What is a reasonable number of frames to allocate to a process? Perhaps more important, how do we justify what is reasonable? What criteria do we use to make such decisions?

In extreme cases, the problems become obvious. If the system allocates too many frames to each process, then just a few processes may reside in memory. That is, the degree of multiprogramming decreases. Remember, memory size is fixed.

As a result, there is more overhead in scheduling processes for execution. Figure 2.42 relates the average time to schedule a process to the number of processes in memory. As the number of processes in memory decreases, the average scheduling time increases. The reason is that all active processes must exist somewhere. If they do not fit in memory, then they must be in secondary storage. Thus, if only a few processes are in memory, then the system must read more of them from secondary storage as it schedules processes for execution. This additional I/O increases the scheduling time.

Figure 2.42 Average time to schedule a process as a function of the number of processes in memory

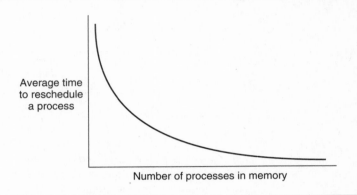

The other extreme occurs when we allocate only a few frames to each process. We can thus increase the number of processes in memory. Then, because a process is already in memory, it can assume control of the CPU more quickly. But, if the allowable number of frames is too small, the page fault rate becomes excessive (remember Figures 2.40 and 2.41). Again, the result is lower productivity.

The graphs in Figure 2.43 show both the page fault rate and the average time to schedule a process as a function of the number of allocated frames per process. The page fault rate graph is from Figure 2.40, while the average scheduling time graph is from Figure 2.42. Remember, if the system allocates only a few frames to a process, more processes fit in memory.

How do we choose a working set size that yields both an acceptable page fault rate and an acceptable average reschedule time? First, we find the minimum number of allocated frames required to give an acceptable page fault rate. We mark this value on the graph as **A**. Then we find the maximum number of allocated frames that give an acceptable reschedule time. We mark it on the graph as **B**. Then, as long as **B > A**, any working set size between **A** and **B** will produce both an acceptable page fault rate and reschedule time.

Figure 2.43 Page fault rate and average reschedule time as a function of the number of allocated frames

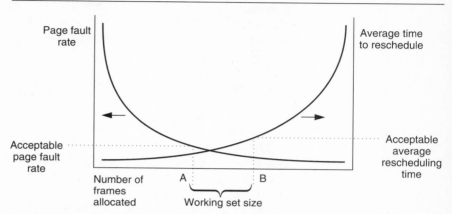

A — Minimal working set size required to produce an acceptable page fault rate.
B — Maximum working set size that still allows an acceptable average rescheduling time.

Model for Finding Working Set Sizes. The graphs in Figure 2.43 are based on averages. System designers must provide specific values. Often, we can compute them from a formula derived from a mathematical model of the system. We will present such a model, and describe rationale on which to compute a working set size.

Let's make the following definitions:

T   = Time needed to read a page from secondary storage.
t   = Time needed to execute a machine language instruction that references a page in memory.
s   = Number of frames allocated to an active process.
$p(s)$ = Average number of page faults per memory access (i.e., the probability of a page fault).

To simplify the model, let us make the following assumptions:

- The system has just one CPU.
- The system can read just one page at a time.
- The system can read a page at the same time a process is running.
- All processes behave similarly; that is, they have similar relationships between page fault rate and the number of allocated frames.

Consider now the page fault rate graph in Figure 2.40. It is constructed from empirical observations of processes in a particular system. In other words, there is no known formula that generates it. The graph is constructed by taking measurements and readings, and plotting points.

However, the field of numerical analysis provides the tools needed to find formulas associated with a given graph. That is, we can determine a function whose graph is a good approximation to it. This means we can find a function that approximates the relationship between the number of allocated frames and the fault rate. However, we will not describe here how to derive such functions. (Don't all cheer at once.)

The page fault rate graph in Figure 2.40 approximates the graph of the following function:

$$p(s) = a2^{-bs}$$

The constants **a** and **b** depend on specific values associated with the graph. Essentially, these constants are used to make minor adjustments in the graph's shape, or rate of descent. We can determine them from the information provided in the model.

Let us now see how to find a formula from which we may determine an approximate working set size. Remember, there are several processes simultaneously in memory. We also assume that each generates page faults at approximately the same rate. Now, if the number of allocated frames is too small, the page fault rate is high. If the page fault rate is too high, the system may not be able to read pages fast enough to keep up. The processes must then wait longer for the system to read and store the needed pages in memory. How can we describe this situation mathematically? Consider the following expression:

$$t/p(s)$$

This expression is the average time between page faults. Think about it. The units of **t** are time (amount required to execute one machine instruction). Since $p(s)$ is a probability function, its units are the number of page faults per machine instruction.

Thus, the units of $t/p(s)$ are:

$$\frac{\text{amount of time to execute one machine instruction}}{\text{number of page faults per machine instruction}}$$

or

$$\text{amount of time to execute one machine instruction} * \text{number of instructions per page fault}$$

or

$$\text{amount of time between page faults.}$$

So, if

$$t/p(s) < T,$$

the time between page faults is less than the time needed for the system to read a page. This means that page faults occur faster than the system can handle them. In other words, the number of allocated frames is too small.

On the other hand, if

$$t/p(s) > T,$$

the time between page faults is longer than the time needed to read a page. Thus, the system could read more pages. So, if we decrease the number of allocated frames, the page fault rate will increase. But, we have already stated that the system can handle the increased I/O. As long as $t/p(s)$ does not drop below T, there is still no more than one process waiting for a page on the average. The advantage is that now more processes will fit in memory.

The ideal is when $t/p(s) = T$. The time between page faults is equal to the time required to read one page. The system is reading pages at its maximum rate, but it still responds quickly enough to the page faults that the processes generate. We therefore define the working set to be the value **s** for which

$$t/p(s) \ = \ T.$$

Equivalently, we can write this as

$$p(s) \ = \ t/T$$

or as

$$a2^{-bs} \ = \ t/T.$$

Solving for **s**, we find

$$
\begin{aligned}
2^{-bs} &= t/(aT) \ <=> \\
-bs &= \log_2(t/(aT)) \ <=> \\
s &= (-1/b)*\log_2(t/(aT))
\end{aligned}
$$

Each variable on the right hand side corresponds to a quantity that can be obtained either through a numerical technique (such as **a** and **b**) or is measurable (such as **t** and **T**).

≡ 2.12 Case Study: Memory Management in a Macintosh

Few personal computers have had the impact of the Apple Macintosh series. The special emphasis on user interface makes these machines easy to learn and use. Their key features are powerful graphic capabilities, pull down menus, windows, and a large family of compatible software.

We have chosen memory management in a Macintosh as a case study for two major reasons. The first is the machine's popularity. Case studies are always much more interesting if the reader is familiar with the products discussed. But there is also a second, more philosophical reason for choosing the Macintosh. Recall that in the early parts of this chapter, we paid little attention to single–user systems. That is because, in general, their memory management is much simpler than in multiuser systems. Operating systems courses generally focus on multiuser systems. Indeed, our previous discussion did almost trivialize the problem. Thus, our aim here is to change any assumptions that memory management in single–user systems is trivial, and show that it may be a complex and demanding task, even in the single–user case.

Note that no case study can ever stand by itself. It cannot provide all the details about a particular system. Rather, it should introduce a product and discuss basic design principles. It should also spark the reader's interest to learn more. For that interested student, many references exist for further study. In the case of the Macintosh, many books provide instruction in software and languages, discuss system design, describe toolbox use, or just provide hints and shortcuts in using its utilities.

To begin, and for a quick review, we have reproduced Figure 2.3 as Figure 2.44 to picture memory in a single–user system. Compared to other systems we have described, there is little complexity. But let's take a more detailed look at the internal memory view of a Macintosh computer.

Figure 2.44 Memory in a single–user system

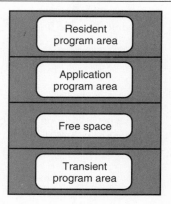

Figure 2.45 shows the contents of memory in a Macintosh. We do not specify a particular model (i.e., Macintosh Plus, Macintosh SE/30, or Macintosh II family). The differences involve details such as the exact locations of regions and specific areas within regions, and we are not concerned with them here. The interested reader should consult texts that deal specifically with the interior of Macintosh [13,14].

Figure 2.45 Internal memory of the Macintosh

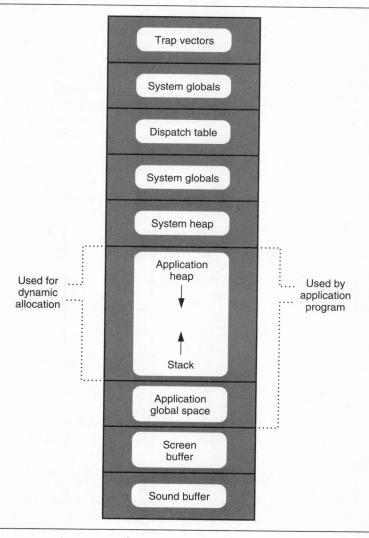

We also do not include a diagram of the ROM (Read Only Memory). It contains many low–level operating system functions such as disk I/O and serial communications. It also contains the routines and user interface toolbox. They are characteristic of the Macintosh. However, the ROM is not essential for the purpose of this section.

Let us now describe the contents of the different areas of memory.

Trap Vectors

The trap vectors are used in conjunction with *traps*. A trap occurs when the CPU detects an abnormal condition during the execution or analysis of an instruction. For example, a trap can be caused by overflow, a reference to an illegal memory address, or divide by zero.

Macintosh associates each trap vector with a particular type of trap. When a trap occurs, the CPU fetches the associated vector. It contains the location of a trap handler routine that responds to the cause of the trap (Figure 2.46).

Figure 2.46 Trap vectors

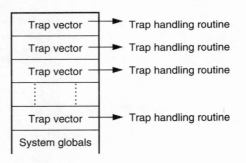

Dispatch Table

Macintosh uses the *dispatch table* to locate toolbox routines through an *emulator trap*. An emulator trap occurs when the CPU does not recognize an instruction.

Some Macintosh high–level languages provide access to the toolbox through procedure calls. See reference book [15] at the end of this chapter. For example, suppose the compiler detects a call to a toolbox routine in the source code. It will generate an instruction with an unimplemented operation code, and an index (the trap number) to an entry in the dispatch table.

When the process runs, the CPU executes its instructions. When it reaches the instruction with the unimplemented code, it accesses a trap vector associated with that special condition (see step 1 in Figure 2.47). The trap vector contains the address of a trap handler called a *trap dispatcher* (step 2 in Figure 2.47). The dispatcher assumes control of the CPU and locates the instruction that caused the trap (Step 3 in Figure 2.47). It then uses the trap number to find an entry in the dispatch table (Step 4 in Figure 2.47). The entry's contents determine the ROM location of the toolbox routine needed by the user (Step 5 in Figure 2.47).

Figure 2.47 Accessing a toolbox routine

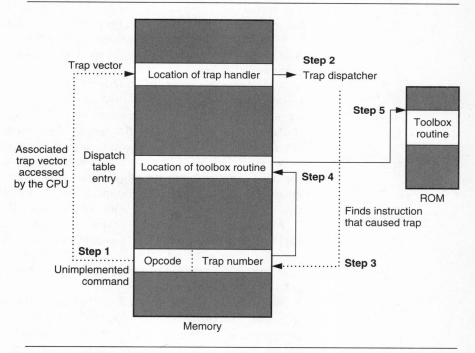

As you might expect, this discussion is incomplete. We have deleted details in the interest of simplicity. (See reference 13 for more thorough description.)

Screen and Sound Buffers

At the high end of memory are the *main screen buffer* and the *main sound buffer*. The main screen buffer contains the bits that define the screen image. The sound buffer defines the sounds that may be produced through the speakers.

System Globals and System Heap

The *system globals* region of memory contains global variables used by the system toolbox. It is reserved for the toolbox's private use. The *system heap* contains data structures needed for system use. They are not discussed further here.

User Memory

The remaining memory contains the *application heap*, the *stack*, and the *application global space*, used by application processes. We spend the rest of the section discussing this area in the context of a Pascal program.

Most of you have probably written programs in Pascal or similar language. As a result, you are familiar with the *scope* of variables. Typically, variables are either *global* or *local*.

A local variable is accessible only by the procedure in which it is declared (or by any locally declared procedures). Macintosh allocates space for local variables whenever a procedure is called. Similarly, when the procedure finishes, Macintosh releases the space. Thus, memory needs change as a program runs, calls various procedures, and returns from them.

A global variable is accessible by the main program and by any procedure compiled along with it. Since program execution begins and ends with the main program, Macintosh maintains the space required for global variables. As far as they are concerned, the program's memory needs are fixed.

When a compiled program is loaded into memory, global variables go in the application global space. Its size depends on the program, but remains fixed once the program enters memory. The application global space also contains other information needed to execute a program properly. For more details, see [13,14] at the end of this chapter.

Whenever a program calls a procedure or function, its memory needs increase. Macintosh creates space for the procedure's local variables, parameters, and return address. When the procedure finishes, these items are no longer needed. Thus, the space is released. Memory needs decrease as procedures and functions finish their tasks.

Macintosh releases the space used for these values in the reverse order in which it was allocated. This is because procedure returns occur in the reverse order of procedure calls. This part of the memory allocation is dynamic, and is implemented through a stack. The memory used corresponds to the *stack* in Figure 2.45. It grows and shrinks as the program runs.

Finally, as anyone who has programmed with dynamic data structures (linked lists or trees) knows, the program may request or release memory at any point during its execution. Space associated with such structures is in the *application heap*. Since these memory needs may grow and shrink arbitrarily, management of the application heap is complex.

Because of the arbitrary way in which Macintosh allocates and releases memory, the application heap can become fragmented. For example, consider the following Pascal code:

```
    :
    :
VAR
  A : ^SomeType1; {pointer to variable of type SomeType1}
  B : ^SomeType2; {pointer to variable of type SomeType2}
  C : ^SomeType3; {pointer to variable of type SomeType3}
  D : ^SomeType4; {pointer to variable of type SomeType4}
  E : ^SomeType5; {pointer to variable of type SomeType5}
    :
    :
Begin
    :
    :
  New(A);
  New(B);
  New(C);
  New(D);
  New(F);
    :
    :
```

In this program, variables A, B, C, D, and E are global pointers, and the program has requested memory space associated with each of them. Each "New" command requests a block of memory. Macintosh will store the block address in a memory location associated with the command's parameter. Since each pointer variable is declared differently, the blocks to which they point may differ in size.

Figure 2.48 shows a possible picture of memory after the CPU has executed all the "New" commands. The locations that contain the addresses are in the application global space. This is because we have declared the variables globally. The blocks to which they point are in the application heap.

Figure 2.48 Dynamically allocated memory

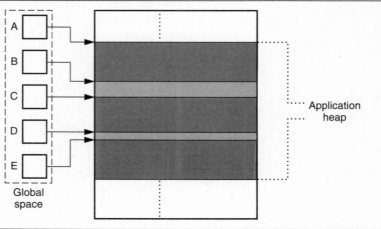

Now, at some point in the program logic, the programmer may decide that the space referenced by the addresses in B and D is no longer needed. That is, the programmer may code the commands

```
Dispose(B);
Dispose(D);
```

Thus, the contents of B and D are now considered undefined, and the space referenced by the addresses previously in them is released. Figure 2.49 shows what memory might look like now. As we see, the newly released memory may consist of blocks too small to be used later. This is very similar to the examples in Section 2.4.

Figure 2.49 Fragmented memory

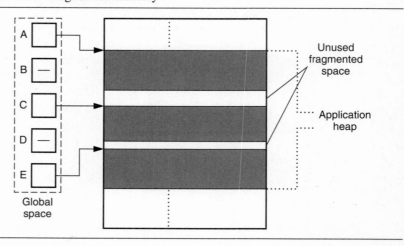

As a result, as the program requests new blocks of memory, the heap becomes larger. However, even if the program releases memory, the heap may not become smaller. Indeed, the application heap in Figure 2.49 is the same size as the one in Figure 2.48. The only difference is that the heap in Figure 2.49 contains unused "holes."

If the programmer had the "New" and "Dispose" commands in a loop, the heap would continue to grow until it ran up against the stack. At this point, the next "New" command would cause an error. The system would respond with a message such as

```
***Memory (system heap) full***
```

This is unfortunate because the heap is full of unused holes.

The solution to this problem is a toolbox routine that compacts allocated blocks. Again, this is similar to the compaction discussed in Section 2.4. Thus, if the system cannot allocate memory because the heap is fragmented, the toolbox routine will compact the blocks (see Figure 2.50).

Figure 2.50 Compacted memory

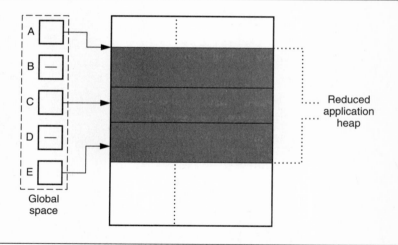

However, compaction leads to another problem. The toolbox routine compacts the blocks as shown in Figure 2.50, but it does not know the location of the pointers used to reference the blocks. As a result, the pointer variables are not changed and do not locate the beginning of the blocks (again, see Figure 2.50). The next memory reference via a pointer variable will be to the wrong location. The result, of course, is that the program references undefined data. And we all know the likely result of that!

≡ Handles

Macintosh has solved this problem through the use of *handles*. Instead of requesting a new *pointer* value, the user requests a new handle value. The toolbox routine allocates a block from the application heap, and creates a *master pointer*, also in the heap (see Figure 2.51). The master pointer points to the beginning of the allocated block. The variables A, B, C, D, and E are no longer pointers; they have become handles.

Figure 2.51 Dynamically allocated memory with handles

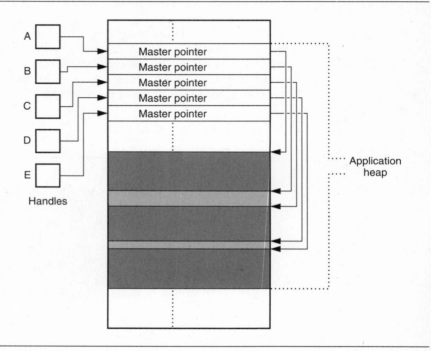

A handle contains the address of the master pointer. The user references each block using a double indirection. That is, the user references the handle, which references the master pointer, which in turn references the block. However, the double indirect reference takes extra time.

If the user releases the blocks associated with handles B and D, then memory is again fragmented as shown in Figure 2.52. The user handles are undefined, and the master pointers may be used for subsequent requests. But, the master pointers are never moved. So even though the ones associated with handles B and D are no longer needed, the other master pointers remain in the same locations.

Figure 2.52 Fragmented memory with handles

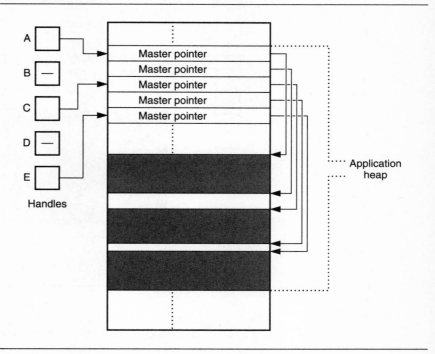

Now suppose the toolbox compacts the remaining blocks. Since it created the master pointers in the first place, it simply changes the addresses in them to correspond to the relocated blocks (Figure 2.53). A reference to any handle still locates the same master pointer; remember, it does not move. But, since the master pointer's value has changed, the reference is to the relocated blocks. The user need never know that relocation has occurred.

As a final note, we mention that the user can request blocks of nonrelocatable memory and store their addresses in pointers. This is a compromise between pointers as described here, and handles. Compaction will not affect the nonrelocatable blocks, only the relocatable blocks are moved. Because of this, however, compaction may not eliminate all fragmented segments. But the program can reference the blocks more quickly, since it needs only one level of indirection.

Figure 2.53 Compacted memory with handles

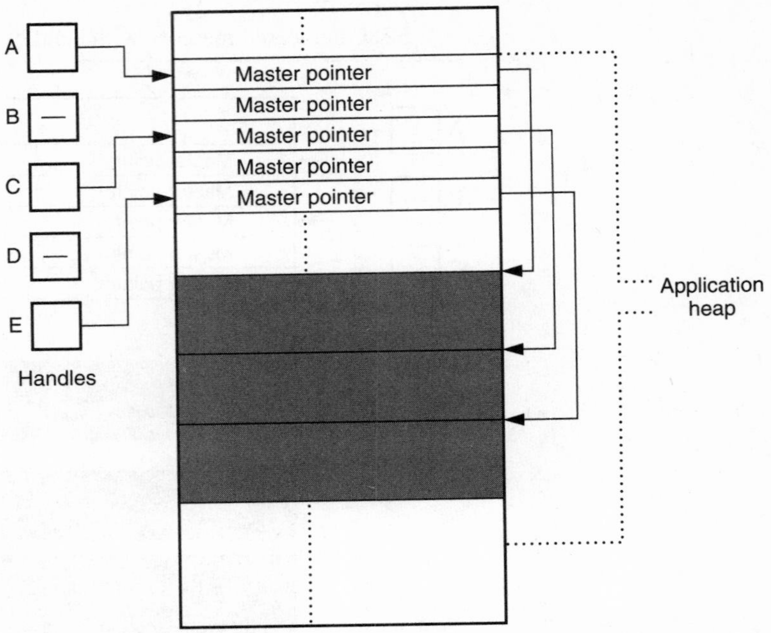

Nonrelocatable blocks are useful if the user does not expect to release many blocks as the program runs. In this case, fragmentation is not a serious problem, and there is no real need for handles. On the other hand, if the user expects to request and release blocks frequently, fragmentation becomes more serious. The problems caused by fragmentation may then be more costly than the use of handles. In this case, the use of handles would be justified.

Specifics on how to use toolbox routines to create handles and nonrelocatable blocks are in references [13,14].

2.13 SUMMARY

In this chapter we discussed the management of a computer's memory in systems ranging from small single–user, single–tasking ones to large multiuser ones. Some major questions in memory management are:

- Where should the system place the code for a process when it is ready to run?

- How does the system make sure that one process does not affect other processes or system routines?
- How does the system efficiently use all available memory?
- What does the system do with a process whose memory requirements exceed   its capacity?

   We described several approaches to memory management. In the simplest one, the system saw memory as fixed sized partitions. The system would then store the code for a process in a partition. Some problems with this were:

- Memory is wasted if the partition size is much larger than a process' needs. This is called fragmentation.
- Processes with memory needs that exceed each partition's size cannot run.

Basically, the underlying problem is that memory is configured in a way that anticipates the process' needs. This is often unrealistic: process' needs vary and are often constantly changing.

   One answer to the problem is to reconfigure memory as processes enter and leave the system. Variable partitioned memory is one such approach. The system creates a partition whenever a process enters. The advantage is that the partition's size matches the process' memory needs exactly. The disadvantage is that when processes (especially small ones) leave the system, the system must coalesce and compact memory periodically. We call this garbage collection. It is necessary to avoid having many small unusable partitions. Variable partitions also do not solve the problem of a process that needs more memory than the total available.

   We then observed that many memory problems are the result of requiring a process' code to reside in a contiguous block of memory. The next step was to break the code into pieces, called segments or pages. Generally, pages are all the same size, whereas segment sizes can vary. However, frequently a segment is a collection of pages.

   When a process is ready to run, the system stores some of its pages in available memory frames. The frames need not be contiguous. The remaining pages stay in secondary storage. If the process needs one of them, the system can retrieve it and store it in memory.

   Again, we had to overcome some problems, such as:

- Users believe that a process' code resides in virtual memory, a single block of contiguous memory locations. How can we bridge the gap between virtual memory and real memory? We called this dynamic address translation.
- When the system must retrieve new pages, what should it do with ones that are already in memory?

• Since code may be in many noncontiguous memory frames, how does the system protect itself and other processes?

The system can implement dynamic address translation and protection through segment and page tables. The system can maintain some of the information from these tables in associative registers. However, the tables can be large, and having many registers is expensive. Thus, a few registers may be used, with the remaining information in the tables. The CPU uses the instruction's virtual address to search the associative registers and, if necessary, the segment and page tables. The CPU then substitutes the real memory address for the virtual address. This happens during execution and is transparent to the user and running process.

Sometimes an instruction references a page or segment not in memory. We call this a segment fault or a page fault. The system must then locate the missing segment or page from the information in the segment or page table. Then the system reads it from secondary storage into memory.

Frequently, the system must limit the number of pages a process may have in memory. What happens if a process has the maximum number of pages in memory and a page fault occurs? In this case, the system must replace a page. The question is, "Which one?" We described several replacement schemes: optimal strategy, random replacement, FIFO, LRU, LFU, and NUR. They varied in effectiveness and implementation cost.

Another question was, "How big should the limit be?" If it is very large, a process occupies more memory than it really needs. The result is that fewer processes reside in memory and system performance suffers. On the other hand, if the limit is too small, a process generates frequent page faults. Again, system performance suffers.

The ideal is to store just enough pages in memory to allow a process to run for a while without generating too many page faults. We called those pages a process' working set. Research has established that well–organized processes tend to reference memory in localized patterns. As a result, they can run efficiently with small working sets. This allows more processes to occupy memory and thereby increases system performance.

Finally, we described memory management in a Macintosh computer. The discussion centered on dynamic memory allocation and relocatable blocks of memory. We saw that if the system allocates and releases memory, dynamically, small unusable "holes" can develop. To avoid this, Macintosh periodically compacts its memory.

A problem occurs when a program uses pointer variables. Variables contain addresses of dynamically allocated blocks, and if the system relocates the blocks, the addresses are no longer valid.

One way to solve this problem is to use handles instead of pointers. A handle points to a system master pointer. The master pointer in turn points to a dynamically allocated block of memory. If the system compacts memory, it also changes the contents of the master pointer. This way, the information is not lost; however, there is extra overhead since an extra memory reference is needed to reference data.

We have covered the essentials of memory management, but not all its aspects. The reader can benefit from consulting other operating systems textbooks (such as references [16–25]) that reinforce concepts described here or deal with memory management at a different level. The serious student should consult at least a few of these to broaden and strengthen his or her perspective.

══════════ **Exercises**

1. How would you declare Table 2.1 as an array of records in a high level language? Write the declaration and logic for a procedure that looks for, and allocates a given partition to a process.
2. Assume Table 2.1 is as described in exercise 1. Write the declaration and logic for a procedure that releases a partition when a specified process finishes.
3. Suppose the operating system has the following view of memory:

   - Memory consists of 800K words.
   - There are 6 partitions, numbered 1 through 6.
   - Partition 1 is 30K, partitions 2 through 4 are 60K each, partition 5 is 150K, and partition 6 is 250K.
   - The resident area is 100K.

   Sketch a diagram of the operating system's view of memory. What would the partition table look like? How big is the transient area?
4. Write the declaration and logic for a procedure that defines the values in registers Hi–Loc and Low–Loc when the process in partition number i assumes control of the CPU. Assume that the partition table (Table 2.2) is declared as an array of records.
5. Suppose that the entries from Table 2.4 are stored as a linked list of records and a new process enters the system. Write the declaration and logic for a procedure that

   - Searches the list looking for a free partition large enough to hold the new process.
   - Updates the free partition entry if the search is successful.
   - Creates an entry for the new allocated partition if the search is successful.
   - Returns an appropriate Boolean value if the search is not successful.

6. Suppose that Table 2.4 is stored as an array of records. Write the declaration and logic for a procedure that searches for entries associated with any two adjacent free partitions. Consider the possibility that two adjacent free partitions do not exist.
7. Suppose that two table entries are located via exercise 6. Write the declaration and logic for a procedure that replaces them with a single entry corresponding to the coalesced partition.

8. Assume an operating system uses a variable partition memory management scheme, and that allocated and free partitions for user memory are currently as shown below.

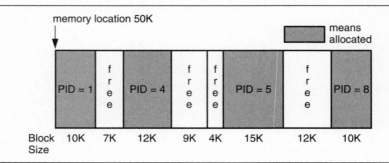

memory location 50K

means allocated

| PID = 1 | free | PID = 4 | free | free | PID = 5 | free | PID = 8 |

Block Size: 10K 7K 12K 9K 4K 15K 12K 10K

Suppose that the operating system uses a table like Table 2.4 to keep track of all partitions.

a) List the table's contents for the above view of memory.
b) How does the table in a) change if the operating system performs coalescing only? Show the new table.
c) How does the table in a) change if the operating system performs compaction only? Show the new table.
d) How does the table in a) change if the operating system performs compaction and then coalescing? Show the new table.

9. Suppose you have an operating system that supports virtual memory. Assume that there is a 100–page virtual memory space and 400 frames of underlying real memory. Every process runs in consecutive pages of virtual memory and always starts on virtual page 50. Suppose the page table is implemented by means of 100 CPU registers. Consider the following table which shows active processes and the frames that each process occupies.

Process ID	Frame Numbers in memory
42	232(D), 279(D),301(P), 329(D)
53	243(P), 261(P), 265(P), 299(D), 300(P), 351(P)

The "D" after a frame number indicates a data frame (i.e., modifiable). A "P" indicates a frame containing instructions (i.e., nonmodifiable). Show the page table entries (including access codes) when each process controls the CPU. Assume within a process' virtual space that all modifiable pages lie before all nonmodifiable pages.

10. Suppose a particular machine language instruction has a 17–bit address field. Suppose also that 8 bits contain the virtual page number. Therefore, the instruction may specify any of 256 virtual pages. Suppose now that memory consists of 4 megabytes of memory and that frames are 0.5K bytes in size. How many frames are there? How can we reference a frame above number 256?

11. Assume we have a segmented/paged memory with associative registers whose contents specify the frame number of a particular page in a particular segment. Suppose also that it takes 50 nanoseconds to search the associative registers. If the page table is normally held in memory and memory access time is 1 microsecond, what is the average amount of time it takes to reference a memory location? Assume that the processor finds the referenced page via the associative map 85% of the time.

12. Assume that a process may have a maximum of 3 pages in memory. Give a sequence of page requests that would make both FIFO and LRU strategies replace the same page on the first replacement. Give another sequence of requests that would make them replace different pages.

13. All things being equal, why do we prefer to replace an unmodified page rather than a modified one?

14. Suppose the following is the sequence of page numbers that a process references as it runs:

   1, 2, 3, 4, 2, 1, 5, 1, 2, 4, 4, 3, 5, 2, 1, 2, 1,

   If only 3 frames are available to the process, show what pages are in memory after each reference if the following strategies are used:

   LRU
   LFU
   FIFO
   optimal strategy

15. Consider the following code to clear an array with 50 rows and 50 columns.

```
For j := 1 to 50 do
    For i := 1 to 50 do
        A[i,j] := 0;
```

Suppose you are given the following:

- The rows are stored in contiguous blocks of memory and the elements in a row are stored in contiguous words.
- Memory consists of frames that hold 250 array elements each.
- Just 8 frames of memory may be allocated to array storage.
- Initially, no part of the array is in memory.

a) Suppose that as page faults occur, the system replaces pages on a FIFO basis. How many page faults does the above code cause?

b) Describe a page replacement strategy that would minimize the number of page faults caused by the above code. How many page faults occur with your strategy in effect?

16. Suppose a computer system has 4 MB (1 MB = 1 megabyte) of memory. The system manages it in fixed sized frames. A frame table maintains the status of each frame in memory. The question is, "How large (how many bytes) should a frame be?" The designers have decided that frame sizes can be only 1K, 5K, or 10K bytes.

4 Mbytes main memory

Which of these choices will minimize the total space unusable by processes due to fragmentation and frame table storage? Assume the following:

- On the average, ten processes will reside in memory. The average amount of unusable space will be 1/2 frame for each process.
- The frame table must have one entry for each frame. Assume that each entry requires 10 bytes.

17. Consider the following section of code:

```
Repeat
     DoSomething;
Until Done
```

Procedure "DoSomething" sequentially accesses the same 10 pages of virtual memory with each call. Suppose the process' working set allows at most 8 of the 10 pages to be in memory simultaneously. Also, suppose none of the 10 pages is in memory initially.

Page accesses by DoSomething

p.1   p.2   p.3   p.10

a) What is the relationship between the number of page faults and the number of calls to "DoSomething" when using the FIFO page replacement strategy? When using the LRU strategy?
b) Assuming these 10 pages are the only ones that can be replaced, describe a replacement strategy that performs better, in this case, than both FIFO and LRU.

18. Many systems allow two or more processes to share common memory. Suppose 1 frame of memory is shared by two processes, A and B. If their virtual memories does not overlap, how can they access the common page?

19. Can two processes reside in the same virtual memory and still share no frames?

══════ **Questions**

1. Consider Figure 2.8 in which the system maintains a single queue of processes for all partitions. Redesign it to show a system that maintains a queue for each partition. Can you think of a situation in which multiple queues are superior to a single queue?

2. A linker relocates the address fields of instructions that reference memory. This is necessary to make the address fields consistent with the process' memory space. Why does this not solve the problems caused by multiprogramming and thus eliminate the need for dynamic address translation?

3. Paging requires more complexity in an operating system. After all, the system must now contend with swapping pages between memory and disk. What are the advantages of storing part of a process' code in secondary storage? Are there situations in which these advantages do not exist?

4. Suppose **n** is the number of pages a process is allowed to have in memory. What happens if **n** is too large? If **n** is too small?

5. Two common paging methods are "demand paging" and "anticipatory paging." In the demand method, when a page fault occurs, only the requested page is read into memory. In the anticipatory method, nearby pages are read into memory also. Consider the discussions on locality and state why anticipatory paging might be sensible. What are its potential disadvantages?

6. Suppose you have responsibility for maximizing the utilization of computing resources for a large–scale multiuser system. Suppose also you are receiving complaints from most users about response and turnaround times. A call to operations reveals that the CPU is being utilized only 20% of the time. Which of the following could be reasons for the poor CPU utilization? Explain why for each that you choose and why not for the others:

   - insufficient memory.
   - frame size is too small.
   - frame size is too large.
   - too much memory.
   1 CPU is not enough.

7. Consider the graphs in Figure 2.43. Can you draw similar ones for B < A? What does this mean in determining a working set size?

8. Suppose you have the following Pascal program written for a Macintosh. Suppose also that the program was working fine for a while, then it started producing absurd results. That is, there has apparently been a loss of data in the linked list. What could have happened?

```
Type
   Link = ^Rectype;
   Rectype = Record
        :
        :
   field descriptions
        :
        :
   End;
```

```
              :
              :
              :
    Var
       First : Link;
              :
              :
              :

       While (some condition) Do
    Begin
       {This loop adds and deletes various records from a
       linked}
       {list beginning at the location specified by FIRST. The}
       {location in First points to a head node}
              :
              :
              :
              :
    End;
```

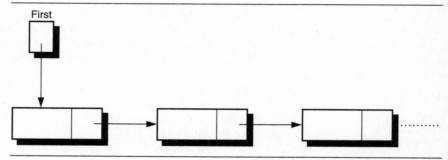

9. What are some advantages and disadvantages of small frames? Large frames?
10. What is wrong with the following declaration? Or is there anything wrong with it? Poorly–designed processes causes more page faults. But high–speed disk drives can find and read data very quickly (times measured in milliseconds). Because of this, additional page faults are just not that significant. After all, who is really going to notice additional milliseconds?
11. Suppose you are a systems programmer receiving complaints from users about poor system response. You suspect that a possible reason may be that the process' working sets are too small but you are not sure. List some questions you would ask the users and some system statistics you would record to help confirm or deny your suspicion.

12. Modify Phase I of the simulator in Appendix A so that paging is allowed. In other words, store only a subset of a process' pages (say 3 or 4) in memory. Then add a segment to the simulator which uses the random number generator to generate page faults. When a fault occurs, Phase I's operating system should replace a page arbitrarily. Make sure no faults occur when all a process' pages are in memory.

==== **References**

1. Gorsline, G. W. *Computer Organization: Hardware/Software*. 2nd ed. Englewood Cliffs, NJ: Prentice–Hall, 1986.
2. Tanenbaum, A. S. *Structured Computer Organization*. 3rd ed. Englewood Cliffs, NJ: Prentice–Hall, 1990.
3. Donovan, J. J. *Systems Programming*. New York: McGraw–Hill, 1972.
4. Beck, L. *System Software: An Introduction to Systems Programming*. Reading, MA: Addison-Wesley, 1985.
5. Brinch Hansen, P. *Operating Systems Principles*. Englewood Cliffs, NJ: Prentice-Hall, 1973.
6. Knuth, D. E. *The Art of Computer Programming*, Vol. 1. Reading, MA: Addison-Wesley, 1968.
7. Denning, P. J. "Virtual Memory." *Computing Surveys* 2, (Sept. 1970):153-189.
8. Bic, L. and A. C. Shaw. *The Logical Design Of Operating Systems*. 2nd ed. Englewood Cliffs, NJ: Prentice-Hall, 1988.
9. Belady, L. A., R. A. Nelson, and G. S. Shedler. "An Anomaly in Space-Time Characteristics of Certain Programs Running in a Paging Environment." *CACM* 12, (June 1969):349-353.
10. Denning, P. J. "The Working Set Model for Program Behavior." *CACM* 11 (May 1968):323-333.
11. ___. "Thrashing: Its Causes and Prevention." *AFIPS Conf. Proceedings* 33 (1968) FJCC:915-922.
12. Naur, P. "The Performance of a System for Automatic Segmentation of Programs Within an Algol Compiler (GIER) Algol." *CACM* 8, (Nov. 1965):671-677.
13. Chernicoff, C. *Macintosh Revealed Vol 1: Unlocking the Toolbox*. Hasbrouck Heights, NJ: Hayden, 1985.
14. ___. *Macintosh Revealed Vol 2: Programming with the Toolbox*. Hasbrouck Heights, NJ: Hayden, 1985.
15. *Turbo Pascal For the Mac. User's Guide and Reference Manual*. Scotts Valley, CA: Borland International, Inc. 1986.
16. Finkel, R. A. *An Operating Systems Vade Mecum*. 2nd ed. Englewood Cliffs, NJ: Prentice-Hall, 1988.
17. Milenkovic, M. *Operating Systems Concepts and Design*. New York: McGraw-Hill, 1987.
18. Deitel, H. M. *An Introduction to Operating Systems*. 2nd ed. Reading MA: Addison-Wesley, 1990.
19. Silberschatz, A., J. Peterson, and P. Galvin, *Operating Systems Concepts*. 3rd ed. Reading MA: Addison-Wesley, 1991.

20. Tanenbaum, A. S. *Modem Operating Systems: Design and Implementation*. Englewood Cliffs, NJ: Prentice-Hall, 1992.
21. Madnick, S. E. and J. J. Donovan. *Operating Systems*. New York: McGraw-Hill, 1974.
22. Lane, M. and J.D. Mooney. *A Practical Approach to Operating Systems*. Boston, MA: PWS-Kent, 1989.
23. Flynn, I.M. and A.M. McHoes. *Understanding Operating Systems*. Pacific Grove, CA: Brooks/Cole, 1991.
24. Davis, W. S. *Operating System: A Systematic View*. 3rd ed. Reading MA: Addison-Wesley, 1987.
25. Turner, R. W. *Operating Systems: Design and Implementations*. New York: Macmillan, 1986.

3

I/O
Processing

3.1 Basic I/O Facilities

How many programmers have ever written a program that reads data from a file or terminal, or writes it to a file or line printer? Your probable response is that most have; however, this is not likely. Commands such as Pascal's Readln or Writeln, or C's Printf and Scanf certainly seem to do I/O, but they do not. Compiled equivalents of them are actually requests that the operating system handle the I/O. Programmers rarely code their own I/O operations. In this chapter we address the following questions: Why don't programmers normally code their own I/O operations? What must the operating system actually do? How does it distinguish I/O to or from different devices?

Providing I/O facilities is one of an operating system's most complex and demanding tasks. Users want to be able to do I/O easily with simple, general commands, and not be concerned with the details of exactly what devices are available and how they work. The operating system must provide the interface between physical I/O and user-level (or logical) I/O.

Physical I/O is very complex in most cases. It does not just involve moving data from one place to another; it requires communication between two completely different electronic devices. This is not easy to achieve. For example, a disk drive is a very different device from memory. To make them exchange information requires complex hardware and software. In fact, there are even large differences among disk drives. Programmers do not normally want to worry about the differences between an 800K floppy disk and a 100 Mb hard disk. They simply want to be able to code a "Read" or "Write" command to transfer data.

I/O Speed

Another complicating factor is that CPUs and other devices work at vastly different speeds. Imagine trying to establish communications between devices when one can "talk" a thousand or a million times faster than the other can "listen." Imagine listening to a recorded lecture played at a thousand times the normal speed.

I/O speeds have increased but so have processor speeds and there is still a large disparity between the two. The CPU and memory are electronic devices. Their speeds depend on electronic clocks, electronic switching circuits, and the speed of electronic signals.

Secondary storage devices often depend on mechanical movements to find and transfer information. Tapes mounted on reels must move past read/write heads. Disks rotate at high rates of speed, and read/write heads must move to different areas. The physical limitations of mechanical operations do not permit data access at electronic speeds.

As a result, a process using the CPU can execute thousands or even millions of instructions in the time it takes to obtain a single piece of information from a secondary storage device. Many could run to completion during this time. In the days of the ENIAC, all the computer's resources were devoted to one process at a time. The execution of a process was a new and unique concept. There were not many applications around.

Figure 3.1 shows a common organization for old computers. One processor handled all aspects of process execution. Even in new systems, if there is just one process, the architecture shown in Figure 3.1 is probably satisfactory. But, as the number of processes grows, the processor becomes overworked, and cannot handle everything.

Figure 3.1 One processor handling all activities

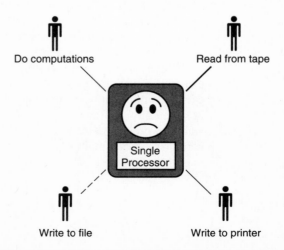

Multiple Process Systems

Many of today's computer systems run multiple processes. If one process requests I/O, there are plenty of others waiting for a chance to run. Imagine the delays if a process monopolizes the CPU getting its own data from a disk or tape file! Many others would be unable to make progress because one process needed something from an external file. Imagine the overall effect if the process needed many records.

Some computer systems use separate processors to do I/O. Figure 3.2 shows an organization in which two processors perform specific operations. When a process needs information from a file, it will ask the secondary processor to obtain it. Meanwhile, this frees CPU for other processes to use. The secondary processor then retrieves the necessary information. At the same time, other processes make progress. Of course the two processors must communicate so each knows what the other is doing.

Figure 3.2 Cooperating processors

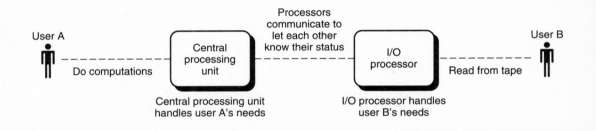

But what does this have to do with operating systems? If they are to manage processes and allow them to run safely and efficiently, they must have the answers to many questions, such as:

- How do the two processors communicate?
- Can the secondary processor handle many I/O devices? If so, how does it keep the information separate?
- How do we handle the speed differential between processors and devices such as disk and tape drives?
- Are two processors enough? If there are more, how should we organize them?

Overview

This chapter discusses several ways of handling I/O activities. Section 3.2 describes some common I/O devices, particularly disk drives and tape drives. It also describes the controllers often used to communicate with them. We will show where the CPU, controllers, and I/O devices fit in a computer system.

Section 3.3 introduces the device driver, an integral part of an operating system. The device driver is software that deals with device specifics. This section also discusses the difference between device-independent and device-dependent parts of I/O activities.

The next three sections discuss different ways of doing I/O operations. Section 3.4 discusses programmed I/O and memory mapped I/O. The approaches are useful in small single-tasking systems and with slow devices.

Section 3.5 discusses interrupt driven I/O, which shares common features with programmed I/O, but removes some of the burden from the CPU. Like programmed I/O, interrupt driven I/O is useful with slow devices.

Section 3.6 discusses Direct Memory Access (DMA). We find that methods suited to slow devices may be inappropriate for fast ones. The concepts of DMA and cycle stealing are introduced. Finally, this section expands on the ideas developed in Sections 3.4 and 3.5 and describes a system with many I/O devices and many controllers. Buffering, multiplexing, and spooling are introduced.

Section 3.7 discusses I/O programming for a DEC VAX running the VMS operating system.

3.2 I/O Devices and Controllers

This section describes some devices (magnetic tapes and disks) used to store files. It also describes other devices that control their operations and how they may be connected. Having a basic understanding of how they operate will help as we describe controlling I/O activities.

Magnetic Tapes

It is hard to imagine anyone being unfamiliar with magnetic tapes. Performers record songs on them, and they are readily available in any music store or department store. Tapes are commonplace items in VCRs and home and car stereo systems. The read/write heads in a tape player sense the signals recorded on the tape's iron oxide surface. The electronics then reproduce music through the speakers.

Tapes used in computer systems are essentially the same as ones used for music. Personal computers can store information on cassettes. Personal computers with high capacity hard disks often use tapes for backups. Larger computers can store information on larger, wider tapes that are mounted on large reels.

Figure 3.3 shows how a tape stores information. It has magnetized "spots" on the iron oxide surface. Their positions along the width of a tape correspond to a binary code for representing information. One row of spots may, for example, correspond to a single character.

Figure 3.3 Magnetic tape

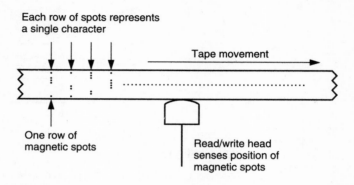

The tape, mounted on a reel or in a cassette, moves past a read/write head. It will either sense the positions of the spots or create new ones. This depends on whether it is reading the tape or writing onto it. A single inch of tape may contain thousands of magnetic spots. Precisely how many spots varies with the hardware used to record and sense data. Densities of 800, 1600, and 6250 BPI (Bytes Per Inch) are common. Rows of spots are combined to form physical records or blocks. (Chapter 6 explores how they relate to the data needs of a process in more detail.)

A reel of tape is mounted on a tape drive. It houses the electronics and mechanisms needed to move the tape and sense the spots. As it causes the reel to rotate, the tape moves past the read/write heads and onto another reel. The drive must generate commands that start, stop, move, and rewind the tape as well as transfer information to and from it. Figure 3.4 is a simplified illustration of a tape drive.

Figure 3.4 Tape drive

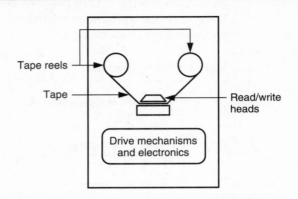

Magnetic Disks

A magnetic disk is a round platter. One or both surfaces are covered with the same iron oxide material that coats a magnetic tape. Each surface is logically divided into concentric circles called *tracks*. They are numbered from 0 through **n**—1, where **n** is device-dependent.

Each track, in turn, is logically divided into sections called *sectors* (Figure 3.5). Within a track, sectors are numbered from 0 through **m**—1, where **m** is also device-dependent.

Figure 3.5 Magnetic disk

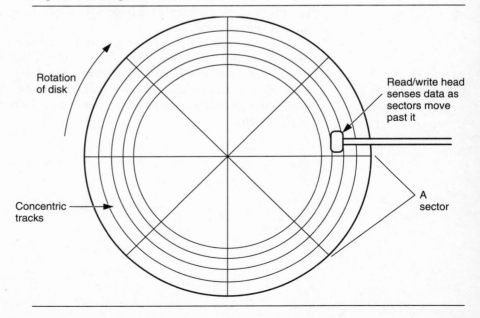

Larger systems have several disks mounted on a spindle to form a *disk pack* (Figure 3.6). The surface of each disk is as previously described. For brevity we will refer to a disk pack even if it contains only one disk.

Figure 3.6 Disk pack

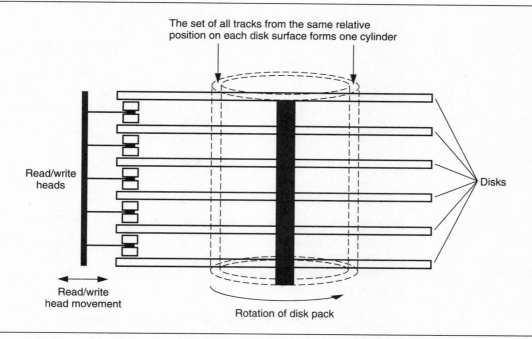

The set of all tracks from the same relative position on each disk surface forms one cylinder

Read/write heads

Disks

Read/write head movement

Rotation of disk pack

A *cylinder* is another logical unit of a disk pack (Figure 3.6). It consists of all tracks from the same relative position across all disk surfaces. The number of cylinders is equal to the number of tracks on a surface. Therefore, cylinders may also be numbered from 0 through $n-1$. Furthermore, if there are k disk surfaces, the tracks within one cylinder may be numbered from 0 through $k-1$.

Typically, a file occupies many sectors. (Chapter 6 discusses file structures and accessibility.) We will assume here that the system stores information on a sector in the same way as on tape. That is, the heads create magnetic spots on the iron oxide coating. The arrangement of spots corresponds to a binary code for information.

Accessing a Disk. There is one major distinction between tapes and disks. A tape drive can access a section of tape only by reading previous sections or "fast forwarding" past them. However, a disk drive can access a sector almost immediately. We can very quickly locate any sector within a disk pack if we know the cylinder number, track number within the cylinder, and sector number within the track.

Locating a Sector. The disks are mounted on a spindle that rotates at high speed inside a *disk drive*, the device that contains the disk pack. The disk drive typically has one read/write head for each surface (Figure 3.6). (Some sophisticated and expensive drives have a head for each track; we will not discuss them here.) The read/write heads are connected to a mechanical arm that moves in and out. By moving the arm, the drive can move a head to a specified cylinder. The track number within the cylinder then determines which head the drive must select to transfer information. As the disk rotates, the specified sector will eventually move past the selected head. When this occurs, the drive can finally transfer the data. Thus, the disk drive must contain the electronics and mechanisms necessary to perform many tasks, including:

- Rotate the disk pack at a constant speed.
- Move the read/write head to a specific cylinder.
- Select a head associated with a track within a cylinder.
- Sense when a particular sector is about to rotate past the head.

However, a programmer who wants to read data from a disk, would prefer just to issue a command such as:

```
READ(file, variables)
```

Somehow, the system must translate this single command into a series of commands that locates the data and controls the electronics and mechanisms of a drive. Obviously, putting all this detail in a high-level language program would be difficult and time consuming.

≡

Buses

Since I/O depends on several components, let us next consider how to connect them. Figure 3.7 shows a possible computer system organization. The major components are the CPU, memory, and external devices such as terminals, disk drives, or printers. Note the figure shows another device called a controller, which will be described shortly.

Components may communicate using a *common bus*, or a set of parallel lines capable of transmitting many bits simultaneously. The number of data bits is often a byte or a word and is system-dependent.

Figure 3.7 Communication among CPU, memory, and devices via a common bus

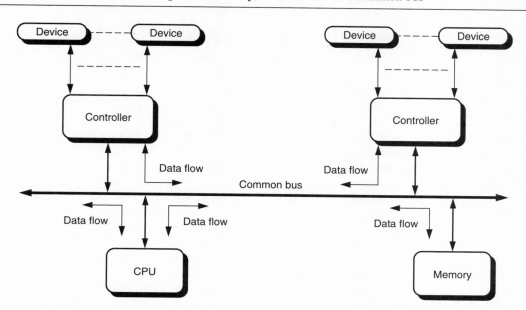

When a component wants to communicate, it signals the bus. Interface circuits (not shown in Figure 3.7) sense whether the bus is available. If one component is transmitting, the interface circuits force other components to wait.

The transmission typically includes data bits, address bits, and control bits. The address bits determine the destination and the control bits manage the transfer. We can think of the common bus as consisting of a data bus, an address bus, and a control bus. Enabling circuits sense the address bits and identify information destined for a particular component. The interfacing circuits then pick up the actual signals.

Many different bus architectures exist, and several texts describe them in detail. (The interested reader should consult references [1-3].)

Controllers

External devices such as terminals, disk drives, or keyboards are usually not connected directly to the bus. Instead, they are connected through *device controllers*. Controllers often can communicate with several devices. They can transfer data to devices and delay operations until devices are ready.

Why is a controller necessary? One reason is to simplify system architecture. If devices communicate directly with the bus, each one needs interface circuits. In practice, for example, we cannot connect a terminal line to a bus with an electrician's "twist connector." It is a slightly more complex job. The interface must sense address bits and determine if a device is busy or not operational. After all, we do not want to send data to a device that is not ready to receive it. Interface circuits can be quite complex.

Now with slow devices such as terminals or printers, relatively little data is transferred. As a result, many interface circuits would be often idle. But, this is not economical. Grouping terminals and using a single controller to communicate with them is less expensive. Since terminals are very slow, a controller can easily handle several of them. Furthermore, we now need only one bus interface.

Another reason to have a controller is to reduce redundancy in electronic components. For example, tape or disk drives must have circuits that move the heads and start and stop tapes. If there are several drives, then these circuits are repeated. An alternative is to put the circuits in a controller and share them among several drives. But is this practical? Yes, because a controller can issue commands to move a head or start a tape much faster than a device can respond. If it had just one device attached, the controller would spend most of its time waiting. With several attached, it has more to do. This is a more efficient use of equipment.

Since the controller contains much of the electronics, the devices can be simpler. They can merely contain the circuits and mechanisms necessary to respond to controller signals.

As a final note, we mention that controllers vary greatly. Some are "dumb," and can only issue simple commands to control basic device movements. Others are "intelligent." Some can actually schedule I/O requests and complete tasks such as data blocking, error detection and correction, and optimization of I/O requests. In some cases, new design technologies put these functions directly into VLSI devices such as disk, tape, or CRT controller chips.

≡ 3.3 Device Drivers

Writing software to control devices requires a lot of detail. The programmer must understand the device's technical specifications. This usually requires careful study of the device's technical manuals. But most programmers do not want to do this, nor should they have to.

≡ Logical Devices

A device's technical specifications are not the only problems to address. For example, what happens if new devices are added to the controller? Must all software be rewritten? What happens when a process that normally writes to a disk drive must write instead to a printer or tape? Must we change the code and recompile it? Most programmers want to take a simplified approach to I/O. They want their programs to handle I/O flexibly and easily.

For example, the following Pascal fragment writes a value **X** to Datafile:

```
Program Test(Input, Output, Datafile);
:
:
Var
 Datafile : SomeFileType;
:
:
Begin
:
:
 Writeln(Datafile, X);
:
:
End.
```

Depending on the system, "Datafile" may actually correspond to a file, a line printer, RAM disk, or even the terminal. The Pascal program does not know or care what device the operating system eventually associates with "Datafile." The program is, therefore, *device-independent*.

The term "Datafile" actually represents a *logical device*. The programmer simply writes to it without concern for its specific characteristics. If the device is a disk file, the programmer need not worry about such details as the number of tracks, sectors, or cylinders. If the device is a line printer, the programmer need not worry about spooling (discussed in Section 3.6). However, it is obvious that some component must worry about the details.

The operating system software that does this is called a *device driver*. It drives, or issues the proper commands to activate a device. The device driver knows all the characteristics of a device necessary to read from or write to the device.

Device drivers are sometimes part of the operating system's kernel or nucleus, the most frequently used part of an operating system. They are resident in memory and are not swapped out as some less frequently used components may be. Sometimes drivers exist as installable routines. When new devices are added, new drivers are too. This approach also allows programmers to write their own drivers and install them when the system is booted. This is useful for systems programmers who want to alter driver software to suit their particular needs. Typically, the operating system maintains a table in which each entry corresponds to a driver. For example, each entry contains the device name, location of driver code, and device attributes. The next question is, "How do drivers fit into the overall scheme of I/O processing?"

Levels of I/O Processing

In general, I/O processing has several levels, illustrated in Figure 3.8. At the highest level is the running process. It contains machine code associated with programmer written READ or WRITE commands. The code does not perform I/O, but it requests it. The next level contains *device-independent* routines. They perform tasks that must be done regardless of the devices accessed. The third level is the *device-dependent* (driver) software which interacts with actual hardware at the fourth level.

Defining several levels like this has a major advantage. User processes and device-independent routines need not be changed when new devices are installed. This, of course, simplifies a computer's ability to expand to take advantage of new technologies.

Figure 3.8 Levels of I/O processing

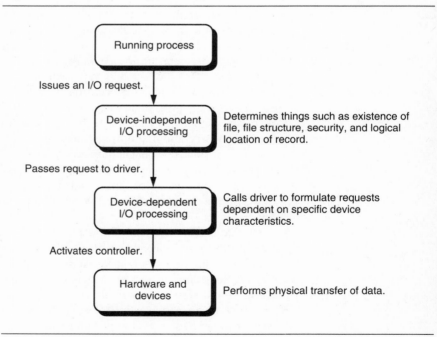

Device-Independent Level. When a running process issues an I/O request, the operating system assumes control of the CPU. Device-independent routines run which examine and begin processing the request. They do several things. For example, they may check whether the process has legitimate access to the requested file or device. If the logical device is a file, they must determine whether it exists and what its structure is. They must determine whether the operation makes sense. (The operating system should not normally allow reading from a line printer or writing to an optical scanner.) Many of these activities involve examining the system and file directories (to be discussed in Chapter 6). Finally, they must format I/O parameters for driver use and pass control to it. Parameters include:

- Memory address to transfer data from (or to).
- Number of bytes to transfer.
- Type of operation.
- Logical device address.
- Device type and name.

Device-Dependent Level. Drivers do the functions appropriate for the particular device. Specifically, what do they do? How do they work? What data structures do they contain?

These are difficult questions because a driver's functions are highly system-dependent. Many driver functions lately are being moved into controller hardware. More intelligent controllers can assume many of the driver's responsibilities. Less expensive computers retain these functions in software. We will discuss some activities of device drivers, but the reader should be aware that the functions may be part of the operating system, a device controller, or a combination.

Driver Functions

Device drivers commonly have two major responsibilities. First, they must prepare for I/O. This requires checking the device status and allocating it, and then initiating the data transfer. The second responsibility is cleanup after the I/O operation. This requires checking the status of the operation (finished or aborted) and responding accordingly. A description of some of the driver functions follows.

Disk Address Calculation (Disk Driver). Computes the exact disk location for a read or write command. Normally, an operating system directory will specify a logical disk address. (We will talk about directories in more detail in Chapter 6.) The important thing here is that the directory indicates the location of a disk sector using a *relative sector number*.

What is a relative sector number? All sectors on a device may be numbered sequentially starting with zero. This makes the directory independent of the disk format (number of sectors per track or number of cylinders per device). Then, if a new drive is installed, the system directories need not necessarily be updated. But the driver must be updated.

In Section 3.2 we saw that to read a sector, the controller must know the cylinder number, relative track number, and relative sector number. These three quantities uniquely determine the disk's relative sector number. If there are **k** tracks per cylinder, and **m** sectors per track, the logical sector number is given by

$$\text{Logical sector number} = \text{cylinder number} * \mathbf{k} * \mathbf{m}$$
$$+ \text{ relative track number} * \mathbf{m}$$
$$+ \text{ relative sector number}$$

When a process wants to read from a file, the operating system must search a directory to find the logical sector number. Since the driver knows the disk characteristics, it can calculate the exact location from that number. It can then give this information to the controller.

Device I/O Scheduling. In general, running processes may generate requests faster than controllers can handle them. In such cases, the list of requests for each device begins to grow. The driver must keep track of them for eventual scheduling. In some cases, the driver may schedule them to optimize disk head movement. (We will discuss disk scheduling in Chapter 6.)

Device Status Check. If a device is not operating, the driver should not direct the controller to access it. Flags describe a device's status.

Transmission Error Check (and Sometimes Correction). Sometimes electrical noise or faulty connections can cause transmission errors. Noise can switch a "0" to a "1" or vice versa. There are algorithms that check transmitted data for errors. Some can also correct the errors.

Error detection and correction techniques vary. Simple *parity bits* can detect errors. More sophisticated techniques such as *Hamming codes* can also correct them. (Discussions of such techniques fall outside the scope of this book; the interested reader should consult references such as [8, 9, 15].)

Creation of Device-Specific Commands. The controller responds to commands the driver sends it. Running processes are unfamiliar with device characteristics and do not know the proper commands. The driver will accept a request from a running process and create commands for the controller. For disk drives, these commands typically involve moving the heads to a cylinder, selecting the correct head, and waiting for the proper sector to rotate past it. For tape drives, they involve fast forwarding, rewinding, starting, and stopping the tape.

Bad Block Determination (Disk Drivers). Normally, a new disk is tested before being put into use. If some sectors are scratched or otherwise damaged, they should not be allocated. If a bad block is detected, the driver records the information. If the operating system tries to allocate the sector, the driver can use another in its place.

Idle Check. If a driver intends to activate a device for I/O, it should ensure that the device is not currently busy. If it is busy, the driver must wait. When the device is available, the driver can instruct the controller to activate it again.

Data Buffering. Data, whether from slow devices such as terminals or fast devices such as disk drives, is often buffered. Programmers often enter commands faster than the operating system can respond, and as a result, often type several commands ahead. In such cases, the commands must be stored temporarily in buffers until the operating system can respond. Processes that request data from a disk file are often swapped out of memory while they wait. The retrieved data must be stored temporarily in buffers until the process is swapped back in.

Control Command Interpretation (Terminal Drivers). Programmers are not professional typists, and make many mistakes. But the mistakes can be corrected by entering certain commands to erase previously typed characters or entire lines. The driver must interpret them and delete characters as necessary.

Echo Print (Terminal Drivers). When drivers receive characters entered from a terminal, they often send them back to the terminal for display. This is called *echo printing*, and allows a programmer to see what he or she types. Also, echo printing may be suppressed to protect typed information such as passwords.

Device Interrupt Servicing. When a device finishes transferring data, or encounters an error, it may notify the CPU via an interrupt (discussed in Section 3.5). Interrupt routines respond and notify the necessary driver. The driver must then determine how the I/O operation completed. For example, was it successful, or did it abort for some reason? Status flags provided by the controller provide this information.

Because many things can go wrong when transferring data, responding to errors can be complex. For example, if a printer is out of paper, turned off, or stolen write operations cannot be done. The driver then reports that an error has occurred and waits for someone to correct the problem.

In other cases, the driver may actually detect a transmission error. When this happens, a common response is to attempt another transmission. If the error was caused by extraneous electrical noise, a retransmission may be all that is necessary. However, the error may also be caused by a faulty medium (e.g., a bad sector on a disk). Usually, several retransmissions are tried. If they are all unsuccessful, a faulty medium is suspected and reported to the user. Other examples of errors include:

- Write to a write-protected disk.
- Invalid sector reference.
- End-of-tape reached.
- Printer is off-line.
- Device is not ready.

Summary of I/O activities

Figure 3.9 summarizes the I/O activities. A process makes an I/O request and normally enters a dormant state, meaning it ceases its activities temporarily. A device-independent routine responds and performs activities unrelated to a specific device. It formats I/O parameters and calls a driver. The driver checks the device's status, performs device-dependent activities, and if possible, initiates the data transfer. Upon completion of the transfer or error, a device interrupt activates an interrupt handler which calls on the appropriate driver. The driver checks the status of the I/O operation and passes the information to the operating system. The operating system then informs the process. If the operation was successful, the operating system resumes the process. If not, the process' next activity depends on its ability to respond to abnormal conditions and the reason the operation was not successful.

Several unanswered questions still remain. How does the driver actually initiate I/O? How does it check status of an operation? What does it do with the data? The answers to these questions depend very much on the system. The next three sections discuss ways to perform physical I/O.

Figure 3.9 Device driver's role in I/O operation

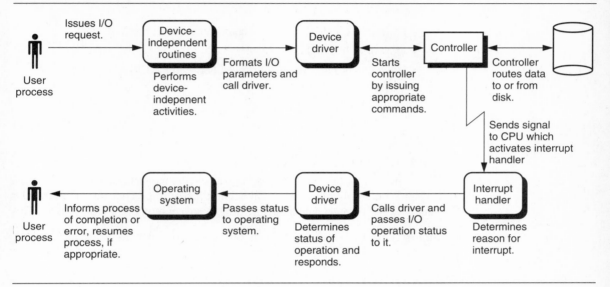

〓〓〓 3.4 Programmed I/O

This section describes physical I/O for slow devices such as line printers, terminals, and keyboards. You may not think of a line printer or a video terminal as a slow device. But compared to disk drives, they are slow. A video terminal's ability to print several hundred characters per second pales in comparison to a disk drive's ability to transfer a hundred thousand characters in the same time.

One approach to physical I/O is *programmed I/O*. In programmed I/O, data is transferred one character at a time, the usual approach for terminals, keyboards, and many printers. Let's suppose that a running process wants to print a character. With programmed I/O, the driver signals the controller that it should write a character. It then sends the character to the controller. The controller, in turn, sends the character to the appropriate device. Reading a character works almost in reverse. The driver signals the controller to read a character. The driver waits until the character arrives and then transfers it to the waiting process.

The term programmed I/O reflects the fact that a driver, running on the CPU, must transfer a character to or from the controller. The driver executes commands to communicate with the controller, and as we will see, waits for the operation to finish. The observant reader may well ask a few questions beyond a general description of programmed I/O. For example:

- How does the driver send the character to the controller?
- How does it signal the controller?
- What about the difference in speed between the CPU and the device, especially if the driver is going to send many characters to the controller?

Controller Registers

To see how programmed I/O works and answer some of the questions, we must examine a controller in more detail (Figure 3.10). If the controller is to transfer data between memory and a device, it must have a temporary storage area. This

Figure 3.10 Device controller with buffer and control/status registers

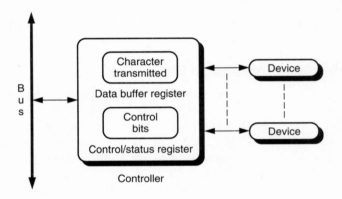

is the *data buffer register* in Figure 3.10.

The controller must also keep track of the type of operation (read or write), its status (completed or uncompleted), and the device involved. For example, the controller must know if the device is busy or inactive. The controller should not send a character to a device that is disconnected, malfunctioning, or turned off.

To maintain such information, the device controller also contains a *control/status register*. Figure 3.11 shows an example register. It shows three one-bit flags. If the READ flag is 1, the controller must read a character from the device and store it in the data buffer register. If the WRITE flag is 1, the controller must write the character in the buffer register to the device. The flags act like on/off switches. Setting a flag to 1 turns the controller on making it start some activity. Finally, if the OPERATION COMPLETE flag is 1, the read or write operation has finished. Zero values have the opposite meanings.

Figure 3.11 Example control/status register

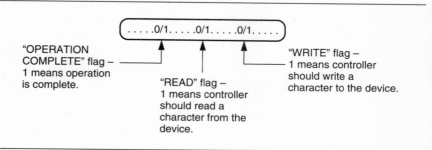

Although a controller can handle several devices, we will assume in this section that it is handling only one. We can then concentrate on issues specific to programmed I/O. We will consider multiple devices in Section 3.6.

Memory-Mapped I/O

Let's consider the first question. How does a driver access a controller register? Well, one way is through *memory-mapped* I/O. Figure 3.12 shows what this means.

Figure 3.12 Memory-mapped I/O

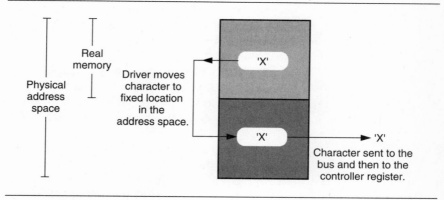

The controller registers are assigned fixed locations within the computer's address space. Note that the address space need not be the same as real memory. The address space is the set of values that may be transmitted on the address bus. There need not be a real memory cell for every address. Indeed, in this case, a reference to an assigned address is transmitted, via the bus, to a controller register and not to a real memory cell. As far as the process is concerned, it is referencing memory. It does not know the references are being routed to a controller instead.

The interesting feature is that a driver can define controller registers simply by moving a character to a fixed memory location. Similarly, it can sense status simply by accessing a fixed memory location. Thus, no special instructions are required to initiate controller actions. To the driver, it is just referencing memory. Bus architecture translates the reference to the controller.

Therefore, to write a character, the driver references the address assigned to the control/status register and sets the WRITE flag to 1. It then moves the character to the address assigned to the data buffer register. If the data is successfully transferred, the OPERATION COMPLETE flag in the control/status register is set to 1.

To read a character we basically reverse the steps. The driver indicates that it wants to read a character by setting the READ flag to 1 in the control/status register. Once the READ flag is set, the controller senses it, reads a character from the device, and stores it in the data buffer register. When the data is transferred, the OPERATION COMPLETE flag is set to 1. The driver can check it by examining the appropriate location. It can then move the character from the data buffer register to memory.

This is an advantage over systems that require special I/O instructions, since it simplifies the I/O process. Drivers reference devices the same way they reference memory. There is also a disadvantage, however. Where they exist, special I/O instructions are usually privileged; that is, they can be executed only by operating system routines (or any with a high enough priority). This provides a level of protection the memory-mapped systems do not have. They must protect the devices by placing the associated locations in a protected part of the address space.

It is surely time for an example. Suppose a driver wants to write a character, X (from location **m**). Suppose location **d** is the data buffer register and location **d**+1 the control/status register. The following pseudocoded program (See Figure 3.13) shows how the process writes X.

```
      Move contents of location m to location d.
      Set WRITE flag in location d+1 to 1.
LOOP: Move contents of location d+1 to a CPU register.
      Test the OPERATION COMPLETE flag in the register.
      If flag is 0, branch to LOOP: {WRITE operation is not
        complete}
      ...next instruction... {WRITE operation is complete}
```

Figure 3.13 Writing character X using memory mapped I/O

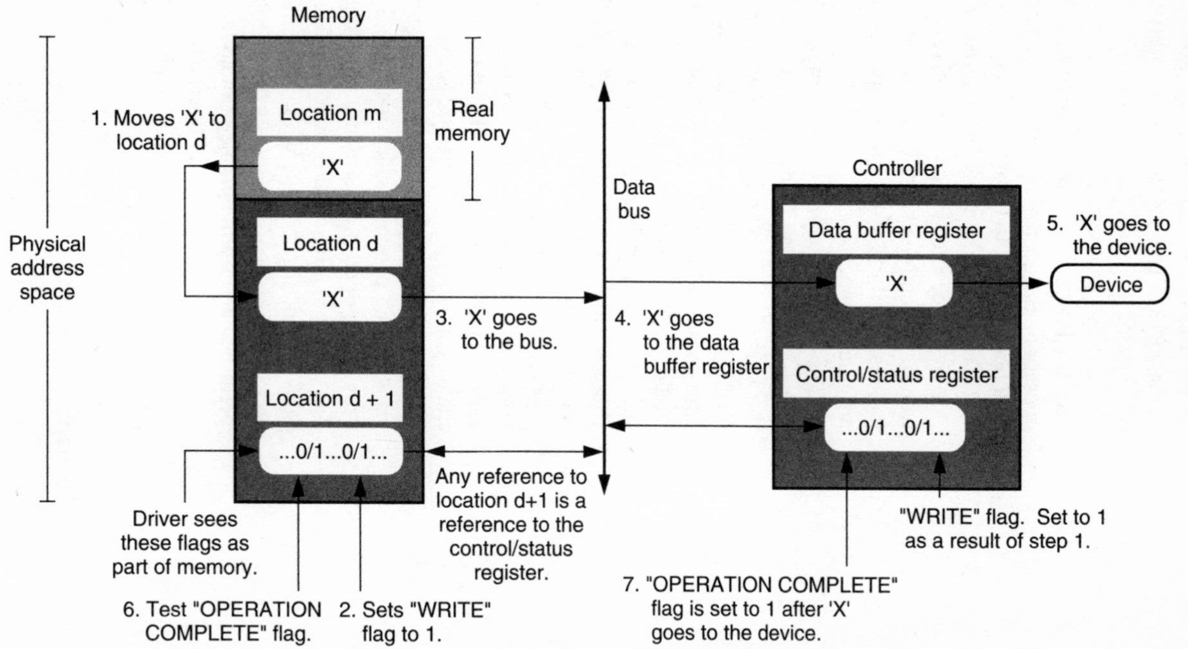

Physical address space

Memory

Real memory

Location m
'X'

Location d
'X'

Location d + 1
...0/1...0/1...

Driver sees these flags as part of memory.

1. Moves 'X' to location d

6. Test "OPERATION COMPLETE" flag.

2. Sets "WRITE" flag to 1.

Any reference to location d+1 is a reference to the control/status register.

3. 'X' goes to the bus.

Data bus

4. 'X' goes to the data buffer register

Controller

Data buffer register
'X'

Control/status register
...0/1....0/1...

5. 'X' goes to the device.

Device

"WRITE" flag. Set to 1 as a result of step 1.

7. "OPERATION COMPLETE" flag is set to 1 after 'X' goes to the device.

The first command moves the contents of location **m** to location **d** (step 1 in Figure 3.13). The second command moves a 1 to the WRITE flag in location **d**+1 (step 2). Because references to location **d**+1 are routed to the control/status register, this sets the WRITE flag in it to 1. From the driver's viewpoint, it has just moved the character X from one memory location to another, a common operation. But in reality, the character has been moved out of memory via the data bus (step 3), to the data buffer register (step 4). Since the controller sees the WRITE flag as 1, it writes the character to the device (step 5).

Now since the device is relatively slow, the driver must wait. We do not want it to continue since it might move another character to the same buffer. If it does this before the previous character has been written, it destroys the previous character.

The third through fifth commands force the driver to wait. The third one moves the contents of **d**+1 (the control/status register) to a CPU register where the driver can examine it. The fourth command tests the OPERATION COMPLETE flag (step 6). If the flag is 0, the operation is not complete. The fifth command will then branch to LOOP.

The driver keeps executing the loop until the OPERATION COMPLETE flag is 1. We call this a *busy-waiting* loop. The controller sets this flag when the character has been written (step 7). At this point, the operation is complete, and it goes on to the next command.

Perhaps the biggest drawback of this I/O method is that the driver must continually test a flag. After issuing a READ or WRITE, it enters a loop that repeats until a flag is set. This monopolizes the CPU for status checking, thus making it unavailable for other activities.

In single-tasking systems, this is no problem. However, it is unacceptable when other processes are waiting. The driver waiting for I/O to finish is preventing other processes from making progress. It is like making a call from a pay phone to a line that is busy and you keep dialing until you no longer get the busy signal. If no one is waiting for the phone you waste only your own time. But, if there many people waiting for the phone, they are likely to become perturbed and tip the phone booth over. The phone becomes inoperative, no one makes his or her call, and Superman has lost his changing room.

The next section describes an alternative approach to busy-waiting.

≣ 3.5 Interrupt Driven I/O

It is awkward to force a driver to examine the control/status register repeatedly to determine when the I/O is complete. It is as unproductive as determining whether someone is calling on the telephone by picking up the receiver every once in a while and listening. This is a useful approach only if you want to snoop on an old-fashioned party line. Clearly, a more sensible approach is to wait for the phone to ring.

Why not use the same concept in programmed I/O? Why should the driver have to examine the control/status register repeatedly? Can the controller simply inform or *interrupt* the CPU when it finishes the I/O operation?

This section focuses on *interrupt-driven I/O*. The driver starts the operation as it did in the last section; however, now it does not check the control/status register. Instead, it waits, freeing the CPU to do other work. When the I/O operation is finished, the controller sends a signal to the CPU that interrupts it. An interrupt handling routine responds which calls the driver back into action. The important concept is that while the driver waits, another process, if available, can make progress.

Figures 3.14a and 3.14b show how both programmed I/O and interrupt driven I/O proceed. These figures assume that a process is writing a character. In Figure 3.14 (a), the driver starts the controller and moves the character to the data buffer register (time t_1). Between t_1 and t_2, two activities occur. The controller writes the character, and the driver persistently asks the controller if it is finished. (Talk about impatience!)

Figure 3.14 (a) Activities with programmed I/O

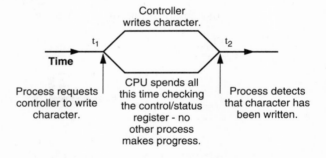

Figure 3.14 (b) Activities with interrupt driven I/O

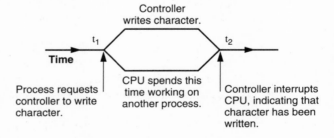

In Figure 3.14 (b), the driver starts the controller and moves the character to the data buffer register (time t_1), and then waits. In this case, between t_1 and time t_2, the controller writes the character while another process uses the CPU. When the controller has finished the I/O (at time t_2) it sends an interrupt signal to the CPU.

As usual, we must answer some questions, such as:

- How does the CPU detect the interrupt?
- If there are many controllers, how does the CPU know which one interrupted it?
- Should certain controllers have a higher priority? If so, how is this implemented?
- What happens to the driver that requested I/O?
- What happens to the interrupted process?

Interrupt Detection

A CPU can detect a controller interrupt through an *interrupt line* (Figure 3.15). The controller interrupts the CPU by sending a signal along that line.

Figure 3.15 Interrupt line

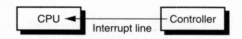

Normally the CPU tests the interrupt line during the instruction cycle. If an interrupt has occurred, the CPU "traps" to a specified location and executes an interrupt service routine. (For more information on interrupt handling, see reference [1, 6].) The fact that the test is part of the cycle allows the CPU to do it quickly.

How does this affect the I/O operation? The following pseudo code shows the example of the previous section (Figure 3.13) with interrupt capability.

```
Move contents of location m to location d.
Set WRITE flag in location d+1 to 1.
Enter a wait state.
...next instruction...      {Write operation is complete}
```

After the driver sets the WRITE flag, it enters a wait state. For now, it is sufficient to say it becomes inactive and waits to be resumed later. (Process states are discussed further in Chapter 4.) Now since it is inactive, another process can use the CPU. The operating system finds one that needs work, and turns the CPU over to it. When the character has been written, the controller interrupts the CPU. It stops working on the current process and executes an interrupt handler. It determines the reason for the interrupt and the driver is resumed at the point where it began the wait. It continues and executes the next instruction.

Despite the difference, interrupt-driven I/O is similar to programmed I/O in that the driver still transfers the character between memory and the controller and gives the controller commands. The most significant issues now are how the CPU handles multiple sources of interrupts.

Identification of Interrupts

The previous discussion is sufficient if just one controller can interrupt the CPU. In this case, the CPU always knows the source of the interrupt. But what if there are many controllers, each of which can generate an interrupt? When the CPU detects one, how does it determine which controller generated it?

We spend the rest of this section describing options for identifying and prioritizing interrupts. However, detailed discussions of interrupts involve flip-flops, timing, logic gates, and circuit design and are best left to texts on computer organization or architecture. The interested reader should consult references [2, 5, 6]. This section describes interrupts from a functional viewpoint without concern for hardware details.

Multiple Interrupt Lines. One way to identify the controller is to use separate interrupt lines. The CPU can then check all lines after executing each instruction.

A problem here is that the CPU architecture depends on the number of interrupt lines, and hence, the number of controllers. This not only creates a more complex architecture but also limits the number of controllers. It also forces CPU designers to work under a constraint unrelated to normal CPU activities.

Multiple Controllers on a Single Interrupt Line. A second option is to connect all controllers to a single interrupt line (Figure 3.16). If any controller generates an interrupt, the CPU detects it by checking the line after executing each instruction.

Figure 3.16 Multiple controllers connected to a single interrupt line

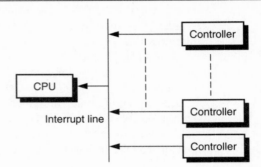

The only problem here is identifying the source of an interrupt. One way is for the interrupt handler to check the "OPERATION COMPLETE" flag in the control/status register of each controller. When it finds one whose value is 1, it has found the controller that generated the interrupt. This is called *software polling*. If more than one controller generated an interrupt, the software stops at the first one it finds. This approach also allows the controllers to be prioritized. The first ones polled have the highest priority. Priorities can be changed simply by changing the order in which they are polled. The drawback to software polling is that it takes time. The CPU must execute a routine to find the source of each interrupt. The time spent is taken from other processes that use the system.

Daisy Chaining. An alternative to software polling is to design hardware that allows a controller to identify itself when it generates an interrupt. One way to do this is illustrated in Figure 3.17. The controllers are connected to a single interrupt line as in Figure 3.16. The difference is that there is another line, the *interrupt acknowledge line*. It starts at the CPU and passes through each controller. This is called *daisy chaining*.

When the CPU detects an interrupt it sends a signal (acknowledgement) along the interrupt acknowledge line. When a controller receives the signal, it responds in one of two ways. If it has not generated an interrupt, it passes the acknowledgement along the line to the next controller in the daisy chain. If it has generated an interrupt, it does not pass along the acknowledgement. Instead, it responds by sending a unique value (sometimes called a *vector*) to the CPU along the bus (not shown in Figure 3.17). The vector is usually either a device identifier or the address of an interrupt handling routine. Either way, an interrupt handling routine responds and reactivates the driver.

Figure 3.17 Interrupt acknowledge line daisy chained through the controllers

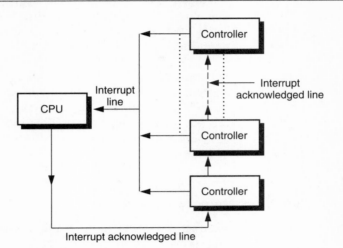

This approach is sometimes called a *vector interrupt* method. As a result, software polling is not needed. Since the polling has been relegated to the hardware, the term *hardware polling* is sometimes used.

Daisy chaining also prioritizes the controllers. If two or more controllers generate interrupts, the ones at the beginning of the interrupt acknowledge line receive the acknowledgement first. Thus, they are serviced first and have the highest priority. In some systems this is a disadvantage since controllers with lower priority may wait for a long time. Daisy chaining is inexpensive to implement, but it is inflexible. Changing the priorities requires connecting the devices in a different order along the interrupt acknowledge line. It is also slow for large system since the acknowledgement sometimes passes through many controllers.

Bus Arbitration. Another method commonly used is *bus arbitration*. A controller must have access to the bus before it can send an interrupt signal. This is done by using additional hardware (commonly VLSI chips) called a *bus arbiter*.

When a controller wants to send an interrupt signal, it first requests access to the bus. It does this by sending a signal along a *bus request line* to the arbiter. When the arbiter grants bus access to the requesting controller, the controller then sends an interrupt signal. When the controller receives the acknowledgement, the controller identifies itself as before.

Controllers may be prioritized by using several bus request lines. If several controllers want to interrupt the CPU simultaneously, each must gain bus access first. If access is requested using different request lines, the arbiter then decides, based on priorities assigned to the lines, who gets the bus. Bus arbitration and prioritizing are discussed in more detail in reference [1, 6].

As we have seen, interrupt driven I/O has an advantage over programmed I/O. The CPU can spend more of its time on useful tasks rather than waiting for a controller to finish I/O. But there remains the problem that a driver must still send the data to the data buffer register; that is, the CPU is still part of the I/O process. This still limits its ability to work on other processes. With today's advances in hardware, you might conclude, "there must be a better way." There is, and we describe it in the next section.

3.6 Direct Memory Access

Interrupt-driven I/O allows multiprocessing. While I/O for one process is in progress, another may be using the CPU. The fact that two processes are active simultaneously increases system productivity. But are we making the best possible use of parallel activities?

Suppose a process must read a data file containing 50,000 characters. If we use the method from the previous section, the driver activates the controller. The CPU is then given to another process while the controller reads the first character. After a while the controller interrupts the CPU. An interrupt handler responds and the driver is resumed. The first character has just been read.

The driver must now activate the controller 49,999 more times and 49,999 more interrupts will occur. Each one, of course, requires an interrupt handler to determine its cause. The net result is a large amount of time spent responding to interrupts and starting the controller. Reading 50,000 characters one at a time makes about as much sense as buying a box of cornflakes and bringing it home one flake at a time.

DMA Controllers

Processes that use fast devices such as tapes and disks often must read or write thousands of characters at a time. The devices and processes can be much more efficient if a block of characters is transferred in each operation rather than a single one.

Direct memory access (DMA) allows the transfer of blocks of characters. It lets the controller access memory on its own. With programmed I/O, the CPU had to transfer each character, and the controller could not access memory independently. Thus DMA-based controller is more sophisticated.

Figure 3.18 shows a DMA controller and a CPU. When a running process must read or write data, the driver activates the controller as before. However, this time the driver does not transfer any data. Instead, it sends the controller the needed information. This includes:

- The operation to be done.
- An address indicating the location in memory it should access.
- The number of characters to transfer.
- The device involved.

Figure 3.18 Direct memory access

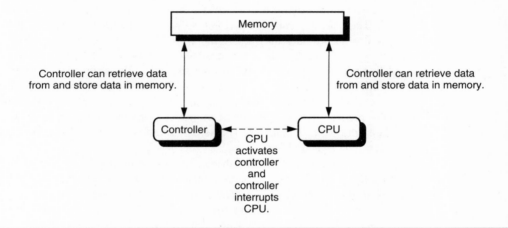

Once the controller receives this information, it begins memory access. If the command was a WRITE, it gets the specified number of contiguous characters beginning at the specified address and writes them to the device. When the controller finishes, it interrupts the CPU. As before, the operating system responds to the interrupt. If the I/O request was a read, analogous actions occur. The advantage, of course, is fewer interrupts. This makes the CPU even more available to other processes. Even if there are no other processes (e.g., single-tasking systems), fewer interrupts still mean better efficiency.

Cycle Stealing. The simultaneous memory accesses by two distinct hardware components does create a new problem. What if they conflict? If the controller and CPU both use the same buses, what happens if both try to access memory at the same time? Even if they use different buses, what happens if they both try to access the same memory module simultaneously? Either way, the result is the same: there is a conflict because the hardware can service only one access at a time.

In such cases, an arbiter gives the controller preference. The CPU is prevented from accessing the bus or memory module for a few clock cycles. In effect, the CPU is delayed. We call this *cycle stealing*, since the controller steals a few cycles from the CPU. Please note that this is not an interrupt as described in the previous section. The CPU has not been interrupted, but rather just delayed. The CPU does not save the current process' status nor does it call an interrupt handler. The delay occurs strictly in hardware.

Buffering. When a driver starts an I/O operation for a process, it must specify a memory location, but which one? It would seem logical to specify the location indicated by the process; however, this is often not done. Rather, the driver often specifies a separate area of memory called a *buffer*. But why not just transfer data between the device and the process' memory?

There are several reasons. First is that what the process requests and what the controller provides may not be the same. For example, suppose a process wants to read a record, such as one declared in a Pascal or COBOL program, from a disk file. Because of a disk's characteristics, the controller actually reads an entire sector containing the record. But where does the controller put the sector's data? It most likely contains much more than the process wanted and the process has no room for it. A buffer (separate area of memory) is used to hold the sector's contents. The actual record is then transferred from the buffer to the process' memory.

It is worth noting that subsequent read requests for records already in the buffer do not cause a physical transfer of data. Since the data has already been read, it need only be moved from the buffer to the process' memory.

There is another reason for buffering. Suppose a process wants to read something. As discussed earlier, it must wait. To provide more room for others, some operating systems may choose to remove a process from memory while it is waiting. Thus, when the data transfer actually occurs, the process may not even be in memory. Similarly, if the process wants to write, there is no need to keep it in memory while the writing occurs. The data may be stored in a buffer and written from there.

We should note that, although buffering is common, sometimes data is transferred directly to or from a process' memory. The advantage is that this eliminates an extra step. But the disadvantage is that part of the process must not be removed from memory, making less memory available to others.

I/O Processors

For fast devices, direct memory access is certainly an improvement over programmed I/O. It would be highly inefficient to transfer large amounts of data one character at a time. But we can still make more improvements.

Consider the fact that even though the controller can transfer data between a device and memory, it cannot act independently. That is, the driver still must give it the proper instructions and information. It does this by writing commands into the controller's registers. This, of course, means that the CPU is still used for I/O details, and takes time that could be used for other processes.

Can we go one step further? If the controller can transfer data at the CPU's command, why can't it execute its own commands to control I/O? Can it be a computer itself? If so, it would relieve the CPU of many I/O specific details and make it still more available to other processes. Such controllers exist, but we generally give them special names. Since they can execute commands, they are processors not unlike the CPU. We call them *I/O processors* or *channels*. When such devices are present, it is called a multiprocessor system. Both the CPU and the I/O processors can execute machine language instructions (although, since the processors differ, so do the instructions). Both have status words and program counters. In short, both may run processes.

We call the commands that an I/O processor executes *I/O commands* (IOC). Sometimes they are called *channel command words*. They contain operation codes, memory references, and flags just like the instructions the CPU executes. The difference is that IOCs control device operations or enable the I/O processor to test device status. Specifically, an I/O processor can issue commands that activate a device controller and sense its status.

We can define a sequence of I/O commands as an *I/O program* (IOP) or *channel program*. IOPs may reside in main memory or they may reside in separate memory associated with the I/O processor. As an I/O processor executes an IOP, it can issue commands to the controller. Thus, it assumes the CPU's role in this regard. The driver no longer must start each I/O operation; it can specify a sequence of I/O operations to be done. Thus, instead of being interrupted after each one, the CPU is not interrupted until after the last of the sequence. The result is higher total throughput.

Figure 3.19 illustrates how the I/O processor fits into system design. This figure shows an I/O processor that communicates with two controllers, but the actual number can vary in practice.

Starting an I/O Processor. A CPU can start an I/O processor by executing a *Start I/O* or SIO command. The SIO command does not contain device specific information. Instead, it makes the I/O processor access a predefined memory location that contains the starting location of the IOP. The I/O processor then executes the program and issues device specific commands to the controller. Once the CPU activates the I/O processor, it runs independently of and in parallel with it.

Figure 3.19 CPU, I/O processor, and controllers

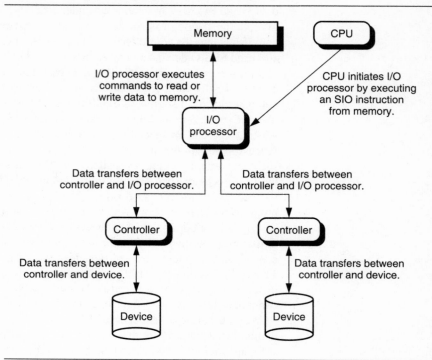

Note that I/O processors generally do not replace controllers. They take over the CPU's job of communicating with controllers. The system now has an extra component that puts an additional level between the software and device characteristics.

I/O Processor Commands

What kinds of commands can the I/O processor execute? For that matter, what kinds of commands can the CPU execute to communicate with the I/O processor? Specific commands are system-dependent, but we will describe common types. (Consult references such as [1, 4, 10, 11] or your computer center's manual for machine specific details.)

Many commands that the I/O processor executes control device operations. The following are some common command types:

Seek. The I/O processor can issue this command to a disk controller. It makes the controller move the disk heads to a specified track.

Write. This command makes the I/O processor transfer data from a specified memory location to a controller. The controller, in turn, transfers the data to the appropriate device. The processor may have to wait for the controller to finish. In many cases, however, it can issue other commands to other controllers while the first one is writing data. This, of course, increases the number of activities that can be in progress simultaneously. The WRITE command must specify the memory location, amount of data, and the device. The controller signals the I/O processor when the writing is done.

Read. This command makes the controller transfer data from a specified device to the I/O processor. Since the transfer takes time, the processor may issue commands to other controllers while it waits for the data. As with the WRITE command, its occurrence is system-dependent. When the controller finishes reading, it signals the I/O processor.

Skip to Next Line or Advance to Next Page. The I/O processor issues these commands to control line printer operations. They are often the result of a user request, such as WRITELN; (skip to next line), or "PAGE" (skip to next page), in a Pascal program.

Rewind. This command rewinds a tape. It is normally used after a tape file has been created or read and the tape is no longer needed. The tape must be rewound before the operator can dismount it.

Sense. This command senses the status of a controller or device. An I/O processor must communicate with the device controller. To do this, it must be able to determine when the controller can receive commands.

CPU I/O Commands

Just as the I/O processor can execute commands that manage the device controllers, the CPU can execute commands designed to communicate with the I/O processor. The commands are often part of the operating system which must start or initiate the I/O processor. Example commands that the CPU can execute to communicate with the I/O processor are:

Start I/O. As described earlier, the SIO command causes the I/O processor to begin executing an I/O program. The SIO command locates the program's start address. After the CPU executes SIO, it may do other things while the I/O program is running.

Halt I/O. This command instructs the I/O processor to suspend an I/O program. This can occur if a higher priority process requires access to the processor. It can also occur if the process requesting the I/O has aborted for some reason. In either case, the I/O operation can be terminated.

Test I/O. This allows the CPU to test the status of an I/O transfer. There may be several things the CPU can test. For example, it can determine the status of an I/O operation; that is, did it succeed or was there a transmission error? If the operation succeeded, how many bytes did it transfer? The CPU can test the status of the device or controller: Is it busy, available, or not operational for some reason? This command usually accesses or defines a *status word* containing flags for each condition.

Processing an I/O request

Some individual components of an I/O system have been described. How do they fit together? What really happens when a user codes a high level READ or WRITE command? Let us follow an example, from start to finish, of a process requesting I/O. Figure 3.20 shows how the components of the I/O system fit together. In this example, we assume that a running process has issued a request to read from a disk file.

However, we also add a word of caution. Specific I/O details are system-dependent. This is a general discussion of common activities in I/O processing. The next section gives a detailed example of a specific system.

Some processes request I/O using a special machine language instruction called a *Supervisory Call* or SVC. When the CPU executes an SVC, a trap, or exception, occurs. The CPU loads a new Program Status Word (PSW) and a new program counter (PC) from a predefined location. The new PC is the starting location of a trap handling routine, an operating system procedure that responds to the trap condition.

After the trap occurs, the trap handling routine is in control of the CPU. The routine determines the reason for the trap and responds accordingly. If the reason was a read request (step 1 in Figure 3.20), the CPU calls a device independent routine (step 1 in Figure 3.20).

Figure 3.20 Actions of driver, I/O processor, and controller

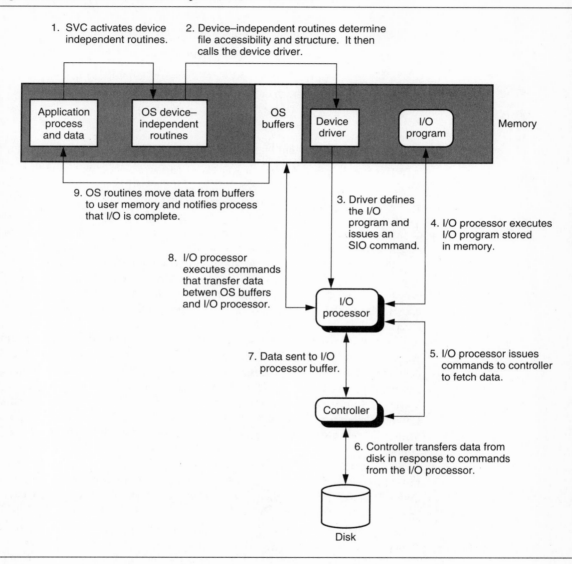

As described in the last section, the device independent routine will:

- Determine whether the referenced file exists.
- Determine if the requesting process has legal access to the file.
- Determine the structure of the referenced file.
- Determine which device has the needed information.
- Determine how much data must be transferred.
- Keep track of the relative position in the file from which new records are read.
- Build a table containing information needed by the device driver.

When the device independent routine finishes, it calls a device driver. The device independent routine passes information needed by the driver in a table. Such a table is sometimes called a *control block*.

In this case the device driver does not communicate directly with the controller (again, this is system-dependent). It does not execute commands that do the actual data transfer. Instead, it defines an I/O program which, when executed, communicates with the controller. The I/O program usually resides in main memory, although it may be in a separate memory used by the I/O processor. In Figure 3.20, the I/O program is in main memory. The device driver places the starting address of the program in a predefined memory location.

Once the device driver has determined the location of the data and has defined the I/O program, it issues an SIO command (step 3 in Figure 3.20). As described earlier, the I/O processor finds the starting address of the I/O program and begins executing it. The CPU is now free to work on other processes.

As the I/O processor executes the I/O program (step 4), it issues commands to the controller to locate and read the requested data. The controller responds to these commands (step 5), controls the device operations, and reads the data (step 6).

The controller transfers the data back to the I/O processor where it waits in a buffer (step 7). Since the I/O processor may be communicating with other controllers, it may not be able to respond immediately. Thus, it must have a place to store data temporarily.

Once the data is in the buffer, the I/O processor can use its DMA abilities to transfer the data to memory (step 8). However, the I/O processor may not move it directly to the process' memory space. In fact, since the process normally waits for I/O, the process may not even be in memory. The system scheduler may have swapped the process out to make room for other processes. As a result, the I/O processor stores the data in a buffer. Once it has stored the data there, its job is done (at least for this request) except for one last detail. It must send an interrupt signal to the CPU.

When the CPU responds to the interrupt, the device driver assumes control. It checks the I/O processor status to determine if the I/O has completed successfully or aborted due to some error. If the I/O succeeded, the driver releases the control blocks associated with the request and calls other operating system routines. They move the data from the buffers to the process' memory space (step 9). The other routines then notify the process that the I/O is complete and that it may use the data.

I/O With Multiple Devices

The previous example shows what happens when one process makes one request to an I/O processor that communicates with one controller. But, in general, many processes make many I/O requests to many I/O processors that communicate with many controllers. With all this simultaneous activity, what keeps the data from colliding?

Data transfers occur in parallel between devices and the I/O processor. The increased level of multiprocessing increases the speed at which I/O requests can be handled. It also increases the processor's complexity. Now it must be able to receive data from several devices and route the data to appropriate buffers in main memory. How does the I/O processor do this?

The answer depends on the processor. There are two types that can handle multiple devices. They are *selector channels* and *multiplexors*. Let's describe multiplexors first.

Byte Multiplexors. First of all, there are two types of multiplexors, *byte multiplexors* and *block multiplexors*. Both can handle I/O for many devices simultaneously. A byte multiplexor transfers data one character at a time to or from its devices, and is often used with slow devices such as terminals or printers. The block multiplexor transfers data one block at a time, and is normally used with fast devices such as disk or tape drives.

Figure 3.21 shows a byte multiplexor. Here we have three users at three different terminals accessing system resources. User 1 is calling on an editor (typing EDIT), user 2 is requesting a compilation (typing COMPILE), and user 3 is executing a program (typing EXECUTE).

The characters that each user types are transmitted to the multiplexor. However, because it can handle characters much faster than any user can ever hope to type, it has ample time to accept characters from multiple terminals and store each in the proper area of memory. That is, it *multiplexes* the characters.

Figure 3.21 Byte multiplexor

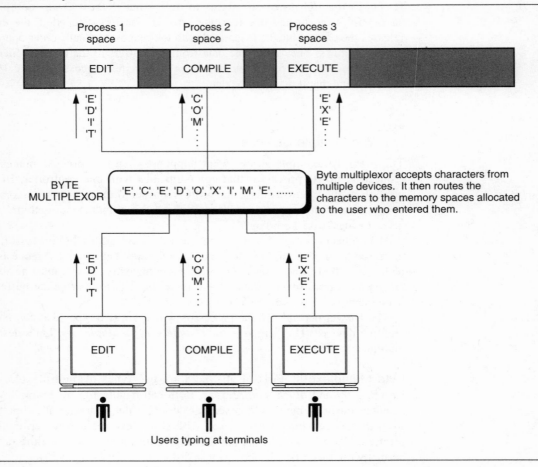

For example, suppose the first user begins by typing E. Before he or she can type the second character, suppose the second and third users each type the first characters of their commands. Thus, the multiplexor receives the characters E, C, and E, from each user's intended command. Similarly, suppose the multiplexor next receives the second characters each user types. Thus, it receives D, O, and X. If the users continue to type in this pattern, the I/O processor receives E, C, E, D, O, X, I, M, E. . . .

The first, fourth, seventh, and tenth characters form the word EDIT. A sequence starting with the second character spells COMPILE. Lastly, a sequence starting with the third character spells EXECUTE. The multiplexor receives the characters in whatever order the users enter them, but it distinguishes which characters belong to whom and stores them in the appropriate memory spaces. To write characters to the terminal, we simply reverse the arrows in Figure 3.21.

An advantage of byte multiplexing is realized by the frustrated user who sees important information scroll off the screen. He or she cannot try to peek under the cover, at least not effectively. Through appropriate control commands, however, the user can freeze the screen image. All printing stops and no more information scrolls off the screen.

The control command blocks transmission to the terminal. That is, the multiplexor stops sending characters to it. The scrolling stops immediately (or quickly enough so it seems immediate). Another control command resumes transmission. The first character to be blocked is the first to be sent when transmission resumes, and the output continues as if it had never been interrupted.

Block Multiplexors. Block multiplexors are similar to byte multiplexors. Figure 3.22 shows one reading multiple sectors from multiple disk drives. The processor works basically the same as in the byte multiplexor. In this figure, each S1, S2, S3, etc., represents a sector of data. Sectors are transferred from each device to the I/O processor. The I/O processor, in turn, receives a sector and routes it to an appropriate process space.

Now sectors indicated by S1, S2, S3, etc. may be transferred simultaneously from a device to the I/O processor. However, there is a delay between the transfers of two distinct sectors from the same drive, especially if they are on different tracks. Remember, once a sector is transferred from a disk, it takes a relatively long time to locate the next one. In general, the read/write heads must physically move to a new track. The I/O processor then transfers the sectors to memory associated with the requesting process.

Selector Channels. Selector channels are like block multiplexors in that they communicate with multiple fast devices. The difference is that once a selector channel begins I/O with a particular device, it dedicates its time to that device until the I/O finishes. A multiplexor may have multiple I/O activities with several devices in progress at the same time.

Although these examples show input, we can illustrate output by reversing the arrows in the figures. Now the data is transmitted from memory and distributed (demultiplexed) to various devices. Terminals, for example, cannot print characters as fast as they can be sent by the I/O processor. The I/O processor therefore transmits a character to one terminal, another character to another terminal, and so on. Because this happens very quickly, the user watching his or her program being printed believes the computer is sending data in an uninterrupted flow.

Figure 3.22 Block multiplexor

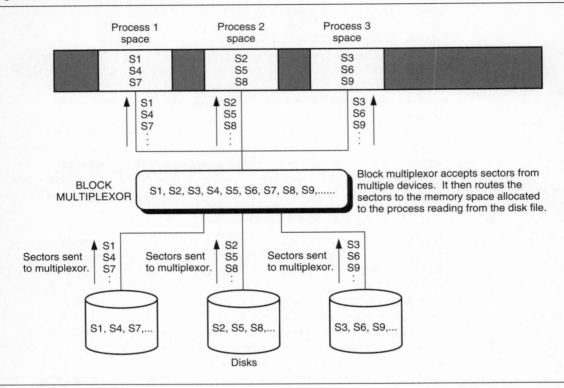

Block multiplexor accepts sectors from multiple devices. It then routes the sectors to the memory space allocated to the process reading from the disk file.

Multiple I/O Processors. A large complex system may have several I/O processors, each communicating with specified devices. Indeed, it is possible to overload the I/O processors. Each one can multiplex data from a fixed number of devices. If you try to attach too many devices, the result is a bottleneck with delays in routing data from the device to memory. This, of course, causes poor response for processes requesting I/O.

If the number of devices is large enough, the system design may warrant multiple I/O processors. The proper number may be difficult to choose and depends on the amount of data traffic and funds available. It also depends on the required response times.

═══
Spooling

Output to many line printers poses a different problem. I/O between many devices and memory is multiplexed or demultiplexed when we assume each device is associated with a single input or output operation. If we apply the same principle to many users sending output to a line printer, we have the situation shown in Figure 3.23.

Figure 3.23 Output demultiplexed to line printer

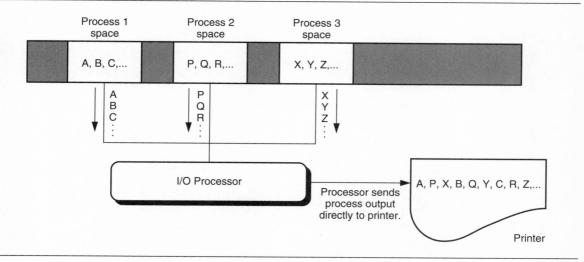

Here, three processes are sending output to a line printer. Process 1's output is A, B, C, . . . ; process 2's output is P, Q, R, . . . ; and process 3's output is X, Y, Z. . . . If the I/O processor demultiplexes the data, the outputs are then mixed together on the paper. This situation is unacceptable. A user would not appreciate a listing of someone's COBOL program right in the middle of the results of some scientific computations or a financial projection.

To avoid this situation, a program command that writes data to a common printer does not actually cause the data to be printed. Instead, it is written to special buffers in a disk file (Figure 3.24). As a result, the user can write from a program without anything being sent to the printer. Everything is written to the file. This is called *spooling*.

Eventually, however, the user expects to see his or her program results. Two events typically cause the data in the buffer to be printed. The first is the user finishing and logging off the system. When this occurs, the operating system tags the appropriate buffers. Their contents are sent to a line printer queue and are eventually printed. The second event is when a user commands the operating system to print the buffers. The data is sent to a printer queue as before.

Figure 3.24 Output spooled to line printer

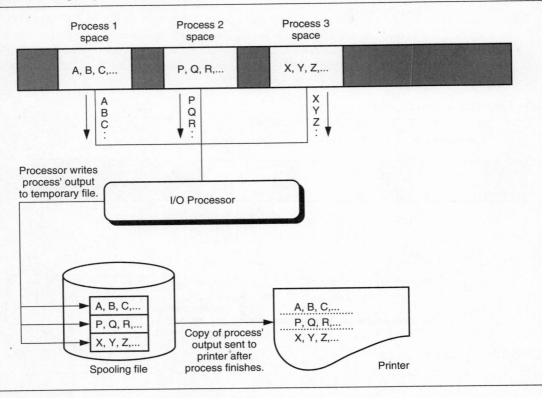

Multiprocessing Hierarchy

We close this section by stating that the number of I/O processors, controllers, and devices varies considerably among systems. Figure 3.25 shows typical connections. The I/O processors have DMA capability and transfer data to and from memory. Each processor, in turn, communicates with device controllers. The figure shows a hierarchical relationship between I/O processors and controllers, but in some cases two distinct processors can communicate with the same controller. Each controller, in turn, governs the actions of specific devices. In general, controllers handle similar devices. In other words, a controller will not usually handle both a disk drive and a tape drive. However, an I/O processor may execute I/O programs for different devices.

Figure 3.25 Multiprocessing hierarchy

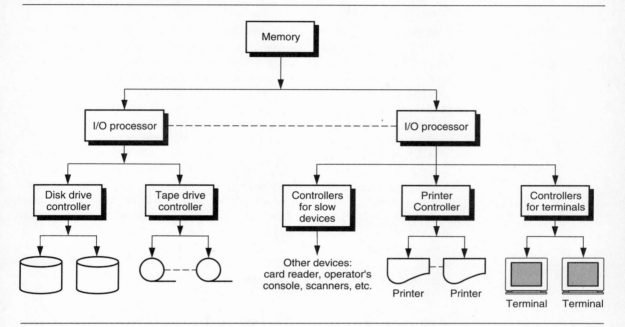

≡≡≡≡ 3.7 Case Study: VMS I/O Processing

The case study here is the VMS operating system for the VAX series of computers manufactured by Digital Equipment Corporation (DEC). Our aim is to describe the components and tables used by VMS in processing an I/O request. A brief description of the VAX series computers follows.

DEC introduced the VAX-11 series in 1978 with the VAX-11/780 processor. Later systems, such as the VAX-11/750 and VAX-11/730, have similar architectures but are smaller and less expensive. The VMS (Virtual Memory System) operating system provides real time, time sharing, and batch processing environments.

The VAX line now consists of a wide range of general purpose computers. For example, the VAX 8800 series are high performance computers that still have complete software compatibility with other VAX systems. 8800 systems contain two CPUs that access 128 Mbytes of shared memory. The smaller VAX 8350 models contain two VAX 8250 CPUs that access up to 32 Mbytes of shared memory.

VMS I/O processing closely follows the methods presented in the previous sections. Indeed it should, since our discussion centered on general principles. This case study exposes you to some of the terminology from a specific system, and relates it to the generalities.

Bus Architectures

Before getting into I/O processing, let's briefly describe VAX organization.

VAX computers use a common *bus*. As stated previously, a bus is a set of parallel electrical lines that connect many devices. Any two devices connected to it may communicate. Typically, an *address bus* carries signals that indicate a location to be referenced. For example, when the CPU needs an instruction, the address of its memory location is sent along the address bus. The memory device receives the address and transmits its contents along a *data bus* back to the CPU. Bits sent along the *control bus* manage the transfer.

VAX architectures differ, depending on the model, but Figure 3.26 shows a typical one. The CPU and memory are normally designed with their own internal bus organization. I/O controllers are commonly attached to a separate bus called the *backplane interconnect* (BI) bus. Slower devices are normally connected to one BI bus and faster devices connected to another. Depending on the architecture, it may be called a *Massbus*, *Unibus*, or *QBUS*. The differences are unimportant here.

Figure 3.26 Typical VAX architecture

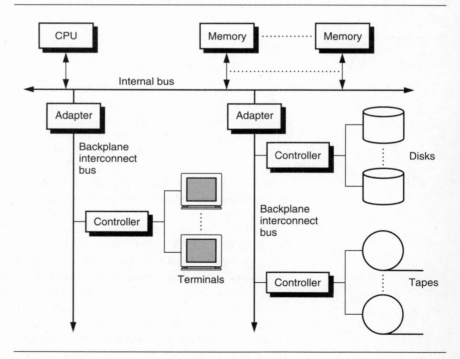

The reason for multiple buses is that the VAX was designed to be compatible with PDP-11 I/O devices, which communicated via older buses. Older buses are slower and have fewer lines than the newer ones. Thus, the VAX designers had two choices in making the bus transition: change the old ones to be compatible with the new ones, or design an adaptor to allow the buses to communicate. The first option would be costly and would make the old ones obsolete (a major problem for every PDP-11 customer). The second option allows advanced devices and communications methods to be added without disrupting existing operations.

≡≡
VMS I/O

We now consider I/O processing under the VMS operating system. The VMS operating system is designed to handle many processes, including real-time ones. It also supports many different types of devices, and as a result, must be able to respond to many I/O requests involving many different devices.

For example, many processes may request I/O involving the same device. Thus, VMS must be able to determine which ones can be handled immediately and which ones must wait. It must define some strategy for packaging requests and storing them for later use by the driver.

In another case, one process may have I/O requests involving many devices. This means that VMS must be able to examine a request, validate it, and locate appropriate devices and drivers. VMS must also be able to determine whether the devices are available.

In yet a third case, device interrupts from arbitrary devices may occur at any time. Several may even occur simultaneously. The asynchronous nature of devices creates many problems, and it is difficult to keep track of events when they occur simultaneously. VMS cannot respond "Sorry I lost your data, I was rather busy at that time." It must respond to every interrupt, regardless of when it happens. It must also be able to determine the status of the I/O operation and locate the appropriate process and driver. It must then look for other requests involving the device that is now available.

As you can see, VMS must respond to many varied events. Each one requires access to different information. Consequently, there are many routines and the database that holds all necessary information is complex.

VMS I/O processing consists of two main parts: device-independent and device-dependent processing. Figures 3-8 and 3-9 outline their primary functions. However, this section examines their VMS analogs in more detail. Specifically, it discusses:

- Device-independent processing (QIO system service)
- Control blocks and tables for I/O processing

- Device drivers
- I/O postprocessing

The interested reader may find more detailed discussions in references [12, 13].

QIO System Service

Let us start from the point at which a running process requests an I/O operation. In response, VMS starts a device-independent routine called the *Queue I/O* (QIO) systems service. QIO has two primary functions. The first is to examine and validate the parameters in the process' I/O request. The second is to build an *I/O Request Packet* (IRP).

Parameters that must be verified include, for example, the type of operation requested (read or write), the address and length of the user memory buffer, and the device or file requested. From them, QIO determines whether the process' request may be processed. For example, is the access permitted? Is the requested operation consistent with the file type or device? The IRP is a specially formatted data structure in which the QIO stores this information along with the process identification number. Since the IRPs have a consistent format, driver routines are simplified somewhat.

Next, QIO distinguishes the IRPs by the device it involves and stores the IRPs in separate queues (Figure 3.27), one for each device. Each queue is accessible using a queue header that is stored in a *Unit Control Block* or *UCB* (discussed shortly). The important thing now is that there is one for each device. When the device driver runs, it responds to the IRP at the front of the queue. Thus, the driver handles the I/O requests in the order of generation.

After QIO queues the IRP it notifies the requesting process and the requesting process may continue. Now, allowing the requesting process to run before the I/O is complete may seem a bit unusual. Indeed most programs with commands such as Pascal's Read(X) assume that X has a value once program control has progressed past the Read(X). However, a process can also be constructed to read values earlier than they are needed in anticipation of their use. This way, rather than spend time waiting, the process can do other things while the operating system is getting the process' data. Of course, the process must check status flags provided by VMS to determine when the I/O operation is complete.

Not all programs work this way. In fact, VMS provides two system commands: QIO and QIOW. The QIO command works as described whereas the QIOW (W for wait) makes the requesting process wait until the I/O operation has finished.

Figure 3.27 QIO creates IRPs for device driver

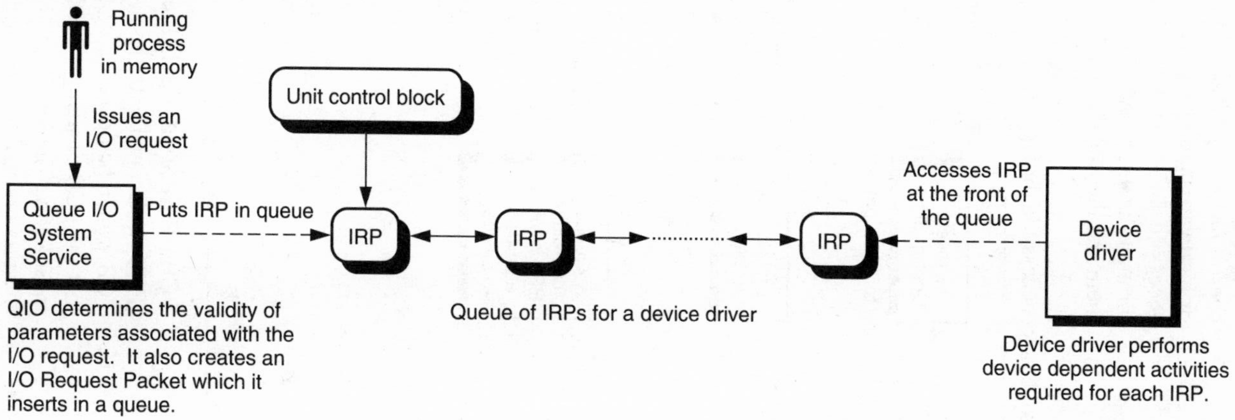

Running process in memory

Issues an I/O request

Queue I/O System Service

QIO determines the validity of parameters associated with the I/O request. It also creates an I/O Request Packet which it inserts in a queue.

Puts IRP in queue

Unit control block

IRP

IRP

IRP

Queue of IRPs for a device driver

Accesses IRP at the front of the queue

Device driver

Device driver performs device dependent activities required for each IRP.

≡≡≡ VMS Control Blocks

Through the IRP, the driver has access to much information stored in many *control blocks*, or tables containing information pertinent to a particular process or hardware component. Figure 3.28 shows some control blocks the driver has access to and how they are related. Most important, they are all accessible through the entity that represents an I/O request: the IRP. Let us now describe them and the role they play in I/O processing.

Figure 3.28 Control blocks accessible through the IRP

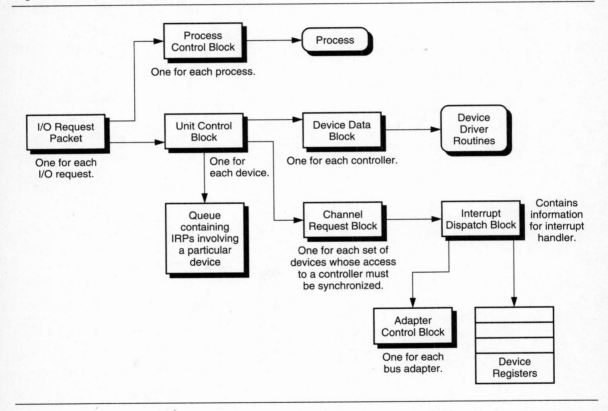

PCB. First of all, the IRP contains the location of the *Process Control Block* (PCB) associated with the process making the I/O request. Every process has a PCB which the operating system uses to keep track of it. For now, let us just say that the PCB contains everything about a running process the operating system must know. The important thing is that, given an IRP, VMS can use it to locate the process making the original request. This is useful after the operation is finished and VMS must locate the process to inform it of the operation's status.

UCB. The IRP also contains the location of a *Unit Control Block* (UCB), and there is one of these for each device. We have already seen that the UCB contains a queue header that locates an IRP list. It also contains the following:

- **Device's characteristics.** For example, what kind of device is it? This is necessary for the device driver to know. After all, disk drives and tape drives differ and the driver must know which type of device it is accessing.

- **Device's status.** For example, is it busy, available, or out of service? If someone spills coffee in a line printer, it must be repaired. If there is no substitute, VMS must know the printer is no longer there. (It can also avoid a heavy ingestion of caffeine and subsequent excessive printing of random numbers.)

- **Driver's context.** If the driver is interrupted its register contents and program counter are stored in the UCB. Upon resumption, the values are restored and the driver continues where it was interrupted.

- **Locations of two other control blocks needed during the I/O process.** They are the *Device Data Block* (DDB) and the *Channel Request Block* (CRB).

DDB. While there is one UCB for each device, there is one device data block (DDB) for each controller. The DDB contains information common to the devices handled by the controller. Remember, a controller handles similar devices. The DDB also locates the device driver.

CRB. The Channel Request Block (CRB) contains the controller's current state. It also indicates which device is currently transmitting data and lists all others that are waiting to transmit. Since a controller handles many devices, it must coordinate or synchronize their activities. The CRB is used for this purpose. It also contains the location of yet another control block, the *Interrupt Dispatch Block* (IDB).

IDB. The Interrupt Dispatch Block (IDB) is actually a logical extension of the CRB. It lists all devices associated with a controller (the CRB lists just those transmitting and waiting to transmit). The IDB also contains the location of the device registers and the location of the UCB for the currently active device. Information in the IDB is used to locate a particular device and driver when an interrupt occurs.

ADP. The IDB also contains the location of one last control block, the *Adapter Control Block* (ADP). Since an I/O request involves transmitting data between the internal bus and I/O buses, the data must pass through an adapter. As a result, VMS provides routines the drivers can call to interface with the adapter. The ADP contains information necessary to convert from one bus architecture to another.

Why use so many control blocks? As stated previously, VMS must be able to respond to a variety of situations and access the information it needs. Once QIO creates an IRP, the status and characteristics of the devices, device types, controllers, drivers, and bus adapters are accessible through the IRP. The important thing is that VMS can find the necessary information at each stage of the I/O process. Now on to the next step, the device driver.

Drivers

The device driver is a process that begins physical I/O operation for a specific device. But if many requests are pending, how does a driver choose one? Recall that QIO creates an IRP for each request. Furthermore, it stores them in a queue accessible through the device's UCB (Figure 3.27). The driver chooses the IRP at the front of the queue, examines its contents, and then begins the I/O operation by writing into the device's registers (accessible through the control blocks in Figure 3.28).

Once the I/O operation begins, the driver suspends itself (ceases execution). Its register contents and program counter are placed in its UCB and the UCB is stored in a wait queue. The UCB remains there until after an interrupt from the device signals that the operation has finished. The wait queue specifies all devices that are busy transferring data. Equivalently, it defines all drivers waiting for a transmission to finish.

Driver Functions. The functions of a driver are device-dependent. Typical ones include:

- Detect and correct errors during I/O operations.
- Handle bad blocks. The driver, along with other VMS routines, is responsible for detecting bad blocks (e.g., damaged disk sectors) and maintaining information about them. If a post I/O routine discovers a transmission error is due to a bad block, it sends the IRP to another routine called the Extended QIO Processor (XQP). The XQP keeps track of suspected bad blocks and sets a flag in the file control block for the affected file. When the file is deleted, XQP creates a process that performs extensive tests to verify a bad block. If one is found, XQP adds it to a bad block file so that it is not allocated again later.
- Respond to cancellations of I/O requests.
- Report device errors to a program responsible for logging them.
- Return the status from a device to the requesting process.
- Respond to interrupts generated by a device when an I/O operation finishes or aborts.
- Create device-specific commands from the information in the IRP.
- Activate a device by writing into its controller's registers.

We should note that later disks called *Digital Storage Architecture* (DSA) have more intelligent controllers that perform some of the device driver's functions (especially error correction, controller operation optimization, and bad block handling).

Driver Tables. In addition to instructions needed to perform its tasks, a driver also contains three tables. They are the *Driver Prolog Table* (DPT), *Driver Dispatch Table* (DDT), and *Function Decision Table* (FDT).

The DPT contains information on the driver's size and identity. This information is needed by the VMS routine that loads the driver into memory for execution.

The DDT sounds like it eliminates all bugs in the system. In reality it contains the addresses of driver entry points associated with the different types of I/O activity permissible on a particular device. Depending on the type of I/O requested, the VMS will use different parts of the driver. The DDT specifies their locations.

Last, the FDT contains a list of valid I/O function codes for a particular device. It also contains the locations of the associated preprocessing routines called *FDT routines*. QIO calls them to validate device-dependent parameters during QIO's verification procedure. For example, they should not let a process read from a line printer.

FDT routines also distinguish between *buffered* and *direct* I/O. Direct I/O transfers data between a device and a process' buffer. Buffered I/O transfers data between a device and a system buffer. I/O requests that take a long time are usually buffered. This allows VMS to remove a process from memory so it does not occupy memory space unnecessarily. Faster transfers may go directly to or from the process' buffer.

For direct I/O, the FDT routines make sure the process' buffers are locked in memory and not swapped out. Recall from Chapter 2 that an operating system often swaps a process' pages out of memory to make room for others. But if data is to be transmitted directly between the process' buffer and the device, then the buffer must not be swapped out. For buffered I/O, the FDT routines must allocate a buffer.

Postprocessing

Previously, we stated that once a driver initiates an I/O operation, it is suspended. The reason is that even though the I/O operation has begun, the driver's responsibilities are not completed. *I/O postprocessing* refers to what the driver must do when the operation has finished. Figure 3.29 describes the postprocessing steps.

When a data transfer finishes, a *device interrupt* occurs (step 1 in Figure 3.29). Recall that an interrupt is a signal from the device controller indicating to the operating system that something has happened. When an interrupt occurs, an

Figure 3.29 Postprocessing after an I/O operation

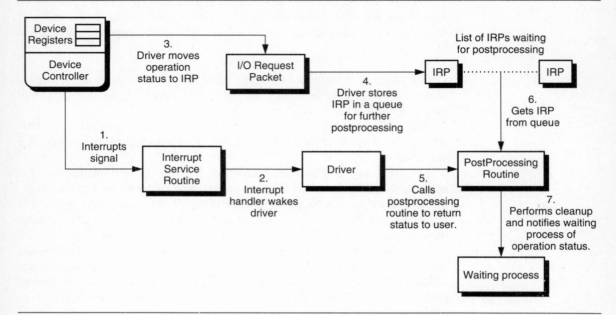

interrupt handler resumes the driver (step 2). The driver then determines the status of the operation. Was it successful or did it abort? The driver gets this information from the device registers and stores it in the associated IRP (step 3). It puts the IRP in an I/O postprocessing queue (step 4) and calls a device independent postprocessing routine (step 5) to finish the I/O request.

The postprocessing routine removes an IRP from the queue (step 6). It then determines from the operation's status how the operation should be completed (step 7). If the I/O ended in an error, the postprocessing routine calls a VMS routine that produces messages and notifies the waiting process.

If the I/O operation ended successfully, the postprocessing routine must determine whether it was direct or buffered. For a buffered read, the postprocessing routine transfers the data to the process' memory space and deallocates the system buffer. For direct I/O, postprocessing unlocks the process buffer pages so they can be swapped out later if necessary. In either case, the postprocessing routine increments the accumulated totals of I/O requests and byte transfers maintained for the process, deallocates the IRP, and proceeds to respond to the next IRP in the queue.

VMS I/O Summary

This section described the major components and tables used in VMS I/O processing. As we saw, I/O processing is complex. There are many tables and control blocks that VMS must access at different stages of I/O. Similarly, there are many VMS components that access tables and control blocks. As we stated previously, this is due to the complex environment that VMS must control and the asynchronous nature of I/O. Many processes making many I/O requests involving many devices create a lot of data traffic. Add this to the fact that interrupts occur randomly and we have the potential for a real traffic jam. Like any congested traffic system, sometimes traffic may flow, sometimes it must wait. VMS must control the flow and not lose any processes.

To help put this discussion in perspective, Figure 3.30 summarizes the major components and their interactions. Also, to help remember the many acronyms we have used, Table 3.1 lists them and what they correspond to. The reader interested in further discussions of VMS or VAX architecture should consult references [12-14].

Figure 3.30 Summary of VMS I/O activities

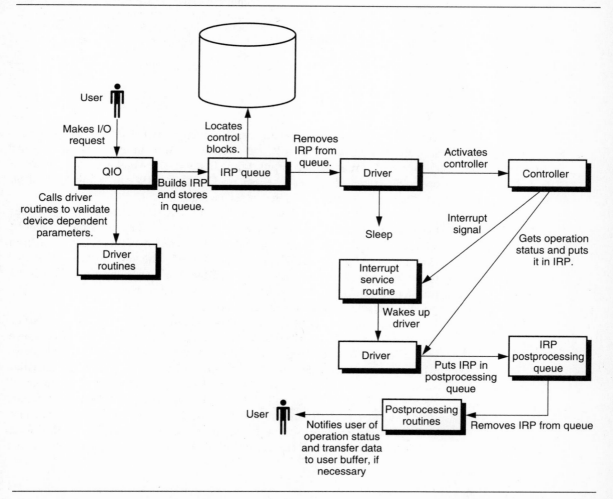

Table 3.1 List of VMS Acronyms

Acronym	Meaning	Use
ADP	Adapter Control Block	Defines characteristics of a bus adapter.
CRB	Channel Request Block	Contains controller information and information about which device is transmitting and which ones are waiting.
DDB	Device Data Block	Contains information common to devices connected to a controller.
DDT	Driver Dispatch Table	Contains locations of driver entry points.
DPT	Driver Prolog Table	Contains a driver's size and identity.
FDT	Function Decision Table	Contains valid function codes and locations of driver preprocessing routines.
IDB	Interrupt Dispatch Block	Locates currently active device and its registers.
IRP	I/O Request Packet	Data structure containing I/O request information.
PCB	Process Control Block	Contains information about a process.
QIO	Queue I/O	Device-independent I/O preprocessing routine.
UCB	Unit Control Block	Contains information about a device and its driver.

≡ 3.8 Summary

This chapter has discussed the general principles of I/O processing. We have seen that commands such as Pascal's Readln or Writeln or C's Printf or Scanf do not really read or write anything. Instead, they make a <u>request</u> to the operating system that data be either read or written. We therefore focused on what happens after a process makes such a request.

Much depends on the device that the I/O request accesses, but all devices have one thing in common: relative to CPU speeds, they are slow. However, some devices are faster than others. Tape drives and disk drives are considered fast devices. The physical operation involved with moving disk heads or rewinding a tape may be slow, but once the data has been located, it can be transferred quickly, a block at a time. Slow devices such as terminals and many printers transmit data one character at a time.

In addition to the hardware components (controllers, devices, I/O processors, and CPU), we also described software components. I/O activity breaks down into several levels. The top level is the user process. It issues an I/O request, which device independent routines examine. The routines perform activities such as determining file accessibility and structure. The next level involves device dependent routines called device drivers. Such routines may calculate disk addresses, check for transmission errors, create device specific commands, and check device status. The driver must be closely in tune with device characteristics. It starts the controller or I/O processor, depending on the system. In some cases, more sophisticated and intelligent controllers have assumed some responsibility from the drivers. Thus, some details of I/O processing have been moved from software to hardware, speeding up the I/O process.

We discussed several approaches to I/O processing: programmed I/O, interrupt driven I/O, and direct memory access. With programmed I/O, the driver issues commands to a device controller to begin data transfer by writing into a controller register. Certain bits in the register tell the controller to transfer data to or from the device. Other bits in the register reflect device status. Thus, the driver must examine them to determine when an I/O operation has been completed.

Issuing commands to the controller and checking its registers uses a lot of time the CPU could be spending on other processes. One way to avoid this is interrupt driven I/O. The driver still issues commands to the controller, but then suspends itself. This frees the CPU for other processes to use. The controller interrupts the CPU when the I/O operation is completed. The driver resumes and finishes its job. The CPU must be able to detect interrupts and identify the responsible device. There are several ways to do this. Interrupt handlers may poll devices, or an interrupt acknowledge line may be daisy chained through the controllers. In many cases, the devices must get control of the bus to identify itself.

In both programmed I/O and interrupt driven I/O, the driver must perform the data transfer. It must move the data between memory and the controller registers. This again takes time that the CPU might otherwise use to work on other processes. Direct memory access allows the controller to transfer the data. Relieved of this duty, the CPU has more time for other activities. Periodically, both the CPU and the controller may try to access common memory, thus creating a conflict. In such cases, the controller has priority and forces the CPU to wait for a few hardware cycles. We called this cycle stealing.

Even with DMA controllers, the driver must still provide detailed commands for the controller. In some cases, separate I/O processors execute I/O programs which issue the commands. The CPU only has to execute a start I/O command that activates the I/O processor. The CPU and I/O processor work simultaneously. The CPU works on other processes, while the I/O processor works on the I/O program and issues commands to the controller.

The extra processor further relieves the CPU of the details of the I/O process. The increase in parallel activity allows more tasks to finish and helps increase throughput in larger systems. The I/O processors themselves may handle multiple controllers. Multiplexors can overlap commands so that controllers may operate in parallel. Selector channels allow communication with multiple controllers, but only one at a time.

Finally, we concluded with a case study of VMS I/O processing. To a large extent, the details were outlined in previous sections. However, the case study gave us a chance to describe some control blocks used to maintain information on aspects of I/O and learn some terminology for a specific system.

Exercises

1. Suppose a CPU can execute a memory referencing instruction in 500 nanoseconds (1 nanosecond=10^{-9} seconds). Suppose also that a disk controller can transfer data from a disk to memory at a rate of 250K characters per second. How many instructions could the CPU execute in the time it takes the controller to transfer one 512(0.5K) byte sector from disk to memory?

2. Assume the parameters in exercise 1, but also assume that on the average it takes 10 ms to move the head to a specified track and 2.5 ms to wait for the proper sector to rotate past it. On the average, how many instructions can the CPU execute in the time it takes to locate a sector of data and transfer it to memory?

3. How many characters per second can a tape drive transfer if the tape moves past the head at 100 inches per second and contains 800 bytes per inch?

4. Consider a disk with the following characteristics:

   - 40 tracks per side
   - 9 sectors per track
   - 512 bytes per sector

   What is the total byte capacity of this disk? Suppose we fix the number of sectors per track and the number of bytes per sector. How many tracks per side are needed to provide a capacity of 1 Mb?

5. Section 3.4 contains a pseudo coded program that writes a single character to a device. Modify it to write 80 characters, one at a time.

6. Write a program analogous to that in Section 3.4 that reads a character from a device.

7. In the same program referenced in exercise 5, there is a command

   > test the OPERATION COMPLETE flag in the register

   Suppose the register has 16 bits and the "Operation Complete" flag is bit 5 (starting from bit 0 at the far right). Write specific language commands that actually test the flag. Use whatever language you know.

8. The example described by Figure 3.13 associated a controller's data and control/status registers with addresses **d** and **d**+1, respectively. Suppose we expand the controller's abilities to include direct memory access. What registers must the controller have? Assign them to consecutive locations starting with location **d**. Pseudo code a driver that writes many characters starting with the one in location **m**. Assume the number of characters to be written is in a location specified by the variable **N**.

9. Suppose a disk pack has 100 cylinders, 10 tracks per cylinder, and 5 sectors per track. Suppose that the logical sectors are numbered as follows:

Logical sector numbers	Physical disk locations
0 through 4	cylinder 0, relative track 0, relative sectors 0 through 4
5 through 9	cylinder 0, relative track 1, relative sectors 0 through 4
10 through 14	cylinder 0, relative track 2, relative sectors 0 through 4
:	:
:	:
44 through 49	cylinder 0, relative track 9, relative sectors 0 through 4
50 through 54	cylinder 1, relative track 0, relative sectors 0 through 4
:	:
:	:
94 through 99	cylinder 1, relative track 9, relative sectors 0 through 4
:	:
:	:

   Assume that successive cylinders contain 50 logically contiguous sectors. Write the formula that relates the logical sector number to the cylinder number, relative track number in a cylinder, and relative sector number in a track.

10. Describe an algorithm a device driver could use to calculate a sector's physical location (cylinder, track, and sector numbers) from the logical sector number. Use the disk characteristics listed in Exercise 9.

11. Repeat Exercise 10 except assume there are **n** cylinders, **k** tracks per cylinder, and **m** sectors per track.

12. Suppose a process makes a request to transfer 500 sectors from a disk. Consider two possible approaches: a DMA controller that reads one sector and interrupts the CPU after reading it; and an I/O processor that handles the operations for all 500 sectors. Suppose it takes 0.5 ms to respond to an interrupt and issue another read. How much time does the CPU save if the second approach is used? How many instructions could it have executed in this time? Assume the CPU can execute one instruction in 500 nanoseconds.

13. Consider a VAX system similar to that in Figure 3.26. Suppose there are 3 identical disk drives, 2 identical tape drives, and 20 identical terminals. Suppose at some instant 20 processes are active and 8 of them are waiting for an I/O operation to finish. How many instances of the following control blocks and tables are there? ADP, CRB, DDB, IDB, IRP, PCB, and UCB.

14. Describe (i.e., list which control blocks and tables must be accessed, and in what order) how VMS would determine the following:
    - Given a particular device, list the IDs for all processes that have an I/O request pending for it.
    - Given an I/O request, is the requested device busy?
    - Given an I/O request, define a controller's control/status registers to initiate I/O.
    - Given an interrupt from a specific device, find the driver for postprocessing.

1. How would you and your fellow students or colleagues be affected if your computer center removed all language compilers from disk and put them on tape?
2. List some examples where storing data on tape makes more sense than storing it on disk.
3. In the pseudo-coded program of Section 3.4, the busy waiting loop exists because we do not want the driver to store another character in the controller's register. The reason is that we do not want the driver to destroy the character before it is actually written. Busy waiting loops are also often necessary when reading a character. What is the reason for this?
4. Checking for interrupts is normally part of the instruction cycle. What is the advantage of doing it this way instead of using a separate machine language instruction?
5. Cycle stealing occurs when the I/O processor and the CPU try to access the same memory module or the same bus simultaneously. Why does the I/O processor normally get priority?
6. Multiplexing allows one I/O processor to communicate with many devices. It also means the I/O processor becomes more complex. What is the main reason for not using one simpler I/O processor per device?
7. VMS I/O is divided into two types, direct and buffered. Which devices are more suitable for buffered I/O? Why? Which devices are more suitable for direct I/O? Why?
8. Distinguish the terms "virtual address space," "physical address space," and "real memory."

≡≡≡≡≡ **References**

1. Stallings, W. *Computer Organization and Architecture: Principles of Structure and Function.* 2nd ed. New York: Macmillan, 1990.
2. Sloan, M. E. *Computer Hardware and Organization.* 2nd ed. Chicago: Science Research Associates, Inc., 1983.
3. Gorsline, G. W. *Computer Organization: Hardware/Software.* 2nd ed. Englewood Cliffs, NJ: Prentice-Hall, 1986.
4. Davis, W. *Operating Systems: A Systematics View.* 3rd ed. Reading, MA: Addison-Wesley, 1987.
5. Tomek, I. *The Foundations of Computer Architecture and Organization.* Rockville, MD: Computer Science Press, 1990.
6. Shiva, S. G. *Computer Design and Architecture.* 2nd ed. Boston, MA: HarperCollins, 1991.
7. Milenkovic, M. *Operating Systems: Concepts and Design.* New York: McGraw-Hill, 1987.
8. Kohavi, Z. *Switching and Finite Automata Theory.* 2nd ed. New York: McGraw-Hill, 1978.
9. Tanenbaum, A. S. *Structured Computer Organization.* 3rd ed. Englewood Cliffs, NJ: Prentice-Hall, 1990.

10. Madnick, S. E., and J. J. Donovan. *Operating Systems*. New York: McGraw-Hill, 1974.
11. Donovan, J. J. *Systems Programming*. New York: McGraw-Hill, 1972.
12. Kenah, L. J., Ruth E. Goldenberg, and Simon F. Bate. *Version 4.4 VAX/VMS Internals and Data Structures*. New York: Digital Press, 1988.
13. Levy, H. M., and R. H. Eckhouse, Jr. *Computer Programming and Architecture: The VAX*. 2nd ed. New York: Digital Press, 1989.
14. *VAX Architecture Reference Manual*. Edited by T. E. Leonard. New York: Digital Press, 1987.
15. Tanenbaum, A. S. *Computer Networks*. 2nd ed. Englewood Cliffs, NJ: Prentice-Hall, 1988.

4

Scheduling

4.1 The Need for Scheduling

Chapter 2 discussed multiprogramming as it applies to memory management. The operating system must satisfy the diverse needs of many users. It also must be efficient. Processes must access resources and execute within a reasonable time. This is more likely if the machine code for a process, or at least part of it, resides in memory. Multiprogramming is the ability to store the code from multiple processes in memory simultaneously.

We must emphasize, however, that multiprogramming does <u>not</u> necessarily mean that many processes execute simultaneously. This is a fact often misunderstood. The codes from many processes may reside in memory simultaneously. However, if there is only one CPU, only one process can run at a time.

Multiprogramming differs from *multiprocessing*. Multiprocessing means that the system has multiple processors. In such cases, more than one activity may proceed at the same time. For example, a system that contains multiple CPUs is a multiprocessor. Each CPU can be executing the code from a separate process.

Multiple CPU systems are not the only multiprocessors. As chapter 3 showed, separate processors called *I/O processors* or *device controllers* often perform I/O. We also saw that once the CPU initiates an I/O operation, the I/O processors and the CPU can operate independently of each other. Again, two or more processors are active at the same time.

Multiprogramming in a single CPU system raises many interesting problems. Multiple processes in memory all want to run—and run immediately! As a computer user, you are surely familiar with the situation depicted in Figure 4.1. You have an unfinished project that was due yesterday. Therefore, you want it to run now. Unfortunately, so do many other people who are also behind in their work (isn't everyone?). With many anxious users and only one CPU, the operating system has a big job.

Figure 4.1 Operating system trying to satisfy all users

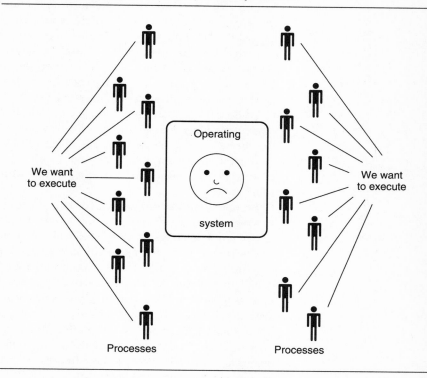

This chapter discusses scheduling strategies that try to resolve the dilemma shown in Figure 4.1. But a list and discussion of scheduling methods is not enough. We must also try to evaluate how well the methods work. Many questions arise that demand answers, such as:

- What algorithms does a scheduling strategy require?
- What data structures does it need?
- What are its goals?
- Does a particular strategy meet system goals?
- Is its implementation efficient? Is it even possible to implement?

There is an old saying, "You can't please all of the people all of the time." We all tire of hearing that said, especially when we are among the displeased, yet nowhere is it more true than in a computer system that must serve many users. A guarantee of service to one user can come only at the expense of others.

Yet, despite this, users still expect the operating system to keep everyone happy all the time. Operating systems designers must expect lots of complaints from users. Designers must be able to defend the design (from the great masses of insignificant gripes), and recognize the validity of a complaint (from a major, paying customer). As users, we must understand that others need the same resources. Our expectations should reflect our knowledge of the system's capabilities. In other words, when we submit a program to run, we should be realistic about the expected response. Of course, after the initial attack of realism wears off, you can always try crying, threats, bribes, or generally obnoxious behavior if you really need to get the work done. In any case, we must be able to evaluate scheduling strategies properly.

To do this, we must understand the organization of a typical multiprocessor. Many scheduling strategies have efficiency and user satisfaction as their goals. But they must also utilize resources effectively. In other words, not only must the operating system make everyone happy, it must do so quickly and cost effectively. The chances of achieving all this with a typical group of users are slim indeed.

Section 2 introduces typical goals of a system scheduler. We will show how striving to meet one goal often detracts from meeting another.

Section 3 describes process states and state transitions. An operating system categorizes processes by the ability to run (state). For example, some processes may be running while others may be waiting for something, such as the completion of an I/O request. Events may then occur which force a running process to stop, or allow a waiting process to begin running. These changes are state transitions and occur frequently as a process moves through the system. These events and the process states are central to a scheduling strategy.

Section 4 presents some scheduling methods. We also discuss tradeoffs among the methods. We will also find that a method that works well in one system may not work well in another.

The last section is a case study of scheduling under IBM's MVS operating system. It will acquaint you with some MVS terminology and show an approach to scheduling in a mainframe environment.

≡≡≡≡≡ 4.2 Scheduling Objectives

Before describing scheduling methods, we must first ask one question: what are an operating system's objectives as it schedules processes?

As stated earlier, the ideal operating system will make every user happy all the time. In reality, however, one user's happiness may come only at the expense of another's. The result is one happy user and one grouchy, complaining beast.

How do we determine whether a scheduling method is fair? How do we measure efficiency? What should a designer strive for when choosing a scheduling method? Certainly, one goal is efficiency. An inefficient system will either cost too much, use too much time, or require too many resources. In any case, it provides a poor return for each dollar spent. When this occurs, the system is no longer a valuable tool.

Throughput

But how do we define efficiency? One way is to measure *throughput*. Throughput is the number of processes that pass through the system per unit of time. A low throughput means that few processes get through. A high throughput means that many do. In the latter case, more users are getting their work done. The obvious conclusion is to try to achieve the largest possible throughput. Or is it?

Suppose the users of a large time shared, multiprogrammed system generate an average of sixty small processes per hour. We define a "small" process as one requiring about one minute to complete. Suppose also that about once every half hour someone generates a large process. We define a large process as one requiring about thirty minutes to complete.

Suppose the operating system allows only the small processes to run. The throughput is then about sixty processes per hour. But, whenever the operating system allows a large process to run, throughput decreases. For each minute spent on a large process, throughput decreases by one. Thus, the operating system will attain the highest throughput by ignoring the large process completely. This is nice for the small processes, but not so nice for the large ones.

The problem, of course, is that our definition of throughput is independent of process size. The system simply looks at the number of completed processes per unit of time. If throughput is the only measure, the most efficient system may ignore some processes. We have thus sacrificed fairness for efficiency. This example shows that fairness may reduce efficiency. It also shows that efficient systems are not always fair.

Responsiveness

Another operating system goal is responsiveness. Interactive users should see quick responses. No one should sit at a terminal for half an hour waiting for a five second program to run. Batch users should also see reasonable response times. Most reasonable people would agree that a large program submitted on

Monday should be returned no later than Tuesday. Even some of the unreasonable ones would agree.

Initially, you might think that responsiveness is the same as throughput. After all, if the system can respond quickly to each process, more of them will pass through. Unfortunately, this isn't always true. We have already seen that an operating system can maximize throughput by giving special attention to short processes and ignoring long ones. But then the long processes do not see a responsiveness system.

Consistency

Consistency is also an important goal. If the demands on the system are the same at 3:00 p.m. as they are at 10:00 a.m., the responses should be about the same. People often plan their schedules around a computer system. They may expect to submit programs and get results by certain times. If the response varies greatly, users never know what to expect. The computer is then like an unreliable person who appears for appointments late or not at all.

Keep Processors Busy

Another goal is that an operating system should keep its resources (for example, I/O processors) busy. They are there to work and should not be idle. If resources stand idle, why were they bought in the first place? (This is the old "slave-driver" school of management made popular by Simon Legree.)

For example, suppose five processes enter the system simultaneously. Four of them (say, processes 2 through 5) execute very little machine code. Suppose, however, they do require the reading of data from secondary storage. The other process (process 1) requires no I/O, but does many calculations. Assume that processes 2 through 5 require 1 ms of CPU time, and that process 1 requires 10 ms. Also assume that the total input for each of processes 2 through 5 requires 50 ms, and that the needed data is on different devices. This way, the reading can be done in parallel.

Which process should the system execute first? Suppose it chooses process 1 (Figure 4.2). During the time that process 1 is running (the interval between **a** and **b** in Figure 4.2), no other activity occurs. The I/O processors are idle, and the other processes do not make any progress.

After 10 ms, process 1 finishes and another process begins (point **b**, time = 10). Suppose process 2 starts running, and uses the CPU for only 1 ms before it issues an I/O request (point **c**, time = 11). The I/O processors handle the request, leaving the CPU available for another process. Suppose process 3 goes next, and it also generates an I/O request after only 1 ms (point **d**, time = 12). Similarly, suppose processes 4 and 5 control the CPU for only 1 ms before each generates an I/O request (points **e** and **f**, times = 13 and 14, respectively).

Figure 4.2 Parallel activities when process requiring no I/O goes first

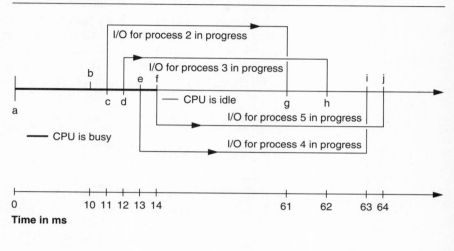

a – All 5 processes enter system, process 1 starts running. (Time = 0)
b – Process 1 finishes. Process 2 begins running. (Time = 10)
c – Process 2 requests I/O. Process 3 starts running. (Time = 11)
d – Process 3 requests I/O. Process 4 starts running. (Time = 12)
e – Process 4 requests I/O. Process 5 starts running. (Time = 13)
f – Process 5 requests I/O. No processes ready to run. (Time = 14)
g – I/O for process 2 is complete. (Time = 61)
h – I/O for process 3 is complete. (Time = 62)
i – I/O for process 4 is complete. (Time = 63)
j – I/O for process 5 is complete. (Time = 64)

After process 5 requests I/O, the I/O processors are simultaneously handling requests from all four processes (2 through 5), and the CPU is idle all this time. Each I/O operation will finish 50 ms after the initial request. Since process 5's request was the last one issued, its I/O operation will be the last one completed.

Because of this, it takes 64 ms for all five processes to finish. (10 ms for process 1, plus 4 ms for each of processes 2 through 5, plus 50 more ms to finish the read process 5 requested.) With this schedule, the operating system is underutilizing the resources. It is ignoring processes 2 through 5 during the first 10 ms. This is unfortunate since, when all the I/O is in progress, the CPU has nothing to do.

Processes 2 through 5 need the CPU only for a short time. Does it make sense to make them wait until after process 1 finishes? Would it not be more efficient to schedule one, or all of these processes, ahead of process 1?

Let's see what happens if we do that. Suppose that the operating system schedules processes 2 through 5, in order of process number, ahead of process 1 (Figure 4.3). Process 2 controls the CPU for 1 ms before generating an I/O request (point **b**, time = 1). Next, process 3 assumes control. It also keeps control for only 1 ms before generating an I/O request (point **c**, time = 2). Processes 4 and 5 act similarly, issuing I/O requests almost immediately (at points **d** and **e**, times 3 and 4, respectively). Thus, after only 4 ms the I/O processors are busy. More important, the CPU has something to do.

Figure 4.3 Parallel activities with process requiring no I/O goes last

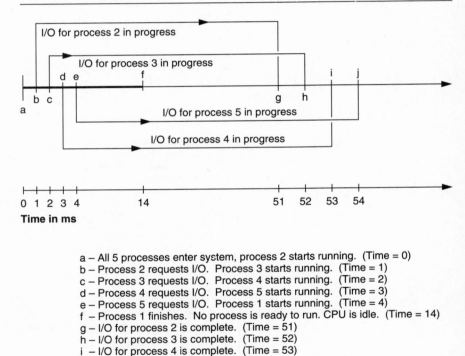

a – All 5 processes enter system, process 2 starts running. (Time = 0)
b – Process 2 requests I/O. Process 3 starts running. (Time = 1)
c – Process 3 requests I/O. Process 4 starts running. (Time = 2)
d – Process 4 requests I/O. Process 5 starts running. (Time = 3)
e – Process 5 requests I/O. Process 1 starts running. (Time = 4)
f – Process 1 finishes. No process is ready to run. CPU is idle. (Time = 14)
g – I/O for process 2 is complete. (Time = 51)
h – I/O for process 3 is complete. (Time = 52)
i – I/O for process 4 is complete. (Time = 53)
j – I/O for process 5 is complete. (Time = 54)

Now, because of the multiprocessing, I/O for all 4 processes is in progress at the same time. Allow 50 ms for all I/O operations to finish, and these processes are completed (point **j**, time = 54). But, since the CPU is available after 4 ms, the operating system can schedule process 1. It can therefore run during the 50 ms in which the I/O processors are working on the I/O requests (between points **e** and **f**). Since process 1 runs in parallel with the I/O processing, all 5 processes finish after only 54 ms, with a savings of 10 ms. Now 10 ms may not seem like a lot. However, let's look at it as a percentage of the time required by all five processes. Using the schedule of Figure 4.2, all processes finished in 64 ms. With the schedule of Figure 4.3, they finished in 54 ms. This represents a percentage time savings of

$$\frac{\text{completion time from Figure 4.2 minus completion time from Figure 4.3}}{\text{time for all processes to finish from Figure 4.2}} * 100$$

$$= \frac{64 - 54}{64} * 100$$

$$\approx 16\%$$

Again, 10 ms may not seem like much, but a nearly 16% reduction in the time needed to complete all 5 processes is significant.

The main point is that, if I/O processors are available, then perhaps the operating system should give special attention to processes that request a lot of I/O. This way more processors are kept busy, and more things get done, resulting in a higher level of multiprocessing.

However, if we take it to an extreme, the approach can prove faulty. For example, suppose instead of 4 processes that issue I/O requests, there is a constant influx of interactive users. Thus, many processes that issue I/O requests enter the system over a period of time. If the operating system always gives them special attention, is the scheduling really fair? What happens to processes like process 1 in the previous example? The operating system will continue to give others special attention at their expense. How long must a process wait before the unfairness to it is more significant than a slight reduction in system efficiency?

Another problem can occur if processes request too much I/O activity. Large queues of requests build up, and the I/O processors are overworked. In that case, perhaps the system should pay a little more attention to processes that use the CPU more heavily.

If the I/O processors are saturated, there is little to gain from generating more I/O requests. The CPU may just as well spend the time on processes that need it. There will be less operating system intervention, and system efficiency will actually increase. Ideally, the operating system should keep each processor busy without overworking it. The way to achieve this depends on the mix of processes in the system.

Priorities

All the above discussion is academic if processes are *prioritized*. In other words, each one is assigned a priority, and the operating system schedules according to it. The system considers high priority processes more important than low priority ones. The earlier considerations apply only when scheduling processes of equal priority.

If a process receives poor attention because of low priority, the system simply considers that a "social" issue beyond its control. That is, life in a prioritized system is unfair; high priority, like rank, has its privileges.

But prioritizing creates problems, too. Who defines and assigns priorities? What are the guidelines? When is a user justified in saying a process is "more important" and therefore deserves a higher priority? What happens if prioritizing runs counter to system efficiency?

Consider the example from Figure 4.2. If process 1 has a higher priority than the other 4 processes, the operating system schedules it first. This occurs despite the fact that it causes poor utilization of resources. The user of process 1 is causing expensive peripherals to be idle. The result is a loss of work, time, and probably money. Frequently, however, the system offsets the losses by charging process 1 a higher price for use of resources.

Real Time Systems

Real time systems constitute another case in which scheduling may run counter to system efficiency. Real time systems must respond to information fast enough to control an ongoing process. Users depend on quick response to avoid impending disasters. Typical applications include nuclear reactors, chemical plants, space probes, aircraft and flight simulators, assembly lines, air traffic control systems, and life support systems. In these cases, a delay in response to an event can be fatal.

In real time systems, quick response has the highest priority. Fairness and system efficiency are less important. In nuclear reactor monitoring, system efficiency is meaningless if we cannot guarantee a quick response. A loss of efficiency is easier to explain than a Three Mile Island or Chernobyl situation.

In summary, scheduling is a complex task. What is fair to one user often turns out to be unfair to another. What is an efficient approach in one system may be entirely inappropriate in another. What works well for one assortment of processes may work poorly for a different collection. There are no constants in scheduling. The method must consider the needs of the processes, system efficiency, existing hardware, and fairness. The problem, as we have seen, is that many of these goals conflict. Often, we cannot attain one without reducing the chances of reaching another.

In the next two sections, we discuss different approaches to scheduling. But we also point out where the approaches are appropriate, and where they may be undesirable. We describe the tradeoffs, when we have a choice among techniques.

4.3 System View of a Process

Scheduling requires careful monitoring of processes as they leave the hands of the user and enter the computer system. The previous section presented scheduling as though the only question was, "Who goes first?" Certainly, this is part of the problem, but there is much more to it.

To describe scheduling fully, we need to understand how the operating system views each process. Let's define the *state* (or status) of a process in terms of its ability to execute. Figure 4.4 contains a *process state diagram*. It shows the states in which a process may exist. These states are common to most systems.

Figure 4.4 Process state diagram

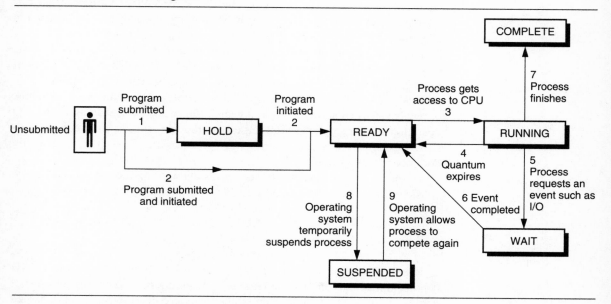

The boxes in the diagram represent the states. The arrows between them represent changes in the state or *state transitions*. Let us discuss the states first.

Process States

The state indicated by ⫪ (or UNSUBMITTED) means that a process is still in the user's hands. As far as the system is concerned, it does not exist as the user has not yet submitted it. The operating system, of course, does not recognize this state. It is just presented as the first step in the life of a process.

The HOLD state means that the process has been submitted. However, the system does not yet allow it to run or compete for system resources. This state occurs when someone submits a process with instructions to start it later. Frequently, a process can run more cheaply during evening hours when system demand is lower. As a result, users often want to save money by running some low priority programs overnight.

Many systems can initiate a submitted process at a specified time, or after a specified amount of time has elapsed. A user can then submit a process during the day with instructions to the operating system that it not be run until later. The user can then go to an all-night party and be assured the program will be done by morning.

The READY state indicates a process that is ready to run. A process in this state is idle, but can run if it gets control of the CPU. In single processor systems, many processes may be ready but waiting; remember, only one can run at a time. This state does not apply to a process that is waiting for I/O.

The RUNNING state indicates a process that is currently in control of the CPU. In a single processor system, just one process is in this state. However, if there is more than one CPU, several processes may be running concurrently.

A WAIT state indicates a process that is waiting for something. For example, it may have issued an I/O request. It cannot run because it is waiting for the I/O operation to be completed. The reason for the wait state is that, compared to CPU speeds, I/O speeds are slow. Thus, a process in the wait state generally does not compete for the CPU.

To see why the distinction between ready and waiting processes is necessary, consider the following program fragment:

$$READ(A,B);$$
$$X := A+B;$$

Recall, from the previous chapter, that the machine code for the READ command may only initiate the read. I/O processors may control the transfer of data while the CPU does something else. Suppose that the process that issued the READ was allowed to compete for the CPU. The operating system could then conceivably allocate the CPU to it before the I/O processors returned values for A and B. When the next command is executed, A and B are undefined. This causes X to be undefined and the program cannot be trusted to produce accurate results.

Processes waiting for I/O may not be the only ones in a wait state. Processes sometimes wait for events caused by other processes. (Chapter 5 describes such events in more detail.) The key point here is that the operating system will not allow any process in a wait state to compete for the CPU.

The SUSPENDED state is similar to the wait state in one respect: the process cannot compete for the CPU. However, it is different in that processes in a wait state may still compete for some resources. For example, the process that has issued an I/O request is, in effect, competing for an I/O processor or I/O controller. The process is idle with respect to the CPU, but it is still making progress.

A process in a suspended state may not compete for any resource. All progress stops temporarily. Processes can be suspended, for example, when too many are in the system. The intense competition for resources may slow the progress of every process. One solution is to suspend some processes so that the system can handle the rest more efficiently. When the heavy competition for resources diminishes, the system can reactivate the suspended processes.

Finally, a process in the COMPLETE state has finished.

State Transitions

A state transition is a change in the state of a process. Certain events may require such a change. From the descriptions of the states, you can probably guess what some of these events are, but let's describe each state transition in Figure 4.4. We refer to the commands needed to submit programs as a *Job Control Language* (JCL). (References 3 and 4 describe JCL extensively.)

1. The transition from UNSUBMITTED to HOLD occurs when a user submits a program with instructions to defer running it until later. As stated previously, the JCL may contain a start or delay time. The program remains in the HOLD state until the appropriate time.
2. The transition from HOLD or UNSUBMITTED to READY occurs when a user submits a program intended to compete for system resources immediately. It also occurs upon startup of a program previously submitted on a delayed basis.
3. The transition from READY to RUNNING occurs when the operating system gives control of the CPU to a particular process. The basis on which the CPU selects the process is an important one and is the topic of section 4.4.

4. The transition from RUNNING to READY occurs when the operating system regains control of the CPU from a process that, if allowed, can still run. For example, some systems define a maximum length of time (*quantum*) for which a process may run without interruption. If the process is still running after the quantum has expired, the operating system regains control of the CPU. It puts the process in the READY state and gives the CPU to the next process in line. This way no one process monopolizes the CPU.

5. The transition from RUNNING to WAIT occurs when the process requests something for which it must wait. For example, we have already seen that a process requesting an I/O must wait until the completion of the I/O operation.

6. The transition from WAIT to READY occurs when a waiting process gets what it needs. For example, the operating system may receive a signal that an I/O operation has been completed. It then moves the waiting process back to the READY state.

7. The transition from RUNNING to COMPLETE occurs when the process finishes. This means either that the necessary tasks have been completed, or the process is guilty of an error and aborts. Either way, as far as the operating system is concerned, the process is finished.

8. The transition from READY to SUSPENDED occurs when there are too many ready processes for adequate service. Any computer system has finite resources, and if the number of processes that compete for them is allowed to increase without limit, the system will saturate like an overcrowded highway, causing the computer version of gridlock and providing poor service for everyone. One way to avoid this is to limit the number of ready processes. Another is to move processes from the ready state to the suspended state whenever response times become bad. Which processes are affected is, of course, another decision the operating system must make.

9. The transition from SUSPENDED to READY occurs when the operating system decides a suspended process can compete for resources again. Presumably, the load has returned to normal levels, and suspension of processes is no longer necessary.

Process Control Blocks

The operating system must maintain information on many processes in a systematic way. A logical question is, "How does it do this?"

The operating system maintains a list of *Process Control Blocks* (or PCBs, not to be confused with any of a variety of carcinogenic chemicals). Basically, there is one PCB for each process. When a process is initiated, the operating system creates a PCB for it and maintains a PCB list. When a process finishes, the system deletes the PCB from the list.

What does the PCB contain? In short, it contains everything the operating system might need to know about the process. Typical fields include the following:

- Process identification number (process ID).

- Process state. As the process undergoes state transitions, the operating system updates its PCB.

- Maximum run time and accumulated run time. As a process runs, the system tracks how much CPU time it uses. Furthermore, the accumulated run time may not exceed the maximum allowable. Otherwise, the operating system aborts the process and provides an error message for the user's benefit. The maximum run time is a system defined parameter and is stored when the PCB is initialized.

- Current resources and limits. They include, for example, number of printer pages, amount of memory, and amount of disk space. As the process runs, it may request more memory, disk space, or printer output. The operating system tracks what is given to each process. When it finishes, the user is often charged according to the cumulative values. Remember, computing resources are not free. Also, if the system detects usage exceeding a maximum value, it can abort the process, and it will print some error message for the user.

- Process priority. The system may schedule a process, or give it access to resources based on its priority. For example, some processes (especially operating system routines) have a high priority that allows them to override the protection mechanisms and access or change tables such as the segment and page tables described in Chapter 2. Applications generally have a low priority that does not allow them to do this.

- Saveareas. If a process stops running temporarily, the system must save the values in the registers. Later, the system can restore the values, and the process can resume execution at the exact place where it stopped.

- Location of process' code or segment table. When the operating system schedules a process to run, the system must know where its code or segment table is located.

═══

Scheduling Levels

Scheduling occurs at *high*, *intermediate*, and *low* levels.

High level scheduling (or job scheduling) determines which programs or jobs gain admission to the system. Operating system routines that do high-level scheduling check a job's JCL. For example, the JCL may specify the following:

- User identification number.
- Limits on execution time, number of printer pages, amount of disk space, or amount of memory.
- Requests for resources such as tape drives, disk files, printers, libraries, and data files.
- Option to start the process at a specified time of day.
- Priority.

A job will be denied entry to the system if its identification number is invalid or if its time or page limit is larger than the system allows. An attempt to reference inaccessible resources (such as a file in another user's account), a low priority, or a delayed starting time will also prevent the job from entering the system. High-level scheduling controls state transitions 1, 2, and 7 in Figure 4.4.

High-level schedulers go through a checklist before allowing a job to enter the system. They simply respond to events, and protect the system's integrity and security. High-level schedulers are needed relatively infrequently. Now a hundred people submitting jobs may not at first seem infrequent, but as we will soon see, it is infrequent when compared to the number of times a low-level scheduler may be needed.

Intermediate-level scheduling determines which processes can actually compete for the CPU. As previously stated, processes that have issued I/O requests may not compete. Sometimes the system will suspend a process when demand is unusually heavy. Intermediate-level scheduling is primarily concerned with state transitions 5, 6, 8, and 9.

Like high-level schedulers, intermediate schedulers are primarily event driven. Events such as an I/O request or completion usually determine which state transitions occur.

Low-level scheduling determines which process in the READY state actually gets the CPU. Low-level scheduling is responsible for state transitions 3 and 4.

In many ways, low-level scheduling is the most difficult to implement. Unlike the other levels, it is not primarily event driven. There are often many processes competing for the CPU, and the low-level scheduler must determine which one gets access. The fact that there are so many alternatives makes the choice difficult.

In time-sharing systems where processes take turns using the CPU, low-level scheduling occurs frequently. If there is a lot of I/O activity, it may be needed as often as once every few milliseconds. Low-level scheduling algorithms must try to allocate the CPU and other resources efficiently. They must also insure a fair response to users. Because of all these requirements, they have received a great deal of attention.

The next section discusses several approaches to low-level scheduling. It considers their appropriateness and effectiveness for different types of computing environments.

≡≡≡≡≡≡ **4.4 Scheduling Strategies**

There are two major categories of low-level scheduling algorithms. They are *preemptive* scheduling and *nonpreemptive* scheduling.

In nonpreemptive scheduling, a process that gains control of the CPU maintains control until it finishes. The operating system will not take control away. Nonpreemptive scheduling has the advantage of simplicity. The operating system gives control of the CPU to a process only when another one finishes. As a result, the low-level scheduler is needed infrequently.

Nonpreemptive scheduling has the disadvantage of unresponsiveness. The process in control of the CPU receives great service, but everybody else must wait. This situation is like having many people waiting for a single public telephone while the user talks interminably. Someone else will get to use the telephone only when this "chatterbox" hangs up.

In preemptive scheduling, a process may not keep control of the CPU indefinitely. After a period, the operating system may decide to take the CPU away from it. The reasons for this vary and we will describe them, but the result is always the same. The processes in the READY state must take turns using the CPU. In short,

"What the operating system giveth, the operating system can taketh away"

In general, the operating system can take control of the CPU away from a running process for several reasons, among which are:

- The process finishes. This could be due to an error, or simply due to the completion of its designated task. In either case, the process leaves the system and is no longer of concern to the low-level scheduler. The operating system then gives control of the CPU to another ready process.

- The process generates a request for which it must wait. This might be an I/O request, a page fault, or a missing segment fault. (Technically, these are also I/O requests.) In this case, the intermediate-level scheduler puts the process in the wait state while the I/O request is processed. When the I/O operation is completed, the intermediate-level scheduler puts the process back in the ready state. During the waiting time, however, the process is of no concern to the low-level scheduler. After the operating system responds to the request, the low-level scheduler gives control of the CPU to another process.

- The process has been executing for a long time. Other processes are not getting a chance to execute, and are becoming "grumpy." The operating system may then decide their interests are best served if it removes control of the CPU from the currently running process. It saves the process' context (e.g., status word, registers, and program counter) so it can resume execution later with no loss of work. In the meantime, one of the other ready processes will get a chance to use the CPU. The maximum length of time the system lets a process run without interruption is an operating system parameter called the *quantum*.

Round Robin Scheduling

A common scheduling technique is a preemptive *round robin* approach. Each process in the ready state has an entry (usually its PCB) in a queue. When the CPU becomes available, the operating system gives control to the process whose PCB is at the front of the queue. That process then begins executing (Figure 4.5).

Figure 4.5 Round robin scheduling

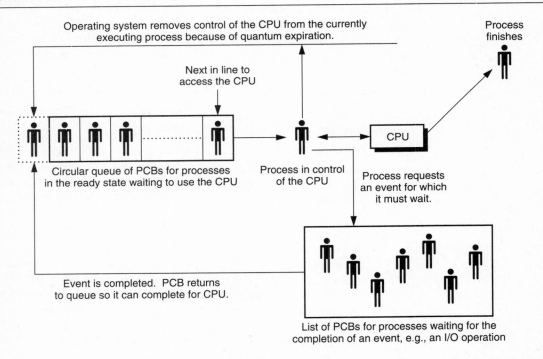

Operating system removes control of the CPU from the currently executing process because of quantum expiration.

Process finishes

Next in line to access the CPU

CPU

Circular queue of PCBs for processes in the ready state waiting to use the CPU

Process in control of the CPU

Process requests an event for which it must wait.

Event is completed. PCB returns to queue so it can complete for CPU.

List of PCBs for processes waiting for the completion of an event, e.g., an I/O operation

The process continues to execute until one of the three events listed previously occurs. At this point, the operating system removes control of the CPU.

If the process has finished, the high level scheduler removes it from the system and deletes its PCB. Usually, the operating system must calculate a summary listing the amount of time and resources used and charge an account.

After that, however, the process no longer exists in the mind of the operating system.

If the process has generated a request for something such as I/O, then the system puts it in the wait state. There is a separate list of PCBs for processes that are waiting. The process will remain in this state until it gets what it needs. If it generated an I/O request, then it waits for an I/O processor to signal the CPU. The intermediate-level scheduler can then remove it from the wait state by deleting its PCB from the wait list. It then puts the PCB at the rear of the queue of Figure 4.5. After a while, the process gets another chance to use the CPU.

If the process does not finish and does not generate a request for which it must wait, the operating system may preempt it. The process may not control the CPU longer than a quantum. If a quantum expires and the process is still executing, the operating system stops it and puts its PCB at the rear of the queue. It then gives the CPU to the process at the front of the queue. The preempted process must wait until every other process in the queue has had a chance to use the CPU. Preemption keeps processes from monopolizing the CPU. No process can execute without interruption for longer than the quantum. Therefore, each process in the ready state gets a chance to use the CPU within a given period of time.

For example, suppose the time quantum is 50 milliseconds, and there are 20 ready processes. Each one is guaranteed a chance to execute within a 1 second period. (1 second = 1000 milliseconds = 50 milliseconds times 20 processes.) Actually, the time is slightly longer because the operating system consumes CPU cycles as it schedules. However, the overhead is generally small compared to the quantum.

Round robin scheduling is most common in systems with many interactive users working at terminals. Universities, banks, libraries, department stores, hospitals, and government agencies are typical environments.

The round robin approach is popular because of the nature of interactive computing. If you are at a terminal trying to run a program, create or edit files, or just enter data into a file, you want your work to progress smoothly and quickly. It is annoying to sit and stare at an inactive terminal for a minute or two before you can type a line of data. On the surface, one or two minutes may not seem like a long time. However, if you do a lot of interactive programming, even ten second delays between system responses try the patience of the hardiest programmers. This is especially true if you have grown accustomed to quick responses.

Of course, you are not the only one expecting a quick response. Everyone expects the same, and the operating system should accommodate. As long as the total number of users is not too large, the system can usually guarantee quick service through a round robin approach.

In the above example, the system responds to each user at least once per second. This is sufficient, since most people cannot enter things faster than that. (It often takes ten seconds just to find the correct key to press.)

Quantum Size. However, round robin scheduling requires some overhead. The operating system must monitor the activities of each process very closely. A built-in timer must interrupt any process that tries to use the CPU longer than a quantum. When such an interrupt occurs, the operating system reschedules and gives control of the CPU to another process. Therefore, there can be a lot of operating system intervention. Since operating system routines typically use the same CPU as the competing processes, the total amount of time available to them decreases.

In addition, the choice of a quantum value is critical. It is a key parameter in round robin scheduling and must be chosen with care. Sometimes a system programmer can even change it to improve overall performance. Let's examine the effect the quantum has on performance.

A small quantum forces the operating system to interrupt processes more frequently. If the quantum is 50 ms, the operating system must preempt a process at least once every 50 ms (or 20 times per second). However, if the quantum is 10 ms, the minimum number of preemptions increases by a factor of 5 (up to 100 times per second). As a result, the additional operating system overhead degrades the performance.

On the other hand, suppose the quantum is 200 ms. In this case, the operating system preempts processes less often (at least 5 times per second), creating less overhead. On the other hand, a process may monopolize the CPU for longer periods. Again, this can decrease throughput and degrade responsiveness.

Consider another example. Suppose the operating system needs 1 ms to do a low level reschedule. If the time quantum is also 1 ms, the situation is as shown in Figure 4.6.

Figure 4.6 Control of the CPU as a function of time

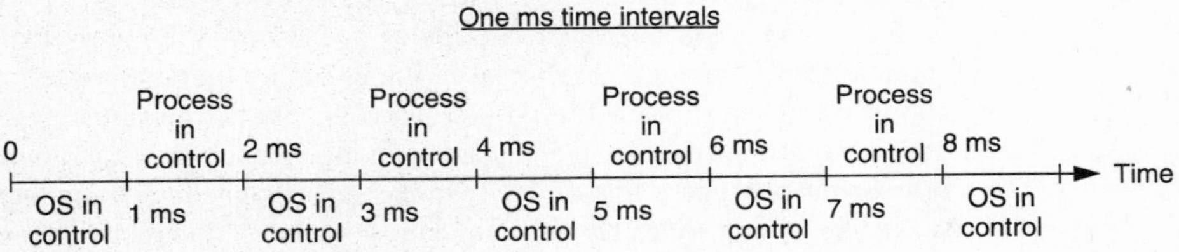

The operating system uses the CPU for 1 ms (from 0 to 1ms), to give control of the CPU to a process. The process then begins running, but executes for no more than 1 ms (from 1ms to 2ms). The operating system then preempts it. The system takes another 1 ms (from 2ms to 3ms) to place the process' PCB at the rear of the queue, and to give control of the CPU to another process. The next process, in turn, also runs for only 1 ms (from 3ms to 4ms).

Can you see what is happening? The operating system and processes alternate using the CPU for 1 ms intervals. The result is that the operating system uses the CPU 50% of the time! During that time no one gets any work done. Small quanta generate excessive operating system overhead. This is like driving your car in low gear. Gears are turning rapidly but you do not get very far.

As the quantum increases, the number of reschedules decreases. The total amount of time that the operating system needs also decreases. Therefore, application processes use the CPU more. The result is that users get more work done. But let's be cautious. This does not necessarily improve user response time.

For example, suppose that 20 processes are in a ready state, and that the operating system requires about 1 ms to do a reschedule. Let us describe two cases. In case **A**, the quantum is 50 ms, and in case **B** it is 100 ms.

In case **A**, there is 1 ms of operating system time for every 50 ms of process time. (This, of course, assumes that each process uses the entire 50 ms allotted to it.) This means that operating system rescheduling routines are active only about 2% of the time. Furthermore, each process is guaranteed a chance to use the CPU about once per second.

In case **B**, there is 1 ms of operating system time for each 100 ms of process time. Operating system overhead is reduced to just 1%. On the other hand, each process is guaranteed a chance to use the CPU only once every two seconds. Overhead time has decreased, but response times have degraded.

Taken to an extreme, large quantum values can cause significant delays for some users. Once a process gets control of the CPU, it can do a lot, but others must wait much longer. In an interactive system, where users expect quick responses all the time, this is unacceptable.

Figure 4.7 shows the relationship between response times and quantum values. Responses are slow when quantum values are small. But they improve as the quantum increases. This is because the main reason for poor response was excessive operating system overhead, which is reduced as the quantum increases. However, as the quantum increases further, responses become slow again. But the main reason for the reduction is now due to the long times during which a process can monopolize the CPU.

The "best" quantum is somewhere in the middle. Its value is difficult to find, because it depends greatly on the number of system users, the time it takes for the operating system to perform a reschedule, and the nature of the executing processes.

Figure 4.7 System response as a function of time quantum

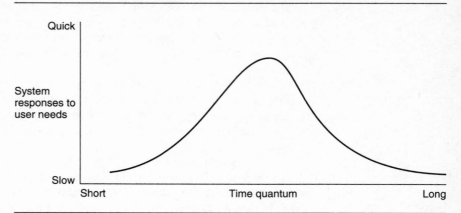

First In First Out Scheduling

Probably the easiest scheduling strategy to implement is *First In First Out* (FIFO). Its nonpreemptive approach is, very simply, "Give control of the CPU to the process that has been in the system the longest." In other words, the earliest arrival gets to use the CPU (see Figure 4.8).

When a process is initialized, the system stores its PCB in the rear of a queue. When the CPU is available, the operating system gives control of the CPU to the process at the front of the queue. The process maintains control until it finishes, and the operating system then gives the CPU to another process.

Figure 4.8 FIFO scheduling

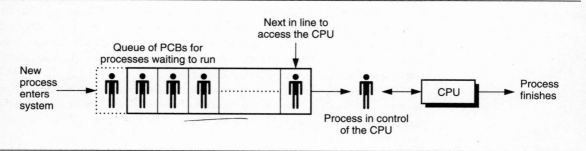

The major advantage of this approach is its simplicity, and this is a feature that should never be undervalued. The operating system reschedules only when absolutely necessary. Overhead, therefore, is small.

FIFO can be unrealistic in many systems. For example, what happens if there is a lot of I/O activity as in highly interactive systems? As we have seen before, a process that issues an I/O request has no use for the CPU until the I/O operation is completed. Why not allow other processes to use the CPU during this time? In this case, preemptive scheduling is best.

Yet, there are cases where FIFO is desirable. Consider a system where most processes do "number crunching." That is, they do many calculations, but very little I/O. Typical applications include fluid dynamics, structural analysis, and image processing. We will demonstrate that, in this case, a round robin approach has no advantage over a FIFO strategy.

Suppose three processes, A, B, and C, all enter the system simultaneously. Suppose also that each requires exactly 1 hour of CPU time. Consider a round robin schedule in which the quantum **Q** is much longer than the rescheduling time. As the processes take turns using the CPU, they progress at about the same rate (Figure 4.9). Therefore, after slightly more than 3 hours, all three have finished.

Figure 4.9 shows the three-hour interval, divided into subintervals of length **Q**. The figure also shows which process is in control during each subinterval.

Figure 4.9   Three processes sharing control of the CPU in a round robin schedule

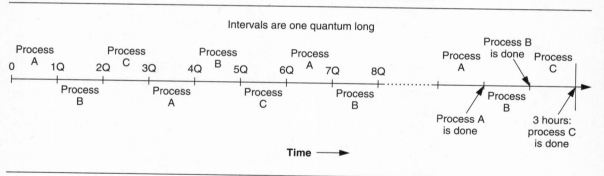

Suppose, instead, we used a FIFO scheduler, and scheduled process A first (Figure 4.10). Since process A needs 1 hour of CPU time and requires little or no output, it will finish in an hour. After it finishes, suppose the operating system gives control of the CPU to process B. B also finishes in one hour. Thus, it has finished 2 hours after entering the system. Finally, process C begins, and after 1 more hour, it also finishes.

Figure 4.10 Three processes using the CPU in a FIFO schedule

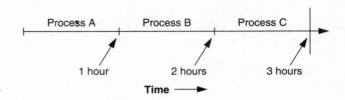

Now compare the results of the two scheduling methods. Table 4.1 shows the turnaround time for each process. It also shows the average turnaround time for all three processes and the number of reschedules done by the operating system.

Table 4.1 Turnaround times and number of reschedules as a function of scheduling approach.

	FIFO	Round Robin
Turnaround time for process A	1 hr.	3 hrs.
Turnaround time for process B	2 hrs.	3 hrs.
Turnaround time for process C	3 hrs.	3 hrs.
Average turnaround time	2 hrs.	3 hrs.
Number of reschedules	3	3 hrs divided by Q (measured in hours)

As the table shows, two processes (A and B) finish much sooner under FIFO. Only process C does not benefit either way. The average turnaround time under FIFO is only 67% of the average under round robin. Furthermore, the round robin values do not reflect the time used by the operating system for reschedules. Thus, they are actually a little worse than shown. If the quantum is 50 ms, there are 72,000 reschedules in 3 hrs. (3,600,000 ms/50 ms). This is a lot of extra overhead for a decrease in performance. Under FIFO, little time is lost since only 3 reschedules occur.

A FIFO scheduler may also be part of a more complex approach, for example, when many systems have a mix of batch and interactive users. Interactive users have short programs to run, need a little information (such as a name or address), or are developing new applications and need quick turnaround. Interactive users at terminals expect almost immediate response from the system. They detect short delays in execution. By contrast, a batch user submits his or her entire program at one time, along with the JCL commands necessary to run it. The JCL may be on a deck of cards, or in some command file. However, after submitting it, the batch user is free to do something else. Unlike the interactive user, he or she need not be present for the process to run. Batch users usually have longer programs to run or want to produce a lot of output. There is no sense waiting at a terminal for a job that will take twenty minutes to run or will generate 1000 address labels or a fifty-page report. Unlike interactive users, batch users will not notice short delays. The operating system can use such facts to provide good service to both types of users.

When batch and interactive processes are mixed, a round robin schedule of all processes is not desirable, especially if there are many batch users. Since they do not need quick responses, why not steal some CPU time from batch processes, and give it to the interactive processes? The batch users may not even notice the difference, and the interactive users will greatly appreciate the improved response.

One way to implement this "Robin Hood" approach is with *batch partitions*. A batch partition is a virtual memory construct that holds a single batch process. (Remember, virtual memory is a view the operating system provides to the user.) There may be several batch partitions, but in this example, we will assume just one.

As processes enter the system, the system distinguishes the batch from the interactive ones. All interactive processes enter the READY state immediately and compete for the CPU. However, the system puts the batch processes in a wait queue for the batch partition (Figure 4.11). Since the partition can hold only one process, all others must wait.

Figure 4.11 Scheduling batch processes along side of interactive processes

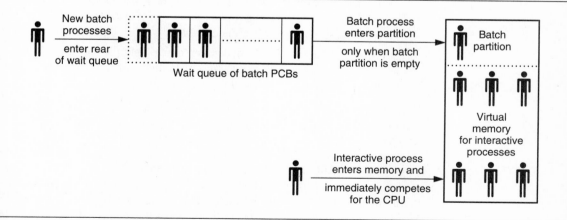

If the partition is empty, the process at the front of the queue is placed in it. The process enters the ready state and competes for the CPU along with the interactive ones. If the partition is full, the process at the front of the queue must wait. The result is a quota system that allows only one batch process to compete for the CPU at a time.

The low-level scheduler is round robin. But no more than one batch process is ever ready. An intermediate-level FIFO scheduler determines which ones enter the ready state.

Note the following about this hybrid approach to scheduling:

- Scheduling batch processes on a FIFO basis means there are fewer ready processes. However, for those, the response times are improved.

- Batch processes suffer longer delays. But as long as the queue does not grow too long, the delays may not be noticeable. Remember, the batch user may be off eating lunch somewhere, or playing racquetball at the YMCA.

- Frequently, batch processes are larger than interactive processes. By allowing only one batch process in memory, more interactive processes can reside there. The transfer of control to a process is faster since there is less swapping. Overall, the system is more efficient.

- This example uses only one batch partition. It is certainly possible to have more. The best number depends on current demands on system resources. If there are few interactive processes, it might be wise to create more batch partitions. In fact, if the number of interactive processes was zero and there was only one partition, the low level scheduler changes from a round robin to a FIFO scheduler (Why?). As we have seen, this is often undesirable.

- There are two ways a system can implement multiple partitions. It can have one queue for all partitions, or one queue for each partition. Processes could be assigned to partitions on a priority basis.

Round robin and FIFO are two common approaches to low and intermediate level scheduling, but they are by no means the only ones. Round robin is most appropriate when users demand quick responses.

Round robin is also appropriate in systems involving batch processes that generate a lot of I/O requests. In this case, we want processes to generate their requests as soon as possible. This keeps the I/O processors active, and decreases the number of processes in the ready state. Since round robin guarantees all ready processes a chance to execute, it increases the chances of generating I/O requests.

FIFO, on the other hand, is best suited to "number crunching" environments, or as part of a more complex scheduling approach such as the one just described. There is nothing to gain by using FIFO in interactive environments or where there is a lot of I/O activity. Similarly, there is nothing to gain by using round robin in a "number crunching" environment.

══

Multilevel Feedback Queues

If all processes are known to be either "number crunching" or I/O intensive, the choice of a scheduling method is simplified. But what happens if the mix varies? Perhaps sometimes there are only "number crunchers" in the ready state, but at other times there are processes that require a lot of I/O. For that matter, what if both are present at the same time?

Computing environments are dynamic, and the types of processes that enter the system may vary tremendously. How can we handle this variety? If we use either round robin or FIFO strategies, there will be times when the scheduler does a poor job. Is there some way a scheduling method can resemble round robin when there is a lot of I/O activity, and then resemble FIFO when there is little or none?

One dual-faceted approach is called *Multilevel Feedback Queues* (MFQ). In it, scheduling depends on the activities currently in progress. The best scheduling approach is dependent on the types of processes in the ready state, and the MFQ system is sensitive to changes in those activities. We call it an adaptive method.

When a lot of I/O activity is in progress, MFQ resembles a round robin scheduler. On the other hand, if little or no I/O activity is in progress, it resembles a FIFO scheduler. MFQ is never completely FIFO, since this would make it unable to respond to changes while a particular process has control of the CPU. But it does perform fewer reschedules by allowing each process to have control of the CPU for longer times.

As the name suggests, MFQ consists of many queues (say, **n** of them). The queues are numbered 1 through **n**, and each one has a priority associated with it. Queue 1 has the highest priority, queue 2 the second highest, and so on. Queue **n** has the lowest priority. The PCB for a process in the ready state is stored in one of the queues. Its priority is determined by the queue in which it resides.

The low level scheduler always schedules by priority. A low priority process will not gain control of the CPU if there is another ready process with a higher priority. If several ready processes have the same priority, and none have a higher one, the scheduler will choose the one at the front of the queue (FIFO).

Whenever a new process is initiated, the system puts it in the READY state and stores its PCB in the first queue. Thus, each new process initially has the highest possible priority. When the CPU is available, the low level scheduler finds the highest priority queue that is not empty. It then gives control of the CPU to the process at the front of that queue. The process then retains control of the CPU until one of the following occurs (see Figure 4.12):

- The process finishes (either gracefully or by aborting).
- The process requests something for which it must wait (for example, an I/O request).
- The quantum expires.

Figure 4.12 Multilevel feedback queueing system

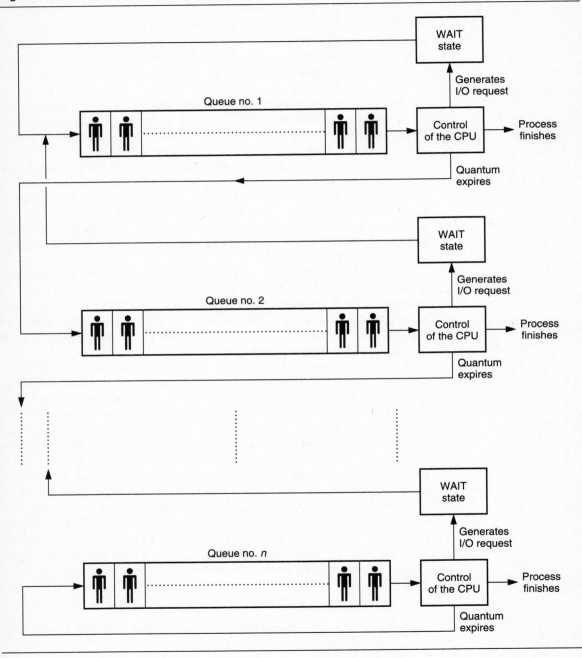

The quantum depends on the queue from which the process was chosen. Typically, each queue has a different quantum. Queue 1 has the smallest quantum, queue 2 the next smallest, and so on up to queue **n**, which has the largest quantum.

Now, consider what happens to each process in each case listed above. If the process finishes, it leaves the system and is no longer considered.

If the process requests something for which it must wait, the intermediate scheduler puts it in the wait state. When the process gets what it needs, it returns to the ready state. But what priority should it get? If its PCB was in the first queue, then the system stores it at the rear of that queue. In other words, the process retains the highest possible priority.

However, suppose the process' PCB was most recently in some other queue, say queue **j**, where **j**>1. In this case, the system stores it at the rear of queue **j**-1. In other words, the system increases the process' priority

Suppose the process does not request anything and does not finish. Then after a quantum has passed, the operating system removes control of the CPU from it. Remember, the quantum value depends on the queue that contained the process' PCB. In this case, the process remains in the ready state. But again, what priority should it get? If the process' PCB was most recently in the **n**th queue, then the system stores it at the rear of the same queue. In other words, it retains the lowest possible priority.

But suppose the process' PCB was most recently in queue **j**, where **j** < **n**. In this case, the system stores it at the rear of queue **j** + 1. In other words, the system lowers the process' priority.

Well, this is all really interesting, but how does it adapt low level scheduling to the types of processes that are ready?

Consider a case where all processes are I/O bound (generate frequent I/O requests) or interactive. They all initially receive the highest priority. Furthermore, because they are I/O bound, the system receives I/O requests frequently. Let us assume the quantum is slightly longer than the average time between I/O requests. As a result, most processes generate I/O requests before the quantum expires.

Now when an I/O request is completed, the process eventually reenters the ready state with the same or higher priority. Therefore, each I/O bound process tends to retain a high priority and generate more I/O requests.

If a process executes for a while without an I/O request, the quantum will expire. In this case, the process remains in the ready state but with a lower priority (unless it already has the lowest priority). But if the process is still I/O bound, it will soon generate more I/O requests and get higher priorities again. This is very close to a round robin schedule among the processes in the first few queues. The quantum of the highest priority queue approximates the optimum value suggested by Figure 4.7.

Suppose now that the entering processes are mainly "number crunching." They may generate few I/O requests, but spend most of their time executing code. Whenever they gain control of the CPU, the quantum will usually expire. As a result, they return to the ready state with a lower priority (unless they already have the lowest priority). If this pattern continues, the processes eventually receive the lowest possible priority.

If all ready processes are "number crunching," they will all eventually get the lowest priorities. Thus, the low level scheduler primarily schedules low priority processes. It becomes a round robin scheduler with a larger quantum than that used for I/O bound processes. The larger quanta are justified, since nothing is gained by frequent rescheduling of "number crunchers." Although the scheduler is still round robin, the large quanta give it more of a FIFO appearance.

Next, suppose there is a mix of I/O bound and CPU bound processes. The I/O bound ones retain high priority, while the CPU bound ones' priority decreases. The scheduler then favors the I/O bound processes over the CPU bound processes. By doing so, it keeps the I/O processors active and increases the degree of multiprocessing. CPU bound processes run only when no I/O bound processes are ready.

Not only is MFQ sensitive to differences among processes, it is also sensitive to changes within a process. For example, a process may start out as I/O bound, but then change to CPU bound. The reverse may also be true: a CPU bound process may begin to issue many I/O requests. When this happens, it gradually receives higher priority. Likewise, an I/O bound process that ceases to generate I/O requests will gradually receive lower priority.

The multilevel queuing system is a flexible method that automatically adapts to the workload and changes in the behavior patterns of processes. If a system has mainly interactive or CPU bound processes, then MFQ is more complex than needed. But in an unpredictable environment, the approach can be productive. In fact, as we will see in chapter 8, it is the scheduling approach used by the VAX/VMS operating system.

Shortest Process Scheduling

The scheduling approaches described so far are best suited to different types of computing environments. However, they all degrade if there are too many processes.

For example, if the scheduler is FIFO, many processes in the queue cause long delays for those near the rear. The delay is particularly annoying for short process waiting behind longer processes. How would you feel about waiting in line at a bank to make a small withdrawal, while the person ahead of you arranges a multimillion dollar mortgage for an office building?

Similar problems can occur with a round robin schedule. If there are too many processes, the scheduler needs more time to cycle through all of them. The result is significantly longer response times.

Is it logical to give a higher priority to short processes to get them out of the system faster? If so, the system can then keep the number of processes competing for resources smaller.

The successes or failures of the previous approaches depend heavily on the type of activity the running processes need. As a result, we distinguished between I/O bound and CPU bound processes, but never distinguished between long and short processes. The above examples suggest that perhaps we should make such a distinction.

There are two strategies that give higher priorities to short processes. They are *Shortest Job First* (SJF) and *Shortest Remaining Job Next* (SRJN). They are similar in that the low level scheduler considers the amount of time needed by a ready process. Simply put, it chooses the one that needs the least time. The two strategies differ in that SRJN is preemptive and SJF is not.

A disadvantage is that both approaches have difficulty answering the question, "How do you know how much time a particular process needs?" It is difficult (in fact, usually impossible) for an operating system to calculate how much time a process needs. However, the person who submitted it will usually have a good estimate. (If not, he or she probably should not be submitting the job.) Such estimates are, in fact, often part of the required JCL. Thus, the low level scheduler can use this estimate to decide which process gets control of the CPU. With SJF, the low level scheduler simply picks the ready process with the shortest estimated run time. Once given the CPU, the process runs to completion.

As we saw earlier, nonpreemptive scheduling creates problems if there are I/O requests. But, if little or no I/O is expected, SJF is viable. Short processes will get great response since they will have the highest priority. System throughput (number of processes passing through the system per unit of time) is impressive. In fact, SJF generates the highest possible throughput. If the objective is to maximize the number of happy users, this method is the best.

But throughput can give a false impression of the system's productivity. Consider the user whose process runs a little longer than many others. The system penalizes it. Indeed, it may face *indefinite postponement* or *starvation*; that is, it may wait forever. As long as shorter processes are coming into the system, the longer ones will not run. To have a process wait for hours, only to see a slightly shorter process enter and leave the system very quickly, may be grossly unfair, particularly if the longer process is yours (or, even worse, mine).

The preemptive version of SJF is SRJN. A process that has control of the CPU may relinquish control if it requests something for which it must wait. If a new process has a shorter estimated run time than that of the currently running process, it gets control of the CPU. Like SJF, SJRN generates high throughput, but it also suffers from the same drawbacks. Longer processes may experience unacceptable delays.

≡≡≡
Starvation

We have seen that the SJF and SJRN methods can cause starvation of longer processes. The MFQ method can also cause starvation of processes in the lower queues. As long as there are ready, interactive processes, the CPU bound ones are ignored. Can we do anything about starvation, or must we live with it as a by-product of a particular method?

One option is to ignore it and hope it causes no serious problems. This is not always an unrealistic approach. For example, under MFQ, interactive processes leave the queues quickly. However, due to the disparity in computing and I/O speeds, it takes much longer for them to return. As a result, it is not unusual to see the high priority queues empty quickly. This, of course, gives the low priority processes a chance to run.

Similar observations may be made for the SJF and SJRN methods. Here, there is an even larger disparity between computing and human processing speeds. It is unlikely that many users can generate short processes more quickly than a CPU can execute them. (We all like to think we are fast, but let's be realistic). In these cases, starvation is rare. Even when it does occur, it will not last long.

Still, saying that events are not likely to happen does not mean they can't happen. Starvation of CPU bound processes under MFQ is more likely as the number of interactive processes increases. Similarly, starvation of long processes under SJF or SJRN is more likely as the number of users increases. In such cases, starvation is a more serious problem.

If we choose not to ignore it, what can the system do? One approach is to suspend some of the ready processes. This reduces the number of processes and minimizes starvation. The system will resume processes when it decides it can handle more.

Another alternative is to recalculate process priorities periodically. The system may do this by using a field, LastTime, in each process' PCB. Initially, the time a process enters the system is stored there. However, whenever a process is preempted, the system changes the field to the preemption time. Under nonpreemptive scheduling, the field never changes. When the system evaluates a process' priority, it examines the value of

$$\text{current time - LastTime.}$$

A large value means the process has been ignored for a long time. If the value increases beyond some threshold value, the system increases priority for that process. Under MFQ, this means putting the PCB in a higher queue. Under SJF or SJRN, this means changing the priority field of the PCB.

You may have noticed that we have not discussed starvation under Round Robin or FIFO. There is a good reason for this: starvation does not occur. (Why?)

═══
Summary

We have discussed five scheduling methods, namely:

1. Round Robin
2. First In First Out (FIFO)
3. Multilevel Feedback Queues (MFQ)
4. Shortest Job First (SJF)
5. Shortest Remaining Job Next (SRJN)

As you probably can surmise from our discussions, none of them is always the best. The simple fact is that each one has strong points and weak points. A scheduling approach that may work well in one system may not work well in another. Each responds to specific situations and achieves different objectives.

Table 4.2 summarizes each approach and points out its advantages and disadvantages.

Table 4.2 Summary of scheduling methods

	Round Robin	FIFO	MFQ	SJF	SJRN
Throughput	not emphasized, but may be low if quantum is too small.	not emphasized.	not emphasized, but may be low if quanta are too small.	high.	high.
Response	shortest average response time, if the quantum is chosen correctly.	may be poor, especially if a long process has control of the CPU.	good for I/O bound, but may be poor for CPU bound processes.	good for short processes, but may be poor for longer processes.	good for short processes, but may be poor for longer processes.
Overhead	low.	the lowest of all the methods.	can be high, needs complex data structures and routines to find the appropriate queue after each reschedule.	can be high, requires a routine to find the shortest job for each reschedule.	can be high, requires a routine to find the minimum remaining time for each reschedule.
CPU bound Processes	no distinction between CPU and I/O bound processes.	no distinction between CPU and I/O bound processes.	receive low priority if I/O bound processes are present.	no distinction between CPU and I/O bound processes.	no distinction between CPU and I/O bound processes.
I/O bound Processes	no distinction between CPU and I/O bound processes.	no distinction between CPU and I/O bound processes.	receive high priority to keep I/O processors active.	no distinction between CPU and I/O bound processes.	no distinction between CPU and I/O bound processes.
Indefinite Postponement	does not occur.	does not occur.	may occur for CPU bound processes.	may occur for processes with long estimated run times.	may occur for processes with long estimated run times.

≡ **4.5 Case Study: Scheduling Under MVS**

There is no question that IBM computers are omnipresent. Businesses, industries, and government agencies around the world use IBM equipment and software for a wide variety of applications such as banking, inventory, and payroll. This section provides a brief exposure to the scheduling concepts and terminology of a major IBM mainframe operating system—MVS. Space does not allow a detailed description of MVS scheduling. The reader interested in further study should consult references [2-12].

≡ Background

MVS (*Multiple Virtual Storage*) is an operating system used on IBM mainframes. It may run on the relatively small 9370 machines, the medium sized 4381 machines, and on the largest 3090 models. Depending on the hardware, it may efficiently support up to several hundred concurrent users. It is the descendant of operating systems developed in the mid-1960s for the System/360.

The earliest IBM System/360 models supported OS/MVT (Multi programming with a Variable number of Tasks). Primarily a batch-oriented system, it gave way to OS/VS2, and eventually to MVS to allow time sharing, multiprocessing, spooling, and sophisticated information management systems. MVS has become a common operating system used in data centers with a high level of resources and needs.

Recall from Chapter 2 that virtual storage is an operating system construct, providing a view of where a process appears to reside in memory. In reality, the operating system stores the process wherever real memory is available. Dynamic address translation during process execution converts memory references from virtual to real locations.

Multiple Virtual Storage allows for multiple address spaces in which processes appear to reside. For example, Figure 4.13 shows a memory containing **n** address spaces. The operating system's view is that each process resides in one of them. In reality, the code and data reside in available frames of real memory or in secondary storage. When a process executes, its page and segment tables implement dynamic address translation.

Figure 4.13 show the use of page and segment tables for each address space. The tables point to the frames containing the process' code and data.

Figure 4.13 Multiple address spaces

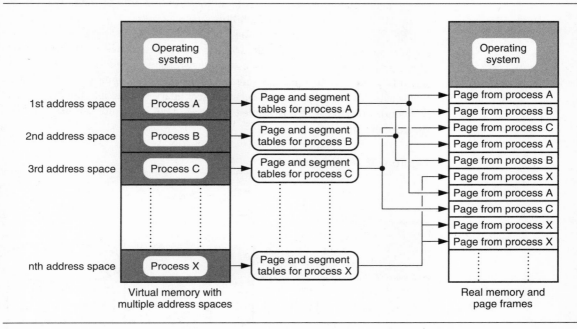

Figure 4.14 shows how MVS organizes real memory. The example involves 12 Mb (Megabytes), a typical size in smaller systems. The resident part of the operating system (sometimes called its *nucleus* or *kernel*) resides in the low end of memory. It occupies .5 Mb, indicated by *System* in the figure.

Figure 4.14 Real memory organization under MVS

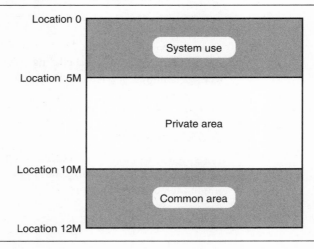

The top 2 Mb of memory contain I/O buffers, transient routines, and control blocks needed as processes run. This is the *common* area of memory. It is not essential to our discussion of scheduling.

The *private* area contains (among other things) the user region. Its frames contain process pages from their working sets. As indicated in our discussions of paging in Chapter 2, a process may reference pages in memory or in secondary storage. If a process references a page in secondary storage, a page fault occurs. MVS swaps pages between secondary storage and the private area of memory (Figure 4.15). If it must replace a page in memory, it uses an LRU replacement strategy.

Figure 4.15 Paging under MVS

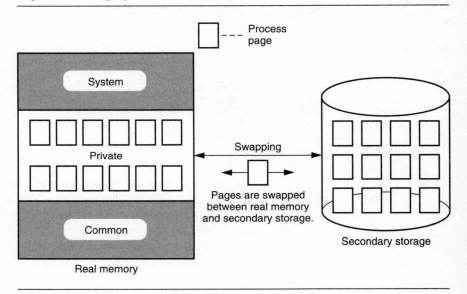

Now that we have provided a few basic facts about MVS, the remainder of the case study will focus on scheduling. We will describe two major components of MVS scheduling: *job management* and *task management*.

Job Management

Let's first define a job. Typically, a job consists of assigning files (called *data sets*), and compiling, linking, and running programs. For example, a payroll job might include the following:

- Locate the file of employee records.
- Find the file containing information from the most recent pay period.
- Run a program to compute gross and net wages for each employee.
- Run a program to sort this information and save it on a file.
- Run a program to print payroll checks.

This one job consists of several file assignments and the running of several programs.

A job submitted to MVS is defined by a set of Job Control Language (JCL) commands. They allow the user to tell MVS what system resources he or she needs. We refer the interested reader to reference [4] for a description of the MVS JCL. We also discuss it in Chapter 8.

The JCL typically does the following (and much more):

- Identifies the user.
- Defines resource limits such as maximum time and maximum memory values.
- Calls compilers or linkers.
- Catalogs files. That is, inserts them into a system catalog for future reference.
- Runs programs.
- Locates data sets (or files).

As we said, a single job may involve compilation, running, and data set assignments for several programs. The execution of a single program within a job is a *job step*. For example, the previously described payroll job has three steps, one for each program it executes. Note that compilation is a job step, as it requires the execution of a program (the compiler).

Lastly, a *job stream* is a sequence of jobs submitted to MVS. The payroll job might be part of a long stream, perhaps including tax reporting, personnel record updating, and general accounting.

The initial aspect of scheduling requires MVS to handle the many jobs submitted to it (job management). Thus, the first question we ask is, "How does it treat them?"

To discuss job management, we focus on three MVS components. They are:

- Job Entry Subsystem (JES)
- Master Scheduler
- Job Scheduler

Job Entry Subsystem

A job may be submitted through JCL typed on cards (no longer common), entered from a terminal, or stored on files (Figure 4.16). Therefore, the first

Figure 4.16 Job entry subsystem

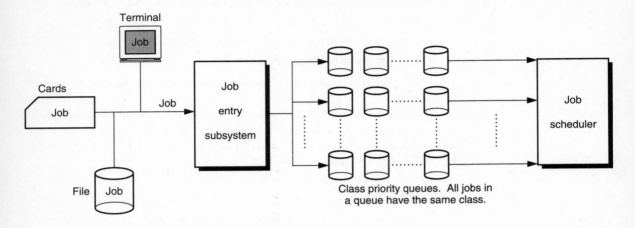

Class priority queues. All jobs in
a queue have the same class.

logical step in scheduling a job is to examine its JCL. The Job Entry Subsystem
(JES) does this.

The JES scans the JCL commands and converts them into internal text that
MVS can read. If it finds any errors, it prevents the job from entering the
system, and prints error messages for the disgusted user.

If it finds no errors in the JCL, JES determines the job's *class* and *priority*,
typically from the first command. Users may define job classes depending on
the type and number of resources needed. MVS knows that jobs with the same
class have similar needs.

The jobs are next put in class priority queues. JES must categorize the jobs
based on class and priority for the job scheduler. They then wait for further
action.

The JES also routes printer output to spooling files. In other words, when a
job step writes data to a printer, the JES places the output in a spooling file (not
shown in Figure 4.16). After the job finishes, the JES sends the spooled output
to a printer. It then releases the space that held the spooled output for later
reuse.

Master Scheduler

The master scheduler has many functions. The one we are most concerned with
here is the role it plays when a job is submitted.

The master scheduler calls an MVS routine that creates an address space for
a job. Not surprisingly, this routine is called the *Address Space Creation
Routine* (ASCR). Remember, as previously stated, MVS must provide each job
with an address space in which to run.

The first step in creating an address space is to construct an *Address Space Control Block* (ASCB). ASCBs define address spaces under MVS. Specifically, each one contains the real memory location of the segment table that running tasks use for dynamic address translation. (An MVS "task" is similar to a process. The difference is not important here.) It also locates control blocks for task in the address space. This is useful when the low-level scheduler looks for a task to schedule for execution. MVS maintains all ASCBs in the common area of memory.

After creating the ASCBs, the ASCR calls the *System Resources Manager* (SRM). It distributes resources among the address spaces in accordance with the installation's requirements. It also optimizes use of the resources.

Depending on available resources, the SRM determines whether the current job should have an address space created for it. Basically, it answers the question, "Based on current resource allocation, can this job access what it needs to execute?" If not, ASCBs are deleted, and the space is released back to the common area. If the SRM decides the job can access the required resources, it returns control to the ASCR. The ASCR in turn calls the *Virtual Storage Manager* (VSM). The VSM allocates and releases virtual storage. It must build the segment and page tables used in dynamic address translation.

Once the tables have been built, the last step for the ASCR is to create the *Region Control Task* (RCT). The RCT is a task that maintains the address space and provides a smooth transition between job steps. Specifically, it spawns subtasks that prepare an address space before the execution of a job step and clean up afterward. We will describe the subtasks shortly.

Before proceeding to the next step, let's quickly review how the components fit together. Figure 4.17 shows the steps described so far. The JES initially scans a job's JCL (step a). If it finds no errors, it puts the job in a class priority queue (step b). The job's class determines the queue and its priority determines placement within the queue. The master scheduler calls the ASCR to create an ASCB (step c). The ASCR next calls the SRM (step d) to determine whether to create an address space. If resources are available, the ASCR calls the VSM (step e) to build the segment and page tables. The net result is that the ASCR has created an address space and another task, the RCT (step f), to control the space. Finally, the job proceeds to the job scheduler (step g).

Figure 4.17 JES and the master scheduler responding to a job

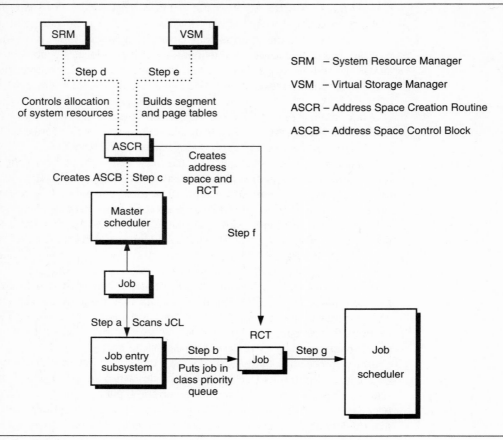

SRM – System Resource Manager

VSM – Virtual Storage Manager

ASCR – Address Space Creation Routine

ASCB – Address Space Control Block

≡≡≡
Job Scheduler

The job scheduler prepares jobs for execution according to their classes and priorities. Remember, Figure 4.17 shows only one job, but there are actually many jobs in many queues. The job scheduler reads and interprets each job step. It uses two components to handle preparation for execution and the smooth transition between steps: the *initiator* and the *terminator* (Figure 4.18).

Although their names sound like movie titles or ominous figures in a mob or guerrilla organization, they are actually harmless routines that create and release space for tables needed in job execution. In particular, the initiator creates the *Job Control Table* (JCT) and *Step Control Tables* (SCT).

Figure 4.18 Initiator and terminator execution

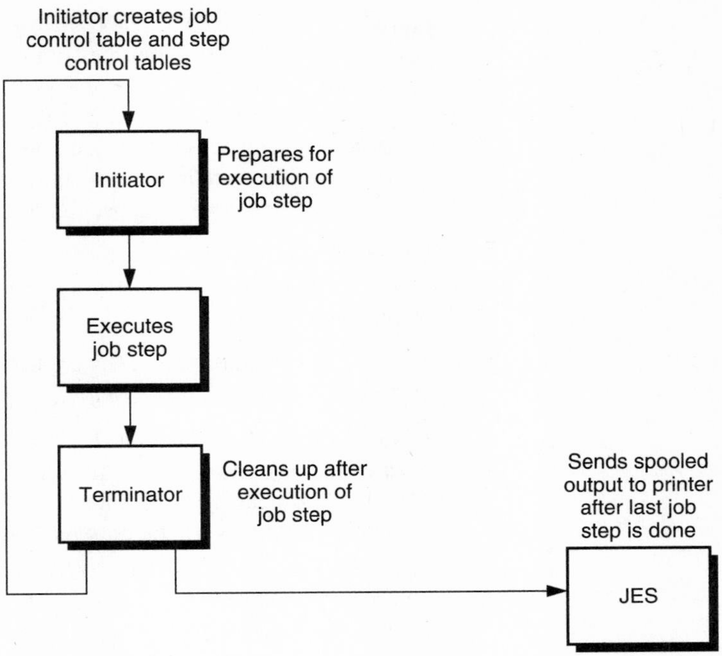

The JCT contains information specified in the job's first JCL command or *job statement*. For example, it includes:

- Class and priority.
- Programmer's name.
- Accounting information such as account number.
- Time limit for the entire job. MVS will not allow accumulated CPU time to exceed this value.
- Message level. Different levels control the amount of information (e.g., list of JCL commands or system messages) that is printed when the job finishes.
- Space limit for the entire job. MVS will not allocate more main memory than this.

The entire job has a single JCT. However, each step has an SCT. Previously, we stated that a job step is the execution of a single program in a job. This may be done by using the JCL *EXEC* command. This command also has options that the initiator puts in the SCTs. For example, these options include:

- Program name.
- Time and space limits like those in the job control table. The ones specified in a job step apply only to the step.
- Condition code test. After the completion of each job step, MVS defines a condition code. Job steps that complete successfully generate different codes than ones that abort. The JCL can then examine the condition code and skip steps that depend on data an aborted step was supposed to produce. The conditional execution of steps helps to avoid compounding errors and useless runs.

Having created the JCT and the SCTs, the initiator next prepares for the execution of the first job step (task). Among the things it must do are the following (Figure 4.19):

- Locate needed data sets. They are defined by the job's JCL.
- Allocate I/O devices needed to transfer data for each data set.
- Build a *Task I/O Table* (TIOT). The TIOT contains the names of the data sets and pointers to File Control Blocks and allocated devices. The File • Control Blocks, in turn, contain descriptions and locations of the data sets. I/O routines use them to read and write.
- Build a Task Control Block (TCB). The TCB resembles the process control block described earlier in this chapter. (We will discuss the TCB shortly in the section on task management.)

Figure 4.19 Initiator operations

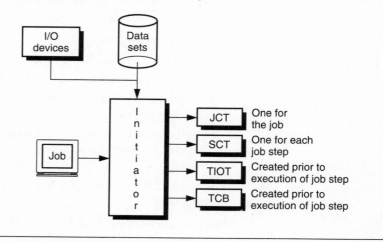

When a job step finishes, the terminator takes over. Among its cleanup work are the following tasks:

- Release devices to make them available for subsequent job steps.

- Associate a *disposition* with data sets used in the job step. In the JCL, a user may specify the disposition of any referenced data set. It indicates, for example, whether a data set should be saved permanently, passed to the next job step for access, or released immediately. The last option usually applies to temporary or scratch files used by several job steps.

- Determine whether the job has other steps. If it does, the terminator examines the job step's *condition code*. As previously stated, the condition code reflects how the step terminated. Typically, if it was successful, the condition code is zero. If it aborted due to an error, the condition code depends on what happened. Now if the condition code is zero and there are other job steps, the terminator returns control to the initiator. (But don't worry. The terminator will be back.) The initiator then prepares for the execution of the next step. If there no more steps, or the condition code dictates that the rest should be skipped, the virtual storage for the job is released. The terminator then passes control to the JES which routes spooled output to the line printer (Figure 4.18). Finally, the job exits the system.

Everything so far has helped prepare a job or job step for execution. The last aspect of scheduling is how the low-level scheduler decides which ready task gets control of the CPU. This is *task management*.

▬▬▬
Task Management

Task management controls the allocation of the CPU, virtual memory, and main memory. The task manager includes a *dispatcher* which recognizes three task states, active, ready, and waiting. An active task is running. It has control of a CPU. A ready task has all the resources it needs and is waiting for the CPU so it may run. A waiting task is waiting for another task (such as an I/O routine) to finish.

Previously, we said that the initiator creates a *task control block* for a job step. At any given time, many jobs are in the system. It follows that many job steps and many TCBs may also exist. Basically, the dispatcher scans the list of TCBs, looking for a ready task. When it finds one, it schedules it for execution. But how does MVS manage the TCBs so the dispatcher can scan them?

The TCBs are accessible through the ASCBs that the ASCR created earlier. Recall that all ASCBs reside in the common area of memory (Figure 4.14) Specifically, they are stored in a subset of the common area called the *System Queue Area* (SQA) (Figure 4.20).

There is an ASCB for each address space. Through it, MVS can access the segment and page tables. It also points to the *Region Control Task* (RCT/TCB). Remember, since the RCT is a task, it also has a TCB. The RCT/TCB marks the beginning of a TCB chain. Each entry in the chain corresponds to a task and specifies its status.

Figure 4.20 Task control blocks and address space control blocks

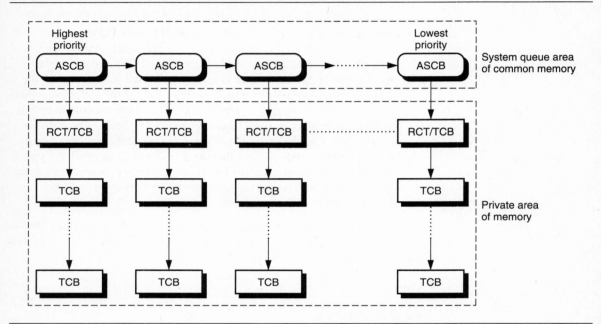

When the dispatcher looks for a task to activate, it scans the TCB chains associated with the ASCBs. It first scans the chain associated with the highest-priority ASCB. If it finds a ready task, the dispatcher gives it control of the CPU. If it does not find one, it searches the TCB chain associated with the next highest-priority ASCB. It continues in order of decreasing ASCB priority until it finds a ready task.

The task then runs until it finishes, issues a request to the operating system, or uses its quantum. The dispatcher then repeats the process. The approach is a hybrid combining elements of priority and round robin scheduling. The preemptive dispatcher forces the tasks to take turns using the CPU. However, a task associated with a low-priority ASCB will run only when there are no ready tasks associated with higher-priority ASCBs.

≡≡≡
MVS Scheduling Summary

We realize that all the acronyms and the number of routines involved make this case study quite imposing. For the benefit of the reader, we have listed acronyms we have used along with their meaning and function in Table 4.3. The key point is that real systems are complex and involve cooperation among many components. We have tried to strike a compromise between vagueness and excessive detail by describing the major routines MVS uses and the events that occur as it schedules jobs and job steps. The scheduling of jobs in a large mainframe environment with heavy demand is a very difficult task.

Table 4.3 MVS scheduling acronyms

Acronym	Meaning	Function
ASCB	Address Space Control Block	Locates segment tables and the first in a chain of TCBs for the address space.
ASCR	Address Space Creation Routine	Creates a process' address space and calls the System Resource Manager and Virtual Storage Manager.
IBM	International Business Machines	One of the world's largest developers and manufacturers of computer hardware and software.
JCL	Job Control Language	Language used to communicate with MVS.
JCT	Job Control Table	Contains information pertinent to a job such as the class, priority, limits, name, and accounting information.
JES	Job Entry Subsystem	Scans a job's JCL before allowing it to enter the system. It also routes printer output to spooling files.
MVS	Multiple Virtual Storage	Operating system designed to run on any of several IBM mainframe computers.
RCT	Region Control Task	Task that maintains an address space and provides a smooth transition between job steps.
RCT/TCB	Region Control Task/Task Control Block	The first in a chain of TCBs for an address space.
SCT	Step Control Table	Contains information pertinent to a job step such as the name, limits, and condition code.
SQA	System Queue Area	Subset of MVS' common area of memory containing ASCBs.
SRM	System Resources Manager	Determines which tasks get system resources.
TCB	Task Control Block	MVS version of a Process Control Block (PCB).
TIOT	Task I/O Table	Contains the names of data sets and pointers to File Control Blocks and devices allocated to a task.
VSM	Virtual Storage Manager	Allocates and releases virtual storage.

4.6 Summary

This chapter discussed the scheduling of processes. We have both defined approaches, and described how well they meet system goals. A scheduling approach should be efficient, fair to users, consistent, responsive and effective in managing resources.

In practice, many goals are contradictory. Trying to achieve one often detracts from achieving another. Any scheduling approach must compromise. For example, an approach should not be maximally efficient at the cost of delaying some users indefinitely, nor should it keep resources occupied at the cost of excessive overhead.

To do scheduling, the operating system recognizes that a process may be in one of several states. Possible states include ready, running, waiting, and suspended. To a large extent, scheduling involves state transitions. High-level schedulers control which programs enter the system, and intermediate-level schedulers control which processes compete for the CPU. The two levels respond mainly to events such as the submission of a job or an I/O request by a running process.

The low-level scheduler determines which processes get control of the CPU. It is active much more frequently than either high- or intermediate-level schedulers. Also, there are many more options for it. As a result, most discussions of schedulers focus on the low level.

We discussed several low-level scheduling strategies: priority, round robin, First In First Out, Multilevel Feedback Queues, and shortest process scheduling. We also described a hybrid approach in which a low-level scheduler was a round robin but an intermediate-level scheduler used FIFO. Each approach had both advantages and disadvantages depending on the types and length of processes. For example, round robin is good when there are a lot of interactive or I/O-bound processes. On the other hand, FIFO is best when the processes are mainly CPU-bound. Multilevel Feedback Queues respond to changing conditions, resembling round robin when there are many I/O-bound jobs, and looking more like FIFO when there are none.

The case study concerned scheduling in IBM's MVS mainframe operating system. The discussion involved defining terms and describing major components of the high- and intermediate-level schedulers. Major components of the intermediate-level scheduler or job manager are:

- Job entry subsystem (JES).
- Master scheduler which includes the address space creation routine, system resource manager, and virtual storage manager.
- Job scheduler which includes the initiator and terminator

The low-level scheduler is part of task management. We described the dispatcher that schedules ready tasks for execution on a priority basis. This case study is incomplete. A thorough description of MVS could occupy an entire book (probably more) by itself. But the case study does illustrate the complexity of scheduling in real systems.

══ **Exercises**

1. Give an example in which round robin scheduling of CPU-bound processes generates a lower average turnaround than a FIFO scheduling.
2. Suppose that CPU-bound processes are scheduled in a round robin manner. If the reschedule time is 2 ms, what quantum will keep the total scheduling time less than 10% of the total time?
3. For the system described in exercise 2, write the percentage in terms of the quantum, **Q**.
4. Suppose the following processes arrive simultaneously and immediately compete for the CPU.

process number	execution time (arbitrary units)
1	6
2	2
3	4
4	8

Consider the following scheduling approaches:

a) Shortest process first (nonpreemptive).
b) FIFO (in the event of simultaneous arrivals, schedule in numerical order).
c) Round Robin with quantum = 1 (start scheduling in numerical order).
d) Round Robin with quantum = 2 (start scheduling in numerical order).

For each approach, answer the following questions:

a) What is the turnaround time for each process?
b) What is the average turnaround time?
c) How much time does each process spend waiting?

5. Give conditions for which a multilevel feedback queue scheduler is equivalent to a round robin one.
6. The following diagram indicates process states. The arrows between the boxes indicate state transitions.

a) For each transition, describe an event that could cause it.
b) Why is there no arrow from the wait to the running state?
c) Why is there no arrow from the ready to the wait state?

7. We discussed the following scheduling methods:
   • Round Robin
   • FIFO
   • Multilevel Feedback Queues
   • Shortest Job First
   • Shortest Remaining Job Next

   Consider a system that must run many types of processes, including large, small, CPU-bound, I/O-bound, batch, and interactive ones. Consider all the following requirements and state which strategy best fulfills all of them. For each remaining strategy, list at least one requirement that is not fulfilled.

    a) The number of interactive processes is relatively small. They should have high priority, but short delays are acceptable.

    b) I/O-bound processes should get high priority to keep I/O processors active.

    c) CPU-bound processes must defer to I/O-bound processes, even if they have been waiting a long time.

    d) When CPU-bound processes are the only ones that are ready, operating system overhead should be minimized.

8. A process is normally charged for the resources and services it uses. Information determining the cost is normally stored in the PCB. List items (beyond those listed in section 4.3) you would expect to find there.

9. Section 4.4 discussed a hybrid approach to scheduling. Specifically, the low-level scheduler used round robin for interactive processes and one batch process. Under what conditions does the low-level scheduler default to FIFO?

10. Why is starvation impossible under round robin and FIFO scheduling?

11. Consider round robin scheduling where there are fewer than 75 ready processes. If the system requires 1 ms to do a reschedule, what quantum will guarantee that each process can run at least once in a 2-second period?

12. Consider the following definitions:

    R = time to reschedule.

    N = maximum number of ready processes.

    T = maximum time during which a ready process must be given a chance to run.

Write the quantum, Q, in terms of R, N, and T.

≡≡≡≡≡≡ Questions

1. Consider a variation on round robin scheduling that provides larger quanta for processes with higher priorities. That is, the quantum is not constant, but varies with process priority. Compare this to a standard round robin method. List some advantages and disadvantages of this variation.

2. A system programmer may adjust the quantum for a round robin scheduler to reflect the kinds of processes in the system. When is it advantageous to increase the quantum? To decrease it?

3. Consider a system with a round robin scheduler and mostly interactive users. Suppose that, on the average, a process runs 10 ms before issuing an I/O request. Which of the following quantum values would you use? Why?

$$Q = 1\text{ms}; Q = 9 \text{ ms}; Q = 11 \text{ ms}; Q = 50 \text{ ms}.$$

4. Suppose a single CPU system uses preemptive scheduling. How can more memory increase overall throughput? After all, only one process at a time can run.

5. When a process issues an I/O request, the operating system places it in a wait state. In some cases, a process can request that this not be done. In what situations is this request reasonable?

6. Suppose you must maximize the efficiency of a large multiuser system. Suppose also you are receiving complaints from many users of poor response and turnaround times. A call to operations reveals that the CPU is in use 99.9% of the time, and that I/O processors are active only 10% of the time. Which of the following could be reasons for the poor responses? Why?

    a) The quantum in the round robin scheduling is too short.

    b) There is insufficient main memory.

    c) There is too much main memory for the operating system to manage. Management routines are using all the CPU cycles.

    d) The CPU is too slow.

    e) Quantum in the round robin scheduling is too long.

7. Consider question 6 again. This time assume the call to operations reveals the CPU is active about 10% of the time and that I/O processors are active about 99.9% of the time. Which of the listed reasons could cause the poor response now? Why?

8. Reconstruct Figure 4.11 for a system with two partitions. When are two partitions better than one?

9. Consider a system with two CPUs. Discuss how you might generalize each of the scheduling methods described in this chapter.

10. Which of the scheduling methods discussed in this chapter could be modified to accommodate a few real-time processes (one which <u>must</u> have a response within a specified period) mixed in with the others. For those you could modify, state how. For those you could not, state why.

11. Implement some different scheduling methods in Phase II of the simulator in Appendix A. Run as specified in Appendix A and compare the results.

References

1. Bic, L., and A. C. Shaw. *The Logical Design Of Operating Systems*. 2nd ed. Englewood Cliffs, NJ: Prentice-Hall, 1988.

2. Deitel, H. M. *An Introduction to Operating Systems*. 2nd ed. Reading, MA: Addison-Wesley, 1990.

3. Davis, W. S. *Operating System: A Systematic View*. 3rd ed. Reading, MA: Addison-Wesley, 1987.

4. Janossy, J. G. *Practical MVS JCL for Today's Programmers*. New York: Wiley, 1987.

5. Yuen, C. K. *Essential Concepts of Operating Systems Using IBM Mainframe Examples*. Reading, MA: Addison-Wesley, 1986.

6. *Basic VS Concepts*, Corporate Training Services, Electronic Data Systems Corporation, 1983.

7. *MVS Concepts and Facilities*, Corporate Training Services, Electronic Data Systems Corporation, 1983.

8. Auslander, M. A., D. C. Larkin, and A. L. Scherr. "The Evolution of the MVS Operating System." *IBM Journal of Research and Development* 25 (No. 5, Sept. 1981):471-482.

9. Considine, J. P., and J. J. Myers. "MARC: MVS Archival Storage and Recovery Program." *IBM Systems Journal* 16 (No. 4, 1977):378-397.

10. Prasad, N. S. *IBM Main Frames: Architecture and Design*. New York: McGraw-Hill, 1989.

11. Case, R. P., and A. Padeas. "Architecture of the IBM System/370." *Communications of the ACM* 21 (No. 1, Jan. 1978):73-96.

12. Gifford, D., and A. Spector. "Case Study: IBM's System/360-370 Architecture." *Communications of the ACM* 30 (No. 4, April 1987):291-307.

5

Concurrency

5.1 What Is Concurrency?

Concurrency has become a major area of computing. The ability to put tremendous computing power in a small chip has allowed multiprocessors to become commonplace. Such systems can do many activities simultaneously. Multiprocessing increases productivity, but also creates many problems.

The power of concurrency is obvious in everyday life. Suppose you move into a new house with fluorescent purple and pink walls. As a result, your first task is to paint the rooms. You can approach the job in two ways.

One way is to dedicate one day to each room (Figure 5.1). On Monday, you scrub and paint the main bedroom. On Tuesday, you do the same to the living room. If your house has six rooms, you will be done on Saturday night. You can then spend Sunday watching the Green Bay Packers on television.

Figure 5.1 One person painting each of six rooms

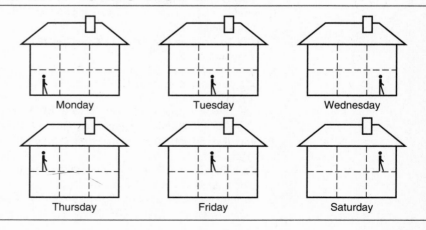

| Monday | Tuesday | Wednesday |
| Thursday | Friday | Saturday |

But you can take another approach (Figure 5.2). Find five good friends, each of whom owes you a favor (or some money). With appropriate incentives (such as free beer), you can get them all over to see your new house. When they arrive, you give them work clothes, and assign each a room. Each can then spend the day scrubbing and painting the walls: the first one to finish gets to paint the bathroom as a bonus. If you proceed this way, all the work is done on Monday and you can all watch the Chicago Bears on Monday night football. What makes the second approach better is obvious. Six people do the work instead of one. All the work is in progress concurrently.

Figure 5.2 Six people, each painting one room

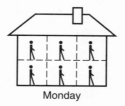

Monday

We have already discussed concurrency in computers. Chapter 3 discussed the advantages of performing I/O in parallel with other activities. Systems with I/O channels have several activities in progress simultaneously. The CPU is working on one process, while the channels work on others. Obviously, using several processors in this way increases throughput.

But concurrent activities can increase system efficiency in other ways. For example, suppose the computer were running simulations, or solving thousands of equations in thousands of unknowns. Such applications occur in flight simulation or in describing air flow past an airplane wing or a helicopter rotor. This type of "number crunching" program is CPU intensive. That is, the CPU spends most of its time doing calculations and requires little I/O.

In this case, I/O channels will not increase execution speed. However, if there were more CPUs, several "number crunchers" might execute at the same time. Perhaps several procedures could run simultaneously. Today, many computers have multiple CPUs. Lower hardware costs have made this a viable solution when a single processor cannot meet the demand.

Another advantage is that CPUs can be dispersed to where the computing needs are. Centralized computing power is not always in an organization's best interests. A large organization may have departments with varied needs. For example, accounting, engineering, or design centers typically have different needs. Thus, placing computing power where the need is and minimizing communications may reduce costs.

For example, each department may have its own processor (Figure 5.3). It may be a mainframe or a personal computer. Suppose each processor can communicate with a centralized database or file server. Each department may then retrieve information and do calculations locally: this way, the departments do not compete for processing time.

Figure 5.3 Multiple CPUs in an organization

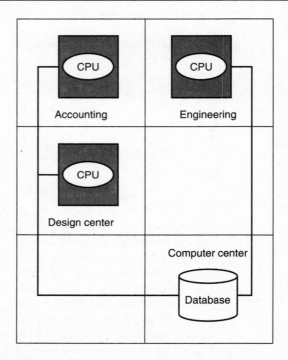

On the other hand, the computing capabilities need not be totally separated. If necessary, CPUs may communicate. Now the way they do this is a significant design issue. In some cases, one CPU may be a *master*. The operating system runs only on it. Such systems are *master/slave* systems. The other CPUs are, of course, the slaves.

In other cases, all CPUs are equivalent; in other words, none is a master. The operating system and any application may run on any of them. This is *symmetrical processing* or *anonymous processing*. It is more complex but more flexible. If one CPU fails, things will slow down, but the effects are not disastrous. In the master/slave organization, if the master CPU fails, nothing works. The systems described above increase throughput globally; that is, since several processors may run several activities simultaneously, the overall throughput increases.

But what about a single process? If it requires two hours of computing time, must it take two hours to run? Can a two hour program finish in one hour? Or perhaps in thirty minutes if enough CPUs work on it concurrently?

Advances in technology make this possible in certain cases. For example, consider a program that contains the following logic:

```
Begin
  Initialize(A);
  Initialize(B);
  Initialize(C);
End;
```

A, B, and C are arrays. **Initialize** is a procedure that clears them. Figure 5.4 shows how long it takes to clear each array using a conventional language and conventional computer. That is, between times t_0 and t_1, we clear array A. Between times t_1 and t_2, we clear array B. Finally, between times t_2 and time t_3, we clear array C.

Figure 5.4 Clearing three array sequentially

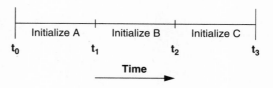

However, there is no reason why we must wait to clear C until after we clear both A and B. The clearing of C is independent of the clearing of the other arrays. For that matter, the clearing of each array is an independent operation. Why not clear all three at the same time?

Until recently, there were two reasons why we could not do this. First, most languages did not allow us to specify independent activities within a program. Historically, programs assume that the computer executes all steps sequentially. The second reason is that to clear three arrays simultaneously requires three processors. Not long ago, multiple processors other than I/O channels were uncommon.

But suppose a language lets you specify independent activities. Suppose also that multiple processors were available to work on a process. Then you could write the following program:

```
CoBegin
  Initialize(A);
  Initialize(B);
  Initialize(C);
CoEnd;
```

CoBegin and **CoEnd** encapsulate independent code, or commands. If the program is compiled and run on a multiprocessor, it can perform the activities as shown in Figure 5.5. In this case, a separate processor clears each array between times t_0 and t_1. Thus, the program has cleared all three arrays by t_1 instead of t_3. This is three times as fast. Such languages do exist. Examples are Ada, Modula-2, concurrent C, and Concurrent Pascal. All allow specification of logically independent commands.

Figure 5.5 Clearing 3 arrays at the same time

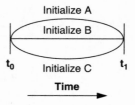

But the ability to perform tasks concurrently also raises many problems. For example, instead of clearing A, B, and C, suppose we initialize A and B by filling them with constant values K and J, respectively. Furthermore, suppose C is initialized as follows:

```
For I := 1 to N do
  C[I] := A[I] + B[I];
```

What happens if the programmer specifies the new initialization procedures as independent? Will it still work? The answer is "Maybe."

Now, to understand the problem fully, you must be aware that if different processors perform different activities, they may not work in synchronization. In other words, they may have different clock speeds, or perhaps one processor is not immediately available. The others may begin their activities sooner, or the last activity is delayed until the processor becomes available. The point is that we must not make any assumptions about the timing with which processors perform their tasks.

Let's examine what can happen if the programmer specifies:

```
CoBegin
    Initialize(A);
    Initialize(B);
    Initialize(C);
CoEnd;
```

Suppose the processor assigned to initialize array C is slower than the ones assigned to A and B. Or suppose the processor assigned to initialize C was busy when the program began and the initialization process for C was delayed. Either way, Figure 5.6 shows how the initialization may occur as a function of time.

Figure 5.6 Positions in C are initialized after positions in A and B

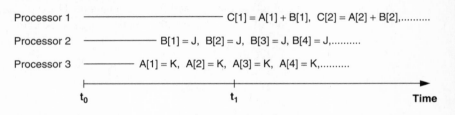

In this case, at time t_1, processor 1 initializes $C[1]$. This is no problem since processors 2 and 3 have already stored appropriate values in $A[1]$ and $B[1]$. Similarly, processor 1 initializes $C[2]$, $C[3]$, and so on. In all cases, processors 2 and 3 have already initialized the required positions in arrays A and B.

But what happens if processor 1 is faster than processors 2 and 3? Figure 5.7 shows how the initialization proceeds in this case. Processor 1 begins to initialize array C first. At time t_1, it initializes $C[1]$. The problem, as you can see, is that neither $A[1]$ nor $B[1]$ have yet been defined. As a result, the value in $C[1]$ is undefined. When all processors have finished their jobs, arrays A and B will be properly defined, but array C will not be because it was initialized too soon. The programmer is in for a surprise when he or she prints or uses the values in C!

Figure 5.7 Positions in C are initialized before positions in A and B

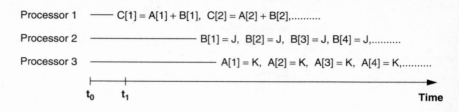

Perhaps even more frustrating is that the program may run perfectly one time, then incorrectly the next. Since the programmer does not control the allocation of processors, he or she never knows what will happen. Perhaps the situation described in Figure 5.6 might happen most of the time. The programmer then believes the program to be correct. Then one day, the case in Figure 5.7 occurs, and the program fails. As you well know, the most frustrating errors come from programs that work most of the time.

The solution to initializing A, B, and C is to recognize that only the initialization of A and B is independent. The initialization of C must occur after that of A and B. Thus, the solution might look like

```
CoBegin
   Initialize(A);
   Initialize(B);
CoEnd;
   Initialize(C);
```

This takes longer than the previous approaches, but at least it is guaranteed to work. Most people are willing to accept the compromise.

Some current research focuses on *massive parallelism*. This means having hundreds, or even thousands, of processors cooperate to compute large programs simultaneously. Applications occur in fluid dynamics, linear programming and in meteorology. They involve millions or billions of computations.

Preview to Concurrency Topics

This chapter introduces some problems for concurrency and examines solutions. Sections 2 through 5 describe how a programmer can isolate code (called a *critical section*) that references shared data. We also show how to guarantee that two critical sections cannot be active concurrently. This is called *mutual exclusion.*

Section 6 introduces the *semaphore*, which does the same thing as the algorithms described in previous sections. It guarantees that two distinct critical sections cannot be active concurrently. The semaphore is much simpler than the algorithms, but it requires the implementation of special *primitive operations*. This section also describes how we can use semaphores to *synchronize* concurrent processes. In other words, how to guarantee the proper sequence if two processes contain events that must occur in a specified sequence. Also, several classic synchronization problems are described.

Next we consider a solution that involves removing the critical section from a program and inserting it into a special operating system construct called a *monitor*. We show how to use a monitor for both mutual exclusion and synchronization.

Section 9 introduces Ada, a language that has received much attention. Ada provides another solution to synchronization and mutual exclusion. We describe two types of Ada tasks, the *caller* and the *server*. When a caller requests something from the server and the server responds, a *rendezvous* has occurred. We will describe the process of suspending and waking up processes to define a rendezvous.

Section 10 describes a serious problem called *deadlock*, which can occur when two processes are both waiting for something only the other can provide. In short, each is waiting for an event that will never occur. Ways to avoid or prevent deadlock will be described. We also will show that the cost of avoiding or preventing deadlock is high, and will also describe ways of detecting deadlock and dealing with it.

Last, we describe a case study of interprocess communication in UNIX. Specifically, we define a UNIX *pipe*. We also describe a program (written in the C language) that can create pipes. This case study illustrates how a popular operating system implements a specific form of interprocess communications.

5.2 Mutual Exclusion

Concurrency with Multiple Processors

The problems illustrated in Section 5.1 show the need for careful planning when implementing concurrent activities. But the solutions may be misleading. There are different levels of concurrency. There is concurrency among processes and among activities (or threads) within a single process. We will discuss processes, but the principles apply to threads as well.

Now if concurrent processes do not share anything, there is no problem. The problem occurs when they access common memory. In this case, one solution is simple: keep the activities sequential. In the example from Section 5.1 we did not initialize array C until after initializing both arrays A and B. But is this always practical?

Suppose we adopt the rule that whenever two processes access common memory, they cannot execute concurrently. For example, once again consider I/O processing. As Figure 5.8 shows, the operating system and channel program cooperate to move data from user memory to external storage. The operating system moves data from user memory to a buffer. From there, the channel moves the data to its destination.

Figure 5.8 Operating system and channel program cooperating to perform I/O

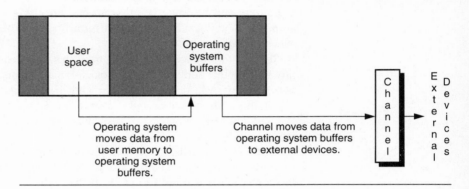

If the user is writing a lot of data, we may describe the activities as

```
Repeat
   Operating system moves data from user area to buffer.
   Channel program moves data from buffer to destination.
Until finished
```

Is this approach sensible? It is logically correct, but it prevents the operating system from moving more data to the buffer until the channel has finished sending the previous data to the destination. But the channel can remove the data quickly. Why should the operating system wait for the data to be sent to its destination? Why not allow it to move the next set of data to the buffer as soon as the channel has removed the previous set? There is no reason why the two processes must occur sequentially.

But they cannot execute concurrently either. What happens if both are called as concurrent processes as shown?

```
Repeat
   CoBegin
      Operating system moves data from user area to OS buffer.
      Channel program moves data from OS buffer to destination.
   CoEnd
Until finished
```

In this case, the channel could move the data from the buffer before the operating system even puts it there. We discuss solutions to this and similar problems in Section 5.8.

Concurrency with One Processor

This illustrates what can happen if two processes run concurrently on two separate processors. However, we can also have concurrent processes with just one processor. In this case, the processes cannot both execute, but they can compete for the CPU at the same time. If two such processes access common memory, problems can still occur.

Consider a case in which the Forest Service wants to track deer movement in a wildlife preserve. One approach is to place motion sensors in strategically located places such as near salt licks, water holes, or documentary filming sites. As shown in Figure 5.9, the sensors are connected to a single computer. Suppose a distinct process monitors each sensor. When a sensor detects a deer, the corresponding process adds 1 to a memory location containing the number of deer. The location is global to all processes.

Figure 5.9 Computer and sensors to detect deer movement

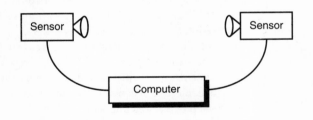

Most of the time, the sensors are inactive, but when a deer crosses one's range, it signals the computer. The corresponding process then adds 1 to the total count. Now the deer-counting processes probably contain a high level language command such as the Pascal statement:

```
NumberOfDeer := NumberOfDeer + 1;
```

Most of the time, the deer count reflects what the sensors detect. But what happens if two deer pass in front of sensors almost simultaneously? The first sensor signals the computer, and its process begins to execute the increment. Now consider what might happen. Remember that high level language commands translate into machine language commands. Suppose that the command

```
NumberOfDeer := NumberOfDeer + 1;
```

translates into

```
LOAD      R,NumberOfDeer
ADD       R,the value of 1
STORE     R,NumberOfDeer
```

Figure 5.10 shows what might happen with unfortunate timing. Suppose that the number of deer is currently 50, and the first sensor detects a deer at time t_0. The first command above loads the number of deer (50) into register R. Then the second command adds 1 to it. Now suppose the second sensor detects a deer at time t_1. It also signals the computer, and the corresponding process responds. What happens if the running process is interrupted?

As shown in Figure 5.10, the signal interrupts the CPU after it executes the ADD command. The operating system then saves the value in register R, currently 51, along with other information. The operating system responds to the interrupt and allows the new process to begin execution at time t_2. The process in control of the CPU loads the value of NumberOfDeer, currently still 50, into register R. It adds 1 to it and stores the sum in NumberOfDeer. At this point, time t_3, NumberOfDeer is 51.

What happens when the previously interrupted process resumes? The operating system restores the register values. The process then resumes execution at time t_4. Since it was interrupted after the ADD command, it executes the STORE command next. The value stored is the one in R (51) when the process was interrupted. Thus, NumberOfDeer is 51.

This situation presents a serious problem. The information in NumberOfDeer is wrong! Furthermore, it is wrong because of a flaw in the system that allows two processes to access common storage at the wrong time. Note that the two processes did not access the common memory at the same time. Unfortunate timing simply caused one process to undermine the other. The real difficulty is that the above example may work 99.99% of the time. Thus, the detection of such errors can be difficult.

But, is 99.99% accuracy sufficient? Instead of counting deer, what if the processes were making airline reservations? What if the processes controlled which train had the right of way on a section of track? What if they counted airplanes in a section of airspace? How would you feel, sitting in an airplane coming in to Chicago's O'Hare Airport, knowing that there is a 99.99% probability that the computer tracking your plane will see it?

Figure 5.10 Sequence of instructions in processes that count deer

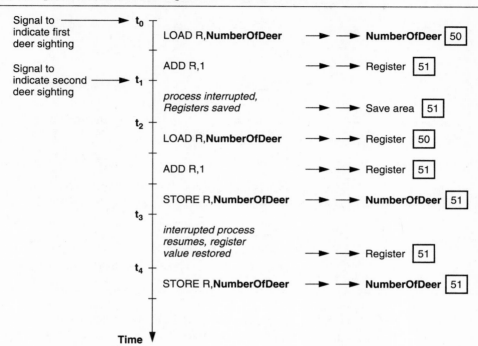

≡≡≡
Mutual Exclusion

Somehow we must allow processes to run concurrently, yet at the same time, prevent concurrent processing of certain sections, called *critical sections*. In other words, suppose concurrent processes access common resources. Then the critical section contains the commands that access these resources. If a process is executing in its critical section, then we must prevent every other process from entering its own critical section. Conversely, we must not allow one process to enter its critical section if any other process is in its own critical section. We call this *mutual exclusion*.

Figure 5.11 shows three concurrent processes. Any part of the code from any of them may run at any time. But we make an exception for the critical sections. If any process is currently executing in its critical section, we must block the others from executing code in their critical sections.

Figure 5.11 Concurrent processes with critical sections

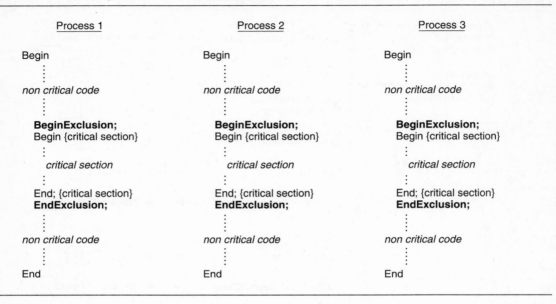

How do we ensure mutual exclusion? What can we do before a process enters its critical section to guarantee it? Must we do something when a process finishes its critical section? In Figure 5.11, each process refers to something called BeginExclusion prior to its critical section. Also, each refers to something called EndExclusion after its critical section. BeginExclusion must do the following:

- Check whether any other process is in its own critical section, and wait if any is.
- Proceed to execute the critical section if no other process is in its own critical section.

EndExclusion must inform all other processes that a process has finished executing its own critical section.

In the deer-counting example, we could use BeginExclusion and EndExclusion as shown in Figure 5.12. Whenever a process wants to execute its critical section, it must first call BeginExclusion. When finished with its critical section, it must call EndExclusion. This prevents the nasty problem shown earlier.

Figure 5.12 Processes to count deer under mutual exclusion

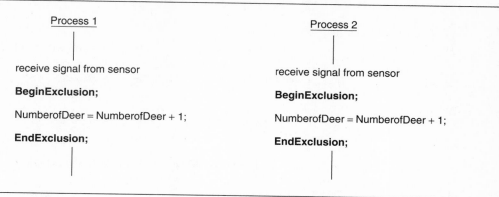

For example, suppose a sensor detects a deer at time t_0. Then process 1 begins to add to the deer count (Figure 5.13). Now suppose a second sensor detects a deer at time t_1. Process 2 also wants to add 1 to the deer count. But the code to add 1 is in a critical section. Thus, process 2 must first call BeginExclusion. Since process 1 is currently executing its critical section, process 2 must wait. When process 1 finishes counting the deer, it calls EndExclusion (at time t_2 in Figure 5.13). This informs process 2 that process 1 is no longer in its own critical section. Process 2 then enters its own critical section at time t_3 and counts the deer. This time both deer are counted because mutual exclusion forced the counts to be executed in strict sequence.

The process BeginExclusion and EndExclusion allows us to guarantee mutual exclusion. But one problem remains. How do we write it? What does it look like? Is it even possible to create it? The task of writing BeginExclusion and EndExclusion is by no means easy, as the next section shows.

Figure 5.13 Instructions to count deer sequenced by mutual exclusion

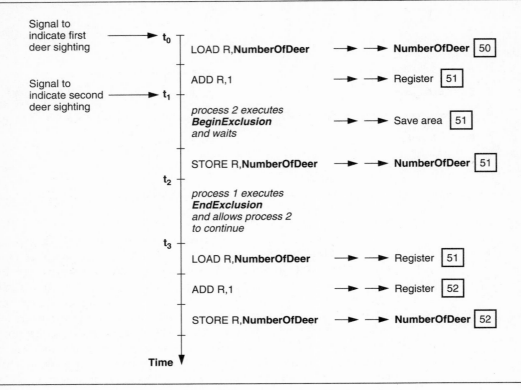

5.3 Software Approaches to Mutual Exclusion

This section examines implementations of BeginExclusion and EndExclusion. We also present pitfalls that occur when dealing with concurrency. Here, we assume only two concurrent processes. Section 5.5 treats the more difficult problem of several concurrent processes.

First Attempt

One way to enforce mutual exclusion is to write BeginExclusion and EndExclusion as shown in Figure 5.14. The idea is simple: declare a Boolean variable Occupied that is global to both processes. Occupied is set to True if either process enters its critical section, otherwise, it is False. Thus, when a process needs to enter its critical section, it checks Occupied to see if the other one is in its critical section.

Figure 5.14 First attempt at mutual exclusion

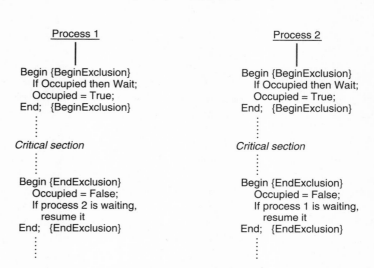

Global variable
Occupied: Boolean; {initially False}

Process 1	Process 2

Begin {BeginExclusion}
  If Occupied then Wait;
  Occupied = True;
End; {BeginExclusion}
	Begin {BeginExclusion}
	  If Occupied then Wait;
	  Occupied = True;
	End; {BeginExclusion}

Critical section	*Critical section*

Begin {EndExclusion}
  Occupied = False;
  If process 2 is waiting,
    resume it
End; {EndExclusion}
	Begin {EndExclusion}
	  Occupied = False;
	  If process 1 is waiting,
	    resume it
	End; {EndExclusion}

To see how this works, suppose process 1 wants to enter its critical section. It first checks Occupied. If Occupied is True, process 1 waits. If it is False, process 1 sets it to True, and then proceeds into its critical section. If process 2 subsequently tries to enter its critical section, it sees Occupied as True and must wait. A symmetric argument can be made if process 2 tries to enter its critical section first.

Now suppose process 1 leaves its critical section. It sets Occupied to False. If process 2 subsequently tries to enter its critical section, it sees Occupied as False and enters its critical section. However, suppose process 2 tried to enter its critical section earlier. It saw Occupied as True and waited. Now, as process 1 leaves its critical section it checks whether process 2 is waiting. Since it is, process 1 wakes it up. Process 2 then sets Occupied to True, and enters its critical section.

We should note that "waiting" and "waking up" may be implemented in different ways. In some cases, a process may wait by defining a condition to be True and entering a loop such as

While condition **Do;**

The semicolon after Do indicates that this logic does nothing except repeatedly check the condition. Once the condition becomes False (presumably set by the other process), the loop stops.

A wakeup could be implemented by simply setting the condition to False. This, of course, assumes the condition uses global variables such as Occupied. One process can then define variables that will wake up another process. In other cases, a wait may be implemented by suspending a process. That is, the operating system puts it in a wait state as described in Chapter 4. A wakeup then corresponds to a state transition from waiting to ready. The details of the implementation of waiting and waking up do not concern us here. To describe approaches to mutual exclusion and associated problems, we need only know that one process can wait and that another can wake it up.

But does the "solution" described in Figure 5.14 work? The simple fact is that it will, most of the time. A problem occurs because the processes reference common memory in BeginExclusion. Both reference Occupied. As we have already seen, unfortunate timing can cause one process to undermine the other.

For example, suppose Occupied is False and process 1 enters BeginExclusion. It sees Occupied as False, and proceeds to set it to True. But it takes time to do this. Suppose process 2 checks Occupied after process 1 checked it but before process 1 set it to True. Then process 2 also sees Occupied as False. Process 1 then continues to set Occupied to True, but this is after process 2 checked its value. Thus, process 2 also sets (redundantly) Occupied to True. Both processes are now in their critical sections.

This is like to two burglars trying to enter the same house (Figure 5.15a and b). Each looks in through the window and sees no one at home. Of course, both are very quiet so neither sees the other. Both enter through different doors. Before long, each burglar is very surprised to discover that he or she is not alone. Next time, take a number. Crime is a crowded occupation these days.

Figure 5.15a Two burglars checking occupancy of house

Looks like nobody's home.   Looks like nobody's home.

Figure 5.15b Two burglars entering house

Hey! What are you doing here?   Hey! What are you doing here?

Second Attempt at Mutual Exclusion

One way to avoid having both processes nearly simultaneously checking Occupied is to use a second condition. In other words, suppose both processes try to enter their critical sections at nearly the same time. They may be prioritized by declaring a global variable Which with a value of either 1 or 2. Both processes must check the value of Which before entering their critical sections. One can proceed, but the other will have to wait.

Figure 5.16 shows how to reference the global variable Which. The code for BeginExclusion in Figure 5.16 is the same as that in Figure 5.14 except for one addition. To allow for the possibility that both processes pass the first test, a second test is inserted to check the value of Which.

Suppose both processes pass the first test as described. If Which is 1, process 1 sees the second condition as False and enters its critical section. Process 2, however, sees the condition as True and must wait. If Which is 2, the reverse happens: process 2 enters its critical section, and process 1 must wait. Since Which is a single value, one process always must wait. Thus, mutual exclusion is enforced.

Unfortunately, there is an undesirable side effect. Can you see it? The two processes can no longer execute independently. They must alternate execution of their critical sections.

To see this, suppose that Which = 1 and that process 2 is not in its critical section. If process 1 executes BeginExclusion, it sees both conditions as False and enters its critical section. When process 1 exits its critical section, it defines Occupied and Which as False and 2, respectively. Suppose process 2 continues to have no need of its critical section. Process 1 may loop back and attempt to reenter its critical section. Occupied is False, but Which is still 2. Process 1 sees the second condition as True and waits, even though process 2 is nowhere near its critical section. The only way to activate process 1 is for process 2 to enter and exit its critical section. This could take a long time. After all, process 2 could be in an infinite loop or could be waiting for a malfunctioning I/O device.

Process 1 suffers from *indefinite postponement*, that is, it must wait for an indefinite time. This solution enforces mutual exclusion, but the cost is very high. Processes may not be able to execute.

Figure 5.16 Second try at mutual exclusion

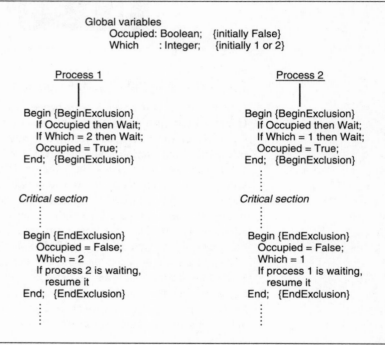

```
Global variables
        Occupied: Boolean;    {initially False}
        Which    : Integer;   {initially 1 or 2}


        Process 1                              Process 2
            |                                      |

    Begin {BeginExclusion}                 Begin {BeginExclusion}
        If Occupied then Wait;                 If Occupied then Wait;
        If Which = 2 then Wait;                If Which = 1 then Wait;
        Occupied = True;                       Occupied = True;
    End;   {BeginExclusion}                End;   {BeginExclusion}
        :                                      :
        :                                      :
    Critical section                       Critical section
        :                                      :
        :                                      :
    Begin {EndExclusion}                   Begin {EndExclusion}
        Occupied = False;                      Occupied = False;
        Which = 2                              Which = 1
        If process 2 is waiting,               If process 1 is waiting,
            resume it                              resume it
    End;   {EndExclusion}                  End;   {EndExclusion}
        :                                      :
        :                                      :
```

≡≡≡

Third Attempt at Mutual Exclusion

A flaw in the second attempt is the use of an integer variable to determine which process can enter its critical section. The integer value allows only one to enter, regardless of what the other one is doing. This constraint is too strong. But we needed something to prevent two processes from simultaneously entering their critical sections. This was obviously a bad approach. So let us return to Figure 5.14 and again look at how two processes can enter their critical sections at the same time.

Two processes can enter their critical sections at the same time because neither "claims occupancy" until <u>after</u> occupancy has been checked. That is, a process defines the global variable Occupied as True after checking its value. What happens if a process claims occupancy before checking for it? In other words, reverse the two statements in BeginExclusion from Figure 5.14.

The first thing you might notice is that when either process sets Occupied to True, it then must wait because Occupied is True. In effect, a process prevents itself from entering its critical section. This fails because there is no distinction of which process is occupying the critical section. A process should be able to distinguish between itself and others.

One way to do this is by using two global Boolean variables, Occupied1 and Occupied2. Occupied1 is True if process 1 is in its critical section and False otherwise. Similarly, Occupied2 is True if process 2 is in its critical section and False otherwise. Thus, a process declares its occupancy of its critical section and then checks to see if the other process has declared its occupancy (Figure 5.17).

Figure 5.17 Third attempt at mutual exclusion

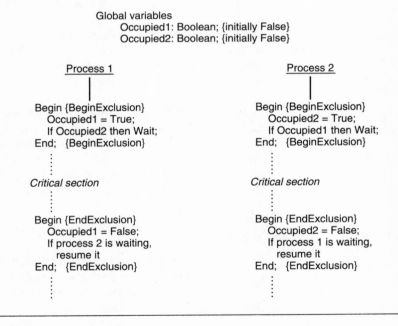

If process 1 is in its critical section and subsequently exits, it sets Occupied1 to False. If process 2 is waiting, process 2 is resumed. The reverse holds if process 2 leaves its critical section. Either process may also loop through its critical section several times if the other in inactive.

This logic enforces mutual exclusion without forcing the processes to take turns entering their critical sections. The only way a process can enter its critical section is if the other process is not in its critical section or trying to enter. For example, process 1 can enter its critical section only if Occupied2 is false. But this can only happen if process 2 has not tried to enter its critical section or it has entered and subsequently exited. Thus, mutual exclusion is guaranteed.

Unfortunately, another problem can occur, albeit only rarely, but can be disastrous when it does. To see what can happen, suppose both processes try to enter their critical sections at or near the same time. The following sequence of events could occur:

```
Process 1 sets Occupied1 to True.
Process 2 sets Occupied2 to True.
Process 1 sees Occupied2 as True and begins to wait.
Process 2 sees Occupied1 as True and begins to wait.
```

What is wrong? Neither process has entered its critical section. Furthermore, neither will—ever! The problem is that each process thinks the other is in its critical section. Each will therefore wait for the other to execute EndExclusion. Since both are waiting, nothing will happen. Thus, both processes will wait forever.

We refer to a situation in which two processes are each waiting for the other to do something as a *deadlock*, or *deadly embrace*. The result is that neither process can continue. Section 5.10 describes solutions to deadlock; they are generally very painful. Usually one process must be terminated, thus losing all or some of the work that it has done. The process must then be rerun. This causes delays and is a serious inconvenience.

≡≡≡≡ 5.4 Dekker's Algorithm

The three tries at producing mutual exclusion in the last section illustrate the complexity of the problem. Each shows a different malady from which a system with concurrent processes can suffer. Each also demonstrates a different type of thinking necessary to solve the problem.

Programmers are familiar with debugging techniques that require precise attention to detail. Debugging depends on statements being executed in an order based solely on the program logic and data. In other words, given the same data, a program executes precisely the same way every time it runs. This knowledge is essential to the use of traces and breakpoints.

Imagine how frustrating it would be if a program might not run the same way twice. How many programmers have complained, "Every time I run my program, something different happens"? Now this statement usually represents a perception rather than a fact. However, when concurrent processes are involved, it <u>may</u> <u>be</u> a fact.

A system with concurrent processes may work most of the time, only to fail at the most inopportune moment. (Of course, when is there an opportune moment for a program to fail? It's like an opportune time to get a traffic ticket.) Then during debugging, the timing that caused the program to fail does not occur, and the program again runs perfectly. This can be very frustrating!

The Dutch mathematician Dekker developed an algorithm (Figure 5.18) that ensures mutual exclusion without undesirable side effects. (Reference [1] describes his algorithm.) It guarantees mutual exclusion for two concurrent, asynchronous processes by using ideas from the previously described algorithms.

Figure 5.18 Dekker's algorithm for solving mutual exclusion

```
Global variables
        Occupied1 : Boolean; {initially False}
        Occupied2 : Boolean; {initially False}
        Which     : Integer;  {initially 1 or 2}
```

```
              Process 1                                        Process 2
                 |                                                |

Begin {BeginExclusion}                         Begin {BeginExclusion}
   Occupied1 = True;                               Occupied2 = True;
   While Occupied2 Do                              While Occupied1 Do
     If Which = 2 Then                               If Which = 1 Then
       Begin                                           Begin
         Occupied1 = False;                              Occupied2 = False;
         While Which = 2 Do; {wait here until            While Which = 1 Do; {wait here until
                        Which is 1}                                     Which is 2}
         Occupied1 = True;                               Occupied2 = True;
       End;                                            End;
End;  {BeginExclusion}                         End;  {BeginExclusion}
   ⋮                                               ⋮

Critical section                               Critical section
   ⋮                                               ⋮

  Begin {EndExclusion}                            Begin {EndExclusion}
     Which = 2;                                      Which = 1;
     Occupied1 = False;                              Occupied2 = False;
  End;  {EndExclusion}                            End;  {EndExclusion}
   ⋮                                               ⋮
```

Dekker's Algorithm is similar to the third solution attempt (Figure 5.17) in that two global Boolean variables indicate occupancy of a critical section. It is also similar to the second solution in that a global integer variable indicates "a turn" or priority. It also resembles the first solution in that each process checks whether a critical section is occupied before trying to enter its own critical section.

There are two major differences from the previous solutions. The first is that the Boolean variables do not indicate whether a process is actually in its critical section. Rather, each indicates that a process wants to enter its critical section. The second major difference is that priority is not enforced rigidly unless both processes try to enter their critical sections at roughly the same time.

The logic behind Dekker's Algorithm works as follows. Before a process enters its critical section, it must:

1. Set its occupancy variable to True. This means it is trying to enter its critical section.
2. Check whether the other process is in or trying to enter its critical section. If not, enter the critical section. If so, proceed to the next step (step 3).
3. If it is the other process' turn to be in its critical section, wait. Set the occupancy variable to False and wait until the other process exits its critical section.
4. Suppose it is the current process' turn to be in its critical section. If the other process is in its critical section anyway, wait until it exits. If, on the other hand, the other process is also trying to enter its critical section it should wait once it detects it is the current process' turn. When that happens enter the critical section.

To see how Dekker's Algorithm implements this logic, examine what happens when process 1 tries to enter its critical section. Figure 5.19 shows a tree structure representing the decisions process 1 makes as it executes the algorithm. This should help you follow the logic in Figure 5.18.

The first command in the BeginExclusion component of Dekker's Algorithm sets the global variable Occupied1 to True (box 1 in Figure 5.19).

Next, process 1 checks the condition of the first While loop. It is actually the global Boolean Occupied2. If it is false (left branch from box 1), the condition on the While loop is False. Consequently, process 1 does not enter the While loop and enters its critical section (box 2 in Figure 5.19). But remember, Occupied2 is False if and only if process 2 is not in or trying to enter its critical section. Thus, process 1 can enter the critical section any time process 2 is not in, or trying to enter, its critical section.

Figure 5.19 Decision tree for process 1 executing Dekker's Algorithm

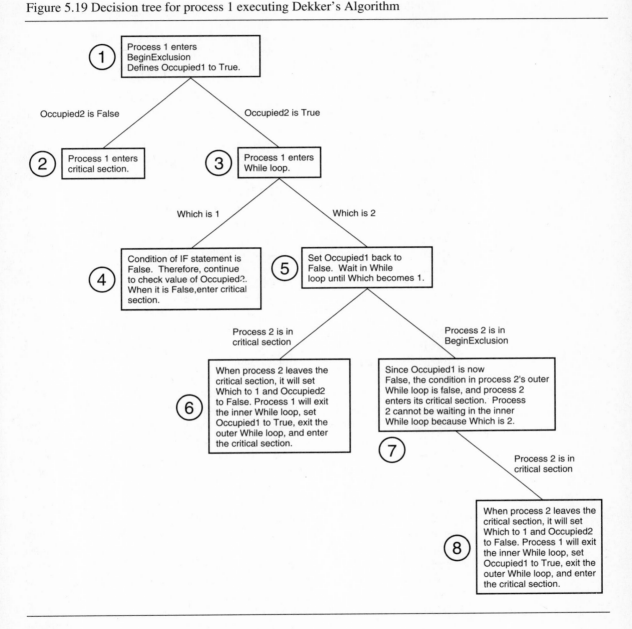

Similarly, process 2 can enter its critical section any time process 1 is not in, or trying to enter, its critical section.

On the other hand, suppose that process 1 sees Occupied2 as True (right branch from box 1). This will mean one of two things: either process 2 has entered its critical section, or it is trying to enter. In either case, process 1 enters the While loop body (box 3 in Figure 5.19).

Once inside the While loop, process 1 checks the integer variable Which. If Which is 1 (left branch from box 3), the statements following the IF statement are ignored. However, since process 1 is still within the While loop, the value of Occupied2 is therefore checked again. As long as it remains True, process 1 just keeps checking. Furthermore, if Which is 1, process 1 cannot change it. Examine the algorithm in Figure 5.18 and you will see that process 1 can set Which to 2 only in EndExclusion. The result is that process 1 is in a holding loop; it does nothing except check Occupied2 and Which repeatedly. Since Which cannot change, process 1 will remain in this loop until Occupied2 becomes False (box 4 in Figure 5.19). Process 1 then enters its critical section. Process 1 is like the persistent salesman who pesters you repeatedly until you finally buy something.

There are only two ways in which Occupied2 can become False. The first occurs when Occupied2 is True because process 2 is already in its critical section. As shown in Dekker's Algorithm, Occupied2 will be set to False when process 2 exits its critical section through EndExclusion. The significance of this is that process 1 cannot enter its critical section if process 2 is already in its own critical section. Thus, mutual exclusion is enforced.

Now suppose that Occupied2 is True because process 2 is trying to enter its critical section. In this case, both processes are trying to enter critical sections at nearly the same time. Since Which is 1 (remember, we are still describing box 4 in Figure 5.19), process 2 will see the condition of the If statement as True. As a result, it will set Occupied2 to False and enter another While loop. It will remain there until Which is set to 2. But the important thing is that process 2 set Occupied2 to False. Process 1 can then enter its critical section. This argument shows that if both processes try to enter their critical sections, Which will force one to back off. Again, mutual exclusion is enforced.

Now return to the point where process 1 entered the first While loop and consider what happens if Which is 2 (right branch from box 3). In this case, process 1 immediately redefines Occupied1 as False. Then process 1 enters a second While loop that does nothing except check Which repeatedly. Remember, Which is 2, so the condition on the second While loop is True. Process 1 will remain there until Which changes to 1 (box 5 in Figure 5.19).

This allows for both processes to try to enter their critical sections at the same time. When this happens, each process makes a global Boolean variable True. Which then determines which process can enter. At box 5 in figure 5.19, Which is 2, so process 2 can enter. This can happen only if process 1 stops trying to enter its critical section. But this is exactly what process 1 does when it sets Occupied1 to False and enters the second While loop.

How long will process 1 execute the inner While loop? It depends on what process 2 does. If process 2 was already in its critical section (left branch from box 5), process 1 remains in the loop until process 2 exits. When this happens, process 2 sets Which to 1 and Occupied2 to False (box 6 in Figure 5.19). At this point, process 1 exits the wait loop. It then makes Occupied1 True. Since Occupied2 was set to False, the condition on the outer loop is false. Process 1 then enters its critical section.

Suppose now that process 2 was trying to enter its critical section (right branch from box 5). Since Which is 2, process 2 is not running in the second While loop. It is, however, still in the first While loop. But because process 1 has made Occupied1 False, process 2 sees the condition on the first While loop change to False. Process 2 then enters its critical section and process 1 must wait until process 2 exits (box 7 in Figure 5.19).

Eventually, process 2 will exit its critical section (right branch from box 7). At this point, process 1 will enter its critical section as previously described (box 8 in Figure 5.19). Note that boxes 6 and 8 correspond to the same events.

The above discussion should convince you that Dekker's Algorithm enforces mutual exclusion. It does not, however, constitute a formal proof of its correctness. Such proofs exist, but are not presented here. For a formal treatment of Dekker's Algorithm, see references [1,2].

5.5 N-Process Mutual Exclusion

Dekker's Algorithm is the first known solution to mutual exclusion for two processes. It is not the only solution. Nor does it easily extend to n processes. More recently, researchers have developed other solutions to mutual exclusion. Some solve the problem for n processes.

Figure 5.20 shows one of these algorithms, developed by Dijkstra [3]. For brevity, we show only the code for process i . Each process has similar code for BeginExclusion. Only variables Status and Which are global; all others are local.

In the algorithm, Dijkstra uses a global array to indicate the status of each process numbered 0 through $n - 1$. This is an extension of the use of Occupied1 and Occupied2 in Dekker's Algorithm. However, there is one important change. Each process may have any of the following status values:

1. A process is idle if it is not executing in or trying to enter its critical section. (The process may be executing noncritical sections, but that is of no concern to us here.)
2. A process is *entering* if it has begun executing BeginExclusion. The process is trying to enter its critical section but has not made it that far.

3. A process is *inside* if it is inside its critical section or has passed a certain point in BeginExclusion. Where this point lies will be specified when we describe BeginExclusion. The status in this case can be misleading since it does not necessarily mean the process is in its critical section. In fact, two or more processes may have a status of *inside*. Still, we will argue that it is not possible for two processes to be in their respective critical sections at the same time. The reader should bear this in mind as we describe the algorithm.

As in Dekker's Algorithm, a global variable Which identifies a specific process. We call it a *favored process*.

Figure 5.20 Solution to mutual exclusion for *n* processes

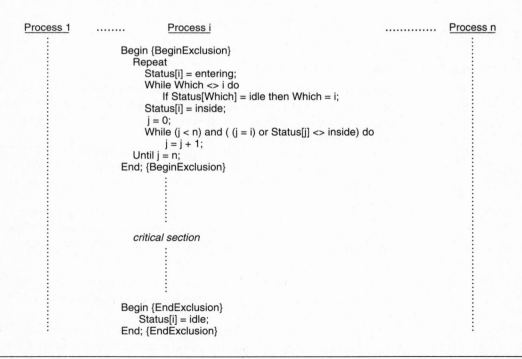

```
TYPE
     ProcessStatus = (idle, entering, inside);
     ProcessNumber = 0 . . n-1;

Global variables
     Status  : Array[ProcessNumber] of ProcessStatus;
                    {initially, all array positions are idle}
     Which   : ProcessNumber
```

Process 1   ....   Process i   .... Process n

```
                          Begin {BeginExclusion}
                            Repeat
                              Status[i] = entering;
                              While Which <> i do
                                   If Status[Which] = idle then Which = i;
                              Status[i] = inside;
                              j = 0;
                              While (j < n) and ( (j = i) or Status[j] <> inside) do
                                   j = j + 1;
                            Until j = n;
                          End; {BeginExclusion}




                            critical section




                          Begin {EndExclusion}
                            Status[i] = idle;
                          End; {EndExclusion}
```

The logic behind this algorithm follows. Before process *i* enters its critical section, it must:

1. Change status from Idle to Entering.
2. If the process i is favored, proceed to step 3. Otherwise, wait until the favored process is Idle. (Note: The favored process may already be Idle.) If this happens, claim the title of favored process and proceed to step 3.
3. Change status from Entering to Inside.
4. If no other process has a status of Inside, enter the critical section. Otherwise, start over from step 1.

To see how the algorithm in Figure 5.20 follows this logic to enforce mutual exclusion, consider what happens if process *i* tries to enter its critical section. As before, a decision tree structure shown in Figure 5.21 should help clarify the logic.

Figure 5.21 Decision tree for process i executing algorithm in Figure 5.20

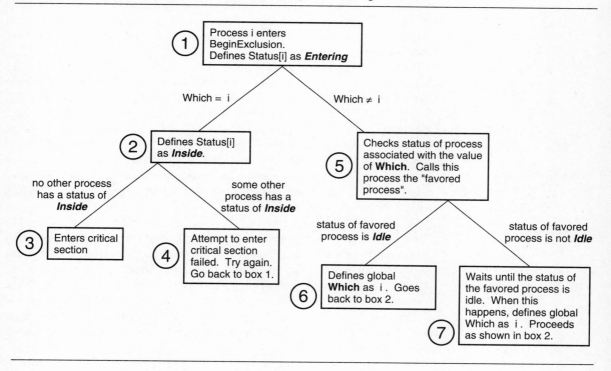

The first thing process *i* does in BeginExclusion is define its status as Entering (box 1 in Figure 5.21). This indicates process *i* is trying to enter its critical section. Keep in mind that other processes may also have just started similar attempts. Thus, they may also have a status of Entering.

Which controls the first While loop in the algorithm. Suppose Which is *i* (left branch from box 1). Then process *i* is favored. It sees the condition on the first While loop as False. Therefore, it bypasses this loop and defines Status[i] as Inside (box 2 in figure 5.21). Although process *i* is not yet actually inside the critical section, it has gotten past the first loop. Suppose, however, process *i* is not the favored process and Which is not *i* (right branch from box 1). Then process *i* enters the While loop. The loop delays its attempt to enter its critical section. The idea is to allow only the favored process beyond this point in the logic.

Of course, if the favored process is currently Idle, there is nothing to gain by forcing process *i* to wait. Therefore, within the While loop, process *i* checks the favored process' status (box 5 in Figure 5.21). If it is Idle (left branch from box 5), process *i* claims the title of favored process by defining Which = *i* (box 6 in Figure 5.21). This will terminate the loop, and process *i* defines its status as Inside (box 2 in Figure 5.21). (Do not forget that other processes could have done this also.)

But the favored process may not be Idle (right branch from box 5). Then process *i* must wait in the While loop until it is idle. The While loop is a holding loop in which process *i* repeatedly checks the favored process' status (box 7 in Figure 5.21). When the favored process becomes Idle, process *i* defines Which = *i*. In other words, process *i* claims the title of favored process and exits the loop. It then defines its status as Inside (box 2 in Figure 5.21). If the favored process is or becomes idle, the first process to detect this becomes the new favored process. Since many processes could be executing in the While loop simultaneously, random chance will determine the next favored process. Which will be the process number.

The analogy of throwing a bone to a pack of hungry dogs is appropriate. The bone is the claim to favored process. The hungry dogs are the processes executing in the While loop. The first one to stake its claim wins. However, the analogy is not perfect. Only one hungry dog can get the bone, but more than one process could get by the first While loop. However, this can happen only if the timing is right. For example, suppose that process 5 is executing in its critical section and that Which = 5. Suppose also that processes 2 and 7 both enter BeginExclusion at nearly the same time. Figure 5.22 shows what could happen at different times.

Figure 5.22 Possible sequence of events as two processes execute inside the While loop of Dijkstra's Algorithm

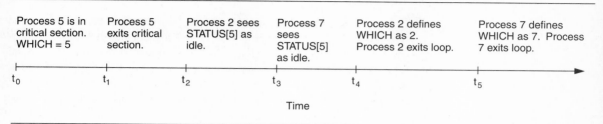

At time t_1 process 5 exits its critical section. Its status is now Idle. Processes 2 and 7 are still executing inside the While loop. At time t_2, process 2 begins executing the If statement inside the While loop. Since Which = 5, process 2 sees Status[5] as Idle. Process 2 proceeds to define Which as 2. But the machine code to do this takes time. There is therefore a lapse between the time process 2 sees Status[5] = Idle and when it defines Which = 2. Suppose during this time, at t_3, process 7 begins executing its If statement. It also sees Status[5] = Idle. It will then proceed to define Which = 7. At time t_4, process 2 defines Which = 2 and exits the loop. Finally at time t_5, process 7 defines Which = 7 and also exits the loop.

As you can see, unfortunate timing allowed both processes to see process 5 become idle at or near the same time. Since both exited the loop, both now have a status of Inside. Other processes could have exited the loop similarly. Which is the process number of the last one to exit. In this case, Which = 7. However processes 2 and 7 have still exited the loop. Something must prevent both from entering their critical sections. This is the purpose of the second While loop.

Suppose a process gets past the first While loop. Suppose also that it is the only process to do so (left branch from box 2). The second While loop contains a counter that allows the process to examine the status of all other processes. If no other process gets past the first loop, no others will have a status of Inside. The compound condition in the second loop will then always be true until j reaches n. When $j = n$, the process exits the second While loop. Furthermore, since $j = n$, the condition on the Repeat loop is true. Thus, the process also exits the Repeat loop and enters its critical section (box 3 in Figure 5.21).

Suppose, as shown in the previous example, that more than one process gets past the first While loop (right branch from box 2). Each one then has a status of Inside. Each also begins executing the second While loop. As a result, each checks the status of all other processes. Each one (with the possible exception of one) will see the status of another as Inside. When this happens, the compound condition is false and that process exits the loop. But when it exits, the value of j will be smaller than n. Because of this, the condition on the

Repeat loop is false. Therefore, the process resumes execution of BeginExclusion at the start (box 4 in Figure 5.21). It changes its status back to Entering and starts all over.

Two processes cannot both increment j up to n. At least one must see the other's status as Inside and exit the loop first. Consider the previous example, where processes 2 and 7 exited the first While loop. Both now enter the second While loop. The status of all other processes is checked in numerical order. Therefore, if the processes are executing at nearly the same speed, process 7 will see the status of process 2 as Inside. It will then resume at the start of the Repeat loop and redefine its status as Entering.

Meanwhile, process 2 is still checking the status of the other processes. When it finally checks the status of process 7, it sees a value of Entering. Therefore, assuming no other processes are involved, process 2 will increment j to n and enter its critical section.

Many processes can get past the first While loop, but at most, one can get past the second loop with $j = n$. All others must start over again. Conceivably, all processes entering the second While loop might have to start over. In the previous example, if process 2 were a little faster, both it and process 7 could check each other's status at nearly the same time. In this case, both would have to start over.

If all processes have to start over, only one will progress beyond the first While loop. Which corresponds to the last process to previously exit the first While loop. In our example, process 7 exited after process 2. Therefore, Which is 7, and process 7 is now favored. As such, it simply bypasses the first While loop. All other processes stay there until process 7 eventually enters and exits its critical section. At this point, the bone is once again thrown to the hungry dogs.

Although Dijkstra's Algorithm enforces mutual exclusion, it may cause *indefinite postponement* of some processes. If several processes execute in the first While loop, random chance dictates which is the first to detect that the status of the favored process has changed. But one process may execute on a slow processor, or it may have a low priority and be frequently interrupted. As such, it may not be as quick as the other hungry dogs. There is no way of telling when it will become the favored process. Conceivably, if there are always other processes trying to enter their critical sections, it may never be favored.

Other algorithms put an upper boundary on how many times a process may start over. This avoids indefinite postponement. For example, Knuth [6] developed an algorithm that guarantees that a process will never start over more than 2^n times (n is the number of processes). DeBruijn's Algorithm [10] guarantees an upper limit of n^2 tries. In Eisenberg and McGuire's Algorithm [5], a process will start over no more than $n - 1$ times.

Another well known algorithm, called Lamport's Bakery Algorithm, guarantees an upper boundary of n -1 tries before a process enters its critical section. It is developed and proved in references [7,11,12]. The interested reader should consult these references. Treatments of software solutions to mutual exclusion also appear in references [4,8,9,13].

≡≡≡≡ 5.6 Semaphores

Most readers will agree that the algorithms presented in the previous sections are complex. Understanding how and why they work is difficult. You must consider all possible sequences of events. Furthermore, the logic grows increasingly complex as the number of processes grows. But ask yourself, "Why is the logic cumbersome and difficult?" Is it because of the problem itself? Oddly enough, the answer is "No." The problem is not inherently difficult. Neither is the logic of a solution inherently difficult.

In fact, look again at the first solution attempt in Figure 5.14. The logic was simple. Before entering your critical section, do the following:

1. Check to see whether any other process is in its critical section.
2. If so, wait until it leaves.
3. If not, enter your critical section.

We saw that this solution did not work. But why not? There was no flaw in the logic. Rather, there was a flaw in its implementation; that is, in the machine language code used to execute it.

We used an analogy of two burglars trying to enter a house at the same time. But the analogy is not perfect. For example, the burglars may have looked into the same house but different rooms. Furthermore, each could enter through a different door.

Figure 5.23 Two burglars trying to enter a very small house at the same time

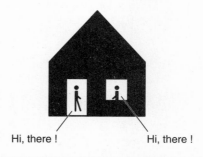

Hi, there !   Hi, there !

But suppose the house was small (Figure 5.23) and had only one room and a single door. In this case, the situation shown in Figure 5.15b cannot happen. Both may try to enter at the same time, but only one can go through the door. Even though they try to enter simultaneously, they must enter in sequence: one must wait while the other enters.

Are there other options for the processes? Consider the following commands from Figure 5.14.

```
If Occupied then Wait;
Occupied = True;
```

These commands normally translate into several machine language instructions. Therefore interruptions may occur between any two of them. But what if the logic translated into a single machine language instruction or were somehow uninterruptible? When a process executes the code it will check the value of Occupied and then either wait or set Occupied to True without interruption. This would force the other process to wait until after the uninterruptible activity is done. The result is that both could not see Occupied as False.

In 1965, Dijkstra [1] introduced the notion of a *semaphore* to enforce mutual exclusion among processes. Railroad buffs might recognize the term: it is a signaling device used to control occupancy of railroad tracks. It allows only one train on a designated section of track at a time. (Can you think of a place where mutual exclusion is more essential?)

Dijkstra introduced the notion of a signaling device into a computer system. He defined a semaphore as an integer variable that may be changed by just two *primitive operations*. A primitive operation is uninterruptible: once it begins, the executing process cannot be interrupted or delayed until it is finished. Primitive operations depend on system design and as such, computer systems must be designed with them in mind.

The primitive operations for a semaphore are P and V and are defined as follows. Let s be a semaphore. Then

$$P(s): \quad \text{If } s > 0 \text{ then}$$
$$s = s - 1$$
$$\text{else}$$
$$\text{suspend process;}$$

$$V(s): \quad \text{If a process is suspended as a result of } P(s), \text{ resume it}$$
$$\text{else}$$
$$s = s + 1;$$

A process that executes a P primitive may have to *wait*. Some texts use Wait or Test instead of P. A process that executes a V primitive may *signal* another process to resume. Some texts use Signal or Increment instead of V. In fact, P and V actually stand for the Dutch equivalents of test and increment, respectively. Again, the uninterruptibility of P and V is essential to all our discussions. Once either begins, it will finish without interruption.

Figure 5.24 shows the solution to mutual exclusion. Logically, it differs little from the attempt in Figure 5.14. The big difference is, of course, that P and V are indivisible.

Figure 5.24 Mutual exclusion with semaphores

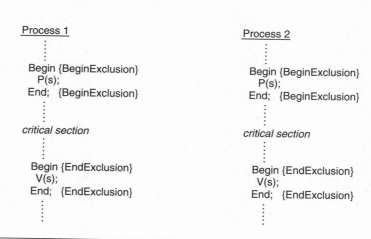

Global variable
s : Semaphore; {initially 1}

Process 1	Process 2
⋮	⋮
Begin {BeginExclusion}	Begin {BeginExclusion}
P(s);	P(s);
End; {BeginExclusion}	End; {BeginExclusion}
⋮	⋮
critical section	*critical section*
⋮	⋮
Begin {EndExclusion}	Begin {EndExclusion}
V(s);	V(s);
End; {EndExclusion}	End; {EndExclusion}
⋮	⋮

Suppose the semaphore s is initially 1. Then suppose process 1 executes P(s). It decrements the semaphore by 1 and then continues into its critical section. Now suppose process 2 executes P(s) before process 1 has left its critical section. Since $s = 0$, process 2 is suspended. The *P* operation prevents process 2 from entering its critical section.

When process 1 eventually leaves its critical section, it executes V(s). The *V* operation finds that process 2 is suspended and signals it to continue. Process 2 then enters its critical section; mutual exclusion has thus been enforced.

Next suppose that processes 1 and 2 both try to enter their critical sections simultaneously. Both therefore try to execute P(s) at the same time. This causes simultaneous references to the semaphore via the primitive operation. The indivisibility of the *P* operation allows only one process to access semaphore s at a time. The other one is delayed until after the first one finishes.

As a result, the other process can access the semaphore only after the first one executes P. But by this time, the semaphore has been decremented and the P operation suspends the other process. Again, mutual exclusion is enforced.

The solution is deceptively easy. We do precisely what we tried to do in Section 5.3, but the difference here is more sophisticated low–level operations. While we cannot know what Dijkstra had in mind, we suspect he decided that if a solution fails because of its implementation rather than its logic, the implementation and not the logic should be changed. The result is an elegant low–level solution to mutual exclusion.

In addition to the simplicity and elegance of semaphores, they have another powerful advantage. The solution shown in Figure 5.24 extends easily to the case of *n* concurrent processes (Figure 5.25). If one process in Figure 5.25 executes P(s) first, all others are forced to wait.

Figure 5.25 Mutual exclusion among *n* processes with semaphores

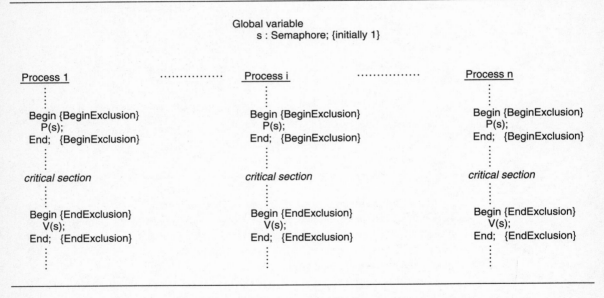

Global variable
s : Semaphore; {initially 1}

Process 1	Process i	Process n
Begin {BeginExclusion} P(s); End; {BeginExclusion}	Begin {BeginExclusion} P(s); End; {BeginExclusion}	Begin {BeginExclusion} P(s); End; {BeginExclusion}
critical section	*critical section*	*critical section*
Begin {EndExclusion} V(s); End; {EndExclusion}	Begin {EndExclusion} V(s); End; {EndExclusion}	Begin {EndExclusion} V(s); End; {EndExclusion}

However, having more than two processes introduces additional complexity in the implementation of P and V. Specifically, if several processes execute P(s) when s = 0, several processes are suspended. Eventually, a process in its critical section will exit and execute the V operation. It will detect a suspended process and resume it: the question is, "Which one?" Some method of prioritizing suspended processes must exist.

One way to prioritize is to queue suspended processes. They can then be resumed in the same order in which they were suspended. Another is to define priorities, and resume processes in order of priority. Either way, this is a problem of implementing the V operation. The discussions that follow are general, and are not concerned with the details.

5.7 Synchronization

The ease with which semaphores enforce mutual exclusion allows us to solve other problems, such as *process synchronization*. We define it as "the forced sequencing of events executed by concurrent asynchronous processes."

To illustrate, suppose processes P_1 and P_2 are executing concurrently and asynchronously. Suppose also that each executes an event (E_1 and E_2, respectively). An event may be a single instruction or a sequence of instructions. Since the processes are concurrent and asynchronous, the events could occur at any time. But as far as order is concerned, there are only three possibilities:

1. E_1 occurs before E_2.
2. E_2 occurs before E_1.
3. E_1 and E_2 are simultaneous.

But what happens if the two events are not independent? What if, for example, E_2 depends on E_1 having already occurred? In this case possibilities 2 and 3 must not happen. How can we guarantee the correct order?

Producer–Consumer Problem

We illustrate by describing the *Producer–Consumer Problem*. It is a generalization of many concurrent programming problems that require synchronization of processes. Specifically, the problem involves two concurrent processes, the *producer* and the *consumer* (Figure 5.26).

Figure 5.26 Cooperating producer and consumer processes

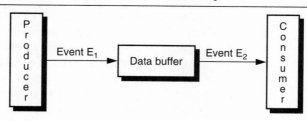

Event E_1 – Producer puts data into buffer.

Event E_2 – Consumer removes data from buffer.

The producer creates or produces data and puts it in a buffer. Event E_1 is the storage of the data. The consumer process, on the other hand, uses or consumes the data. Event E_2 is the reading of data from the buffer.

Assume these processes are concurrent. If E_2 occurs before E_1, the consumer will have accessed an undefined buffer. It will then not generate the expected result. If E_1 and E_2 are simultaneous, mutual exclusion is violated. Two concurrent processes have accessed common memory and the results are unpredictable.

If the consumer is to generate correct results, it must use correct data. If it expects to obtain data from a buffer, the contents must be defined. In other words, the producer must first store the data there. That is, event E_1 must occur before E_2.

The code in Figure 5.27 shows how to do this using semaphores. Here, s is a semaphore. However, this time its initial value is zero instead of one. In Figure 5.27, the consumer contains the primitive P(s) prior to E_2. We also see that the producer contains the primitive V(s) after E_1.

Figure 5.27 Synchronization of the producer and consumer processes using semaphores

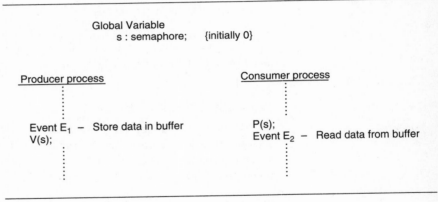

Global Variable
    s : semaphore;   {initially 0}

Producer process

Event E_1 — Store data in buffer
V(s);

Consumer process

P(s);
Event E_2 — Read data from buffer

Now suppose the producer tries to execute E_1 first. It places data in the buffer, and the V operation increases s to 1. If the consumer subsequently tries to execute E_2, P(s) decrements s to 0 and the event occurs. The consumer then has the desired data. The events occur in precisely the required order.

However, suppose the consumer tries to execute E_2 first. When it executes P(s), s is 0. As a result, it is suspended. The consumer cannot retrieve the undefined buffer. Furthermore, the consumer remains suspended until the producer stores something in the buffer and executes V(s). When this happens, the V operation resumes the consumer. It then proceeds to execute E_2 and retrieves the data. Again, events occur in precisely the required order.

If the processes try to execute their respective events simultaneously, the consumer is suspended. The P operation suspends it until after event E_1 occurs.

The code in Figure 5.27 shows how to use a semaphore and primitives to synchronize the producer and consumer. If the producer produces one set of data and the consumer consumes it, the code works. But there is a more general problem. What if the producer produces many sets of data? What if the consumer consumes many sets? The chapter on I/O showed that operating system routines may store many sets of data in buffers for consumption by channel programs.

For example, if E_1 is inside a loop, what happens if the producer executes E_1 several times in succession? The first time, it simply puts some data in the buffer. The second time, though, it puts new data in the same buffer, destroying the old data. If the consumer did not execute E_2, the old data is lost forever. In actuality, the statement, "Event E_1 must occur before event E_2" is not strong enough. We really should say, "Events E_1 and E_2 must alternate, beginning with E_1." But now the code in Figure 5.28 does not work.

Circular Buffer Problem

The producer-consumer problem is actually a special case of the more general *Circular Buffer Problem*. In it (Figure 5.28), a producer stores data consecutively in a set of n buffers numbered 0 through n-1, starting with buffer zero. Similarly, a consumer retrieves data from consecutive buffers one at a time, starting with buffer zero. An example of a producer and consumer relationship is the cooperation of operating system I/O routines and channel programs described in Chapter 3. In response to a user request to write data, operating system routines (producers) place data in special buffers. Channel programs (consumers) then transmit it to device controllers.

We assume the producer and consumer keep storing and retrieving data indefinitely. Thus, when the producer stores data in buffer n-1, it is not finished. The producer continues to create and store data, but where?

This depends on what the consumer does. If it has been active, it has emptied some buffers. Therefore, the producer may use those buffers for new data. In this case, the producer continues to store new data beginning with buffer zero. Buffer zero logically follows buffer n-1. Because of this, we call the data structure circular.

Figure 5.28 Producer and consumer accessing a circular buffer

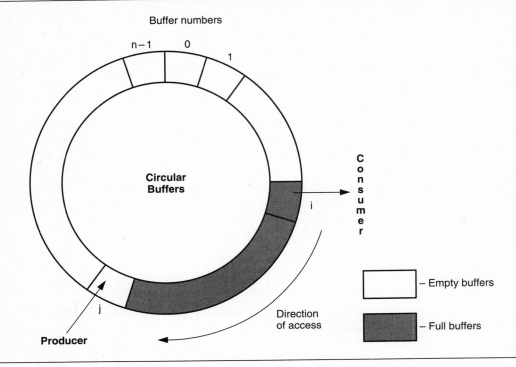

A problem occurs if the producer stores data faster than the consumer retrieves it. The number of unused buffers decreases, and eventually all buffers become full. If this happens, the producer must stop. There is no place to store any more until a buffer is emptied. A similar problem can occur if the consumer retrieves data faster than the producer stores it. In this case, the number of unused buffers increases and eventually all buffers become empty. If this happens, the consumer must stop retrieving data, since there is no more to retrieve.

In the circular buffer problem, storage and retrieval of data are the events to be synchronized. However, the synchronization is more complex than in the producer-consumer problem. There is no need to alternate storage and retrieval of data. The producer may store several sets of data before the consumer becomes active. Similarly, if the producer has stored several sets of data, the consumer may retrieve them all while the producer is temporarily inactive.

The synchronization requirements for the circular buffer problem are as follows. The producer and consumer may store and retrieve data concurrently and independently, subject to the following constraints:

1. The consumer may not consume more than the producer has produced. In other words, the consumer may not read an empty buffer.
2. The number of data buffers filled by the producer may not exceed by more than *n*, the number emptied by the consumer. In other words, the producer may not store more data if no buffers are empty.

Figure 5.29 contains a solution to the circular buffer problem. It uses two distinct semaphores called Occupied and Empty. We use two because there are two reasons for suspending a process. First, we suspend the producer if there are no empty buffers. Second, we suspend the consumer if there are no full buffers.

Figure 5.29 Synchronization of the producer and consumer accessing a circular buffer processes using semaphores

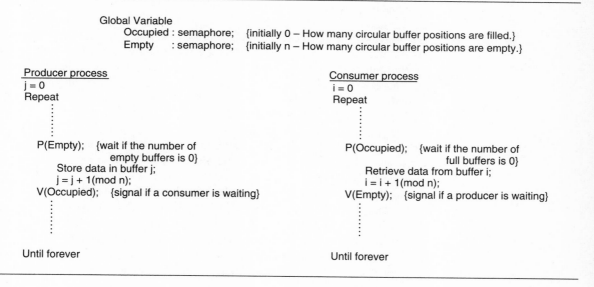

Global Variable
    Occupied : semaphore; {initially 0 – How many circular buffer positions are filled.}
    Empty   : semaphore; {initially n – How many circular buffer positions are empty.}

Producer process
j = 0
Repeat
    ⋮

    P(Empty); {wait if the number of
                 empty buffers is 0}
      Store data in buffer j;
      j = j + 1(mod n);
    V(Occupied); {signal if a consumer is waiting}
    ⋮

Until forever

Consumer process
i = 0
Repeat
    ⋮

    P(Occupied); {wait if the number of
                  full buffers is 0}
      Retrieve data from buffer i;
      i = i + 1(mod n);
    V(Empty); {signal if a producer is waiting}
    ⋮

Until forever

Occupied and Empty can be anything between zero and *n*, inclusive. Sometimes we refer to them as *counting semaphores*. (Those that can have only values of zero and 1 are sometimes called *binary semaphores*.) Counting semaphores serve a double purpose. Their values determine when processes will be suspended, but they also indicate how many full or empty buffers there are. For example, Occupied is the number of full buffers. Initially, of course, its value is zero. Empty is the number of empty buffers. Initially, its value is *n*, the total number of buffers.

In Figure 5.29, the producer must execute the primitive P(Empty) before storing data in a buffer. Since Empty is initially n, this primitive can be executed as many as n times in succession. Each time, it reduces the value of Empty by 1. Therefore, if P(Empty) is executed n times without V(Empty) being executed, Empty decreases to zero. This means that all n buffers are full. Any additional attempts to store data causes P(Empty) to be executed. But when this happens, the producer is suspended. The producer will remain suspended until the consumer executes V(Empty). But this happens only after the consumer has emptied a buffer. This makes it available to the suspended producer.

If the producer and consumer run concurrently, P(Empty) and V(Empty) decrease and increase the semaphore Empty as they access the buffers. Only if the producer produces too much and Empty decreases to zero will P(Empty) suspend the producer.

Similarly, the consumer must execute P(Occupied) before reading a buffer. The producer, in turn, executes V(Occupied) after storing data in a buffer. As before, Occupied increases and decreases as the producer and consumer access the buffers. If the consumer consumes too much, Occupied decreases to zero. If this happens, the consumer is suspended if it tries to empty another buffer. Initially, Occupied is zero. Therefore, the consumer cannot access a buffer before the producer has stored something in it.

The variables i and j in the producer and consumer processes of Figure 5.29 are local integer variables that keep track of the buffer numbers each process accesses next. The modulo arithmetic allows them increase from 0 to n-1 and then revert back to 0.

Sometimes a third semaphore s is used to enforce mutual exclusion of the code that the producer and consumer use to access the buffer. However, the way we have stated the problem, another semaphore is unnecessary. There is nothing wrong if the producer stores something in buffer j at the same time as the consumer retrieves something from buffer i unless i and j are the same. If they are not, the two processes are not referencing common memory. Therefore, mutual exclusion is unnecessary.

On the other hand, if $i = j$, the two processes will reference common memory and mutual exclusion is necessary. But the current primitives in Figure 5.29 prevent this. To see why this is so, think about the conditions required for i and j to be equal.

The values of i and j can be equal in only two cases—after the producer has stored data in the last remaining empty buffer (Figure 5.30), or after the consumer has retrieved data from the last remaining full buffer (Figure 5.31).

According to Figure 5.30, the producer fills the buffers in clockwise order. Therefore, if only one buffer is empty, one of two cases must hold. Either $j=i$-1, or $i=0$ and $j=n$-1. Either way, if the producer fills buffer j, it then adds 1 (modulo n) to j. The result is $i = j$. All buffers are then full.

Figure 5.30 Producer storing data into last remaining available buffer

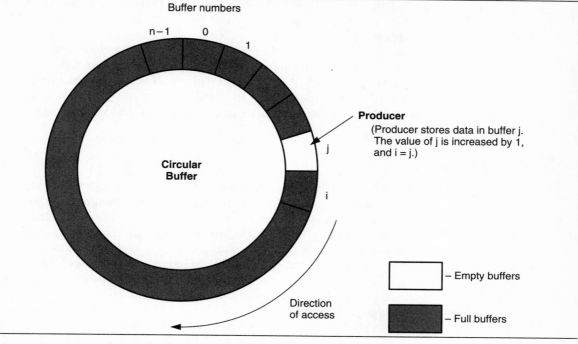

Buffer numbers

Producer
(Producer stores data in buffer j.
The value of j is increased by 1,
and i = j.)

Circular
Buffer

Direction
of access

— Empty buffers

— Full buffers

Figure 5.31 Consumer retrieving data from last remaining full buffer

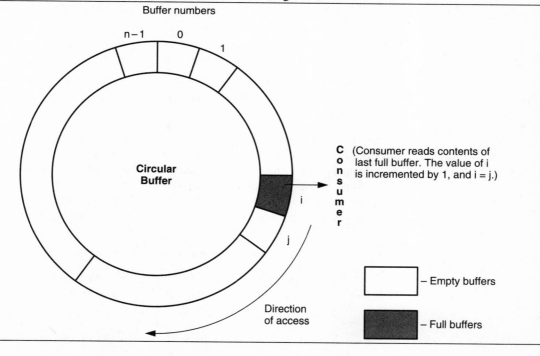

Buffer numbers

Consumer
(Consumer reads contents of
last full buffer. The value of i
is incremented by 1, and i = j.)

Circular
Buffer

Direction
of access

— Empty buffers

— Full buffers

If only one buffer is full (Figure 5.31), then again one of two cases must hold. Either $i=j-1$, or $j=0$ and $i=n-1$. Again either way if the consumer empties buffer i, it adds 1 (modulo n) to i. The result once again is $i=j$. All the buffers are then empty.

We can summarize by stating that the only way the producer and consumer can try to reference the same buffer simultaneously is when $i=j$. But, this means the buffers are all full or all empty. If they are all full, the producer is already prevented from storing data. If they are all empty, the consumer is already prevented from reading data. In either case, mutual exclusion is assured.

≡ 5.8 Monitors

The previous sections have discussed several solutions to mutual exclusion among concurrent processes. The solutions allowed concurrent processes to share common data without interfering with each other. They also allowed the synchronization of processes that run independently, except for certain events.

Of course Dekker's Algorithm must be included in processes that require it. With semaphores, no coding other than the insertion of a primitive operation is necessary. Either way, a system built with either semaphores or algorithms guarantees mutual exclusion when it is needed; or does it?

Strangely, the answer is both "yes" and "no," just like the answers in a political debate. Mutual exclusion algorithms or semaphores guarantee mutual exclusion, but only when they are used! This seems like a strange and perhaps obvious statement: in reality, it is not.

Any system based on mutual exclusion algorithms or semaphores is susceptible to one major problem: the algorithm or primitive must be built into each process' code. Therefore, those who write the code must remember to insert them. This is error-prone for two reasons:

1. People forget things.
2. People may ignore rules to gain a performance advantage or violate security.

Everything we have described requires the programmer to specify critical sections, since there is no formal declaration of them. But sometimes programmers forget things. Therefore, a system built with either semaphores or algorithms cannot guarantee mutual exclusion. Someone may simply forget, or omit primitives or algorithms. If you forget something in a program, it fails. But what happens if you forget something in the design of an operating system? The answer is simple: the operating system fails. In such cases

"Where goes the operating system, so go the processes."

Even if no one ever forgot to insert mutual exclusion primitives, there is still a danger of deliberate omissions. One aim might be sabotage. Or perhaps the programmer feels underpaid, overworked, or politically or socially disaffected. Any secure system must be able to protect itself against mistakes and sabotage.

To avoid such problems, we must make mutual exclusion mandatory. One way to do this is to place critical sections in an area accessible to only one process at a time. The processes then reference the code in a way that automatically enforces mutual exclusion. This requires a formal specification of critical sections.

We refer to the special areas as *monitors*. Dijkstra first suggested them in 1971, and Hoare [14] and Brinch Hansen [15, 16] further developed and implemented them in a programming language. A monitor is a construct that may contain code that references shared data. On the surface, it looks like a collection of data types, data structures, and procedures, all under a monitor heading. But a monitor is much more. It does contain procedures and variables, but the procedures are special. If concurrent processes call different procedures in a monitor, the monitor forces the processes to execute them in sequence. Two procedures within the same monitor cannot be active simultaneously. Calling protocols defined by the language enforce this automatically.

Therefore, rather than coding a critical section within a process, we may code it as a monitor procedure. The code is therefore not duplicated. When a process must reference shared data, it calls a monitor procedure. Compiler generated code that transfers control to a monitor procedure guarantees mutual exclusion.

In this way, a monitor differs greatly from a simple collection of procedures. Its nature is to enforce mutual exclusion rigidly among processes trying to execute its procedures. To emphasize this difference, we shall henceforth refer to a monitor procedure as a *procedure entry*. Brinch Hansen uses this terminology describing concurrent Pascal [17].

Figure 5.32 shows a possible structure for a monitor. It also shows processes that can call procedure entries. Every monitor has a name and may include many procedure entries. The code for each entry has access to any global variable declared under the monitor heading. The design of the language prohibits direct access to these variables by other processes. Each monitor may also have code to initialize global variables.

Figures 5.33a and 5.33b illustrate the difference between the way a monitor and semaphores enforce mutual exclusion. Figure 5.33a shows *n* concurrent processes. Each has a critical section that references shared data. Assume the critical section is duplicated in each process. Then the optional semaphores and primitive operations enforce mutual exclusion. However, if a primitive is removed, there is no longer any guarantee of mutual exclusion.

Figure 5-33b shows the same *n* processes, but here a monitor contains the common critical section. Whenever a process needs access to its critical section, it calls a procedure entry. Mutual exclusion cannot be avoided. The only way a process can access shared data is indirectly through the procedure entry. But the monitor enforces mutual exclusion of its procedure entries.

Figure 5.32 General structure of a monitor

MONITOR MonitorName;

List of global variables accessible
by all monitor entries;

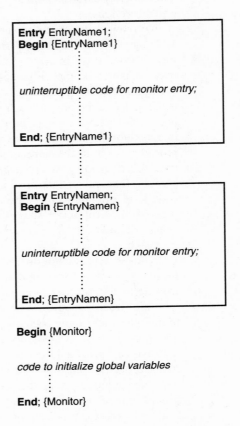

```
Entry EntryName1;
Begin {EntryName1}
          ⋮

uninterruptible code for monitor entry;
          ⋮

End; {EntryName1}
```

```
Entry EntryNamen;
Begin {EntryNamen}
          ⋮

uninterruptible code for monitor entry;
          ⋮

End; {EntryNamen}
```

Begin {Monitor}
          ⋮

code to initialize global variables
          ⋮

End; {Monitor}

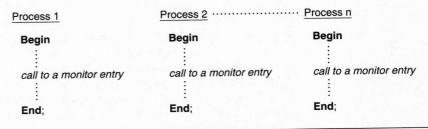

Process 1	Process 2 ⋯⋯⋯⋯⋯ Process n

Begin   **Begin**   **Begin**
  ⋮   ⋮   ⋮

call to a monitor entry   *call to a monitor entry*   *call to a monitor entry*
  ⋮   ⋮   ⋮

End;   **End;**   **End;**

Figure 5-33a *n* processes with an optionally defined critical section

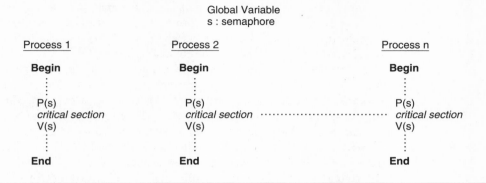

Global Variable
s : semaphore

Process 1	Process 2	Process n
Begin	**Begin**	**Begin**
P(s)	P(s)	P(s)
critical section	*critical section* ·························	*critical section*
V(s)	V(s)	V(s)
End	**End**	**End**

Figure 5.33b *n* processes with critical section inside a monitor

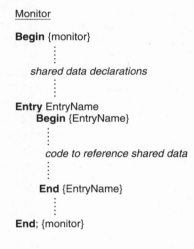

Monitor

Begin {monitor}

    shared data declarations

Entry EntryName
    Begin {EntryName}

        code to reference shared data

    End {EntryName}

End; {monitor}

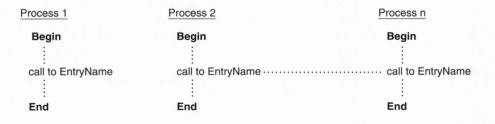

Process 1	Process 2	Process n
Begin	**Begin**	**Begin**
call to EntryName	call to EntryName ·························	call to EntryName
End	**End**	**End**

≡≡≡
Circular Buffer

Monitors can also synchronize events. For example, once again consider the circular buffer problem where a producer and consumer each have critical sections that reference a circular buffer (Figure 5.29). We can define monitor entries to synchronize access to the circular buffer.

Before describing specific entries, we must introduce a new type of variable often used by monitors. For procedure entries to synchronize events, there must be suspension and wakeup procedures. Processes that call procedure entries may be suspended for many reasons. This was certainly true of the producer and consumer; each had to be suspended if certain conditions occurred.

Within a monitor, we may define *condition variables*. They are usually associated with conditions that cause suspension or wakeup of a process. Specifically, a condition variable may be an argument in two special commands, Delay and Continue (some use Wait and Signal) defined as follows. Suppose C is a condition variable:

DELAY(C):   Makes the monitor suspend the process that made the entry call. The monitor stores information about the suspended process in a data structure (often a queue) associated with condition variable C.

CONTINUE(C): Makes the monitor resume a process represented in the data structure associated with C (if one exists). It resumes execution of procedure entry code immediately following the point where the monitor suspended it. The process that called the procedure entry causing execution of the CONTINUE command exits.

If the data structure is a queue, processes are resumed in the order in which they were suspended. In fact, in the language Concurrent Pascal, condition variables are called queues. Other types of data structures may be used to allow for process priorities. We are not concerned with the order of resumption. We only note that the monitor resumes a process that it previously suspended.

Figure 5.34 shows a solution to the circular buffer problem using a monitor. In this case the monitor has just two procedure entries, PutIn and TakeOut. The producer puts data in the circular buffer using the entry PutIn. Similarly, the consumer will remove data through the entry TakeOut. Parameters may be specified in entry calls, as in normal procedure calls.

Figure 5.34 Synchronization of the producer and consumer accessing a circular buffer processes using a monitor

```
Monitor  circular-buffer;
    buffer    : Array[0..n-1] of thing; {circular buffer.  "thing" represents an
                                           unspecified data type}
    i         : integer;              {position in the buffer accessed by the consumer, initially 0}
    j         : integer;              {position in the buffer accessed by the producer, initially 0}
    Fullbuf   : condition             {condition variable indicating whether all buffers are full}
    Emptybuf : condition;             {condition variable for indicating whether buffers are empty}
    Occupied : integer;               {initially 0 - How many circular buffer positions are filled}


{*********************************************************************************}
{This procedure entry puts data in position j of the circular buffer}
{*********************************************************************************}
Entry PutIn(SomeData : thing);
    Begin   {PutIn}
      If Occupied = n then
          Delay(Fullbuf);
      Store SomeData in position j of buffer;
      j = j+1 (mod n);
      Occupied = Occupied + 1;
      Continue(Emptybuf);
    End;   {PutIn}


{*********************************************************************************}
{This procedure entry reads data from position i of the buffer}
{*********************************************************************************}
Entry TakeOut(SomeData : thing);
    Begin   {TakeOut}
      If Occupied = 0 then
          Delay(Emptybuf);
      remove SomeData from position i of buffer;
      i = i+1 (mod n);
      Occupied = Occupied – 1;
      Continue(Fullbuf);
    End;   {TakeOut}


Begin   {Monitor}
    i = 0;
    j = 0;
    Occupied = 0;
End;   {Monitor}
```

Producer Process	Consumer Process
Repeat	Repeat
⋮	⋮
PutIn(SomeData);	TakeOut(SomeData);
⋮	⋮
Until forever	Until forever

Both producer and consumer contain loops in which they call the procedure entries. Since we can make no assumptions about how frequently they make calls, we must prevent either from making too many accesses to the buffer. Suspension and resumption of the processes is done within the monitor.

The monitor itself manages the data and associated bookkeeping variables. The circular buffer is declared globally (global only to the procedure entries and monitor) within the monitor. Variables i and j keep track of which buffer positions the producer or consumer accesses next (Figure 5.28). Variable Occupied specifies how many buffer positions contain data. If Occupied is zero, the monitor must suspend the consumer if it calls TakeOut. Condition variable Emptybuf is associated with this event. If Occupied is n, the monitor must suspend the producer if it calls PutIn. Condition variable Fullbuf is associated with this event.

Whenever the producer must store data in the circular buffer, it calls PutIn. (Figures 5.34 and 5.35). The code in this entry examines Occupied. If Occupied = n, the entry executes Delay(Fullbuf). The monitor immediately suspends the producer and stores information about it in a data structure associated with Fullbuf. The monitor will resume the producer only when it executes Continue(Fullbuf). But this happens only after the consumer has called TakeOut and the monitor empties a buffer.

Figure 5.35 Suspending and resuming producer and consumer

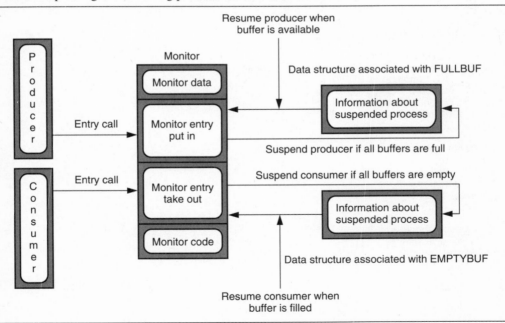

Whenever the consumer must read the circular buffer, it calls TakeOut (Figures 5.34 and 5.35). The code in this entry examines Occupied. If Occupied = 0, it executes Delay(Emptybuf). The monitor suspends the consumer and stores information about it in a data structure associated with Emptybuf. The monitor resumes the consumer only when it executes Continue(Emptybuf). But this happens only after the producer has called PutIn and the monitor has filled a buffer.

Readers & Writers Problem

Monitors may also synchronize events in a more difficult case called the *Readers and Writers Problem.* It is a generalization of the circular buffer problem. The circular buffer problem has a single producer and consumer storing and retrieving data. Furthermore, the consumer retrieves data in the same order in which the producer stores it.

In the readers and writers problem (Figure 5.36), there are many producers (called writers) and many consumers (called readers). In addition, instead of a circular queue, the processes access a shared database. Readers may access but not change data. Writers, however, can change data or add new data.

Figure 5.36 Readers and writers accessing a shared database

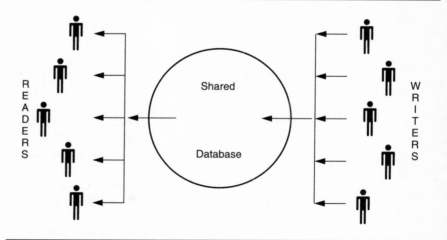

Readers may access the data in any order. They do not necessarily read it in the order in which the writers stored it. Furthermore, many readers may read the same data. A common example is an airline reservation system. The readers are examining flights between cities. The readers are not booking flights, they are just looking at the schedule. The writers, on the other hand, are making reservations: they are changing the database. In this problem, there is nothing wrong with multiple readers accessing the database. After all, they are just looking at its contents. However, we can run into trouble if a writer is also active (Figure 5.37).

Figure 5.37 Update problem when a reader and writer are both active

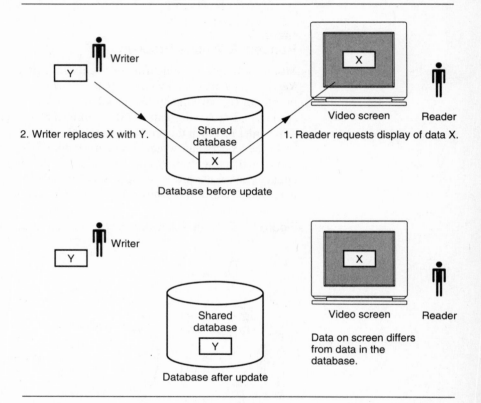

To see this, suppose a reader accesses data (step 1 in Figure 5.37) from the database. The system usually displays it on a video terminal. But what happens if, while the data is displayed on the screen, a writer changes it (step 2 in Figure 5.37)? Now the screen is no longer an accurate reflection of the database. The system becomes unreliable.

For this reason, we should not allow both a reader and a writer to access common data simultaneously. Similarly, we should not allow two or more writers to access data simultaneously. Therefore, the question is, "Can we use monitors to allow multiple concurrent readers, and at the same time enforce mutual exclusion whenever a writer is active?" The answer to this question is "Yes." However, before describing the solution, we must carefully state our goals. Unclear goals can cause problems. For example, suppose the goals of the monitor are to:

1. Allow a reader access to the database if no writer is active, but deny a reader access if a writer is active.
2. Allow a writer access only if no readers or other writers are active.

These goals certainly seem to be what is needed. But examine their ramifications very carefully. Suppose at some point only readers are active. If more readers request access, the monitor allows it. Now suppose a writer requests access. Because of goal 2, the monitor denies access and suspends the writer. Meanwhile, more readers continue to request access. Since no writer is active (remember, the writer is waiting), more readers continue to access the database. All this time, the writer is waiting, and waiting, and waiting.... As long as readers make requests, the writer will wait. The monitor prevents the writer from accessing the database as long as readers want to examine it. The writer suffers from indefinite postponement.

In an airline reservation system this means you can see the flight you want, but you cannot reserve a seat on it. Airline profits suffer, despite enormous demand. You miss your flight to the Caribbean and must be content to spend your vacation watching reruns of "Gilligan's Island."

One way to correct this is to have the monitor prevent more readers from accessing the database after a writer requests access. Therefore, suppose we change goal 1 to:

1. (revised) Allow a reader access to the database if no writer is active or waiting for access. Otherwise, deny a reader access.

With this revised goal, Figure 5.38 contains a monitor solution to the Readers and Writers Problem.

The monitor contains two condition variables, Reader and Writer. The data structure associated with Reader contains information about readers who must wait for a writer to finish. The data structure associated with Writer contains information about writers who must wait for all current readers to finish. A third variable, NumOfReaders, contains the number of active readers.

The monitor has three entries. A writer who wants to access the database must call WriteToDatabase. If no other procedure entry is active, the monitor executes the entry. It then checks the number of active readers. If there are none, the monitor writes the data into the database. Otherwise, it suspends the writer, and stores information about it in the Writer data structure. The monitor has thus prevented the writer from changing to the database while readers are still active.

Figure 5.38 Mutual exclusion of readers and writers using monitors

```
Monitor  Readers&Writers;
    Reader          : condition;    {condition variable to suspend readers}
    Writer          : condition;    {condition variable to suspend writers}
    NumOfReaders : integer  ;       {initially 0 - How many readers in the database}


{*********************************************************************************}
{This monitor entry allows a reader to begin reading from the database if no writer is active or waiting}
{*********************************************************************************}
Entry StartRead;
    Begin    {StartRead}
       If (data structure associated with Writer is nonempty) then
          Delay(Reader);
       NumOfReaders = NumOfReaders + 1;
       Continue(Reader);
    End;  {StartRead}


{*********************************************************************************}
{This monitor entry allows a reader to finish reading from the database.  If the reader is the last one to
 finish, the monitor will resume a writer if one is waiting}
{*********************************************************************************}
Entry FinishRead;
    Begin    {FinishRead}
       NumOfReader = NumOfReader − 1;
       If (NumOfReader = 0) then
          Continue(Writer);
    End;  {FinishRead}


{*********************************************************************************}
{This monitor entry allows a writer to write to the database if it is not being used}
{*********************************************************************************}
Entry WriteToDatabase(SomeData : AnyType);
    Begin    {WriteToDatabase}
       If (NumOfReader <> 0) then
          Delay(Writer);
       write SomeData to the database;
       If (data structure associated with Reader is nonempty) then
          Continue(Reader)
       else
          Continue(Writer);
    End;  {WriteToDatabase}


Begin {Monitor}
    NumOfReaders = 0;
End. {Monitor}
```

Any Reader Process

Repeat
   ⋮

  StartRead;
  read data from database
  FinishRead
   ⋮

Until forever

Any Writer Process

Repeat
   ⋮

  WriteToDatabase(SomeData);
   ⋮

Until forever

After the monitor writes the data, it resumes a reader if one is waiting; if not, it resumes another writer if one is waiting. The monitor prefers a reader over a writer. There are usually more readers than writers, so this reduces the average wait time.

To see the advantage of preferring readers, consider the alternative. Suppose the monitor preferred waiting writers. Whenever a writer finished, the monitor would resume another if one were waiting. When it finished, the monitor would resume yet another if one is waiting, and so on. Readers cannot access the database until there are no more writers, and under the assumption of more readers than writers, the list of waiting readers could grow very long.

Since the monitor actually writes to the database, mutual exclusion is guaranteed. Suppose a writer is executing a procedure entry, and a second writer or another reader calls an entry. The monitor will not respond until it finishes with the first writer.

Next, suppose a reader requests access to the database by calling StartRead. The monitor examines the Writer data structure. If it is empty, the monitor adds 1 to NumOfReaders, thus tracking the number of readers accessing the database. If the data structure is not empty, a writer is waiting. Thus, in accordance with revised goal 1, the monitor suspends the reader. It stores information about the reader in the Reader data structure.

At the end of the StartRead entry, the monitor executes Continue(Reader). At first glance, this seems peculiar. But to see its use, suppose a writer calls WriteToDatabase. If readers are active, the monitor suspends it. Subsequently, the monitor will also suspend readers who call StartRead. Eventually, the writer will access the database and finish. When it finishes, the monitor resumes one waiting reader. But what about others? They have all been waiting for the writer to finish: should they not all be resumed? When the first reader is resumed, it finishes StartRead, causing the monitor to resume the next reader. This reader, in turn, causes resumption of the following one, and so on. The monitor resumes all readers until none are waiting.

When a reader finishes, it calls FinishRead. The monitor code there decrements NumOfReaders by 1. At this point, the monitor checks NumOfReaders. If it is zero, the monitor executes Continue(Writer) In other words, if a writer is waiting and no more readers are accessing the database, the monitor resumes the writer. If there are no writers waiting, the Continue command has no effect, and the monitor and database are idle until the next request.

A monitor is a powerful mutual exclusion tool. Yet, it is no more powerful than a semaphore. Ben-Ari [2] shows that a monitor can simulate a semaphore. Conversely, he also shows that semaphores can simulate a monitor. Therefore, an application using one can also use the other. However, a system built around monitors can be more secure. As long as all critical sections are placed in the monitor, mistakes are less likely. A programmer could forget to insert a semaphore primitive, and because mutual exclusion is then not guaranteed, system security could be destroyed. A monitor enforces mutual exclusion automatically.

5.9 Multitasking in Ada

The previous section showed how to construct monitors to enforce mutual exclusion among processes or to synchronize independent processes. The monitor is a construct in a particular programming language. We defined critical sections and stored them as procedure entries. If processes must be synchronized or need access to shared data, they do so through the monitor. This means the monitor must be accessible to all processes. A monitor is most easily implemented if its code is stored in common memory and is executed by a central CPU.

Many multiple CPU systems have a central CPU. It is a *master* and all other CPUs are *slaves* (Figure 5.39). All user or application programs run on either the slave or master CPU. However, operating system routines may run only on the master. All CPUs have access to common memory (solid lines in Figure 5.39). In such systems, a monitor is most easily implemented by storing it in common memory and running it on the master CPU.

Figure 5.39 Master/slave CPU system with common memory

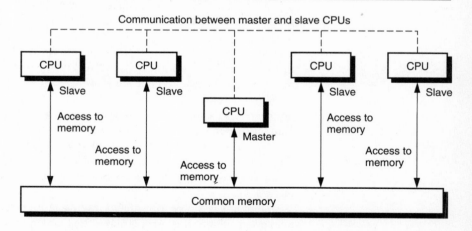

But many computer systems do not have common memory or a single master CPU. They may consist of many independent systems, each with one or more CPUs and its own memory (Figure 5.40).

Figure 5.40 Independent computer with occasional need to communicate

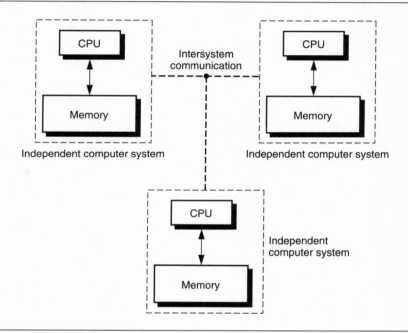

Figure 5.40 shows three separate computers. Each has a CPU and memory and runs its own operating system. However, the computers may have to communicate occasionally to synchronize processes or access shared data. A monitor does not easily lend itself to such systems. It is central, but there is no central physical resource. Where should the monitor code be stored? On which CPU will it run? These design questions are difficult to answer.

On such systems, a different form of process communication may be desirable. Ada is a programming language that supports parallel activities occasionally needing synchronization. We refer to these activities as *tasks*. They are part of a process that may execute in parallel with other tasks. Sometimes one task must provide information to another; at other times, a task may not continue until another has generated an event.

Callers and Servers

Suppose that two independent tasks must communicate. They may execute on different computers as shown in Figure 5.40. In Ada, the following occurs:

- The first task, the *caller*, asks to communicate with the second task. The caller makes the request by referencing a named *entry*.
- The second task, the *server*, must be ready and willing to accept the request.
- If the server cannot accept the request, the caller must wait until it does.
- If the server can accept it, communication is established. We call this a *rendezvous*. What happens next depends on the nature of the tasks.

In this section examples will illustrate how each task contributes to the rendezvous and what happens after it occurs. (For a more detailed discussion of Ada consult references such as [18, 19].)

Before discussing multitasking, we first describe some of Ada's syntax. Anyone familiar with Pascal should have little difficulty understanding this brief introduction. Figure 5.41 shows the basic outline of an Ada program.

Figure 5.41 Syntax outline of an Ada program

```
task      task name     is
    :
    declaration of entries, if any exist, in this task
    :
end;

task body      task name      is
    :
    variable declarations for this task
    :
begin
    :
    task code
    :
    :
end
```

The first line is the name of the task. After it come the declarations of the entries. Server tasks contain entry points that other tasks may call. Their names must appear here. The task body follows. Like a Pascal procedure, it contains variable declarations and code. It may have logic structures like those in Pascal, entry calls, or code that accepts entry calls from other tasks.

We now give a simple example of a single caller and a single server to illustrate the rendezvous: the problem from section 5.2 in which processes detect deer in a wildlife preserve. For simplicity, we assume that deer are counted at only one location (marked by a large "Deer Crossing" sign that all well–educated deer obey). There is only one process to detect deer and one to count them.

Figure 5.42 shows two Ada tasks. The first one, CountDeer, counts the number of deer detected by other tasks. It has one entry called Increment. Other tasks may call upon it.

Figure 5.42 The Ada solution to counting deer

```
task    CountDeer   is                  task    SightDeer;
   entry increment;
end;                                     task body    SightDeer    is

task body    CountDeer    is             begin
   NumofDeer : integer;                     loop
                                               wait until a deer is detected
begin                                          increment;
   NumofDeer = 0                           end loop;
   loop                                 end    SightDeer;
      accept increment do
         NumofDeer = NumofDeer + 1;
      end increment
   end loop;
```

The second task, SightDeer, responds to a sensor signal when a deer is sighted. It then calls Increment. Consider what happens when the sensors detect a deer and SightDeer calls Increment. There are two possibilities.

The first one (Figure 5.43) occurs when the server is currently incrementing the number of deer in response to a previous call. Suppose the caller makes an entry call at time t_1. Because the server is busy, it cannot respond. That is, it cannot accept calls until it finishes incrementing. Therefore, the caller task must wait. The server's code contains an *accept* command. It cannot respond to an entry call until it executes the Accept. Accept specifies the name of an entry call. When the server finishes incrementing NumOfDeer, the loop brings the logic back up to the Accept command. Suppose this occurs at time t_2 as shown in Figure 5.43. Once the server executes Accept, it can respond to the caller's request. The rendezvous succeeds.

Now, the server executes all commands associated with the Accept command. While this occurs, the caller waits. The associated commands lie between the Accept and the End. In Figure 5.42, there is only one associated command, NumOfDeer = NumOfDeer + 1. The rendezvous remains in effect until all associated commands have been executed. Suppose this occurs at time t_3. The rendezvous is then over. The caller and server both resume independent execution.

Figure 5.43 Timing of events when entry call occurs before it is accepted

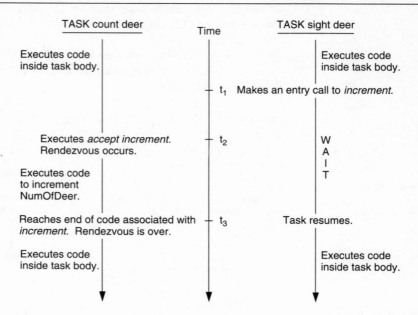

The second possibility when the sensors detect a deer, occurs when a call is accepted before it is made. (Talk about sitting by the telephone, anxiously awaiting a call!) Suppose the server executes the Accept Increment command at time t_1 (Figure 5.44). If a deer has not yet been sighted, the server should certainly not increment the number of deer, and as a result, it waits.

The server waits until a task calls Increment. Suppose the caller sights a deer and calls Increment at time t_2. Since the server has already executed the Accept command, it responds to the call immediately. The rendezvous has now been made.

At this point, the processes proceed as before. The caller waits while the server executes the code associated with the Accept. When the server finishes incrementing the number of deer (time t_3 in Figure 5.44), the rendezvous is over. As before, both tasks resume independent execution.

Figure 5.44 Timing of events when entry call occurs after it is accepted

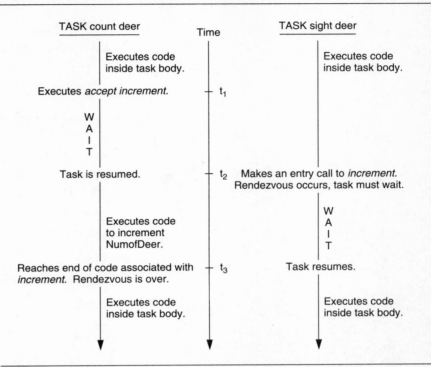

Conditional Accepts

As stated earlier, a server may have many entries. It must have a declaration for each one. The code inside its task body may contain an Accept command for each entry. However, we face a potential problem in coding Accept commands. For example, we may code them as shown in Figure 5.45. But can you see a problem with coding them this way?

Remember that the tasks that make entry calls execute, with the exception of entry calls themselves, independently of the server. The server thus cannot know in advance when the tasks will make calls. Any task may make any call at any time, yet the code for the server in Figure 5.45 accepts entry calls in order from Entry1 through Entry-n.

What happens if a task calls Entry2 before there is a call to Entry1? The server has executed Accept Entry1. Since no call to Entry1 has yet been made, the server waits. This is in spite of the fact that a process has called Entry2 and has requested a response. The server is not responding to the caller's needs.

Figure 5.45 Server containing multiple entries

```
task      taskname    is
  :
  declaration of entries in this task
  :
end;

task body    taskname    is
  :
  variable declarations for this task
  :
begin
  loop
    :
    :

    accept entry1
      :
      code associated with accept
      :
    end entry1;

    accept entry2
      :
      code associated with accept
      :
    end entry2;
      :
      :
    accept entry-n
      :
      code associated with accept
      :
    end entry-n;
  end loop;
end.
```

How can we make the server execute Accept commands in any order? This is not an unusual requirement. Most languages have logic that allows commands to be executed out of sequence. This is called conditional execution, and it is usually implemented with an If statement.

Ada has a structure that lets a server execute Accept commands in any order. It is the Select statement (Figure 5.46).

Figure 5.46 Ada select statement

```
                                        :
                                        :
                            select
                                When Condition1 =>
                                    Accept Entry1
                                        :
                                        entry code
                                        :
                                    End Entry1;
                            or
                                When Condition2 =>
                                    Accept Entry2
                                        :
                                        entry code
                                        :
                                    End Entry2;
                        or
                            :
                            :
                            :
                        or
                                When Condition-n =>
                                    Accept Entry-n
                                        :
                                        entry code
                                        :
                                    End Entry-n;
                        else
                                other logic
                        end select;
```

A Select statement may contain many Accept commands. A Boolean condition may be associated with each one as Figure 5.46 shows. In Ada, these conditions are called *guards*. Each guard is either True or False. This, of course, depends on values associated with variables within it. If a guard is True, it is said to be *open*. The server may execute only Accept commands that follow an open guard or that have no associated guard. When an Ada task reaches a Select statement, it does the following:

- Identifies all open guards.
- Identifies all Accept commands that have open guards or no guards.
- Determines which of those Accept commands are for entries to which a call has been made.
- Selects one for execution.
- Executes the selected command and initiates the rendezvous.

The format for the Select command in Figure 5.46 has an *else* clause. If there are no open guards, the Select executes code associated with the *else*.

Through Select commands, the server is busy as long as other tasks call the entries. The server will not wait for an entry call that has not occurred if another caller requests its assistance at another entry.

Readers and Writers

Let us consider the Readers and Writers Problem again. Suppose many Ada tasks want to read or write to a shared database. As before, we want to ensure that a writer has exclusive access. We want to design an Ada server that will write to the database at a writer's request and keep track of the number of readers. Figure 5.47 contains the code.

The server in Figure 5.47 has three entries. They are StartRead, FinishRead, and WriteToDatabase. If a reader task, also shown in Figure 5.47, wants to read from the database, it calls StartRead. The server increments the number of readers, and the reader then reads from the database. When it is done, it calls FinishRead. The server then decrements the number of Readers.

When a writer task, also shown in Figure 5.47, wants to write to the database, it calls WriteToDatabase. The code for this entry then writes data (specified in the parameter SomeData).

How does the server decide when to accept or reject entry calls? The Select statement discriminates among requests. The server in Figure 5.47 contains a Select statement with 3 Accept commands. Two have guards, and the third does not.

Accept StartRead is protected by the guard when WriteToDatabase'count = 0. The apostrophe defines an *attribute* in Ada. Attributes may be associated with entries by means of an apostrophe followed by a keyword. In this example, WriteToDatabase'count is an attribute associated with the entry WriteToDatabase. It represents the number of tasks that have called WriteToDatabase and are waiting to rendezvous.

As you can see, the server only accepts a call to StartRead if WriteToDatabase'count is zero. In other words, a reader can rendezvous with StartRead only when no writer has requested a rendezvous with WriteToDatabase. As long as no writer is trying to access the database, the server accepts reader requests. Once a writer has requested a rendezvous, the server will accept no more calls to StartRead. This allows all readers to finish eventually so that the writer may safely access the database. Accept FinishRead has no guard. Thus, the server always accepts calls to it. This is what we want. There is no reason to prevent a reader from finishing. Accept WriteToDatabase is protected by the guard when NumOfReaders = 0. The server will accept a writer's request for a rendezvous only when there are no active readers.

Figure 5.47 Ada solution to the readers and writers problem

```
task Readers&Writers is
    entry StartRead;
    entry FinishRead;
    entry WriteToDatabase
end;

task body Readers&Writers is
    NumOfReaders : Integer;

Begin
    NumOfReaders = 0;
    loop
        select
            when WriteToDatabase' count = 0
                accept StartRead;
                    NumOfReaders = NumOfReaders + 1
                end StartRead;
            or
                accept FinishRead
                    NumOfReaders = NumOfReaders − 1
                end FinishRead;
            or
                when NumOfReaders = 0
                    accept WriteToDatabase (SomeData : AnyType);
                        Write SomeData to the Database;
                    end WriteToDatabase;
        end select
    end loop
end.
```

```
task reader;

task body reader is

begin
    loop
        :
        :
        StartRead;
            Read data from database
        FinishRead;
        :
        :
    end loop;
end reader
```

```
task writer

task body writer is
    SomeData : AnyType;
begin
    loop
        :
        :
        WriteToDatabase(SomeData);
        :
        :
    end loop;
end writer;
```

Suppose that several readers are active and no writer has requested a rendezvous. The server accepts calls to StartRead and FinishRead as readers make them. However, once a writer calls WriteToDatabase, the guard protecting accept StartRead is closed. The server will accept no more calls to StartRead. This prevents more readers from accessing the database. Now the writer has requested a rendezvous with WriteToDatabase, but if there are still active readers accessing the database, the server cannot yet establish it.

In fact, the only entry calls the server can accept are ones to FinishRead. Therefore, as readers finish and rendezvous with FinishRead, the server will eventually decrement NumOfReaders to zero. At this point, there are no more active readers and the guard when NumOfReaders = 0 is open. The writer has its rendezvous with WriteToDatabase, and the server writes the data.

Despite our discussion, there is a small problem with the solution in Figure 5.47. Can you spot it? What happens if a second writer requests a rendezvous with WriteToDatabase while the first writer is waiting for its rendezvous to end? What happens when the rendezvous between the first writer and WriteToDatabase is completed?

If the second writer calls WriteToDatabase, it will wait because the server is already in a rendezvous. However, when the rendezvous is over, the server will examine which entry calls can be accepted. Since a second writer has requested a rendezvous, the guard protecting StartRead is closed. Furthermore, there are no readers, so no calls to FinishRead are pending. The server therefore accepts the call to WriteToDatabase.

If yet another writer requests a rendezvous, the same events will occur. Readers are blocked from accessing the database as long as there is a writer requesting or in a rendezvous. The readers may suffer indefinite postponement. Can you think of a way to solve this problem?

5.10 Deadlocks

The previous sections have simplified many examples to remove irrelevant details. This allowed us to concentrate on a specific concept such as mutual exclusion. Unfortunately, such simplifications often hide or eliminate actual problems. In this section, we consider more realistic situations and the additional difficulties that can arise.

Mutual Exclusion of Readers and Writers by Page

To illustrate, reconsider the Readers and Writers Problem and the monitor solution described in Figures 5.36 through 5.38. The problem as stated in Figure 5.36 was simplified. We insisted that no reader may be active if a writer is active. In general, this is a sound restriction, however, we may not want to enforce it across the entire database. In other words, if a writer is active, do we really want to deny a reader access to everything? Consider an airline reservation database. If an agent is booking a flight from New York to Boston, should we prevent someone else from looking at flights from Tokyo to Honolulu? Of course not.

A database is often divided into regions called *pages*. Pages contain collections of records, and they are usually stored separately in secondary storage. Databases often contain many thousands of pages. If a writer is accessing one page, we certainly do not want to block a reader from every other page in the database. Yet, we still need mutual exclusion to prevent a reader from reading the page to which the writer has access.

One solution is to enforce mutual exclusion by page. For example, we may change the goals from Section 5.8 for a solution to the Readers and Writers Problem as follows:

- Allow a reader access to a database page if no writer is writing to it or waiting for access to it. Otherwise, deny a reader access to the page.

- Allow a writer access to a page only if no readers or writers are currently accessing it.

The monitor solution for the revised problem is similar to the one in Figure 5.38. That solution used two condition variables to control access to the entire database. Also, a counter kept track of the number of readers. The revised solution (Figure 5.48) uses two condition variables to control access to each page and a counter for each page to keep track of the number of readers accessing it.

The major differences between the monitor in Figure 5.38 and the one in Figure 5.48 are the following:

- Reader, Writer, NumOfReaders, and WriterBusy are arrays with page numbers as subscripts.
  Procedure entries StartWrite and FinishWrite replace the entry
- WriteToDatabase in Figure 5.38. In the original problem, we required that no more than one writer be active in the entire database. We did this by inserting the code to write to the database inside the entry.
- WriteToDatabase. The monitor did not allow more than one writer to be active.
- The revised problem allows many writers to be active as long as they are accessing different pages. Therefore, if a writer wants access to a database page, it calls StartWrite. If the number of readers accessing the page is not zero (NumOfReaders[page#] <> 0) or another writer is accessing the page (WriterBusy[page#] = True), the monitor suspends the writer. If no reader or writer is accessing the page, the monitor sets

Figure 5.48 Mutual exclusion of readers and writers, by page numbers, using monitors

```
Monitor Readers&Writers;
   Reader          : array[1..n] of condition;        {condition variable array to suspend readers}
   Writer          : array[1..n] of condition;        {condition variable array to suspend writers}
   WriterBusy      : array[1..n] of boolean;          {array of boolean values to indicate active writer on a page}
   NumOfReaders : array[1..n] of integer;             {initially all 0's - How many readers in a database page}

{* * * * * * * * * * * * * * * * * * * * * * * * * * * * * * * * * * * * * * * * * * * * * * * * * * * *}
{This monitor entry allows a reader to begin reading from a database page if no writer is active
   on it or waiting for it.}
{* * * * * * * * * * * * * * * * * * * * * * * * * * * * * * * * * * * * * * * * * * * * * * * * * * * *}
Entry StartRead(Page#);
   Begin {StartRead}
     If (data structure associated with Writer [Page#] is nonempty)  or WriterBusy[page#] then
      Delay(Reader[Page#]);
      NumOfReaders[Page#] = NumOfReaders[Page#] + 1;
      Continue (Reader [Page #]);
   End; {StartRead}

{* * * * * * * * * * * * * * * * * * * * * * * * * * * * * * * * * * * * * * * * * * * * * * * * * * * *}
{This monitor entry allows a reader to finish reading from a database page.  If the reader is the last one to
       finish, the monitor will resume a writer if one is waiting.}
{* * * * * * * * * * * * * * * * * * * * * * * * * * * * * * * * * * * * * * * * * * * * * * * * * * * *}
Entry  FinishRead(page#);
   Begin {FinishRead}
     NumOfReaders[page#] = NumOfReaders[page#] − 1;
     If (NumOfReaders[page#] = 0) then
      Continue(Writer[page#]);
   End; {FinishRead}

{* * * * * * * * * * * * * * * * * * * * * * * * * * * * * * * * * * * * * * * * * * * * * * * * * * * *}
{This monitor entry allows a writer to start writing to a database page if it is not being used.}
{* * * * * * * * * * * * * * * * * * * * * * * * * * * * * * * * * * * * * * * * * * * * * * * * * * * *}
Entry  StartWrite(Page#);
   Begin {StartWrite}
     If (NumOfReaders[Page#] <> 0)  or WriterBusy[Page#] then
      Delay(Writer[Page#]);
     WriterBusy[Page#] = True;
   End; {StartWrite}

{* * * * * * * * * * * * * * * * * * * * * * * * * * * * * * * * * * * * * * * * * * * * * * * * * * * *}
{This monitor entry allows a writer to finish writing to a database page.  The monitor will resume either a
       waiting reader or writer.}
{* * * * * * * * * * * * * * * * * * * * * * * * * * * * * * * * * * * * * * * * * * * * * * * * * * * *}
Entry  FinishWrite(Page#);
   Begin  {FinishWrite}
     WriterBusy[Page#] = False;
     If (data structure associated with Reader[Page#] is nonempty) then
     Continue(Reader[Page#])
     else
     Continue(Writer[Page#]);
   End; {FinishWrite}

End. {Monitor}
```

Any Reader Process	Any Writer Process
Repeat	Repeat
⋮	⋮
StartRead(Page#);	StartWrite(Page#);
read data from database	*write data to database*
FinishRead(Page#);	FinishWrite(Page#);
⋮	⋮
Until forever	Until forever

WriterBusy[page#] to True. The writer leaves the procedure entry and writes to the database. If another writer subsequently tries to access the page, the monitor suspends it.

- When a writer finishes with a page, it calls FinishWrite. The monitor sets WriterBusy[page#] to False. If readers are waiting to use the page, the monitor will resume them. If not, the monitor will resume a writer if one is waiting.

This problem is more realistic than the one described in Section 5.8, but more realism causes difficulties. For example, suppose two writers call the monitor as shown in Figure 5.49. Suppose they make the calls in the following order:

- Writer 1 calls StartWrite to request access to page 17. It is available, and the monitor grants the access.
- Writer 2 calls StartWrite to request access to page 23. It is available, and the monitor grants the access.
- Writer 1 calls StartWrite to request access to page 23. The monitor checks WriterBusy[23]. Since it is True, the monitor suspends writer 1.
- Writer 2 calls StartWrite to request access to page 17. The monitor checks WriterBusy[17]. Since it is True, the monitor suspends writer 2.

Figure 5.49 Two writers that have become deadlocked

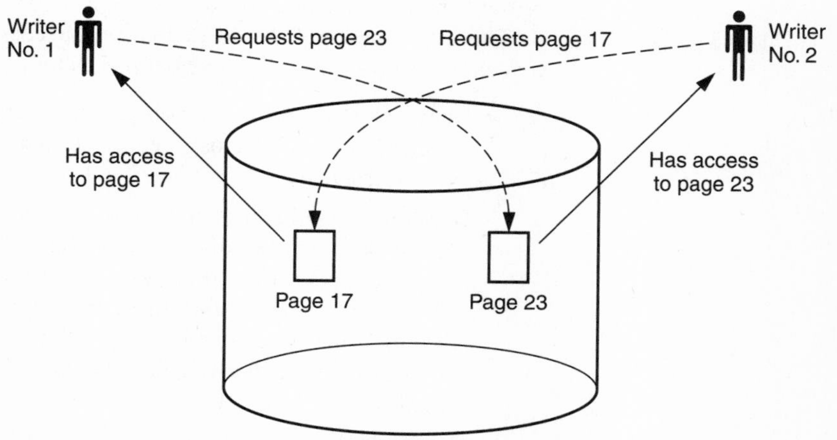

Can you predict the result? The monitor has suspended writer 1 and will not resume it until writer 2 finishes with page 23. The monitor has also suspended writer 2 and will not resume it until writer 1 finishes with page 17. Each writer must execute an event to make the other resume. Unfortunately, since the monitor has suspended both, neither can do so. Thus, both will remain suspended forever. We call this painful event a *deadlock* or *deadly embrace*. A deadlock can occur when multiple processes request access to common resources. The resources may be database pages or devices such as tape drives. How can an operating system deal with the problem?

Aspects of Deadlock

Before describing how an operating system might deal with deadlock, let's first ask the question, "What are the aspects of deadlock?" This is an important question, as deadlock can be discussed from many different perspectives.

We must first consider the type of resources involved. We may classify resources as either *serially reusable* or *consumable*. Serially reusable ones are fixed in number, and each can be allocated to just one process. When a process finishes with it, the resource is released back into the system pool. Examples include memory, disk storage, files, peripherals, and shared processors. By contrast, consumable resources may be created or eliminated (consumed) depending on activities. For example, a producer may create resources to which consumers request access. After the consumer uses them, they may not be reused. The resources are not released back into the system pool; instead, they have been consumed. Examples include data or messages from processes intended to be read or used just once. This chapter deals only with serially reusable resources. (Reference [33] discusses consumable ones.)

The key aspects of deadlock that we discuss are *prevention, avoidance, detection*, and *recovery*. They are defined as follows:

- **Deadlock Prevention**. The operating system constrains resource sharing to make deadlock impossible. As we shall see, the constraints are often very restrictive.

- **Deadlock Avoidance**. This differs from deadlock prevention in that deadlock is theoretically possible, given the right (or wrong?) sequence of requests. However, the operating system examines all requests carefully. If it sees that the allocation of a resource creates the risk of deadlock, the system denies access, thus avoiding the issue. We will describe a deadlock avoidance method called Dijkstra's *Banker's Algorithm*.

- **Deadlock Detection**. Some operating systems may use neither prevention nor avoidance mechanisms. Thus, if a deadlock occurs, it must be detected, but how? In the example of Figure 5.49, neither process knows it is deadlocked. The operating system sees each in a Wait state, a common situation. How can the system detect that the waits are permanent?

- **Deadlock Recovery**. What should be done after the operating system detects a deadlock? The processes cannot remain deadlocked forever. The operating system must resolve the problem.

Let us now discuss each area in more detail.

Deadlock Prevention

To prevent deadlock, we must first understand why and when it occurs. In 1971, Coffman et al. [21] wrote that four conditions are necessary for deadlock to happen:

Mutual exclusion. The resources must be shared in a mutually exclusive way; that is, if a process has access to a resource, no other process may access it until it is released (Figure 5.50a).

Figure 5.50a Mutual exclusion of resources among processes

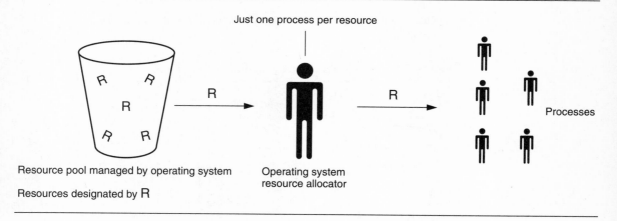

Just one process per resource

R →

R →

Processes

Resource pool managed by operating system

Resources designated by R

Operating system resource allocator

Non-preemption. If the operating system has allocated a resource to a process, it cannot remove the resource until the process finishes with it. The process must release the resource voluntarily (Figure 5.50b).

Figure 5.50b Non-preemption of resources from processes

Hold and request. A process may retain control of resources while obtaining others (Figure 5.50c).

Figure 5.50c Hold and request condition for processes

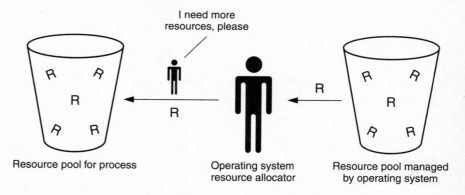

Circular wait. A list of processes, each of which wants a resource that its successor has, while the last one wants a resource that the first one has (Figure 5.50d).

Figure 5.50d Circular wait condition of resource requests

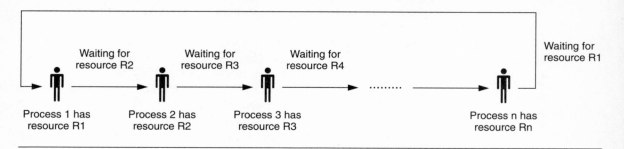

Since these are necessary conditions, one can prevent deadlock by simply removing one condition [20]. We now consider the consequences of removing each condition.

Removing Mutual Exclusion. We have already described what can happen if mutual exclusion is not enforced. The activities of one process may affect the progress of another. This is precisely why so much time has been spent explaining the need for mutual exclusion. Thus, that condition must not be removed.

Removing Non-preemption. What happens if we remove the *non-preemption* condition? The mutual exclusion mechanisms can then forcibly remove a resource from a process. This may be undesirable for a few reasons (besides the typical screams of angry users!).

The first is that processes cannot depend on consistent resource allocation. Users have difficulty planning since they cannot predict when resources may be taken away from them. You may compare the situation to business planning under an unstable and capricious government.

Second, the system becomes more complex. It must have an arbiter to decide whether it should remove a resource from a process if another one requests it. The system may need built-in priorities assigned to processes.

Third, the accuracy of a process may be compromised. For example, what happens if a process is accessing a shared file and a second process requests it? Suppose the operating system seizes the file from the first process and allocates it to the second. If the second one begins to write to it, it may destroy what the first one wrote. When the first one gets the file back, it will find its information changed.

In summary, removing the *non-preemption* condition can cause scheduling problems and can introduce inconsistencies in day to day activities. It can also cause processes to lose data if extra care is not taken. This can be a costly solution to deadlock.

Removing Hold and Request. How can we remove this condition? There are two ways. The first is to force the process to give up all resources whenever it requests more. Unfortunately, this violates the *non-preemption* condition. The other way is to forbid a process from making requests at different times; in other words, make it request whatever is needed all at once.

What is wrong with this? To illustrate, suppose a writer process from the *readers and writers* problem needs access to several database pages. It must request them all at once. However, it can write to just one page at a time. The result is that the other pages are unavailable to other processes even though the writer is not actually using them.

In general, if it must request all resources at one time, a process ends up needlessly controlling some resources for long periods without actually using them. This decreases resource availability.

Another problem is that a process may be postponed indefinitely. Suppose it needs access to many resources. They must all be available at once before the process can run. But there is no guarantee that all of them will ever be available simultaneously. The result is that the requesting process may wait for an event that may never occur.

Removing Circular Wait. The last chance of preventing deadlock without severe side effects lies in removing the *circular wait* condition. Unfortunately, this also has its price.

Recall that for a circular wait to occur, a circular list of processes must exist. Each has requested a resource that its successor has. Each also has a resource that its predecessor wants. How can we prevent such a list from forming?

Consider the final request that completes the cycle in Figure 5.50d. Without loss of generality, suppose it was process n requesting resource 1. After all, we can always renumber processes and resources in our diagram to make this true. We must determine how to prevent the last request from occurring until another process releases its resource and causes a break in the potential cycle.

There are several possibilities. One is to forbid a process from requesting resources at different times. However, we just rejected this approach when discussing the removal of the *hold and request* condition.

Another is to allow a process access to only one resource at a time. If it wants access to another, the process must give up the one it has. This solution is undesirable for processes that may read from multiple files or copy data from one device to another. Such processes need access to multiple resources simultaneously.

Still another way is to force processes to request resources in a specified order. For example, the system might do this by numbering the resources and requiring that a process always request them in numerical order. In this case, process n would not be in the list of Figure 5.50d. It could not have requested and obtained resource R_n before requesting resource R_1 and thus could not cause the deadlock.

Unfortunately, any numbering of resources may be counter to a process' needs. For example, suppose one process wants to copy data from tape to disk and another wants to copy from disk to tape. The two processes need the resources in reverse order. If the system requires them to conform to a fixed order, say disk drive first, the process that needs the tape drive first has a problem.

Again we see that trying to prevent deadlock by eliminating a necessary condition causes significant problems. From this we conclude that deadlock prevention is impractical in many systems and that we must seek other ways of dealing with the issue.

Deadlock Avoidance

Deadlock avoidance differs from prevention in that it does not make deadlock impossible. Instead, the idea is to reject requests that create a potential for deadlock. We clarify this statement by an example using an avoidance method called *Dijkstra's Banker's Algorithm* [1].

The algorithm applies to cases involving multiple indistinguishable resources. The usual examples are tape drives or spooling files. A system may have many drives, or files and processes generally do not care which ones they get.

Suppose many processes are writing to a shared printer using a spooling file (see spooling in Chapter 3). Suppose the file is fixed in size and is divided into pages. Thus, as processes write, the operating system allocates pages and stores the process' output on them temporarily. When a process finishes, its pages are released. A deadlock can occur if all the pages are currently allocated and each process needs access to at least one more. In this case, none can finish. Therefore, none releases any pages, and the system is deadlocked. How can we avoid this situation?

Dijkstra's Banker's Algorithm distinguishes between *safe* and *unsafe* states. They are defined as follows:

A state is *safe* if the operating system can guarantee sufficient resources for all processes to request eventually what they need and finish without deadlock occurring. In a safe state, the system can always avoid deadlock by rejecting requests selectively.

A state is *unsafe* if, regardless of system response, processes can make requests that cause a deadlock. An unsafe state does not mean that deadlock is imminent. It does mean the system cannot guarantee that deadlock will not occur. In an unsafe state, the system is at the mercy of chance requests; it cannot avoid deadlock if the wrong sequence occurs.

For example, suppose four processes are currently executing in a system with fourteen spooling pages (small, we know, but better than an example with hundreds of processes and thousands of spooling pages). Consider the case where Figure 5.51a shows the number of allocated pages and the maximum number each process needs.

Figure 5.51a Processes with spooling pages in a safe state

	Current Number of pages allocated	Maximum Number of pages needed
Process-1	2	4
Process-2	3	6
Process-3	1	6
Process-4	4	8

14 pages in the system
4 pages are unallocated

Here four pages are currently available and the system is a safe state. Can you see why?

Since four pages are available, process 1, 2, or 4 could request its maximum number of pages and finish. For example, suppose process 1 requests two more pages to reach its limit and finishes. Figure 5.51b then shows the page allocations.

Figure 5.51b Processes with spooling pages after process 1 finishes

	Current Number of pages allocated	Maximum Number of pages needed
Process-2	3	6
Process-3	1	6
Process-4	4	8

14 pages in the system
6 pages are unallocated

Now any process could request pages up to its maximum and finish. Suppose process 3 requests five more pages and finishes. Figure 5.51c then shows the page allocations.

Now only processes 2 and 4 remain. As before, either could request and receive up to its maximum number of pages and finish. Afterward, only one process would remain. Finally, it too could request and receive the pages needed to finish.

Figure 5.51c Processes with spooling pages after process 2 finishes

	Current Number of pages allocated	Maximum Number of pages needed
Process-2	3	6
Process-4	4	8

14 pages in the system
7 pages are unallocated

The fact that we presented a sequence of requests that allowed all processes to finish does not, in itself, indicate a safe state. The situation in Figure 5.51a could lead to a deadlock if the operating system were not careful.

For example, what happens if process 3 requests the 4 available pages? If the operating system allocates them, Figure 5.52 shows the result: all pages are allocated. What happens if each process subsequently requests 1 more page without releasing any it currently holds? Each process is suspended, waiting for a page to become available. Since all pages are allocated, the system is deadlocked.

Figure 5.52 Processes with spooling pages in an unsafe state

	Current Number of pages allocated	Maximum Number of pages needed
Process-1	2	4
Process-2	3	6
Process-3	5	6
Process-4	4	8

14 pages in the system
0 pages are unallocated

The situation described in Figure 5.52 need not lead to deadlock. One process could finish without requesting more pages and release what it holds. This would allow others to finish and thus avoid deadlock, but the operating system cannot depend on that. More important, it cannot guarantee that the remaining processes will not all request another page. As such, the situation in Figure 5.52 is an unsafe state. Deadlock is not inevitable, but the system cannot guarantee that it will not occur.

Here is the major difference between the cases in Figure 5.51a and Figure 5.52. The case in Figure 5.52 is unsafe because the system cannot guarantee that deadlock will not occur. The case in Figure 5.51a is safe because the system can make that guarantee. It simply has to refuse the request that leads to the case of Figure 5.52. An operating system using the Banker's Algorithm would refuse it.

Specifically, suppose a process requests resources. The operating system answers the following question, "If I allocate the requested resources, is the result a safe state?" The algorithm refuses any request that produces an unsafe state. By remaining in a safe state, the operating system can always guarantee that, no matter what requests are made, deadlock will not occur. Whereas again, in an unsafe state, the operating system cannot provide such a guarantee. The next question is, "How does the operating system determine if a state is safe?" We now describe Dijkstra's Bankers Algorithm.

Dijkstra's Banker's Algorithm. Whenever a process requests a resource, the operating system "pretends" to allocate it. In other words, it examines the result of allocating the resource. But it does not actually make the allocation, at least not yet. After creating the pretend situation, the operating system tries to find a scenario in which each process eventually requests and receives the maximum number of resources it needs to finish. If such a scenario exists, then there is still a way for the processes to get their resources and finish. The operating system then allocates the requested resources.

If no scenario can be created, the pretend situation is unsafe. The operating system refuses to allocate the requested resources. The requesting process is then suspended until such time as the resources can be safely allocated. Figure 5.53 shows Dijkstra's Banker's Algorithm. This is applied to the situation in Figure 5.54a. At first glance, the situation may seem to be a safe state. There are enough pages for process 1 to finish. If it finishes, there are enough pages for process 2 to finish. However, the algorithm proves that, after process 2 finishes, deadlock may be unavoidable. Let us see why.

First, we describe how the algorithm works. It creates a list L of active processes and defines the variable *Available* as the number of available resources. The algorithm contains a main loop. In each pass, the operating system pretends to allocate the maximum number of resources to some process so that it may finish. The system chooses a process by examining all *claims*. The *claim* is the difference between the number of resources allocated to the process and the maximum number it may request.

Figure 5.53 Dijkstra's Banker's Algorithm

```
        ⋮
Var
  Safe      : Boolean;
  Available : Integer;   {Number of available resources}
  {Number of processes}

Begin
  Safe :=True;
  Define L to be a temporary list of all active processes;
  Available := number of currently available resources;
  Repeat
    If there is a process in L for which Available ≥ Number of unclaimed  resources by that process  Then
      Begin
          Delete the process from the list, L;
          Available := Available + number of resources held by the deleted process;
      End
    Else
        Safe := False;
    Until (L is empty) Or (Not Safe)
End;
```

Figure 5.54a Processes with spooling pages in an unsafe state

	Current Number of pages allocated	Maximum Number of pages needed
Process-1	1	2
Process-2	2	4
Process-3	2	7
Process-4	1	6

7 pages in the system
1 page is unallocated

Inside the loop, the algorithm compares each process' claim with *Available*. Suppose there is a process whose claim is less than or equal to *Available*. The algorithm increments *Available* by the number of resources currently held by that process and removes the process from the list. This represents a situation in which the process requests and receives all remaining resources it needs and subsequently finishes and releases its resources.

The iterations continue until the list is empty or until every process in it has a claim larger than *Available*. In the first case, the algorithm has detected a way for every process to get its maximum number of resources and finish. This means the algorithm began with a safe state, and the pending request is acceptable. Thus, the operating system allocates the requested resources.

On the other hand, suppose at some point every process in the list has a claim larger than *Available*. Then the algorithm began with an unsafe state. The system cannot guarantee that any of the current processes can finish. Each could request the maximum number of resources. If that happens, the operating system must put each into a wait state. The result is deadlock!

We now illustrate the algorithm using the example in Figure 5.54a. It initializes *Available* = 1 and the list contains all 4 processes. During the first pass of the loop, only process 1 has a claim not exceeding the number of available pages. Thus, there are sufficient resources for process 1 to finish. If process 1 finishes, the system returns its pages to the available pool. Therefore, the algorithm increases the number of available pages to 2 and removes process 1 from the list. Figure 5.54b shows the allocations afterward.

Figure 5.54b Processes with spooling pages in an unsafe state after process 1 finishes

	Current Number of pages allocated	Maximum Number of pages needed
Process-2	2	4
Process-3	2	7
Process-4	1	6

7 pages in the system
2 pages are unallocated

During the second pass, only process 2 has a claim less than or equal to the number of available pages. This means that process 2 could finish. As before, the algorithm adds the number of pages held by process 2 to *Available* and removes it from the list. Figure 5.54c shows the allocations afterward.

Now the algorithm finds that every process in the list has a claim exceeding the number of available pages. As before, this does not mean that deadlock is inevitable. However, if each process asserts its claim, deadlock will occur. Since the operating system has no control over a process asserting its claim, the system is in an unsafe state. The algorithm sets the Boolean variable *Safe* to False and terminates the loop. Since the algorithm detected an unsafe state, the operating system refuses any request that leads to the situation in Figure 5.54a.

Figure 5.54c Processes with spooling pages in an unsafe state after process 2
finishes

	Current Number of pages allocated	Maximum Number of pages needed
Process-3	2	7
Process-4	1	6

7 pages in the system
4 pages are unallocated

Although the Banker's Algorithm appears in most operating systems texts, it has limitations. It requires that all processes state the maximum number of resources needed. It also requires that the resources be multiple indistinguishable occurrences of a single type. References [13] and [22] at the end of this chapter present a variation of the algorithm that applies to multiple occurrences of several types of resources. Again, however, the occurrences of any one type are indistinguishable.

Unfortunately, this does not solve the deadlock problem described in the Readers and Writers Problem. There a process requested something specific—a database page. In such a case, solving the deadlock problem is more difficult. On the other hand, there are cases where there are far more resources than processes. In such cases, although deadlock is possible, in practice it seldom occurs. It may therefore be more efficient to dismiss prevention or avoidance schemes and simply deal with deadlock when it happens. This leads us to deadlock detection.

═══
Deadlock Detection

Suppose we have a system in which deadlock can occur. That is, there are no schemes to prevent or avoid it. In short, whenever a process requests a resource, deadlock could occur. We now must answer two questions:

- How can the system detect a deadlock?
- If deadlock occurs, what does the system do about it?

One way to detect deadlock is through a *resource allocation digraph*. Before we describe what this is, we briefly discuss graphs and digraphs, subjects typically covered in a data structures class.

Graphs and Digraphs. A graph is a pair of sets G = (V,E). The set V consists of *vertices*. A *vertex* is a point or a node corresponding to a specific piece of information in a system. The set E consists of *edges*. An edge is a pair (v,w), where v and w are vertices. An edge often defines some relationship between v and w.

Sometimes the vertices in an edge are *ordered*, and may be written as <v,w>. The ordering means that <w,v> and <v,w> differ. This often corresponds to cases where the relationship between two elements differs, depending on order.

For example, we may say that *A* is the sister of *B*. But, asuming that both *A* and *B* are female, this is precisely the same as saying that *B* is the sister of *A*. The relationship between *A* and *B* is independent of order. The "sister" relationship goes both ways. However, we may also say that *X* is the mother of *Y*. But this does not mean that *Y* is the mother of *X*. The "mother" relationship only goes one way.

When order is implied, we refer to a *directed edge* instead of an edge. Also, instead of the term *graph*, we use the term *directed graph* or *digraph*.

Digraphs may be represented using points for vertices and arrows for the directed edges. For example, consider the digraph with the set of vertices

$$V = \{ v_1, v_2, v_3, v_4, v_5, v_6 \}$$

and

$$E = \{ <v_2,v_1>, <v_1,v_3>, <v_3,v_2>, <v_2,v_4>, <v_4,v_5>, <v_3,v_5>, <v_5,v_6> \}$$

A pictorial representation is Figure 5.55. Here the arrow that represents a directed edge always points to the second vertex.

Another topic in a data structures class is a *path*. It is a sequence of edges $<w_1,w_2>, <w_2,w_3>, <w_3,w_4>, \ldots, <w_{k-1},w_k>$, where w_i is a vertex, for i = 1 through k. Note that the second vertex in one edge is the same as the first vertex in the next edge. This may be interpreted in a pictorial representation as following the arrows through a set of vertices. For example, the sequence of edges $<v_1,v_3>, <v_3,v_5>, <v_5,v_6>$ is a path in the digraph of Figure 5.56. The path goes from v_1 to v_3 to v_5 to v_6.

A *cycle* is a path $<w_1,w_2>, <w_2,w_3>, <w_3,w_4>, \ldots, <w_{k-1},w_k>$ in which $w_1 = w_k$. It has the same starting and ending points. The path $<v_2,v_1>, <v_1,v_3>, <v_3,v_2>$ from the digraph of Figure 5.56 is a cycle.

Figure 5.55 Digraph representation

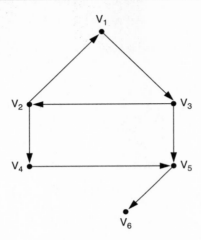

≡≡≡
Resource Allocation Graph

Digraphs may represent many different types of information. Of particular interest to us here is their use to represent resource allocation. Such a digraph is called the *resource allocation digraph*.

For example, suppose four processes are contending for six resources. We may represent each process and resource by a vertex in a resource allocation digraph. The vertices representing processes may be labeled P_1 through P_4. The ones representing resources may be labeled R_1 through R_6. Edges are added and deleted from the digraph as processes request, obtain, and release resources.

To illustrate, suppose process P_i requests a resource R_j. If R_j is currently allocated, P_i must wait. If this happens, we add an edge $<P_i,R_j>$ to the digraph. Thus, an edge of the form $<P_i,R_j>$ means that process P_i is waiting for resource R_j. But what if resource R_j is available? We can then allocate it to P_i. In this case we add the edge $<R_j,P_i>$ to the digraph. If P_i was previously waiting for R_j, we also delete the edge $<P_i,R_j>$. Thus, an edge of the form $<R_j, P_i>$ means that resource R_j is allocated to process P_i. Last, suppose process P_i finishes with resource R_j and releases it. We then delete the edge $<R_j,P_i>$ from the digraph.

Consider the digraph in Figure 5.57. It represents allocation information after the following events:

- Resources R_1 and R_2 have been allocated to P_1. (Edges $<R_1,P_1>$ and $<R_2,P_1>$)
- Resource R_3 has been allocated to process P_2. (Edge $<R_3,P_2>$)

- Resource R_4 has been allocated to process P_3. (Edge $<R_4,P_3>$)
- Process P_3 has requested and is waiting for resource R_3. (Edge $<P_3,R_3>$)
- Process P_4 has requested and is waiting for resource R_1. (Edge $<P_4,R_1>$)

Figure 5.56 Resource allocation digraph with no deadlock

	Resources allocated to process	Resources requested by process
Process-1	R1, R2	none
Process-2	R3	none
Process-3	R4	R3
Process-4	none	R1

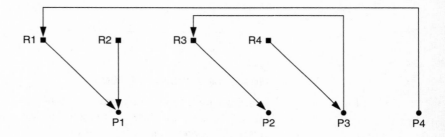

At this point, there is no deadlock. The waiting processes (P_3 and P_4) are waiting for resources allocated to running processes. They can release the resources, allowing P_3 and P_4 to finish.

But what happens if P_2 requests resource R_4? We must insert the edge $<P_2, R_4>$ into the digraph (Figure 5.57). This creates a cycle ($<P_2,R_4>$, $<R_4,P_3>$, $<P_3,R_3>$, $<R_3,P_2>$). Its edges indicate that process P_2 is waiting for resource R_4, which is allocated to process P_3. At the same time, process P_3 is waiting for resource R_3, which is allocated to process P_2. In short, processes P_2 and P_4 are each waiting for something the other has: they are therefore deadlocked.

We can detect a deadlock by examining the resource allocation digraph. If it has a cycle, deadlock exists. This is a direct result of the circular wait condition necessary for deadlock. The operating system may use various algorithms to detect cycles in a digraph. Such algorithms are normally covered in a data structures class, and we do not discuss them here. The important thing is that if a cycle exists, the processes represented by its vertices are deadlocked. If no cycle exists, there is no deadlock.

Figure 5.57 Resource allocation digraph with deadlock

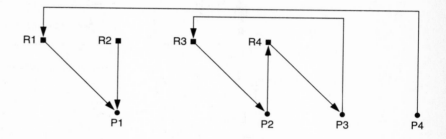

	Resources allocated to process	Resources requested by process
Process-1	R1, R2	none
Process-2	R3	R4
Process-3	R4	R3
Process-4	none	R1

Deadlock Recovery

Now that we know how to detect a deadlock, one last question remains: What do we do if deadlock occurs? Unfortunately, the answers to this are simple but painful.

One possibility is simply to abort a process and remove the resources allocated to it. This eliminates the cycle, and consequently, the deadlock, at the expense of the process. But what if it had been running for an hour and was just about to finish when the operating system aborted it? We must be able to answer serious questions about which process the operating system should abort. For example, who is responsible for the loss of work? You may be facing some very unhappy users, who know some very aggressive attorneys.

Another possibility is to do a *rollback* on a process. This means removing all resources currently allocated to it. The process loses all updates made through the use of these resources and suffers a loss of work, however, it is not aborted. The system does force it back into its state prior to the request and allocation of the removed resources. This might correspond to initial startup or to a *checkpoint* in the process logic. A checkpoint occurs when a process voluntary releases all resources.

For example, consider two processes that access pages from a common database as shown in Figure 5.58. Both hold copies of several pages in buffers. Process 1 wants access to page 54, a page held by process 2. Similarly, process 2 wants access to page 23, a page held by process 1. Suppose process 2 has made the request that caused the deadlock. Since it caused the deadlock, one solution is to roll it back.

Figure 5.58 Two deadlocked processes holding copies of database pages

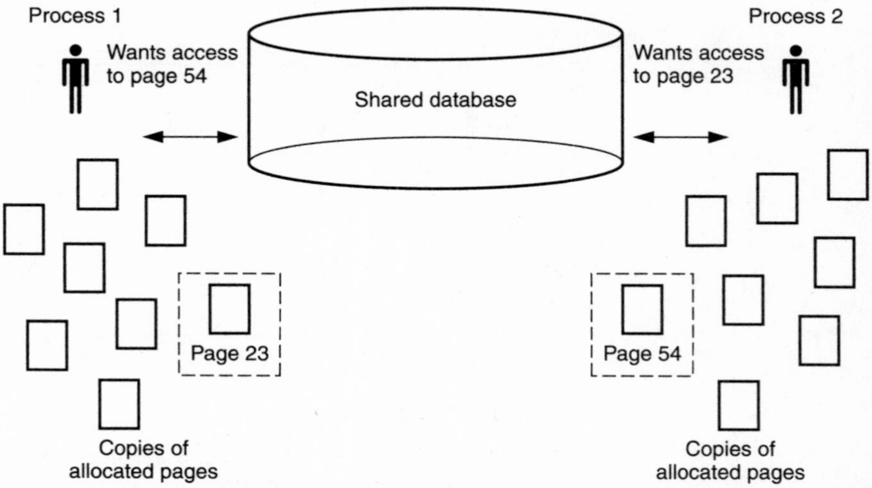

This means that all pages currently held by process 2 will revert to their values prior to being requested by process 2. In many databases, the software maintains a journal to reflect changes. It may then use the journal to restore the original information.

Why doesn't the system just remove page 54 from the process and restore it? The problem is that updates on page 54 may have depended on updates made to the other pages. More important, the changes on page 54 may have been part of an update of information stored on several pages. If we restore one page but not the others, we make the database inconsistent.

For example, we may have added a record to page 54 that a record on another page points to. If we restore page 54 to its original image, what does that other record point to? If these records were part of a linked list, the list is then broken. Since the system cannot determine the interdependencies of the data, the only viable solution is to guarantee consistency by restoring all pages. The process is forced to run again later.

As you can see, deadlock can be very painful. Restoring the contents of many pages means a loss of work. The process must be run again, reproducing all its transactions. This is a waste of both system time and the user's time.

But each process can minimize potential loss of work through the use of checkpoints. As stated previously a checkpoint is where a process voluntary releases all database pages. The software then writes the changes to the database. Thus, a rollback will cause a loss of work back to the start of the process or the most recent checkpoint. A process does itself a favor by releasing all pages periodically. Not only will this minimize the loss of work, but it will also reduce the possibility of deadlock in the first place. If a process holds fewer pages, it is less likely to get caught in a deadlock. Any process that holds on to pages for long periods is asking for trouble.

5.11 Interprocess Communication in UNIX—Pipes

In 1974 Ken Thompson and Dennis Ritchie [30] described an operating system called UNIX they had developed at Bell (now AT&T Bell) Laboratories. The most important thing about UNIX was its portability. Before UNIX, operating systems were typically developed for specific machines. In fact, many of them were written in assembly language. This meant that they were almost impossible to transport to other architectures. Most of UNIX, however, is written in a high–level language called C. Since C is machine–independent, UNIX is portable. Today, it runs on many different architectures.

UNIX is noted for its layered design. It does not process commands directly. A layer of software called the *shell* lies between the user and the operating system kernel (Figure 5.59). A user entering UNIX commands interacts with the shell. It interprets commands and issues system calls to the kernel for processing. The kernel is the resident part of the system that implements the calls.

Another important feature of UNIX (and the focus of this case study) is a *pipe*, which allows processes to communicate. Specifically, a pipe allows the output of one process to serve as the input to another. UNIX has many different forms of interprocess communications [24–29]. However, the pipe concept is immediately visible to all users. Use of a pipe also streamlines a complicated sequence of commands.

We will focus on pipes and show how to create them using system calls. This will allow us to describe briefly some of UNIX's unique features and to introduce the C language. (Chapter 8 contains a more detailed description of UNIX.)

Figure 5.59 UNIX operating system structure

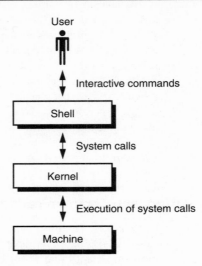

Shell Commands

To understand the need for pipes, we first examine simple shell commands and describe what a user must do to meet more complex needs. The following commands are a simple set that someone might use:

ls   Lists the names of all files in the user's current directory. (Chapter 6 describes directories and their structure in detail.) For now, just think of a directory as a collection of files.

pr   Prints the contents of specified files. The result is a formatted printout. The command 'pr' produces headings with date, time, page number, and file name.

wc -w   Counts the number of words in a specified file. The option -w limits wc to words, rather than lines or characters.

The UNIX shell has many other commands. However, this short list is enough to understand and describe the use of pipes.

I/O Redirection

Perhaps one of the more difficult things for programmers to adjust to is that an operating system command is just a call to invoke a process. That is, the user may see commands as different from processes. But, UNIX sees them all as processes. The command "ls" actually invokes a process that reads the user's directory and prints the names of all files. The command "pr" invokes a process that reads and prints the contents of a collection of files. Like user–written programs, these processes read data, do something with it, and produce output.

Unless otherwise specified, each process generally reads from and writes to default devices or files. For example, suppose the user is logged on to a video terminal and types the command

```
ls
```

UNIX reads from the current directory and prints the file names on the screen. By default, "ls" reads from the current directory and writes to the screen. Similarly, suppose the user types the command

```
pr filename1, filename2
```

The process "pr" reads the filenames as they are entered from the keyboard and writes their contents on the screen. The input for pr comes from the keyboard and its output goes to the screen.

Sometimes the user may want to reroute the output or obtain input from somewhere other than a terminal or directory. In UNIX, the user may easily *redirect* input or output with the symbols > and < . For example, the command

```
ls > fname
```

writes the list of file names in file *fname* rather than on the screen. Similarly, the command

```
wc-w < fname
```

counts the number of words in file *fname*.

Now suppose the user wants to count the number of files in the current directory. He or she can do this by executing the process ls and redirecting the output to a file. The next step is to use wc (Figure 5.60) to count the number of words in the file. Since each word is the name of a file, wc actually counts the number of files in the directory. The processes ls and wc communicate through I/O redirection.

To accomplish this, the user can type

```
ls       > fname
wc  -w   < fname
rm         fname
```

Figure 5.60 Process communication by I/O redirection

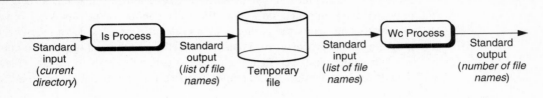

To count the files, the user first redirects the output of ls to a file *fname*. Afterward, *fname* contains the names of the files in the user's directory. The user can next specify *fname* as the input to wc. UNIX will print the number of files in *fname*. Last, since *fname* was only needed temporarily, the user removes it from the directory with "rm".

Pipes

Is there an easier way? Can we activate both processes simultaneously and connect the output of ls directly to the input of wc? The answer is "Yes," and UNIX uses a pipe to do it. Figure 5.61 shows how. Very simply, the pipe connects two processes. The first one writes into it and the second process reads from it. UNIX makes sure the second process waits until after the first process has written. Only then will it allow the second process to read. Similarly, if both processes contain a loop in which each reads or writes into the pipe, UNIX will not let the first process write into a full pipe or the second read from an empty pipe.

Figure 5.61 Process communication by pipes

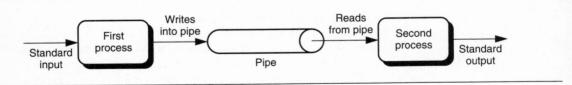

A UNIX user can easily connect the two processes ls and wc with a pipe. He or she need only type

```
ls | wc-w
```

For example, suppose the current directory has three files *f1*, *f2*, and *f3*. Figure 5.62 shows what happens when the user types the command above.

UNIX activates both processes and creates a pipe connecting them. It allows process ls to execute and send its output, *f1, f2,* and *f3* into the pipe. When ls finishes its output, UNIX allows wc to execute. Process wc reads its information from the pipe, counts the number of words (file names), and prints the number on the screen.

Figure 5.62 Connecting shell commands ls and wc by pipes

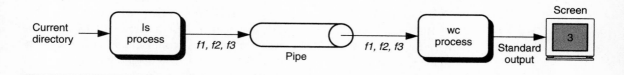

Pipes may also allow more than two processes to communicate in sequence. In general, shell commands may be written as

```
ShellCommand1 | ShellCommand2 | ShellCommand3 |...| ShellCommandn
```

UNIX activates all specified processes and creates pipes connecting the standard output of one to the standard input of the next one in the list. UNIX makes sure that no process actually runs until the prior one has written into the appropriate pipe.

But how does UNIX actually create a pipe? How does it ensure that the output of one process becomes the input of another? We will first provide background information that gives insight into how UNIX works.

UNIX File Descriptors

The first thing we need concerns the way in which UNIX maintains information on files. As before, we provide just enough detail to describe how pipes are created. (Chapter 8 discusses UNIX file management further.)

UNIX maintains information on user files in several tables. One is a table of *file descriptor values.* Specifically, as in most systems, users may name files. When a user wants to access a file, he or she must first open it with the command

```
fdesc = open(fname, mode)
```

Here *fname* is the file's name and *mode* is the access type (0 for reading, 2 for writing, or 1 for reading and writing). In response to this command, UNIX looks for the file. If the user has not violated any security, it returns a *file descriptor value*, a nonnegative integer. If, for some reason, UNIX cannot locate the file, it returns a value of -1. Subsequent references to the file such as reading and writing must specify the descriptor value. UNIX then uses the value to access the file. For example, the UNIX command to read is

```
read(fdesc, buffer, size)
```

As you might guess, *fdesc* is the file descriptor, *buffer* is the buffer where UNIX stores the input data, and *size* is the number of bytes to read.

But what is the file descriptor value actually? Each user of UNIX has a *file descriptor table*. When UNIX executes an "open" command, it creates an entry in the table. Thus, the table contains an entry for each open file. The descriptor value references a table entry. Subsequent "read" or "write" commands cause UNIX to access the table entry associated with the file descriptor value.

UNIX normally reserves the first three entries (descriptors 0, 1, and 2) in the file descriptor table for the default input and output files. Unless otherwise specified, processes will read from and write to file descriptors 0 and 1, respectively. File descriptor 2 is used to write error messages (standard error).

Each entry in the file descriptor table contains the location of an entry in a *system file table*. As with the file descriptor table, UNIX creates an entry in the system file table whenever a user issues an "open" command (Figure 5.63). This table contains information on all currently open files (not just those for one user). For example, since most reading in UNIX is sequential, an entry in the system file table contains the relative position of the last byte read from the file. This way, when another read occurs, UNIX will resume reading at the next byte position.

A system file table entry also contains the location of an *inode* for a file. The inode is actually an entry in another system table called the *ilist* or *inode table*. Each inode contains a description of a file. There is an inode for each file, regardless of whether it is open or closed. Specifically, it contains information such as

- file size;
- time of creation, last access, and last update;
- protection bits;
- actual disk address.

For the purpose of pipe creation, the reader need only know a few things. One is that I/O is done through file descriptors. Second is that file descriptors provide access to files. Finally, is that descriptors 0 and 1 are a process' standard input and output.

Figure 5.63 UNIX file access tables

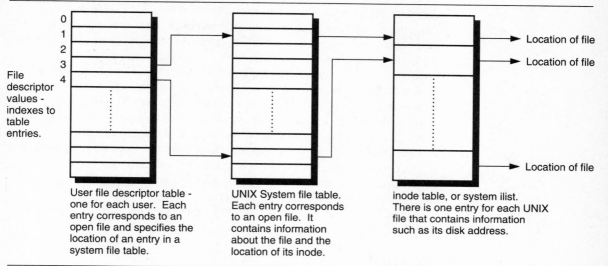

File descriptor values - indexes to table entries.

User file descriptor table - one for each user. Each entry corresponds to an open file and specifies the location of an entry in a system file table.

UNIX System file table. Each entry corresponds to an open file. It contains information about the file and the location of its inode.

inode table, or system ilist. There is one entry for each UNIX file that contains information such as its disk address.

Location of file

Location of file

Location of file

Forks and Execs

Two items remain before we describe how pipes are created. They are the *fork* and *execl* system calls. The UNIX shell uses them to process user commands. As we shall see, they are also used to create pipes. The system call

```
procid = fork()
```

duplicates the process that made the call (Figure 5.64). That is, the UNIX kernel creates a second process with identical code: both run and compete for resources. Literally, two processes now exist where there was previously only one (a computer mitosis or cell division). The process that called *fork* is the *parent*. The one that UNIX creates is the *child*.

Figure 5.64 System fork call

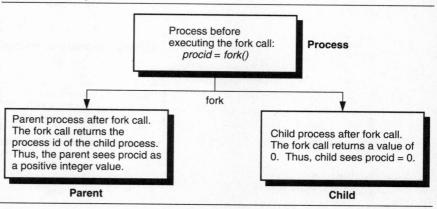

Process before executing the fork call: *procid = fork()*

Process

fork

Parent process after fork call. The fork call returns the process id of the child process. Thus, the parent sees procid as a positive integer value.

Child process after fork call. The fork call returns a value of 0. Thus, child sees procid = 0.

Parent

Child

This probably seems peculiar to most readers. When the *fork* call is complete, the parent continues to execute code. The child also begins to execute the same code at the same point in the process as the parent. Since it is a new process, the child seems to start in the middle. In practice, as we shall soon see, the child process takes a different logical path than the parent's. The *fork* is often the first step in the creation of a process that responds to a user request.

When the *fork* is complete, the call returns a different value in each process. In the child, it returns to zero. In the parent process, it returns the child's process identification number (procid). For our purposes, we need only know that the fork call returns a nonzero value. At this point, both child and parent execute code that follows the fork call. Both may test the value of *procid* and execute accordingly. We should note that a *fork* call returns a value of -1 if an error occurs. (For more information about errors, consult one of the UNIX references listed at the end of the chapter.)

A *fork* system call is not the only way to initiate a new process. The system call

```
execl(fname, argument list)
```

also initiates a new process (Figure 5.65) called the *successor*. UNIX overlays the successor over the one that made the call. The effect is to replace one process with another. The successor has the same identification number as the caller. Technically, because of this, UNIX does not actually create a new process. More accurately, it gives an existing process a new identity. You might say it has done major plastic surgery.

The code associated with the successor process is in the file *fname* specified in the *execl* command. The argument list provides options that are not needed here. As we will see, UNIX uses a *fork* followed by an *execl* to create new processes.

Figure 5.65 System execl call

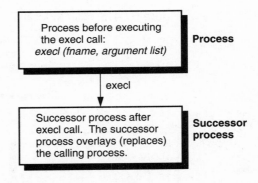

When the UNIX shell interprets commands, it calls *fork* and *execl*. The examples that follow use commands written in the C programming language. Remember, UNIX is written in C. The shell interprets and executes commands as follows:

```
:
read shell command
:
If (fork() == 0)
    execl(fname, argument list)
:
```

When the shell reads a command, it calls fork to split into two identical processes, parent and child (Figure 5.66). The condition following *If* compares the value that fork() returns with zero. When the parent (the shell) executes, it sees the value as nonzero. As a result, it ignores the execl command.

Figure 5.66 Shell using fork and execl commands to execute shell command

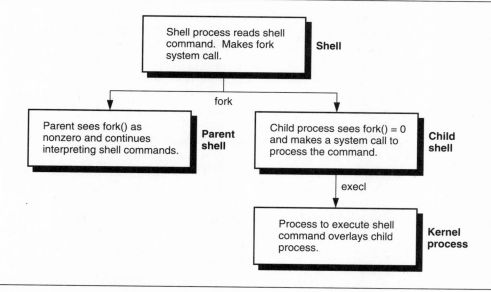

However, in the child (a clone of the shell) fork() returns a zero value. Therefore, the child calls execl. The code to execute the shell command is in file *fname*. The child process thus takes on a new identity; that of the kernel process that executes the shell command. The shell and the kernel process now run concurrently. The shell remains to interpret other commands that other users may enter. The successor kernel responds to the shell command.

≡≡
Pipe Creation

To show how UNIX creates pipes, we consider an example described in reference [29]. Suppose we want to write a function *popen(cmd, mode)*, that does the following:

- Creates a process to execute the *cmd* command. We refer to it as the *cmd* process.
- Creates a pipe so that the *cmd* process either reads from or writes to the pipe depending on the specified mode.
- Returns a file descriptor value for the end of the pipe that the *cmd* process does not use.

Why on earth would we want such a function? We do this for establishing interprocess communication. For example, suppose we issue the function call

```
fout = popen("pr", WRITE).
```

This function creates a process that executes the "pr" command. It also defines a pipe between that process and the one making the call. Variable *fout* corresponding to the write end of the pipe. The pipe's read end is connected to the standard input of the process that will execute the "pr" command. The calling process can write using *fout* as the file descriptor and its output is piped to the process that executes the "pr" command.

The C function that does this is in Figure 5.67. We now describe how it works. More complete descriptions of C are in references such as [31–32].

Line 0 brings in definitions required to use the standard input/output library. Lines 1 and 2 define meaningful symbolic names for 0 and 1. The C preprocessor interprets them and replaces them with the values 0 and 1 wherever they appear. Line 3 defines a macro *tst*. The preprocessor will replace any reference to it by its code, along with parameter substitutions. The macro compares the value of *mode* with READ, and returns either *a* or *b*. Specifically, if *mode* = READ, it returns *b*. If not, it returns *a*. The variables *a* and *b* are parameters in a reference to the macro. Lines 4 and 7 declare variables popen_pid and *mode* as integers. Line 5 contains the formal declaration of the function *popen* along with its formal parameters. Line 6 declares variable *cmd* as a pointer to a character string.

Lines 9, 14, 21, and 26 delimit compound C statements. The { is similar to Begin in Pascal: similarly, } is similar to End in Pascal.

Line 10 declares variable *p* as an integer array with two elements, p[0] and p[1].

The *pipe* system call in lines 11 and 12 actually creates a pipe (remember, a pipe is a file) and assigns an inode to it. The system call also stores file descriptors in p[0] and p[1] used to locate associated file table entries to read

Figure 5.67 C program to create a pipe

```
(0)      #include <stdio.h>

(1)      #define READ   0
(2)      #define WRITE  1
(3)      #define tst(a, b) (mode == READ ? (b) : (a) )
(4)        static int popen_pid

(5)      popen(cmd, mode)
(6)      char *cmd
(7)      int mode

(9)      {
(10)       int   p[2]

(11)       if (pipe(p) < 0)
(12)           return(NULL);
(13)       if ( (popen_pid = fork() ) == 0)
(14)         {
(15)           close (tst(p[WRITE], p[READ] ) );
(16)           close (tst(0, 1) )
(17)           dup    (tst(p[READ], p[WRITE] ) );
(18)           close (tst(p[READ], p[WRITE] ) );
(19)           execl("/bin/sh", "sh", "–c", cmd, 0);
(20)           exit(1);
(21)         }
(22)       if (popen_pid == –1)
(23)           return(NULL);
(24)       close(tst(p[READ], p[WRITE] ) );
(25)       return(tst(p[WRITE], p[READ] ) );
(26)       }
```

from or write to the pipe (Figure 5.68). The pipe system call also returns a value of -1 if an error such as too many open files occurs. Line 12 protects against this kind of error.

Figure 5.68 File descriptors associated with the read and write ends of the pipe

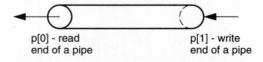

p[0] - read
end of a pipe

p[1] - write
end of a pipe

At line 13, the process forks to create a child process with the same code as in Figure 5.67. The value *fork* returns is stored in *popen_pid*. It is then compared to zero. If it is zero, the process executes statements 15 through 20. Since only the child sees *popen_pid* = 0, only it executes these statements. The parent process skips them and resumes execution at line 22. The child eventually becomes the process that executes *cmd* (line 19).

To more clearly describe lines 15–18, assume the mode is READ. Then every reference to the macro *tst(first, second)* returns *second*. Thus, in this case lines 15–18 are logically the same as

```
close(p[READ])
close(1)
dup(p[WRITE]
close(p[WRITE])
```

The first command closes the read side of the pipe that was just created. Remember, if the mode is READ, *popen* must connect the write end of the pipe to the standard output of the new process and return the read end of the pipe. For this reason, the child *popen* closes the read end since it is only supposed to write into the pipe.

The next two commands are the conventional way to associate a pipe descriptor with the standard output of the child process. File descriptor 1 corresponds to a process' standard output (Figure 5.69a). The command close(1) closes the standard output (Figure 5.69b). The next command duplicates the file descriptor p[1] and copies it into the lowest numbered available entry in the file descriptor table. Since we just closed descriptor 1, this command stores the descriptor of the WRITE side of the pipe into table position 1. The standard output for this process is now the WRITE side of the pipe (Figure 5.69c). The last command then closes the file descriptor p[WRITE]. There is no need to have two file descriptors associated with the WRITE side of the pipe.

Figure 5.69a Child process with standard output and pipe

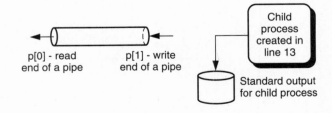

Figure 5.69b Child process after standard output is closed

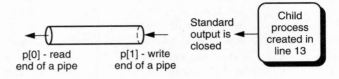

p[0] - read
end of a pipe

p[1] - write
end of a pipe

Standard
output is
closed

Child
process
created in
line 13

Figure 5.69c Child process after p[1] replaces file descriptor 1

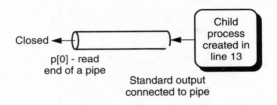

Closed

p[0] - read
end of a pipe

Child
process
created in
line 13

Standard output
connected to pipe

Finally, at line 19, the child calls *execl*. The kernel uses the first three parameters and the last one to locate the shell ('sh' is the shell) and to interpret the arguments properly. When *popen* executes line 19 UNIX overlays it with the process to execute command *cmd*. The *cmd* process assumes the child's characteristics such as its standard output. But since the standard output has been connected to the pipe, the *cmd* process writes to the pipe just as we desired (Figure 5.70). Furthermore, since the *cmd* process has overlaid the child, lines 20–25 no longer exist in the child. If an error occurs in line 19, of course, the new process is not created. In this case, the lines remain, and line 20 simply terminates the process.

Figure 5.70 Shell overlays child process

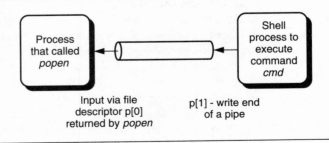

Process
that called
popen

Shell
process to
execute
command
cmd

Input via file
descriptor p[0]
returned by *popen*

p[1] - write end
of a pipe

Meanwhile, as the child *popen* creates the process to execute *cmd*, the parent *popen* continues executing at line 22 (remember, it skipped lines 14 through 21). Lines 22–23 return a NULL value if the *fork* call erred and returned a value of -1. If the *fork* executed as expected, line 24 closes p[WRITE]. Since the child is writing to the pipe, the parent has no need for the pipe's write end. Line 25 returns the value in p[READ]. (Remember, if the mode is READ, *tst* selects the second parameter.) The process that initially called *popen* gets the file descriptor associated with the READ end of the pipe. It may then read from the pipe and can read whatever the *cmd* process writes into it. Of course, UNIX ensures that it will not read from the pipe until after the *cmd* process has written into it.

To finish this example, recall that we described previously how a user can create a pipe between commands com1 and com2 by typing

```
com1 | com2
```

Of course, as we now know, the UNIX kernel actually creates the pipe. If a user types this, the shell proceeds similar to *popen* to fork and create a process for each of com1 and com2. The first process closes its standard output and duplicates the write side of the pipe in file descriptor 1. The second process closes its standard input and duplicates the read side of the pipe in file descriptor zero. Both processes call *execl* to make the kernel execute the commands com1 and com2. Command com1 then writes into the pipe, com2 reads from the pipe, and the user's needs have been met.

≡ 5.12 Summary

This chapter has presented many new ideas. The problem of concurrency is real and is the subject of much research. This chapter has defined concurrency and has described the problems that can occur with concurrent processes.

Specifically, we defined the critical section of a process as the code that references shared data. When processes are concurrent, we must ensure that they do not execute within their critical sections at the same time. We called this mutual exclusion. We also showed several examples where the activities of one process could otherwise interfere with the activities of another. Since operating systems often consist of many concurrent processes, we do not want the components to interfere with each other. The result, quite simply, is an operating system that will not work.

The most important question answered was, "How do we prevent processes from concurrently executing within their critical sections?" Several algorithms were examined to explain the problems in enforcing mutual exclusion. Dekker's Algorithm is one solution. The reader new to the ideas of concurrency is likely to find it complex. Trying to consider the timing of concurrent processes is a new experience.

But Dekker's Algorithm does not easily extend to more than two processes. Thus, we examined another algorithm that enforced mutual exclusion among many processes. Many such algorithms exist. Some guarantee that a process trying to execute its critical section will never be delayed too long. The complexity of these algorithms makes them very difficult to implement in practice. Thus, we discussed other simpler and more elegant approaches.

One such approach was the use of semaphores and the primitive operations P and V. On the surface, the two primitives are simple. But the key to their viability is in implementation. A primitive must be uninterruptible. If we can guarantee this, the primitives can easily be used to enforce mutual exclusion. They provide a very elegant, although low–level, solution to a nasty problem. They are especially useful because they generalize very easily from just two processes to many processes.

We also looked at how semaphores can synchronize events from two concurrent processes. We can use blocking to suspend a process that tries to execute an event too soon. We can use signaling to indicate when the process may resume. In systems with many concurrent processes, suspension and signaling are common events. A disadvantage of semaphores is that their use is voluntary. We must depend on the integrity and memory of a programmer to insert them before and after critical sections. Unfortunately, not everyone has integrity or a good memory. One misplaced or omitted semaphore compromises the whole idea of mutual exclusion. Thus, we considered other approaches.

One approach involves using monitors. A monitor is an operating system construct that contains the critical sections of programs. They are removed from the processes and placed in the monitor. Processes then reference them through procedure entry calls. By definition, a monitor enforces mutual exclusion among processes that reference its entries. Thus, mutual exclusion is guaranteed. Some programming languages that support concurrency allow the specification of a monitor.

We described several problems in which a monitor can provide synchronization. The producer–consumer problem, the circular buffer problem, and the readers and writers problem are typical examples requiring different levels of synchronization. Through condition variables, the monitor can suspend and signal processes to synchronize events.

Monitors work best when they can be centrally located. Since all processes access the monitor, it is central to all discussion and analysis. But many systems lack a central component. The Ada language, heavily promoted by the US Department of Defense, provides an approach to process cooperation in decentralized systems. Ada tasks may consist of callers and servers. Caller tasks call server tasks for various reasons. If a server responds, a rendezvous occurs.

If the server does not respond, the caller waits. A single server may respond to the calls of many tasks, as needed.

One serious problem associated with concurrency is deadlock. The management of concurrent processes can cause two of them to be suspended, each waiting for the other to do something. We may want to avoid or prevent such situations, because the solution to deadlock often requires one process to lose much of the work it has done.

We discussed several ways of preventing deadlock. Typically, this involves removing one of four conditions necessary for deadlock to occur. The conditions are mutual exclusion, non-preemption, hold and request, and circular wait. Unfortunately, the removal of any of these conditions causes costly side effects.

Another approach to deadlock is to allow all four conditions to exist, but to implement avoidance algorithms. In other words, examine requests by concurrent processes. If the operating system determines that one request creates the risk of deadlock, the system refuses to honor it. An algorithm known as Dijkstra's Banker's Algorithm was discussed. However, it applies only to cases where processes request one of several resources of a given type.

We discussed ways to detect and remove deadlock. We described the resource allocation digraph and referred to algorithms that can detect cycles in a digraph and consequently deadlock in a system. If a deadlock is detected, the process that caused it is usually aborted or rolled back to a previous state. Either way, it loses work. However, frequent checkpoints in a process can minimize such losses.

We described a way in which the UNIX operating system handles interprocess communication. We showed how a user can create concurrent processes that communicate through pipes. We also described the system calls *fork* and *execl* and how the shell uses them to interpret commands and call the kernel to execute the commands. We ended the case study by showing how the shell responds to a user command to create a pipe between the output of one process and the input of another.

Exercises

1. Consider the following logic that multiplies two n x n matrices **A** and **B**:

```
For i := 1 to n do
    For j := 1 to n do
        Begin
            C[i,j] := 0;
            For k := 1 to n do
                C[i,j] := C[i,j] + A[i,k] * B[k,j]
        End;
```

If n = 2 rewrite it to make maximum use of parallelism. That is, minimize the number of arithmetic operations that must be made sequentially. Use the "cobegin" and "coend" constructs.

2. Suppose there are three asynchronous, concurrent processes, each of which executes an event:

```
Process 1              Process 2              Process 3
    :                      :                      :
    :                      :                      :
 repeat                 repeat                 repeat
    :                      :                      :
    :                      :                      :
 event-1                event-2                event-3
    :                      :                      :
    :                      :                      :
Until forever          Until forever          Until forever
```

Define semaphores and use *P* and *V* primitives so the events always occur in the order:

```
event-1
event-2
event-3
event-1
event-2
event-3
    .
    .
    .
    .
    .        '
    .
    .
    .
```

3. Consider an extension of the Producer-Consumer Problem defined as follows:
   a. There are two producer processes and one consumer process. The processes execute concurrently and asynchronously.
   b. Each process contains a critical section that triggers an event.
   c. The consumer process cannot execute its critical section until <u>both</u> producers have executed their respective events.
   d. Neither producer may loop through its critical section until after the consumer has executed its event. An exception is made for the producers' first pass.
   e. Both producers may execute their events simultaneously.

```
Process Producer1    Process Producer2    Process Consumer
  :                    :                    :
  :                    :                    :
repeat               repeat               repeat
  :                    :                    :
  :                    :                    :
  critical section     critical section     critical section
  :                    :                    :
  :                    :                    :
Until forever        Until forever        Until forever
```

Define semaphores and use *P* and *V* primitives to enforce mutual exclusion and synchronize the processes.

4. Consider another extension of the Producer-Consumer Problem defined as follows:
   a. There are two consumer processes and one producer process. They execute concurrently and asynchronously.
   b. The producer may not write into the buffer until after both consumers have read from it. An exception is made for the first write.
   c. Neither consumer may read the contents of an undefined buffer.
   d. Neither consumer may read the same contents twice in succession.
   e. Both consumers may execute their events simultaneously.

```
Process Producer     Process Consumer 1   Process Consumer 2
  :                    :                    :
  :                    :                    :
Repeat               Repeat               Repeat
  :                    :                    :
  :                    :                    :
  Place data into      Get data from        Get data from
  buffer               buffer               buffer
  :                    :                    :
  :                    :                    :
Until forever        Until forever        Until forever
```

Define semaphores and use P and V primitives to enforce mutual exclusion and synchronize the processes.

5. We have shown that if *s* is a semaphore, the following enforces mutual exclusion:

```
        :
        :
      P(s)
      critical section;
      V(s)
        :
        :
```

Suppose P(s) and V(s) were replaced by calls to monitor entries *P* and *V*, respectively. Write these entries so this example still enforces mutual exclusion.

6. Consider the monitor solution to the Readers and Writers Problem shown in Figure 5.38. One monitor entry is used for writing. Change the solution so that each writer must call two monitor entries, StartWrite and FinishWrite.

The writer will then do the writing in between calls to the entries. The entries are analogous to StartRead and FinishRead. Make sure your solution meets the same goals as the solution in Figure 5.38.

7. Figure 5.47 contains an Ada solution to the Readers and Writers Problem. Unfortunately, this solution can cause the readers to suffer indefinite postponement. Revise it so that when a server finishes a rendezvous with a writer, it will accept any pending calls to StartRead. Make sure your solution does not indefinitely postpone writers waiting for a rendezvous.

8. Apply Dijkstra's Bankers Algorithm to the situation shown below. Is the state safe?

	Current Number of pages allocated	Maximum Number of pages needed
Process 1	4	10
Process 2	2	4
Process 3	1	2
Process 4	1	4
Process 5	4	10

13 pages in the system
1 page is unallocated

9. Consider the following resource allocation graph. Give an example of a request that deadlocks all 4 processes. Give one that deadlocks just two processes.

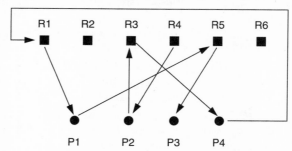

10. Write equivalent code for the process in Figure 5.67 if the mode is WRITE.

11. Write C commands to create a pipe and initiate two processes in response to the user input

```
com1 | com2
```

≡≡≡≡≡ Questions

1. Suppose two process P_1 and P_2 each contain the following high level language commands in a loop:

$$\text{Numres} = \text{Numres} + 1$$
$$\text{If Numres} = 50 \text{ Then Numres} = 0$$

Suppose also that both share the variable Numres and that both are active. Even with only one CPU, explain how Numres may never be reset to zero.

2. In the second try at enforcing (Figure 5.16) mutual exclusion, explain how the processes could deadlock if the test for Occupied were removed?

3. Consider the following software "solution" to mutual exclusion for two processes:

```
Type
    Turntype = (One, Two, Either); {User defined enumerated
    type}
Var
    Turn : Turntype ; {This is global to both processes}
Processi {i is one or two}
    :
Var
Ours, Theirs:Turntype; {Local to Process-i. In process-1,
    Ours=One and Theirs=Two. In process 2, Ours=Two and
    Theirs=One}
Begin {Processi}
    :
  Begin {BeginExclusion}
    If Turn = Theirs Then
        Wait
    Else
        Turn = Ours;
  End; {BeginExclusion}
  :
  Critical Section
  :
  Begin {EndExclusion}
    If other process is suspended Then
        Begin
          Turn = Theirs;
          resume other process
        End
    Else
        Turn = Either;
  End {EndExclusion}
    :
End. {processi}
```

The idea is to allow entry into a critical section only if it is "our turn" or "either turn." The "Either" value avoids the requirement that processes must alternate entry into their critical sections. Initially, Turn = Either. Does this work?

4. Explain how the Producer-Consumer Problem is a special case of the circular buffer problem.

5. Consider the following software "solution" to mutual exclusion for two processes:

<u>Process 1</u>   <u>Process 2</u>

```
Begin {BeginExclusion}              Begin {BeginExclusion}
  Flag[i] = True;                     Flag[i] = True;
  While Turn <> i Do                  While Turn <> i Do
  Begin                               Begin
    If Flag[j] Then Wait;               If Flag[j] Then Wait;
    Turn = i;                           Turn = i;
  End {While}                         End {While}
End; {BeginExclusion}               End; {BeginExclusion}
    critical section                    critical section
Begin {EndExclusion}                Begin {EndExclusion}
  Flag[i] = False;                    Flag[i] = False;
  Resume the other process;           Resume the other process;
End; {EndExclusion}                 End; {EndExclusion}
```

Suppose the following are global to both processes:

```
Flag : array[1. .2] of Boolean; {Initially False}
Turn : 1. .2; {Initially 1 or 2}
```

Assume that for each process, i and j are local. In process 1, i = 1 and j = 2. In process 2, i = 2 and j = 1. What can go wrong?

6. Dekker's Algorithm (Figure 5.18) enforces mutual exclusion for two processes. What undesirable event can occur if the first statement in EndExclusion is deleted? What undesirable event can occur if the second occurrence of the statement Occupied1=True (for process 1) and Occupied2=True (for process 2) are both deleted from BeginExclusion?

7. The monitor solution to the Readers and Writers Problem shown in Figure 5.38 requires the readers to call procedure entries StartRead and FinishRead. But the reader actually does the reading. Explain how the reader can misuse the entries so that the monitor can no longer enforce mutual exclusion.

8. Suppose we replace the monitor entries StartRead and FinishRead in Figure 5.38 with a single entry ReadtoDatabase which reads from the database. Are there any undesirable side effects?

9. Consider the following monitor solution to the Circular Buffer Problem:

```
Monitor circular-buffer;
   buffer : Array[0..n-1] of thing; {circular buffer.
   "thing" represents an unspecified data type}
   i : integer; {position in the buffer accessed by the
                   consumer, initially 0}
   j : integer; {position in the buffer accessed by the
                   producer, initially 0}
   FullBuf : condition; {condition variable for when all
                          buffers are full}
   EmptyBuf : condition; {condition variable for when all
                          buffers are empty}
   Occupied : integer; {initially 0 - How many circular
                          buffer positions are filled}
{***********************************************************}
{This procedure entry will place data into position j of
 the buffer}
{***********************************************************}
ENTRY PutIn(SomeData : thing);
   BEGIN {PutIn}
(1) If Occupied = n then Wait(FullBuf);
(2) Store SomeData into position j of buffer;
(3) j = j+1 (mod n)
(4) Occupied = Occupied + 1;
(5) Signal(EmptyBuf);
   END; {PutIn}
{***********************************************************}
{This procedure entry removes data from position i of the
 buffer}
{***********************************************************}
ENTRY TakeOut(SomeData : thing);
   BEGIN {TakeOut}
(6) If Occupied = 0 then Wait(EmptyBuf);
(7) remove SomeData from position i of buffer;
(8) i = i+1 (mod n);
(9) Occupied = Occupied - 1;
(10) Signal(FullBuf);
   END; {TakeOut}
BEGIN {Monitor code to initialize values}
   i = 0;
   j = n-1;
   Occupied = 0;
END; {Monitor}
```

Describe undesirable side effects for each of each of the following changes:

a. Remove line 9.

b. Remove line 4.

10. The following is an Ada solution to the Readers and Writers Problem from Figure 5.47:

```
task Readers&Writers is
  entry StartRead;
  entry FinishRead;
  entry WriteToDatabase
end;

task body Readers&Writers is
  NumOfReaders : integer;

Begin
  NumOfReaders = 0;
1 loop
2   select
3     when WriteToDatabase'count = 0
4       Accept StartRead;
5         NumOfReaders =NumOfReaders + 1
6       end StartRead;
7   or
8       Accept FinishRead
9         NumOfReaders =NumOfReaders - 1
10      end FinishRead;
    or
      when NumOfReaders = 0
        Accept WriteToDatabase (SomeData : AnyType
          Write SomeData to the Database;
      end WriteToDatabase;
    end select
  end loop
end.
```

Suppose you replace the entries StartRead and FinishRead with one entry, Reader, and replace lines 4 through 10 with the following:

```
Accept Reader(SomeData: AnyType)
  NumOfReaders = NumOfReaders + 1;
  read SomeData from the database;
  NumOfReaders = NumOfReaders - 1;
end Reader;
```

Assume now that all tasks that want to read call Reader. Are there any undesirable side effects from the change?

11. State the 4 conditions necessary for a deadlock to occur. Suppose the resources are pages in a shared database. Why is it important to allow each condition?

12. Explain how processes in a spooled system can deadlock. Recall the discussions in Chapter 3 on spooling.
13. Consider a system which has 4 identical resources shared by 3 separate processes. Each process requires no more than 2 resources. When a process requests a resource, the operating system allocates any available resource. If none is available, the process waits. Is deadlock possible in this system? If so, indicate a sequence of requests which results in a deadlock. If not, which of the 4 conditions necessary for deadlock does not exist in this system?
14. Repeat question 13, but assume each process requires no more than 3 resources.
15. The project simulator in Appendix A generates random events to which an operating system must respond. Create a phase IV in which some random events correspond to processes requesting and releasing a set of resources R1 through Rn. Phase IV's operating system should allocate and release resources, suspend and resume processes, and be able to check for deadlock.
16. The Banker's Algorithm of Section 5.10 assumed the resources were a single type. Modify the Banker's Algorithm if each of the resources is one of two types. Can you generalize further by assuming each of the resources is one of m types.
17. Investigate the capabilities of your system and determine whether it allows you to run two processes concurrently. For example, you can do this under VAX VMS using a Lib$Spawn system call. If you can, write two programs where the first sends the second a message and the second responds. Then generalize to where the first sends the second a series of messages and waits for an acknowledgement of each.

References

1. Dijkstra, E.W. "Cooperating Sequential Processes." Reprinted in *Programming Languages*, edited by F. Genuys. Academic Press, 1968.
2. Ben–Ari, M. *Principles of Concurrent Programming*. Englewood Cliffs, NJ: Prentice–Hall,1982.
3. Dijkstra, E.W. "Solution of a Problem in Concurrent Programming Control," *Communications of the Association for Computing Machinery* 8 (September 1965):569.
4. Brinch Hansen, P. "Distributed Processes—a Concurrent Programming Concept." *Communications of the Association for Computing Machinery* 21 (November 1978):934–941.
5. Eisenberg, M. A., and M. R. McGuire. "Further Comments on Dijkstra's Concurrent Programming Control Problem." *Communications of the Association for Computing Machinery* 15 (November 1972):999.
6. Knuth, D. "Additional Comments on a Problem in Concurrent Programming Control." *Communications of the Association for Computing Machinery* 9 (May 1966):321–322.
7. Lamport, L. "A New Solution of Dijkstra's Concurrent Programming Problem." *Communications of the Association for Computing Machinery* 17 (August 1974): 453–455.
8. Peterson, G.L. "Myths about the Mutual Exclusion Problem." *Information Processing Letters* 12 (June 1981):115–116.

9. Ricart, G., and A.K. Agrawala. "An Optimal Algorithm for Mutual Exclusion in Computer Networks." *Communications of the Association for Computing Machinery* 24 (January 1981):9–17.

10. deBruijn, N.G. "Additional Comments on a Problem in Concurrent Programming and Control." *Communications of the Association for Computing Machinery* 10 (March 1967):137–138.

11. Lamport, L. "Proving the Correctness of Multiprocess Programs." *IEEE Transactions on Software Engineering* SE-3 (February 1977):127–143.

12. Lamport, L. "A New Approach to Proving Correctness of Multiprocess Programs." *ACM Transactions on Programing Languages and Systems* 1 (1979):84–97.

13. Silberschatz, A., J. Peterson and P. Galvin. *Operating System Concepts*. 3rd ed. Reading MA:Addison–Wesley,1991.

14. Hoare, C. A. R. "Monitors, An Operating System Structuring Concept." *Communications of the Association for Computing Machinery* 17 (October, 1974): 549–557. Erratum in *Communications of the Association for Computing Machinery* 18 (February 1975):95.

15. Brinch Hansen, P. "The Programming Language Concurrent Pascal." *IEEE Transactions on Software Engineering* SE-1 (June 1975):199–207.

16. Brinch Hansen, P. *Operating System Principles*. Englewood Cliffs, NJ: Prentice–Hall, 1973.

17. Brinch Hansen, P. *The Architecture of Concurrent Programs*. Englewood Cliffs, NJ: Prentice–Hall, 1977.

18. Gehani, N. *Ada: An Advanced Introduction*. 2nd ed. Englewood Cliffs, NJ: Prentice–Hall, 1989.

19. Barnes, J. *Programming in Ada*. 3rd ed. Reading, MA: Addison–Wesley, 1989.

20. Havender, J. W. "Avoiding Deadlock in Multitasking Systems." *IBM Systems Journal* 7 (1968):74–84.

21. Coffman, E. G., M. J. Elphick, and A. Shoshani. "System Deadlocks." *Computing Surveys* 3 (June 1971):67–78.

22. Tanenbaum, A. S. *Operating Systems: Design and Implementation*. Englewood Cliffs, NJ: Prentice–Hall, 1987.

23. Zobel, D., and C. Koch. "Resolution Techniques and Complexity Results with Deadlocks: A Classifying and Annotated Bibliography." *Operating Systems Review* 22 (January 1988):52–72.

24. Sobell, M. G. *A Practical Guide to the UNIX System*. Menlo Park, CA: The Benjamin/Cummings Co., 1984.

25. Shaw, M. C., and S. S. Shaw. *UNIX Internals: A Systems Operations Handbook*. Blue Ridge Summit, PA: Tab Books Inc., 1987.

26. Kernighan, B. W., and R. Pike. *The UNIX Programming Environment*. Englewood Cliffs, NJ: Prentice–Hall, 1984.

27. Bach, M. J. *The Design of the UNIX Operating System*. Englewood Cliffs, NJ: Prentice–Hall,1986.

28. *UNIX Programmer's Manual*. Revised and expanded version Vol. 1. Bell Telephone Laboratories, Inc., Holt, Rinehart, and Winston, 1983.

29. *UNIX Programmer's Manual* Seventh ed., Vol. 2. Bell Telephone Laboratories, Inc., Holt, Rinehart, and Winston, 1983.

30. Thompson, K., and D. M. Ritchie. "The UNIX Time Sharing System." *Communications of the Association for Computing Machinery* 17 (July 1974): 365–375.

31. Kernighan, B. W., and D. M. Ritchie. *C Programming Language*. 2nd ed. ANSI version, Englewood Cliffs, NJ: Prentice–Hall, 1988.

32. Banahan, M. *The C Book: Featuring the Draft ANSI C Standard*. Reading, MA:Addison–Wesley, 1988.

33. Bic, Lubomir, and Alan C. Shaw. *The Logical Design of Operating Systems*. 2nd ed. Englewood Cliffs, NJ: Prentice–Hall, 1988.

6

Auxiliary
Storage
Management

6.1 Overview

Previous chapters described how an operating system treats processes. Chapter 2 showed how a system manages code and data for processes as they compete for memory. Chapters 3 and 4 described how to do I/O and schedule processes for execution. Chapter 5 described how processes communicate and synchronize their activities. All these chapters discussed how the operating system deals with active processes.

We have not considered another important component of an operating system. How does it find the code and data that a process needs to run? Where and how is the code and data stored? At any time, hundreds of processes may be active simultaneously, but what about programs that are not currently active? Where are their code and data? There may be tens of thousands of files on disk or tape. If someone wants to run a program or a process wants a specific data file, how does the operating system find it?

Chapter 3 briefly described the physical components of a disk pack or magnetic tape. A hard disk, for example, typically has a capacity measured in *megabytes* (one million bytes or 1MB). A disk pack with a 1 gigabyte capacity is not unusual. Furthermore, a system may have several such packs. What does this mean to the average user?

The average user logs on to a computer and begins to edit a file. He or she types a command, and the operating system locates the file. Usually, this occurs quickly, but think about what the operating system must do. It has to locate a small file within over a billion bytes of storage. It is difficult to appreciate the difficulty of this task because few of us really understand how big a billion is: well, it is big. (For example, a billion seconds spans almost 32 years; or if you earn $100 per hour, 24 hours per day, and 365 days per year, you would need almost 1150 years to earn a billion dollars. The only thing against which a billion seems small by comparison is the Federal deficit.) The operating system must truly find the proverbial "needle in a haystack," yet, it does this efficiently.

But finding the file is only part of its job. The operating system must also provide security. Files that contain sensitive information demand strict security. How can the operating system guarantee that a file does not fall into the wrong hands? How can it prevent someone from accessing your latest (potential) best–seller program and copying it, or worse yet, destroying it?

The ability to obtain information quickly and securely raises interesting questions. How does a system find all the sectors for a given file? If several processes simultaneously request information from different sectors, how does the system decide what to do first? How does it decide which sectors to use when a process creates a file or adds to it? How does a system decide which processes can request information on which sectors? Answers to these questions are part of our discussion of "Auxiliary Storage Management."

Section 6.2 discusses record formats and how they are stored on a disk or tape. It distinguishes blocked and unblocked records and discusses pros and cons of each.

Section 6.3 discusses low–level scheduling of accesses to disk sectors. We will find that a controller will not always handle requests in the order it receives them. In fact, we will see that doing this can degrade the response tremendously and tax the hardware. (I wonder if Congress has thought of that?)

The fourth section discusses file and account directories. They allow the system to find a user's files and provide security. Directories take various forms, ranging from simple linear structures to complex hierarchical ones.

Section 6.5 describes file structures. The way in which a system accesses information depends greatly on the file structure. We will find that many files have a simple structure. Their users are often limited in the types of manipulations they can request. Other file structures are more complex, allowing users a wider range of options.

Section 6.6 covers file security. We will discuss protection methods such as passwording, encryption, and I/O modes.

Last, Section 6.7 provides a case study of MS–DOS disk management. We describe the organization of MS–DOS directories and files. We also discuss how MS–DOS uses directories and tables to access files.

≡≡≡≡≡ **6.2 Physical and Logical Records**

≡≡≡
Record Formats

The first order of business is to describe the difference between a *logical record* and a *physical record*. A logical record is a unit of information created by a programmer. For example, in Pascal you can make the following declaration:

```
EmployeeRecord=Record
   Name : character string declaration ;
   Yearsservice : Integer;
   Salary : Real;
End
```

You are defining a unit of information called EmployeeRecord that contains an employee's name, number of years service, and salary. You may then pass the record as a parameter to procedures, or transfer it to or from a file as a unit. For all intents and purposes, the system treats each record separately.

In reality, however, the system does not necessarily treat a record as a unit. Frequently, it groups several records into a contiguous unit called a *physical record*. A logical record is just a subset of a physical record.

For example, suppose the employee record is organized as shown in Figure 6.1. If the name requires 32 bytes and the salary and years service fields each require 4 bytes, the record requires 40 contiguous bytes.

Figure 6.1 Employee Record

Employee name	Years of service	Salary
32 bytes	4 bytes	4 bytes

However, instead of storing one record on a disk or tape, the system may group several into a physical record, and then store the record. Subsequent reads would actually read a physical record and, consequently, several logical records at a time. For example, if a physical record consisted of 400 bytes, Figure 6.2 shows how the system packs the records.

Figure 6.2 Physical record containing 10 logical records

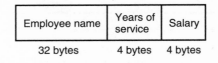

| rec 1 | rec 2 | rec 3 | rec 4 | rec 5 | rec 6 | rec 7 | rec 8 | rec 9 | rec 10 |

First employee record (40 bytes) Second employee record (40 bytes) — Tenth employee record (40 bytes)

Why would a system do this? It seems like added work to deviate from the user's perception. However, there are good reasons to group logical records. The first reason is to reduce the amount of information the system must maintain. Consider another example. Chapter 2 discussed page sizes and fragmentation. We argued that we could eliminate fragmentation by using frames containing one memory word. But then the number of frames the operating system must maintain becomes huge. The same tradeoff applies here. Suppose a file contains 10,000 student records. If the system stores each one separately, it must keep track of 10,000 pieces of information. However, suppose it stores them as physical records consisting of 10 logical records. Now the system needs just 1000 pieces of information. We have reduced the number of items the system must maintain by 90%.

Unblocked Records. A second reason to group logical records is based on how storage devices work. Suppose the file is on a tape. If the system stores logical records separately, Figure 6.3 shows a typical section of tape. Logical records appear consecutively with large gaps of tape in between. We say the records are *unblocked*. But why are the gaps there?

Figure 6.3 Unblocked records stored on tape

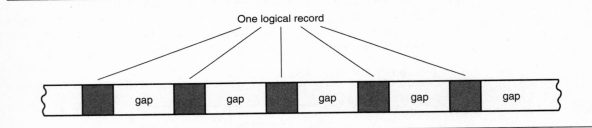

When a process executes a command to read a tape record, the controller must first start the reel moving. The tape must accelerate to a certain speed before the drive can read the data accurately. (Consider what happens if you load a music cassette into a player with dirty drive mechanisms. The tape may move too slowly, and the music is "garbled." Similarly, a computer tape moving too slowly causes data to be read incorrectly.)

If a head is at rest in a gap, then, as the tape begins to accelerate, only the gap moves past it. If the gap is the correct size, the logical record moves by the head just as the tape has accelerated to the required speed. The drive can then read the record correctly.

The gaps may be much larger than the size of a logical record. Therefore, if the system stores the records as shown in Figure 6.3, the tape consists mostly of gaps. Furthermore, if a process wants to read several records, the controller must schedule multiple requests and start and stop the tape repeatedly. This slows reading considerably.

Blocked Records. But suppose the system stores the records as shown in Figure 6.4. Here the records are *blocked*. There are fewer gaps, and less tape is wasted. Also, once the tape accelerates, the drive can read several logical records without stopping. Thus, the drive transmits the information faster and the controller can schedule fewer requests. Of course, the operating system must now have a buffer large enough to hold the physical record. This puts a limit on how large a physical record can be.

Figure 6.4 Blocked records stored on tape

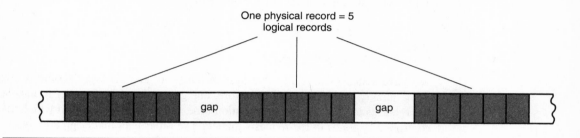

One physical record = 5 logical records

Grouping logical records is also useful for disk files. Chapter 3 showed that magnetic heads read and write information to one sector at a time. Suppose that each sector is 400 bytes long. If we store one logical record per sector, we waste 90% of it (assuming the employee record from before). If we group 10 logical records into a single physical record, we use the entire sector. Furthermore, we can read 10 logical records with one "sector read." Otherwise, this would require 10 reads and would take 10 times as long.

The numbers used above are just an illustration. In general, suppose x is the number of bytes per logical record and y is the number per physical record. Then $z = y$ DIV x is the number of logical records per physical record. If there is a remainder, we can take one of two approaches. One is to store an extra fraction of a logical record in each physical record, thus eliminating waste. The other is to allow some waste in each physical record, thus not splitting logical records over two disk sectors. Which approach is better depends on the system and the file structure.

If n is the number of logical records per file, the number of physical records is at least $((n-1)$ DIV $z) + 1$. We say at least here because the actual number depends on the file's structure. Additional overhead may be necessary. We discuss file structures briefly later in this chapter.

≡≡≡≡≡ 6.3 Disk Access Scheduling

Tapes and disks differ in one major way: access to tapes is sequential. The drive cannot read from the middle of a tape without fast forwarding or rewinding through a section. Reading from a disk need not be sequential. The controller can move the read/write head to any track and wait until the sector rotates past it. This ability raises questions that a controller must answer and decisions that it must make.

Specifically, if many processes want to read information from a disk pack, how does the controller handle them? Remember, the mechanisms of a disk drive limit how fast data can be transmitted. Thus, processes can easily generate requests faster than the controllers can move the heads and transmit or store data. It is not unusual for many processes to issue I/O requests in the time it takes the controller to find and transmit one sector of data. If this happens, which request should the controller honor first?

≡≡ Reading/Writing a Sector

We have stated many times that system hardware and software should do its work quickly and efficiently. Therefore, one goal is for the controller to handle I/O requests to minimize total execution time. Now, does the order in which the controller responds to the requests matter? The order may matter greatly, but to see why, we must first describe how the controller finds the data and transmits it.

Suppose a process has issued a request to read data from a sector. The controller must do the following:

- Move the read/write head to the track on which the sector lies.
- Wait for the beginning of the sector to rotate to the head.
- Read the sector as it rotates past the head.

Seek Time. Let's now discuss each action in more detail. Figure 6.5 shows a rotating disk and read/write head. Suppose the head is currently at track *A*. Next the controller receives a request to read a sector on another track, say *B*. The controller must issue a command to move the head from track *A* to track *B*. The drive mechanisms then physically move the head. The time necessary to move it to a new track is called *seek time*.

Figure 6.5 Read/Write head moving to a new track

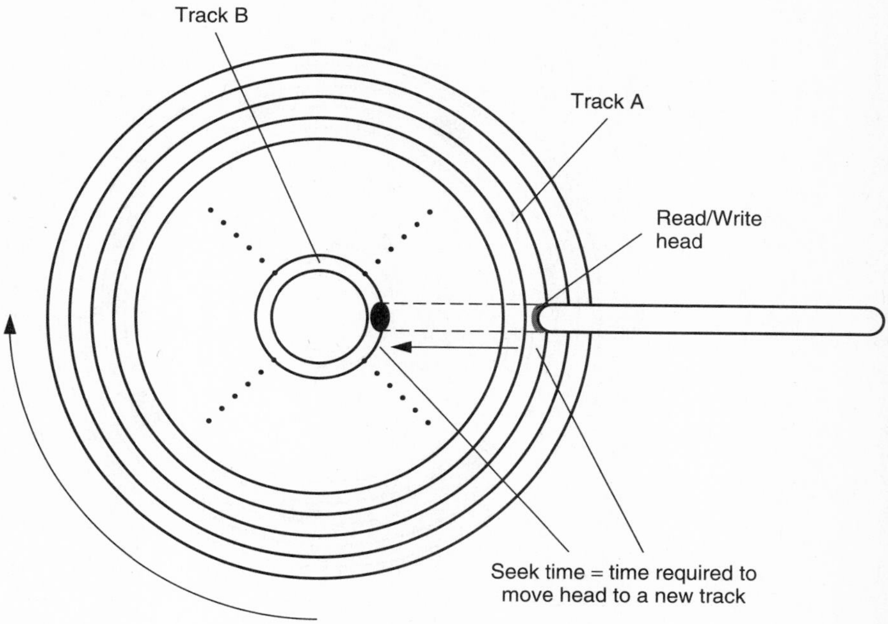

Latency Time. Now suppose the head is at the correct track. But where is the sector? Figure 6.6 shows a case where it is on the far side. The drive must wait until the beginning of the sector rotates to the head. There are usually notches or holes on a disk that mark the beginning of a sector. The drive has sense mechanisms that detect when the notch or hole rotates to a certain point. This means the sector has rotated to the head, and the drive may now read it. The time required for a sector to rotate to the head is the *latency time*.

Transmission Time. The last step requires the drive to sense and transmit information back to the controller. The time required is the time it takes for a sector to rotate past a head, or *transmission time*. Therefore, if T is the total time needed to find and read a disk sector,

$$T = \text{seek time} + \text{latency time} + \text{transmission time}$$

Some drives contain a read/write head for each track. Their seek time is zero since no head movement is needed. In this chapter, we consider only drives containing one head per disk surface. There are certainly enough of them to justify the discussion.

Figure 6.6 Desired sector rotating toward head

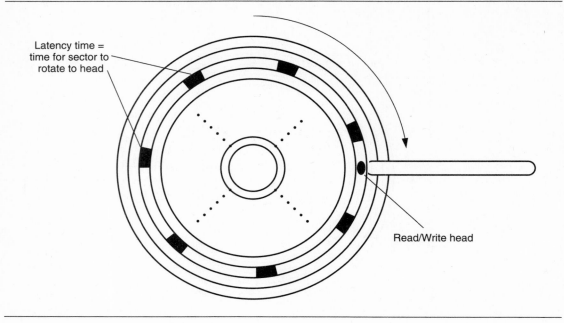

How can we minimize the time needed to find and read data? The seek time is by far the most significant factor. The head must accelerate from rest, move to the desired track, and decelerate back to rest. The starting and stopping accounts for most of the time. This may all occur in milliseconds. But when instruction execution time is in microseconds, even a millisecond is a long time. If we can minimize seek time among many I/O requests, we can significantly decrease the total time needed to find and transmit data.

But how do we minimize seek time? If only one read is pending, there is little the controller can do. But suppose there are many read requests pending. The controller can make many different choices. We illustrate by giving several approaches to the problem.

≡ FIFO Scheduling

The first approach to minimizing seek time is to do nothing; in other words, the controller simply responds to requests in the order it receives them. The value of this approach is its simplicity, a factor not to be underestimated in system design. The controller need not execute any clever algorithms. However, there is a disadvantage illustrated by the read requests in Figure 6.7. Suppose the characteristics of the disk are as follows:

- It has 1000 sectors (numbered 0 through 999) per surface.
- It has 10 sectors per track.
- Tracks are numbered 0 (innermost) through 99 (outermost).
- Given a sector, we can find its track from the formula

$$TrackNumber = sector\ number\ \text{DIV}\ 10;$$

Figure 6.7 Controller receiving many requests for a sector read

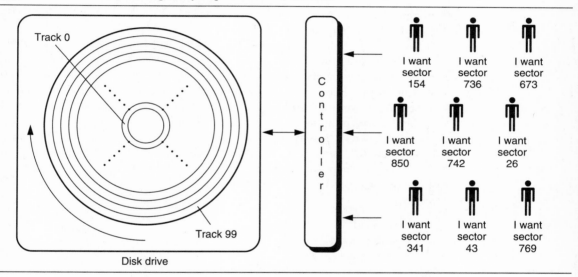

These assumptions simplify the calculations. Consider what happens if processes make the requests of Figure 6.7 in the order shown in Table 6.1.

Table 6.1 Example requests for disk reads

Request Number	Sector Number	Track Number	Track Distance
1	154	15	-
2	736	73	58
3	673	67	6
4	850	85	18
5	742	74	11
6	26	2	72
7	769	76	74
8	341	34	42
9	43	4	30

The track distance for each request is the difference between its track number and that of the previous request. It is proportional to the distance the heads must move and affects the seek time. In this example, the average track distance is about 39. "So what?" you say. How do we know whether this is good? After all, we have nothing with which to compare it. So, let's consider another approach.

Shortest Seek Time Scheduling

Suppose that the controller receives all nine requests at about the same time. Suppose it was initially idle and responds to the first one in Table 6.1 immediately. Now suppose that after the drive has transmitted data from sector 154, all other requests are pending.

Which one should the controller honor next? Does it make sense for it to move the head from track 15 to track 73? The head will pass by tracks 34 and 67. Since there is data on them, would it not make sense for the head to stop, wait for the sector, and transmit the data? For that matter, would it not be more sensible to get data from tracks 4 and 2, since they are relatively close to the current head position?

Consider an analogy. Suppose a deliveryman was working in the area shown in Figure 6.8. Suppose he had to make deliveries to City Hall, the grocery store, the butcher shop, and a department store. Would you make the deliveries in the following order?

Butcher shop
City Hall
Grocery store
Department store

This would obviously waste a lot of time and gasoline not to mention adding to air pollution. To reduce driving distance, a more logical choice would be to make deliveries in the following order:

Grocery store
Butcher shop
Department store
City Hall

The *shortest seek time first* (SSF) method of scheduling disk accesses tries to minimize seek time. The controller can do this by processing requests in an order that minimizes track distance between them. That is, given a current track number, it moves the head to the closest track for which there is a request pending. Therefore, if it processed request 1 from Table 6.1 first, it would process the remaining requests in the order shown in Table 6.2. Now the average track distance is just 12.

Figure 6.8 Local map used for running errands

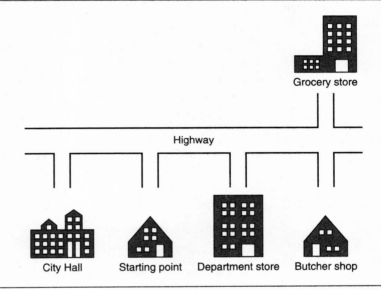

Table 6.2 Disk accesses scheduled using shortest seek time first

Request Number	Sector Number	Track Number	Track Distance
1	154	15	-
9	43	4	11
6	26	2	2
8	341	34	32
3	673	67	33
2	736	73	6
5	742	74	1
7	769	76	2
4	850	85	9

Analysis of Shortest Seek Time. Shortest seek time scheduling minimizes track distance and, consequently, the average seek time. Unfortunately, it creates a problem. SSF may work to the detriment of some processes. Specifically, the controller favors requests near the middle of the disk over those at the edges.

For example, suppose the head is currently at track k and two requests are pending. One is for track zero and the other for track i. We will show that the controller is unlikely to honor the request for track zero first. We will further show that, as additional requests occur, the probability of the request for track zero being honored gets even lower.

Suppose that track numbers k and i are random. That is, we assume that requests occur randomly, and with equal probability for all tracks. Thus, i and k can be any integer between 0 and 99 inclusive.

The question we ask is, "If the head is currently at track k, what is the probability that the controller will reference track zero next?" Since the controller minimizes seek time, we can rephrase the question as, "What is the probability that track k is closer to track zero than to track i ?"

Since the distance between tracks is proportional to the difference between their track numbers, we therefore seek the probability that $|k-0| \leq |k-i|$ or equivalently, $k \leq |k-i|$. If both tracks are equidistant from track k, we will assume the controller gives track zero preference.

Probability theory shows that we can compute an event's probability from the formula

$$\text{probability of event} = \frac{\text{number of outcomes favorable to the event}}{\text{number of possible outcomes}}$$

In this case, an outcome is a specific pair of values for i and k. There are 10,000 possible outcomes (100 possible values of i multiplied by 100 possible values of k). We can determine the number of outcomes producing $k \leq |k-i|$ from Table 6.3.

Table 6.3 Values of i and k for which $k \leq |k-i|$

Value of k	Values of i for which $k \leq |k-i|$	Number of favorable outcomes
99	0	1
98	0	1
97	0	1
⋮	⋮	⋮
50	0	1
49	0,98,99	3
48	0,96 through 99	5
47	0,94 through 99	7
46	0,92 through 99	9
⋮	⋮	⋮
1	0, 2 through 99	99
0	0 through 99	100

The number of outcomes producing $k \leq |k-i|$ is the sum of entries from the last column of Table 6.3. The sum is 2649. Therefore, the probability that $k \leq |k-i|$ is 2649/10,000 or approximately .265. If k is between 50 and 99, the probability drops to a mere .01.

More important, consider what happens generally. Suppose that the head is currently on track k and there are n requests for accesses pending. Also suppose the requests are for tracks 0, i_1, i_2, i_3,..., i_{n-1}. The probability that the controller will process track zero next is equal to the probability that

$$k \leq |k-i_1| \text{ and } k \leq |k-i_2| \text{ and } k \leq |k-i_3| \text{ and,..., and } k \leq |k-i_{n-1}|.$$

Call this probability P_{n-1}. Again, if we assume that i_1 through i_{n-1} are random and independent of one another, P_{n-1} is the product of the probabilities of each inequality. But we have already shown that the probability of one inequality occurring is .265. Therefore, $P_{n-1} = .265^{n-1}$. Table 6.4 shows values for P_{n-1} and $1-P_{n-1}$ as a function of n. Here, $1-P_{n-1}$ is the probability that the controller will <u>not</u> access track 0 next.

Table 6.4 Probability of accessing track zero next

n	P_{n-1} (probability of accessing track 0 next)	$1-P_{n-1}$ (probability of not accessing track 0 next)
2	.2650	.7350
3	.0702	.9298
4	.0186	.9814
5	.0049	.9951
6	.0013	.9987
7	.0003	.9997

These probabilities apply to the controller's first choice. If we assumed that new requests are generated regularly, a more detailed analysis would show that the probability of choosing track zero with successive choices remains very low. Given this information, you can begin to see how the controller may indefinitely postpone requests for track zero.

Although we have discussed the problem of a request for track zero, the logic applies to a request for a track at the disk's outer edge also. In conclusion, requests for tracks near the middle receive better service than for ones near the edges.

Shortest Seek Time — Preferred Direction (Scan)

Shortest seek time is a classic example of improving overall statistics at the expense of some requests. This strategy is unfair and causes performance to depend on the almost random factor of sector location. How can we improve the situation?

One approach would be simply not to store data on the innermost or outermost tracks. Then, for example, requests for data on track 0 would never occur. Unfortunately, there are two serious problems with this approach. First, it wastes part of the disk surface. Why leave perfectly good tracks unused? Second, oddly enough, it does not even help solve the problem. Suppose, for example, we choose not to use tracks 0 through 4. Then track 5 becomes the innermost track. Everything we stated earlier about track 0 is now true for track 5. We have accomplished nothing.

A better strategy is to apply shortest seek time but require the heads to move in a *preferred direction*. The preferred direction is either inward (toward track zero) or outward. When processing read requests, the controller will do the following:

- Choose the closest request in the preferred direction.
- If no such request exists, change the preferred direction and choose the closest request in the new direction.

To show how this works, consider again the I/O requests in Figure 6.7. Suppose the controller has just finished with track 15 and the preferred direction is outward. Table 6.5 shows the order in which it handles the requests.

Table 6.5 Disk accesses using shortest seek time first in a preferred direction

Request Number	Sector Number	Track Number	Track Distance
1	154	15	-
8	341	34	19
3	673	67	33
2	736	73	6
5	742	74	1
7	769	76	2
4	850	85	9
9	43	4	81
6	26	2	2

After handling the request for track 15, the controller next chooses the one for track 34. Track 4 is actually closer but it is not in the preferred direction. The controller keeps moving the heads outward, getting data from tracks 67, 73,

74, 76, and 85. Since there are no requests for tracks above 85, it changes the preferred direction. It next processes the request for track 4 and finally for track 2.

In this case, the average number of tracks the heads must move to process a request is approximately 19. This is larger than that achieved using shortest seek time first, but it is still considerably better than the FIFO approach. Furthermore, requests for low-numbered or high-numbered tracks will receive much better response. For example, as the heads move outward, the controller will ignore requests for low-numbered tracks until the preferred direction changes. Thus, these additional requests do not affect the response to requests for high-numbered tracks.

This method also goes by the name *elevator algorithm*. The analogy is to an elevator in a tall building. It has a preferred direction, picking up passengers as it moves up or down. What would happen if it always went to the nearest floor where people were waiting? Obviously, those on the top floor would wait a long time. Of course, if you are on the observation deck in Chicago's Sears tower, you can always relax and enjoy the view!

Circular Scan

A variation on the scan approach is *circular scan* (C–Scan). Whereas scan provides more consistent service than shortest seek time, it still gives some requests better service than others. Suppose that T is the average time needed to process all requests before changing preferred direction. Suppose also that the controller starts at the innermost tracks. As Figure 6.9 shows, it eventually moves the head to the outermost tracks at approximately time T. The preferred direction changes, and the heads begin moving inward. They reach the innermost tracks at time $2T$. On the average, the heads are at the innermost tracks at times $2T$, $4T$, $6T$, etc., and at the outermost tracks at times T, $3T$, $5T$, etc. But the heads pass the middle track at approximately times $.5T$, $1.5T$, $2.5T$, etc.

In other words, requests for data on inner or outer tracks may experience delays of up to $2T$. However, requests for data on middle tracks will generally experience waits no longer than T. The controller gives them better service.

In C–Scan, the preferred direction never changes. When there are no requests pending in the preferred direction, the controller quickly moves the heads back to the opposite end of the disk and continues in the same direction. Figure 6.10 shows head movement using C–Scan with a constant "outward" preferred direction.

Figure 6.9 Head movement using the scan approach

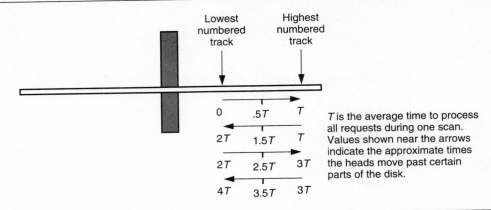

T is the average time to process all requests during one scan. Values shown near the arrows indicate the approximate times the heads move past certain parts of the disk.

Figure 6.10 Head movement using the circular scan approach

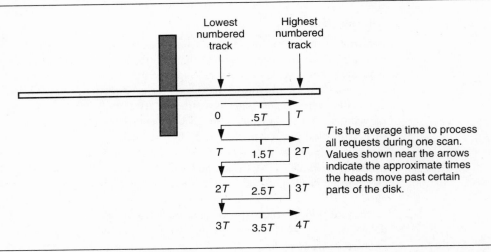

T is the average time to process all requests during one scan. Values shown near the arrows indicate the approximate times the heads move past certain parts of the disk.

With C–Scan, the heads pass over inner, middle, and outer tracks approximately once every *T* time units. The controller treats all parts of the disk equally. There is, of course, slightly less efficiency than with the scan method. An extra delay occurs when the drive has read data from the outermost track for which a request was pending. Suppose this was track *k*. The controller then moves the head back to the innermost track for which a request is pending. Thus, in this instance, the head moves to the track furthest away from track *k*. The scan approach would have moved the heads to the track closest to *k*. But this occurs only when the heads must reverse direction, and the extra delay is not great.

Note that circular scan is inappropriate for elevators. If the preferred direction were always up, the people leaving the observation deck in the Sears Tower would get an exciting trip as the elevator free falls to the ground.

Rotational Delays

Reducing seek time does the most to speed up the response to I/O requests. This is because seek time is the most significant part of the time required to find and transmit a sector of data. But what about latency time? Can we do anything to minimize the amount of time needed to read several sectors from the same track?

For example, consider the disk surface shown in Figure 6.11. There are five sectors per track. For simplicity, we have numbered them 1 through 5. Suppose the controller has just read data from sector 4, and there are two more requests for data on this track. If they are for sectors 1 and 2, which one should the controller read first?

Figure 6.11 Reading 5 sectors from a track

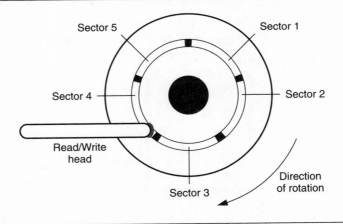

When the controller moves the heads to different tracks, it has control over the direction. However, once it has moved the heads, it must wait until the desired sector rotates past the heads. The direction of rotation is fixed, and thus, it would seem sensible simply to read the first desired sector that reaches the head. In the example of Figure 6.11, this means the controller should read sector 2 before sector 1.

Let us calculate how much time it takes to read the two sectors in either order. Suppose the controller reads sector 2 first. Since it has just read data from sector 4, it must wait for sector 3 to rotate by the head before it can read sector 2. After it reads sector 2, it can read sector 1. This can all be done in the time it takes the disk to make 3/5 of a revolution.

How long will it take to read the sectors in reverse order? To read sector 1 first, the controller must wait for both sectors 3 and 2 to rotate past the head. It must then wait for sector 2 to come around again before reading it. This requires the disk to rotate 1 and 2/5 of a revolution from the position shown in Figure 6.11.

It appears that the controller can halve the latency time by reading sector 2 first. But this logic works only if the controller can read two contiguous sectors without any rotational delay in between. Many controllers cannot. Let's see why.

Error Detection for Disk Reads. Figure 6.12 shows a problem that can occur any time we transmit data. A disk drive must sense a sequence of bits stored in a sector. It then sends the bits to the controller. However, what happens if some interference affects the bit string and changes a "1" to a "0"? As a consequence, the controller receives different data than the drive sent.

Figure 6.12 Loss of data integrity during transmission

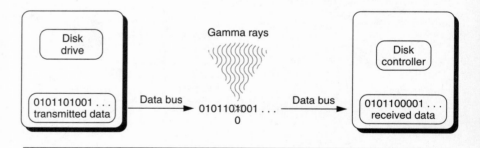

Many things can actually cause data transmission errors. Examples include unusual electrical fields caused by electrical storms, fluctuations in line voltages, a rat with metal braces chewing through a cable, or faulty communication lines. The result is that the received data differs from what was sent. How can we recover the correct data? Some controllers contain error detection or correction logic. The following are common techniques.

- Define a *parity bit* for each word. It makes the number of 1's always even (even parity) or odd (odd parity). If a bit changes, the number of 1's changes, thus making the parity incorrect.

- Define a *checksum* for each block of words. It is the numeric sum of all other words. If some change during transmission, the checksum will usually be wrong.

- *Hamming codes.* Hamming codes can be used not only to detect errors but also to correct them.

For more detailed discussions of these methods, consult references [1–3].

All error-detecting techniques have one thing in common. It takes time to validate the transmitted data. What does this mean in terms of sequencing sector reads from a single track?

Suppose that in the example of Figure 6.11, the controller verifies everything it reads. If it reads sector 2 first, it must verify the integrity of the data. By the time it does this, sector 1 has probably already begun to rotate past the head. In fact, depending on the rotational speed of the disk and the execution time of the error detection algorithm, sector 1 may have already rotated completely past the head. Either way, the controller must wait for it to come around a second time. In this case, the disk must rotate 1 and 3/5 of a revolution for the controller to read both sectors. This is actually longer than the 1 and 2/5 revolutions required when the controller read sector 1 first.

If the verification algorithm requires less time than 3/5 of a revolution takes, a better choice in this example is to read sector 1 first. The drive must wait 3/5 of a revolution to read sector 2, but if the controller must verify what it reads, the wait occurs anyway.

Sector Interleaving

Sometimes the controller cannot choose the order in which to read sectors from a given track. For example, suppose we want to read the first five physical records or blocks of a sequential file. Since sequential files must be read sequentially, there is no choice of which sector to read first. We must first read the one that has the first block, read the one that has the second block, and so on.

However, when the operating system first creates the file, the controller may store its blocks to minimize rotational delays in later reads. That is, the controller may deliberately skip sectors when writing consecutive blocks.

To illustrate this, suppose the disk with five sectors per track takes 0.01 seconds (10 ms) per revolution. Suppose also that error detection takes 3 ms. Read time plus verification time for one sector is 5 ms. During verification, 1.5

sectors rotate past the head. Thus, the controller cannot read the next two sectors without waiting for a full revolution. The best it can do is read every third sector.

What the controller should do is place consecutive blocks two sectors apart. We call this 2:1 *interleaving*. That is, we store consecutive blocks every third sector. Figure 6.13 shows the arrangement of five consecutive blocks using 2:1 interleaving. The controller stores the first block in sector 1, then skips sectors 5 and 4. (Don't forget which direction the disk is rotating.) It then stores the second block in sector 3. Similarly, it skips sectors 2 and 1, then stores the third block in sector 5. It finishes by storing the fourth and fifth blocks in sectors 2 and 4, respectively.

Figure 6.13 Blocks stored using 2:1 interleaving

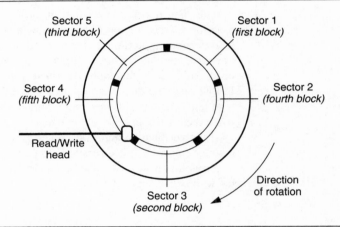

As a final note we should mention that any interleaving ratio can be used. Specifically, n:1 interleaving stores consecutive blocks every $n+1$ sectors. That is, we store a block, skip n sectors, store the next block, skip n sectors, and so on.

But n:1 interleaving does not always work well. What happens if we use 2:1 interleaving on a disk where each track contains 6 sectors (Figure 6.14)? In this case, suppose we start by placing the first block in sector 1. We then skip sectors 6 and 5 and store the second block in sector 4. If we proceed similarly, we must next skip sectors 3 and 2 and store the third block in sector 1. But we already stored the first block there. Thus, 2:1 interleaving does not work if there are 6 sectors per track.

Figure 6.14 2:1 Interleaving on a 6-sector track

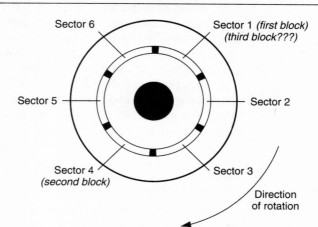

In general, if there are k sectors per track, n :1 interleaving can use all of them only if n +1 and k have no common factors. That is, they are relatively prime. In the first example, 2:1 interleaving works for 5 sectors per track because 2+1 (or 3) and 5 have no common factors. But since 2+1 (or 3) and 6 have a common factor of 2, 2:1 interleaving cannot use all sectors when there are 6 per track.

Describing what happens generally with n :1 interleaving for k sectors per track requires the application of mathematical group theory. We will leave a proof of the above claim to those who are more mathematically inclined.

══ 6.4 Account and File Directories

A typical large computer has hundreds or thousands of users. Each user in turn, may have hundreds of files in his or her account. A little arithmetic shows that an operating system must be able to maintain tens or hundreds of thousands of files. Some systems are even larger. This section answers the following questions:

- How does the system keep track of all the files?
- How does the system keep track of all the users?
- How does it prevent unauthorized users from logging on?
- How does it prevent authorized users from gaining unauthorized access to other files?

Actually the operating system keeps track of things the same way a well–organized programmer keeps track of different modules. It stores pertinent information in disk files. It simply maintains files of information about users and their files. The operating system maintains this information in *directories*. If the information is about user accounts, we call it an *account directory*. If it is about user files, we call it a *file directory*.

Computers have different types of directories, containing different information. This section discusses a simple directory structure known as a *flat directory* or *linear directory*. We will later discuss a more popular approach called a *hierarchical directory*.

Flat directories

In a flat directory, the operating system simply maintains a list of authorized accounts in a file. The computer center assigns each user an account number. The operating system keeps the account numbers in an *account directory*. Only authorized personnel can add to this directory or update its entries. Otherwise, someone could create a bogus account number and allow unauthorized users to access system services.

Figure 6.15 shows a typical flat account directory. Basically, it is a sequential file with one record per account. A large account directory will occupy many disk sectors. They may not all lie on contiguous tracks. Therefore, pointers stored in them must link logically consecutive sectors. The links allow the system to search several sectors to locate a specific account record.

Figure 6.15 Flat account directory

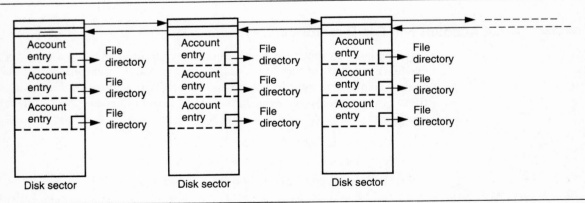

An account record typically contains the following information:

- Account number.
- User name.
- Passwords.
- Priority level.
- Limits such as CPU limits or memory limits. They indicate the maximum amount of a given resource this account may use. For example, if the CPU limit is five minutes, a program running in this account may not exceed five minutes of CPU time.
- Location of a file directory.

When a user wants to log on to the system, he or she turns on a terminal and waits for a message asking for an account number. After the user enters the account number, the system reads it and searches the account directory. The search produces one of two results. The system either finds an entry with the given account number or it does not. If it does not find an entry, it reports that the account number is invalid. The system usually gives the user another chance to enter a valid account number.

If the system found an entry for the account number, it may check for a password. It it does, it asks the user to enter the password and compares it with the one stored in the account entry. If they match, the system will now accept commands from the user. In other words, the user has logged on successfully. Of course, if the password does not match, the system complains. It will not accept commands until the user enters both a valid account number and a valid password (if required).

File Directory. Once a user has logged on, he or she may create, access, or delete files. The system will store information about the files in the account's *file directory*. This directory is again another file that the operating system uses. The operating system stores its location in the entry for the user's account number. Figure 6.16 shows a typical file directory. Like the account directory, it is a system file. It has an entry (record) for each file in a particular account.

A file entry typically contains the following information:

- File name.
- File size (number of bytes or disk sectors).
- File structure. This is necessary in systems that allow different file structures.
- Creation date.
- Date of the last update.
- Expiration date.

- Password. Some systems allow passwording of files to provide additional protection.
- Other accounts that may read this file or write to it.
- Actual disk location of the beginning of the file.
- Current position in file if user is currently reading its records sequentially.

Figure 6.16 Flat file directory

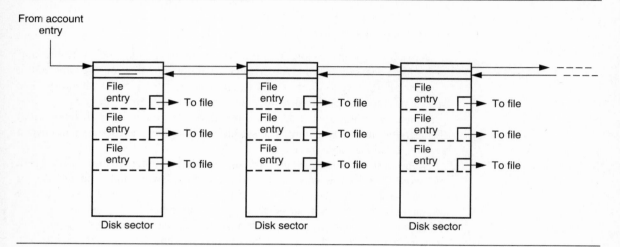

One important thing to note is that the file entry and the file are different. The entry contains information about the file, including its location, but the file entry and the file are separate entities.

When a user enters a command to list all files, the system searches the directory and prints the names of each file in it. If a user calls an editor to change a file, the system locates it through the directory. If the user creates new files, the system inserts new entries into the directory. The new names appear in subsequent requests for file listings. If a user deletes a file, the system deletes the corresponding directory entry.

An interesting note here is that deletion may not actually erase the file. That is, all the system may do is delete the reference to it and free the sectors it occupied, but it does not actually erase. Since the system deleted the references, the user can no longer access the file through conventional means.

But "disk dumps" or other system software can display the contents of unallocated disk sectors. Even sectors that have been reallocated may not be fully used. Thus, old data may still be there. In fact, there are file recovery software and services such as those provided by the popular Norton Utilities that, in some cases, may recover files. This is good if the old data is valuable information lost accidentally through human error or computer failure. However, it can also cause a breach of security or privacy if the old data was classified or confidential. More secure systems clear all sectors occupied by a deleted file. This is comparable to shredding old printouts rather than just tossing them in the garbage. (However, we do not recommend shredding your disks.) Unfortunately, such systems are unforgiving of accidental deletions of important files.

Another tradeoff is that clearing sectors requires disk writes. Remember, clearing a disk sector is the same as writing zeros (or some other constant) to it. Thus, greater security requires more overhead. In cases involving many file deletions (such as student accounts in a university), this overhead can be significant.

Hierarchical Directories

Flat directories provide a simple way of managing account and file information. Unfortunately, they do not always organize the information well, particularly if there is a lot of it. A top–down approach is preferable. As in programming, top–down design uses a hierarchical organization. Professionals have long recognized hierarchical organization as a good way to manage information. Let's see why.

If a user enters a command to list files in a directory, the system prints all the names. If there are just a few files, the user can quickly see what he or she wants. But what if the directory contains hundreds of files? This is too much for a person to absorb or for a screen to hold. Most of it is probably irrelevant (at the moment), anyway. Good information management provides the user with only what he or she needs.

Another problem with a flat directory is that the user must assign different names to each file. Again, this is no problem if there are just a few files. But creating unique names for hundreds of files is a significant task. You often end up with long file names with elaborate prefixes or suffixes just to keep them different. The result is confusion and a lot of extra typing and mistakes.

A hierarchical directory is like the common hierarchical organization of businesses, government agencies, or institutions. There are different levels, as shown in Figure 6.17. At the top is the *root directory*. A user logged into it will generally see only the entries at the next or second level.

But a level may contain other things besides file entries. It can also have *subdirectories* that contain the next level of entries. A subdirectory is itself a directory that may contain file entries and subordinate subdirectories. A user can log into a subdirectory and examine its contents.

Figure 6.17 Hierarchical directory format

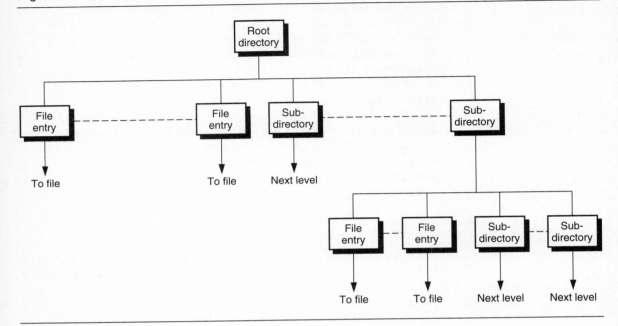

One advantage is that a user logged into a subdirectory sees only what's in it. By defining and naming subdirectories appropriately, the user may enter different places in the hierarchy. If the user groups files belonging to a specific application in a subdirectory, he or she can work just within that subdirectory. This effectively prevents all other information in the directory from cluttering the user's environment. That is, the system hides information irrelevant to current needs. For example, business PC users may have separate directories for word processing documents, spreadsheets, databases, and accounting records. A user need not be concerned with spreadsheet files while writing a letter or updating a mailing list. It is almost like having a separate computer for each distinct task.

To illustrate hierarchical directories, suppose a bookstore keeps all its information on a PC. The materials include a publisher list and files of book titles. However, instead of storing all titles on one file, they are separated by type. For example, paperbacks are separated from hardcovers. Fiction is separated from nonfiction. Horror books are separated from funny ones. Figure 6.18 shows a possible hierarchical arrangement.

Figure 6.18 An example of a hierarchical directory

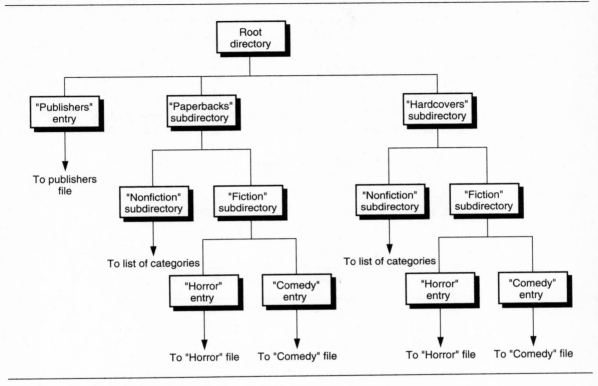

When a user logs on, the directory shows that he has access to a publisher list and two subdirectories called "Paperbacks" and "Hardcovers." To access the "Paperbacks" subdirectory, he enters a command that makes it the current (working) directory, effectively ignoring the other directory.

Once in the "Paperbacks" subdirectory, the user sees entries for subdirectories "Nonfiction" and "Fiction." To print all "Fiction" titles, he makes "Fiction" the working directory. Once in it, he has access to files "Horror" and "Comedy" which contain book titles. Similarly, the "Hardcovers" subdirectory contains entries for subdirectories "Nonfiction" and "Fiction." As before, the "Fiction" subdirectory contains files "Horror" and "Comedy."

Note that there are two files named "Horror" and two named "Comedy." Since they are in different directories, this is allowed. Also, there are two subdirectories named "Fiction" and two named "Nonfiction." Again, because they are in different directories, this is allowed. The user does not have to create distinct names for each file. He simply organizes the information as if he were placing it in folders inside a file cabinet.

Use of Icons in Hierarchical Directories. The beauty of a hierarchical organization is that the user need not even explicitly be aware of it. Some systems such as Macintosh and Windows use *icons* (graphic images) to represent files and subdirectories.

For example, a picture of a folder may represent a subdirectory, and a different image may represent a file. Figure 6.19a shows the view of a user logged into the root directory of Figure 6.18. The folders "Paperbacks" and "Hardcovers" correspond to the subdirectories of Figure 6.18. A folder indicates there is additional information inside it. The other image represents a data file.

Figure 6.19a View from root directory using icons

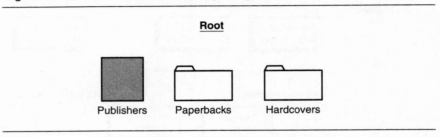

The user may open (enter) the "Paperbacks" folder (subdirectory) and see what it contains. Figure 6.19b shows the view.

Figure 6.19b View from "Paperbacks" subdirectory of root directory

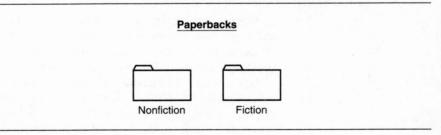

Once in the " Paperbacks" folder, the user sees folders for "Nonfiction" and "Fiction." They represent two additional subdirectories. If the user opens the "Fiction" folder, he or she sees two images indicating the two files "Horror" and "Comedy" (Figure 6.19c) which contain book titles.

Figure 6.19c View from "Fiction" subdirectory of "Paperbacks" subdirectory

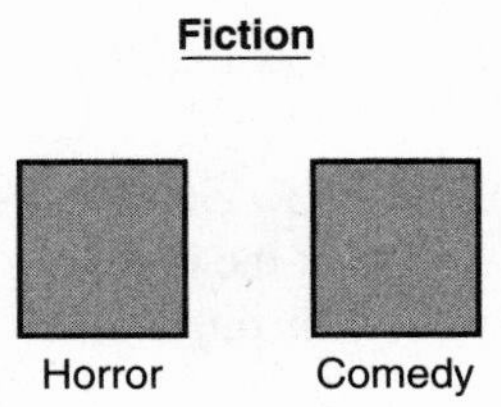

Fiction

Horror   Comedy

A hierarchical organization is well suited to the user who has many files for distinct applications. At any time, he or she can enter the appropriate subdirectory and effectively block out everything not associated with it. This greatly simplifies the view of accessible information. It is the computerized version of "tunnel vision" or picking a particular file cabinet or drawer.

Sharing Hierarchical Directories. Hierarchical directories are also helpful when several users share accounts. In a flat directory all users see the same files. They not only must develop elaborate naming mechanisms, but they must also avoid conflicts. No two people can use the same file name. Otherwise, one could accidentally erase or corrupt another's file.

In a hierarchical directory system, several users may log into the same root directory. Each one can then create his or her own subdirectory. When working in the subdirectory, the user need not be concerned with file names in other subdirectories. For all intents and purposes, each has his or her own directory.

But the hierarchical organization allows users to share files. One can enter another's directory if he or she needs access to specific files. Users can work in their own areas or in shared directories, as the need dictates. Herein lies a major advantage of hierarchical directories over flat directories. The ability to share files is particularly important when many people are working on a joint project such as a large software system, a long report, or a new product.

The author remembers an experience with 3 students who were working together to create a database in a flat directory system. During their testing, they came across a problem and brought it to their instructor. The instructor asked, "Are you sure you all gave your files distinct names?" The first student and second student said yes. The third student just looked around and said, very quietly, "Uh–oh."

Directory Paths. As we discuss hierarchical directories, the inquisitive reader may ask the following questions:

- How does the operating system handle multiple files with the same names?
- How can a user in one subdirectory reference a file in another, especially if the file name is duplicated? How does the operating system distinguish the files?

The file directory of Figure 6.18 contains two files called "Horror." But they are in different subdirectories. Does the system actually see two files with the same name? For each name that a user assigns to a file or subdirectory, the system maintains a prefix. It is the *path name* from the root to the current directory. The path name from the root to a subdirectory is the concatenation of all subdirectory names in between, separated by a symbol such as a back–slash. Thus the path name "root\Paperbacks\Fiction" specifies the "Fiction" subdirectory in the "Paperbacks" subdirectory. Similarly, the path name "root\Hardcovers\Fiction" specifies the "Fiction" subdirectory in the "Hardcovers" subdirectory.

When the user references a file in the current subdirectory, the operating system prefixes it with the path name. Thus, although the user may refer to two files by the name "Horror" the system does not. For example, suppose the user is currently in the "Fiction" subdirectory in the "Paperbacks" subdirectory and references the file "Horror." The system references the file "root\Paperbacks\Fiction\Horror." If the user is in the other "Fiction" sub-directory and references "Horror," the system references "root\Hardcovers\Fiction\Horror." The system has distinct names for the two files. In general, when a user references a file, he or she need not specify the path name. If not, as the previous example showed, the system assumes the path name leading to the current subdirectory as a default.

However, a user can reference a file in another subdirectory by explicitly specifying the path name. He or she need not change working directories. This can save programming steps. For example, a user logged into the "Paperbacks" subdirectory can reference a file called "root\Hardcovers\Fiction\Horror." This reference tells the system the user wants a file in another subdirectory.

Systems ranging from personal computers to supercomputers use hierarchical directories. Designers have recognized the advantage of this kind of organization. Section 6.6 describes how MS–DOS supports a hierarchical directory structure. Also, Chapter 8 discusses the Unix implementation of hierarchical directories.

===== 6.5 File Access Techniques

The previous section described how an operating system tracks accounts and files. We saw two different directory structures. Through a directory, operating system routines can find a disk file. There are questions, however, that directories do not answer. For example, how can we read records after locating the file? How can we store new records in a file?

The answers to these questions depend on the file's *structure*. The structure is the relationship between the logical organization of records and the physical organization. The way a user perceives data is not necessarily the way the system actually stores it. For example, the fact that a user can retrieve records sequentially does not mean they are stored that way. In fact, we shall see that sometimes the actual records are stored randomly. The file's structure dictates how the system stores and removes information.

This section discusses three common access techniques: *sequential access, direct access,* and *indexed* or *keyed access.* Sequential access allows the system to handle records sequentially. Direct access allows it to handle them through the specification of their relative position in the file. Indexed or keyed access allows the system to handle them by specifying a predefined value. The value is often a field (called the *key field*) of the desired record.

The three access techniques represent common capabilities required in many applications. Of course, this section can only introduce management techniques. Additional material is in file structures textbooks such as reference [5].

Sequential Access

The simplest access technique is the sequential method. Simply put, it means the user can access records sequentially; that is, the first read gets the first record. The second read gets the second record and so on. If the user wants the twenty fifth record, he or she must read the previous twenty-four.

File structures that provide only sequential access have many limitations, but the internal storage structure is simple. Sequential files are useful as backups (copies) or as temporary storage moving data between applications. In both cases, users are unlikely to probe the file in detail. They are more likely just to load or move all or a large part of it.

Tape files are always sequential. A tape's characteristics simply do not allow reading in any other way. Generally, the system groups records into blocks and stores them consecutively as Figures 6.3 and 6.4 illustrate.

The system may also store disk files sequentially. However, it is often impractical to store records in consecutive disk sectors. Even if the system found enough consecutive sectors to hold the file, what happens if we add records? We would need to leave extra sectors available for growth or rearrange all the sectors so they are consecutive again. This would lead to fragmentation and waste. A better approach is necessary in a dynamic environment where sectors are frequently allocated and released in random patterns.

Consequently, some systems will link the disk sectors assigned to a file. Figure 6.20 shows one way to do this. The system stores as many records in a sector as will fit. It stores excess records in other sectors. But where are they?

Figure 6.20 Sequentially stored records

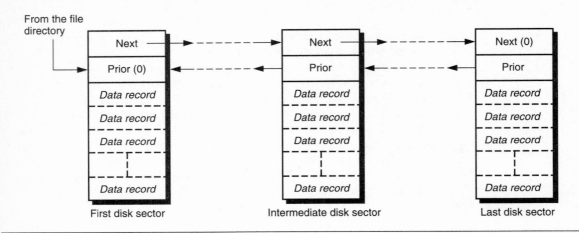

The system does not use the entire sector for data storage. Instead, it uses several bytes to indicate the next and previous sectors. The system can then store groups of records consecutively in a sector, and it can treat the sectors as nodes in a linked list. Thus, each sector may lie anywhere on the disk. The file directory contains a pointer to the first sector.

The sequential nature of this structure is a direct result of the links. The system cannot read records from the second sector until after it has read the first sector. Remember, it does not know where the second sector is until it finds out from the first sector. Note that the system need not read every record in sequence. But it must read the sectors in sequence to reach one containing a desired record. But, as we saw previously, reading the sector is the most time consuming part of reading a record anyway.

Direct Access

There is a major disadvantage of sequential files in applications that require a lot of searching for records. Typical examples are credit card verification, banking transactions, and membership renewals. The operations are usually simple; finding the correct records in essentially random order is most of the work. If the file has many records, it occupies many sectors. Each search will require reading a long sequence of sectors. The controller must process and schedule each read request. The wait for scheduling, seek time, and latency time for each read all make the search time consuming.

A common alternative, especially in personal computers, is direct access. Direct access files allow sequential processing of records, but are not limited to it. If a user wants the fiftieth record in a file, he or she need not read the first forty-nine. The user codes a command with a parameter specifying the fiftieth record.

For example, consider a high–level language command:

```
GET filenum,recnum
```

The integer value for *recnum* is a relative record number in the file. On executing this command, the system retrieves the contents of the record and stores it in a buffer. If *recnum* is 50, the system retrieves the fiftieth record. Furthermore, it does this without reading the first forty-nine records.

How does the system find a specific record without reading all the previous ones? The method we describe is generalized. However, the concepts are common and provide a natural introduction to the MS–DOS case study at the end of the chapter.

Figure 6.21 shows how a system may find a record, based on its relative position in the file. When the system creates the file, it uses whatever disk sectors are available. However, in contrast to the previous example, it does not link the sectors. We may consider them to be at random locations.

Recall that the file's directory entry contains information about it. The last section described some information that may be in the entry. Of particular use to us now is the record size and the addresses of allocated sectors. Figure 6.21 shows sector addresses stored consecutively in the directory entry. The first address is that of the first sector, the second address is the address of the second sector, and so on.

Figure 6.21 Directly accessible records

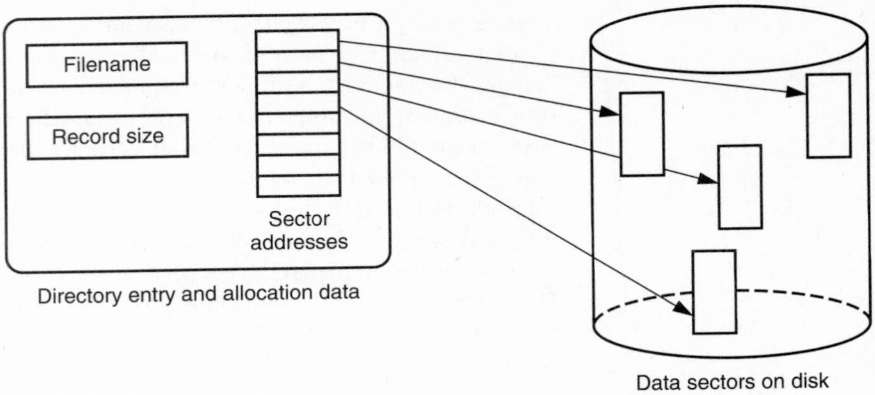

Directory entry and allocation data

Data sectors on disk

In some cases, the entry may not contain actual sector addresses but a sector number instead. Still, the system can use the information it does contain to determine or calculate the sector addresses. This is a system-dependent process. The key point is that the entry information can lead us to any desired sector. For simplicity, we assume the entry contains the actual addresses.

To see how the system finds a specific record, assume that it stores records consecuti ely in a sector. The number that fit in a sector depends on the size of both the sector and the record.

To illustrate, suppose a sector holds 512 bytes and a record is 64 bytes. The number of records that fit in a sector is given by the formula

$$\text{\# records on a sector} = (\text{capacity of one sector}) \text{ DIV } (\text{size of one record}) \quad (6.1)$$

We use the Pascal notation "DIV" for integer division. Here, the number of records per sector is 512 DIV 64 or 8. Therefore, records numbered 1 through 8 are in the file's first sector. Call it logical sector 1. Records 9 through 16 are in logical sector 2, and so on. You may always calculate the logical sector number from the logical record number as follows:

$$\text{Logical sector number} = (\text{logical record number} - 1) \text{ DIV } (\text{\# records on a sector}) + 1 \quad (6.2)$$

In the current example, Equation 6.2 reduces to

$$\text{Logical sector number} = (\text{logical record number} - 1) \text{ DIV } 8 + 1$$

You should convince yourself that this is correct. Choose a few logical record numbers and determine the logical sectors in which they reside.

Once we have computed the logical sector number, there remains the matter of choosing the correct record in the sector. Since the system stores records consecutively in a sector, we need the record's position. Assume the position of the first record in a sector is 1. We can calculate the position from the equation

record position =
    (logical record number - 1) MOD (# records per sector) + 1   (6.3)

The MOD operation, like the Pascal MOD operator, calculates an integer remainder. As before, you should do this calculation with a couple of examples to get familiar with the process.

Now, when a program requests a specific logical record, the system does the following:

- Determines the logical record size from the file directory.
- Determines the sector capacity, a system–defined parameter.
- Calculates the number of records per sector using Equation 6.1.
- Calculates the logical sector number using Equation 6.2.
- Finds the logical sector address from information in the directory entry.
- Calculates the position of the record within the sector using Equation 6.3.
- Moves the record to a buffer.

Let's see how this process works for specific numbers. Suppose we want to retrieve the contents of logical record 50. As before, assume that the sector capacity is 512 bytes and each record is 64 bytes. Now let's go through the steps and see what values we get:

Step 1: The logical record size is assumed to be 64 bytes.
Step 2: The sector capacity is assumed to be 512 bytes.
Step 3: Equation 6.1 yields 512 DIV 64 = 8 records per sector.
Step 4: Equation 6.2 yields 49 DIV 8 + 1= 7 as the logical sector number. Thus, the fiftieth record is in the seventh sector.
Step 5: The system finds the seventh sector's address from the directory.
Step 6: Equation 6.3 yields 49 MOD 8 + 1= 2 as the position of the record in logical sector 7. Thus, the fiftieth record is the second record in the seventh sector. (Almost sounds like playing the horses.)
Step 7: Move the record to a buffer.

As Table 6.6 shows, logical record 50 is indeed the second record in logical sector 7.

Table 6.6 Logical record and logical sector numbers

Logical Record Numbers	Logical Sector Numbers
1 – 8	1
9 – 16	2
17 – 24	3
25 – 32	4
33 – 40	5
41 – 48	6
49 – 56	7

Access by Index Value

For large files, direct access can save a lot of time compared to sequential access. The simple fact that the system does not need to read each sector physically to find its successor reduces overhead significantly. As a result, direct access files are quite powerful.

Yet there is a disadvantage to direct access. The user must specify the position of a record in the file, but he or she may not always know this or want to be bothered with it. For example, when you withdraw money from a bank, the teller must access your account. He or she is unlikely to know the relative position of your account in the bank's files. Instead, he or she knows only your account through an account number. Thus, the next question is, "Can the system find a record in a file if it knows just one of its fields?" We call this field the *key field* or *index field*.

The answer is "Yes," and there are a number of ways to do it. One way is for the system to maintain an internal table that associates a record's index field value with the record's position in the file. We can then proceed as before.

Another way is to use a *hash function* to calculate a location within a file, based on the index field's value. The user supplies the field's contents, and the system uses it to calculate the disk address of the sector containing the record. The system can then search the sector for a record that has the index field specified by the user.

Yet another way is to use a directory with entries containing a specific index value and the location of the record within the file. This is similar to a book index in a book that allows you to look up an entry and find the location (page number) where it is discussed. You need not search an entire book to find something, but you usually must search the page that the index referenced.

Files Indexed by B-trees. Some systems access records through a hierarchical structure of index values called *B-Trees*. This type of file organization is important because it allows an individual record to be accessed quickly and also allows it to be accessed sequentially, in order of key field.

Figure 6.22 shows a general organization of a file based on a B–Tree structure. Each node is actually a disk sector. The system stores all records in sectors corresponding to leaf nodes in the B–Tree. Furthermore, leaf nodes contain *only* records, and all are at the same level of the tree. We call them *data nodes*.

Figure 6.22 B-Tree structure with index nodes and data nodes

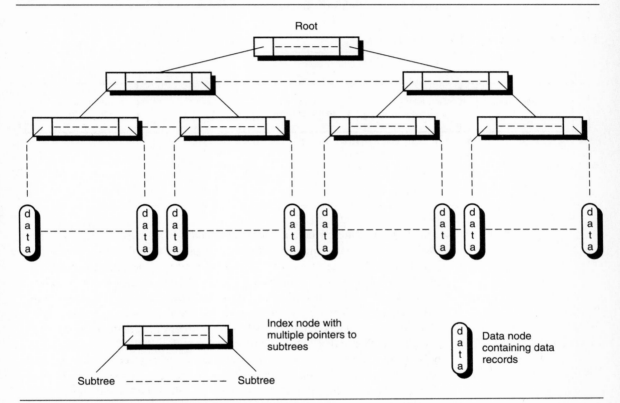

The system stores records in a data node according to the value of their key fields or indexes. Furthermore, it organizes data nodes (leaf nodes) so the records are in increasing order of index value from left to right in the figure. The leftmost data node contains records with the smallest index values, and the rightmost node contains ones with the largest index values.

Nonleaf nodes do not contain data records. Instead, they contain index values and pointers to the child nodes at the tree's next level. We call them *index nodes*. Each index node may have many children. However, the number of children normally lies between $k/2$ and k, where k is an integer. We call this a *B–Tree of order k*. This requirement simplifies insertion and deletion algorithms.

Figure 6.23 describes index nodes in more detail. This particular node has exactly k children. Each child is the root of a subtree that contains some of the tree's data nodes. We label the subtrees T_j for $j = 1$ through k. Because of the ordering of the records by index value, the following discussion shows how we may define the fields of an index node.

Figure 6.23 Structure of B-Tree index node

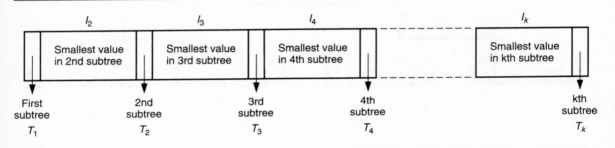

Let T_j be a subtree, where j is between 1 and k-1 inclusive. Each record from a data node in T_j has a smaller index value than any record from a data node in T_{j+1}. That is, T_1 contains records with smaller index values than the ones in T_2. Tree T_2 contains records with smaller index values than the ones in T_3, and so on. This fact is critical in storing and retrieving data records from the structure.

Besides child pointers, each index node also contains up to k-1 index values. In fact, it has one index value for each subtree except T_1. The first value, in field I_2, is the smallest index value in any record stored in data nodes in subtree T_2. The second value, in field I_3, is the smallest one in any record stored in data nodes in T_3. In general, for any value of j between 2 and k inclusive, the index value, in field I_j, is the smallest value in any record stored in data nodes in the jth subtree. This, of course, assumes there is a jth subtree. If not, there is no index value, and the corresponding field is unused.

To locate a record containing a specific index value, the system first examines the root index node. The information in each index node indicates which subtree contains the desired record if it exists. The following partially pseudocoded program describes the logic to locate a record in a data node of a B–Tree:

```
Procedure FindRecord(filename, IndexValue,...);
{"filename" is the file's name and "IndexValue" is the
desired record's index value}
Begin
  Locate the root index node from the file directory entry
  for "filename";
  Repeat
    If there is a j, 2 ≤ j < k, for which value in
      Iⱼ ≤ IndexValue < value in Iⱼ₊₁ then
      locate the node that is the root of subtree Tⱼ
    Else if IndexValue < I₂ value in then
      locate the node that is the root of subtree T₁
    Else if value in Iₖ ≤ IndexValue then
      locate the node that is the root of subtree Tₖ ;
  Until the located node is a data node;
  Search the current data node for the desired record. If
  it is not there, it is not in the file. If it is, return
  it or its location via other procedure parameters.
End;
```

This hierarchical structure of index values is especially powerful for very large files containing tens or hundreds of thousands of records. Let us see how this works by considering the example of Figure 6.24.

Suppose that record lengths and sector capacities allow the system to store just ten records per sector (data node). Also assume that the index field and pointer fields allow ninety-nine index values and 100 pointers per sector (index node). Now suppose that we want to store 100,000 records with index values i_1, i_2, through $i_{100,000}$. Furthermore, suppose that

$$i_1 < i_2 < i_3 <, \ldots, < i_{100,000}.$$

To store 100,000 records at ten records per sector, the system will require 10,000 data nodes (sectors). In this example, each index node can have up to 100 children. Therefore, let us group the 10,000 data nodes into groups of 100. All data nodes in a group have the same index node as a parent. Thus, there are 100 index nodes at the level immediately above the data nodes. Index nodes, in turn, may also have a common parent. In this case, the common parent of all 100 index nodes is the root node. Thus, we have a B–Tree with three levels, two levels of index nodes and one of data nodes.

Figure 6.24 B-Tree containing records indexed on values i_1 through $i_{100,000}$

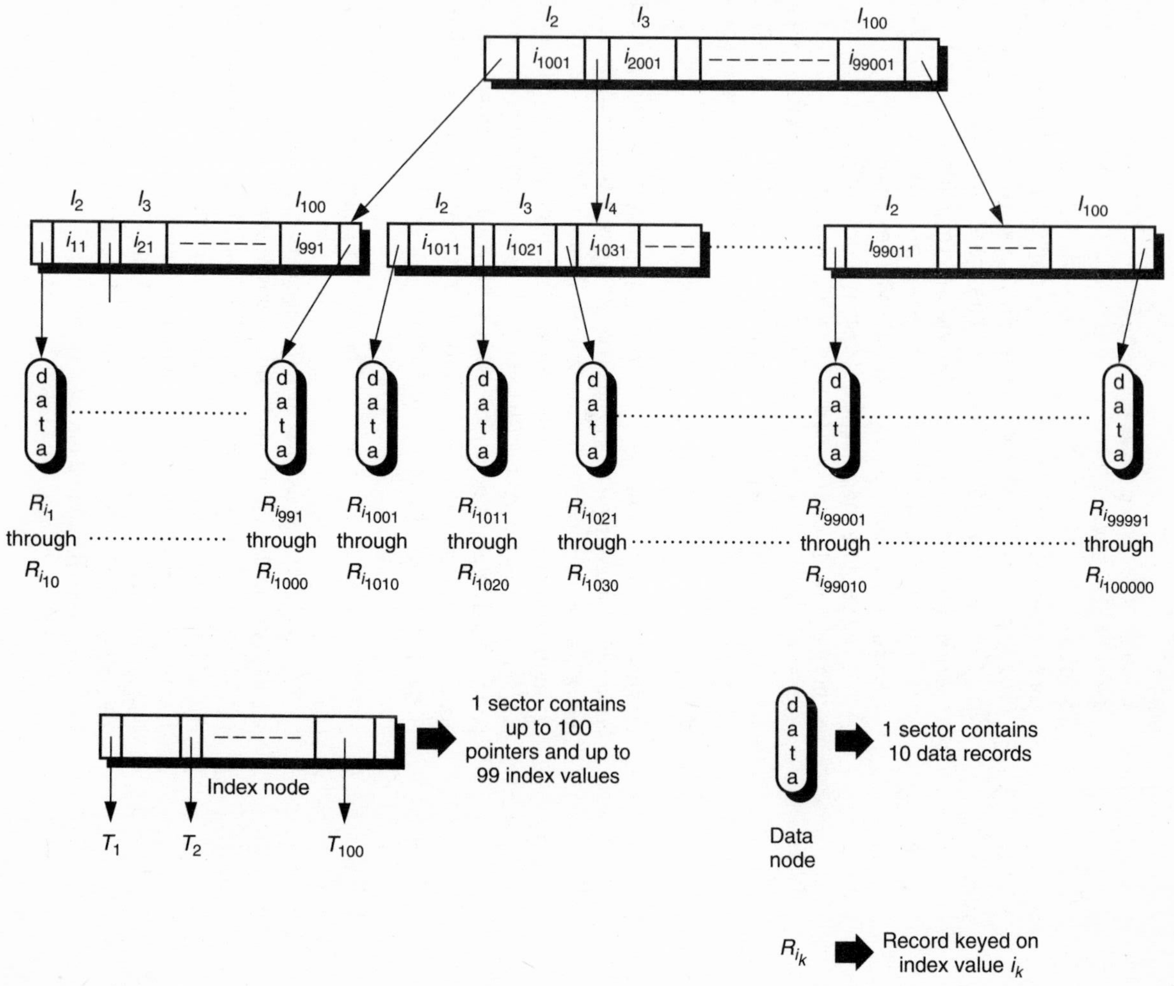

We can access the records with index values i_1 through i_{1000} via the leftmost subtree of the root node. The first index value stored in the root node is the smallest value of any record in the second subtree. Since records with index values i_{1001} through i_{2000} are in the data nodes of the second subtree the first index value stored is i_{1001}. Similarly, the second index value, stored in the root node is i_{2001}, and so on.

Suppose we want to find the record with index value i_{1025}. The system locates the root index node and determines that $i_{1001} \leq i_{1025} < i_{2001}$. The system next locates the second child of the root node. It also is an index node. For it, the system determines that $i_{1021} \leq i_{1025} < i_{1031}$. Next, the system locates the third child of the current index node. However, it is a data node containing records with index values i_{1021} through i_{1030}. The system may now search it and find the record with index value i_{1025}.

In this example, the system can find any of 100,000 records with just three sector reads. That is impressive! How many of you can find one of 100,000 books in a library without looking at more than three cards in the catalog? If your card catalog system is not computerized, you invariably will scan through dozens of cards before finding the one you want.

What makes this technique so powerful is that the B–Tree is very wide but shallow; that is, there are few levels and each node has many children. In this case, there are 100 nodes at the second level. There are 100^2, or 10,000 nodes at the third level. This allows access to any of 100,000 records. A fourth level could have up to 100^3 or 1,000,000 nodes. It would allow access to 10,000,000 (that's right, ten million) records with just 4 sector reads.

As you might expect, this structure does involve some overhead. The example requires 101 disk sectors to be used for index nodes. Of course, with 10,000 data nodes, the 101 index nodes represent only a 1% increase in the total number of sectors required. Insertion and deletion algorithms deal mainly with maintaining the structure of the index node. Specific algorithms to add and delete records appear in many data structures or file structures textbooks such as references [5, 21, 22, 25].

═══════ **6.6 Security**

The availability of peripherals that can hold large amounts of information is a significant factor in the growth of computer systems. Early computers did little more than just compute or calculate. The use of a computer as an "information manager" was nonexistent. Now, in some cases, they do very little computing: Computers are information managers. Their main function is to store, retrieve, and generally manage large amounts of information. This is feasible only because peripherals such as high–speed disk drives can hold the information.

Information is readily available to the software that needs it. It is easily transported from one location to another. In this era of "user friendly" systems, information is easily accessible to a user who knows how to get it: but therein lies a major problem. What if we don't want that user to get that information? Marketing strategies and productivity demand that information be easy to access, yet security sometimes demands that it be difficult to access, at least for some people. These two requirements are constantly in conflict.

For example, a university registrar may use a database to track registration records. They include student, course, and faculty information. The personnel office may use the same database to manage payroll and fringe benefits for faculty. The system should allow the registrar's office access to faculty information needed to process registration records. However, registrar personnel have no business accessing salary or fringe benefit information. How can we prevent an authorized user from the registrar's office from accessing certain parts of faculty record? This section describes some measures used to make a system more secure.

Common Sense

Oddly enough, one effective security measure has nothing to do with sophisticated software or clever coding algorithms. It is, in fact, common sense. Here are some easy ways to avoid common but nasty problems.

Create Backups. You have just finished an important project and have all the code on a floppy disk. You decide to celebrate and put your books and disks in your car during a weekend vacation. While you celebrate, your car bakes in the Arizona desert sun. When you retrieve your disks, they are blobs of hot, black plastic. Too bad you didn't make copies before you left.

Lock Up Valuable Data. You work for a research firm that has just completed months of gathering important secret data such as the president's Christmas card list. The data is on a tape in your desk drawer. When you return from lunch, you find your desk has been searched and the tape is gone. Too bad you didn't lock your desk or put the tape in a locked vault. Could all these fresh reindeer droppings mean that Santa Claus was the culprit or are they just a ruse?

Change Passwords Frequently and Use Imaginative Ones. You frequently must log on to a time sharing system and for convenience you use the password M–I–N–E since it is easy to type. One day as you log on, a colleague who is jealous of your recent successes (such as getting the

"Employee of the Month" parking space), sees you type your password. A short password is easy to spot, particularly if you tape it to the front of your terminal. When you come back from vacation, you find that someone has been in your account and tampered with important work. You wish you had used a more complex password, taped it to the inside of your locked desk, and changed it more often.

Keep Your Mouth Shut. One day during lunch, you have a couple of potent orange sodas to drink. You and your associates discuss unusual passwords. Your current one is clever and becomes part of the conversation. The next day, when you log on to the system, you find that all your files have been deleted. They can be restored through system backups, but one contains information needed for a meeting with your manager in ten minutes. No more three orange soda lunches for you!

The above scenarios describe problems you can avoid with a little common sense and care. Always make copies of important data. Even if you are careful with disks or tapes, there is no guarantee that malfunctioning drives will not destroy them. Major computer centers regularly copy user files as a precaution against such problems. Keep sensitive data in secure locations. By definition, sensitive means there are people who should not see it. Keep passwords secret and use ones that are not easy to guess. You may as well not have a password if you do not guard it or it is obvious.

A recent story described a company that was concerned about security in their data processing department. They hired an investigator to look around to test their security. He claimed that he had to take pictures for use in company advertising. He received a lot of cooperation as people logged on and helped shield the terminal screens from reflective lights. He found one secure room, the one that held the coffee money. Security is difficult enough to guarantee when all involved are careful. It is impossible to guarantee if people are careless and loose–lipped.

═══

Disk Erasures

One common way to breach security is to discard information carelessly. Old computer printouts fed through a paper shredder are virtually impossible to piece back together. But what about deleted disk files? Section 6.3 shows that each user has a directory the system can use to find disk space allocated to his or her files. If a user deletes a file, is it really gone? Not necessarily. In some cases, deleting a file really means deleting the directory entry. In other words, the system deletes the reference to the file. Figures 6.25a through 6.25c show what can happen in such systems.

Figure 6.25a shows a user's directory with an entry for an "important file." It contains important data, such as payroll information or the office football pool. At some point, user *A* decides she no longer needs the file and deletes it.

Figure 6.25a User *A*'s directory before "important file" is deleted

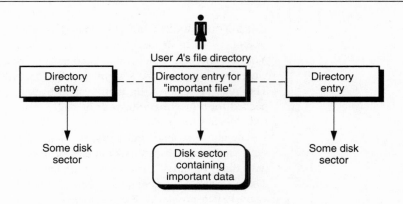

Figure 6.25b shows what the system may do. It has deleted the directory entry to "important file." As far as user *A* is concerned, it is no longer there. The sector containing the data is marked as available. As such, the system can allocate it to another file when needed. But, the data is still there. If the computer is an IBM PC, the master spy need only invest in an inexpensive copy of the Norton Utilities to recover it. In practice, the system may actually hand over the data, just as if it had been paid off.

Figure 6.25b User *A* deletes important file

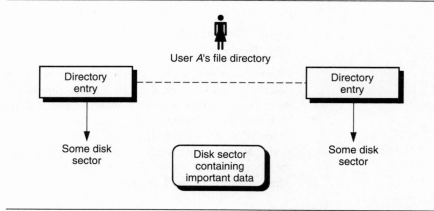

Suppose that user *B* creates a new file. The system looks for unused sectors it may allocate. Figure 6.25c shows what happens if the system allocates the sector with important data to user *B*'s file.

Figure 6.25c User *B* allocated sector with important data

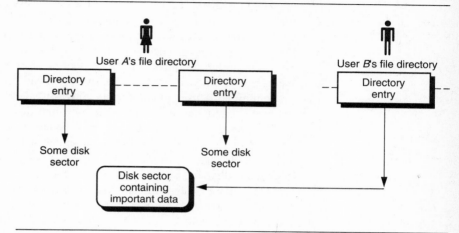

User *B* now has a disk sector containing the important data. Of course, if user *B* fills the sector with his own data, the important data will be destroyed. But what if *B* uses only part of the sector? Then part of the important data is still there. User *B* can use any utility routines that dump disk sectors to retrieve it.

Now, the fact that user *B* has access to important data is due to chance. He happened to create a file at the right (or wrong?) time. Consequently, the system allocated the sector. But the fact that security is breached due to chance is usually small consolation. This is especially true if your payroll record is in the file, and *B* finds out you make a lot more than he does. *B* can create a lot of problems by simply posting the last payroll on the company bulletin board.

How can the system prevent this? Some systems erase sectors they release due to file deletions or name changes. If the data is destroyed, the situation described in Figure 6.25 cannot occur.

Restricted Accesses

Disk erasures prevent unauthorized access to logically deleted data. But how can we prevent unauthorized access to other data? How can you stop someone from examining your files? In some cases, you may want to allow others to see your files but not change their contents.

For example, three and a half inch disks have a switch in one corner that can write protect the contents. Programs can read the disk but not write on it. This keeps users from accidentally overwriting important code or data. Imagine accidentally entering a command to erase a disk when the switch is not set.

On time shared systems, the file directory entry may contain a list of accounts that have access. If anyone tries to access the file from an unauthorized account, the system intervenes and prevents it. The user who created the file may specify accounts that have access to it. File directory entries may also contain passwords assigned to a file at creation. Anyone who tries to access the file must enter the password. The user who created the file defines the password. As with accounts, file passwords should be changed periodically.

Sometimes a user may want to allow only limited access to a file. For example, airline reservation systems must allow agents to access flight information. It should also allow them to make some changes such as booking or cancelling reservations. However, it should not allow them to change flight information such as arrival or departure times, or worse yet, cancelling or adding unauthorized flights.

Finally, a user may want a program to have different access rights to a file at different points. One part may create or update a file, whereas another part only reads it. In the latter case, the user may disallow write privileges to prevent accidental changes caused by program errors.

Files may have *access modes* assigned at the time they are opened. An access mode indicates allowed types of accesses. Typical modes are:

- **Read**. The file can only be read. An attempt to change will produce an error message or cause the program to abort.

- **Write**. The file can only be written, and (generally) read as well.

- **Execute**. The file can be loaded into memory and executed. However, it cannot be read or changed.

≡

Locks and Keys

Access modes are especially useful in database systems where many users have access to many different types of records. A database designer can assign an access mode to each record and perhaps even to each field. The latter ability allows a user access to some fields of a record but not others.

Some systems work on a *lock and key* basis; that is, a designer assigns lock values to records and fields. He or she also defines a password that users must have to access the database. But the designer may also associate key values with a given password. They are normally invisible to the user. However, when he or she tries to access a given field, the lock value associated with it must match a key value associated with the password.

For example, suppose a university database contains records with assigned lock values of the following types:

Faculty = Record	Lock Value = 1
Name : Character String;	Lock Value = 1
Department : Character String;	Lock Value = 1
Salary : Real;	Lock Value = 3
End;	

Student = Record	Lock Value = 2
Name : Character String;	Lock Value = 2
Credits : Integer;	Lock Value = 4
GPA : Real;	Lock Value = 4
FinancialAidRcvd : Real;	Lock Value = 5
End;	

The fields are all self explanatory, but what do the lock values mean? Suppose there are three major users of the database: the registrar, financial aids office, and personnel office. Each has needs and requires access to different data.

For example, the registrar must have access to faculty records with the exception of the "Salary" field and to student records with the exception of the "FinancialAidRcvd" field. Furthermore, it must be able to update the student "Credits" and "GPA" fields. The personnel office needs access to the entire faculty record and should be able to update (preferably increase) the "Salary" field. Finally, the financial aids office must have access to the "Name" and "FinancialAidRcvd" fields of the student record and be able to change the "FinancialAidRcvd" field. The last ability is particularly important when the football quarterback needs a new car in a hurry.

The database designer assigns locks to the records and fields as indicated earlier. The reason is to control access to information by different users. Furthermore, the designer defines passwords and associated key values for the three major users as follows.

Registrar	Personnel	Financial Aids
PASSWORD = "p1"	PASSWORD = "p2"	PASSWORD = "p3"
KEYS = 1(R), 2(R), 4(W)	KEYS = 1(R), 3(W)	KEYS = 2(R), 5(W)

The "R" (read) or "W" (write) after each key value indicates access mode.

The registrar can read anything with a lock value of 1 or 2, and write anything with a lock value of 4. Thus, the registrar can read the entire faculty record except "Salary." This is because "Salary" has a lock value of 3, and password *p1* has no associated key value of 3. Furthermore, the registrar can read the entire student record except "FinancialAidRcvd." (Why?) In addition, the key value of 4 has an associated write mode. This means the registrar can change the "Credits" and "GPA" fields, exactly as the designer wanted.

The personnel office can read anything with a lock value of 1 and change anything with a lock value of 3. Thus, the personnel office can read the entire faculty record and can alter the "Salary" field, but it cannot access the student record at all.

Can you determine what the financial aids office may access?

There are good reasons why the system controls access to files instead of allowing the users to read or write them directly. This allows users to define many different protection mechanisms. The system then acts as an enforcer making sure that no unauthorized accesses occur.

Encryption

Despite all measures for protecting files, there are still people who are clever enough to overcome them. To believe a system provides an absolute guarantee of privacy is wishful thinking. There will always be someone who considers defeating security measures to be an exciting challenge. Sometimes he or she can meet the challenge. A computer center director once remarked about a person who can defeat the system's security, "If he works for us, fire him; if not, hire him." (The thought applies to "she" and "her" also.)

An additional security measure is to store data in an altered format. We call this *encryption* or *ciphering*. That is, when an authorized user stores data in a file, a procedure changes its format. Anyone gaining unauthorized access to the data sees only the altered format.

Of course, if an authorized user wants to read the data, another procedure must restore its original form. We call this *decryption* or *deciphering*.

Figures 6.26a and 6.26b show a simple encryption/decryption process. Suppose we want to store the message SECRET DATA in a file in encrypted form. That is, we want to change it into something that appears to be nonsensical (of course, many classified documents have that characteristic even without encryption). Recall that a system stores characters in a code, say ASCII. Figure 6.26a shows the ASCII hexadecimal version of each character in the message.

Figure 6.26a Simple encryption method (add 1)

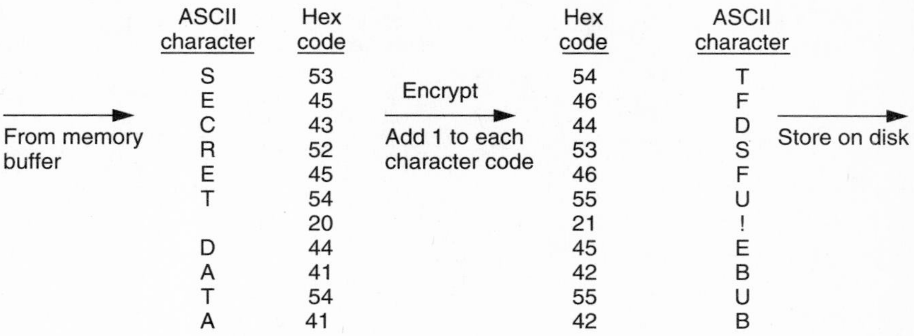

	ASCII character	Hex code		Hex code	ASCII character	
	S	53		54	T	
	E	45	Encrypt	46	F	
	C	43		44	D	
From memory	R	52	Add 1 to each	53	S	Store on disk
buffer	E	45	character code	46	F	
	T	54		55	U	
		20		21	!	
	D	44		45	E	
	A	41		42	B	
	T	54		55	U	
	A	41		42	B	

We can encrypt the message by adding 1 to each code. The result is that each character is replaced by another. This is called a *subsitution* or *Caesar cipher*. The following Pascal–like program does this.

```
Procedure Encrypt;
Var
   X : Char;
   I : Integer;
Begin
   Repeat
      Get X from memory buffer;  {Get a character from the
                                  memory buffer}
      I := Ord(X);              {Calculate the hex code for
                                  the ASCII character in X}
      X := CHR(I+1)            {Assign a new ASCII
                                  character corresponding to
                                  the hex code I+1}
      Write(file, X);          {Write the encrypted ASCII
                                  character to the file}
   Until buffer is empty
End.
```

The result of adding 1 to the hex code of each character in the message SECRET DATA is TFDSFU!EBUB. That looks like the acronym for some government agency, cancer–causing chemical, or airline baggage destination, depending on how large a tip you gave.

To read the data, we must first decrypt it. If we encrypted it by adding 1 to the hex code for each character, we decrypt by reversing the process. That is, we subtract 1 from each hex code. Figure 6.26b shows the message as read and decrypted.

Figure 6.26b Simple decryption method (subtract 1)

	ASCII character	Hex code		Hex code	ASCII character	
	S	53	Decrypt	54	T	
	E	45		46	F	
	C	43	←	44	D	
←	R	52	Subtract 1	53	S	←
To memory buffer	E	45	from each	46	F	Retrieve from disk
	T	54	character code	55	U	
		20		21	!	
	D	44		45	E	
	A	41		42	B	
	T	54		55	U	
	A	41		42	B	

In this case decrypting is easy, as the following program illustrates.

```
Procedure Decrypt;
Var
   X : Char;
   I : Integer;
Begin
   Repeat
      Read(file, X) ;              {Read a character from the
                                    file}

      I := Ord(X);                 {Calculate the hex code
                                    for the ASCII character in
                                    X}

      X := CHR(I-1)                {Assign a new ASCII
                                    character corresponding to
                                    the hex code I-1}

      Put X in the memory buffer;  {put the decrypted ASCII
                                    character in the buffer}

   Until end-of-file
End.
```

The problem with the Caesar cipher is that it is easy to break. It preserves character sequences which cryptanalysts analyze to break them. For example, messages encrypted with the previous scheme would contain many sequences of the form "FS," the encrypted form of the common sequence "ER." However, a message would rarely contain the sequence "RK," the encrypted form of "QJ."

Another technique involves encrypting and decrypting at the bit level. To encrypt, a bit string representing one or more characters is exclusively OR'd with another string (key). If the encrypted string is subsequently exclusively OR'd with the key, the original string is restored. That is, suppose D is a bit string and K is the key. Then the encrypted string E is formed using $E = D \oplus K$. To decrypt, compute $E \oplus K$. But

$$E \oplus K = (D \oplus K) \oplus K = D \oplus (K \oplus K) = D \oplus (0\text{-string}) = D$$

For example, suppose $D = 1101\ 1101$ and $K = 0100\ 0111$. Then

$$E = D \oplus K = 1101\ 1101 \oplus 0100\ 0111 = 1001\ 1010$$

and

$$E \oplus K = 1001\ 1010 \oplus 0100\ 0111 = 1101\ 1101 = D$$

If each character is encrypted using the same eight-bit key, character sequences are again preserved. Alternatives include encrypting multiple characters simultaneously using a longer key, or using a different key for each character. The method of encrypting each character using a different key is a Vernam cipher and is the only proven unbreakable code. However, in the latter case, key distribution is a problem as authorized users must know every key that was used.

The encryption algorithms described here are only examples. Other very sophisticated schemes involve the factoring of large prime numbers. By large, we mean up to 200 digits and more! Some codes are very difficult to decipher. (The reader interested in such schemes should consult references [23,24].)

Viruses

Of course, there is no foolproof method of guaranteeing privacy. This has been reaffirmed by the proliferation of computer viruses in recent years. A virus is a code segment that attaches itself to executable files and does unpredictable things. They often find their way into a system and make unauthorized changes in a program or data. In many cases, the virus is inserted into an application and destroys a tiny portion of the program or data every time it runs. These, of course, are the most dangerous ones.

A virus that wipes out a file or floods the system with extraneous files is troublesome and often illegal, but backups usually minimize its effects. Such viruses are also often easy to detect using special software that looks for them.

The ones that make subtle changes are often more difficult to detect. Sometimes they are not detected until after they have made many changes. In such cases, the unauthorized changes also make their way into the backups. If undetected for too long, the files and backups are all infected and the effects are disastrous.

There are some secure systems and some that recent experience has shown are not so secure. We have just touched on a difficult current research topic. The interested reader will find additional material in references [8–13]. A good operating system design provides many options for controlling access and protecting sensitive data. But frequently the best design in the world cannot overcome carelessness. A fascinating article about an intruder into a secure computer system is in reference [26]. This serious accounting of a real–life investigation often reads like science fiction.

6.7 Case Study: MS–DOS Disk Management

So far, we have presented the general principles of directories and file and disk management. This section shows how the principles apply to MS–DOS, a popular operating system for personal computers. Most readers have probably used MS–DOS and will find this case more relevant and more interesting than systems studied only from books. Also, there are many popular books about MS–DOS and its file management (see references [14-20]). Furthermore, the interested reader can almost surely get access to an MS–DOS computer to check an actual implementation and investigate further.

MS–DOS Directories

Let us first describe the directory structure as seen by the user. MS–DOS uses a hierarchical structure as discussed in Section 6.3. Through simple commands, the user can create files, directories, and subdirectories. Once in a subdirectory, a user can reference any file in it by name. The user can also reference a file in another directory by using its name prefixed by a list of the subdirectories leading to it in the directory structure. This is like the path name described in Section 6.3. Let us illustrate with examples.

MS–DOS has commands to create, delete, and change directories. They are *MKDIR*, *CHDIR*, and *RMDIR* for *make directory*, *change directory*, and *remove directory*. When a user initializes a disk, MS–DOS automatically creates a *root directory*. It is the root (base) of the hierarchy. As such, the user accesses everything through it. Upon initialization, a disk contains only the root directory. There are no files or subdirectories until the user creates them.

The user can create a new subdirectory with the command

`MKDIR` *subdirectory name*

The name may have a prefix (such as B:), indicating a disk drive. The user must specify the subdirectory name which may include a path or a sequence of subdirectory names. They indicate how to reach a terminating subdirectory. MS–DOS puts the new subdirectory there.

For example, consider the sample directory from Figure 6.18. The bookstore manager decides to keep a list of book reviews. Suppose each review is in a word processor file and the manager wants to group them according to the type of book. The first step in doing this is to enter the command

`MKDIR \Paprbcks\Fiction\Reviews`

Note that "paperbacks" has been abbreviated as "Paprbcks." This is to maintain consistency with an MS–DOS requirement that file and directory names contain eight or fewer characters. MS–DOS responds by creating a new subdirectory "Reviews." Furthermore, MS–DOS puts it in the "Fiction" subdirectory, which in turn is in the "Paprbcks" subdirectory. The first backslash indicates that the path starts at the root directory. Figure 6.27 shows the resulting structure. The new subdirectory is enclosed by dotted lines.

Figure 6.27 MS–DOS hierarchical directory after creating subdirectory reviews

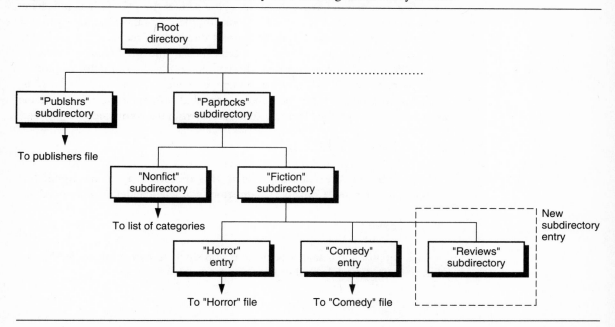

To simplify the figure, we did not include the subdirectory for hardcover books. We assure the reader that MKDIR did not affect it. Note that the new subdirectory contains no files. This is to be expected, since the manager has not had a chance to create any. As she finds reviews for paperback fiction books, she will add them to the directory. Of course, she can also create "Review" directories elsewhere in the hierarchy for other reviews.

The manager is not always required to specify the entire path for a subdirectory. For example, suppose she was currently working in the "Fiction" subdirectory of the "Paprbcks" subdirectory. She could then enter the command

```
MKDIR Reviews
```

By default, since she did not specify a path, MS–DOS assumes the current subdirectory. As a result, this command has the same effect as the previous one. MS–DOS creates a new subdirectory as shown in Figure 6.27.

But how do you enter the "Fiction" subdirectory? Initially, a user enters at the root directory. The command *CHDIR* changes working directories. Its format is

```
CHDIR subdirectory name
```

Once in a subdirectory, there are many MS–DOS commands that operate on files. The user may reference a file through a path or through a file name alone. In the latter case, MS–DOS normally looks for the file in the current directory.

For example, suppose you enter the root directory of the structure of Figure 6.27. If you subsequently want to access files in the subdirectory "Fiction" under "Paprbcks" you could type the pathname \Paprbcks\Fiction\ ahead of each file name. But this is time consuming, especially if you type slowly. Most people would rather enter the subdirectory and reference the files by name alone. You can enter the "Fiction" subdirectory with the command

```
CHDIR \Paprbcks\Fiction
```

Now you can reference any file in this directory by name alone. For example, to enter the "Comedy" subdirectory you would enter the command

```
CHDIR Comedy
```

Last, suppose the manager decides to stop stocking horror books. To dispose of it, she must first delete all its files, and then remove it with

```
RMDIR Horror
```

Note that this form assumes she is currently in the "Fiction" subdirectory. Remember, references to files or subdirectories without a path name default to the current directory.

As a precaution, MS–DOS lets you remove only empty directories. Imagine the grief if you accidentally removed a subdirectory that contained dozens of files and subdirectories. Unless you had backups, all would be lost and you would never want to see a computer again.

Disk Allocation

Now that we understand the structure of directories, let us consider how MS–DOS stores them on a disk and how it finds a file. In this chapter, we have often stated that operating systems generally store files over many sectors. MS–DOS is no exception. But how does it actually find the data for a particular file?

MS–DOS Disk Organization. MS–DOS supports many different types of disks with different capacities and structures. There are single–sided disks and double–sided ones. There are low–density disks and high–density ones. There are floppy disks and hard disks. They have different numbers of tracks and sectors, and different sector sizes. While the specifications for different types of disks vary, the basic techniques used to manage information are similar.

Our discussion focuses on just one disk format. This allows us to provide concrete examples. Format changes do not affect the basic structures: some numbers change, but that is about all.

This section assumes a double–sided 5 1/4" disk containing 40 tracks per side. We also assume 9 sectors per track and 512 (.5K) bytes per sector. Track 0 is the one nearest the edge of the disk (see Figure 6.28), and track 39 is nearest the center. Since the disk is double–sided, there are actually two track 0's, one on each side. However, for simplicity we will assume that each track contains 18 sectors from both sides of the disk.

MS–DOS numbers sectors consecutively. On our sample disk, we calculate how many there are by multiplying the number of sectors per track by the number of tracks. Thus, there are 18 * 40 = 720 sectors. MS–DOS therefore numbers them from 0 through 719. Sectors 0 through 17 are on track 0. Sectors 18 through 35 are on track 1, and so on. If there are .5K bytes per sector, our example disk has a capacity of .5K * 720 or 360K bytes. Table 6.8 shows how MS–DOS uses the sectors.

Figure 6.28 5 1/4" disk format, 9 sectors per track and 40 tracks per side

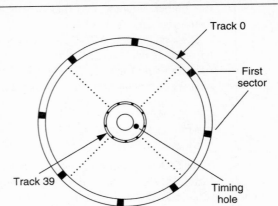

Table 6.8 Sector allocation of a 5 1/4" double-sided disk with 9 sectors per track

Sector #	Contents
0	Bootstrap record
1 - 2	First File Allocation Table (FAT)
3 - 4	Second File Allocation Table (FAT)
5 - 11	Disk directory entries
12 - 719	Data

The bootstrap record appears in most disks and is used to start up applications software. It contains a bootstrap program that has just enough instructions to read essential code for an application. It also contains disk characteristics such as the number of bytes per sector or sectors per track. Whenever a disk is inserted into a drive, the bootstrap program is locked into memory. It then locates and loads an application program, which then runs. The bootstrap record is not essential to our discussions, and we will not consider it further.

Sectors 1 and 2 contain the *File Allocation Table* (FAT for short). MS–DOS uses the FAT to locate the actual sectors assigned to a file. In a previous example (Figure 6.21), we assumed that sector addresses were part of the file directory. In this case, the directory entry locates the FAT, which contains disk sector addresses. We will describe the actual structure of the FAT shortly.

Sectors 3 and 4 contain a copy of the FAT. It is so critical to proper management of files and disk space that MS–DOS keeps a copy in the event of damage. If the original FAT is unusable, MS–DOS can use the copy to reclaim the files.

Directory entries are in sectors 5 through 11. As described in Section 6.3, each file has an entry in a directory. As already stated, the entries do not contain actual file locations, but rather point to a FAT location that refers to file locations.

Last but not least is the data. All data sectors and unused sectors are in the range 12 through 719. Whenever MS–DOS creates a new file, it looks for unused sectors there. Similarly, when it deletes a file, it returns the sectors to the pool of unused sectors. MS–DOS accesses these sectors through the FAT.

However, MS–DOS does not always allocate individual sectors to a file. If a file requires disk space, MS–DOS allocates a *cluster* of sectors to it. Double-sided disks, as we have described, commonly have two consecutive sectors per cluster. Higher capacity disks will normally have more.

Thus, if a file requires a sector for data storage, MS–DOS will actually allocate two sectors. This seems wasteful, especially if the file does not need or use the extra sector. But because MS–DOS allocates the sector to it, no other file can use the sector. Why does MS–DOS do this?

The answer is based on economy of scale. If MS–DOS were to allocate one sector at a time, it would have to keep track of 720 sectors. Thus, the FAT would have to contain at least 720 entries. However, if it allocates sectors in clusters of two, it must keep track of only 360 clusters. Thus, the FAT requires only 360 entries, occupying less disk space. This of course means more space for data files. Clustering makes more sense as the number of sectors on a disk grows. MS–DOS does not have to keep track of as much, and the FAT need not be so large.

Typically, on double–sided disks, cluster 0 consists of sectors 0 and 1. Cluster 1 consists of sectors 2 and 3. In general, cluster j consists of sectors $2*j$ and $2*j+1$.

MS–DOS Disk Directory

Let us now see how MS–DOS uses the directory and FAT to manage disk space. Each entry in the directory is 32 bytes long. Thus, MS–DOS can store up to 16 directory entries per sector. Since it uses 7 sectors for directory entries, there is room for up to $7*16$ or 112 entries. Table 6.8 shows the format of a directory entry.

Bytes 0 through 10 contain the file name and an optional extension. Remember, MS–DOS allows file names up to eight characters long. Shorter names are blank padded at the end. The file name extension is often used to indicate types, such as backup file (extension BAK), assembly language source file (extension ASM), or object code from an assembler or compiler (extension OBJ). We will discuss filenames and extensions in more detail in Chapter 8.

Table 6.8 Format of a file directory entry

Byte #	Purpose
0 through 7	File name
8 through 10	File name extension
11	Attribute vector
12 through 21	Reserved for future use
22 through 23	Time of creation or last update
24 through 25	Date of creation or last update
26 through 27	First cluster number and location of first FAT entry
28 through 31	Size of file (in bytes)

Byte 11 contains up to eight 1–bit flags that indicate special status (or attributes). Suppose we number the bits in the attribute byte as follows:

$$b_7 b_6 b_5 b_4 b_3 b_2 b_1 b_0$$

Among the bit flags are:

$b_0=1$: Indicates a "read only" file. It cannot be opened for writing or updating.

$b_1=1$: Indicates a "hidden file." Its name will not appear in normal directory listings.

$b_2=1$: Indicates a "system file" such as MSDOS.SYS and IO.SYS (see Chapter 8).

$b_4=1$: Indicates a subdirectory rather than a file.

Bytes 22 and 23 contain the time of day when MS–DOS created or updated the file. The time is a 16–bit integer derived from the formula

$$\text{Time of day} = \text{Hours} * 2^{11} + \text{Minutes} * 2^5 + \text{Seconds DIV 2}$$

Let us explain the formula. The time of day consists of hours (between 0 and 23), minutes (between 0 and 59), and seconds (between 0 and 59). Since hours ranges from 0 through 23, we need 5 bits to represent the number of hours. If we multiply the number of hours by 2^{11}, we effectively put 11 zeros to the right of its binary representation. In effect, this defines the 5–bit value for hours as the leftmost 5 bits of a 16–bit word (see Figure 6.29).

Similarly, we need 6 bits to store a minute value between 0 and 59. Suppose we multiply minutes by 2^5, and add the product to the shifted hours value. In effect, minutes ends up in the middle 6 bits of a 16–bit word.

Figure 6.29 Time of day in an MS-DOS directory entry

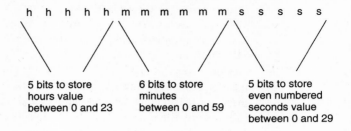

h   h   h   h   h   m   m   m   m   m   m   s   s   s   s   s

5 bits to store
hours value
between 0 and 23

6 bits to store
minutes
between 0 and 59

5 bits to store
even numbered
seconds value
between 0 and 29

This leaves only 5 bits for seconds. Since it ranges from 0 to 59, this is not enough. To make it fit, MS–DOS drops the least significant bit, thus keeping time only to the nearest even–numbered second. An odd value is truncated, not rounded. The 5–bit representation can be obtained either through integer division by 2 or through a right shift.

For example, suppose MS–DOS creates a file at 1:24.30 p.m. (13:24.30 in international or military 24–hour time). Thus, we have

$$
\begin{aligned}
\text{Time of day} \quad &= \text{Hours} * 2^{11} + \text{Minutes} * 2^5 + \text{Seconds DIV } 2 \\
&= 13 * 2^{11} + 24 * 2^5 + 30 \text{ DIV } 2 \\
&= (01101_2) * 2^{11} + (011000_2) * 2^5 + (011110_2) \text{ DIV } 2 \\
&= 0110100000000000_2 \\
&\quad + 01100000000_2 \\
&\quad\quad + 01111_2 \\
&= 0110101100001111_2
\end{aligned}
$$

The date of file creation or last update is in bytes 24 through 25. MS–DOS stores it as a 16–bit integer derived from the formula

$$
\text{Date} = (\text{Year-1980}) * 2^9 + \text{Month} * 2^5 + \text{Day}
$$

Can you explain the rationale behind this formula? Bytes 28 through 31 specify the size of the file in bytes. Finally, bytes 26 and 27 locate the first cluster of sectors containing the file's data. The next question is "How does MS–DOS locate all the clusters?"

File Allocation Table

Recall from previous discussions that for double–sided disks MS–DOS allocates sectors in clusters of two. Most important now is the fact that MS–DOS numbers clusters starting with 0. Thus, if there are 720 sectors, MS–DOS numbers clusters from 0 through 359. Once MS–DOS knows a cluster number, it can calculate the sector numbers. The first one in a cluster is the cluster number times 2. The second one is just the next logical sector. From there, it can calculate the track number and relative sector number. So MS–DOS can find any file if it can find all the clusters allocated to it.

Since files may occupy varying numbers of clusters, MS–DOS stores the numbers as a linked list. Each node in the list is actually an entry in the FAT. The directory entry for the file contains the first cluster number and the location of the first node.

For example, suppose that MS–DOS has allocated clusters 23, 31, 44, and 33 to a file. Figure 6.30 shows the logical representation of the cluster number list.

Figure 6.30 Linked list of cluster numbers for a file

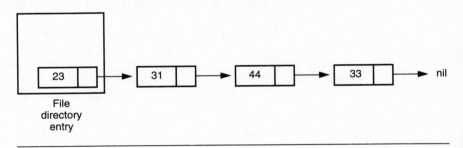

File
directory
entry

The manner in which MS–DOS implements the linked list is rather interesting. Each FAT value serves two purposes. It indicates not only a cluster number, but also the FAT entry where MS–DOS can find the next cluster number. Figure 6.31 shows the implementation of the linked list from Figure 6.30.

Bytes 26 and 27 of the file directory entry contain 23, the first cluster number. Also the next cluster number is in FAT entry 23. That entry contains 31. So cluster 31 is the second cluster associated with the file. Furthermore, the third cluster number is in FAT entry 31. That entry indicates that cluster 44 comes next and that FAT entry 44 contains its successor. Finally, FAT entry 44 indicates that cluster 33 is the fourth one associated with the file. Since the file occupies no more clusters, FAT entry 33 contains a special marker (-1).

Figure 6.31 Linked list of cluster numbers using FAT entries

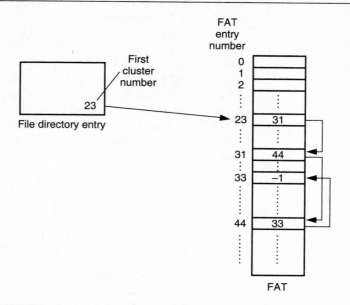

If a FAT entry contains 0, the corresponding cluster is unallocated. When MS–DOS must allocate a cluster, it searches the FAT to find an entry containing 0. This entry is then linked into the list of cluster numbers for the file. Note that using 0 to indicate an unallocated cluster causes no conflict since MS–DOS never allocates cluster 0. Remember, MS–DOS uses cluster 0 (sectors 0 and 1) itself (see Table 6.7). As you can see, the FAT entries are actually nodes in many linked lists, each starting in a directory entry.

Locating FAT Entries. Figure 6.31 shows each FAT entry associated with a particular file. But the implementation is not as straightforward as it might seem. Note that each FAT entry must be able to store a value as large as 359. Higher density disks have more clusters and consequently larger numbers. Thus, their largest FAT entry exceeds 359. The point is that FAT entries need more than one byte, since a byte is limited to 255 as its largest value.

If each FAT entry were 2 bytes, its largest value would be 2^{16}-1 or 65,535. This is easily enough to hold any cluster number we need. However, MS–DOS only uses 1 1/2 bytes for each entry. Since 1 1/2 bytes is 12 bits, it can hold cluster numbers as large as 2^{12}-1 or 4095. The advantage of using 12 bits rather than 16 is that the FAT entries are smaller. Thus, the FAT requires less space, leaving more room for files. The disadvantage is the awkwardness of handling 12–bit units. Let us explain.

Since each FAT entry occupies 1 1/2 bytes, MS–DOS stores two consecutive entries in 3 consecutive bytes. Thus, given an entry number, the first thing MS–DOS must do is identify the two corresponding bytes in the FAT sector. It then loads the two bytes into a register. But only 12 of the 16 bits are the actual FAT value. The question is which 12 bits? A complicating factor is that the microprocessor stores 2-byte integers in memory with the least significant byte first and the most significant byte second. Thus, a hexadecimal number such as $ABCD_{16}$ appears in two consecutive bytes as shown in Figure 6.32. We call this *byte reversal*.

Figure 6.32 Storage of a two byte hexadecimal number ABCD

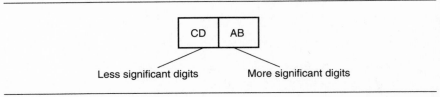

The question is, "Given the FAT entry number, how do we find the data?" Since each entry occupies 1 1/2 bytes (3 hexadecimal digits), MS–DOS must do the following:

- Multiply the FAT entry number by 1 1/2 (and truncate any fraction) to determine a relative byte location within the sector.
- Load the 16–bit number beginning at that location into a register.
- If the entry number is odd, ignore the least significant hexadecimal digit. We do this by shifting the value 4 bits right.
- If, on the other hand, the initial FAT entry is even, ignore the most significant hexadecimal digit. We can eliminate it by doing a logical AND with the 2–byte value and $0FFF_{16}$.

Now that you are probably thoroughly confused, let's clarify this with an example. Consider the FAT in Figure 6.33. Remember, each entry is 12 bits (or 3 hexadecimal digits) long. This is why we show all FAT values as 3 hexadecimal digit numbers. We do not show the first ten FAT entries (0 through 9), nor do we show the first 15 bytes (remember the 2:3 ratio of FAT entries to bytes). As the figure shows, the value in FAT entry 10 is 112_{16}. However, if you look in the FAT sector in Figure 6.33, you will probably have a difficult time finding it. But let's see what happens if we follow our procedure.

Figure 6.33 Relationship between logical contents of the FAT and the actual contents of its sector

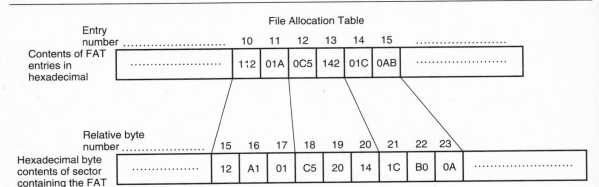

Multiply the FAT entry (10) by 1 1/2 to get 15. Next load the two–byte number beginning at relative byte 15 into a register. The two bytes contain 12_{16} and $A1_{16}$, respectively. But remember, the first byte is less significant and the second byte is more significant. So, when MS–DOS loads the two bytes into a register, it reverses them. Thus, the register contains $A112_{16}$. Since the entry number is even, we logically AND $A112_{16}$ and $0FFF_{16}$. This clears the most significant digit and leaves us with 0112_{16} as desired.

Now consider FAT entry 11. If we multiply 11 by 1 1/2 and truncate the result, we get relative byte 16. The two bytes at that location contain $A1_{16}$ and 01_{16}, respectively. Next, load them into a register, which therefore contains $01A1_{16}$ (remember the byte reversal). Since the entry number is odd, we shift the value $01A1_{16}$ right 4 bits. The rightmost hexadecimal digit disappears, and we get $001A_{16}$ just as desired.

To further clarify this confusing process, you should repeat the steps for FAT entries 12 through 15.

This description should give you a general idea of how MS–DOS manages information on a disk. As previously stated, if we consider disks with different capacities, the numbers change but the basic concepts stay the same. We will discuss MS–DOS further in Chapter 8.

═══════ **6.8 Summary**

This chapter described how an operating system manages information in secondary storage such as tape or disk. Initially, we distinguished between physical and logical records. This is necessary because devices usually treat data in fixed size blocks or physical records. However, the user must be able to define the type and size of record best suited to a particular application.

Tapes group several logical records as one physical record. Doing this means fewer interrecord gaps are necessary to separate records. The result is more efficient use of space. Another advantage is that we can read many logical records faster. This makes I/O processing faster and more efficient.

A disk contains concentric tracks, consisting of sectors. A disk sector is analogous to a physical record on a tape. We may store many logical records in one sector. The exact number depends on the sector's capacity and the record's size. Large files may require many sectors.

At any time, a disk controller may have many read requests pending. How it responds to them may greatly affect system efficiency. Before reading a sector, the disk controller must move the head to the correct track, wait for the sector to rotate to it, and read. The times required are the seek time, latency time, and transmission time, respectively.

The controller should minimize the amount of head movement, but not to the extent of ignoring certain requests. We discussed several methods of scheduling track accesses. They were FIFO, shortest seek time first (SSF), scan, and circular scan. The FIFO method does not try to minimize head movement and the SSF method may cause indefinite postponement of some requests. The scan and circular scan methods are compromise solutions that reduce head movement, while still preventing indefinite postponement.

The controller can also reduce latency time by interleaving consecutive sectors within a track. Depending on the rotation speed of the disk and the time required to do error checking, we may store logically consecutive sectors separated by one or more physical sectors. Thus, suppose the controller must read two logically consecutive sectors. By the time it has read and verified the first sector, the second one has rotated close to the head. This means less rotational delay.

An operating system keeps track of files through a directory. File directories may consist of a linear list of entries or a hierarchical arrangement. The latter allows for subdirectories that group related files. A user working in a subdirectory can shut out the details of other subdirectories. This simplifies the view of accessible files.

The way in which a system stores and accesses records in a file is a topic for an entire course. File structure and access methods range from sequential through indexed using a complex hierarchy of index values. Sequential files require little overhead but provide few access options. A user wanting a particular record must read all the ones ahead of it. Direct files allow a user to request any record by specifying its relative position. The user can access it without reading all its predecessors. Some systems allow a user to access a record by specifying the contents of a key or index field. Access in this way is a powerful technique but requires more overhead.

Security has become a widely discussed topic. The proliferation of software and hardware have created enormous demands for computer systems. System users want easy access to software and data without having to learn or use a complex programming language. They simply want their computer systems to do a job in response to a few simple, straightforward commands. However, easy access can be a disadvantage, especially if it applies to the wrong people. Computer systems often contain important, sensitive data that only certain people should see. Major security issues deal with how to prevent the wrong people from accessing it.

Simple common sense provides a great deal of basic security. Users must lock up important disks and keep backups of important data. They should choose passwords that are not obvious, keep them secret, and change them regularly. But despite common sense precautions, devious people can still overcome security measures. We must use special techniques to protect information. For example, systems can erase disks when information is no longer needed. Designers may restrict access to files to let users see but not change data. Complex encryption algorithms may scramble data to make it incomprehensible to unauthorized observers.

The last topic of this chapter was the case study of MS–DOS, a popular operating system for personal computers. It supports a hierarchical directory structure. The directory has an entry for each file and subdirectory on a disk. MS–DOS allocates disk space in clusters or groups of sectors. Given a cluster number, MS–DOS can locate the sectors associated with the cluster. Thus, it maintains disk allocation information as a linked list of cluster numbers. Nodes in the linked list are actually entries in a File Allocation Table (FAT). Each file directory entry contains a pointer to an entry in the FAT. From there, MS–DOS can follow the list to access each cluster associated with a file.

≡≡≡≡≡ **Exercises**

1. Consider a disk and drive with the following characteristics:
   - Rotational velocity of 100 revolutions per second.
   - Five sectors per track.
   - The controller reads one sector at a time.
   - The controller requires 2 ms to verify the accuracy of a sector after reading it.
   - Sectors are physically numbered within a track as shown below.

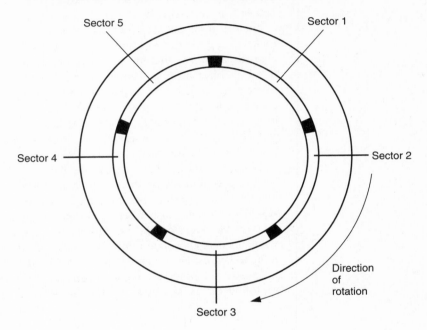

   Suppose a file requiring 5 sectors is to be stored on the disk. If we want to store it on one track, how should it be divided to minimize the latency time (rotational delay) required to sequentially read and verify it? Assume the first part of the file (logical sector 1) is stored in physical sector 1.

   How much time does it take (in ms) to sequentially read and verify all 5 logical sectors? Show your calculations and reasoning.

2. Suppose there are 12 sectors per track. Find values for n between 1 and 11, inclusive, for which n :1 interleaving will use all sectors on a track.

3. Suppose there are 13 sectors per track. Find values for n between 1 and 12, inclusive, for which n :1 interleaving will use all sectors on a track.

4. Consider the following list of disk I/O requests.

Request Number	Sector Number
1	548
2	123
3	459
4	156
5	645
6	818
7	825
8	843
9	239

If they are processed in the order shown, compute the average track distance using the FIFO, scan, and circular scan methods. Assume the same disk characteristics as in Table 6.1.

5. Repeat the development leading to Table 6.4, assuming 50 tracks per disk surface instead of 100.

6. Write a program that allows a user to enter an account number and searches a predefined list. (You may think of the list as an array or linked list of records.) If the number is not found, print an appropriate message and request another entry. Allow no more than 5 retries. If it is found, check to see if a password exists within the list entry. If so, then prompt the user to enter a password.

7. Consider the bookstore directory structure of Figure 6.18. Suppose the manager wants to reorganize so that all books are primarily categorized as either nonfiction or fiction. Within each category, they should be further classified as "horror," "comedy," etc. Only after that should a distinction between paperbacks and hardcovers be made. Draw the hierarchical directory suitable for this arrangement.

8. Suppose a direct access file consists of sectors with 1024 byte capacity. Suppose also that records are 32 bytes long. On which logical sector do the following logical records lie? What is the relative record number in the sector?

   Logical record 42
   Logical record 131
   Logical record 32
   Logical record 512

9. Create a B–tree file structure using the following information:

   There are 100 records.
   Each data node contains 4 records.
   Each index node contains up to 5 pointers.
   The i th record has index value i^2.

10. Consider the following records:

```
Employee = Record
  Id        : Integer;         {identification number}
  Name      : Characterstring; {employee name}
  ProjectId : Integer;         {id number of secret
                                project assigned to
                                employee}
  Clearance : Integer;         {employee clearance
                                level}
  Salary    : Real;            {employee salary}
End;

Project = Record
  ProjectId : Integer;         {secret project
                                identification number}
  Clearance : Integer;         {minimum employee
                                clearance level for
                                access to technical data}
  Funds     : Real;            {project funds}
  TechData  : CharacterString; {name of file containing
                                technical data}
  EmpId     : Integer;         {identification of
                                employee in charge of
                                project}
End;
```

Each employee works on a project and has a clearance level allowing or restricting access to technical data. Each project requires a certain clearance level for access to its data. Four departments need access to parts of each record. They are the personnel, research & development, security, and technical support. Their access needs are as follows:

Department	Record: Field needed and access type -R (read) or W (write)
Personnel	Employee: name, Id, and salary (W)
Research & development	Employee: name, Id (R), ProjectId (W) Project: ProjectId, funds, and EmpId (W)
Security	Employee: Id (R) and clearance(W) Project: ProjectId (R), clearance (W)
Technical support	Employee: Id and clearance (R) Project: ProjectId (R) and TechData (W)

Assign locks and passwords with keys to allow minimum accessibility and still meet the needs.

11. Consider the following message:

    KYZJ TFLIJV ZJ VRJP

    Each nonblank character was encrypted using

    encrypted character = CH[(OR(original character) + k) mod 26]

    OR is a function that maps the characters A through Z to the integers 0 through 25, respectively. CH is a function that maps the integers 0 through 25 to the characters A through Z, respectively. Also, k is an integer. To make life easier, we did not encrypt blanks. Decode the message by determining the value of k and creating a decryption algorithm. (Hint: Note that J appears frequently in the coded message and the sequence ZJ appears twice.)

12. Write programs to encrypt and decrypt secret messages using the algorithm described in problem 11.

13. Show a sequence of MKDIR commands to create the hierarchical directory structure of Figure 6.27.

14. Consider the formula MS–DOS uses to store the date of file creation in the directory:

    Date = (Year-1980) $*$ 2^9 + Month $*$ 2^5 + Day

    Draw a figure similar to Figure 6.29 and show where the values appear in a 16–bit word. How would MS–DOS store the following dates: Jan. 14, 1990 and Dec. 7, 1989.

15. Show the FAT entries that specify allocation data for the following three files:

File Name	Clusters Allocated
Accounts	95,25,82, and 86
Invntry	89,91, and 18
Ledger	19,37,84, and 79

16. Refer to Figure 6.33 and show how MS–DOS obtains the values associated with FAT entries 12 through 15.

17. Assume the following FAT entries. Determine the relative byte numbers and hexadecimal byte contents in the FAT sector corresponding to them.

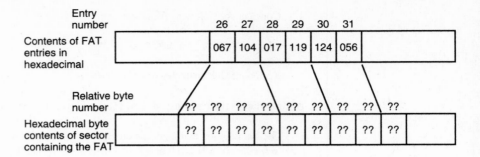

Questions

1. In what cases would the FIFO scheduling of track accesses be appropriate?
2. What effect does the number of logical records per block have on the size of memory buffers? Explain.
3. Describe the process by which MS–DOS would locate a record given its relative position in the file. Consider the sector and logical record sizes. Assume all allocation units, except possibly the last one, contain the maximum number of records.
4. When analyzing the SSF method of track accesses, we assumed that the controller receives requests as fast as it processes them. Why is this a reasonable assumption? After all, processes can normally make I/O requests much faster than they can be processed.
5. Sector interleaving can reduce the latency time between sector reads from a single track. Considering a typical disk rotation speed, it will save a few milliseconds between reads. Why is interleaving important? After all, who will notice a change of a few milliseconds?

References

1. Gorsline, G.W. *Computer Organization Hardware/Software*. 2nd ed. Englewood Cliffs, NJ: Prentice–Hall, 1986.
2. Kohavi, Z. *Switching and Finite Automata Theory*. 2nd ed. New York: McGraw–Hill, 1978.
3. Tanenbaum, A.S. *Structured Computer Organization*. 3rd ed. Englewood Cliffs, NJ: Prentice–Hall, 1990.
4. Walter, R.K. *Introduction to Data Management and File Design*. Englewood Cliffs, NJ: Prentice–Hall, 1986.
5. Folk, M.J., and B. Zoellick. *File Structures: A Conceptual Toolkit*. Reading, MA: Addison–Wesley, 1987.
6. Salzberg, B.J. *Introduction to Database Design*. New York: Academic Press, 1986.
7. Date, C.J. *Introduction to Database Systems*, Vol. 1, 5th ed. Reading, MA: Addison–Wesley, 1990.
8. National Research Council. *Computers at Risk: Safe Computing in the Information Age*. Washington, DC: National Academy Press, 1991.
9. Gasser, M. *Building a Secure Computer System*. New York: Van Nostrand Reinhold, 1988.

10. Donning, Peter, ed. *Computers Under Attack*. Reading, MA: Addison–Wesley, 1990.

11. Lobel, J. *Foiling the System Breakers: Computer Security and Access Control*. New York: McGraw–Hill, 1986.

12. Moultin, R.T. *Computer Security Handbook: Strategies and Techniques for Preventing Data Loss or Theft*. Englewood Cliffs, NJ: Prentice–Hall, 1986.

13. Bic., L., and A.S. Shaw. *The Logical Design of Operating Systems*. 2nd ed. Englewood Cliffs, NJ: Prentice–Hall, 1988.

14. Norton, P., and R. Wilton. *Programmer's Guide to the IBM PC and PS/2*. Redmond, WA: Microsoft Press, 1988.

15. *The MS–DOS Encyclopedia*. Redmond, WA: Microsoft Press, 1987.

16. O'Day, K. *Understanding MS–DOS*. Indianapolis, IN: Howard Sams & Co., 1988.

17. Wolverton, V. *Running MS–DOS*. 3rd ed. Redmond, WA: Microsoft Press, 1988.

18. Duncan, R. *Advanced MS–DOS Programming*. 2nd ed. Redmond, WA: Microsoft Press, 1988.

19. Simrin, S. *The Waite Group's MS–DOS Bible*. 2nd ed. Indianapolis, IN: Howard Sams & Co., 1988.

20. Angermeyer, J. et al. *The Waite Group's MS–DOS Developer's Guide*. 2nd ed. Indianapolis, IN: Howard Sams & Co., 1989.

21. Aho, A.V., J.E. Hopcroft, and J.D. Ullman. *Data Structures and Algorithms*. Reading, MA: Addison–Wesley, 1983.

22. Horowitz, E., and S. Sahni. *Fundamentals of Data Structures in Pascal*. Rockville, MD: Computer Science Press, 1982.

23. Lakshmivarahan, S. "Algorithms for Public Key Cryptosystems: Theory and Practice," *Advances in Computers*. 22, Edited by M.C. Yovits. New York: Academic Press, 1983.

24. Rivest, R.L., A. Shamir, and L. Adleman. "A Method for Obtaining Digital Signatures and Public–Key Cryptosystems." *Communications of the ACM*. 21 (February 1978).

25. Tenembaum, A. M., and M. J. Augenstein. *Data Structures Using Pascal*. 2nd ed. Englewood Cliffs, NJ: Prentice–Hall, 1986.

26. Stoll, C. "Stalking the Wily Hacker." *Communications of the ACM*. 31 (May 1988): 484–497.

7

Modeling

7.1 Evaluation Methods

You are now aware that an operating system is just a program. Granted, it is large and complex. Nevertheless, it is still a program. Like any other, it must be tested thoroughly to verify that it works correctly. Most operating systems go through a period of "on-site" or "beta" testing as well (besides the usual period of testing by frustrated buyers of a new version). But is it enough for an operating system to work correctly?

No, the market demands much more. An operating system must be maintainable and expandable to meet the challenges of new technologies, faster and more capable peripherals, and new user and application needs. Furthermore, it must also be efficient. The operating system should perform its tasks quickly to avoid causing excessive overhead.

The key word here is efficiency. Is the operating system efficient? But just what does that mean? To determine it, we must have something to measure. But what can we measure about an operating system? What indicates whether a program is efficient?

There are many measures of program efficiency. For example, sorting algorithms have been evaluated extensively because of their importance in many applications. Simple bubble or exchange sorts are adequate for small amounts of data, whereas more complex methods such as quicksort or heapsort are necessary for large databases.

We measure the efficiency of sorting algorithms by determining how many iterations or comparisons they require. We can then compare the values. For further discussion, see references [7-9]. But an operating system is much more complex than a sorting algorithm. (That is a candidate for understatement of the year.) A sorting algorithm's input is a list of elements that we can analyze and categorize. An operating system's input consists of requests by users to compile or run programs; create, modify, or delete files; and use resources. The requests may occur at any time and are random as far as the system is concerned. Thus, the input is a sequence of random requests for random services. How can we analyze such requests? How can we categorize them? How can we measure the responses?

Queuing Theory

Fortunately, there are mathematical tools for dealing with random events. They are part of a branch of statistics called *Queuing Theory*. Simply put, *Queuing Theory* is the study of waiting in lines or queues. Waiting in line has become a commonplace, annoying fact of life. Figure 7.1 shows a typical situation at a bank, government agency, or ticket window. People who require service wait in line for it. The people who wait are *customers*. Those who provide the service are (cleverly!) *servers*.

Figure 7.1 Customers waiting in a queue for service

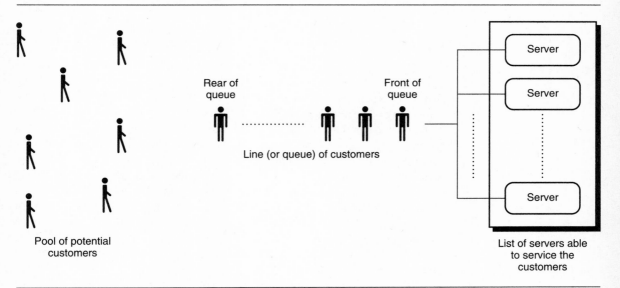

Designers must analyze the techniques an operating system uses before actually writing the codes. Reference 10, for example, describes the planning behind the development of Microsoft's OS/2. Designers must thoroughly understand the environment in which the system will work. Queuing Theory provides a way to define the environment mathematically. Its formulas allow us to predict likely responses and wait times. We will describe statistics it can generate, and we will develop equations for them.

Let us return to Figure 7.1. It is a simple representation of many places where people often wait in line. The location may be a fast food restaurant, a movie theater, a gasoline station, a supermarket, a bookstore, a doctor's office, a hospital, a stadium, a government office, or an amusement park. Waiting in line is a worldwide phenomenon that occurs regardless of economic, political, or social philosophy.

But Figure 7.1 also represents many situations in a computer system; only the terminology changes. Lines become queues. I/O requests wait in queues until device controllers respond. Processes wait in queues to gain access to a CPU. Users wait in queues to get access to special equipment such as an express terminal or a laser printer. Batch programs wait in queues to enter a system and compete for resources. Can you think of other examples?

At this point, it does not matter whether the customers are I/O requests, processes, users, or batch programs. It also does not matter whether the servers are device controllers, CPUs, express terminals, or schedulers. We only care that customers wait for a server to serve them.

Measurables

Figure 7.1 represents a queuing system we must analyze. What do we want to know about it? If you were waiting in line, what would you want to know? The first and perhaps most obvious question is, "When will I be served?" That is, "How long is the average wait?" We call this the *average* or *expected wait time*.

But averages can be misleading. For example, suppose there are ten customers. If one waits an hour and the other nine wait just five minutes, the average wait time is 10.5 minutes. Just sum the wait times for all customers and divide by ten. An average wait time of 10.5 minutes might not sound too bad. In fact, for 90% of the customers, it is more than double the actual value. But that is small consolation to the customer who must wait an hour, particularly if he or she is waiting for an ambulance, the fire department, a police response, or a bathroom on an airplane.

An average value is just a single measure. It says nothing about the distribution of wait times. Other statistics indicate how many customers experience long waits. Stating that the average wait time is 10.5 minutes gives one picture of a system. But stating that 10% of the customers must wait at least an hour gives an entirely different picture. Surely you would have many angry people if the wait was for baggage after an airplane flight arrived. Thus, a second useful statistic is the percentage of customers who experience long wait times.

Average values can be misleading for another reason. Suppose in the same example that the first nine customers did not wait at all but the tenth one had to wait an hour. In this case, the average wait time is six minutes, but it does not reflect the fact that 90% of the customers did not wait at all.

A third useful statistic is the probability that a customer must wait. Another way to describe this is as the probability that all servers are busy. We assume, of course, that servers are not watching television or playing cards when there are customers. In other words, a customer must wait only if all servers are busy.

A fourth important statistic is the average number of customers in the queue. Designers must know how much space to set aside for lines. In airports, for example, this number determines how large waiting rooms must be and how much lobby area must be roped off for ticket lines. In computer systems, it determines how much memory must be allocated to queues and how large counters must be.

A fifth useful quantity is the probability that servers are idle. If they are idle much of the time, perhaps there are too many. Then we can reduce costs by removing some of them. On the other hand, if servers are never idle, maybe there are too few. We may have to examine other statistics such as average time in the queue or percentage of customers who experience long waits.

Simulations

Although this chapter focuses on modeling and queuing theory, we must mention another method of evaluation: *simulation*. In general, a simulation is a computer-programmed model of something. It is designed to behave as much like the real system as possible.

You are probably familiar with simulators as learning tools or games. For example, driver education programs often use simulations to create the experience of driving a car without turning the instructor's hair gray prematurely. You sit behind a wheel and watch events (on a screen) just like those you will encounter on a road. You, of course, must respond by turning the wheel, braking, or taking some other action. Astronauts, pilots, and air traffic controllers also train using simulators (although much more complex ones). For some reason, few airlines like to have raw beginners flying real jumbo jets or directing traffic over a busy airport.

An operating systems designer may work with mathematical models initially. But all models depend on assumptions whose accuracy must be tested eventually. Thus, a prototype operating system must be tested. The best test is in the marketplace, subject to real-world conditions. However, few customers are enthusiastic about buying a completely untested system.

The next best test is to create a situation that is as much like the real world as possible. This might include writing a simulator program using random numbers to represent real-world events. The association of numbers with events is based on probability distributions. The simulator feeds the "events" to the prototype and it responds. Of course, people monitor the events, record the responses, and take measurements. If the simulator is accurate, the prototype's behavior is a good indicator of how it will perform in the real world.

Appendix A contains an example simulator. It is part of a project in which you write an operating system designed to respond to certain events. Simulated events include process creation, process errors, I/O requests, I/O completions, wait and signal primitives, and process completion.

As systems grow more complex, mathematical models become increasingly difficult to create and, as a result, less practical. Consequently, simulations play a key role in the development of complex systems such as computer networks, databases, communications networks, and of course, operating systems. Because of its complexity, few textbooks deal with simulation in any detail. However, there are several articles that discuss specific simulators.

For example, reference [15] discusses the Time Warp Operating System for a hypercube processor. Simulations are constructed that run under it. Reference [16] discusses fault simulation in distributed systems. Such simulations are used to examine digital circuits under faulty conditions. Finally, the entire October 1990 issue of the *Communications of the ACM* [17] is devoted to simulation. It contains articles discussing, for example, simulation of on-line scheduling, networks, and a semiconductor manufacturing line.

Chapter 7 Preview

The reader of this chapter should be comfortable working with complex equations. Some familiarity with calculus is helpful, but not necessary. We use its techniques to develop some equations. Thus, a background in calculus is necessary to understand the derivations, but not to apply the equations.

The second and third sections describe the mathematics of Queuing Theory. We will categorize one type of queuing system and introduce terminology and symbols used later. We will also derive formulas for quantities we will define. The reader of these two sections should have at least a basic knowledge of limits, as taught in a calculus course. The equations we generate provide a foundation for the fourth and fifth sections. The reader unfamiliar with calculus can simply proceed to Section 7.5. It assumes the derived formulas and focuses on applications rather than theory.

The fourth section generates equations for and defines an M/M/c queuing system. Specifically, we generate equations for estimating the following quantities:

- Expected waiting time.
- 90th percentile of expected waiting time (time exceeded for only 10% of the customers).

- Probability that a customer must wait.
- Expected number of customers in a queue at a given time.
- Probability that all servers are idle.

There are other performance measures, and the interested reader can consult the references [1, 3, 5, 11-13]. However, this list contains common measurements that analysts and customers alike often want to know.

The M/M/c system is relatively simple and allows us to introduce analytic techniques without getting too involved in mathematics. Other queuing systems exist, but we do not describe them here.

The fourth section's goal is to illustrate the role of quantitative analysis in computer science. Computer science is not just writing and verifying programs, despite the importance of those activities. In this chapter, we derive formulas for several measures. The derivations are not easy, but they are accessible to a student with a little calculus. We will not derive formulas for others that are more complex or go beyond the scope of this book. Our goal is to introduce Queuing Theory, not to overwhelm you with it. That is the purpose of Queuing Theory textbooks.

The fifth section contains two case studies. We use the equations developed in the fourth section to answer real-life questions. We will find that Queuing Theory often contradicts what seems intuitively obvious. This will show the danger of assuming what "should" be true.

We will also see that some queuing statistics are paradoxical. For example, a system may have long waits for customers even though servers are idle much of the time. This situation is common in the analysis of operating systems.

≡≡≡ 7.2 Poisson Processes

One goal of this chapter is to generate equations we can use to calculate the statistics described in the previous section. We must first start with some assumptions about the system. This section describes them.

Many different types of queuing systems exist. They differ in part according to the assumptions we make about arrival patterns and service rates. To generate equations, we must make assumptions about system behavior. Otherwise, we have nowhere to start.

The first assumption we make is about arrival patterns of customers. For example, do they arrive at regular intervals? Do they arrive in groups or one at a time? An assumption of regular intervals makes the analysis easier; unfortunately, it is unrealistic in most cases. For example, people do not submit programs to a time-sharing system at regular intervals. They submit them when they are ready. If the user population is large, the system must be able to accept programs submitted at arbitrary and random times.

One categorization of arrivals is the *Poisson (or random) arrival pattern (or process)*. Be careful, the term "process" here refers to any sequence of events not necessarily involving computers at all. For a discussion about other types of assumptions, the interested reader should consult references [1, 3, 5, 12].

To some, the phrase "random pattern" may seem to be a contradiction in terms. A pattern often suggests repetition. But queuing analysts have observed that random events exhibit patterns. Let us explain.

Consider the queuing system of Figure 7.1. Assume that two customers never arrive simultaneously. This assumption is characteristic of a Poisson arrival pattern. Another way to state this is to assume that the first customer arrives at time t_0, the second one at time t_1, and so on. In general the $i+1$st customer arrives at time t_i. The values t_0, t_1, etc. are ordered as shown:

$$0 < t_0 < t_1 <, \ldots, < t_i < t_{i+1} <, \ldots$$

The value of t_i is the *arrival time* of the $i+1$st customer. The values of t_i and t_{i+1} may be arbitrarily close, but they are never the same.

Exponential Distribution of Arrival Times

Define the *interarrival time* as the elapsed time between the arrivals of two consecutive customers. Specifically, define the ith interarrival time τ_i as

$$\tau_i = t_i - t_{i-1}$$

The Poisson arrival process categorizes the interarrival times. Specifically, an arrival process is Poisson if they are *exponentially distributed*. Mathematically, this means that if λ is the average arrival rate (number of customer per unit time) and $P(t)$ is the probability that an arbitrary interarrival time is less than t, then

$$P(t) = 1 - e^{-\lambda t}$$

At this point, you should ask two questions. The first is "What does this mean?" The second is "Where did this equation come from?" Let's first worry about what it means before we describe its origin.

Look at the graphs in Figure 7.2. They show the function $P(t) = 1 - e^{-\lambda t}$ for two values of λ. In both cases, when $t=0$, $P(t)=0$. That is, there is zero probability (impossibility) that an interarrival time is 0. This is consistent with our definition of interarrival times: they are always positive.

Figure 7.2 $P(t) = 1 - e^{-\lambda t}$ for different values of λ

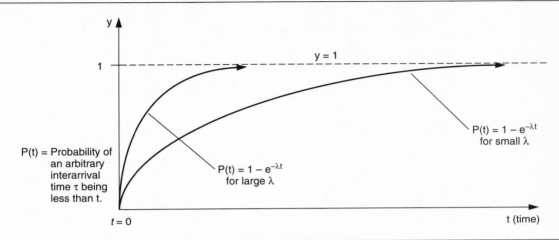

Both graphs in Figure 7.2 approach the horizontal line $y = 1$ as t increases. That is, the value of $P(t) = 1 - e^{-\lambda t}$ approaches 1. But, for larger λ, it approaches λ faster. For smaller l, $P(t)$ increases slower. What does this mean?

If customers arrive frequently (large λ) the probability is low that long periods will elapse between arrivals. Remember, a large value of λ means many customers arrive per unit of time. Let us think of this another way. Suppose that τ is an arbitrary interarrival time. Then as t increases, the probability that τ is larger than t decreases. Equivalently, the probability that τ is smaller than t increases, approaching certainty.

In calculus, we write this as

$$\lim_{t \to \infty} P(t) = 1$$

For smaller values of λ, we make the same statement. The difference is, that as t increases, the probability that τ is smaller than t does not increase as quickly.

Let us illustrate the probabilities with an example. Suppose a queuing system has customers randomly arriving at a rate of one every two minutes. Assume the interarrival times are exponentially distributed. The rate of one customer every two minutes is equivalent to $\lambda = .5$ customers per minute. The probability function is therefore

$$P(t) = 1 - e^{-\lambda t} = 1 - e^{-.5t}$$

Table 7.1 shows $P(t)$ evaluated for selected values of t.

Table 7.1 $P(t) = 1 - e^{-.5t}$

t	$P(t)$
0	0
1	.393
2	.632
3	.777
4	.865
5	.918
:	:
:	:
10	.993
:	:
20	.99995

Remember, we are not assuming that customers arrive at regular two-minute intervals. We assume that they arrive randomly at a rate of one every two minutes. There is a big difference that may not be obvious at first. In fact, Table 7.1 helps illustrate the difference.

For $t = 1$, $P(t)$ is .393. This means there is a .393 probability of an interarrival time being less than one minute. That is, nearly 40% of the interarrival times are less than one minute or, equivalently, nearly 40% of the customers arrive within one minute of the previous customer

If $t = 5$, $P(t) = .918$. That is, almost 92% of the interarrival times are less than five minutes. This also means that about 8% exceed 5 minutes. Finally, nearly 99.995% of the interarrival times are less than 20 minutes. This is a far cry from stating that customers arrive at regular two-minute intervals. Conceivably, twenty minutes or more may elapse between arrivals. Although the probability of .00005 makes this unlikely, it can happen!

The probability function does not tell us when customers will arrive. It does, however, provide information about the random arrival process. Note that Table 7.1 also indicates that nearly 14% of the customers arrive four or more minutes after the previous customer. (Can you see how we know this? What does the entry for $t = 4$ tell us?) Combine this with the fact that about 40% of the customers arrive within one minute of the previous customer and we see that arrivals occur in bunches. This is characteristic of random arrivals.

Derivation of the Exponential Distribution

Now that we have explained the significance of $P(t)=1-e^{-\lambda t}$, let us explain its origin. Did it just mysteriously appear from the bottom of a magician's hat or is there a logical reason for this function? Contrary to popular belief, there is a logical reason for it. The following discussion assumes familiarity with calculus, particularly the idea of a derivative. Those unfamiliar with calculus may skip it.

How can we go from the statement "customers arrive randomly at a rate λ" to the conclusion that "interarrival times are exponentially distributed"? We do it in two steps. First, we define a function $P_n(t)$ that represents the probability that n customers arrive during a period of length t. We then use it to generate $P(t)$.

Consider the function $P_1(h)$. It is the probability that one customer arrives in a period of length h. According to [1], a necessary requirement for a Poisson process is that

$$P_1(h) = \lambda h + o(h). \tag{7.1}$$

The expression "$o(h)$" represents a term that becomes insignificant as h approaches zero. More explicitly, we say that a function $f(h)$ is $o(h)$ if

$$\lim_{h \to 0} \frac{f(h)}{h} = 0$$

If h is small, $o(h)$ is even smaller and $P_1(h)$ is approximately equal to λh.

There is a rationale behind Equation 7.1. It says that we can approximate $P_1(h)$ by the linear term λh. Graphically (see Figure 7.3), we are approximating the graph of $P_1(h)$ by a straight line graph of λh. In practice, we can always use a straight line to approximate part of a continuous curve, especially a very small part. A small part of any curve often resembles a straight line.

Figure 7.3 Linear approximation of $P_1(h)$

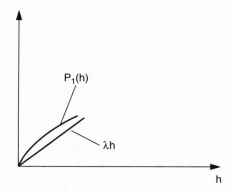

To illustrate, consider the case in which λ is .5 customers per minute. If h is six seconds (0.1 minutes), the probability that a customer will arrive during period h is about one tenth of .5 or .05. That is, $P_1(h)$ is approximately $\lambda h = .5 * .1 = .05$.

Another requirement in [1] for a Poisson process is that

$$P_2(h) + P_3(h) + P_4(h) + \ldots = o(h) \tag{7.2}$$

What does this mean? Remember, $P_i(h)$ is the probability that exactly i customers will arrive during a period h. Theory says that the probability that any of a set of mutually exclusive events will occur is the sum of the probabilities of each event. Here, the events are the arrivals of a specified number of customers. This sum, therefore, is the probability that 2 or more customers will arrive in a period h. Since, by assumption, this is negligible for small h, the sum is $o(h)$.

Since $P_0(h)$, $P_1(h)$, $P_2(h)$, . . . represent the probabilities of all possible events, and the events are all mutually exclusive, their sum must be 1. That is,

$$P_0(h) + P_1(h) + P_2(h) + P_3(h) + \ldots = 1$$

Solving for $P_0(h)$, gives

$$P_0(h) = 1 - P_1(h) - (P_2(h) + P_3(h) + \ldots .)$$

Substituting from Equations 7.1 and 7.2, gives

$$\begin{aligned} P_0(h) &= 1 - (\lambda h + o(h)) - o(h) \\ &= 1 - \lambda h + o(h) \end{aligned} \tag{7.3}$$

Note that the o(h) terms do not cancel, since they may be different. But if both become insignificant as h approaches 0, the difference also becomes insignificant. Thus, the difference between two $o(h)$ terms is an $o(h)$ term.

Now let us derive $P_0(t)$ for any t. Consider the expression $P_0(t + h)$. It is the probability that no customers will arrive before time $t + h$. But it depends on two mutually distinct events. They are:

- No customers arrive before time t (period t).

- No customers arrive during the period from t to $t + h$ (period h).

Theory states that the probability of two mutually distinct events both occurring is the product of their probabilities. Therefore,

$$\begin{aligned} P_0(t + h) &= P_0(t) * P_0(h) \\ &= P_0(t) * (1 - \lambda h + o(h)) \\ &= P_0(t) - \lambda h * P_0(t) + o(h) * P_0(t) \end{aligned}$$

Subtracting $P_0(t)$ from each side gives

$$P_0(t+h) - P_0(t) = -\lambda h * P_0(t) + o(h) * P_0(t)$$

Next divide by h to get

$$(P_0(t+h) - P_0(t))/h = -\lambda * P_0(t) + (o(h) * P_0(t))/h$$

Now take the limit as h approaches zero. The left hand side of the equation is $P'_0(t)$, the derivative of $P_0(t)$. The first term on the right hand side is independent of h and is unaffected by the limit. The second term contains the factor $o(h)/h$ which approaches zero as h approaches zero. Therefore, the second term disappears when we take the limit. We are thus left with

$$P'_0(t) = -\lambda * P_0(t)$$

The solution to this equation is $P_0(t) = Ke^{-\lambda t}$, where K is a constant. But, we already know that $P_0(0) = 1$. Equivalently, $P_0(0) = Ke^{-\lambda 0} = K = 1$. Thus, we have

$$P_0(t) = e^{-\lambda t} \tag{7.4}$$

Through a similar argument found in reference [1], one can show that in general

$$P_n(t) = \frac{e^{-\lambda t}(\lambda t)^n}{n!} \tag{7.5}$$

Finally we can derive $P(t)$. Let t be any value, and let h be an arbitrarily small interval. Consider the expression

$$P(t+h) - P(t)$$

It is the probability that an arbitrary interarrival time is less than $t + h$ minus the probability that it is less than t. The result is the probability that it lies between t and $t + h$. But an interarrival time between t and $t + h$ depends on two mutually distinct events. They are:

- No customers arrive during period t.
- One customer arrives between t and $t + h$ (an interval of length h).

The probability of the first event is $P_0(t)$. The probability of the second event is $P_1(h) = \lambda h + o(h)$. Multiplying the probabilities gives us

$$P(t + h) - P(t) = P_0(t) * P_1(h) = P_0(t) * (\lambda h + o(h))$$
$$= P_0(t) * \lambda h + P_0(t) * o(h)$$

As before, dividing each side by h gives

$$(P(t + h) - P(t))/h = P_0(t) * \lambda + P_0(t) * o(h)/h$$

Also as before, if we take the limit as h approaches 0, the left hand side becomes $P'(t)$ and the the right hand side becomes $P_0(t) * \lambda$. (Think about this. The argument is similar to the previous one.) Thus,

$$P'(t) = P_0(t) * \lambda$$

Since $P_0(t) = e^{-\lambda t}$, we have

$$P'(t) = \lambda e^{-\lambda t}.$$

The solution to this equation is $P(t) = K - e^{-\lambda t}$, where K is a constant. To find K, we evaluate the equation at $t = 0$. By the definition of $P(t)$ (Figure 7.2), $P(0) = 0$. This is equivalent to stating $K - e^{-\lambda*0} = 0$. But, $K - e^{-\lambda*0} = K - e^0 = K - 1 = 0$. Thus $K = 1$ and we have the equation

$$P(t) = 1 - e^{-\lambda t} \tag{7.6}$$

≡≡≡≡≡ 7.3 Birth and Death Rates

The previous section described the Poisson arrival pattern for customers arriving at a queue. If the customers are processes, the arrivals are equivalent to *creations* or *births*. We then call λ the *birth rate* of the processes.

But to answer the questions posed earlier, we need to know more. After all, how long a process must wait in a queue depends not only on how many are likely to enter the queue but also on how long the service takes. When a server finishes with a customer or process, it leaves the system. We call this its *death* (exit would be less dramatic). We denote the *death rate* (number of deaths per time unit)by μ.

In this section, we further categorize a queuing system by considering both its birth and death rates. We will also extend the results of the previous section to a more complex model.

In the previous section, we assumed the birth rate λ was fixed. This is not always true. As anyone who has studied population dynamics knows, birth rates may vary. They may depend on the current population or the current *state* of the system. Similarly, the death rate may depend on the current state of the system.

In some cases, the birth and death rates depend not only on the current state, but also on previous states (history) as well. If the rates depend only on the current state and not on the history, we say the model is a *Markov Process*. In this section, we assume the birth and death rates depend only on the system's current state. Our main objective here is to generate a formula for the probability of the system being in a given state.

State Transitions

Let us start by describing the *state transition diagram* (Figure 7.4) for a system. As we stated, a system can be in any one of many possible states. If our system is like the one in Figure 7.1, we can define each state by the number of customers. The customers may be in the queue or with a server. Thus, state zero means that no customers are in the system. State 1 means exactly one customer is in the system. In general, state i means that i customers are in the system. If there are n servers, state i, where $i \geq n$, means that all servers are busy and that any arriving customers must wait. We assume that scheduling guarantees that customers never wait if a server is available.

Figure 7.4 State transition diagram showing birth and death rates

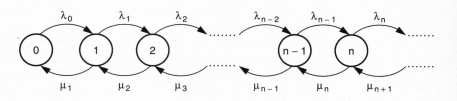

A *state transition* is the way in which the system changes states. In this section we assume only two types of transitions. The first goes from state i to state $i+1$, for $i \geq 0$. It is a birth and occurs whenever a customer enters the system. The other is from state $i+1$ to state i, for $i \geq 0$. It is a death and occurs whenever a server finishes with a customer and the customer leaves the system. We are assuming that two births or two deaths never occur simultaneously.

The circles in Figure 7.4 represent the states, and the arrows indicate possible transitions. Each arrow is marked with λ_i or μ_i for some value of i. Here we assume the birth rates are not constant but, in fact, depend on the current state.

Thus, λ_i is the birth rate for a system in state i. Similarly μ_i is the death rate for a system in state i. As we shall soon see, the probability of any state transition depends on either the birth or death rate. Now that we have defined the state transition diagram, what can we do with it? How does it help us analyze a system?

Steady State Systems

Analyzing a system involves estimating likely activity within it. For example, are long lines likely or will servers frequently be available? The first situation may indicate too few servers. The second may indicate too many. The reader should beware of oversimplifying the situation. It is possible for both situations to occur; that is, the system may frequently have long lines and idle servers (although not simultaneously). We will see such a case later. A system may be a complex mixture, as births and deaths occur in random patterns.

Basically, in terms of the state transition diagram, we want to know the probability of the system being in state i, for $i \geq 0$. To do this, define $P_i(t)$ as the probability of the system being in state i at time t. $P_i(t)$ is a generalization of the similarly named function in the last section. There, $P_i(t)$ was the probability that i customers would arrive by time t. If no deaths occur during t, this is the same as the probability that the system is in state i at time t. Including death rates makes $P_i(t)$ more complex.

$P_i(t)$ also is more complex because birth rates are not constant but depend on the state of the system. In fact, finding a general formula for $P_i(t)$ is very difficult [1], and we do not attempt it here. However, we will generate a *steady state* formula.

What do we mean by steady state? A system is in *steady state* (also called *stationary* or in a state of *equilibrium*) if its state no longer depends on time. That is, $P_i(t)$ becomes independent of t. If a system approaches steady state, it will usually do so only after a long time. In such cases, we write

$$\lim_{t \to \infty} P_i(t) = p_i$$

Thus, if we assume this limit exists (and we will), p_i is the probability that a steady state system is in state i.

Let us illustrate the meaning of steady state through an example. Suppose a computer (and its users) has suffered through an extended period of down time. When it finally starts up, many events cause it to behave erratically. For example, because of the down time, many people are anxiously waiting to submit programs. When the system starts working again, they will probably all submit them at roughly the same time. This can cause unusual system behavior, as the large number of nearly simultaneous submissions is not typical of the normal workload. Many processes need to execute immediately. Many may make I/O requests in a short time. Initially, all I/O controllers are idle. It will take a while for the system to settle into its normal mode of operations.

After the system has been running for a while, the workload will presumably return to normal. Now if nothing special happens, the system will enter a steady state. For example, its behavior after six hours is likely to be the same as after eight hours. Thus, the probability that the system is in a specific state is, for all intents and purposes, constant.

In terms of state transitions, steady state means that the probability of a transition from state i to state $i + 1$ is equal to the probability of one from state $i + 1$ to state i. Essentially, the number of processes in the system remains relatively constant, and births and deaths are equally likely. Remember that every process begins with a birth and ends with a death. Again, major exceptions occur at startup and shutdown. Startup involves many births but few deaths, and shutdown is the opposite.

Let us now ask the question, "What is the probability of the system being in state i ?" In other words, can we find a formula for p_i ? In particular, what is the probability of the system being in a state i, where $i \geq n$? That is, what is the probability that arriving customers must wait?

A transition from state i to state $i + 1$ depends on two events. The first is that the system must be in state i. The second is that a birth must occur. Consider a small time interval of length h. The probability of a transition from state i to state $i + 1$ equals the probability of the system being in state i initially (p_i) times the probability of a birth during the interval $(\lambda_i * h + o(h))$. The latter expression is from the previous section. Therefore, the probability of a transition from state i to state $i + 1$ is

$$p_i * (\lambda_i * h + o(h))$$

Similarly, we may write the probability of a transition from state $i + 1$ to state i as

$$p_{i+1} * (\mu_{i+1} * h + o(h)).$$

Thus, the steady state assumption gives the following equation

$$p_i * (\lambda_i * h + o(h)) = p_{i+1} * (\mu_{i+1} * h + o(h))$$

which is equivalent to

$$p_i * \lambda_i * h + p_i * o(h) = p_{i+1} * \mu_{i+1} * h + p_{i+1} * o(h)$$

If we divide each side, by h, we get

$$p_i * \lambda_i + p_i * o(h)/h = p_{i+1} * \mu_{i+1} + p_{i+1} * o(h)/h$$

If we now take the limit as h approaches zero, the two terms with $o(h)$ disappear. We are left with

$$p_i * \lambda_i = p_{i+1} * \mu_{i+1} \quad \text{for } i = 0, 1, 2, \ldots$$

or equivalently

$$p_{i+1} = (\lambda_i / \mu_{i+1}) * p_i \quad \text{for } i = 0, 1, 2, \ldots$$

Since p_{i+1} can be expressed in terms of p_i for each i, we can therefore write p_i in terms of p_0 as follows. For $i = 1$, we get

$$p_1 = (\lambda_0 / \mu_1) * p_0$$

For $i = 2$,

$$p_2 = (\lambda_1 / \mu_2) * p_1$$

Substituting the formula for p_1 gives

$$p_2 = (\lambda_0 * \lambda_1)/(\mu_1 * \mu_2) * p_0$$

For $i = 3$,

$$p_3 = (\lambda_2 / \mu_3) * p_2$$
$$= (\lambda_0 * \lambda_1 * \lambda_2)/(\mu_1 * \mu_2 * \mu_3) * p_0$$

We can continue this, but a pattern is emerging. In general, for any i,

$$p_i = \frac{\lambda_0 * \lambda_1 * \lambda_2 * \ldots * \lambda_{i-1}}{\mu_1 * \mu_2 * \mu_3 * \ldots * \mu_i} * p_0 \tag{7.7}$$

Thus, we can define p_i in terms of p_0. Of course, this is useful only if we can determine p_0. One more observation will allow us to do that.

Since p_i, for $i = 1, 2, 3, \ldots$, are the probabilities of the mutually exclusive and exhaustive states of the system, they must sum to 1. Therefore,

$$p_0 + p_1 + p_2 + \ldots + p_i + \ldots = 1 \tag{7.8}$$

Now, if we use Equation 7.7 for each p_i, Equation 7.8 changes to

$$p_0 + \frac{\lambda_0}{\mu_1} * p_0 + \frac{\lambda_0 * \lambda_1}{\mu_1 * \mu_2} * p_0 + \cdots$$

$$+ \frac{\lambda_0 * \lambda_1 * \lambda_2 * \ldots * \lambda_{i-1}}{\mu_1 * \mu_2 * \mu_3 * \ldots * \mu_i} * p_0 + \cdots = 1 \qquad (7.9)$$

Since p_0 appears in each term, we can factor it out to get

$$p_0 * (1 + k_1 + k_2 + \ldots + k_i + \ldots) = 1$$

where

$$k_i = \frac{\lambda_0 * \lambda_1 * \lambda_2 * \ldots * \lambda_{i-1}}{\mu_1 * \mu_2 * \mu_3 * \ldots * \mu_i} \text{ for } i = 1, 2, 3, \ldots \qquad (7.10)$$

Now we can solve for p_0 as

$$p_0 = 1/(1 + k_1 + k_2 + \ldots + k_i + \ldots) \qquad (7.11)$$

Finally (and we do mean finally), if we put the formula for p_0 from Equation 7.11 into Equation 7.7, we get

$$p_i = k_i * p_0$$

or, equivalently,

$$p_i = k_i /(1 + k_1 + k_2 + \ldots + k_i + \ldots) \text{ for } i \geq 0 \qquad (7.12)$$

Thus, if we know the birth and death rates of the steady state system, we can calculate the probability that it is in state i for any $i \geq 0$. This is not a calculation you would care to do by hand, but a computer has no trouble with it.

We realize that some may find these formulas horrendous. However, the development of general equations is seldom easy. We generate them to show the reasoning behind the calculations in the next sections. At this point, you should mentally file the equations away for further use. We will consider cases that require their use. We will also make assumptions that simplify the equations and allow us to calculate interesting quantities.

≡≡≡≡≡ **7.4** *M/M/c* **Queuing Systems**

The previous two sections mainly provide a basis for a mathematical model of a queuing system. We can use the equations to estimate useful quantities. We still have to see how to do this.

In the first section we mentioned several quantities we want to estimate. For the benefit of the reader, we repeat them here. They are:

- The probability that all servers are idle.
- The probability that a customer will have to wait.
- Expected number of customers in a queue at a given time.
- Expected wait time for a customer in a queue.
- Wait time which 10% of the customers exceed (90th percentile wait time).

In this section we generate equations used to estimate some values. We will give references for those we do not generate.

The literature [1, 3, 5, 12] describes many types of queuing systems. In this section, we describe only one type, the *M/M/c* system. The name *M/M/c* queuing system comes from the *Kendall Notation*; it is based on system parameters and assumptions. *M/M/c* means there are *c* identical servers. It also means the interarrival and service times are exponentially distributed. Recall that this means if $P(t)$ is the probability of an interarrival time being less than t, and $Q(t)$ is the probability of a service time being less than t,

$$P(t) = 1 - e^{-\lambda t}$$

and

$$Q(t) = 1 - e^{-\mu t}$$

where λ is the average arrival rate and μ is the average service rate.

≡≡≡
Probability of All Servers Idle

Let us now find expressions for our measures. We start by generating the formula for the probability that all servers are idle.

As previously stated, interarrival times are exponentially distributed. However, here we assume the birth rates do not depend on the number of customers in the system. This is often reasonable. For example, the number of processes entering a system does not necessarily depend on the number of processes currently in it. This assumption helps simplify some equations generated in Section 7.3.

In particular, Figure 7.5 shows the state transition diagram for an *M/M/c* system with a constant birth rate. Note the changes from Figure 7.4. Since the birth rate does not depend on the number of customers, it is a constant λ. But this is just a special case of Figure 7.4 where $\lambda_n = \lambda$ for all n.

Figure 7.5 State transition diagram showing birth and death rates for an *M/M/c* system

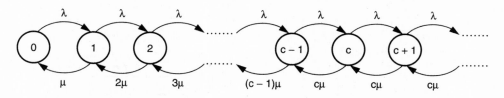

However, the death rate does depend on the number of customers in the system. Again, using the previous example, the number of processes finishing certainly depends on the number in the system. More specifically, the death rates μ_n, for $n \geq 0$, depend on the number of processes currently receiving service. All this says is that more processes will finish per unit of time if there are more servers (processors).

Now, since μ is the average customer service rate (death rate), $\mu_n = n * \mu$ as long as $n < c$. Remember, μ is actually the death rate when there is one server. If there are two servers, the death rate is twice as large. If there are three servers, it is three times as large, and so on. We assume that all servers provide equal rates. If there are c servers, the death rate cannot exceed $c * \mu$. We therefore define the death rates as

$$\mu_n = \begin{cases} n * \mu & \text{if } n < c \\ c * \mu & \text{if } n \geq c \end{cases}$$

The terminology is a bit gruesome here, particularly when the servers are doctors in an emergency room. The only nice part here is that "dead" customers can always be reborn to wait in still another queue. As this is a secular textbook, we deny all religious implications.

From this assumption, we can now generate formulas for two desired measures. They are the probability that no servers are active and the probability that all are busy and that a new customer must wait.

From Equation 7.10, we have

$$
k_i = \frac{\lambda_0 * \lambda_1 * \lambda_2 * \ldots * \lambda_{i-1}}{\mu_1 * \mu_2 * \mu_3 * \ldots * \mu_i} =
\begin{cases}
\dfrac{\overbrace{\lambda * \lambda * \lambda * \ldots * \lambda}^{i \text{ factors}}}{\mu * 2\mu * 3\mu * \ldots * i\mu} & \text{if } i < c \\[3em]
\dfrac{\overbrace{\lambda * \lambda * \lambda * \ldots * \lambda}^{i \text{ factors}}}{\underbrace{\mu * 2\mu * \ldots * c\mu}_{c \text{ factors}} * \underbrace{c\mu * \ldots * c\mu}_{i-c \text{ factors}}} & \text{if } i \geq c
\end{cases}
$$

$$
=
\begin{cases}
\dfrac{\lambda^i}{i! * \mu^i} & \text{if } i < c \\[2em]
\dfrac{\lambda^i}{c! * \mu^i * c^{i-c}} & \text{if } i \geq c
\end{cases}
\qquad (7.13)
$$

Now, using this definition for k_i in Equation 7.11, we get

$$
p_0 = (1 + k_1 + k_2 + \ldots + k_i + \ldots)^{-1}
$$

$$
= \left[\sum_{i=0}^{c-1} \frac{\lambda^i}{i! * \mu^i} + \sum_{i=c}^{\infty} \frac{\lambda^i}{c! * \mu^i * c^{i-c}} \right]^{-1}
$$

$$
= \left[\sum_{i=0}^{c-1} \frac{\lambda^i}{i! * \mu^i} + \frac{\lambda^c}{c! * \mu^c} \sum_{i=c}^{\infty} \frac{\lambda^{i-c}}{\mu^{i-c} * c^{i-c}} \right]^{-1}
$$

$$= \left[\sum_{i=0}^{c-1} \frac{\lambda^i}{i! * \mu^i} + \frac{\lambda^c}{c! * \mu^c} \sum_{i=0}^{\infty} \frac{\lambda^i}{\mu^i * c^i} \right]^{-1}$$

$$= \left[\sum_{i=0}^{c-1} \frac{\lambda^i}{i! * \mu^i} + \frac{\lambda^c}{c! * \mu^c} \sum_{i=0}^{\infty} \left(\frac{\lambda}{\mu * c} \right)^i \right]^{-1}$$

Be careful! We used several algebraic tricks to simplify each step. Examine them carefully.

Now, we may write the infinite sum in the last step as

$$\sum_{i=0}^{\infty} \rho^i$$

where $\rho = \lambda/(\mu*c)$. Calculus shows that this sum converges if $| \rho | < 1$. Given fixed values for λ and μ, we can always find a value of c for which this is true. Furthermore, calculus shows that under this condition the sum converges to $1/(1-\rho)$.

If we substitute this for the infinite sum, we finally have our first formula. So without further delay, we proudly present the formula for the probability that no servers are active. It is:

$$p_0 = \left[\sum_{i=0}^{c-1} \frac{\lambda^i}{i! * \mu^i} + \frac{\lambda^c}{c! * \mu^c * (1-\rho)} \right]^{-1} \tag{7.14}$$

═══

Probability of All Servers Busy

Not only does Equation 7.14 allow us to calculate one desired measure, it also allows us to generate a formula for another one; the formula for the probability that all servers are busy and that an arriving customer must wait. We follow the example of reference [1] and use the notation $C(c, \lambda / \mu)$ to represent the probability that all servers are busy. The formula we will generate is called *Erlang's C Formula* or *Erlang's Delay Formula*.

The easiest way to get a formula for $C(c, \lambda/\mu)$ is from Equation 7.8. Now the probability that all servers are busy is 1 minus the probability that they are not all busy. All servers busy means there are c or more customers, and not all servers busy means there are fewer than c customers. Therefore, in terms of Equation 7.8, this is the same as writing

$$C(c, \lambda/\mu) = p_c + p_{c+1} + p_{c+2} + \ldots =$$
$$1 - (p_0 + p_1 + p_2 + p_3 + \ldots + p_{c-1}) \qquad (7.15)$$

But from Equation 7.12, we have $p_i = k_i * p_0$ and from Equation 7.13, we have $k_i = \lambda^i/(i! * \mu^i)$ for $i < c$. We can thus write $p_i = p_0 * \lambda^i/(i! * \mu^i)$ for $i < c$. If we substitute this into Equation 7.15 and factor out p_0, we end up with

$$C(c, \lambda/\mu) = 1 - p_0 * [1 + \lambda/\mu + \lambda^2/(2! * \mu^2) + \lambda^3/(3! * \mu^3) + \ldots$$

$$+ \lambda^{c-1}/((c-1)! * \mu^{c-1})]$$

or

$$C(c, \lambda/\mu) = 1 - p_0 * \left[\sum_{i=0}^{c-1} \frac{\lambda^i}{i! * \mu^i} \right] \qquad (7.16)$$

Furthermore, we can simplify the summation inside the brackets. To see how, look at Equation 7.14. If we multiply each side of it by the bracketed expression in Equation 7.14, we get

$$p_0 * \left[\sum_{i=0}^{c-1} \frac{\lambda^i}{i! * \mu^i} + \frac{\lambda^c}{c! * \mu^c * (1-\rho)} \right] = 1$$

This is nice because we can now divide each side by p_0 and then subtract the second term inside the brackets from each side of the equation. This gives us the following simpler expression for the summation

$$\sum_{i=0}^{c-1} \frac{\lambda^i}{i! * \mu^i} = 1/p_0 - \frac{\lambda^c}{c! * \mu^c * (1-\rho)}$$

We can now substitute the right hand side of this equation for the summation in Equation 7.16 to get

$$C(c, \lambda/\mu) = 1 - p_0 * \left[1/p_0 - \frac{\lambda^c}{c! * \mu^c * (1-\rho)} \right]$$

$$= \frac{p_0 * \lambda^c}{c! * \mu^c * (1-\rho)} \tag{7.17}$$

We now have a formula for the second measure. Equation 7.17 gives the probability that all servers are busy and that an arriving customer must wait. We have two formulas down and three to go.

Expected Number of Customers

The third formula we derive is for the expected number of customers in the queue. We will denote it by L_q. By definition, the expected number of customers in a queue is a weighted average of the number of customers in it. We can calculate a weighted average of any collection of values by summing the product of each and its probability of occurrence. Therefore, in this case we have

$$L_q = \sum_{i=0}^{\infty} (i \text{ customers in the queue})*(\text{probability that } i \text{ customers are in the queue})$$

$$= \sum_{i=0}^{\infty} i * p_{i+c} \tag{7.18}$$

Note that the probability that i customers are in the queue is p_{i+c}, the probability that $i + c$ customers are in the system. Remember, there are i customers in the queue only if all servers are busy. But this occurs only when there are c customers being served. Since there are i customers in the queue and c being served, there are $i + c$ customers in the system.

Now, from Equations 7.11, 7.12, and 7.13, we may write p_{i+c} as

$$p_{i+c} = p_0 * \lambda^{i+c} / (c! * \mu^{i+c} * c^i)$$

Remember, in Equation 7.13, we have replaced i with $i + c$. Also, since $i + c \geq c$ we use the part of 7.13 that contains the '$c!$' factor. We can further simplify the above equation as follows:

$$p_{i+c} = p_0 * \lambda^{i+c} / (c! * \mu^{i+c} * c^i)$$

$$= p_0 * [\lambda^c / (c! * \mu^c)] * [\lambda^i / (\mu^i * c^i)]$$

$$= p_0 * [\lambda^c / (c! * \mu^c)] * [\lambda / (\mu * c)]^i$$

$$= p_0 * [\lambda^c / (c! * \mu^c)] * \rho^i$$

where again $\rho = \lambda / (\mu * c)$

Substituting this expression for p_{i+c} into Equation 7.18, we get

$$L_q = \sum_{i=0}^{\infty} i * p_0 * \frac{\lambda^c}{c! * \mu^c} * \rho^i$$

$$= p_0 * \frac{\lambda^c}{c! * \mu^c} * \sum_{i=0}^{\infty} i * \rho^i$$

$$= p_0 * \frac{\lambda^c}{c! * \mu^c} * \rho * \sum_{i=0}^{\infty} i * \rho^{i-1}$$

$$= p_0 * \frac{\lambda^c}{c! * \mu^c} * \rho * \sum_{i=0}^{\infty} \frac{d(\rho^i)}{d\rho}$$

In the last version, $d(\rho^i)/d\rho$ is the derivative of ρ^i with respect to ρ. This is the same as is $i * \rho^{i-1}$. As before, we assume the infinite sum converges. We also assume the infinite sum of derivatives is the derivative of the infinite sum. (This is not an assumption to take lightly, but to verify it is far outside the scope of this book.) We therefore have

$$L_q = p_0 * \frac{\lambda^c}{c! * \mu^c} * \rho * \frac{d\left(\sum\limits_{i=0}^{\infty} \rho^i\right)}{d\rho}$$

$$= p_0 * \frac{\lambda^c}{c! * \mu^c} * \rho * \frac{d\left(\dfrac{1}{1-\rho}\right)}{d\rho}$$

$$= p_0 * \frac{\lambda^c}{c! * \mu^c} * \frac{\rho}{(1-\rho)^2}$$

$$= \rho * p_0 * \frac{\lambda^c}{c! * \mu^c * (1-\rho)^2}$$

Finally, $L_q = \rho * C(c, \lambda/\mu) / (1-\rho)$ (7.19)

The last step uses Equation 7.17. We now have the formula for the third desired measure, the expected number of customers in the queue.

≣

Expected Wait Time (Little's Formula)

The next measure we find is the expected wait time for a customer. We denote it by W_q. Since we have already found an expression for L_q, finding one for W_q is easy. But, we must reference a well known result in queuing theory called *Little's Formula*. In reference [2], Little shows that under certain conditions which we have assumed, the following formula holds:

$$L_q = \lambda W_q$$

That is, the expected number of customers in the queue is the product of the expected wait time and the arrival rate. Since we have already found a formula for L_q and λ is a given parameter, we can easily solve for W_q:

$$W_q = L_q / \lambda$$

$$= \rho * C\,(c, \lambda / \mu) / [\, \lambda *(1-\rho)]$$

But since $\rho = \lambda / (\mu * c)$, we have

$$W_q = C\,(c, \lambda / \mu) / [\, \mu *c *(1-\rho)] \qquad (7.20)$$

This derivation was much easier than its predecessors thanks to Little.

90th Percentile Wait Time

We are almost done with this section. Just one last formula remains. The measure we denote by $\pi_q(90)$ is the 90th percentile wait time in the queue. In other words, 90% of the customers wait less than $\pi_q(90)$. Of course, this means 10% of the customers wait longer.

We will not show the derivation of the formula for $\pi_q(90)$. (Don't everyone cheer at once.) The derivation is longer and more complex than the previous ones. If you are interested, consult a reference on Queuing Theory, such as [1]. In this section, we simply present the formula.

The formula for the the 90th percentile wait time is

$$\pi_q\,(90) = \ln\,[10* C\,(c, \lambda / \mu)\,] / [\, \mu *c *(1-\rho)] \qquad (7.21)$$

We now have obtained the five formulas for the measures we wanted to find. They are Equations 7.14 (probability that no servers are busy), 7.17 (probability that all servers are busy and that an arriving customer must wait), 7.19 (the expected number of customers in the queue), 7.20 (the expected wait time for a customer in the queue), and 7.21 (the 90th percentile wait time in the queue).

These formulas represent sophisticated mathematics and statistics, and apply only under certain model assumptions. Different models require different assumptions, and of course, produce different formulas for performance measures. We leave them to texts on Queuing Theory and advanced operating system modeling. We will use the formulas generated here in case studies in the next section.

==== **7.5 Case Studies**

We have used considerable space developing theory and formulas to estimate performance measures in a queuing system. If you have read the previous sections, you understand where the equations originated. Even if you have not read them, you can still benefit from this section. However, you must believe (on faith) that our formulas adequately describe the measures. You should also be comfortable working with complex expressions.

Our first case study is a queuing system with only one server. It is a good starting place because our equations become much simpler with just one server ($c = 1$). Equations 7.22 through 7.26 are Equations 7.14, 7.17, 7.19, 7.20, and 7.21 rewritten and simplified with $c = 1$. We will not derive the simplified equations here, but we suggest that you do so (see the Exercises at the end of the chapter). The equations are deceptively simple.

$$p_0 = 1 - \rho \tag{7.22}$$

$$C(c, \lambda/\mu) = \rho \tag{7.23}$$

$$L_q = \frac{\rho^2}{1 - \rho} \tag{7.24}$$

$$W_q = \frac{\rho/\mu}{1 - \rho} \tag{7.25}$$

$$\pi_q(90) = \frac{\ln(10*\rho)}{\mu - \lambda} \tag{7.26}$$

=====
Case Study 1: A Shared Laser Printer

A manager of a company's graphic design department has approved funds for a laser printer in the downtown office. All the department's employees will share it to produce high quality copies of their artwork. They all have access to it via PCs connected to a local area network. When an employee needs a laser copy, he or she enters the proper command, and the document is queued for printing.

Since the manager is not in charge of a large department, she approved purchase of only one laser printer (Figure 7.6). Unfortunately, she has been receiving complaints from employees that they must wait nearly half an hour for their designs. Similarly, the technical support person has stated that long queues are indeed forming and that employees are using the time in extended coffee breaks where they solve most of the world's problems. (Perhaps all is not lost.)

Figure 7.6 Queuing system with customers and one laser printer

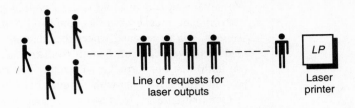

Line of requests for
laser outputs

Laser
printer

The manager is frequently out of the office, but the few times she has passed
by the printer, it was idle. Furthermore, the summary of printer output for each
eight-hour day shows an average of 64 requests occurring at random times.
They require an average of about 5 minutes to print. Thus, there are about 8
requests per hour and about 40 minutes per hour of printing. Since the printer is
idle one-third of the time, the manager is obviously perplexed. Can you analyze
the situation and help her?

Solution. Suppose you examine the employee records and verify that the
submission of requests is a Poisson process. That is, the interarrival times (times
between submissions) are exponentially distributed. Your preliminary analysis
also verifies that the average printing time is about 5 minutes and that printing
(service) times are exponentially distributed. In short, the situation is an M/M/1
queueing system. Let us now begin the analysis.

Since there are 64 requests per eight-hour day, they arrive at the printer
randomly at an average rate of 8 per hour. If we use minutes as our time unit,
the average arrival rate is

$$\lambda = (8 \text{ requests/hour})*(1 \text{ hour/60 minutes}) = 2/15 \text{ requests per minute.}$$

The expected service time is 5 minutes per request. This means one server
(printer) could handle 12 requests per hour on the average. Therefore, the
average service rate is

$$\mu = (12 \text{ requests per hour})*(1 \text{ hour/60 minutes}) = 1/5 \text{ (or 0.2) requests per}$$
$$\text{minute.}$$

Since $c = 1$,

$$\rho = \lambda/(\mu c) = \lambda/\mu = (2/15)/0.2 = 2/3$$

Therefore, from Equation 7.22, we find

$$p_0 = 1 - \rho = 1 - 2/3 = 1/3.$$

Now remember that p_0 is the probability that no servers are busy. In this case, it is the probability that the printer is idle. Indeed, there are no requests being processed one-third of the time. It seems strange that such long lines can be forming. But let us continue.

From Equation 7.23, we have

$$C\,(c, \lambda\,/\mu) = \rho = 2/3$$

There is a 2/3 probability that an arriving request must wait. Since the printer is busy two-thirds of the time, this makes sense. Let's go on.

Equation 7.24 tells us that

$$L_q = \rho^2/(1-\rho) = (2/3)^2/(1-2/3) = 4/3$$

Thus, the expected number of requests in the queue is 4/3. Averages are not always integers, even though the actual values must be.

Equation 7.25 yields the average waiting time in the queue. It is

$$W_q = (\rho\,/\mu)/(1 - \rho) = [(2/3)/0.2]/(1 - 2/3) = 10 \text{ minutes}$$

Thus, on the average, requests wait 10 minutes before printing begins.

Finally, the 90th percentile wait time is, from Equation 7.26,

$$\pi_q\,(90) = \ln(10*\rho)/(\mu - \lambda) = \ln(10*2/3)/(1/5 - 2/15) \cong 28.4 \text{ minutes}$$

This means that 10 percent of the requests wait half an hour or more for about 5 minutes worth of printing.

The situation is anomalous. The printer is busy only 2/3 of the time, yet about 10% of the requests wait nearly half an hour. Much of this is due to the fact that requests arrive at random. If they arrived at evenly spaced intervals, the wait times would be much shorter. But of course the manager cannot schedule when employees need printed output. Since the interarrival times are exponentially distributed, requests tend to occur in bunches (as random numbers often do). The result is long waits. Anyway, we have convinced the manager that there is a problem. The next step is to solve it. What can we do?

An obvious solution is to buy a second printer. Of course, the manager is a little nervous about approving more funds (as all good managers should be). Will it really solve the problem and reduce excessive waiting? The question the manager may well ask is, "What will the average and 90th percentile waiting times be with the second printer?"

You can easily answer the question. All you must do is use an M/M/2 queuing system and generate the equations. The values of λ and μ are, of course, unchanged. However, since the number of servers is 2 ($c=2$), ρ now becomes

$$\rho = \lambda /(\mu\, c) = (2/15)/(0.2*2) = 1/3$$

Using Equations 7.14, 7.17, 7.19, 7.20, and 7.21 and the new values of ρ and c, we obtain the following performance measures.

p_0 (probability that neither printer is busy) $= [1 + \lambda /\mu + \lambda^c /(c\,!* \mu^c *(1-\rho))]^{-1}$
$$= [1 + (2/15)/0.2 + (2/15)^2/(2!* 0.2^2*(1-1/3))]^{-1} = 0.5$$

$C\,(c, \lambda/\mu)$ (probability that a request must wait) $= p_0* \lambda^c /(c\,!* \mu^c * (1-\rho))$
$$= 0.5*(2/15)^2/ (2!* 0.2^2*(1-1/3)) = 1/6$$

L_q (Expected number of waiting requests) $= \rho* C\,(c, \lambda /\mu)/ (1-\rho)$
$$= (1/3)*(1/6)/(1-1/3) = 1/12$$

W_q (Expected wait time for a printer) $= L_q / \lambda = (1/12)/(2/15) = 5/8$ minutes
$$= 37.5 \text{ seconds}$$

$\pi_q\,(90)$ (90th percentile wait time) $= \ln(10* C\,(c, \lambda/\mu))/(\mu *c *(1-\rho))$
$$= \ln(10* 1/6)/(0.2 *2*(1-1/3)) \cong 2$$
$$\text{minutes}$$

Thus, only the crabbiest employee will complain of long waits. If the manager can afford to buy two laser printers, the problem is solved.

As a side note, the assumption that the arrival rate of 8 requests per hour applies to the entire day is probably unrealistic. Many employees may spend the first half hour in the morning pumping coffee into their systems to wake up (on Monday mornings, it may be much longer). Many may spend the last hour of the day thinking about the evening. If lunch hours are staggered, midday requests will be less frequent. A better approach might be to define queuing systems for different periods; that is, we might use one system for off-peak hours and another for busier parts of the day. See Questions at the end of the chapter.

═══
Case Study 2: Master Scheduler

A company is buying a new computer. Its employees mainly run simulation programs that require a lot of CPU time and little I/O. The company has decided on a system that schedules programs on a FIFO basis (Figure 7.7).

Figure 7.7 Queuing system with many programs and multiple CPUs

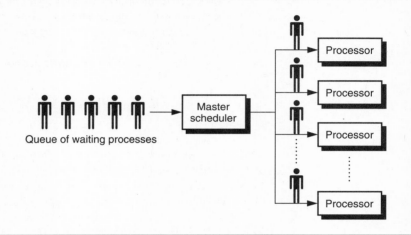

Company employees generally submit about 100 programs per day. Furthermore, they work independently and at different times (including an entire shift of seldom seen "nightowls"). As a result, they submit programs at random times. The programs themselves require an average of about one hour of CPU time. Furthermore, the run times are exponentially distributed.

It takes no genius to realize that getting 100 hours of computing time in a twenty-four-hour day will require more than one processor. In fact, the company will need at least five processors. (Four will provide a maximum of 96 hours of computing per day. We will ignore the amount of processor time required by the operating system.)

But simply buying enough processors is not sufficient. The employees' time is very valuable, and the company insists they not be delayed by long waits. In fact, the company requires that the new system provide at most ninety-minute turnaround for 90% of its employees. That is, the system must process 90% of the programs within a ninety-minute period.

Analyze this system and determine how many processors the company should buy.

Solution. Let us proceed as before to calculate the arrival and service rates. Now, we assume that employees submit 100 programs per day. This means that 100 customers arrive at the master scheduler (Figure 7.7) per day. Therefore, the arrival rate is

$$\lambda = 100/24 \cong 4.2 \text{ customers per hour}$$

Since each program requires about an hour of CPU time, the expected service time is one hour per customer. Thus, one CPU could service one customer per hour on the average. Therefore, the average service rate is

$$\mu = 1 \text{ customer per hour}$$

We also have

$$\rho = \lambda/(\mu c) \cong 4.2/c$$

We do not yet know the value of c. After all, it is the number of processors and that is what we must find.

We have not generated a formula to find c given other constraints, and we will not do so here. Our approach is simply to calculate values from Equations 7.14, 7.17, 7.19, 7.20, and 7.21 using $c = 5, 6, 7, \ldots$. We stop when Equation 7.21 yields a value of 0.5 hours or less. (Remember, Equation 7.21 provides only the waiting part of the turnaround time.) We will then have found a value for the number of processors needed to provide ninety-minute turnaround for 90% of the employees.

We have written a Turbo Pascal program (Figure 7.8) that calculates p_0, $C(c, \lambda/\mu)$, L_q, W_q, and $\pi_q(90)$. We list it here for students who want to calculate statistics of their own and to help with the Questions section at the end of the chapter.

The program produced the results (rounded to two significant digits) in Table 7.2. The units of time are all hours.

Table 7.2 Queuing statistics generated from the program in Figure 7.8

c	p_0	$C(c, \lambda/\mu)$	L_q	W_q	$\pi_q(90)$
5	0.0099	0.62	3.1	0.74	2.2
6	0.014	0.33	0.74	0.18	0.65
7	0.015	0.16	0.24	0.056	0.17

Figure 7.8 Program to calculate queuing statistics

```
Program Demo(Input, Output, Outfile).

Var
    Lambda      :Real;       {λ - Average arrival rate}
    Mu          :Real;       {μ - Customer service rate}
    C           :Integer;    {c - Number of servers}
    Rho         :Real;       {ρ - Server utilization}
    P0          :Real;       {p₀ - probability no servers are busy}
    Lq          :Real;       {Lq - Expected number of customers in the queue}
    Wq          :Real;       {Wq - Expected wait time for a customer in the queue}
    Piq         :Real;       {πq(90) - 90th percentile wait time in the queue}
    BigC        :Real;       {C(c, λ/μ) - Probability that an arriving customer must wait}
    Outfile     :Text;       {Text file to hold queue statistics}
{***************************************************************************************************}
Function Factorial(N : Integer) : Real,
                                { ───── Calculates N!───── }
Var
    Temp : Real,
    I       : Integer;

Begin {Factorial}
    Temp := 1;
    If N > 0 Then
      For I := 1 To N Do
        Temp := Temp*I;
    Factorial := Temp,
End;
{***************************************************************************************************}
Function Powerof(N : Integer; X : Real) : Real;
                                { ───── Calculates Xᴺ───── }
Var
    Temp : Real,
    I       : Integer;

Begin {Powerof}
    Temp := 1;
    If N > 0 Then
      For I := 1 To N Do
        Temp := Temp*X;
    Powerof := Temp,
End;
{***************************************************************************************************}
Function FindP0(Lambda : Real; Mu : Real; C : Integer; Rho : Real) : Real;
                                { ───── Calculates P₀ ─────}
Var
    I       : Integer;
    Sum : Real,

Begin {FindP0}
    Sum := 0;
    For I := 0 to C − 1 Do
      Sum := Sum + Powerof(I, Lambda/Mu)/Factorial(I);
    Sum := Sum + Powerof(C, Lambda/Mu)/(Factorial(C)*(1 − Rho) );
    FindP0 := 1/Sum;
End;
```

Figure 7.8 Cont.

```
{*****************************************************************************}
Function FindBigC(Lambda : Real; Mu : Real; C : Integer; Rho : Real;
                  P0 : Real) : Real;
                            {————— Calculates C(c,λ/μ)—————}
Begin
    FindBigC := P0*Powerof(C, Lambda/Mu)/(Factorial(C)*(1 – Rho) );
End;
{*****************************************************************************}
Function FindLq(Rho : Real; BigC : Real) : Real;
                            {————— Calculates Lq————— }
Begin
    FindLq := Rho*BigC/(1 – Rho);
End;
{*****************************************************************************}
Function FindWq(Mu : Real; C : Integer; Rho : Real; BigC : Real) : Real;
                            {————— Wq————— }
Begin
    FindWq := BigC/( Mu*C*(1 – Rho) );
End;
{*****************************************************************************}
Function FindPiq(Mu : Real; C : Integer; Rho : Real; BigC : Real) : Real;
                            {————— Calculates πq(90)—————}
Begin
    FindPiq := Ln(10*BigC)/(Mu*C*(1 – Rho) );
End;
{*****************************************************************************}
Begin {Main}
    Rewrite{Outfile, 'Qstats');
    Writeln(Outfile,'C' : 3, 'P0' : 10, 'BigC' : 10, 'Lq' : 10, 'Wq' : 10, 'Piq' : 10);
    C := 4,
    Lambda := 100/24;
    Mu := 1;
    Repeat
        C := C + 1;
        Rho := Lambda/(Mu*C),
        P0 := FindP0(Lambda, Mu, C, Rho);
        BigC := FindBigC(Lambda, Mu, C, Rho, P0);
        Lq := FindLq(Rho, BigC);
        Wq := FindWq(Mu, C, Rho, BigC);
        Piq := FindPiq(Mu, C, Rho, BigC);
        Writeln(Outfile, C :3, P0 :10:4, BigC :10:4, Lq :10:4, Wq :10:4, Piq :10:4);
    Until Piq < 0.5;
    Close(Outfile);
End.
```

As stated, the company needs at least five processors to provide 100 hours of computing time per day. The problem, according to Table 7.2, is that with five processors, the average wait (W_q) is nearly 3/4 of an hour. Add it to the average run time, and the average turnaround time is nearly 1 and 3/4 hours. In fact, 10% of the employees will experience a wait of almost 2.2 hours and a turnaround time of 3.2 hours. These values far exceed the company's goals of ninety-minute turnaround time for 90% of the employees.

If the company buys six processors, the wait times improve dramatically. But 10% of the programs still wait in the queue approximately 40 minutes (.65 hours) or more.

When we increase c to 7, we get the desired results. The 90th percentile wait time is approximately .17 hours or about 10 minutes. The average time in the queue is about .056 hours or 3.4 minutes. Also at $c = 7$ there is only a .16 probability that an employee will have to wait at all and the expected number of processes in the queue is only .24. So the solution you give to the president of the company is to buy seven processors.

Now let's consider a possible response to your suggestion. Suppose that the ever skeptical president of the company thinks that seven processors is overkill. The reason you suggest so many, he reasons, is that every employee competes for the same processors. Since there are 100 employees, that is a lot of competition.

Would it not make more sense just to buy the minimum five processors and assign each employee to one of them (Figure 7.9)? That is, we could assign each employee to a group of 20 users. Then we could assign each group to one processor. As a result, each employee competes with just 19 others for a processor. With much less competition, there should be less waiting time.

Figure 7.9 20 Programs per processor or 5 M/M/1 queuing systems

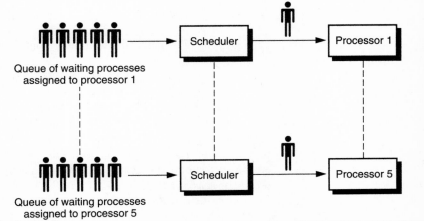

Queue of waiting processes
assigned to processor 1

Queue of waiting processes
assigned to processor 5

Besides making proposals, an analyst must also respond to counterproposals or arguments. What is your answer in this case?

Well, suppose we have 5 groups of 20 employees competing for a processor. This corresponds to 5 separate queuing systems with one server each. The average service rate, μ, remains the same, but the arrival rate changes. Here, the average arrival rate for each system is

$$\lambda = 20 \text{ employees}/24 \text{ hours} = (5/6) \text{ employees/hour}$$

Since this is an M/M/1 system, we can use the simpler equations from 7.22 through 7.26. Also, since $c = 1$,

$$\rho = \lambda/(\mu c) = \lambda/\mu = (5/6)/1 = 5/6$$

Therefore, from Equation 7.22, we find the probability that no servers are active.

$$p_0 = 1 - \rho = 1 - 5/6 = 1/6$$

From Equation 7.23, we have the probability that an employee must wait.

$$C(c, \lambda/\mu) = \rho = 5/6$$

Equation 7.24 gives the expected number of programs in the queue as

$$L_q = \rho^2/(1 - \rho) = (5/6)^2/(1-5/6) = 4\ 1/6$$

The average waiting time in the queue, from Equation 7.25, is

$$W_q = (\rho/\mu)/(1 - \rho) = [(5/6)/1]/(1 - 5/6) = 5 \text{ hours (Wow!)}$$

Finally, the 90th percentile wait time, from Equation 7.26, is

$$\pi_q(90) = \ln(10 * \rho)/(\mu - \lambda) = \ln(10*5/6)/(1 - 5/6) \cong 12.72 \text{ hours (Double Wow!)}$$

The wait times are incredibly long! Again, they are caused by the fact that random arrivals tend to occur in bunches. The only way to get 20 hours of processor time in a twenty-four-hour day with little waiting is to schedule program submissions carefully. But this runs counter to the assumption that employees submit programs at random. Assigning employees to a single processor is asking for disaster.

In conclusion, the solution to the company's problem is to buy seven processors and allow any employee to use any available processor. The M/M/7 system that we modeled shows performance measures within the stated guidelines.

===== **7.6 Summary**

This chapter has shown one way to model real-world systems. The idea is to estimate system performance before implementation. Otherwise, if a system fails to perform as expected, it may well be too late for changes. Modeling allows us to examine a wide variety of implementations quickly, inexpensively, and unobtrusively.

Queuing Theory lets us create mathematical models of waiting in line for service. Many such models exist. In part, we can categorize the systems by assumptions about customer interarrival times and service times. The M/M/c queuing system assumes that customer interarrival times and service times are exponentially distributed. These are common patterns in random behavior.

The measures that characterize a queuing system also depend on the birth and death rates of the customers. One can make many assumptions about them. Our discussions have assumed constant birth rates but death rates that depend on the system's state.

These assumptions allow us to develop equations that provide estimates of certain performance measures. The main ones we computed were:

- The probability that all servers are idle.
- The probability that a customer must wait.
- Expected number of customers in a queue at a given time.
- Expected wait time for a customer.
- 90th percentile wait time.

The equations we generated require some calculus. We hope this shows the student that there is a place for mathematics in computing. Moreover, there is a need for mathematics in computing as pointed out in a well-known article by Ralston [14]. But even if you do not care to generate the equations, you should be able to apply them. If we have convinced you that there is more to computer science than writing, documenting, and verifying programs, we have met our goals for the chapter.

===== **Exercises**

1. Suppose a queuing system has customers arriving randomly at a rate of one every 5 minutes. Also suppose the interarrival times are distributed exponentially. What is the probability that an interarrival time will be less than 5 minutes? 10 minutes? 20 minutes? What percentage of customers arrive within 1 minute of the previous one?
2. Consider the queuing system in exercise 1. Suppose the service times average about 4 minutes and are distributed exponentially. If there is one server, calculate the following performance measures:
   - The probability that all servers are idle.
   - The probability that a customer must wait.

- Expected number of customers in a queue at a given time.
- Expected wait time for a customer.
- 90th percentile wait time.

Repeat these calculations for 2 servers.

3. With $c = 1$, simplify Equation 7.14 to produce Equation 7.22. Similarly, simplify Equations 7.17, 7.19, 7.20, and 7.21 to produce Equations 7.23, 7.24, 7.25, and 7.26, respectively.

4. Consider the laser printer problem of Section 7.5. Calculate the same performance measures with 80 requests per eight-hour day. Consider the cases with 1 printer and with 2 printers.

5. Consider the laser printer problem of Section 7.5. Suppose you determined that although there are 64 requests per eight-hour day, the request rate varies dramatically at different times. In fact, your records show that the number of requests depends on time of day as indicated below:

9:00 AM to 11:00 AM ——— 20 requests with random interarrival times
11:00 AM to 1:00 PM ——— 10 requests with random interarrival times
1:00 PM to 5:00 PM ——— 34 requests with random interarrival times

Model each time interval with an M/M/1 queuing system and calculate performance measures. Next, model each period with an M/M/2 queuing system and calculate performance measures.

6. Consider the second case study in Section 7.5, especially the part involving separate M/M/1 systems. That is, there are multiple processors and each employee runs programs on only one of them. Assume also that each processor is assigned to an equal (or nearly equal) number of employees. For example, if there are 6 processors, two of them are assigned to groups of 16 employees. The other 4 are assigned to groups of 17 employees. How many processors are necessary to achieve a maximum turnaround of 1.5 hours for 90% of the employees?

7. Consider the computer center of a college or university. Between 8:00 AM and 6:00 PM, approximately 100 students spend a half hour on the average at a terminal working on their assignments. Assume also the time spent is exponentially distributed. Since students have varied schedules, they work at random times. How many terminals should the computer center have so that 90% of the students less than 15 minutes? What is the average wait time for a terminal?

8. Suppose a disk controller receives I/O requests randomly at a rate of 20 per second. If the requests average 20 ms for processing, calculate the 5 performance measures listed in Exercise 2.

9. Repeat Exercise 9, but assume the frequency of I/O requests doubles and an additional controller is purchased.

═══════ **Questions**

1. Suppose you have a queuing system with 2 identical servers. Which of the two following cases will have smaller average wait times? Why?
   - All customers compete for either of the servers.
   - Half the customers compete for one server and the other half compete for the other one.
2. Consider an M/M/1 queuing system. In general, what happens to the 90th percentile wait time if the arrival rate doubles? What happens to the average wait time? For this question, consider the relative sizes of λ and μ.
3. Consider an M/M/1 queuing system for which the arrival rate is 60 customers per minute and the average service rate is 2 seconds. If we try to calculate the 90th percentile wait, $\pi_q(90)$ evaluates to a negative number. Explain this phenomenon.

═══════ **References**

1. Allen, A. O. *Probability, Statistics, and Queuing Theory with Computer Science Applications.* New York: Academic Press, 1978.
2. Little, J. C. D. "A Proof of the Queuing Formula: L = λW." *Operations Research* 9 (May 1961):383-387.
3. Kleinrock, L. *Queuing Systems, Volume I : Theory.* New York: Wiley, 1975.
4. Kleinrock, L. *Queuing Systems, Volume II : Computer Applications.* New York: Wiley, 1976.
5. Kobayashi, H. *Modeling and Analysis: An Introduction to System Performance Evaluation Methodology.* Reading, MA: Addison-Wesley, 1978.
6. Brinch Hansen, P. *Operating Systems Principles.* Englewood Cliffs, NJ: Prentice-Hall, 1973.
7. Baase, S. *Computer Algorithms: Introduction to Design and Analysis.* 2nd ed. Reading, MA: Addison Wesley, 1988.
8. Knuth, D.E. *The Art of Programming, Vol. III: Sorting and Searching.* Reading, MA: Addison-Wesley, 1973.
9. Horowitz, E., and S. Sahni. *Fundamentals of Data Structures in Pascal.* 2nd ed. Rockville, MD: Computer Science Press, 1987.
10. Letwin, G. *Inside OS/2.* Redmond, WA: Microsoft Press, 1988.
11. Walrand, J. *An Introduction to Queuing Networks.* Englewood Cliffs, NJ: Prentice-Hall, 1988.
12. Clarke, A. B., and R. L. Disney. *Probability and Random Processes: A First Course with Applications.* 2nd ed. New York: Wiley, 1985.
13. Muntz, R.R. "Performance Measurement and Evalation." *Encyclopedia of Computer Science and Engineering.* Edited by A. Ralston and E. D. Reilly. New York: Van Nostrand Reinhold, 1983.
14. Ralston, A. "Computer Science, Mathematics, and the Undergraduate Curricula in Both." *American Mathematical Monthly* 88 (July 1981):472-484.
15. Jefferson, D., et al. "Distributed Simulation and the Time Warp Operating System." *Operating Systems Review* 21 (November 1987):77-93.
16. Markas, T., M. Royals, and N. Kanopoulos. "On Distributed Fault Simulation." *Computer* 23 (January 1990):40-54.
17. *Communications of the ACM* 33 (October 1990), entire issue.

8

Case Studies: MS–DOS, UNIX, VMS, and MVS

This chapter describes four operating systems in some detail: MS-DOS, UNIX, VMS, and MVS. Why did we choose them? The main reason is that readers are likely either to have used them already or to encounter them in the future. A case study might as well deal with a popular, widely used system.

What is the purpose of a case study? There are two major ones. The first is to show working implementations of the ideas discussed in this book. Case studies provide a bridge between theory and practice. They also show how concepts that we have studied separately are integrated into actual working systems. Remember, operating systems must perform all the tasks described in the previous chapters.

The second purpose is to help you master actual systems at a professional level. You now have the tools necessary to do this. Computer scientists generally must deal with many operating systems during their careers. They must take the theory they have learned and apply it to mastering systems that are both complex and idiosyncratic. The case studies show the approach required, although we skip a level of detail due to lack of space and time.

8.1 MS-DOS

Let us start with MS-DOS. It runs on personal computers, particularly the IBM PC and PS/2 lines and the many PC clones or compatibles. We will not distinguish the many different versions of MS-DOS, nor will we distinguish MS-DOS from PC-DOS, the version used on IBM PCs. Instead, we discuss general MS-DOS principles.

As with many operating systems, MS-DOS users must either start (*boot*) the system from a floppy disk or install it on a hard disk. The operating system is not an intrinsic part of the computer.

Starting MS-DOS

When you first start MS-DOS, it identifies itself with a brief copyright message, asks for the date and time, (if your system does not provide them automatically), and displays its basic prompt in the form

C>

The letter indicates the current drive. It will usually be C if your computer has a hard disk. This is the system prompt. It means that MS-DOS has been loaded in memory and is ready to process commands. Obviously, MS-DOS is neither talkative nor particularly user-friendly. The current drive, the one that commands access by default, is all the information it provides automatically. There is no status, no list of commands, and no friendly messages.

You can change drives by typing the new one's name, followed by a colon. For example, typing

B:

makes B the current drive. MS-DOS computers typically refer to floppy disk drives as A and B and hard disk drives (or RAM disks, logical drives that are actually just areas of memory) as C, D, E, F, G, and H. What you may use depends on your computer's configuration.

MS-DOS Files

Now, the first thing users usually want to do is create and manage files. Thus, you must know how to name files and how to operate on them.

Let us start with naming conventions. MS-DOS file names may have up to eight characters. Valid characters are letters, numbers, and some special characters such as the underscore, hyphen, percentage sign, dollar sign, ampersand (&) and number sign (#). Embedded spaces are not allowed, nor are most punctuation marks (commas, periods, semicolons, colons, etc). Table 8.1 shows legal and illegal characters.

Table 8.1 Legal and illegal MS-DOS filename characters

Legal Characters				Illegal Characters				
A-Z	a-z	0-9		?	/	\	.	,
!	@	#	$	;	:	"	=	*
%	^	&	(	<	>	+	space	
)	_	{	}					
'	~	-						

MS-DOS also lets you add three characters as an *extension* to the file name. It is optional but helpful to indicate what type of information the file contains. For example, a user may create a file with the name

PROG-1.ASM

The file name is PROG-1 and the extension is ASM. The extension ASM identifies the file as an assembly language source program. Other common extensions appear in Table 8.2:

Table 8.2 Some common MS-DOS filename extensions

Extension	Description
.BAK	Backup files in editors or word processors. When you use the editor to change a file, it keeps a backup copy. This is in case the changes were a mistake and the user wants to undo them.
.BAT	Batch files, a file containing commonly used MS-DOS commands.
.COM	Command file, a binary file that the user may execute under MS-DOS. It contains process code ready to execute. MS-DOS calls it a *memory image format*. This means MS-DOS stores the code in memory without alteration. COM files often contain operating system routines that go in fixed memory locations.
.EXE	Executable binary file. Such files also contain machine code. The main difference between EXE and COM files is that the code in EXE files must be relocated when it is loaded into memory. EXE files are usually the result of compiling and linking programs written in a high-level language.
.OBJ	Object code, the result of compiling or assembling a source program. Normally the file name is the same as the one containing the source code.
.SYS	System file. It contains an attribute (See Section 6.7) that hides it from directory lists.
.$$$	Temporary files.

Other common extensions are BAS for BASIC programs, DOC for word processing documents, DBF for database files, WKS for spreadsheets, TXT for text, PRN for printed output, DAT for ASCII data files, and NDX for index files [1-8].

Users may keep their files in hierarchically organized directories, as described in section 6.6. Here we will only mention the following key points:

- The user may reference any file in any directory. Files in the current (working) directory may be referenced by name alone. Others require a path, a sequence of subdirectory names that leads to the desired directory. A backslash (\) separates subdirectory names. A leading backslash indicates the root directory.

- The user can create, change, and delete directories using the commands MKDIR, CHDIR, and RMDIR, respectively. Only empty directories can be deleted.

MS-DOS components

MS-DOS has four major components:

Boot Loader
MSDOS.SYS
IO.SYS
COMMAND.COM

The boot loader occupies a fixed sector (usually the first) on an MS-DOS disk. When you turn the system on and insert a disk in a drive (or rely on a hard disk), the computer's hardware automatically reads the disk's first sector. If the disk is bootable, that sector contains a boot record.

The boot record contains a small program that finds and reads other MS-DOS components from the disk and stores them in memory. It then transfers control to MS-DOS. At this point, part of MS-DOS is in memory and it is ready to respond to commands. As the boot loader is no longer needed, MS-DOS components often overwrite it.

The other three components of MS-DOS are in files MSDOS.SYS (sometimes called MSDOS.COM or IBMDOS.COM), IO.SYS (sometimes called IBMBIO.COM or HPBIOS.COM), and COMMAND.COM. Figure 8.1 shows where they reside in memory. Let us now describe them.

COMMAND.COM

Let us start with COMMAND.COM. It responds to commands entered from the keyboard. It is the primary interface between the user and MS-DOS. Because of this, it is sometimes called the *shell, console command processor (CCP),* or *command interpreter.*

Figure 8.1 Memory map of MS-DOS major components

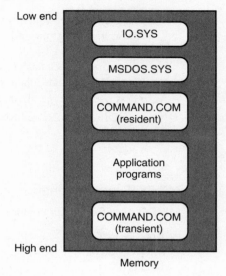

COMMAND.COM displays the prompt when MS-DOS is ready to accept commands. When you type a command and press the RETURN key, it analyzes your entry. In part, it is a text processor that interprets commands and responds accordingly. (We note that commands are not always entered from the keyboard. We will see an alternative shortly when we discuss batch files.)

As Figure 8.1 shows, COMMAND.COM consists of two components, the *internal (resident)* and *external (transient)* parts. (There is actually a third called the *initialization component*, but we do not discuss it here.) There is a good reason to distinguish the internal and external parts. MS-DOS has many commands. If all the code needed to respond to them were in memory, there would be less room for anything else, such as applications programs. On the other hand, if all of it were left on disk, MS-DOS would have to access the disk for every command. The result would be slow responses. Neither is appealing.

But there is a compromise. MS-DOS keeps the code for often used commands in memory, thus providing a quick response. This is the internal part of COMMAND.COM. It stays in memory at all times. Some internal MS-DOS commands can be found in Table 8.3:

Table 8.3 Some internal MS-DOS commands

Command	Description
CHDIR	Changes current directory.
CLS	Clears the screen.
COPY	Copies a file.
DEL (ERASE)	Deletes a file.
DIR	Lists the files in a directory.
MKDIR	Creates a new directory.
PATH	Specifies path to search for MS-DOS transient commands.
RENAME	Renames a file.
RMDIR	Removes a directory.
SET	Defines a string as equivalent to another.
TIME	Displays or changes the time of day.
TYPE	Displays ASCII file contents.
VERIFY	Sets (VERIFY ON) or clears (VERIFY OFF). If it is on, MS-DOS verifies that it can read back what it wrote.

The external part of COMMAND.COM lies in a higher area of memory. It contains code for less frequently used commands. MS-DOS stores it in memory only when needed. Furthermore, if an application subsequently needs the memory occupied by the external part, MS-DOS will overlay it. If the user later repeats an external command, MS-DOS must read its code from disk and store it in memory again.

If you work on a personal computer, you may notice that certain commands make the disk drives run; others do not. The ones that do are external commands such as those listed in Table 8.4:

Table 8.4 Some external MS-DOS commands

Command	Description
CHKDSK	Checks how much disk space is in use and how much is available. It also checks for discrepancies or inconsistencies in the directory.
CIPHER	Reads and encrypts or decrypts the contents of a file. The user must specify a ciphering key.
DISKCOMP	Compares two disks and determines whether they are identical.
DISKCOPY	Copies disks.
FORMAT	Formats a disk.
MORE	Displays output one screenful at a time.
PRINT	Prints hardcopy of ASCII files.
SEARCH	Searches a directory for a specified file name. If the file exists SEARCH prints its path name.
SORT	Sorts data from files into ascending or descending order. It can display the sorted data or write it to another file.
TREE	Displays the path names for all subdirectories on the current disk. With appropriate options, the user can also disply the names of files inside each subdirectory.

Batch Files. Commands need not always be entered from the keyboard. In fact, entering common commands repeatedly is often a nuisance, especially when they have several parameters. Most users prefer to store them somewhere. When needed, they can be retrieved and given to MS-DOS.

To do this, the user can create a file containing commonly used commands. The file is called a *batch file* and has the BAT extension. Then whenever the user wants to execute the commands, he or she simply enters the filename. MS-DOS responds by executing each of the commands in the file. By storing commonly used commands in batch files, the number of keystrokes (and typing errors) is reduced.

To illustrate, suppose you want to run a program that creates a data file, sort it, and print it on the screen. You might type the following:

```
A>progname
A>SORT file1,file2
A>TYPE file2
```

Instead of entering all three commands each time, the user can store them on a file named DISPLAY.BAT. Then to create, sort, and display the data, the user types

```
A>DISPLAY.
```

MS-DOS supports a special batch file known as AUTOEXEC.BAT. When a file with this name exists in a root directory, MS-DOS automatically executes its commands upon startup. For example, suppose you write a simple program that prints the following message:

"Good day my Lordship. My humble CPU circuits are waiting to respond to your every command."

If your AUTOEXEC.BAT file contains the command to run this program, the message appears every time you boot the system. Naturally, your friends are impressed as you have obviously established superiority over the mighty computer.

AUTOEXEC.BAT files, of course, can be used for any commonly used startup procedure. For example, maybe you routinely use your PC for spreadsheet, database, or word processing. Then commands to change the default drive and run the application may be put in AUTOEXEC.BAT. Thus, on booting the system, the application is ready to run.

Batch files can do more than simply execute the same set of MS-DOS commands each time. For example, a PAUSE command halts execution of the batch file until the user presses a key. This is helpful if a command requires a new disk. By putting the PAUSE before the command, the user has time to insert a new disk. When it has been inserted, the user presses a key and execution continues.

Another useful command is 'IF'. Like its counterpart in Pascal, it contains a condition. If the condition is true, a command (listed with IF) is executed. If not, it is ignored. This is useful to avoid commands that try to create files that already exist, or commands that reference nonexistent files. For example, suppose the batch file DISPLAY contains

```
IF NOT EXISTS %2 SORT %1, %2
```

Here, %1 and %2 are replaceable parameters. The user, when entering the batch file name, also enters additional file names. The batch file then sees %1 and %2 corresponding to the file names in the order they are typed. This is similar to formal parameters in a high-level language procedure assuming the values of the actual parameters.

Thus, suppose the user enters

```
DISPLAY file1, file2
```

When control reaches the IF command, it checks to see if *file2* (%2) exists. If it does, the SORT is not executed. If not, the SORT is executed and it creates *file2*.

Batch files provide many elements of programming logic found in languages such as Pascal, COBOL, and FORTRAN. The ability to specify parameters and provide conditional execution allows the user to create flexible and powerful batch files.

MSDOS.SYS

As previously stated, when a user enters a command, COMMAND.COM interprets it and takes action. COMMAND.COM calls routines in MSDOS.SYS that perform the command. MSDOS.SYS contains the nucleus or kernel of MS-DOS.

For example, MSDOS.SYS contains file and disk management routines. However, it includes only the *hardware independent* parts. One of its major functions is to interface between COMMAND.COM and the *hardware dependent* IO.SYS (Figure 8.2). For example, suppose you enter a command that requires I/O. COMMAND.COM analyzes it and calls MSDOS.SYS to process it logically.

Figure 8.2 MS-DOS command execution

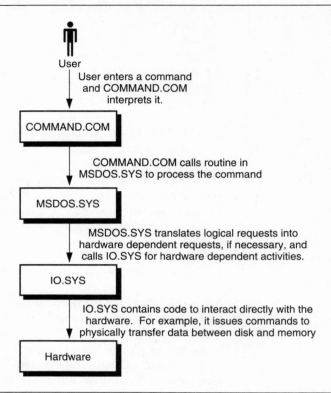

Routines in MSDOS.SYS maintain directory information and the file allocation table (although IO.SYS actually reads them from disk and writes them back after MSDOS.SYS has changed them). MSDOS.SYS executes directory searches if the user wants to look for a file. It adds to the directory or deletes from it. It also blocks and unblocks data that moves between an application program's logical records and physical disk sectors.

If MSDOS.SYS needs data from an external source such as a disk, it calls routines in IO.SYS. They contain specific disk formats or other device characteristics and can issue commands to physically transfer data between the device and memory.

=====
IO.SYS

As noted, the routines in IO.SYS are hardware dependent. For example, they issue specific commands to read or write data.

In some systems, notably the IBM PC, IO.SYS communicates with the ROM BIOS which does many low-level I/O operations [5]. The ROM BIOS is software permanently stored in the computer's ROM (read only memory). As such, we can think of it as firmware because of its close association with an actual machine. Some people do not consider the ROM BIOS to be part of the operating system.

If the ROM BIOS exists, IO.SYS is largely an interface between it and MSDOS.SYS. It consists of many branch commands that transfer control to routines for keyboard input, serial I/O, printer I/O, etc. (Specific details of the ROM BIOS are in reference [5].) The ROM BIOS is machine-dependent. Non-IBM compatibles use a different BIOS than the copyrighted ones used in IBM PCs and PS/2s.

The ROM BIOS also contains self-test routines that run whenever the machine is turned on, which test internal circuits to see whether they are working properly. The ROM BIOS also reads the boot record from a bootable disk.

Next we will describe the major functions of the I/O system. Whether these functions are in ROM is not our concern here.

IO.SYS receives general commands from MSDOS.SYS. It translates them to instructions that are device-dependent. To illustrate, suppose MSDOS.SYS issues a command to print characters on the CON logical device. IO.SYS must first determine that CON is the console. After that it must consider the screen's physical characteristics. For example, how fast does it display characters? How many rows and columns does it allow? What is the current cursor position? Routines in IO.SYS then issue commands that physically transfer the characters to the console.

If instead, IO.SYS receives a command to write to a disk, it must consider physical disk characteristics. For example, it must translate a logical sector number specified in the file allocation table to a specific disk surface, track number, and sector number. It would then issue the necessary commands to physically transfer a block of data.

Device Drivers. IO.SYS contains the system's standard device drivers. We say "standard" because a user can define his or her own drivers. We will discuss this shortly when we talk about the CONFIG.SYS file. There are two types, character and block drivers. Character drivers handle character oriented I/O for devices such as the screen, keyboard, or printer. Not surprisingly, the block drivers handle block oriented I/O for devices such as disk drives. MS-DOS identifies device drivers by assigned names, such as:

- AUX or COM1, the device attached to the first serial port, usually a printer or modem.
- CON, the keyboard and screen.
- PRN or LPT1, the device attached to the first parallel port, usually a parallel printer.
- LPT2 and LPT3, the second or third attached parallel device.
- COM2, the second attached serial device.
- CLOCK$, the real-time clock.

MS-DOS maintains all its drivers in a linked list. When a user requests an I/O operation, MS-DOS searches the list to find the correct driver. It then calls the driver to perform the physical data transfer.

How are the drivers organized? Each one contains three main sections, a *device header*, a *strategy routine*, and an *interrupt routine*. The device header contains information about the driver, such as (Figure 8.3):

- Location of the next driver. Remember, drivers are stored in a linked list.
- Logical device name.
- Bit vector containing device attributes, such as character or block orientation and whether it is the standard input or output device (described later).
- Location of the *strategy routine*.
- Location of the *interrupt routine*.

Figure 8.3 Device driver components

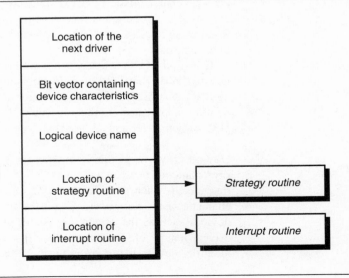

We will describe the strategy and interrupt routines shortly. But first we must discuss another data structure called the *request header*. When a process makes an I/O request, MS-DOS creates a request header. It contains information such as:

- Command code, specifying the type of operation requested. For example, it could be input or output (with VERIFY ON or OFF), a buffer status check, an initialization, or an exchange of control information between a process and a driver. More details are in references [1-2].
- Unit code for a particular device.
- Bit vector, containing error codes such as:

  a) No paper in the printer.
  b) Attempt to write to a write protected disk.
  c) Device busy.
  d) Requested sector not found.
  e) Unrecognized command code.

- Data area that may contain

  a) Number of bytes (character drivers) or sectors (block drivers) to transfer.
  b) Buffer address.
  c) Sector number requested.
  d) Result of a device status check.

After MS-DOS creates the request header, it passes it to the driver's strategy routine. The routine has one responsibility: save the address of the header. It is needed later when the interrupt routine runs. It then returns control to MS-DOS which next calls the interrupt routine. Note that MS-DOS does not pass the request header directly to the interrupt routine, so that the queuing and processing of requests are separated.

The interrupt routine does the actual work. The first thing it does is save the CPU registers. It then locates the request header saved by the strategy routing. It finds the command code and determines the operation to be performed. Finally it calls a procedure to process the request.

When the interrupt routine finishes, it puts the operation status in the request header and returns control to MS-DOS. MS-DOS then determines the results of the request and returns them to the original caller.

CONFIG.SYS. Sometimes the drivers may not meet the needs of the user. The user may have some nonstandard devices. Perhaps the user has simply found a better way to handle I/O for a particular application. In such cases the user does not have to use the existing drivers. He or she may modify or even add other drivers.

The user does this through the CONFIG.SYS file. When MS-DOS boots, it examines the main directory for a file named CONFIG.SYS. If found, it reads and processes commands from the file. Typically, the commands alter the existing MS-DOS configuration. For example, they may be used to change the number of buffers or the maximum number of open files. There is also a command to locate and install new drivers.

Suppose the user puts the command

```
DEVICE = filename
```

in CONFIG.SYS. The specified file must contain a valid device driver. During booting, MS-DOS examines the file's contents and calls an initialization procedure. The procedure determines device characteristics and performs necessary startup functions. Afterwards the driver is inserted in the driver list. The driver is then installed.

I/O Redirection, Pipes, and Filters

We end the case study of MS-DOS by describing how it executes I/O redirection, pipes, and filters.

Section 5.11 discussed I/O redirection and pipes in UNIX. Basically, they work the same in MS-DOS. Since MSDOS.SYS is device-independent, it can perform I/O through *standard input* and *standard output* devices. That is, by default I/O requests may specify STDIN (standard input) and STDOUT (standard output). The routines in IO.SYS determine which physical devices correspond to the names. As in UNIX, we can redefine the standard input and output devices, called *I/O redirection*.

For example, the MS-DOS command

```
DIR
```

displays the contents of the current directory on the screen, the default standard output device. To print the directory, you enter

```
DIR>PRN
```

This command changes the standard output device of "DIR" from the screen to the printer. The output has been redirected.

In general, you can enter

```
DIR d:pathname > filename
```

The "d:pathname" option indicates the pathname to a specified directory on a disk in drive "d." MS-DOS will write its contents in filename. The symbol ">" redirects output from the default standard output device (the screen).

Similarly, to sort the data in a file, you can use the MS-DOS command SORT. Since the standard input device is the keyboard, you redirect the input by entering

```
SORT < filename
```

The option "< *filename*" makes MS-DOS sort the data in *filename*. In other words, you have redirected the input from the default standard input device (keyboard) to the specified file. We have not redirected the output, so MS-DOS will display it on the screen.

The SORT command is an example of a *filter*. A filter is a command that reads information from the standard input device, transforms it, and writes it to the standard output device (Figure 8.4). In a sense, the MS-DOS command reads and filters (changes) the data before writing it.

Figure 8.4 Filter operation

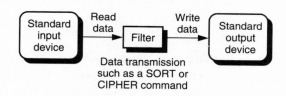

SORT is not the only filter. Others are:

- CIPHER reads data from the standard input device, encrypts it, and writes the results to the standard output device. The user must specify the ciphering key.
- FIND reads from the standard input device and searches for a specified character string.
- MORE reads from the standard input device and displays the data on the standard output device one screenful at a time.

Last, pipes can connect the standard output of one command to the standard input to another. This is especially useful in tasks that involve multiple commands. Pipes may allow you to specify them with one keyboard entry.

A user can create a pipe between com-1 and com-2 by entering

com-1 | com-2

The vertical bar (|) defines the pipe (Figure 8.5). MS-DOS executes the first command, **com-1**. However, instead of sending output to the standard output, it sends it to a pipe (actually, an MS-DOS created file).

Figure 8.5 Pipe connections

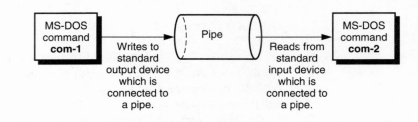

Next, MS-DOS executes the second command, **com-2**. Instead of getting data from the standard input device, it gets the data from the pipe.

For example, suppose you want to display the directory of a disk. Suppose also that it contains so many entries that they will not fit on the screen. You want to display them one screenful at a time. To do this, enter

```
DIR | MORE
```

DIR normally displays the current directory on the screen. However, here the command routes the entries into a pipe. MORE is a filter that normally gets data from the standard input device and displays it one screenful at a time. But here it gets data from the pipe. Since the data there are just the directory entries, MORE displays them one screenful at a time.

This concludes the case study of MS-DOS. References [1-8] contain much more information about it.

≡≡≡≡≡ 8.2 UNIX

Our second case study is the UNIX operating system. Contrary to what you might think, UNIX is not an operating system; rather, it is a family of operating systems. First described in 1974 by Thompson and Ritchie [9], it has become one of the most widespread systems.

Many versions of UNIX exist. It runs in slightly different forms on computers such as the PDP-11, UNISYS 1100 series, VAX-11/780, IBM 370, and personal computers and workstations based on the Motorola MC68000, Intel 8086, and other microprocessors. Two popular versions of UNIX are System V, produced by AT&T, and the BSD system, developed at the

University of California at Berkeley and popularized by Sun Microsystems. Our examples and descriptions deal with UNIX System V. This section covers UNIX's file system, memory management, view of a process, process synchronization, and input/output.

UNIX Design

Figure 8.6 shows the layered design characteristic of UNIX. At the top level are the users or applications software. Requests from processes are handled by the second layer called the *UNIX Shell*. It accepts and interprets commands and calls the UNIX Kernel to execute them. The kernel is resident in memory and performs standard functions such as scheduling, memory allocation, and synchronization.

Figure 8.6 UNIX structure

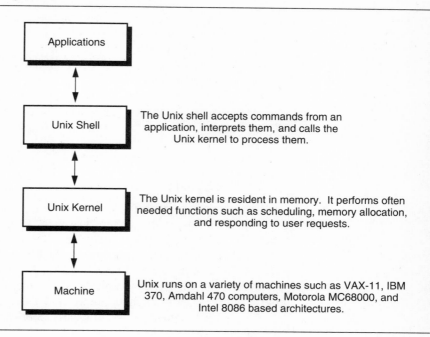

The Unix shell accepts commands from an application, interprets them, and calls the Unix kernel to process them.

The Unix kernel is resident in memory. It performs often needed functions such as scheduling, memory allocation, and responding to user requests.

Unix runs on a variety of machines such as VAX-11, IBM 370, Amdahl 470 computers, Motorola MC68000, and Intel 8086 based architectures.

Table 8.5 Some UNIX commands

Command	Function
at	Initiates a job at a specified time.
cat	Concatenates files.
cd	Changes directories.
cp	Copies files.
grep	Searches a file for a specified character string.
help	Asks UNIX for help.
kill	Terminates a process (non-violence advocates may prefer to rename it something kinder and gentler).
ls	Lists the entries in the current directory.
mail	Allows users to exchange messages.
mkdir	Creates directories. (Directories are discussed later, but they are essentially the same as those described for MS-DOS.)
pr	Prints files.
ps	Reports the status of a process.
rm	Deletes files.
rmdir	Removes directories.
sleep	Causes the execution of another command to be delayed for a specified period of time.

Table 8.5 contains some UNIX commands. (Complete lists of UNIX commands appear in references [13-14].)

The shell can read commands from a terminal or from a file called a *shell script*. Commands in the file are executed by typing the file name. As with MS-DOS, this is a convenient way in which to execute commonly used commands.

UNIX File System

Let us begin by describing the UNIX file system. Like MS-DOS, UNIX provides each user with a hierarchical view of files and directories. Each user has a root directory that may contain files and other subdirectories. Each subdirectory, in turn, may contain more files and subdirectories. On the surface, the hierarchical directory structures of MS-DOS and UNIX differ very little. Therefore, we will spend our time describing the storing, accessing, and sharing of files.

A UNIX file system consists of 4 parts: *boot block*, *super block*, *data blocks*, and an *inode list*.

- Boot block. The boot block contains a bootstrap record used to initialize the operating system. It is typically in the first disk sector. If UNIX has been booted from another disk, the boot record is not used.

- Super block. The super block contains fields describing the file system, such as its size, number of free inodes, number of free data blocks, and the location of the free space.
- Data blocks. The data blocks contain the file's data. Block sizes vary, but a typical value is 512 bytes (0.5K bytes). We will assume this size here.
- UNIX inodes. There is one inode for each file. The list of inodes, also called the *ilist*, provides access to files and defines the directory structure. Inodes also allow users to share files. Basically, the inode locates the file's data blocks. But be careful! This does not mean that it contains the locations of all the data blocks. We will explain.

Keep in mind that files vary in size and UNIX must provide access to different sized files. But the way it does this is rather unusual.

Section 6.7 describes how MS-DOS keeps track of data blocks (clusters) by using a linked list of FAT entries. UNIX provides access to all data blocks in a file through a single inode. Providing access to files ranging from just a few bytes in size to megabytes is quite a challenge. Figure 8.7 illustrates how to use an inode to access a file's data blocks.

An inode has up to thirteen pointers. The first ten contain the locations of the file's data blocks. If there are fewer than ten blocks, UNIX uses as many pointers as needed. Thus, the first ten pointers can locate up to 5K (10 blocks times 0.5K per block) of data.

But files can grow much larger than this. Instead of linking multiple inodes, UNIX uses an indirect approach.

The eleventh pointer contains the location of an *indirect block*. The indirect block contains up to 128 entries, each of which may contain the location of another data block. Thus, the indirect block can specify the locations of up to 128 more data blocks. This one additional block allows files as large as 5K + 64K = 69K bytes. But wait, this is not all.

The twelfth inode pointer contains the location of a *second indirect block*. It has another 128 entries, but each of them may contain the location of another indirect block. Thus, there may be another 128 indirect blocks. Each, in turn, may contain the locations of up to 128 data blocks.

Thus, the second indirect block allows UNIX to access up to 128*128 = 16384 more data blocks or 8192K more bytes of data. A file can now grow to 69K + 8192K = 8261K bytes or 8.261 megabytes (MB). This is larger than most users need, but not big enough for large databases. Fortunately, there is one more pointer in the inode. It contains the location of a *third indirect block*, and guess what it does?

Figure 8.7 UNIX access to data blocks

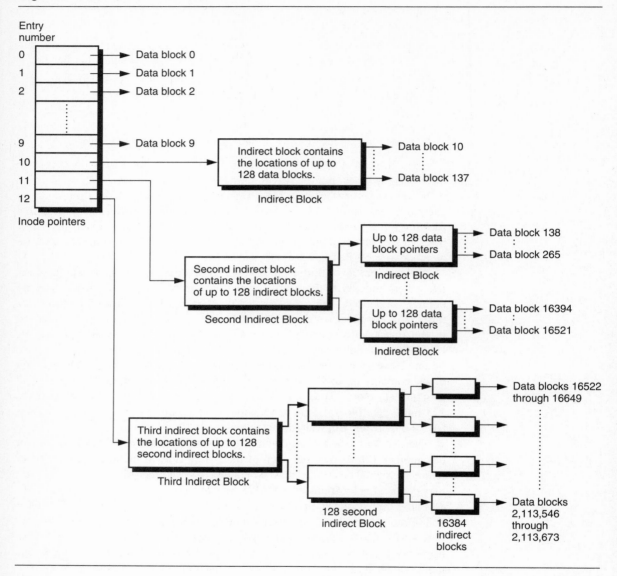

The third indirect block contains the locations of up to 128 more second indirect blocks. Each of them, as described before, contains the locations of up to 128 more indirect blocks, and can locate up to 16384 more data blocks. (Don't forget to look at Figure 8.7 to help clarify all this.) Since the third indirect block can locate up to 128 second indirect blocks, it can provide access to as many as 128 * 16384 = 2,097,152 data blocks. This allows for an additional 1,048,576K bytes or just over 1 gigabyte (1 GB = 1 billion bytes) of data. Thus, UNIX files can grow no larger than 1.056837 GB. Oh well, we can't have it all.

Basically, the inode is the root of a hierarchical structure in which data blocks are leaf nodes. It differs from the B-tree structures of Section 6.4 in that the leaf nodes are not necessarily all at the same level.

≡≡≡
System Tables

The inodes provide only part of what is needed to access files. For example, you might ask, "How does UNIX even find an inode for a particular file?"

The first step is to examine the *file descriptor table*. We discussed it briefly in Section 5.11. Each user has one file descriptor table, and it has one entry for each open file. The first three entries, numbered 0, 1, and 2, correspond to the standard input, output, and error devices. That is, unless otherwise specified, all input, output, and error reporting defaults to the corresponding files.

A user, of course, can open more files. If he or she does so, UNIX creates more entries in the file descriptor table. Primarily, each entry points to an entry in the *system file table*. The system file table contains one entry for each open file. It differs from the file descriptor table in that it has entries for <u>all</u> open files for all users. UNIX keeps the system file table in memory for quicker access. Primarily, its entries contain the following information:

- Location of the inode.
- Whether the file is open for reading, writing, or both.
- The relative position of the last transfer. This allows sequential access. UNIX initializes it to 0 if the file is opened for reading, and to the file length if it is opened for writing. Thus, read requests normally start at the beginning, and write requests start at the end.
- The number of file descriptor table entries that point to it. This allows the kernel to know how many processes may be sharing an open file.

Figure 8.8 shows an example UNIX file system with three processes that have opened several files. We call them fileA, fileB, and fileC. Other files may be open, but we do not show them to simplify the diagram. The first process has access to all three files. The second one has access only to fileB, and the third one has access only to fileC. Thus, processes 1 and 2 share fileB and processes 1 and 3 share fileC. We have also shown an inode for a closed file to emphasize that the system file table points only to open files.

Figure 8.8 Sample UNIX file system

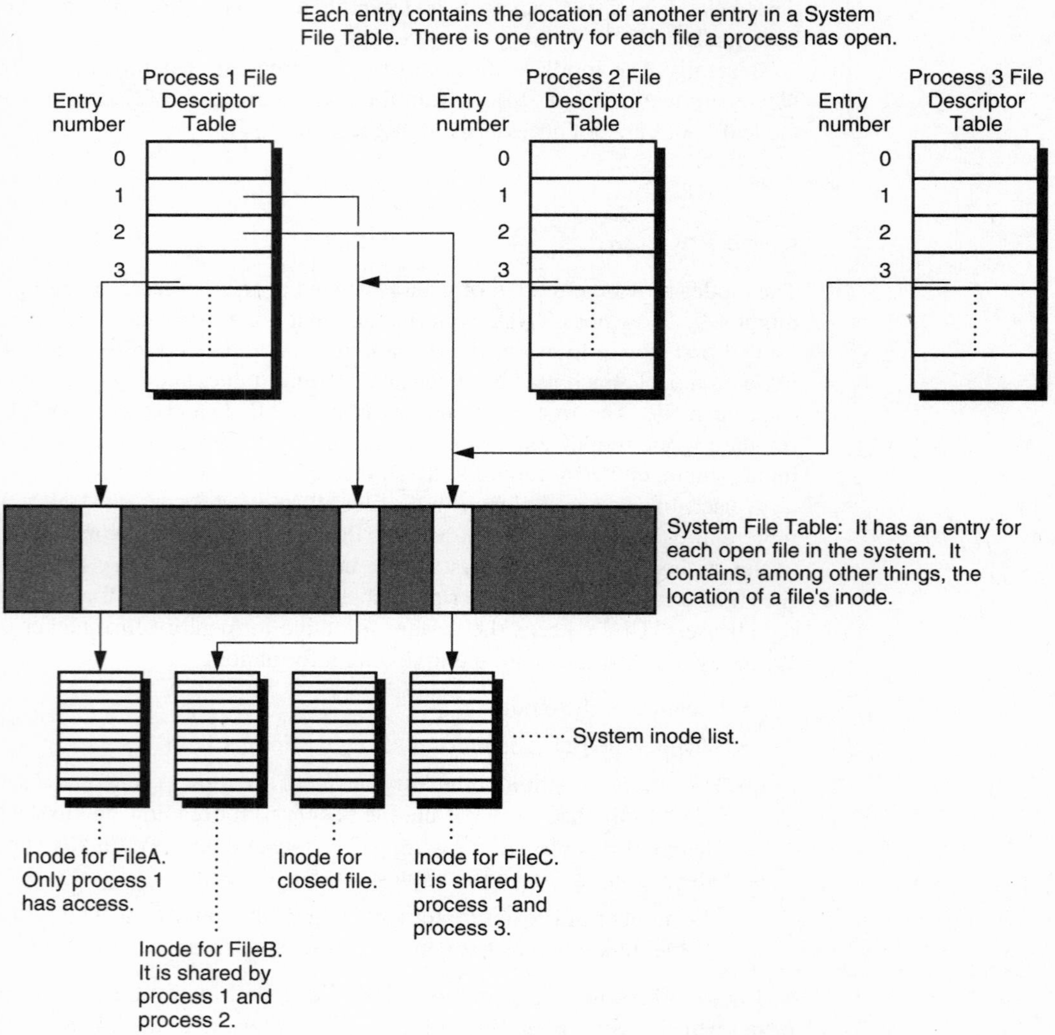

Each entry contains the location of another entry in a System File Table. There is one entry for each file a process has open.

System File Table: It has an entry for each open file in the system. It contains, among other things, the location of a file's inode.

System inode list.

Inode for FileA. Only process 1 has access.

Inode for closed file.

Inode for FileC. It is shared by process 1 and process 3.

Inode for FileB. It is shared by process 1 and process 2.

When a process wants to read or write a file, it must specify the descriptor number. UNIX does the rest of the work of finding the file's data.

UNIX Directories

We have already said that UNIX maintains a hierarchical directory structure. A logical question is, "How do the inodes define a directory structure?" Well, thanks for asking. Like Tolstoy's historians, textbook writers specialize in "answering questions that no one has asked them."

Basically, UNIX sees a directory as just another file. The difference is in the contents of the data block. In a data file, the data blocks contain (reasonably enough) data. However, in a directory, they contain the names of entries and the locations of their inodes.

There are also two extra entries in directory's data block. One is for the directory itself, denoted by (.), and the other is for its parent directory, denoted by (..). In a special case, the parent of the root directory is the root directory.

We can clarify this through an example. Suppose a university professor has created the directory structure shown in Figure 8.9. The root directory contains three entries, one file and two subdirectories. The file contains the professor's resume in case he either is awarded the Nobel Prize or is fired for moral turpitude (unlawful cohabitation with an underage computer).

Figure 8.9 Example UNIX file directory

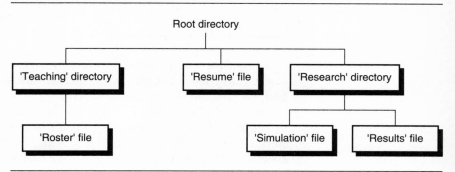

The subdirectory "Teaching" contains just one file, a class roster for a course the professor teaches. The "Research" subdirectory contains two files. The first ("Simulation") contains the source code for a research program, the second ("Results") contains data the program has recently produced. How do the inodes define the structure?

Figure 8.10 shows how. It contains the *ilist* or list of inodes. UNIX numbers each inode and can reference one by its *inode number*.

Figure 8.10 Inodes and data blocks for the sample directory

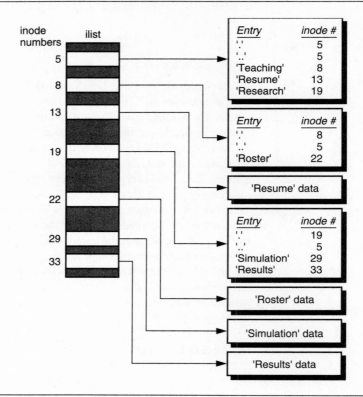

Suppose the root directory is a file with inode 5. The actual location of the root directory inode is stored in the process address space which we describe later. For now, we focus on the directory.

Since inode 5 corresponds to a directory, the associated data block contains its entries and the special entries (.) and (..). In Figure 8.10, the (.) and (..) entries both contain 5. This tells UNIX the current entry is also the root directory. The other three entries contain the names "Teaching," "Resume," and "Research." The inode numbers are 8, 13, and 19, respectively.

Inode 13 points to a data block containing the resume text. Inodes 8 and 19 point to data blocks defining the subdirectories "Teaching" and "Research." This is consistent with the structure of Figure 8.9.

Let's look at the data block referenced through inode 19. It contains four entries. The (.) entry contains 19, the inode for the current subdirectory. The (..) entry contains 5. This, of course, is the inode for the root directory (also the parent of the "Research" subdirectory). The other two entries correspond to the "Simulation" file (inode 29) and the "Results" file (inode 33). Examination of inodes 29 and 33 show they do indeed point to the "Simulation" and "Results" files, respectively. Again, this is consistent with the structure of Figure 8.9.

The remaining inodes and data blocks contain similar information. In summary, the data blocks associated with a file contain data. No surprise there. The ones associated with a directory contain the inode numbers of other directories and files. The reader should follow the rest of Figure 8.10 to determine that the data structures actually describe the structure of Figure 8.9.

System Calls Fork, Exec, Wait, and Exit

As we have done throughout this text, UNIX also defines a process as an executing entity. Four system commands are particularly important to a UNIX process: *fork*, *exec*, *wait*, and *exit*. Through them, UNIX creates, redefines, and kills processes, and puts them to sleep. Let's take a look at each command and see what it does.

Fork Command. Every UNIX process is created with the system *fork* call. (There is one exception; the very first process that exists when UNIX is first booted.) In other words, every process must be created by another process.

When a process calls *fork*, the kernel creates a new process (Figure 8.11). The caller is the *parent*, and the new process is the *child*. The child is almost identical to the parent. Its address space has the same commands (including the *fork* call) and it begins execution at the next command, just where the parent resumes execution.

Figure 8.11 System fork call

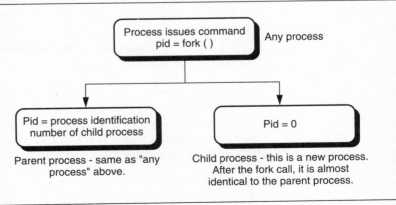

Parent process - same as "any process" above.

Child process - this is a new process. After the fork call, it is almost identical to the parent process.

This probably seems strange. Indeed, the child seems to come from nowhere and starts doing exactly what its parent is already doing (I guess it is typical of all children). It is like the magical brooms that keep multiplying in The Sorceror's Apprentice. Perhaps the term "child" is misleading: "clone" might be a better word because parent and child have the same commands. However, as we will see, the child often subsequently takes on a new identity.

The *fork* call also returns an integer (in each process). In the parent, it returns the child's process identification number. However, in the child, it returns 0. Typically, the parent (and consequently the child) contains code that tests the value returned by the *fork* call. The code then makes another system call (such as an *exec*) if the *fork* call returns 0. Now the parent and child become different, rather than being two clones doing the job of one. (There is a detailed example in Section 5.11.)

Exec Command. When a process calls *exec*, the kernel redefines the process. It does this by replacing the contents of its address space with an executable file. The exec call contains parameters that locate the executable file. In effect, it completely redefines a process by giving it new commands and data.

The user might think a new process has appeared. But, to UNIX, it is still the same old process, just redefined. The redefined process is the *successor* to the one that called *exec* (Figure 8.12).

Figure 8.12 System exec call

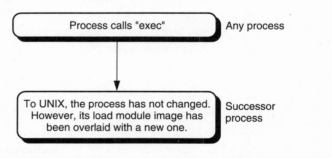

Process calls "exec" — Any process

To UNIX, the process has not changed. However, its load module image has been overlaid with a new one. — Successor process

Wait Command. In some cases, the parent waits for the child to finish by executing a conditional *wait* system call. (Under what condition should the parent execute *wait*? Don't forget, if the parent has the *wait* command, so does the child initially.) UNIX puts the parent in a wait state until the child finishes. Then UNIX wakes up the parent. This is a form of process synchronization.

Exit Command. Last is the system command *exit*. When a process calls exit, UNIX terminates it. The process no longer competes for resources.

Process States

Each process may be in one of many states, most of which appear in Figure 8.13. With the exception of a few additional states and transitions, this diagram is similar to Figure 4.4.

The ready and wait states resemble those described in Chapter 4. However, UNIX also distinguishes between processes in memory and those that have been swapped to secondary storage.

A running process may be in either the *user mode* or the *kernel mode*. The two have different priority levels. A user mode process has access only to what the UNIX kernel allows. Normally, this is the process' data, instructions, and open files. Specifically, it cannot access kernel data or routines. In kernel mode, a process has access to kernel data and instructions. It may also execute *privileged* instructions. For example, instructions to start I/O or change processor status may be privileged. Not all architectures have privileged instructions.

Basically, a process is in user mode when it is executing commands in a user program. A process is in kernel mode when it is executing commands in the kernel. A process may go from user to kernel mode when it makes a system call or if its time quantum expires. It then enters the kernel mode in order to take appropriate action. Conversely, when a system call has completed, the process returns to the user mode.

When a process calls *fork*, the child first enters a *created* state. When it is ready to run, it moves to a ready state and competes for the CPU with all other processes.

Last, when a process calls *exit*, it enters the *zombie* state. As the name indicates, this is a peculiar condition. The process no longer competes for resources, nor is there any address space associated with it: in effect, it does not exist. Technically, however, it still has an entry in the kernel's process table (described shortly). It is gone, but not quite forgotten.

When a process calls *exit*, the parent receives a signal (how do we know it has a parent?). It responds by collecting information the child may have left such as the reason for its demise and some run time statistics. The parent then removes the child's entry from the kernel's process table. The child is now gone and forgotten. Not even a picture on the mantelpiece remains. This not quite as disgusting as animals that eat their young or their parents, but it is close. UNIX has little use for traditional family values, despite its nomenclature.

Process Table

UNIX keeps track of all processes through a *process table* which has an entry for each process. The only time a new entry is added is when a process calls *fork*.

Figure 8.13 UNIX process state transitions

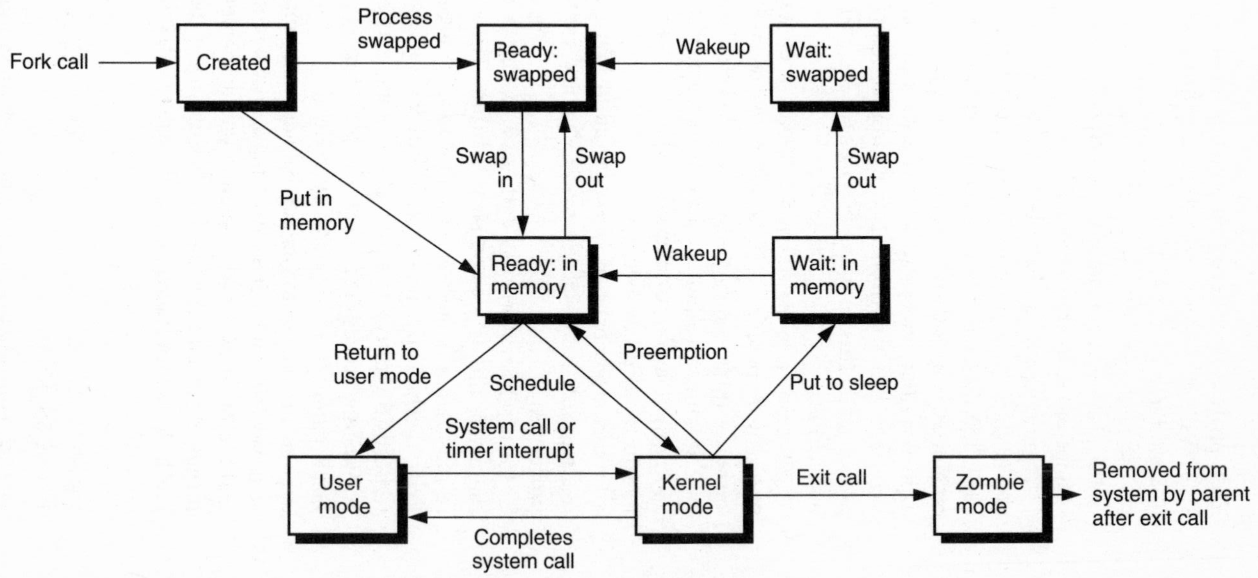

A process table entries contains *static* information. It is fixed in size and describes the process throughout its life cycle. The table must always be accessible to the kernel and resident in memory. Each entry includes the following:

- Process identification number.
- Amount of time the process has been resident in memory.
- Accumulated CPU time.
- Current state.
- Parent's process identification number.
- Priority.
- Information that allows the kernel to find the process and its *u area*.

Process *U Area*

A process' *u area* (user area) is basically an extension of its process table entry. The u area contains information that the process needs as it runs, including the following:

- Locations of the current and root directories.
- Entries in the user file descriptor table.
- I/O parameters such as the number of data bytes to transfer and the location of the buffer.
- Limits on the size of the process and the number of files it can create.
- Information on how the process should respond to signals. We will describe them later when we talk about process synchronization.
- Information that allows the kernel to locate the *per process region table*.

Per Process Region Table

The per process region table contains information about the process' address space. Depending on the UNIX implementation, the table may be in the process table, the u area, or in a separate location entirely. Figure 8.14 shows the per process region table in a separate location.

UNIX divides the virtual address space into *regions*. The per process region table provides dynamic address translation, and allows processes to share memory. Let's see how.

A process normally consists of three regions: the *code (or text) region*, *data region*, and *stack region*. The code region contains the process' code or instructions. The per process region table contains information that prevents the process from writing in its code region. Thus, the region is write protected and not modifiable. The data region contains the process' data and is modifiable.

Figure 8.14 Process table, process u area, per process region table, and kernel region table entry

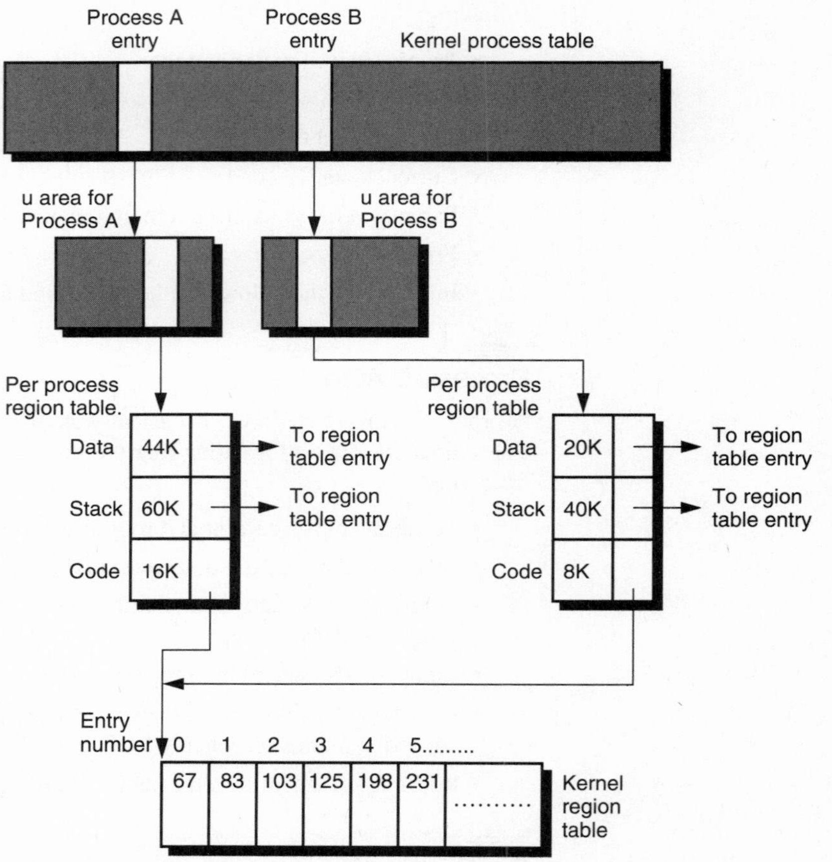

The stack region is also modifiable. It holds parameters when the process calls functions, and register values when the process is interrupted. The stack region grows and shrinks as the process runs.

The process references its regions through virtual addresses. The per process region table plays a role in address translation. Primarily, it contains the starting virtual address of each region. It also contains information used to locate an entry in a *kernel region table*. Reference [11] discusses this table in more detail. For our purposes, we will assume its entry keeps track of active regions. We also assume that memory consists of frames. Thus, in Figure 8.14, the kernel region table entry contains the frame numbers in the region.

Figure 8.14 shows how two processes (A and B) can share memory. According to process A's per process region table, its code, data, and stack reside in regions starting at locations 16K, 44K, and 60K, respectively. Similarly the code, data, and stack for process B start at virtual addresses 8K, 20K, and 40K, respectively.

An entry in the per process region table points to the page table for the region (kernel region table). Figure 8.14 shows only the one for the code region. Furthermore, it shows that the code regions for both processes have the same kernel region table.

Thus, references to the code regions of either process are translated to the same real locations.

To see this, suppose that frames contain 1K bytes. When process A makes its reference, its region table is accessed. For example, a reference to virtual address 20K corresponds to the code region starting at location 16K. Furthermore, since the frame sizes are 1K, the code region consists of pages starting at virtual addresses 16K, 17K, 18K, etc. Thus, virtual address 20K corresponds to the fifth virtual page in the code region. Using the kernel region table, this is actually frame 198 (fifth entry in the kernel region table).

Similarly, we can translate the virtual reference for process B. For example, a reference to virtual address 12K corresponds to the fifth page of a region that starts at virtual address 8K. But because the code region table entry points to the same kernel region table, the real memory reference is again to frame 198. Thus, even though the virtual addresses of the processes differ, they translate to the same frames.

═══

Interprocess Communication

UNIX has seven mechanisms for handling interprocess communications or IPC. They are *pipes*, *messages*, *semaphores*, *shared memory*, *synchronization signals*, *process tracing*, and *death of child*. Section 5.11 discussed pipes in detail, so we will not devote additional space to them. However, we will briefly describe the other mechanisms.

Messages. Processes can transfer messages to and from other processes. By executing system calls, a process can leave a message in a queue from which another process can retrieve it. The main commands are *msgsnd* ( ) and *msgrcv* ( ).

UNIX stores messages in memory and uses *message headers* to locate them. A message header is a structure that contains the message's location, type, and size. UNIX organizes the headers in linked queues and uses a *queue header* to locate the beginning of each of them. Figure 8.15 shows three linked queues containing message headers. Each header specifies the location of a message stored in a buffer.

Figure 8.15 UNIX message queue

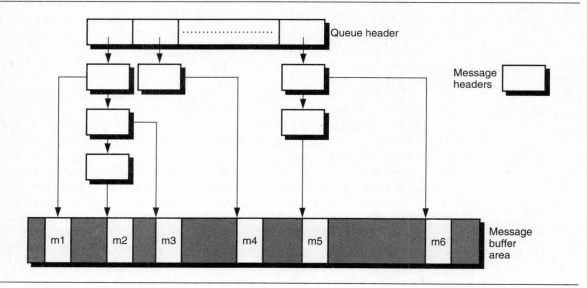

To send a message, a process executes the command

msgsnd(*argument list*)

The arguments are:

- The queue descriptor. It locates a queue header and specifies which message queue to access.
- The message's location and size.
- Flags that specify what the kernel should do if the message overflows its storage space.

Msgsnd causes the UNIX kernel to store the specified message in the buffer area and to create and insert a new message header at the front of the specified queue. If any other processes were in a wait state because that particular queue was empty, UNIX moves them to the ready state. Presumably, they were waiting for a message, and can now proceed.

If, on the other hand, there is no more room in the queue, the kernel puts the process in a wait state. It remains there until another process removes a message from the queue. If a flag in the *msgsnd* call specified the process should not wait, the system command returns an error.

A process can receive a message by making the call

```
size = msgrcv(argument list)
```

The arguments are:

- Queue descriptor.
- Location and size of the message storage area.
- Flags that specify what the kernel should do if the queue is empty.
- Message type.

Msgrcv directs the kernel to look for a message of a particular type in the specified queue. If it finds the message, it copies the message to the specified address, removes the header from the queue, and frees the buffer area. It returns the number of bytes in the message.

If the queue was empty, the kernel puts the process in a wait state. It remains there until another process sends a message to the queue.

In both commands, the kernel ensures that the process has access rights to the queue and that the message lengths do not exceed defined limits. If there are problems, the kernel returns an error condition.

Semaphores. A UNIX semaphore is basically similar to the ones described in Chapter 5, but there are a few extra features. Specifically, a UNIX semaphore consists of four parts. They are:

- Semaphore value.
- PID of the last process that operated on the semaphore.
- Number of processes waiting for the semaphore value to increase.
- Number of processes waiting for the semaphore value to decrease to 0.

The main system command that operates on a semaphore is *semop( )*.

UNIX maintains a structure similar to the one it uses for messages. That is, there is an array of headers, each of which points to an array of semaphores (see Figure 8.16).

Figure 8.16 UNIX semaphores

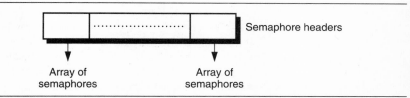

When a process wants to operate on a semaphore, it makes the system call

```
value = semop(argument list)
```

The arguments are:

- Semaphore array identifier.
- A pointer to an operation list. The list consists of elements indicating a semaphore operation. Each element contains a semaphore entry number, the actual semaphore operation (stored as an integer), and flags.
- Number of elements in the operation list.

Semop directs the kernel to change semaphore values in a designated array in accordance with the operation list. If the kernel is interrupted while changing values, it will restore all semaphore values, and restart the call later. Thus, the kernel will make all requested changes, or none, i.e., the *semop* call is indivisible. This is consistent with the semaphore operations described in Chapter 5.

We said that the operation list contains integer values that specify operations. The kernel responds to the values as follows:

- If the integer is 0, the kernel examines the specified semaphore. If the semaphore value is also 0, the kernel proceeds to the next element in the operation list. If not, the kernel adds 1 to the number of processes waiting for the semaphore to be 0. It reverses previous semaphore operations done in this system call, and puts the process in a state waiting for the semaphore value to become 0.
- If the integer is positive, the kernel adds it to the semaphore value. It wakes up any processes that were waiting for the value to increase. This is similar to the *V* operation in Chapter 5, but more general.
- If the integer is negative, the kernel asks, "What is the sum of the integer and the semaphore value?" If it is greater than or equal to 0, the kernel performs the addition. If, afterward, the value is 0, the kernel wakes any processes waiting for that condition. However, if the result is negative, the kernel does not do the addition. Instead, it reverses previous semaphore operations done in this system call, and puts the process in a state waiting for the semaphore value to increase.

The semaphore operations are generalizations of those discussed in Chapter 5. How would you modify the above definitions to make them equivalent?

Shared memory. Figure 8.14 shows how processes may share memory. All that is necessary is to map their regions to the same kernel region table entry. A process may do this by making the system call

```
address = shmat(argument list)
```

The arguments are:

- Identifier specifying an entry in a shared memory table. Each entry locates a shareable region (kernel region table entry).
- Virtual address that the process wants to use to reference the region.
- Flags that specify the access mode for the region.

This call makes the UNIX kernel attach a specified region to a process' virtual memory. The kernel returns the virtual address of the region. The address may not be the one the process requested. Sometimes a different virtual address is returned to avoid overlap with other regions.

Figure 8.17 Two processes using shmat( ) to attach the same region

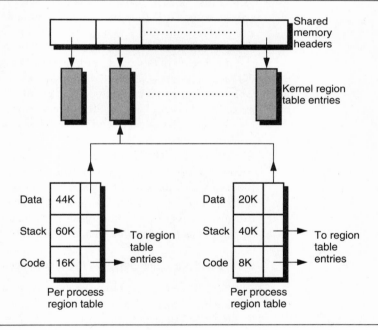

Figure 8.17 shows an example in which two processes call *shmat* with the same identifier. The kernel returns a value of 44K to one process and a value of 20K to the other. Either process may now write data to the region for the other to read.

When a process no longer needs to share memory, it may call *shmdt*( ). It detaches the region specified by a virtual address.

Death of Child. Previously, we described the *fork* call that creates a new process. The new process is the child, and the caller is the parent. Sometimes the parent may want to sleep or wait until the child finishes. In such cases, the parent may issue the system call

```
procid = wait(address)
```

The *wait* command makes the kernel check whether the process has children in the zombie state. If it has no children at all, the kernel returns an error. If there are children, but none are in the zombie state, the process goes into a wait state until it receives a signal (described shortly). If there is a child in the zombie state or when the parent receives a signal, the kernel stores the child's exit status code in memory associated with the specified address. The kernel also adds the CPU time the child accumulated to fields in the parent's u area, and removes the child's entry from the process table. The process ID of the zombie child is returned in *procid*. There must be some psychological significance to all this weird terminology, but it is surely beyond the scope of an OS textbook.

Remember that a child process enters the zombie state after it calls *exit*. *Exit* makes the kernel close all files, release allocated resources, free the process' regions and memory, and send a signal to the parent. A status value is returned.

Synchronization Signals. Processes may use signals to indicate the occurrence of specific events. Generally, a process may send a signal to other processes, and may wait for the receipt of a signal. The three system calls we describe here are *signal( )*, *kill( )*, and *pause( )*. Basically, they send signals, cause a process to wait for a signal, and specify what it should do if it receives a signal. Let us first describe what a signal is.

Normally, a signal indicates the occurrence of an event, such as:

SIGPIPE: An attempt to write to a pipe in which no one is reading.
SIGCLD: A child process has died.
SIGSYS: An error has occurred during a system call. For example, it may request more resources, but the caller has used up its allocation.
SIGBUS: Bus error.
SIGTRAP: Trap or exception. For example, a process may have tried to execute a privileged instruction, or write into a read only segment.

Each signal has an associated value that may be specified as an argument in a system *signal( )* call. There are 19 signals in Release 2 of UNIX System V. You can find details on them in references [11, 14].

A process issuing a system *signal* call will execute

```
oldfctn = signal(sigvalue, fctn)
```

It specifies what to do if a particular signal arrives. The normal choices are: exit, ignore the signal, or execute a particular function. The parameter *sigvalue* identifies the signal. The parameter *fctn* specifies a function to call on receipt of the signal. A *fctn* value of 1 means the process should ignore certain signals. The value that *signal* returns specifies the function in the most recent signal call with *sigvalue*.

A process may send signals through the system call

```
kill(procid, sigvalue)
```

The second parameter specifies the signal. For example, when a child process exits, it signals the parent with SIGCLD (symbolic equivalent of 18).

The first parameter is either the ID number of a process or a *process group ID*. The process group ID identifies a group of recipient processes. Normally, they are related.

Finally, a process that calls *pause( )* simply suspends execution until it receives a signal. The signal, of course, must be one that the process has not chosen to ignore or the pause will be eternal.

Process Tracing. Process tracing normally used in debugging, involves the *ptrace( )* system call. A process to be traced is spawned by a system *fork( )* call from within a debugger. The *ptrace( )* system call is used to send signals between the parent (debugger) and child (traced) process.

The *ptrace( )* call has the following parameters:

- Specification of certain commands such as read or write.
- Identification number of the traced process.
- Virtual address location within the child process.
- Integer data value.

Normally, both the debugger and child call *ptrace( )*.

After the debugger spawns a child, it will normally wait for the child to awaken it. Remember that the spawning of a child does not mean it begins execution immediately. It must call *exec* to execute the process to be traced. Upon return, the child enters a special trace state and sends a signal to wake up the debugger. The child then waits for the debugger to issue another command.

When the debugger wakes up, it calls *ptrace( )* and waits for the child to respond. Meanwhile, the kernel verifies that there is a child process with the specified ID number. It then copies the command, address, and integer data into a special trace data structure and wakes up the child. The child then executes the specified command and wakes up the debugger (again). Depending on the command, the child may reenter the trace state or resume execution.

≡≡

Input/Output

We finish the case study of UNIX by describing its I/O system and device drivers. The UNIX kernel typically treats all I/O as byte streams. That is, it treats its files as a contiguous collection of bytes. This simplifies the device independent component of I/O, as distinctions among file types are unnecessary. UNIX device drivers handle device specific operations.

The first step in file I/O is to issue the system call

```
filedesc = open(filename, mode)
```

The UNIX kernel searches its file system for the named file. If it finds the file, it makes an entry in the system file table and the user file descriptor table (Figure 8.8). It returns the file descriptor value. If it does not find the file, it returns a value of -1. *Mode* specifies whether the file is opened for read or write privileges or both.

A process reads using the call

```
howmany = read(fd, buffer, number)
```

The first parameter is the file descriptor returned by *open*. The buffer specifies where to store the data, and number is how many bytes are requested. The kernel returns the number actually transferred.

The write command has the form

```
howmany = write(fd, buffer, number)
```

and works essentially in reverse.

Generally, I/O occurs between processes and two types of devices. They are *block* (such as disk and tape drives) and *character* (such as terminals and printers) oriented devices. As described in Chapter 3, a device driver called by the kernel handles the specifics for a particular device.

Block Drivers. Block drivers execute basic functions for a device. A disk driver will, in some cases, determine sector numbers on a disk, control the movement of the disk heads, and schedule disk accesses. Specific operations depend on how much the controller does. In some cases, controllers do much of the work. Whatever they don't do, the driver must.

The UNIX kernel treats file systems as logical devices. It does not deal with the devices themselves. When a process issues an I/O request involving a device such as a disk, it specifies a file descriptor number. Through the file descriptor and system file tables, the kernel locates an inode. The inode, along with a *logical device number*, determines the file.

The logical device number consists of two parts: a *major device number* and a *minor device number*. The major device number specifies an entry in a *block device switch table*. This table contains pointers to all block drivers that use the system buffer cache (described shortly). When a process requests I/O, the kernel accesses the table to locate the driver.

The minor device number specifies one of several identical devices or a particular *partition* (or *section*) on a disk. A partition is a set of sectors that contains a file system. UNIX allows the division of a disk into several partitions. Consequently, one disk may contain multiple file systems. System tables define the disk partitions and the sector numbers at which they begin. Thus, whereas the major device number specifies the driver, the minor device number specifies the file system.

Block drivers may perform *unbuffered I/O* or *buffered I/O*. Unbuffered I/O allows data transfer directly to or from a process' virtual space. Its pages must be locked so they are not swapped out of memory.

Buffered I/O uses a *system buffer cache*, a set of buffers within the kernel. The kernel manages them in a free list, and allocates and deallocates them when they are needed for I/O. Process output will go from a virtual space to the buffer cache before being transferred to a device. Similarly, process input is stored in the buffer cache before going to the process' virtual space. This allows process code to be swapped while it is waiting for I/O and improves the efficiency of the I/O system.

Terminal Drivers. Terminal drivers are like block drivers, except that they transmit data a character at a time. But there is often one major difference in the mode of transfer. For example, during a read a block driver will transfer the data to a buffer. Does a terminal driver work the same way? Surprisingly, the answer is sometimes "No."

For example, most users are far from skilled typists. They often make many typing mistakes. They may type characters and then enter backspace or delete keys to erase them. Sometimes they even need to erase entire lines.

Terminal drivers may use *line discipline modules* that interpret sequences of characters entered from a terminal. Typically, the module runs in either a *canonical mode* or a *raw mode*.

In a canonical mode, the module receives a sequence of characters from a terminal and interprets control characters to alter the input. Examples include pressing a "backup" or "erase" key. However, such actions do not actually delete characters, at least not yet. Since they have been typed, they have already been transmitted. Pressing a "backup" or "erase" key sends another character. The line discipline module intercepts it and acts according to its value. When the code for the "return" key is sent, the altered string is transferred to a buffer.

For example, consider the scenario in Figure 8.18. The user intends to type PASCAL MYFILE. However, he or she makes a few mistakes. Pressing the backspace key (indicated by <), deletes the prior character. What the terminal sends is PASCS<AL MNF<<YFILE. The line discipline module uses "<" as a signal to delete the prior character. The string "<<" deletes the two prior characters.

Figure 8.18 Line discipline module interpreting terminal entries

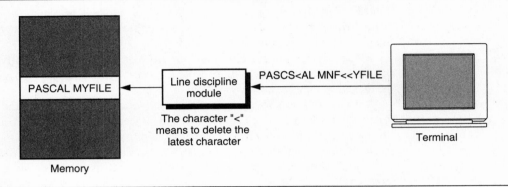

In a raw mode, the line discipline module does no conversions. It simply accepts whatever is sent. What a dangerous way to live.

Another difference in terminal drivers is in how they buffer characters. Since characters arrive very slowly and in small numbers, a buffer cache is not used. Instead, the driver keeps the characters in a linked list of blocks called a *clist*. The blocks are called *cblocks*. Each cblock basically contains an array of characters. However, since the number can vary, it also contains a pointer to the first and last characters. Furthermore, since one cblock may not be enough, each one also contains a pointer to another cblock. Figure 8.19 shows the format of a cblock.

Figure 8.19 Cblock format

Location of next cblock	Location of first character in this cblock	Location of last character in this cblock	⋯⋯List of characters⋯⋯

When a user enters characters from a terminal, they are placed in the cblocks in the driver's clist. For example, consider the terminal session in Figure 8.20. The user is typing the command "pr file1a, file2a." The initial characters, starting with p, r, (blank), etc., are stored in the first cblock. If cblocks hold seven characters (a small number used only for illustration), the first one is full when the programmer types "pr file."

Figure 8.20 Clists used to buffer terminal entries

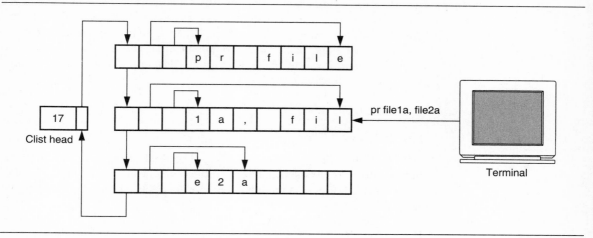

When the programmer continues by typing 1, a, etc., a second cblock is allocated and the characters are stored there. In this case, the second cblock also fills, and a third one is needed. When the programmer has entered the entire command, the third cblock contains the last three characters. The clist head contains the location of the first cblock and the total number of characters.

As the kernel removes characters from the clist, it adjusts the pointers. Also the number of characters (in the clist head) decreases. When the kernel removes all the characters, it returns the cblock to an available pool.

Each terminal driver typically has three clists. One contains output data, another contains input data prior to translation by the line discipline module, and the third contains the translated or *cooked data* that the line discipline module creates.

━━
Other Reading

This concludes the case study of UNIX. The interested reader should certainly consult additional references such as those listed at the end of the chapter. Depending on your interests you may want to consult certain references.

For instance, reference [13] contains many examples of UNIX commands and how to use the system to perform various tasks. Reference [11] contains details on the UNIX's inner workings. The author presents numerous algorithms describing how UNIX carries out many of its tasks.

≡≡≡ 8.3 VMS

The VMS operating system runs on VAX computers. As in previous case studies, we will not distinguish among its many versions. We will discuss some VMS commands, memory management, dynamic address translation, process structure, scheduling, interprocess communication, and deadlock. We do not discuss I/O, since it was treated in Chapter 3. The reader may refer to references [18-20] for additional information.

≡≡ Directories and Files

VMS, like the other systems we have described, provides a hierarchical directory structure. At the user level, it differs little from the structures of UNIX and MS-DOS. A user logs on in the root directory, and can create a hierarchy of files and subdirectories.

A file name takes the following form:

```
[dir1.dir2.....dirn]filename.extension;versionnumber
```

The sequence of directory names inside the brackets defines the path from the root to a particular subdirectory. Thus, if the "Simulations" file of Figure 8.9 were a VMS file, its name would be

```
[rootname.Research]Simulations
```

Each file also has an extension that describes its type. VMS commands often need not specify the extension. For example, if the file Prog1.Pas contains Pascal source code, we compile it by typing

```
$Pascal Prog1
```

The Pas extension need not be specified. If the compilation succeeds, the compiler creates a file named Prog1.Obj. The Obj extension means Object module. To link the module, the user issues the command

```
$Link Prog1
```

In this case, the extension Obj is assumed. If the link succeeds, the linker creates a file named Prog1.Exe. Finally, to run the program, the user types

```
$Run Prog1
```

In all cases, $ is the *DCL (Digital Command Language) prompt.*

Backups. Each VMS file also has a version number. On creation, a file has the name *filename.extension*;1. This is the first, or initial, version. If someone edits the file, the new version is *filename.extension*;2. The file *filename.extension;1* still exists and is unchanged. It is analogous to the .Bak file created by many word processors.

However, in VMS, subsequent changes generate versions 3, 4, and so on. Thus, the user can keep many levels of backups. Usually, an installation will allow only one or two to avoid clutter. Thus, if you edit a file for the seventieth time, you will not have seventy different versions. If you are allowed two backups, you will have only versions 70, 69, and 68.

If you do many compilations or linkings, you will end up with multiple versions of the object and load modules as well. Obviously, unless you clean house frequently, the result is many useless and confusing files.

An easy way to delete extraneous files is with the command

```
$Purge
```

It deletes all but the most recent versions of every file in your directory.

Subdirectories. As in other systems, you may enter any subdirectory and reference files without specifying the complete subdirectory path. The command to enter a subdirectory is

```
$Set default [subdirectories list].
```

A minus sign (-) may be used instead of a subdirectory list. It indicates the parent of the current directory.

If a user forgets his or her current directory, the command

```
$Show Default
```

displays it as a subdirectory list.

Wildcards. A user may reference a group of files with the wildcard *. An asterisk in the filename, extension, or version number means "all." For example, the command

```
$Delete *.Obj;*
```

deletes all files with extension Obj, regardless of their names or version numbers.

Name Substitutions

Another feature of VMS allows its user to substitute simple names for complex commands. For example, we could define the *Cleanup* as

```
Cleanup :== Delete *.Obj;*, *.Exe;*
```

This equates *Cleanup* to deleting all Obj and Exe files. Later, when the user enters the command

```
$Cleanup
```

VMS will perform the deletion.

Other VMS Commands

Obviously, there are many other VMS commands. Table 8.6 summarizes the previous ones and shows some other common ones.

Table 8.6 Some VMS commands

Command	Function
Append	Concatenates two or more files into a single file.
Assign	Establishes one character string as equivalent to another.
Copy	Copies files.
Create/Directory	Creates a directory.
Deassign	Cancels assignment made via the "Assign" command.
Delete	Deletes a file or directory.
Directory	Lists directory contents.
Help	Asks VMS for a list of DCL commands or information about a particular command.
Mail	Calls mail facility and allows users to send and receive messages.
Password	Allows a user to define or change a password.
Phone	Calls phone facility. Users can make and receive calls, thus establishing a two-way conversation.
Print	Prints one or more files on the system default printer.
Rename	Renames a file. Can also move a file from one directory to another.
Set Default	Establishes a directory as current.
Set Prompt	Defines a message or character as the system prompt.
Show Users	Displays information on all current interactive users.
Type	Displays a file on the terminal.

Command Files

You can also define a *command* file (one with a "Com" extension). This is similar to the MS-DOS batch files and the UNIX shell scripts. Command files normally contain a sequence of DCL commands. Typing @filename is sufficient to make VMS execute everything in filename.Com.

Some installations give each user a file named Login.Com. VMS executes it automatically whenever the user logs on. Users may store definitions in it, and effectively define their own DCL commands. Each user can thus create a friendly working environment. This is similar to the Autoexec.Bat files of MS-DOS.

File Protection

You may reference files from another user's directory. All you need is the appropriate sequence of directories and the file name. But your references are limited by the file's protection levels.

Files are protected through access modes. VMS allows four access modes: *R* (read), *W*(write), *E*(execute), and *D*(delete). These may be used in any combination to limit access to a file. Note that one mode does not imply another. For example, write access does not imply read access. Therefore, to allow read and write access to a file, you must give it an *RW*(*R* and *W* mode). (Can you think of a situation in which you might allow someone to write to a file, but not read it? This sounds like the security situation in which a document is classified at a level higher than its author can access.)

VMS assigns default modes to new files. The default settings are installation-dependent. However, you can define your own protection modes through the command

```
$Set Protection = (category : mode) filename
```

The *category* defines to whom the access mode applies. There are four possibilities. The first category is *system*. It includes very few people. Typically, they are systems programmers and perhaps installation directors who assign directories to users. The default modes for *system* are *RWED*.

Another category is *owner*. The owner of a file is the person who created it. For most files, the default modes are *RWED*. However, for a directory, the default is *RWE*. This means that, by default, even the creator of a directory cannot delete it. However, you may override the default by typing

```
$Set Protection=(Owner:D) name of directory file
```

The third category is a *group*. All VMS users are assigned a *user identification code* (UIC), which contains two parts, the *group code* and the *member code*. Users with the same group code form a group. Thus, the *group* category defines the access modes for the group. The normal default for the group is *RE*.

The last category is the *world* or all VMS users. The normal world default is no access whatsoever. However, an instructor may allow his or her students access to a file by entering

```
$Set Protection=(World:R) filename
```

If you forget the current protection settings for a file, you can type

```
$Dir/Protection
```

"Dir" lists all files in the current directory. The "Protection" qualifier shows their protection levels.

Help

One of VMS' nicest features is its online help. You may seek help on the use of DCL commands by typing

```
$Help command
```

VMS responds with a brief explanation of the command, and lists the available qualifiers. You can then enter a qualifier to get more information. This is especially useful when one forgets a command's syntax, or possible qualifiers.

Virtual Addressing

Virtual addresses are 32 bits long. Each one (Figure 8.21) includes a 2-bit segment number, a 21-bit virtual page number, and a 9-bit byte offset.

Figure 8.21 VMS virtual address

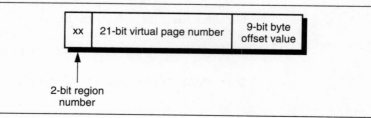

Virtual memory contains 2^{32} bytes, divided into four regions (Figure 8.22). The two high-order bits in a virtual address specify the region. Each region contains 2^{30} bytes.

Figure 8.22 VMS virtual memory

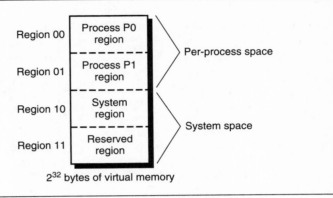

2^{32} bytes of virtual memory

The system regions (numbers 10 and 11 binary) are for system use. Region 10 contains operating system routines and tables. Region 11 is reserved for future use.

Address Translation. All processes that run in the system space use the *system page table* for address translation. The mechanics are very similar to those described in Chapter 2. When a process is running in system space, VMS uses two special registers to describe the system page table. The *System Base Register* (SBR) contains its physical address, and the *System Length Register* (SLR) contains the number of entries.

Figure 8.23 shows the mechanics of address translation in system space. The virtual page number is added to the SBR. The result is the physical address of a page table entry. This entry, in turn, contains the frame number. The frame number is then concatenated with the byte offset to form the physical address.

The other two regions (numbers 00 and 01 binary) define the *per-process space*. Region 00, also called the program or P0 region, contains the executable code in a user process. Region 01, called the control or P1 region, contains system maintained process data such as user and system stacks and message sections. In fact, both regions are actually stacks. The P0 region begins at virtual address 0, and grows upward. The P1 region begins at location $2^{31}-1$, and grows downward.

Figure 8.23 Address translation in the system region

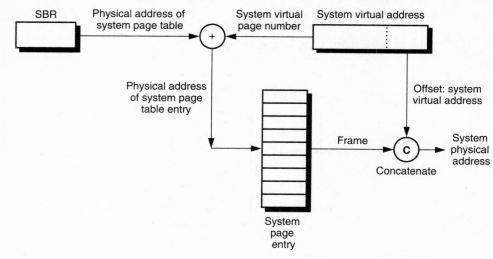

Each process running in these regions has its own page tables, one for each region. VMS uses four registers to maintain their location and size. They are the P0 and P1 page table Base Registers (P0BR and P1BR) and Length Registers (P0LR and P1LR).

However, dynamic address translation is more complicated in these regions, because the base registers do not contain the physical address of the page table. Instead, each contains a system virtual address of the page table. This causes more complex translation mechanics. Let us explain using the P0 region as an example. Figure 8.24 should help you follow the discussion.

The page number from a process' virtual address is added to the P0BR. But it contains a system virtual address of the P0 page table. Therefore, the result is the system virtual address of a P0 page table entry. This address must then be translated to a physical address using the SBR. Therefore, this address' page number is added to the SBR. The sum is the physical address of a system page table entry. Its contents are then concatenated with the byte offset from the virtual address of the P0 page table entry. The result is the physical address of the P0 page table entry. Finally, that entry is concatenated with the byte offset from the original virtual address, giving the final physical address. (As Groucho Marx said in <u>Duck Soup</u>, "Why, a four-year-old child could understand this report. Run out and find me a four-year-old child. I can't make head or tail out of it.") Address translation for region P1 is similar.

Figure 8.24 Address translation for the P0 region

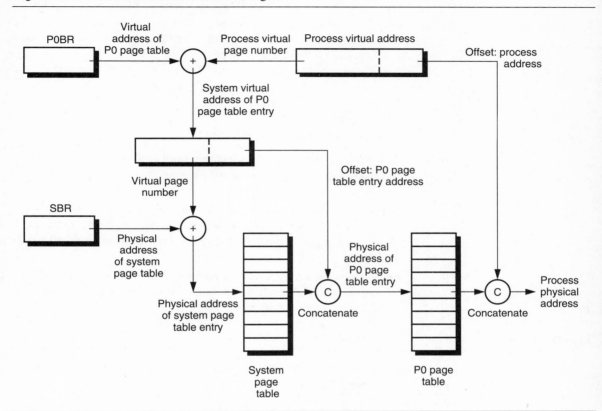

To save time on repeated references, hardware buffers (called *translation buffers*) remember the most recently referenced physical pages. When an address translation occurs, the physical page number is stored in a translation buffer. Subsequent references to the same virtual page are translated faster.

Access Modes

A running process does not always get every virtual page it requests. VMS defines access modes for all running processes. They are *user mode*, *supervisory mode*, *executive mode*, and *kernel mode*. Access to a virtual page depends on the process' access mode, which is checked during address translation. Most applications, including user processes, compilers, linkers, debuggers, and editors, run in user mode. Supervisor mode defines a higher privilege. For example, software for command interpretation runs in supervisor mode. The executive mode has still a higher privilege. Many operating system routines, such as the record management system, run in executive mode. The most privileged mode is the kernel mode. Scheduling, I/O processing, and memory management run in kernel mode.

Page Table Entries

Each page table entry contains the following:

- Modify bit, 1 means the virtual page has been updated.
- Physical frame number of the virtual page. Meaningful only when the valid bit (described next) is 1.
- Valid bit, 1 means the virtual page is in memory. It also means the modify bit and physical frame number fields contain valid information. When the valid bit is zero, VMS uses the other fields to locate the page in a file.
- Access codes. Four bits define accessibility to a virtual page, depending on a process' access mode. Figure 8.25 shows how the access code defines access to a virtual page.

Figure 8.25 Access codes for each process mode

Access code	Accessibility for each process mode			
	Kernel	Executive	Supervisor	User
0010	W	N	N	N
0011	R	N	N	N
0100	W	W	W	W
0101	W	W	N	N
0110	W	R	N	N
0111	R	R	N	N
1000	W	W	W	N
1001	W	W	R	N
1010	W	R	R	N
1011	R	R	R	N
1100	W	W	W	R
1101	W	W	R	R
1110	W	R	R	R
1111	R	R	R	R

W = Write and read access

R = Read access only

N = No access

═══

Memory Management

There are two main components in VMS memory management: the *pager* and the *swapper*. The pager responds to page faults. It determines the disk location of the page and initiates the read. The swapper responds to process state transitions. It swaps processes between memory and secondary storage to keep the highest priority executable processes in memory. Let us now take time to expand these ideas.

Working Set and Paging. Each process may have a limited number of virtual pages in memory. They form its *resident set* or *working set*. Working set dynamics are similar to those described in Chapter 2. During address translation, the valid bit is checked to see if the virtual page is in memory. If not, a page fault occurs. The pager then determines the page's disk location from the page table entry and initiates a read.

If the working set limit has not been reached, the pager finds an empty frame. The page is read into it, and the pager updates the page table. However, if the limit has been reached, a page must be replaced. But which one? As Chapter 2 showed, there are several replacement strategies.

VMS replaces pages on a FIFO basis. Now Chapter 2 showed that this strategy does not consider heavily referenced pages. As a result, it can make poor choices. However, VMS maintains additional data structures to minimize their effects.

When VMS replaces a page, it determines whether it has been modified. If not, VMS puts it at the end of a *free page list* (Figure 8.26). This list maintains physical pages available for use. When a process needs a page, VMS allocates it from the front of this list.

If the page has been modified, VMS puts it at the end of the *modified page list*. This is similar to the free page list except that the pages must be written back to secondary storage, before they are given to another process.

Because VMS puts the replaced page in one of the two lists, the page is still in memory. Therefore, if the process subsequently requests a replaced page, VMS can retrieve it with no physical I/O. This assumes, of course, that the page is still in the list. But, since VMS allocates free pages from the front of the list, a replaced page is likely to remain in memory for a while.

The page list acts like a cache memory. Paging occurs between the process' working set and the system lists, but no I/O occurs. But the cache does not keep the page indefinitely. Eventually, if it is not reclaimed, it will move to the front of the list. VMS will then allocate it to another requesting process as a free page.

If the replaced pages are modified, there are additional savings. If a modified page is replaced and subsequently referenced, two physical I/O operations are

Figure 8.26 Free and modified page lists

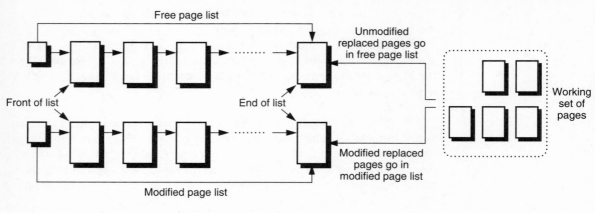

A referenced page from either list goes back into
the process' working set

saved. VMS does not write the page when it is replaced, and does not read it
when it is referenced. In fact, a modified page may be replaced and referenced
many times with no intervening I/O.

Yet another advantage is that the modified page list allows VMS to *cluster*
its I/O. That is, instead of writing one page at a time, VMS may write many
with one I/O call. When the list of modified pages becomes long, VMS will
write several pages from it. Pages in contiguous virtual memory of a process
may be written to consecutive disk locations. This reduces the total time for I/O.

Pages are not always removed from the working set. System services allow
pages to be *locked*. Locked pages are always valid. That is, as long as the
process is resident, they will be in the working set. However, if a process is
swapped out of memory, its working set, including locked pages, is also
swapped.

Swapping and the Process Header. The working sets of all executable
processes may not all fit in memory simultaneously. In such cases, VMS may
remove some of them (*outswap*), and load others (*inswap*). This is necessary
when the highest priority executable process (discussed later) is not resident in
memory. Then the swapper is needed.

Much of the information the swapper needs is in the *process header* or PHD
(Figure 8.27). VMS maintains a PHD for each process, and stores its location in
the PCB. The PHD contains the P0 and P1 page tables. They grow toward each
other as the working set increases.

Figure 8.27 Process header

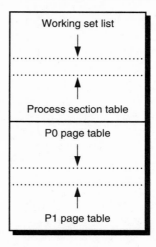

The PHD also contains the *working set list* and the *process section table*. The process section table contains information about the location of files, called *section files*, that contain process pages. Each entry contains information used to locate a file. Multiple entries allow the memory manager to locate pages from different section files.

The working set list describes the valid entries of the page table. Its entries are stored in three consecutive areas of the PHD (Figure 8.28). The PHD also contains pointers that locate these areas. The first area contains entries for pages permanently locked in memory by VMS. They are always part of the working set. They include the kernel stack, process header, and parts of the P1 page table.

The second area contains entries for pages a process has locked in memory. A process may, for example, lock pages containing logic that must quickly respond to certain events. This is especially true of real time processes.

The third area contains entries for swappable pages. This is the dynamic part of the working set list. Entries are stored in a circular queue to facilitate the FIFO page replacement strategy. The PHD contains pointers to the front and back of the queue. Each entry of the working set list contains the following:

- Virtual address of the page.
- Lock bit, set if the page is locked in memory.
- Valid bit, indicates the current entry is in use (contains valid information).
- Type field, determines the type of page, such as a process page, system page, global read-only page, global read/write page, or page table page.
- Modify bit, indicates if a page has been changed.

Figure 8.28 Working set list

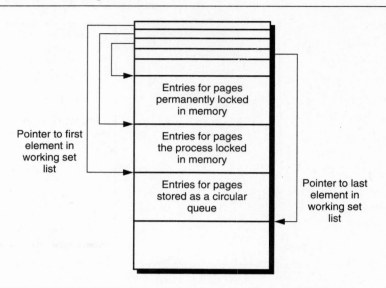

Process Control Blocks

VMS maintains information on each process through a process control block (PCB). Actually, there are two PCBs, a *hardware PCB* and a *software PCB*.

The hardware PCB defines the hardware context of a process when it is not running. It contains information such as the contents of the general registers and program status word and the locations and size of the P0 and P1 page tables. When a process is running, a *process control block base register* points to the hardware PCB. If it is interrupted, the contents of CPU registers are stored there. This, of course, preserves the process context. When it resumes execution, the contents of the hardware PCB are reloaded in the registers. The process resumes exactly where it was interrupted.

The software PCB contains the process priority and base priority (described shortly), location of the PHD, process state, number of pages in the working set, and link fields. The scheduler uses the link fields to maintain PCBs in a linked list.

The following discussions consider only the software PCB. Because of this, we will refer to it as the PCB.

Scheduling

VMS uses priority scheduling; that is, it schedules for execution the resident process with the highest priority.

The scheduling data structure resembles the multilevel feedback queue described in Chapter 4. Initially, VMS gives each process one of 32 possible priorities. This is the *base priority*; it is stored in the PCB. As the process runs, events may cause its priority to change. Its *current priority* is also stored in the PCB. Normally, VMS will not allow the current priority to fall below the base priority.

The data structure in Figure 8.29 shows how VMS schedules by priority. It maintains an array of headers, one for each priority. Each header points to the first in a list of PCBs. The current priority of a process determines the list in which its PCB resides. That is, if a process has a current priority p, its PCB is in the linked list starting at the pth header. When a process changes priority, VMS moves its PCB to a different list.

Figure 8.29 Software PCBs ordered by priority

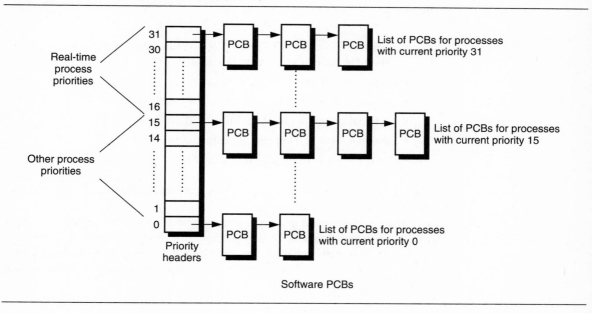

Scheduling is simple. VMS examines each list, starting from the highest priority, until it finds one that is not empty. It then chooses the process whose PCB is at the front of the list. The chosen process then begins running. It runs until it makes a request for which it must wait, or until it is preempted. Either way, the next process is chosen from the highest priority nonempty list.

Reasons for preemption depend on the type of process. VMS defines two types. Processes with a priority between 16 and 31, inclusive, are real-time processes. Those with a priority below 16 are normal processes. Real-time processes must respond to real-time events. Consequently, they must have a high priority. Normal processes include time sharing and batch processes; small delays in them are not dangerous.

A real-time process is preempted only when one with a higher priority reenters the ready state. A real-time process must never wait for another with a lower priority.

A normal process is preempted for the same reason. However, it also runs in a time-sharing mode, and is preempted if its time quantum expires. If there are no real-time processes, the ones with the highest priority will execute in round robin fashion. A process runs only when there is none with a higher priority.

There is another important difference between normal and real-time processes. The priorities of real-time processes do not change: their current priority is always the same as their base priority.

The current priority for a normal process changes with time. Events, such as those listed below, cause priority to increase or decrease. However, remember that the priority can never fall below the base priority or exceed 15. (The latter would turn a normal process into a real-time process.)

- Quantum expiration. The priority is decreased by 1, and the PCB is placed at the rear of the next lowest list.
- Completion of I/O. Priority increase of 2.
- A requested resource becomes available. Priority increase of 2.
- Terminal output is complete. Priority increase of 4.
- Terminal input is complete. Priority increase of 6.
- Process is created. Priority increase of 6.

The list sounds like a child's board game with magic squares that tell you how much to move your piece.

Because of these events, highly interactive processes get higher priorities, whereas compute-bound processes get lower priorities. The system is sensitive to changes in process behavior. Compute-bound processes that start doing more I/O increase in priority. I/O-bound processes that begin intensive computations decrease in priority.

≡≡≡

Process States

VMS processes are in one of four main states: running, wait, computable resident, or computable outswapped.

A process in a computable state is not waiting for anything. It is ready to run. VMS distinguishes between those in memory (resident) and those not in memory (outswapped). A process must be in the computable resident state before it can be scheduled for execution.

Processes in the wait state are waiting for a resource or event. There are different classes of wait states, depending on the reason why the process is waiting. The system scheduler maintains a queue for each class. A PCB for a waiting process is in one of these queues. Typical classes are:

- Page fault wait state. A process enters this state when it generates a page fault.

- Free page wait state. A process may request additions to its working set. VMS will allocate pages from its free list for that purpose. However, if the free list is empty, the process must wait.

- Collided page wait state. Suppose several processes reference a shared page not in memory. The first one enters the page fault wait state, but the others enter the collided page wait state. They enter the computable state when the page is read.

- Common event flag wait state. An event flag (described shortly) is a bit used to signal the occurrence of an event. Processes waiting for an event that has not yet occurred are in this state.

═══

Interprocess Communications

The simplest form of interprocess communications involves an *event flag*. It is a bit that indicates the occurrence of an event. Each flag is part of a 32-bit cluster called an *event flag cluster*. Each process may access four clusters, numbered 0 through 3. Clusters 0 and 1 contain *local event flags*. They are stored in the PCB and are used only by the process. Clusters 2 and 3 contain *common event flags*. They are used for interprocess communication and are stored in a system maintained *Common Event Block* (CEB). We will describe the operations on the common event flags.

Common event flags are used to synchronize cooperating processes. A process may clear or set flags, or it may wait on certain flags. VMS provides system services through which each process may access flags in the CEB.

The system may have many CEBs (Figure 8.30). A process with the proper authority may create a CEB by using a system routine. Actually, VMS creates the CEB and stores it in a list. VMS uses a CEB header to locate the first one in the list. Each CEB has a name, and all references to it must contain that name.

Before any process can access the flags in a CEB, it must first *associate* with it. This means the process makes a system call ($ASCEFC), specifying the CEB name. A system routine looks for the named CEB in the list. If it does not find the CEB, then it creates one. It puts the name and UIC of the requesting process in the CEB, and stores the CEB in the list.

Figure 8.30 Common event blocks and associated PCBs

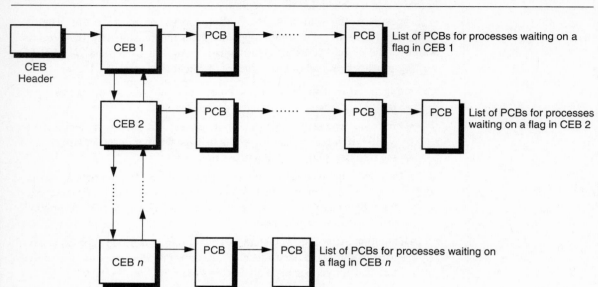

If the system finds the CEB, it stores its address in the PCB and increments a counter inside the CEB. The counter contains the number of processes currently associated with the CEB. Once the process has associated with a CEB, it may make other system calls, such as:

- $WAITFR. If the specified flag is set, control returns to the process. If not, the process enters a state waiting for the flag to be set. VMS stores the PCB in a list associated with the CEB (Figure 8.30). It also stores the flag for which the process is waiting in the PCB.
- $WFLOR. It is similar to $WAITFR, except that the process checks the logical OR of several event flags. That is, if any of them is set, control returns to the process. Otherwise, it waits for any of the flags to be set. VMS stores the list of flags for which the process is waiting, in the PCB and puts it in the list.
- $WFLAND. It is similar to $WFLOR, except that it uses the logical AND of several event flags. If the flags are not all set, the process will wait until they all are.
- $SETEF. This sets an event flag, often at the completion of an I/O or othersystem service request. A system routine must search the list of PCBs associated with the CEB, and move appropriate processes to a computable state. The state transition depends on whether a process was waiting for one event flag or a logical OR or AND of several flags.
- $CLREF. This clears an event flag.

Mailboxes

VMS processes may use a mail facility to send messages. One process sends a message to another's *mailbox*. Mailboxes are logical I/O devices that may be read or written through the VMS I/O system. Depending on the processes, the messages may be buffered in memory or stored in files.

Mail allows interactive users to exchange messages. A user can send a message by typing the command

```
$Mail filename
```

The *filename* is a file containing the message. VMS responds by asking the user for a directory to which the message should be sent. The user then enters the directory or specifies a file containing a list of directories. The latter is a *mail list* or *distribution list*.

The mail facility reads the file and sends it to each specified directory. Each user directory contains a message queue. New messages are inserted at the end of the queue (Figure 8.31), and the user can read messages from the front.

A user can read a message by entering the command

```
$Mail
```

Figure 8.31 Sending mail messages

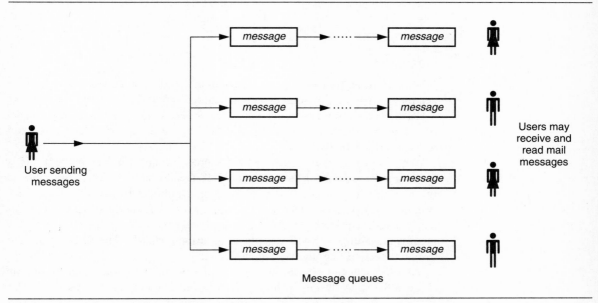

Message queues

VMS responds with a "Mail>" prompt. Subsequent "Read" commands allow the user to read each message in the queue. Messages can be erased with "Delete," or moved to another file with "Extract." For example, the following sequence of commands reads a message and stores it in file *filename*.

```
$Mail
Mail>Read
:
message is displayed on screen
:
>Extract filename
```

Shared Memory

Processes may share memory through *global sections*. A global section is a memory area that is mapped into the address space of one or more processes. One process may send information or messages to another by writing in its global section. The two processes normally agree on synchronization techniques such as event flags. This, of course, prevents a process from reading messages before they have been sent.

VMS maintains a global page table in the system virtual space. In fact, it is a logical extension of the system page table. The table is used much like the system page table or the process page table.

Resource Sharing and Deadlocks

VMS provides a lock management system that allows processes to synchronize access to resources. Resources include shared memory, files, and devices. As VMS allocates resources, it must also detect deadlocks. The major components of resource allocation and deadlock detection are the *Lock Block* (LKB) and *Resource Block* (RSB).

When a process wants access to a resource, it requests a *lock* on it. If this is the first such request for the resource, VMS creates an RSB. The RSB contains the name of the resource, access mode, and pointers to two additional lists (Figure 8.32) of LKBs. One list (lock granted list) represents locks that VMS has granted. The other (lock wait list) represents lock requests for which a process is waiting. We will describe both of these shortly. The RSB defines the resource; there is one for every requested resource.

All RSBs in the system are in one of several lists that VMS maintains (Figure 8.33). A system *resource hash table* contains all list headers. The system uses a hash function and the resource name to determine the list in which to store the RSB.

Figure 8.32 An RSB and its lists of LKBs

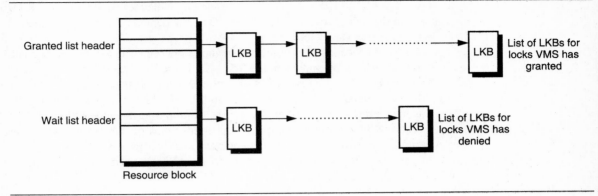

Figure 8.33 Resource hash table and RSBs

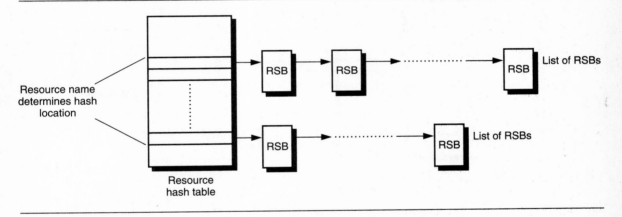

When a process requests a lock, VMS also creates an LKB. It identifies the type of lock requested. Each LKB contains a *lock mode* that determines the level of shareability. If two locks are *compatible*, the two requesting processes may share the resource. If they are *incompatible*, then they may not. There is one LKB for every lock a process requests.

Suppose a process requests a lock for a resource. VMS uses the resource name to find a header in the system hash table. It searches the list for the appropriate RSB. If VMS does not find it, it creates one.

Next, VMS creates a new LKB. It then locates a list header in the RSB for the *lock granted list*. It searches the list and examines the lock modes in each LKB. If they are all compatible with the lock mode of the new LKB, then it is put in that list. VMS grants the lock, and the process uses the resource. However, if VMS finds an LKB with an incompatible lock mode, the new LKB is put in the *lock wait list*. In this case, VMS has denied access to the resource, and the process must wait.

All LKBs for locks that a process requests are connected to the PCB. Each PCB has a header that points to the first LKB in the list. The first LKB points to the second, and so on. The LKB also contains a field that indicates whether VMS has granted the lock. Thus, given an LKB, VMS can find the PCB for the requesting process. As we shall see, this is useful for deadlock detection.

Figure 8.34 shows an example of the connections of the various blocks. In this example, two processes have requested locks on resources. Process 1 has requested a lock on resource R1, and process 2 has requested a lock on resource R2. Both have been granted.

Figure 8.34 Relationships among PCBs, RSBs, and LKBs

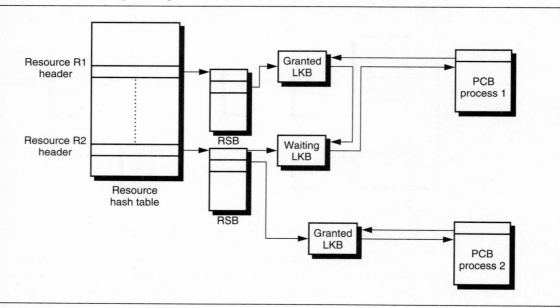

Process 1 has also requested a lock on resource R2. In this case, the lock mode is incompatible with the mode in the LKB of R2's granted list. Thus, it is put in the wait list. Process 1's PCB contains a header linking the two LKBs.

From Chapter 5, we know that deadlock occurs when there is a circular list of processes, each requesting a resource granted to the next one in the list. How does VMS detect deadlock? When does it decide to look for one?

VMS does not check for deadlock at every request for a resource. That would be time consuming. However, when a LKB is put in a wait list, it is also put in a *lock timeout queue*. If VMS eventually grants the lock, the LKB is removed from the queue. If an LKB remains in the queue for a long time, VMS suspects that a deadlock may have occurred. In particular, if a lock for an LKB at the front of the queue is not granted in a specified amount of time, the lock request *times out*. If this happens, VMS suspects a deadlock and starts an algorithm designed to detect it.

The algorithm is recursive. The idea is to first save the ID of the process whose lock request has timed out. Then, it examines all LKBs blocking the lock request. Each corresponds to a process with access to the requested resource.

Each of these processes, in turn, may be waiting for another resource. Thus, the algorithm looks at each process' LKB that represents a denied lock request. The LKBs exist because there are other LKBs blocking that request. Each corresponds to a process with access to a resource, and the algorithm looks at each one.

The algorithm repeats the pattern described in the previous paragraph. If it eventually finds a process with the same ID as the one it started with, deadlock exists.

When the algorithm detects deadlock, another routine examines all processes involved in the circular wait. It chooses one that has the lowest *deadlock priority*. This is a value assigned to each process for deadlock resolution.

Once the process is chosen, VMS returns an error code to it. The process must then resolve the deadlock by removing some (or all) of its lock requests.

═══
Acronym Summary

This section contains many acronyms which always makes reading more difficult. For convenience, Table 8.7 contains the acronyms used and what they stand for.

Table 8.7 VMS acronyms

Acronym	Meaning
CEB	Common Event Block
DCL	Digital Command Language
LKB	LocK Block
PCB	Process Control Block
PHD	Process Header
P0BR	P0 Base Register
P0LR	P0 Length Register
P1BR	P1 Base Register
P1LR	P1 Length Register
RSB	ReSource Block
SBR	System Base Register
SLR	System Length Register
VAX	Virtual Address eXtension
VMS	Virtual Memory System

≡≡
Other Reading

References [17-20] contain further coverage of VAX computers and the VMS operating system. Reference [17] contains a case study similar to ours. It covers different topics and provides a broad overview. Reference [20] integrates discussions of VAX hardware with VMS software. It contains more detail than reference [17], but not as much as [18-19].

≡≡≡≡≡ ## 8.4 MVS

The fourth case study is MVS. Recall from Section 4.5 that MVS is one of IBM's most popular operating systems. It runs on a variety of models, including the largest IBM system 370 mainframes. Coverage of a mainframe operating system is appropriate since the three other systems, MS-DOS, UNIX, and VMS generally run on smaller computers.

Section 4.5 gave a brief history of MVS. MVS is the result of many years of operating system evolution, starting with OS/360 in the mid-1960s. Today, it is one of the most powerful and complex operating systems.

MVS was originally designed as a batch operating system. The language used to communicate with it is the *Job Control Language* (JCL). In the early days, JCL commands were submitted on punch cards. Today they are typically stored on files. Users then submit them to the scheduler (Figure 8.35). Once submitted, they are stored in a class queue to await further scheduling.

Figure 8.35 MVS batch program submission

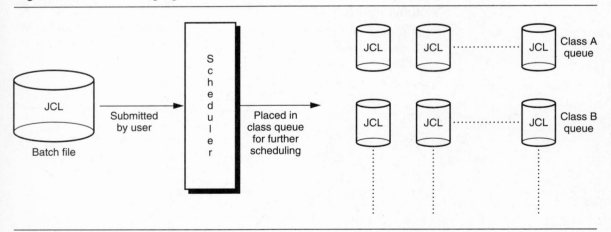

This does not mean MVS has no interactive ability. Indeed, it does. Programming tools such as *Time-Sharing Option* (TSO) provide interactive compiling, editing, and debugging capabilities. However, we focus just on MVS here and do not discuss TSO or any other tools or utilities. Also, since scheduling was the main focus of Section 4.5, we do not discuss it any further.

Our approach is to first discuss some preliminaries on disk organization and files. They are prerequisites for the next topic, the JCL. The JCL is a complex language and books have been written on it. It also provides a framework in which to discuss some of MVS' functions. Last, we discuss MVS' major components, data management, address translation, memory management, and I/O support.

Disk Organization

MVS maintains disk space similar to that described in Section 3.2. It defines tracks and cylinders as allocations units. However, it does not divide a track into sectors. The smallest allocation unit is a track. Track capacities and the number of cylinders vary. For example, IBM 3330 disks have 808 tracks of about 13K bytes each. Newer 3380 disks can have 1770 tracks of almost 50K bytes each.

However, this does not limit physical I/O to one track at a time. An MVS programmer must define physical records or blocks. They are stored on a track and separated by a gap (Figure 8.36). The gaps and physical records are similar to those on magnetic tape. Most important is that MVS physically reads one physical record at a time.

Figure 8.36 Physical records in a track under MVS

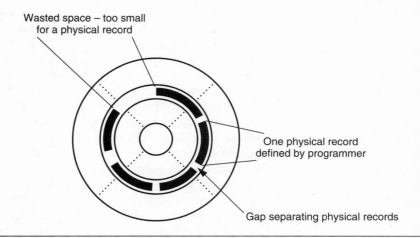

Wasted space – too small
for a physical record

One physical record
defined by programmer

Gap separating physical records

Physical record sizes vary and constitute an important parameter. Small ones mean many gaps and more wasted disk space. Large ones mean fewer gaps, and require large buffers, but large ones do not always mean less waste. Another consideration is how well they "fit" a track. For example, if a physical record and gap require 10K, then 5 of them will fit in a 50K track. However, if we increase the record size so they require 11K each, only 4 will fit in a 50K track. Furthermore, there is an extra 6K (50K minus 4 times 11K) of wasted track space. Figure 8.36 shows a large section of track that is too small for another physical record. (We should note that MVS does provide for variable-sized records. This makes the organization more complex and we do not discuss it.)

Each physical record actually has three parts: *count*, *key*, and *data blocks*. They also are separated by gaps (Figure 8.37). The key block contains a character string that identifies the data. The count block contains information about the physical record such as the data and key block lengths. The data block, of course, contains the data.

Figure 8.37 Count-Key-Data format under MVS

Partitioned Data Sets

The three previous case studies all provide hierarchical directories: MVS does not. It provides primarily a linear structure. However, it does support a structure called a *Partitioned Data Set* (PDS). It can simulate a two-level hierarchy.

A *data set* is the same as a file. Each data set has a name (*Data Set Name* or DSN) with as many as 44 characters. In a DSN, letters, digits, and certain symbols may appear in groups consisting of 1 through 8 contiguous characters. Each group is separated by a period. In other words, each DSN has the form X.Y. ... .Z, where X, Y, and Z are groups of 1 through 8 characters each. Each group is called a *qualifier* or *node*. Through naming conventions alone, a programmer can simulate hierarchical file lists by using the same leftmost qualifiers and different rightmost ones.

There are several types of data sets which we will describe later. The one of concern now is the partitioned data set, also called a *library*. It is a special data set consisting of two parts. The first part is a *data area*. It consists of separate and independent data sets or *members*. The second part is a *directory*. It contains an entry for each member. The directory is similar to that of the other case studies. Each entry contains the member's creation and last modified date, size, name, and location (Figure 8.38).

Figure 8.38 MVS partitioned data set

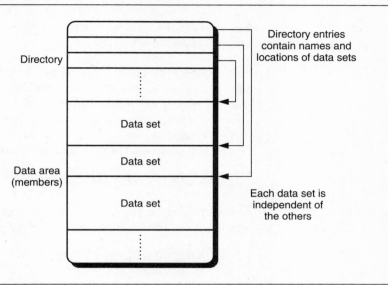

To MVS, a PDS is just another data set. But, a programmer can reference a member of a PDS through the naming convention

X.Y. ... **.Z**(DSN)

The name of the PDS is **X.Y.** ... .**Z**, and DSN represents the member's name. A programmer can add members to a PDS, remove them, or modify them. The PDS provides the equivalent of a two-level hierarchy.

Job Control Language

We are now ready to discuss the JCL. JCL statements have many options. This, of course, gives the user a lot of choices, but it can also be confusing. This is especially true since some options are used only rarely. This section provides an overview of three common JCL statements. It does not cover all the options. More extensive treatments of JCL are in references [6, 21-22].

Recall that programming in batch mode requires the programmer to code all the statements in advance. This, of course, is a major difference from interactive programming, where the programmer can enter commands depending on the operating system's response to a previous command. This is one of the reasons for the language's complexity.

The three statements we discuss are: The JOB, EXEC, and the DD statements. Primarily, they identify the *job* (set of JCL statements) and define its specifications, execute programs, and describe and assign data sets. Each program execution is called a *job step*.

Job Statement. Each job contains a sequence of statements. Each one is preceded by two slashes (//) to distinguish it from a line of data or other symbol. The first one is the JOB statement, and the last one is a dummy statement, indicated by two slashes alone. This is a carryover from the old days when all JCL was coded on punched cards. The last card contained just the two slashes.

The JOB statement has the following format:

```
//jname JOB parameter-list
```

The job name is "jname" and the parameter-list defines the job's specifications. The following are some of the parameters:

- Programmer Name. Defines who receives the job upon its completion. The name may appear on a banner page if the job is sent to the printer.
- CLASS=job-class. Defines the job class. Each class corresponds to jobs with similar needs. For example, jobs using tape drives may have one class, whereas those needing disk files and a printer may have another. The class is denoted by a single letter. Each installation defines its own classes appropriately to schedule more efficiently. This means that class A at one installation may not be the same as class A at another. Section 4.5 describes how the class affects scheduling.
- MSGLEVEL=(i,j). Defines the number and type of messages printed with the job's output. For example, MVS may print all JCL statements on the file (i=2), all JCL statements and those from another referenced JCL file (i=1), or just the JOB statements (i=0). Also, MVS may print allocation messages only if the job *abends* (ends abnormally or aborts), j=0 or in all cases (j=1).
- Time=(m, s). Defines the maximum allowable CPU time for the job. It is specified in minutes (m) and seconds (s).
- Account-name. Defines the account against which charges are billed.
- PRTY = n. Defines the job's priority. This parameter determines the job's initial position in its class queue (see Section 4.5).

EXEC Statement. This statement is used to execute load modules or to compile programs (e.g., execute a compiler). It is also used to execute JCL statements in another file. Which one it does depends on the form of the statement and how data sets are assigned. Data set assignments are discussed after the EXEC statement. The EXEC statement defines a job step and has two forms:

```
//step-name EXEC PGM=prog-name parameter-list
```

or

```
//step-name EXEC proc-name parameter-list
```

The "step-name" is the name of the job step. Naming steps is useful for conditional execution of JCL. Later JCL statements may refer to a step name to determine if it was completed successfully. Options exist that make MVS skip statements if it was not.

The difference between the two forms is in the part following EXEC. In the first form, "prog-name" refers to a program's load module. It must have been created in a previous job step or be stored in a library. Either way, MVS stores it in memory and transfers control to it. The second form refers to *cataloged procedures*. A procedure is a data set containing JCL statements. A cataloged procedure means that its location is accessible through a system catalog. It is a system maintained PDS, and we will discuss this later. For now, it is enough to say the second form makes MVS find the procedure using the PDS and execute its statements.

This is a convenient way to perform common tasks. The statements needed to assign data sets and call a compiler or linkage editor may be stored on a file and cataloged. Any programmer wishing to use them need simply EXEC the procedure.

As with the JOB statement, there are many parameters. Among them:

- COND = (value, condition, step-name) allows conditional execution. MVS maintains a *condition code* that quantifies the completion status of each job step. Zero values mean the step completed successfully, whereas nonzero values indicate an error. Usually, larger numbers indicate more serious errors. It is a lot like receiving demerits when you misbehave: the worse your behavior, the more you get.

    Since certain steps depend on the successful completion of previous ones, MVS allows a step to be tested. The step-name indicates which one. The specified value is then compared to that step's condition code. The second parameter indicates the type of comparison. Usual comparisons are the familiar GT (greater than), EQ (equal to), LT (less than), GE (greater or equal), LE (less or equal), and NE (not equal). If the comparison is true, the step is skipped. For example, COND=(0, LT, STEP1) means skip the current step if 0 is less than the condition code from STEP1. Alternatively, execute the current step only if STEP1 returned a zero condition code.

- REGION = size specifies the maximum memory that the current step may use.

- TIME = (m, s) defines the maximum amount of CPU time the current step may use.
- PARM = parameter passes parameters to programs or cataloged procedures. This is common when compiling programs. A programmer passes parameters that, for example, specify whether listings are to be produced. Parameters can also be passed to application programs that are set up to receive them. The application program performs different functions depending on the parameters it receives. For more details on the PARM option, see reference [21].

DD Statement. The DD statement is perhaps the most widely used JCL command. Its primary function is to associate logical files (e.g., filenames that appear in source code) with actual data sets, and to describe them. This is necessary for proper execution of a job step. The DD statement for a job step appears after the EXEC statement. Its format is

```
//DDname DD parameter-list
```

The DDname specifies the logical file. As usual, there are many parameters possible. They include:

- DSN = dataset-name. Specifies the actual data set to be associated with the logical file.
- DISP = (a, b, c). Specifies how MVS handles the file before and after the job step. The first subparameter indicates the file status before the step. For example, the job step may create a file. In this case, the file does not yet exist (a=NEW). In other cases, the file already exists (a=OLD). Sometimes files are in a library for shared use (a=SHR).

    The second subparameter tells MVS what to do with the file after the step completes normally. Common options are to keep the file (b=KEEP), delete it (b=DELETE), enter it in the system catalog (b=CATLG), remove it from the catalog (b=UNCATLG), or simply pass it to the next job step (b=PASS). (Some have suggested other values to increase programmer options. For example, b=DRACULA would give each data set an extra byte, or b=OLDMACDONALD would create a file using EIE I/O.)

    The third subparameter tells MVS what to do with the file if the step abends. For example, if a job step is to create and catalog a file, the parameter may look like

    ```
    DISP=(NEW, CATLG, DELETE)
    ```

- SPACE = (type, amount). Tells MVS how much space a new data set may use. Unlike many operating systems, MVS requires the programmer to estimate and specify its maximum size in advance. Limits are defined in units of track (type=TRK), cylinder (type=CYL), or block (type=block size). A block is the same as a physical record. In the latter case, MVS will automatically determine the maximum number of tracks or cylinders and allocate accordingly. The second subparameter specifies how many. For example, SPACE=(TRK,10) defines a limit of 10 tracks, and SPACE=(5000,10) defines a limit of ten 5000-byte blocks.

A problem with using TRK and CYL options is the programmer may not really know what he or she is getting. This is because track and cylinder capacities vary. As a result, programmers often use the BLOCK option. MVS determines the capacities and calculates how many tracks or cylinders are needed for the requested blocks. (An interesting analogy in reference [21] to requesting tracks or cylinders describes entering a butcher shop and ordering a side of an animal. Since you haven't specified if you want a turkey, cow, or a stegosaurus, your spouse's large family may be surprised when they show up at a holiday dinner to feast on a fat cornish hen.)

What happens if the data set's size exceeds the limit? To address this question, MVS allows "amount" to be written as an ordered pair (*primary*, *secondary*). The primary value is the initial limit. If the data set grows to exceed it, MVS assigns more. The secondary value specifies how much more. For example, SPACE=(5000, (10, 2)) defines an initial limit of ten 5000-byte blocks. If all ten become full, MVS increments the allocated space by two 5000-byte blocks at a time. It will continue to allocate additional space until a system defined limit is reached.

- VOL = SER = serial#. Specifies the identity (*volume*) of a storage media. This is common with tapes. Be careful to distinguish this from specifying a device. For example, specifying which drive you want is one thing: specifying which tape you want on it is another. Most data centers have many tapes that may be mounted on a drive. The programmer specifies which one by stating its serial number. Volumes sometimes apply to removable disk media, but they are less common.

- LABEL = (position, type). Specifies the data set's position on a tape volume and the *label type*. The position is needed when a volume contains several data sets. If the volume contains just one data set, the position need not be specified. Each data set has a label which describes it. For example, a label contains the DSN, logical and physical record lengths, and creation date. Labels have different formats and MVS must know which one is on a tape. By default, data sets are written with "IBM standard labels" (type=SL). But, some tapes are not labeled (type=NL) and others have ANSII standard labels (type=AL). Other options exist, but their use has diminished over the years.

- UNIT = device. Specifies the device type. This is not needed if the data set already exists and is cataloged, or the data set is a VSAM file (described later). The UNIT can specify an actual channel and devices address or a specific device type (such as a 3380 disk unit). However, installations commonly define device groups. For example, UNIT=TAPE typically means any of a group of tape drives, or UNIT=SYSDA means any of a group of disk drives.

- SYSOUT = A. Used for printer output. It directs printed output to a spooling file for eventual printing. This, of course, allows several users to use the same printer. The character "A" is just one of several print class spools. The others are not relevant to this discussion.

- DCB = (subparameter-list). Describes the data set. DCB is an acronym for *Data Control Block*. It is a table MVS uses to maintain necessary information about a data set. Some program coded information is stored in the DCB. But it has other things normally specified in the subpara-meterlist. This allows changing a data set's description without recompiling a program.

  Each subparameter has the form "key-word=value." For example, "LRECL= size" specifies the number of bytes in a logical record. "BLKSIZE=size" specifies the block size. (Recall previous discussions on the importance on block size.) "RECFM=type" indicates the record format. Single letters define four possible record formats: fixed length (F), variable length (V), undefined length (U), and variable length ANSI records (D). These formats can also be further qualified with other descriptors. Examples include fixed length blocked records (FB) and variable length blocked records (VB). As before, there are other subparameters (in fact, over 30 of them), but these are the most common.

- AMP=('subparameter-list'). AMP (*Access Method Parameter*) was added as a DD parameter when VSAM files were introduced. VSAM files (discussed later) are a complex structure with powerful access abilities. Subparameters include AMORG which identifies the data set as VSAM. Others include specifying the number of data buffers (BUFND=number) and their size (BUFSP=size).

It is, no doubt, time for an example. Figure 8.39 shows part of an MVS job. The first line contains the JOB statement. It contains the account, programmer name, and so on. They are as described previously.

The second line shown contains the EXEC statement. (We include the possibility of other statements preceding it, but they do not concern us.) The step (named STEPN) calls for the conditional execution of a load module named FIRST. The COND parameter does not contain a step name. In this case, it refers to the most recent step. Its form means the step should be skipped if 0 is less than the previous step's condition code (i.e., the previous step abended).

Figure 8.39 Sample MVS job

```
//SAMPLE   JOB  ACCN1234, 'W. A. SHAY', CLASS=A, MSGLEVEL=(1,1)
                    :
                    :
//STEPN    EXEC PGM=FIRST, COND=(0,LT)
//STEPLIB  DD    DSN=SHAY.COBOL.TEST, DISP=SHR
//FILEIN   DD    DSN=PAYROLL, UNIT=SYSDA,
                    DISP=(OLD, KEEP),
//FILEOUT  DD    DSN=REPORT, UNIT=TAPE,
                    DISP=(NEW, CATLG),
                       DCB=(LRECL=80,BLKSIZE=8000, RECFM=FB),
                    VOL=SER=1234,
                    LABEL=(,SL)
                    :
                    :
  / /
```

MVS uses the third line to locate the load module. It requires load modules to be in a PDS or library. Thus, if it is a private library, the programmer must specify its name. The third statement specifies it as "SHAY.COBOL.TEST" and that it is shared.

The next 7 lines contain two DD statements. The DDnames "FILEIN" and "FILEOUT" correspond to logical files. For example, if the source were a COBOL program, the SELECT/ASSIGN clause specifies them. Inspection of the source code would reveal statements of the form

```
SELECT . . . ASSIGN TO FILEIN
SELECT . . . ASSIGN TO FILEOUT
```

The real data set names are PAYROLL as the input file, and REPORT as the output file. The input file exists and must be kept (DISP=(OLD, KEEP)). The program is creating and cataloging a new data set, REPORT (DISP=(NEW, CATLG)). The input file is on a disk unit associated with SYSDA (installation defined). The output file is to be written on tape using standard labels. The volume's serial number is shown. Each logical record has 80 bytes and there are 100 of them (8000 bytes) in a fixed length block.

MVS Organization

Studying the JCL provides a nice overview of MVS and its resources. But, now let's examine some of its internal functions and data structures. We start with MVS' address space (Figure 8.40). It consists of three main parts: *system*, *private*, and *common areas*.

Figure 8.40 MVS address space

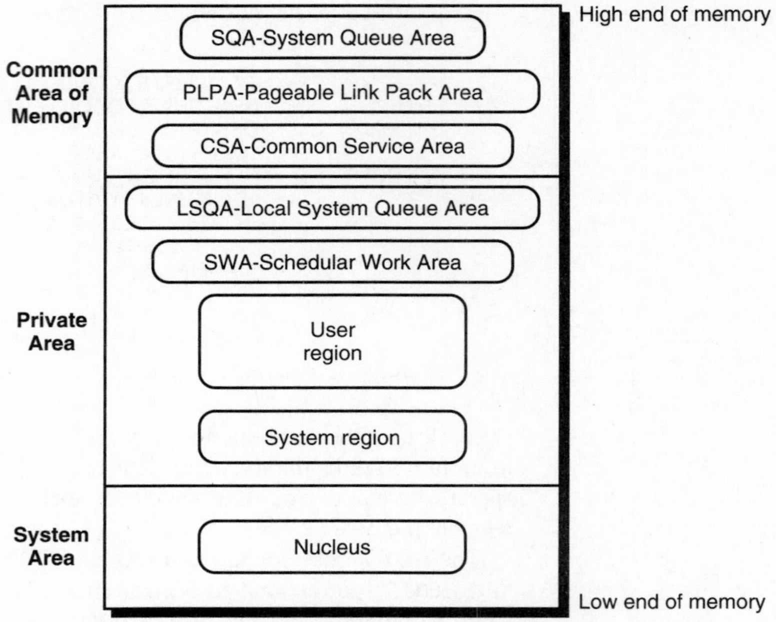

System Area. The system area contains the nucleus and resources needed by all tasks (processes). For example, it contains:

- Frame table (discussed later).
- Unit Control Blocks (UCBs) and Data Extent Blocks (DEBs) (also discussed later).
- Communication Vector Table (CVT). It locates important control blocks, routines, and tasks.
- Frequently used MVS routines. They include some interrupt service routines, scheduling functions, and recovery management routines (discussed later).

Common Area. Like the system area, the common area contains system routines and control blocks. The difference is that the system area contains the most important control blocks and most frequently used routines. The common area has three parts: the System Queue Area (SQA), Pageable Link Pack Area (PLPA), and Common Service Area (CSA).

The SQA contains page tables for both the system and common areas. It also contains the Address Space Control Blocks (ASCBs). Recall from Section 4.5

that they locate the a task's segment and page tables and the task control block. The SQA is fixed in memory and cannot be swapped.

The PLPA contains less frequently used interrupt service routines and I/O support routines. Each installation can also store certain commonly used functions there. PLPA routines are re-entrant. This means that they cannot be changed and may be shared by many tasks. The PLPA may be paged in, but is not paged out.

The CSA is part of every task's virtual space. Its primary function is for storing shared data. Tasks, running in different virtual spaces, can access data stored there because their spaces overlap in the CSA. The CSA is paged in and out of memory as needed.

Private Area. The private area contains data and routines unique to a task and its virtual address space. It has 4 parts: the Local System Queue Area (LSQA), Scheduler Work Area (SWA), user's region, and the system region.

The LSQA contains the segment and page tables for address translation. It also contains Task Control Blocks (TCBs) and control blocks needed by the Region Control Task (RCT) (see Section 4.5).

The SWA contains other control blocks that are needed between a task's initiation and its finish. Section 4.5 described some of them such as the Job Control Table (JCT) and Step Control Table (SCT). It also contains control blocks built from the DD statements. They include the *Step Input/Output Table* (SIOT) and *Job File Control Block* (JFCB) (discussed later).

The user region contain user programs (tasks) and I/O buffers. Finally, the system region contains functions that do work for an address space. This includes the RCT and memory dump functions.

System Data Sets

Operating systems normally reside on a disk or disk pack. Some of the operating system must be stored in memory before the computer can be used. With personal computers, this is called booting. MVS calls this process *SYStem GENeration* (SYSGEN). The disk containing MVS routines and data is called the *SYStem RESidence volume* (SYSRES). The contents of SYSRES depend on the installation. However, the following data sets are common:

- SYS1.NUCLEUS contains routines that form the MVS nucleus.
- SYS1.SVCLIB contains the supervisory call (SVC) routines that are not part of the nucleus.
- SYS1.LOGREC contains information about software and hardware errors that occur after SYSGEN (we discuss this shortly under Recovery Management).

- SYS1.PROCLIB is a PDS containing cataloged procedures designed for system functions.
- SYS1.LINKLIB is another PDS containing other useful MVS utilities. For example, a common utility, named IEBGENER, provides copy and backup facilities. It is also used to add members to a PDS.
- Master catalog is used to locate programmer cataloged data sets.

Recovery Management

Data set SYS1.LOGREC provides a useful function. When an applications program errs, the system usually aborts it. But what happens if an operating system routine errs? Many systems simply stop when software or hardware errors occur. Most of us have probably had the experience of having a personal computer simply stop responding. MVS, in its mainframe environment, must minimize system failures. It contains *recovery management* routines that respond to certain errors and keep the system running. The SYS1.LOGREC data set is used by two routines: the *Recovery Termination Manager* (RTM) and the *Recovery Management Support* (RMS).

The RTM deals primarily with software errors. They include I/O errors, invalid SVCs, and abnormal ends of system routines. It handles errors by logging them in SYS1.LOGREC and passing control to appropriate recovery routines. The important thing is that they try to keep the system running in spite of the error.

The RMS deals primarily with hardware errors. It contains several routines designed to perform hardware checks. For example, a *machine check handler* responds to interrupts caused by a CPU malfunction. It retries the instruction being executed when the error occurred. If the retry is unsuccessful and the task was critical, MVS informs the operator and enters a wait state. Otherwise, it terminates the task.

Another example is a *Dynamic Device Reconfiguration* (DDR). Suppose a tape volume is mounted on a drive and then it fails. The DDR swaps the bad drive for another. This allows the operator to remount the tape on the other drive.

Recovery management in general is very difficult. This is because errors (especially software ones) are often detected long after damage has occurred. Recovery often requires the establishment of copies of all current data structures. This is difficult in a mainframe environment where changes are frequent. Periodic backups of selected structures can help to maintain retrievable information in the event of a failure.

═══
Data Management

Data management is the routines and methods used to locate and maintain information on data sets. Perhaps the logical place to start is with a description of how MVS manages its disk space. We know from Section 6.3 that operating systems use directories to keep track of files and free space on a disk. MVS refers to its disk packs as volumes and to the directories as a *Volume Table Of Contents* (VTOC).

Each VTOC entry (called a *Data Set Control Block* or DSCB) is a 140-byte record that describes a volume's data set. The DSCBs are linked together. There are 7 possible formats for a DSCB:

- Format 0. Unused DSCB, created when a VTOC is initialized. MVS uses them when adding new data sets to the volume.

- Format 1. Describes the first 3 extents (another IBM terminology for contiguous disk space) for a data set. Each data set occupies 1 or more extents.

- Format 2. Used for indexes on ISAM (indexed sequential) files. These are no longer common.

- Format 3. Describes the remaining extents for the data set initially described by a format 1 DSCB.

- Format 4. Describes the VTOC itself. Remember, the VTOC is also a data set.

- Format 5. Describes free space (up to 26 extents).

- Format 6. Describes extents shared by multiple data sets.

Data Set Organization. MVS supports several data set organizations. Among them are:

- Partitioned. These have been described previously.

- Physical sequential. Records are stored sequentially. They must be accessed in the order they are stored.

- Indexed sequential. MVS manages a hierarchical list of index values, each of which uniquely identifies a record. MVS can use an index value to locate a particular record without searching through all the previous ones. It can also use the index list to process the records in sequence (order of index value).

- Direct. The programmer decides how to organize the records and where to store them. Records may be accessed in sequence or in any other order. However, the programmer must specify the location of each record to be stored or accessed.

Access Methods. An access method is the collection of routines that carry out a user's I/O request. Many are available, some of which were developed for old systems but retained in MVS for compatibility reasons. The following are some access methods:

- BSAM (*Basic Sequential Access Method*) processes records sequentially. Programmers get or store physical records. They must do their own blocking or unblocking. Readers with knowledge of IBM assembly language might be familiar with READ and WRITE macros that read and store them.

- QSAM (*Queued Sequential Access Method*) processes logical records sequentially. System routines block and unblock records. Assembly language programmers use GET and PUT macros to read and store logical records.

- QISAM (*Queued Indexed Sequential Access Method*) creates indexed sequential data sets. It also updates existing records and adds new ones to the end of the data set, but it does not add new records randomly.

- BISAM (*Basic Sequential Access Method*) gets, modifies, and adds records randomly to an index sequential data set. It also deletes records. However, "deleted" records are often just "tagged" and not physically removed.

- BPAM (*Basic Partitioned Access Method*) processes the directory in a PDS when new members are added to or deleted from it. This is in contrast to BSAM or QSAM which normally processes the individual member's data.

- BDAM (*Basic Direct Access Method*) stores and retrieves records given their locations in the data set.

- VTAM (*Virtual Telecommunications Access Method*) provides the software to a host node in IBM's *Systems Network Architecture* (SNA). SNA defines the rules and protocols for a distributed computer network.

VSAM. One other access method warrants more space due to its impact on MVS users. It is the *Virtual Storage Access Method* (VSAM). Designed as a replacement for ISAM, it is a powerful and flexible access method suitable for many uses, including complex databases.

VSAM can interact with three types of data sets: *Entry-Sequenced Data Sets* (ESDS), *Key-Sequenced Data Sets* (KSDS), and *Relative Record Data Sets* (RRDS). ESDS, RRDS, and KSDS data sets are similar to sequential, direct, and indexed sequential organizations, respectively.

VSAM stores ESDS records in the order they are submitted. It then returns the relative position of it to the user. The user can retrieve the records in sequence or, if desired, can create his or her own index and use the relative position for later access. The user can read, delete, or modify records, given the relative position. However, new records are always added to the end of the data set.

In an RRDS data set, the user specifies a relative record number. VSAM then stores the record in that position. Using the relative record number, the user may access the records sequentially or directly.

VSAM maintains KSDS data set records in order of a record's key (index) field (*primary key*). It does this using a hierarchical directory of key values. This is similar to the index directories of ISAM files. Like ISAM, it provides access to a record quickly, given its key value. However, one important difference is the way in which the directory changes as new records are added to and deleted from the data set.

The VSAM index structure is based on a B-tree organization. Each entry in the lowest level points directly to a *control interval* (group of physical records) containing the record. Each entry in the higher levels, points to one in the next lower level. Also, VSAM maintains a number of levels so that the root of the hierarchy is contained in a single track. This is similar to the structures of Section 6.5 and Figure 6.22.

As new records are added to or deleted from the data set, the B-tree grows or shrinks accordingly. However, entries that point to control intervals are always on the same level and the root is always in a single track. ISAM directories are clumsier. Furthermore, deleted records are actually removed, rather than simply being "tagged" as deleted.

VSAM can also create an *alternate index*. This allows access to a record using a field other than the primary key field. This is useful when records may be identified in one of several ways. For example, an employee record may be identified using a social security number or the employee's name. Unlike the primary key, the alternates need not identify a record uniquely. (There may be ten Johnny Smith's but each has a unique social security number.)

Cataloged Data Sets. Now let's consider what happens when a programmer catalogs a data set. Recall that MVS has a master catalog on the SYSRES volume. Like any data set, it is accessible through the SYSRES VTOC (Figure 8.41). The master catalog has one entry for each cataloged data set. It may contain the data set's name or just part of it. Recall that a data set name consists of qualifiers separated by periods. The master catalog contains the leftmost qualifier. The remaining qualifiers are stored on an extension of the master catalog called the *Control Volume* (CVOL).

The entries in the CVOL can locate the data set or another CVOL. Figure 8.41 assumes just one CVOL. An advantage of separating the qualifiers is to create a hierarchical structure. That is, a single entry in the master catalog can represent many cataloged data sets as long as their names have the same leftmost qualifier. This is especially helpful when there are many such data sets.

Figure 8.41 illustrates locating a cataloged data set. First, MVS locates the master catalog through the SYSRES VTOC. It then searches it for the leftmost qualifier in the data set's name. In this case, the master catalog entry locates the VTOC of another volume containing the CVOL. Searching the CVOL for the rest of the data set name produces an entry that locates yet another volume's

Figure 8.41 Locating an MVS cataloged data set

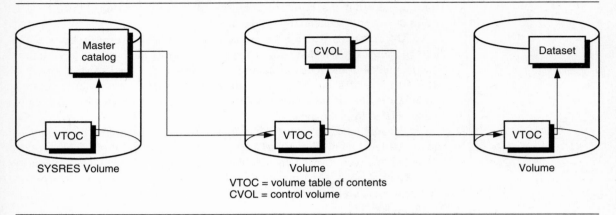

VTOC = volume table of contents
CVOL = control volume

VTOC. Finally, the volume containing the data set is found. The last step is to search the volume's VTOC for the data set. If it is a load module, the data set can then be stored in memory and run.

Address Translation

Now, how does a running task reference real memory? MVS address translation is similar to that described in Section 2.8. Each task's virtual space is segmented and each segment is divided into pages. When a task runs, its pages (some of them) are in real memory frames. MVS locates some of them using special associative registers. The larger System/370 machines call them *Translation Lookaside Buffers* (TLBs) (Figure 8.42). During instruction execution, the CPU searches them for the segment and page numbers in the virtual address. If found, it replaces them with the real frame number found in a TLB.

Figure 8.42 MVS translation lookaside buffer

Segment number	Page number	Frame number

If they are not found, the CPU accesses the segment table (Figure 8.43). Its location is stored in another register called the *Segment Table Origin Register* (STOR). Again, the method is similar to that of Section 2.8. The segment number determines a segment table entry and it contains the address of a page table for that segment. The page number determines a page table entry. Each entry contains an "invalid bit" field. If it is 0, the page is in memory and the entry contains the frame number. If it is 1, the page is not in memory. A page fault occurs and MVS gets the page from disk storage. When a new page is stored in memory, its segment and page numbers are placed in a TLB along with the frame number in which it is stored.

Figure 8.43 MVS dynamic address translation

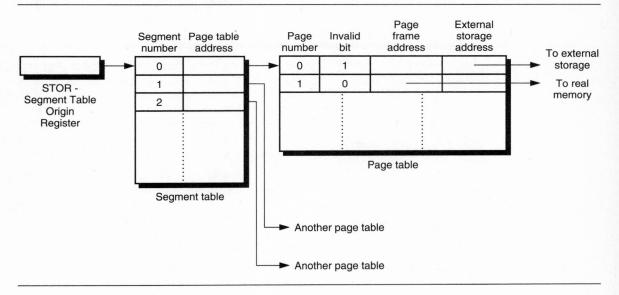

Replacement Strategies

Two replacement strategies are worth discussing. First is when a new entry is placed in a TLB. If they are all filled, MVS must replace one of them. Second is when a new page is stored in memory. If the task's maximum memory allocation is reached, MVS must replace a page.

TLB replacement is similar to the LRU strategy of Section 2.9. If a new entry must replace an existing one, MVS chooses the TLB entry not referenced for the longest time. Note that this is not the same as removing the page from memory. It may still be there. It is just not accessible through the TLB.

When MVS swaps pages in, it uses a combination of the LRU and NUR strategies. Recall that LRU replaces the page not referenced for the longest time and NUR replaces one not used "recently." To maintain information on pages, MVS maintains a frame table in its nucleus. This table has an entry for each real memory frame (Figure 8.44). It contains the task ID, segment and page number of the frame, its status (available or occupied), and tag fields indicating whether it has been recently referenced or modified. These last two fields are the same as the reference and dirty bits of the NUR strategy of Section 2.9.

Figure 8.44 Frame table entry

Frame number	Task id	Segment and page numbers	Frame status	"Recently referenced" field	"Modified" field	Interval count

As with NUR, MVS periodically resets each reference bit to 0. When it does this, it also increments the counter. Thus, it counts the number of consecutive periods during which a frame is not referenced. When a frame is referenced, two things happen. The reference bit is set to 1 and the counter is set to 0. If several periods pass with no reference to a frame, the counter increases. The larger the counter, the longer a page has not been referenced. When MVS replaces a page, it chooses one with the largest counter.

Memory Protection

Memory protection is done using locks and keys. Each task has a 4-bit key value. When the task is running, the key is stored in the *Program Status Word* (PSW). Each frame has a 4-bit protection lock associated with it. When a task accesses a frame, its 4-bit key must match the 4-bit lock. Otherwise, an exception occurs and the task faces termination.

MVS also distinguishes page accesses and updates. It does this using a fifth bit (*fetch bit*) associated with each frame. If it is 1, the keys and locks must match only for write operations. Thus, protection is overridden for read operations. However, if it is 0, they must match for both read and write operations.

Input/Output

Our final topic is MVS I/O processing. Because of the mainframe environment, it is complex. Fortunately, we have already discussed much of what is necessary in Section 3.6. MVS uses channels and channel programs to do the actual data transfer. MVS builds control blocks and provides access methods which respond to the user's request. We have already described the access methods, now let us describe some of the control blocks.

Control Blocks. Several control blocks are essential for I/O processing. They are:

- *Unit Control Block* (UCB). MVS has 1 for each device. All UCBs are in the MVS nucleus. They are used for device allocation and for controlling and synchronizing I/O operations. Each one contains the device type, its address (channel and device number), and several status fields.
- *Job File Control Block* (JFCB) lists a job's data sets and their characteristics. Characteristics include the buffer size and length, DD name, data set name, organization, disposition, location, logical record length, and block size. The JFCB is built from the DD statement parameters and a data set's DSCB.
- *Data Control Block* (DCB) is another critical block. There is one for each device a task is accessing. Primarily, it describes the data set and includes the access method, record format, and block and logical record lengths.
- *Data Extent Block* (DEB) is an extension of the DCB but is not accessible to the programmer. It locates both the DCB and the UCB.
- *Step I/O Table* (SIOT) lists the DD name and the device type for each data set.
- *Task I/O Table* (TIOT) provides I/O support routines with data set names and the locations of the UCBs and JFCBs.

I/O Steps. Prior to executing a task, MVS routines build the JFCB, SIOT, and TIOT. This is part of task scheduling and was partly discussed in Section 4.5. MVS then locates the data sets and, if possible, allocates the devices.

When the task is ready to issue an I/O request, it issues an OPEN which executes an SVC (supervisory call, a command causing an MVS routine to run). MVS routines complete the building of the DCB, which was partially built in the source code. The control blocks now provide necessary information for subsequent I/O requests.

Eventually, the task issues an I/O request in the form of another SVC. The way MVS and its channels handle I/O is similar to that described in Section 3.6 and Figure 3.20. Figure 8.45 is similar to Figure 3.20 and shows the primary activities.

Figure 8.45 MVS I/O activities

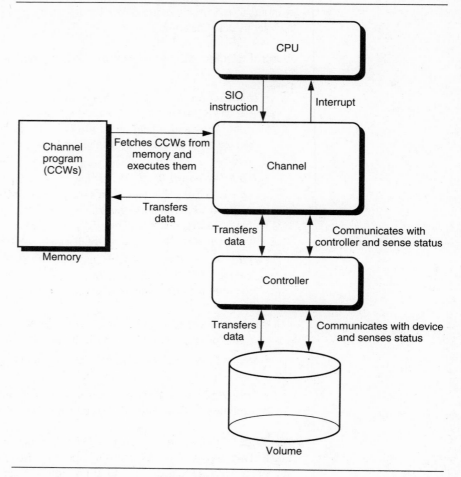

After the SVC, appropriate access methods build a channel program. Afterward, MVS schedules the I/O and uses an SIO instruction to start the I/O operation. The channel begins executing, getting its commands (CCWs or Channel Command Words) from specified memory locations. It communicates with the appropriate controller which transfers data between it and the device. When the transfer is complete, the channel interrupts the CPU. MVS determines the status of the operation and passes it to the task. The task now sees the operation as complete.

≣≣≣
Acronym Summary

Every description of IBM software or products has many acronyms. As with the other case studies, this makes reading difficult. To help make it easier, Table 8.8 contains a list of acronyms that appear in this section and their meanings.

Table 8.8 MVS acronym list

Acronym	Meaning
ASCB	Address Space Control Block
BDAM	Basic Direct Access Method
BISAM	Basic Indexed Sequential Access Method
BPAM	Basic Partitioned Access Method
BSAM	Basic Sequential Access Method
CCW	Channel Command Word
CSA	Common Service Area
CVOL	Control Volume
CVT	Communication Vector Table
DCB	Data Control Block
DD	Data Definition
DEB	Data Extent Block
DSCB	Data Set Control Block
DSN	Data Set Name
ESDS	Entry-Sequenced Data Set
IBM	International Business Machines
ISAM	Indexed Sequential Access Method
JCL	Job Control Language
JCT	Job Control Table
JFCB	Job File Control Block
KSDS	Key-Sequenced Data Set
LSQA	Local System Queue Area
MVS	Multiple Virtual Storage
PDS	Partitioned Data Set
PLPA	Pageable Link Pack Area
QISAM	Queued Indexed Sequential Access Method
QSAM	Queued Sequential Access Method
RCT	Region Control Task
RMS	Recovery Management Support
RRDS	Relative Record Data Set
RTM	Recovery Termination Manager
SCT	Step Control Cable
SIO	Start I/O
SIOT	Step I/O Table
SQA	System Queue Area
STOR	Segment Table Origin Register
SVC	Supervisory Call
SYSGEN	SYStem GENeration
SYSRES	SYStem RESidence
TIOT	Task I/O Table

TCB	Task Control Block
TLB	Translation Lookaside Buffer
TSO	Time-Sharing Option
UCB	Unit Control Block
VSAM	Virtual Storage Access Method
VTAM	Virtual Telecommunications Access Method
VTOC	Volume Table Of Contents

Further Reading

This case study, by necessity, has omitted many details. MVS is an extremely large and complex operating system and is impossible to describe in a few pages. In fact, it's probably impossible to describe using a lot of pages (or maybe even at all). Some references do provide more details. For example, Kudlick [26] has more about data set organizations and access methods. It also contains descriptions of low-level assembly language instructions and macros. Davis [6] discusses IBM mainframe systems. Neither reference describes MVS, but both and reference [22] consider OS, MVS' predecessor. Janossy [21] has complete descriptions of the three JCL statements described here. Stallings [27] describes I/O processing from a computer organization perspective. Finally, no reference would be complete without Madnick and Donovan [25]. It is an old but classic text centered around IBM systems.

8.5 Summary

This chapter contained discussions of four operating systems: MS-DOS, UNIX, VMS, and MVS. These are systems which the reader is likely to see or has seen. Some of the topics covered are common to several systems. For example, the first three support hierarchical directories. The commands differ, but the concept of creating directories containing files and other directories is the same. Another shared concept is the use of files to store frequently used commands. MS-DOS calls them batch files, UNIX calls them shell scripts, and VMS calls them command files. For MVS, it is a primary form of communication. These files may also contain logic to conditionally execute commands.

MS-DOS Summary

MS-DOS contains 4 major components: Boot loader, MSDOS.SYS, IO.SYS, and COMMAND.COM. The boot loader, typically on a disk's first sector, is a small program read into memory upon startup. This program then reads other MS-DOS components into memory. COMMAND.COM contains logic that responds to user commands and consists of two parts. The internal (resident) part contains logic to process commonly used commands and the external (transient) part responds to lesser used ones.

MSDOS.SYS contains the MS-DOS kernel and the hardware-independent components. It perform functions such as directory maintenance, directory searches, and record blocking. IO.SYS contains hardware-dependent logic. It uses device drivers to transfer data physically between a device and memory.

Drivers. Two types of drivers, block and character, were discussed. The drivers, organized in a linked list, contain three main sections: device header, strategy routine, and interrupt routine. The header contains driver information. The strategy routine saves the address of a request header, another record containing information related to a particular I/O request. The interrupt routine does the work associated with the I/O operation.

If desired, a user can define his or her own drivers by putting a DEVICE command in the CONFIG.SYS file. The command must specify a file containing a valid device driver. Upon startup, MS-DOS installs the new driver in its list.

I/O Redirection. Last, we described I/O redirection, pipes, and filters. Options on MS-DOS commands can redefine the standard I/O devices. A user can also connect the standard output of a process to the standard input of another. This is useful when passing data through several commands.

═══

UNIX Summary

File System. The UNIX file system contains four parts: The boot block, super block, data blocks, and inodes. The boot block is similar to the MS-DOS boot loader. The super block contains information about the file system such as its size, number of free inodes, and number of free data blocks. Data blocks contain, obviously, data. An inode (one for each file) provides access to the data blocks. Specifically, it contains pointers to data and indirect blocks. Together they define a hierarchical structure with data blocks as leaf nodes. Files can grow as large as 1 gigabyte.

The inodes are located through the system file table which has an entry for each open file. Each entry, in turn, is located through a file descriptor table. Each user has one and there is an entry for each open file a user has. By having several file descriptor table entries locate the same system file table entry, users can share files.

System Commands. Perhaps most characteristic of UNIX are the system commands fork, exec, wait, and exit. The fork command creates a new process called the child. The calling process is the parent. This is often followed by an exec command which redefines it. The wait command allows a parent process to wait for its child to finish. When the child finishes, it calls the exit command which sends a signal to the parent.

Process Modes. Processes run in one of two modes: user and kernel mode. Most processes run in user mode. UNIX keeps track of its processes through a process table. Each entry has information such as the process ID, accumulated CPU time, and priority. Each process also has a u area which is an extension of the process table. It contains information a running process needs such as the location of the current and root directories, I/O parameters, and process limits. It may also contain the per process region table, which has information about the process' address space.

Interprocess Communication. UNIX has seven mechanisms for interprocess communication. They are pipes, messages, semaphores, shared memory, synchronization signals, process tracing, and death of child. Pipes allow the output of one process to be treated as input to another. Messages can be sent and received through a message queue. Semaphore operations can put processes to sleep or wake them. Synchronization signals can send signals upon the completion of certain events. Shared memory allows processes access to common memory. Process tracing is used to define a wait and signal protocol between a debugger and a traced process. Finally, the death of child allows a waiting parent to resume upon the demise of a child.

Drivers. UNIX also has block and character drivers. Block drivers may perform buffered or unbuffered I/O. Unbuffered allows data transfer to or from a process' locked pages. Buffered I/O allows a process to be swapped by transferring data to or from system buffers.

Terminal drivers are an example of character drivers. Typically, they use line discipline modules that operate in either a canonical or raw mode. In canonical mode, they interpret control characters such as the backspace key. In raw mode they simply translate what the user types. Terminal drivers use clists to store characters as they are transmitted between the terminal and process. Each clist has several cblocks. Each cblock, in turn, contains some of the characters being transmitted.

═══
VMS Summary

Virtual Addressing. VAX virtual addresses are 32 bits long. An address contains a region number (2 bits), virtual page number (21 bits), and an offset (9 bits). Address translation for processes in the system region (region 10) is similar to that described in Chapter 2. A System Base Register (SBR) points to a page table and the virtual page number specifies an entry. However, address translation in the per-process space (region 00 or 01) involves extra steps. Page table registers (either P0BR or P1BR) contain the virtual address of a page table. Thus, a translation must occur just to find the page table. Once located, the process' virtual memory reference is translated into a real one.

Process modes. Process may run in one of four modes. They are, in order from lowest to highest privileged: user, supervisory, executive, and kernel mode. Each page table entry contains a 4-bit access code that defines accessibility to a page depending on the process mode.

Memory Management. Memory management has two main parts: the pager and swapper. Since VMS allows each process a working set, page faults are inevitable. When they happen, the pager responds by determining the location of the page and initiating the read.

If a page must be replaced, VMS uses the FIFO strategy. However, it minimizes effects of bad replacements choices by placing the pages in a free or modified page list. The result is that pages are replaced but not really removed from memory. If they are referenced again soon, no additional I/O is needed.

The swapper swaps the working sets when they don't all fit in memory. It uses a process header (PHD) that, in turn, contains the working set list and process section table.

Process Control Blocks. VMS maintains two Process Control Blocks (PCBs) for each process, a hardware PCB and software PCB. The hardware PCB contains the process context after it is interrupted. The software PCB contains process information such as the PHD location, process state, and priority.

Scheduling. VMS schedules using a variation of the multilevel feedback queues discussed in Chapter 5. It defines 32 priorities, half of them (16-31) for real-time processes. When normal processes run and events occur, their priority changes. However, a normal process never falls below a given base priority nor rises above 15.

Interprocess Communication. We also discussed interprocess communication. Processes use system calls to set, clear, or test common event flags stored in Common Event Blocks (CEBs). System calls are similar to the *P* and *V* primitives discussed in chapter 5. They are more flexible as they can perform a logical AND or OR of flag values.

Resource Sharing. Resource sharing and deadlock detection are done by maintaining a complex relation between Lock Blocks (LKBs) and Resource Blocks (RSBs). VMS creates an RSB for each resource requested by a process. It also creates an LKB for each request. The RSBs are in several lists located through a resource hash table. Each RSB is also the header for two lists of LKBs. One list corresponds to honored requests, the other to denied requests. All LKBs for a process are linked to its PCB. If a cycle consisting of RSBs and LKBs exists, deadlock has occurred.

When VMS creates an LKB, it puts the LKB in a lock timeout queue. If it remains in the queue a long time, VMS initiates a cycle detection algorithm to look for deadlock. If a deadlock is found, VMS returns an error code to one of the involved processes. The process must then resolve the deadlock by removing some or all of its requests.

MVS Summary

MVS is the most complex of the four case studies. In part, this is because MVS runs on very large systems. It is also due to the fact that, as MVS has evolved, it has had to maintain compatibility with its predecessors.

Disks and Directories. Where many systems allocate disk space by sectors, MVS allocates by tracks and cylinders. As a result, the smallest allocation unit is quite large. This is because MVS often manages large data sets. This is a consequence of a mainframe environment. It is also the only one of the four case studies that does not support hierarchical directories. However, it does support partitioned data sets which resemble a two-level hierarchy, and the format for data set names can be used to simulate hierarchies.

JCL. The language used to communicate with MVS is the Job Control Language (JCL). Three statements are commonly used: the JOB, EXEC, and DD statements. The JOB statement defines a job and some of its limits. The EXEC makes MVS execute load modules or other JCL files. The DD statement defines data sets and their characteristics.

Organization. MVS' address space is divided into three parts: system, common, and private areas. The system area contains the nucleus, the common area contains less frequently used routines and control blocks, and the private area is used for tasks and their virtual space. Prior to SYSGEN, MVS resides on the system residence volume (SYSRES). Some of its common data sets are SYS1.NUCLEUS, SYS1.SVCLIB, SYS1.LOGREC, SYS1.PROCLIB, SYS1.LINKLIB, and the master catalog. The NUCLEUS, SVCLIB, and LINKLIB data sets contain nucleus and non-nucleus routines: LOGREC is use for recording errors, and PROCLIB and the master catalog are used for cataloged data sets.

Recovery Management. MVS must make efforts to continue running in spite of occasional software or hardware errors. It has a recovery termination manager which responds to software errors and recovery management support which responds to hardware errors. Certain hardware errors can be handled by reconfiguring or reallocating. However, other hardware errors and software errors often cause a loss of critical data. In such cases, recovery requires reloading lost data or, in a severe case, a new SYSGEN. The latter is disruptive to all users. The former option can sometimes be done more quickly, but backups must be available. This adds overhead.

Data Management. Because of its mainframe environment, data management is complex. MVS support four data set organizations: partitioned, physical sequential, indexed sequential, and direct data sets. It also provides numerous access methods including BSAM, QSAM, QISAM, BISAM, BPAM, BDAM, VTAM, and VSAM. Some of these, such as BISAM, QISAM, and BSAM are not common, but exist for compatibility with older systems. VSAM is one of the most common access techniques, having the ability to interact with three types of data sets: entry-sequenced, key-sequenced, and relative record data sets.

Memory Management. Memory management is similar to that described in Sections 2.8 and 2.9. Tasks consist of segments and tables. Address translation is done using either Translation Lookaside Buffers (TLB), or segment and page tables. The TLB is searched first. If a page is not found, the segment and page tables are searched. MVS replaces TLB entries using a LRU strategy and replaces memory pages using a NUR/LRU hybrid approach. Last, memory protection is done by matching 4-bit locks and keys.

I/O. MVS I/O is similar to that in Section 3.6. It uses channels and channel programs to handle data transfer. The I/O data base requires many control blocks to locate and describe data sets, allocate peripherals, and synchronize access. MVS builds most of them prior to the task's execution. When a task issues a request, access methods build a channel program. MVS then starts the I/O using an SIO instruction. The channel handles the transfer and interrupts the CPU upon its completion.

≡≡≡≡≡≡ **Exercises**

1. To what type of files do the following MS-DOS file extensions typically correspond?

   `FOR COB TMP DVD LST`

2. Which of the following are legal MS-DOS filenames?

   `My_File, 9-20-89.Txt, File_#1, File:1, First_File,`
   `Rec.File, Data.XXX, 9/20/89.Txt`

3. Are the following MS-DOS internal or external? Give a brief description of each one.

   `DATE, PROMPT, FIND, BACKUP, ASSIGN, ECHO`

4. Write the commands for an AUTOEXEC.BAT file that automatically prints your directory files in alphabetical order whenever MS-DOS is booted.

5. Write commands for a batch file that sorts the contents of one file and stores the results on another. The commands must not be executed if the first file does not exist or the second file does.

6. Use MS-DOS pipes to satisfy the following request with one command:
   Print all the files in the current working directory one screenful at a time and in alphabetical order.

7. Which of the following are determined by MSDOS.SYS and which by IO.SYS:
   - Determine existence of a file.
   - Determine sector number containing data to be read.
   - Convert sector number to a track number and relative sector within the track.
   - Delete file from a directory.
   - Transmit data between a disk sector and a memory buffer.
   - Read a directory from a disk.
   - Block logical records into physical records.
   - Allocate disk space to a file.

8. Indicate, via a diagram similar to that in Figure 8.7, how UNIX provides access to each of 10,000 records in a file. Assume each data block contains 10 records. What is the total number of blocks used?

9. Show file descriptor table entries and system file table entries for files shared by processes as follows:
   - FileA shared by processes 1, 3, and 5
   - FileB shared by processes 2, 3, and 4
   - FileC shared by processes 1 and 5
   - FileD shared by all five processes

10. Show the inode lists and data nodes (similar to that in Figure 8.10) for the following directory structure:

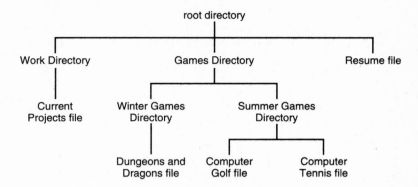

11. Suppose a UNIX process contains the following:

```
pid = fork()
if condition Wait
```

The intent is for parent to wait until the child finishes. What should the condition be? Remember that the spawned child also has the above code and should not wait.

12. Modify the definition of UNIX's *semop* command so it is consistent with the primitive operations P and V discussed in Section 5.6.

13. Suppose a UNIX user has typed

```
mkdir dir1/dir2/dir3
```

What does the clist look like after the kernel has removed the character 1? Assume each cblock contains 7 characters.

14. Solve the Producer-Consumer Problem from Section 5.7 using the UNIX semop command.

15. Suppose that VMS processes have requested resources and they have been allocated as follows:

   - R1 and R2 have been allocated to P1.
   - R3 has been allocated to P2.
   - R4 has been allocated to P3.
   - P4 has requested R1.
   - P2 has requested R4.
   - P3 has requested R3.

   Assume that all locks are incompatible and show the VMS structure containing the PCBs, LKBs, and RSBs. Does deadlock exist?

16. How many pages does each VMS virtual region contain?

17. Assume the following:

   - The system virtual address of the P0 page table is page 500, offset 50.
   - The physical address of the P0 page table is page 50, offset 50.
   - The physical address of the system page table is page 5, offset 0.

Suppose a VMS process makes a reference to page 10, offset 25 in its P0 region, that is translated to frame 465, offset 25. Show the contents of necessary registers and table entries and describe the translation process.

18. Solve the Producer-Consumer Problem from Section 5.7 using the VMS event flag operations.

19. Suppose VMS processes need access to a page as follows:

mode	access type
kernel	read and write
executive	read and write
supervisory	read only
user	none

What must the page's access code be?

20. Which of the following DISP parameters for the MVS DD statement are reasonable?

- DISP=(NEW,DELETE,CATLG)
- DISP=(NEW,CATLG,UNCATLG);
- DISP=(OLD,KEEP,KEEP);
- DISP=(NEW,DELETE,DELETE);
- DISP=(OLD,DELETE,DELETE);

21. Assume a disk track has a 50K byte capacity and that its physical records are separated by 0.5K byte gaps. Suppose we want to store 10 of them per track. What is the largest permissible physical record? What percentage of the track is unused due to the gaps? Repeat these questions to store 5 physical records per track.

22. An IBM 3380 disk drive has 47,476 bytes per track, 15 tracks per cylinder, and 1770 cylinders. What is the total disk capacity?

23. Write MVS JCL statements that meet the following requirements:

- Execute a sort program named SORT on a library named DP101.PROD.COBOL.
- The program reads records from a disk file named DP101.DATA.EMPREC, sorts them, and writes them to another file named DP101.STDATA.EMPREC.
- The input file exists and must be kept.
- The output file is new. It should be cataloged if the sort is successful and deleted if the program abends.
- The output file should be on a tape with standard labels. Its records should be fixed length blocked. Each logical record has 80 bytes and they should be grouped 15 to a block.

24. Code an EXEC statement that executes a cataloged procedure named ERR.REPORT, but only if a previous job step named STEP5 returned a condition code of 4 or more.

≡≡≡ Questions

1. Why must the MS-DOS boot loader always occupy the same sector on a disk? (The answer also applies to any boot loader.)
2. If COMMAND.COM is primarily an interface between the user and MS-DOS, why have it at all? That is, why not eliminate it and have the user enter commands to the kernel directly?
3. Resident and transient commands are separated to keep frequently used ones in memory and less frequently used ones on disk. However, some microcomputers support several megabytes of memory. With this much memory, why worry about separating them?
4. In UNIX, which processes have parents? Explain.
5. Why do UNIX inodes contain entries ".." and "."?
6. Can you think of a case where a VMS file might have access mode *W* (write) but not *R* (read)?
7. Which VMS commands discussed under *interprocess communication* are most closely related to Dijkstra's P and V primitives? Describe similarities and differences between them and the primitives.
8. VMS processes are given a base priority and as soon as they are created they get a priority boost of 6. Why not let them start at their base priorities?
9. What will the following VMS command do for you?

   `$Delete *.*;*`

10. The VMS access code is four bits long. This means there are 16 (2^4) possible access codes. However, there may be three types of access (write, read, and none) for each mode. Since there are four modes, there are 81 (3^4) possible combinations. This means that 65 (81-16) combinations cannot be described via the access codes. Why is this not a problem?
11. Suppose an MVS installation uses only one type of disk drive. Give reasons why the block option is still preferable on the DD statement's SPACE parameter.
12. Is the following statement true? On an IBM disk, smaller physical records sizes always mean more wasted space per track.
13. Consider KSDS and RRDS data sets for VSAM. Both provide access to a record without reading previous ones. How do they differ? Which is likely to be faster?

≡≡≡ References

1. Simrin, S. *The Waite Group's MS-DOS Bible*. 2nd ed. Indianapolis, IN: Howard Sams & Co., 1988.
2. Angermeyer, J., et al. *The Waite Group's MS-DOS Developer's Guide*. 2nd ed. Indianapolis, IN: Howard Sams & Co., 1989.
3. Wolverton, V. *Running MS-DOS*. 3rd ed. Redmond, WA: Microsoft Press, 1988.
4. Duncan, R. *Advanced MS-DOS Programming*. 2nd ed. Redmond, WA: Microsoft Press, 1988.
5. Norton, P., and R. Wilton. *Programmer's Guide to the IBM PC and PS/2*. Redmond, WA: Microsoft Press, 1988.
6. Davis, W. S. *Operating Systems: A Systematic View*. 3rd ed. Reading, MA: Addison-Wesley, 1987.

7. *The MS-DOS Encyclopedia.* Redmond, WA: Microsoft Press, 1987.
8. O'Day, K. *Understanding MS–DOS.* Indianapolis, IN: Howard Sams & Co., 1988.
9. Ritchie, D. M., and K. Thompson. "The UNIX Time-Sharing System." *Communications of the ACM* 17 (July 1974):365-375.
10. Silberschatz, A., J. Peterson, and P. Galvin. *Operating System Concepts.* 3rd ed. Reading, MA: Addison-Wesley, 1991.
11. Bach, M. J. *The Design of the UNIX Operating System.* Englewood Cliffs, NJ: Prentice-Hall, 1986.
12. Kernighan, B. W., and R. Pike. *The UNIX Programming Environment.* Englewood Cliffs, NJ: Prentice-Hall, 1984.
13. Poole, P. C., and N. Poole. *Using UNIX by Example.* Reading, MA: Addison-Wesley, 1986.
14. Bourne, S. R. *The UNIX System V Environment.* Reading, MA: Addison-Wesley, 1987.
15. Sobell, M. G. *A Practical Guide to the UNIX System.* Menlo Park, CA: The Benjamin/Cummings Co., 1984.
16. Rochkind, M. J. *Advanced UNIX Programming.* Englewood Cliffs, NJ: Prentice-Hall, 1985.
17. Deitel, H. M. *An Introduction to Operating Systems.* 2nd ed. Reading, MA: Addison-Wesley, 1989.
18. Kenah, J. K., Ruth E. Goldenberg, and Simon F. Bate. *Version 4.4 VAX/VMS Internals and Data Structures.* New York: Digital Press, 1988.
19. *VAX Architecture Reference Manual.* Edited by T. E. Leonard. New York: Digital Press, 1987.
20. Levy, H. M., and R. H. Eckhouse, Jr. *Computer Programming and Architecture: The VAX.* 2nd ed. New York: Digital Press, 1988.
21. Janossy, J. G. *Practical MVS JCL for Today's Programmers.* New York: Wiley, 1987.
22. Trombetta, M., and S. C. Finkelstein. *OS JCL and Utilities.* Reading, MA: Addison-Wesley, 1984.
23. Yuen, C. K. *Essential Concepts of Operating Systems Using IBM Mainframe Examples.* Reading, MA: Addison-Wesley, 1986.
24. Auslander, M. A., D. C. Larkin, and A. L. Scherr. "The Evolution of the MVS Operating System." *IBM Journal of Research and Development* 25 (Sept. 1981):471-482.
25. Madnick, S. E., and J. J. Donovan. *Operating Systems.* New York: McGraw-Hill, 1974.
26. Kudlick, M. D. *Assembly Language Programming for the IBM Systems 360 and 370 for OS and DOS.* 2nd ed. Dubuque, IA: W. C. Brown, 1983.
27. Stallings, W. *Computer Organization and Architecture: Principles of Structure and Function.* New York: Macmillan, 1987.

Operating Systems Project: A Pascal Based Simulator for Running Processes

A.1 Phase I: Memory Management

This book explains what an operating system must do and what methods it uses. This appendix describes a project that allows you to write a small operating system.

To be more exact, you can write part of an operating system. After all, even small operating systems contain thousands of program lines. The largest ones contain over one million lines of code. Obviously, even the harshest taskmaster could hardly expect a semester or quarter project to involve writing more than just part of an operating system. Besides, reading and grading one million lines of code could take a while.

The project is machine-independent. It does not ask you to write any low–level or machine-specific functions. Instead, it deals mainly with scheduling, memory management, and process synchronization. The processes are generated randomly, make random requests for services, require a random number of memory frames, and generate wait and signal calls randomly.

An obvious problem is, "Where do we get processes for your operating system to manage?" Rather than begging computer installations to donate their old processes, we have written a Pascal based simulator that mimics the activities and requests typical of real processes. At the end of each section in this appendix is the source code for these Pascal procedures.

Real operating systems transfer control of the CPU to a process. Instead in this project, your operating system calls one of these procedures. The net result is that it yields control of the CPU and the events that follow are external to your operating system.

In real life, processes make requests and events occur to which an operating system must respond. Through parameters, the simulator mimics all of this. Your operating system must respond accordingly.

This project has three phases. Phase I deals mainly with memory management and low–level scheduling. You should be ready to work on Phase I after reading Chapter 2. The second phase is more complex. It involves high-level and intermediate-level scheduling, I/O requests, and process swapping. Chapter 4 explains what you must know to work on Phase II. Finally, Phase III introduces process synchronization covered in Chapter 5. We list several events for which processes issue wait and signal calls.

Let us first describe the use of the simulator. At this stage, we restrict the simulated environment significantly. This lets you focus on the design of logic and data structures needed to manage memory properly. Your operating system should do the following (See Figure A.1):

- Detect when a new program is submitted.
- Read the code and run time limits.
- Determine the number of pages.
- Store the pages in a file to await placement in memory and eventual scheduling.
- Read program pages from the file and store them in memory frames when there is room. The file should act like a queue. That is, you read programs from it in the same order in which you put them there.
- Between program submissions, perform round robin scheduling among the processes in memory. Remember, when your operating system chooses a process for execution, it calls the Pascal simulator, which then models the process's activities.

Submitting programs

The first question you should ask is, "Where do we get programs from?" Figure A.2 outlines where. In this project, we define a program as having two parts, a maximum CPU time limit and code. The time limit is an integer in unspecified units (say seconds).

The code is just a character string. This may seem odd, but think about it. For the most part, an operating system does not care what the code looks like (as long as it does not do anything naughty). It simply treats the code as data to be stored in memory. Since program code varies in length, we need a variable length data structure to represent it. Character strings work nicely.

Figure A.1 Program submission and round robin scheduling

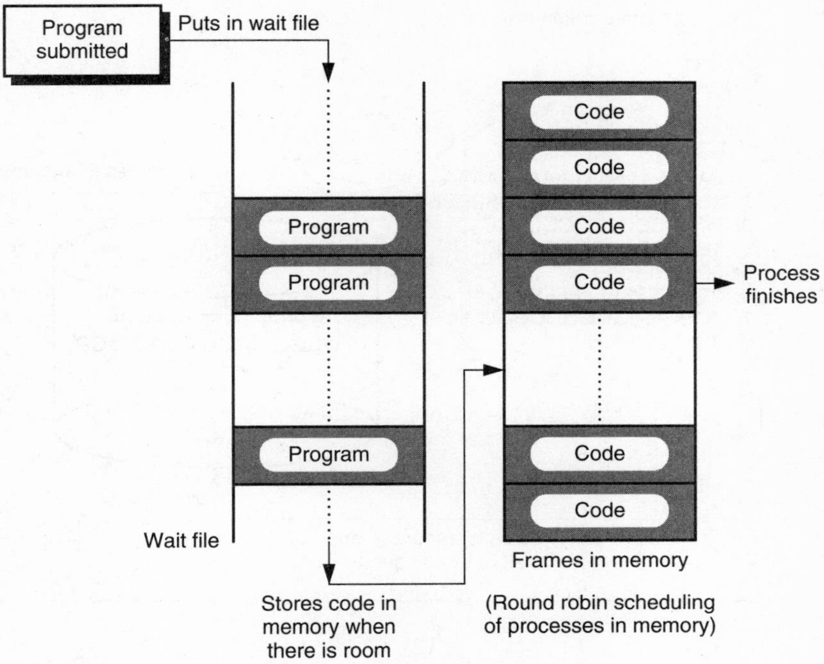

Thus, when a program is submitted, your operating system reads a number (the maximum time limit), followed by a character string (the code). It divides the character string into groups of four or fewer characters and stores them in a file (queue) and eventually stores it in memory. Figure A.2 shows eight programs that have been submitted. The code for each is a string consisting of repetitions of a single character. Programs 6, 7, and 8 are still in the wait file. Programs 3 and 5 are in memory. Programs 1, 2, and 4 are not in the wait file or in memory. This means they have finished and no longer exist as far as the operating system is concerned.

Figure A.2 Simulated program code stored in simulated memory

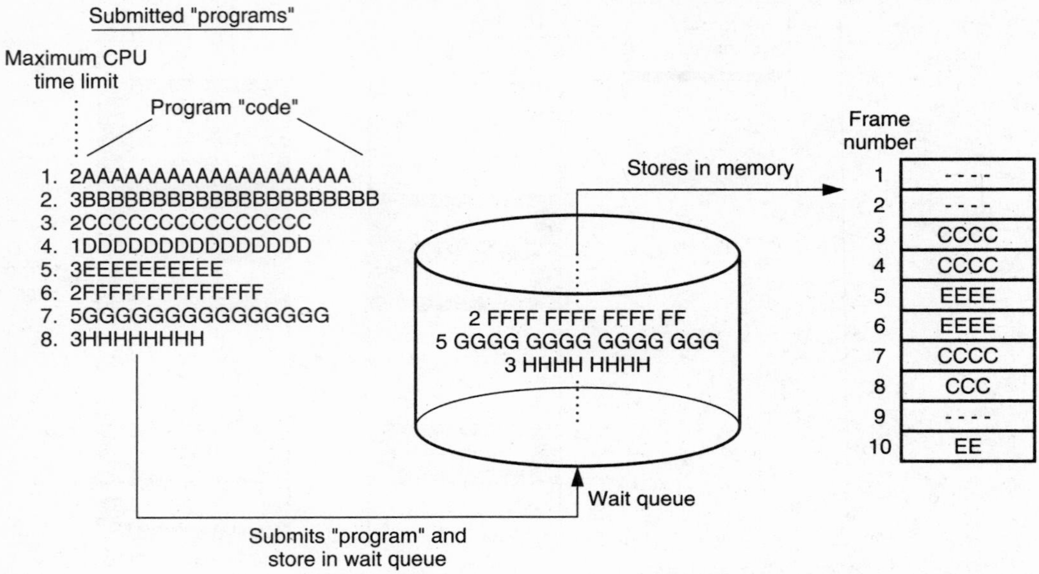

Storing Program in Memory

The next question should be, "How do we simulate memory?" In this project, we define memory as an array in which each position is a frame. Each frame can hold one page. We assume each one has a capacity of four characters.

Of course, the frames are small! However, a major goal of Phase I is to manage frames. Their size is unimportant. As long as you do not try to store the code from two programs in the same frame, you are off to a good start. Initially, the array positions should contain blank characters.

Let's look again at Figure A.2. When your operating system first reads a character string (the program code), it should divide it into substrings of four characters each (corresponding to program pages) before storing it in a file. Whenever there are enough blank array positions (frames) available, your operating system must store the substrings in them. (For simplicity, we assume that all or none of a process' code is in memory.)

Figure A.2 shows how "memory" might appear if programs 3 and 5 were still in it and programs 1, 2, and 4 had finished. The figure shows a memory with just ten frames. The operating system has not put program 6 (string of Fs) in memory because there are not enough empty frames to accommodate it.

Your operating system can track available frames through a frame table. Figure A.3 shows an example table representing the frames in Figure A.2. It contains only ten entries, but you can easily increase its size.

Figure A.3 Sample frame table

Frame number	Occupied/free	Proc_id
1	Free	- -
2	Free	- -
3	Occupied	3
4	Occupied	3
5	Occupied	5
6	Occupied	5
7	Occupied	3
8	Occupied	3
9	Free	- -
10	Occupied	5

List of processes in memory
Process 3 occupies frames 3, 4, 7, and 8
Process 5 occupies frames 5, 6, and 10

Round Robin Scheduling

Another major function of your operating system in Phase I is to schedule processes in memory for execution using a round robin approach. Thus, it must be able to repeatedly choose a process and allow it to run. We can loosely code this function as:

```
Repeat
  Choose a process in memory using round robin scheduling;
  Allow the process to run;
Until an event occurs
```

The loop describes round robin scheduling and execution of processes until an event occurs. In Phase I, the event could be:

- An interrupt that indicates a new program has been submitted. Your operating system should then place its code in the file. If the file was previously empty, your system should determine whether the code can fit in memory, then it should resume the round robin scheduling.

- A process finishes either by completing its work or by exceeding its maximum time limit. At this point, the operating system should remove it from memory and update its tables. Since this makes some frames available, your system should check to see if the first program in the wait file will fit in memory. It should store as many programs in memory as will fit. Then it should resume round robin scheduling.

Figure A.4 contains a general flowchart of the logic. Executer is the Pascal simulator. Whenever your operating system schedules a process for execution, it must call Executer. We will soon describe Executer, but we must discuss some data structures first.

Figure A.4 Scheduling in Phase I

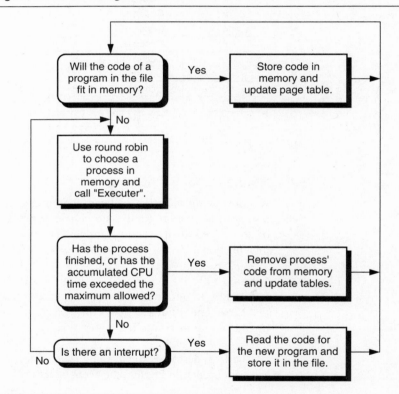

Data Structures

Some data structures must be exactly as shown for consistency with the process simulator. They may be changed only if corresponding changes are made in the simulator. Necessary data structures are:

1. PCB List. This table or linked list has an entry for each process currently in memory. Each PCB should be a record, declared as follows:

```
Ar8 = Array[1..8] Of Integer;
PCB = Record
ProcId    :Integer; {Process identification number}
ProcSize  :Integer; {Number of frames needed to store
                        process' code}
MaxTime   :Integer; {Maximum run time — in milliseconds}
Frames    :Ar8;     {Frame numbers containing process'
                        code}
CpuTime   :Integer; {Current accumulated run time — in
                        milliseconds}
End;      {PCB record}
```

The process simulator contains a parameter of type PCB. Therefore, the PCB must have exactly this form.

2. Frame Table. It has an entry for each frame. Each entry contains a Boolean field indicating whether the frame is occupied. Another field has the identification number of the process whose code is in that frame. A suggested format for the frame table is in Figure A.3.

3. Wait File. It holds submitted "programs". Each entry should contain:

   - program ID.
   - maximum allowable CPU time.
   - program size (number of pages).
   - program code (substrings).

   You may use whatever file types your system allows. However, it is easier to use a file structure that allows access to any entry by specifying the process ID. Keyed files, direct files, or indexed files are fine. You can use consecutive files, but they require more work since you must develop logic to find and delete specific records.

4. Entry File. It contains all programs that will eventually be submitted. Keeping them in a file is easier than entering them by hand. Henceforth, when we say "a program is submitted," your operating system should read one from the entry file. The "programs" are as in Figure A.2. You can create your own for the simulation.

5. Main Memory. A table whose entries represent the real memory frames that your operating system manages. As already stated, you may assume that each frame is only 4 bytes long. Remember, each "program" consists of a character string representing code. Thus, your operating system must divide the string into units of four characters or less, and store them in available frames. Initially, assume 24 frames.

6. Free Frames. A variable representing the number of free frames.

7. Clock. A variable representing <u>clock</u> time. You should initialize it to zero. It will increase as your operating system schedules and executes processes. You may think of clock units as milliseconds. Note: In some systems, Clock is a predefined Pascal function, so you must use a variable name such as clockx.

Startup

Initially, there are <u>no</u> processes to schedule and execute, so your operating system is idle. The simulator contains a procedure Idle, declared as follows:

```
Procedure Idle(Var Clock : Integer;
               Var Seed  : Integer);
```

Idle contains a random number generator used to generate increments of clock time. It simulates idle time until a program is submitted. Initially, your operating system should call Idle. After the call, it can read the first submitted "program."

Procedure Idle uses the parameter Seed to generate random numbers. You should initialize Seed to an arbitrary value and not refer to it again. This is not a true random number generator, but you can actually use its properties to your advantage. If you start with the same Seed value, the simulator will generate the same "random numbers." This consistency is helpful in debugging your operating system.

The Simulator

Finally, we can discuss the simulator. Your operating system schedules a process to run by choosing a PCB from the PCB list. It must transfer control to the procedure Executer declared as follows:

```
Procedure Executer(Var Process    :PCB;      {Process control
                                                block}
                     Var Interrupt:Vector;    {Interrupt
                                                vector}
                     Var Clock      :Integer; {Clock-maintains
                                                "real time" in
                                                milliseconds}
                     Var Quan       :Integer; {Time quantum
                                                used for round
                                                robin scheduling}
                     Var Seed       :Integer);{Input to random
                                                number generator}
```

Process is a PCB as previously described. It defines the process whose execution the procedure simulates. The parameter Interrupt is a record declared as type

```
Vector = Record
           NewProc  : Boolean;  {True means a new program has
                                  been submitted}
           ProcDone : Boolean;  {True means the currently
                                  running process is done}
End; {Interrupt record}
```

Executer contains random number generators used to increment Clock, and produce True or False values for each field of Interrupt. If upon return from Executer, NewProc is True, an interrupt has occurred and a new program is waiting to be submitted. If ProcDone is True, the current process has finished and your operating system should remove its code from memory and update all tables accordingly. Both fields may be True simultaneously.

Before returning to the operating system, the simulator increases Clock by a value between 1 and Quan. (Actually at this stage of the project, the increment is Quan unless the ProcDone field of Interrupt returns a value of True. This will change in Phase II.) The clock increment represents the amount of CPU time the process has just used. Upon return from Executer, your operating system should add the clock increment to the CpuTime field of the PCB. This allows you to track the accumulated execution time for each process. Don't forget to initialize CpuTime to zero.

If, upon return from Executer, the total accumulated CPU time for the process exceeds the maximum allowed (don't forget the maximum allowed was specified in seconds and a conversion is necessary), your operating system should abort it. In any case, when a process finishes, your operating system should clear the frames that contained its code. Last, if at any time there are <u>no</u> processes to execute, your operating system should call Idle, and read a new program upon rewriting.

Output

Once you have compiled and run your operating system, how do you know if it works? For the most part, you must carefully examine what happens as new programs enter and old ones finish. To help with this, your operating system should produce the following output:

1. Whenever a program is submitted, print the ProcId, maximum time allowed, code (character string), and current clock time.
2. Whenever a process finishes, print the ProcId, accumulated execution time, reason for termination (completion or excessive accumulated CPU time), current clock time, and turnaround time. (Turnaround time is the difference between the submission time and termination time.)
3. After the entry of every fifth program into memory (ProcId's 5, 10, 15, etc.) print the contents of all data structures (including the wait file).

When program 50 finishes, your operating system should stop (something must terminate the project.) At this point, print the following:

1. Current clock value.
2. Total idle time.
3. Total clock time spent on processes (application time).
4. Total operating system overhead time. (Whenever the operating system gets a new program, finishes one, performs a reschedule (calls Executer), or stores code in memory, it should add 1 to the clock. This will account for CPU time the operating system uses to perform its functions.)
5. Percentage of operating system overhead. Compute it with the formula

$$\frac{100 * \text{overhead time}}{\text{overhead time} + \text{application time}}$$

6. Number of reschedules performed and the average number per minute.
7. Average number of free frames (accumulated prior to each call to the procedure Executer).
8. Average turnaround time over all processes that have passed through the system.

Test the first phase with QUAN values of 50, 100, 200, and 400. Also rerun it with the number of frames set to 32, 40, and 48 (with QUAN = 50). For the other runs, print <u>only</u> the results at termination. How do the different runs compare?

══

Important Notes

Later phases will require you to revise your program. Be sure to design and document it so you can implement changes easily.

Since the project ends when program 50 finishes, you need only create 50 programs for the entry file. However, the simulator will continue to generate occasional True values for the interrupt vector's NewProc field. Your operating system should ignore them after 50 programs have been submitted.

The simulator has two random number generators named Num. One works on machines with 32-bit integers, the other works on machines with 16-bit integers. On some machines, you may be able to declare 32-bit integers using a Longint type. Check your manuals. If 32-bit integers are not available, use 16-bit integers. In any case, Seed should initially be less than half the Pascal Maxint value.

Program for Phase I simulation

```
Module name;

Type
  AR8 = Array[1..8] of Integer;
      {***********************************}
      {*******Process Control Block******}
      {***********************************}
  PCB = Record
    ProcId   : Integer;    {Process identification number}
    ProcSize : Integer;    {Number of pages required to
                             store process' code}
    MaxTime  : Integer;    {Maximum run time — in
                             milliseconds}
    Frames   : Ar8;        {Frame numbers containing
                             process' code}
    CpuTime  : Integer;    {Accumulated run time — in
                             milliseconds}
  End; {PCB record}
      {*************************}
      {****Interrupt vector*****}
      {*************************}
  Vector = Record
    NewProc  : Boolean; {True means a new program has been
                         submitted}
    ProcDone : Boolean; {True means the currently running
                         process is done}
  End; {Interrupt record}
```

```
                    {*******************************}
                    {****Random number generator****}
                    {****assumes 32-bit integers ****}
                    {*******************************}
        Function Num(Var Seed: Integer): Integer;

            {*********************************************************}
            {This function generates random numbers between 0 and 99.}
            {The sequence depends on Seed. The same initial value of }
            {Seed produces the same set of random numbers each time.}
            {This function works on machines with 32-bit integers.  }
            {*********************************************************}
        Var
            X      : Real;
            Rseed  : Real;
            N      : Integer;
        Begin {Random Number generator}
            Seed := 37915* Seed + 13849;
            Seed := Seed Mod 32768;
            Rseed := Seed;
            X := -Ln((Rseed+1)/32768);
            N := Trunc(X*25173);
            N := N Mod 100;
            Num := N;
        End; {Random Number generator}
                    {************************************}
                    {****Random number generator**********}
                    {****assumes 16-bit integers**********}
                    {************************************}
        Function Num(Var Seed: Integer): Integer;

            {*********************************************************}
            {This function generates random numbers between 0 and 99.}
            {The sequence depends on Seed. The same initial value of}
            {Seed produces the same set of random numbers each time.}
            {This function works on machines with 16—bit integers.  }
            {*********************************************************}
```

```
Var
   X     : Real;
   Rseed : Real;
   N     : Integer;
Begin {Random Number generator}
   Seed := 137* Seed + 53;
   Seed := Seed Mod 128;
   Rseed := Seed;
   X := -Ln((Rseed+1)/128);
   N := Trunc(X*97);
   N := N Mod 100;
   Num := N;
End; {Random Number generator}


Procedure Executer(Var Process   :PCB;        {Process control
                                               block}
                   Var Interrupt:Vector;     {Interrupt vector}
                   Var Clock     :Integer;   {Clock -
                                               maintains "real
                                               time" in
                                               milliseconds}
                   Var Quan      :Integer;   {Time quantum
                                               used for round
                                               robin scheduling
                                               should be greater
                                               than or equal to
                                               50}
                   Var Seed      :Integer); {Input to random
                                               number generator}


   {*******************************************************}
   {This procedure simulates the execution of the process  }
   {specified in the formal parameter list. The procedure  }
   {will randomly define each field of the interrupt vector}
   {to True or False. It will also increment the Clock by a}
   {value no larger than Quan.                             }
   {*******************************************************}
   {

Var
   Temp   : Integer; {Temporary variable}
```

```
     I     : Integer; {Loop control variable}
     Weight : Integer; {Weight is proportional to Quan. As
                        Quan increases, Weight increases the
                        probability of certain events
                        occurring}
Begin {Executer}
        {*********************************}
        {*********Intialize data**********}
        {*********************************}
  Weight:= Quan Div 50;
  Interrupt.NewProc := False;
  Interrupt.ProcDone := False;
        {*********************************}
        {*****Test for a new process ******}
        {*********************************}
  If Num(Seed) <= 5*Weight Then
    Interrupt.NewProc := True;
       {***************************************************}
       {Test whether the running process has finished. As }
       {the CpuTime increases, there is a higher          }
       {probability of the process finishing              }
       {***************************************************}
  Temp := (Process.MaxTime - Process.CpuTime) Div 10;
  For I := 1 to Weight do
    If Num(Seed) > Temp Then
      Interrupt.ProcDone := True;
       {****************************************************}
       {Increment the clock by a value no larger than Quan }
       {****************************************************}
  If Interrupt.ProcDone Then
    Clock := Clock + (Num(Seed)*Weight) Mod Quan
  Else
    Clock := Clock + Quan;
End; {Executer}

Procedure Idle(Var Clock : Integer;
               Var Seed : Integer);
Begin {Idle}
  Clock := Clock + Num(Seed);
End; {Idle}

End. {Module}
```

≡≡≡≡ A.2 Phase II: Process Scheduling

In Phase I, the major items of concern were:

1. Understanding how the simulator works and what its parameters mean.
2. Making sure your operating system stores process code in appropriate frames.
3. Low–level scheduling of processes in memory.

In itself, Phase I is a very simple operating system. There were many restrictions on it and the processes, such as:

1. Once your operating system stored a process' code in memory, it stayed there until the process finished.
2. Newly submitted programs had to sit in a wait file until sufficient memory became available. Memory was freed only when a process finished. In some cases, programs waited a long time before they could begin running.
3. There was no mechanism for I/O requests. We simply pretended they never happened. There was no intermediate–level scheduling.

≡≡ Phase II Goals

The goals of Phase II are to:

1. Eliminate the wait queue status of the file.
2. Distinguish between processes in a <u>ready</u> state (those that are competing for the CPU), and ones in a <u>wait</u> state (those that have issued an I/O request and are waiting for its completion).
3. Allow round robin scheduling among all ready processes, not just those in memory.

≡≡ Swapping

Goal 3 says that all <u>ready</u> processes should execute in a round robin fashion, regardless of where their codes reside. Of course, there is no guarantee that their code will even fit in memory, so your operating system must introduce swapping. That is, when your operating system chooses a process before a call to Executer, it must make sure its code is in memory. If not, then your operating system must store it in memory. If there are a enough frames available, this is easy. But, if not, your operating system must select another process, remove its code from memory, and store it in a swap file.

Swapping is easier if the file is keyed, direct, or indexed. Then the process identification number can serve as the key or relative position. When your operating system later schedules the process for execution, it can retrieve the necessary information through the process identification number, delete it from the swap file, and store it in memory.

If your file system does not allow records to be deleted (such as in consecutive files), you can use a "tag" field in each record. It can indicate whether the record has been "deleted." This is not ideal, but it serves our purposes.

Phase II PCB

To account for the additional process states, you must change the Process Control Blocks described in Phase I to the following form:

```
Ar8 = Array[1..8] of Integer;
PCB = Record
  ProcId     : Integer;    {Process identification number}
  ProcSize   : Integer;    {Number of frames needed to
                             store process' code}
  MaxTime    : Integer;    {Maximum run time — in
                             milliseconds}
  Frames     : Ar8;        {Frame numbers containing
                             process' code, if it is in
                             memory}
  CpuTime    : Integer;    {Accumulated run time—in
                             milliseconds}
  Resident   : Boolean;    {Indicates whether process' code
                             is in memory}
  DiskLoc    : Integer;    {Disk location of process' code,
                             if it is not in memory}
  IOReqs     : Integer;    {Total number of I/O requests
                             made}
End;
```

The PCB has three new fields: resident, DiskLoc, and IOReqs. The resident field specifies whether the process' code is in memory. If it is, the field is True. If not, it is false. The field DiskLoc contains the "disk location" of the process' code (if it is not in memory). More specifically, this field can hold a key value used to find the code in a file. You might store the code keyed on the process identification number. You can then store the Pid in DiskLoc. The field IOReqs contains the total number of I/O requests the process has made. We will describe shortly how Executer simulates an I/O request.

Phase II Simulator

We have changed Executer to reflect the additional features of Phase II. You should declare it as follows:

```
Procedure Executer (Var Process   : PCB;        {Process
                                                  controlblock}
                    Var Interrupt : Vector;     {Interrupt
                                                  vector}
                    Var Clock     : Integer;    {Clock -
                                                  maintains
                                                  "real
                                                  time"in
                                                  milliseconds}
                    Var Quan      : Integer;    {Time quantum
                                                  used for
                                                  round robin
                                                  scheduling}
                    Var Seed      : Integer;    {Input to
                                                  random
                                                  number
                                                  generator}
                    Var IOList    : Overhead;   {List of
                                                  processes
                                                  waiting for
                                                  the comple-
                                                  tion of I/O}
                    Var ProcMix   : Real);      {Percentage
                                                  of I/O
                                                  versus CPU
                                                  bound
                                                  processes}
```

Executer has two new parameters, IOList of type Overhead and ProcMix of type Real.

The type Overhead is declared as

```
Ar30 = Array[1..30] of Integer;
Overhead = Record
   Number   : Integer; {Number of processes waiting for
                        the completion of I/O}
   ProcId   : Ar30;    {Id's for processes waiting for
                        the completion of I/O}
End; {Overhead}
```

The fields of Overhead help the simulator track processes that generate I/O requests. The simulator also uses them to determine which processes can be activated after an I/O completion. Your operating system need not deal with this record. Just make sure you put in the parameter list. Do not alter the contents of the fields, but do initialize the Number field to zero. Also be sure to declare IOList in your main program.

The last parameter, ProcMix, allows you to indicate the type of processes your operating system will manage. You should give it a value between 0 and 1. A value of 0 means that all processes are CPU-bound (they will never generate an I/O request). A value of 1 means that all processes are I/O-bound (an I/O request occurs every time you call Executer). A value between 0 and 1 means the processes are between I/O- and CPU-bound. The larger the value, the more frequently they generate I/O requests. The simulator uses ProcMix to control the frequency with which it generates I/O requests.

We have still not answered the question, "How does the operating system know when a process generates an I/O request?" Well, there is no time like the present. To simulate I/O requests, we have expanded the Interrupt vector of Phase I. We now define it as follows:

```
Vector = Record
  NewProc : Boolean;      {TRUE means a new program has been
                           submitted}
  ProcDone: Boolean;      {TRUE means the currently running
                           process is done}
  IOReq   : Boolean;      {TRUE means the current process has
                           issued an I/O request}
  IODone  : Integer;      {Whenever an I/O operation is
                           completed, this field specifies the
                           ID of the waiting process }
  Abort   : Boolean;      {TRUE means the current process has
                           aborted}
End; {Vector}
```

Whenever your operating system calls Executer, it must check each field of the interrupt vector. Figure A.5 is a rough flowchart of the required low-, intermediate-, and high-level scheduling.

If the IOReq field is TRUE, the current process has just issued an I/O request. At this point, your operating system should switch it from the ready state to the wait state. You may keep two separate PCB lists, one for each state.

Figure A.5 Scheduling in Phase II

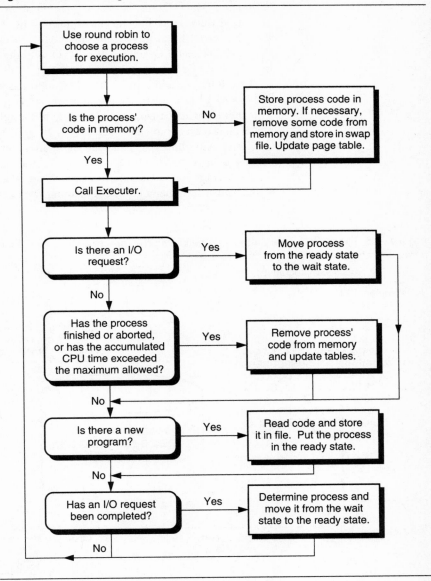

Next, your operating system must determine if the process should be terminated. Three things can cause this: an abort, completion, or accumulated execution time exceeding the maximum allowed. In the first two cases, you should remove the process from the system. In the last case, the process may also have made an I/O request. If so, wait until the I/O finishes before removing it.

If the IODone field is not 0, an I/O request has been completed. The contents of IODone are the identification number of the process that made the request. You should switch it from the <u>wait</u> state to the <u>ready</u> state. If IODone is 0, no request has been completed.

Figure A.6 shows an example of memory and the swap file after eight programs have been submitted. Three of them (numbers 1, 2, and 4) have finished. Their code is neither in memory nor in the swap file. Three others (3, 5, and 8) reside in memory. The remaining two are in the file.

Figure A.6 Example memory allocation and swap file, processes 1, 2, and 4 have finished

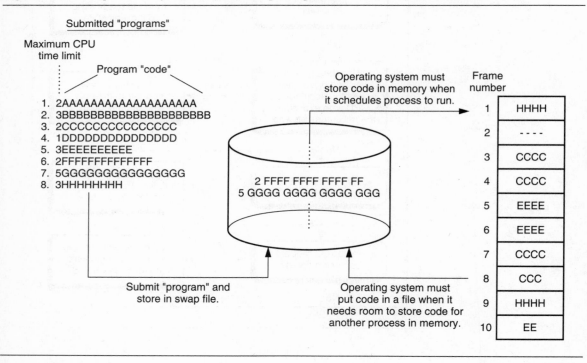

Figure A.7 shows the PCBs associated with these processes. Note that we have not shown every field. The resident field is true for processes 3, 5, and 8. For them, the Frames field specifies which frames contain the "code." For processes 6 and 7, the DiskLoc field contains the ProcId. This value can be used to locate the "code" in a disk file.

Figure A.7 Example list of PCB's (from Figure A.6)

PCB list (not all fields shown)

ProcId	ProcSize	Frames	Resident	DiskLoc
3	4	3, 4, 7, 8	True	- -
5	3	5, 6, 10	True	- -
6	4	- -	False	6
7	4	- -	False	7
8	2	1, 9	True	- -

List of processes in memory

Process 3 occupies frames 3, 4, 7, and 8.
Process 5 occupies frames 5, 6, and 10.
Process 8 occupies frames 1 and 9.

List of processes in the swap file

Process 6 accessible through key value 6.
Process 7 accessible through key value 7.

Idling

Finally, if there are no ready processes, your operating system should call Idle. As before, it just passes time until something happens. For Phase II, we declare it as

```
Procedure Idle( Var Clock      : Integer;
                Var Seed       : Integer;
                Var Interrupt  : Vector;
                Var IOList     : Overhead);
```

Upon return from Idle, an interrupt flag will be set, and your operating system should proceed as described above.

Overhead time

When you make your runs, you should account for the clock time your operating system needs. To do this, compute overhead time as in Phase I. That is, add 1 to the clock time each time a reschedule (call to Executer) occurs, a new program enters the system, or a program finishes. Also, add 1 to the clock for every ten I/O requests. This accounts for the time the operating system spends processing I/O requests. We assume that I/O processors do most of the

I/O work. That is why we only increase the clock by 1 for every ten requests. Don't forget, count the storage of process code in the swap file, or the loading of it into memory as an I/O operation.

Output

To determine whether your operating system is working, produce the following output:

1. Whenever a program is submitted, print the ProcId, maximum time allowed, code that is to be stored in memory, and current clock time.
2. Whenever a process finishes, print the ProcId, accumulated execution time, reason for termination (completion, abort, or excessive accumulated CPU time), current clock time, number of I/O requests, and turnaround time.
3. Whenever a process generates an I/O request, print its identification number and the current clock time.
4. When a process is activated after an I/O completion, print its identification number and the current clock time.
5. After every 5000 milliseconds (clock = 5000, 10000, 15000, etc.), print the following:

   a) PCBs for processes in a <u>ready</u> state.
   b) PCBs for processes in a <u>wait</u> state.
   c) Contents of the swap file.
   d) Contents of memory.
   e) Contents of the page table.

In Phase II, the project ends when fifty processes have exited the system. When this happens, print the following:

1. Current clock value.
2. Total idle time.
3. Total clock time spent on processes (application time).
4. Total operating system overhead time.
5. Percentage of operating system overhead. Compute it with the formula

$$\frac{100 * \text{overhead time}}{\text{overhead time} + \text{application time}}$$

6. Number of reschedules performed and the average number per minute.
7. Average number of free frames (accumulated prior to each call to the procedure Executer).

8. Average turnaround time over all processes that have exited the system.
9. The total number of swaps the operating system has performed.
10. The total number of I/O requests made.

Run your operating system with ProcMix values of 0, .25, and .50. Use Quan = 50 and 24 frames. Also with ProcMix =.25 and Quan = 50, run it with 24, 32, 40, and 48 frames. As before, compare the statistics generated for different numbers of frames and values of ProcMix. Display the statistics in a table. A column should represent one statistic. A row should represent a run with a specified number of frames, ProcMix, and Quan value.

Program for Phase II Simulation

```
Module name;

Type
  Ar8=Array[1..8] of Integer;

      {****************************************** }
      {********Process Control Block *********** }
      {****************************************** }
  PCB = Record
    ProcId   : Integer;    {Process identification number}
    ProcSize : Integer;    {Number of pages required to
                            store process' code}

    MaxTime  : Integer;    {Maximum run time — in
                            milliseconds}

    Frames   : Ar8;        {Frame numbers containing
                            process' code}

    CpuTime  : Integer;    {Accumulated run time — in
                            milliseconds}

    Resident : Boolean;    {Indicates whether process' code
                            is in memory}

    DiskLoc  : Integer;    {Disk location of process' code,
                            if it is not in memory}

    IOReqs   : Integer;    {Total number of I/O requests
                            made}

  End; {PCB record}
```

```
         {************************}
         {****Interrupt vector****}
         {************************}
Vector = Record
    NewProc  : Boolean;      {TRUE means a new program has
                              been submitted}
    ProcDone : Boolean;      {TRUE means the currently
                              running process is done}
    IOReq    : Boolean;      {TRUE means the current process
                              has issued an I/O request}
    IODone   : Integer;      {Whenever an I/O operation has
                              completed, this field specifies
                              the waiting process}
    Abort    : Boolean;      {TRUE means the current process
                              has aborted}
END;

         {********************}
         {*****Overhead*******}
         {********************}
Ar30 = Array[1..30] of Integer;
Overhead = Record
    Number : Integer;        {Number of processes waiting for
                              an I/O completion}
    ProcId : Ar30;           {Process IDs for processes
                              waiting for an I/O completion}
End; {Overhead}

         {********************************* }
         {****Random number generator****** }
         {****assumes 32-bit integers****** }
         {********************************* }
```

```
Function Num(Var Seed : Integer): Integer;

  {**********************************************************}
  {This function generates random numbers between 0 and 99.}
  {The sequence produced depends on Seed. The same value   }
  {of Seed produces the same set of random numbers each    }
  {time. This function works when implemented on machines  }
  {with 32-bit integers.                                   }
  {**********************************************************}
Var
  X      : Real;
  Rseed  : Real;
  N      : Integer;

Begin {Random Number generator}
  Seed := 37915*Seed + 13849;
  Seed := Seed Mod 32768;
  Rseed := Seed;
  X := -Ln((Rseed+1)/32768);
  N := Trunc(X*25173);
  N := N Mod 100;
  Num := N;
End; {Random Number generator}


Procedure FindProc( Var Seed      : Integer;
                    Var IOList     : Overhead;
                    Var Interrupt  : Vector);
{**********************************************************}
{Determines which process has been waiting for an I/O     }
{operation that has finished. Called in Executer and in   }
{Idle                                                     }
{**********************************************************}
Var
   Pos : Integer; { Subscript to locate process waiting for
                    I/O operation that has finished}


Begin {FindProc}
   Pos := Num(Seed) MOD IOList.Number + 1;
   Interrupt.IODone := IOList.ProcId[Pos];
   While Pos < IOList.Number Do
     Begin
       IOList.ProcId[Pos] := IOList.ProcId[Pos +1];
       Pos := Pos +1;
     End; { While }
   IOList.Number := IOList.Number - 1;
End; {FindProc}
```

```
Procedure Executer ( Var Process  :PCB;      {Process control
                                               block}
                      Var Interrupt:Vector;  {Interrupt
                                               vector}
                      Var Clock    :Integer; {Clock-main-
                                               tains "real
                                               time" in
                                               milliseconds}
                      Var Quan     :Integer; {Time quantum
                                               used for round
                                               robin
                                               scheduling}
                      Var Seed     :Integer; {Input to random
                                               number
                                               generator}
                      Var IOList   :Overhead;{List of
                                               processes
                                               waiting for I/O
                                               to be
                                               completed}
                      Var ProcMix :Real);    {Indicates
                                               percentage of
                                               I/O versus CPU-
                                               bound
                                               processes}

  {***********************************************************}
  {This procedure simulates the execution of the process  }
  {specified in the formal parameter list. It randomly    }
  {defines each field of the interrupt vector as TRUE or   }
  {FALSE. It also increments the Clock by the local        }
  {variable Clockinc                                       }
  {***********************************************************}

Var
  Done     : Boolean;  {Used to prevent certain events
                        from occurring simultaneously.}
  Temp     : Integer;  {Temporary variable}
  I        : Integer;  {Loop control variable}
  Weight   : Integer;  {Proportional to Quan. As Quan
                        increases, Weight increases the
                        probability of certain events
                        occurring}
  Clockinc : Integer;  {Time increment for the Clock}
```

```pascal
Procedure ProcInList;

{*********************************************************}
{Puts a process that makes an I/O request in the list of}
{processes that have made requests Local to Executer    }
{*********************************************************}
  Begin {ProcInList}
    Interrupt. IOReq := True;
    Done := True;
    With IOList Do
      Begin
        Number := Number +1;
        ProcId[Number] := Process.ProcId;
      End; {With}
    Clockinc := 50*(I-1) + Num(Seed) MOD 50;
  End; {ProcInList}

Begin {Executer}
      {***********************}
      {****Initialize data****}
      {***********************}
  Weight := Quan DIV 50;
  With Interrupt Do
    Begin
      NewProc  := False;
      IOReq := False;
      ProcDone := False;
      Abort := False;
      IODone := 0;
    End; {With}
  Done := FALSE;
  Clockinc := Quan;
      {***********************************}
      {******** Test for I/O completion ***}
      {***********************************}
  If (IOList.Number > 0) Then
    Begin
      I := 0;
      While (I < Weight) AND (Interrupt.IODone = 0) Do
        Begin
          I := I + 1;
          If Num(Seed) < Trunc(100*ProcMix) Then
              FindProc(Seed, IOList, Interrupt);
        End; { While }
    End; {If}
```

```
      {*************************** }
      {**** Check for abort ****** }
      {*************************** }
If Num(Seed) = 5 Then
  Begin
    Interrupt.Abort := TRUE;
    Done := TRUE;
  End;
      {*******************************}
      {***** Test for I/O request ****}
      {*******************************}
If (Not Done) AND (ProcMix > 0.1) AND (IOList.Number < 30)
Then
  Begin
    I := 0;
    While (I < Weight) AND (Not Done) Do
      Begin
        I := I+1;
        If Num (Seed) <= Trunc(100* ProcMix) Then
          ProcInList;
      End; { While }
  End; {IF}
      {*********************************** }
      {***Check for process completion**** }
      {*********************************** }
If Not Done Then
  Begin
    Temp:= (Process.MaxTime - Process.CpuTime) DIV 10;
    I := 0;
    While (I < Weight) AND (Not Done) Do
      Begin
        I := I + 1;
        If Num(Seed) > Temp Then
          Begin
            Interrupt.ProcDone:= TRUE;
            Done := True;
            Clockinc:= (Num(Seed)* Weight) MOD Quan;
          End; {If}
      End; {While}
  End;
```

```
        {************************ }
        {** Increment clock ****** }
        {************************ }
   Clock := Clock + Clockinc;
   Weight := Clockinc DIV 50 + 1;


        {*****************************}
        {*****Test for a new program**}
        {*****************************}
   If Num(Seed) <= 5* Weight Then
      Interrupt.NewProc := TRUE;
End; {Executer}

Procedure Idle(Var Clock     : Integer;
               Var Seed      : Integer;
               Var Interrupt : Vector;
               Var IOList    : Overhead);

Var
   Pos : Integer;

Begin
   With Interrupt Do
     Begin
        NewProc := False;
        ProcDone := False;
        IOReq := False;
        IODone := 0;
        Abort := False;
     End; {With}
   Clock := Clock + Num(Seed);
   If (IOList.Number = 0) Then
      Interrupt.NewProc := True
   Else
      FindProc(Seed, IOList, Interrupt);
End;

End. {Module}
```

≡≡≡≡ A.3 Phase III: Process Synchronization

Phase III is very similar to Phase II. The only difference is that it adds synchronization among processes that wait for and signal the occurrence of certain events. We assume three such events represented by

```
EventType = (Event1, Event2, Event3);
```

   and

```
SemArray = Array[EventType] of Integer;
```

   Your operating system should use a variable of type SemArray to track occurrences of each event. Initially, nothing has happened, so you should initialize the values to zero. A variable of type SemArray is an array of semaphores.

For Phase III, we declare procedure Executer as follows:

```
Procedure Executer (Var Process    :PCB;       {Process
                                                control block}
                    Var Interrupt :Vector;    {Interrupt
                                                vector}
                    Var Clock      :Integer; {Clock -
                                                maintains
                                                "real time" in
                                                milliseconds}
                    Var Quan       :Integer; {Time quantum
                                                used for round
                                                robin
                                                scheduling}
                    Var Seed       :Integer; {Input to
                                                random number
                                                generator}
                    Var IOList     :Overhead;{List of
                                                processes
                                                waiting for
                                                I/O to finish}
                    Var ProcMix    :Real);    {Percentage of
                                                I/O versus CPU
                                                bound
                                                processes}
                    Var Primitive :EventRec); {Used to
                                                block and
                                                wake up
                                                processes
                                                for an event}
```

The only new parameter is Primitive of type EventRec. The simulator uses it to return wait and signal primitives to your operating system. The type EventRec is declared as

```
EventRec = Record
  Wait : Boolean;      {True means the current process has
                        issued a wait on an event}
  Signal : Boolean;    {True means the current process has
                        issued a signal on an event}
  Event : EventType; {Indicates the event involved}
End; {EventRec}
```

After any call to Executer, the current process may have issued a Wait or Signal for an event. A TRUE value in the field indicates which one has occurred. If either is True, Event (Event1, Event2, or Event3) specifies the event.

Now, if the Wait field is True, your operating system should determine whether the specified event has occurred. If it has, you should decrement its semaphore by 1.

On the other hand, if the event has not occurred (semaphore = 0), you should remove the process from the ready state. You should place it in a wait queue associated with the event. There should be a queue for each event.

If the Signal field is True, your operating system should determine if any processes are waiting for the event. If there are some, it should return the process at the front of the queue to the ready state. The corresponding semaphore should not change. If there are no processes waiting, your operating system should add 1 to the semaphore.

Overhead

Compute operating system overhead time as before. That is, add 1 to the clock time each time a reschedule (call to Executer) occurs, a new program enters the system, a program finishes. Also, add 1 to the clock for every ten I/O requests (and swaps). In addition, add 1 to the clock each time a job has to wait for an event or is reactivated after an event occurs.

Output

You should output the following:

1. Whenever a program is submitted, print the ProcId, maximum time allowed, code that is to be stored in memory, and current clock time.

2. Whenever a process finishes, print the ProcId, accumulated execution time, reason for termination (completion, abort, or excessive accumulated CPU time), current clock time, number of I/O requests, and turnaround time.
3. Whenever a process generates an I/O request, print its identification number and the current clock time.
4. When a process is activated after an I/O completion, print its identification number and the current clock time.
5. Whenever a Wait or Signal occurs, print the process ID of the issuer and the current clock time.
6. After every 5000 milliseconds (clock = 5000, 10000, 15000, etc.), print the following:

   a) PCBs for processes in a <u>ready</u> state.
   b) PCBs for processes waiting for I/O.
   c) Contents of the swap file.
   d) Contents of memory.
   e) Contents of the page table.
   f) PCBs for processes waiting on each event.

As in Phase II, the project ends when fifty processes have exited the system. When this happens, print the following:

1. Current clock value.
2. Total idle time.
3. Total clock time spent on processes.
4. Total operating system overhead time.
5. Percentage of operating system overhead. As before, it is

$$\frac{100 * \text{overhead time}}{\text{overhead time} + \text{application time}}$$

6. Number of reschedules performed and the average number per minute.
7. Average number of free frames (accumulated prior to each call to the procedure Executer).
8. Average turnaround time over all processes that have passed through the system.
9. The total number of swaps the operating system has performed.
10. The total number of I/O requests made.
11. The total number of Wait and Signal calls processed.

Program for Phase III simulation

Module *name*;

Type
```
  Ar8=Array[1..8] of Integer;
      {*****************************************}
      {********Process Control Block ***********}
      {*****************************************}
  PCB = Record
    ProcId     : Integer;   {Process identification number}
    ProcSize   : Integer;   {Number of pages required to
                             store process' code}
    MaxTime    : Integer;   {Maximum run time — in
                             milliseconds}
    Frames     : Ar8;       {Frame numbers containing
                             process' code}
    CpuTime    : Integer;   {Accumulated run time — in
                             milliseconds}
    Resident   : Boolean;   {Indicates whether process' code
                             is in memory}
    DiskLoc    : Integer;   {Disk location of process code,
                             if it is not in memory}
    IOReqs     : Integer;   {Total number of I/O requests
                             made}
  End; {PCB record}


      {************************}
      {****Interrupt vector ****}
      {************************}
  Vector = Record
    NewProc  : Boolean;   {True means a new program has
                           been submitted}
    ProcDone : Boolean;   {True means the current process
                           is done}
    IOReq    : Boolean;   {True means the current process
                           has issued an I/O request}
    IODone   : Integer;   {Whenever an I/O operation
                           finishes, this field contains
                           the ID of the waiting process}
    Abort    : Boolean;   {True means the current process
                           has aborted}
  End; {Vector}
```

```
        {********************}
        {*****Overhead*******}
        {********************}
Ar30 = Array[1..30] of Integer;
Overhead = Record
   Number : Integer;        {Number of processes waiting for
                              I/O to be completed}
   ProcId : Ar30;           {IDs for processes waiting for
                              I/O to be completed }
End; {Overhead}


        {**********************}
        {***** EventRecord*****}
        {**********************}
EventType = (Event1, Event2, Event3);
EventRec = Record
   Wait   : Boolean;        {True means the process has
                              issued a wait for an event}
   Signal : Boolean;        {True means the process has
                              signalled the completion of an
                              event}
   Event  : EventType;      {If either the Wait or Signal
                              field is TRUE, this field
                              specifies the event}
End; {Overhead}


        {********************************}
        {****Random number generator*******}
        {****assumes 32 bit-integers*******}
        {********************************}
Function Num(Var Seed : Integer): Integer;

{**********************************************************}
{This function generates random numbers between 0 and 99.}
{The sequence produced depends on Seed. The same value of}
{Seed produces the same set of random numbers each time.}
{This function works on machines with 32-bit integers.  }
{**********************************************************}
```

```
Var
  X       : Real;
  RSeed   : Real;
  N       : Integer;

Begin {Random Number generator}
  Seed := 37915* Seed + 13849;
  Seed := Seed Mod 32768;
  RSeed:= Seed;
  X := -Ln((Rseed +1)/32768);
  N := Trunc(X*25173);
  N := N Mod 100;
  Num := N;
End; {Random Number generator}

Procedure FindProc( Var Seed : Integer;
                    Var IOList : Overhead;
                    Var Interrupt : Vector);
  {********************************************************}
  {Determines which process has been waiting for an I/O   }
  {operation that has finished. Called in Executer and in }
  {Idle.                                                  }
  {********************************************************}
Var
  Pos : Integer;    {Subscript to locate the process
                     waiting on I/O operation that has
                     finished}

Begin {FindProc}
  Pos := Num(Seed) MOD IOList.Number + 1;
  Interrupt.IODone := IOList.ProcId[Pos];
  While Pos < IOList.Number Do
    Begin
      IOList. ProcId [Pos]:= IOList. ProcId [Pos +1];
      Pos := Pos +1;
    End; {While}
  IOList. Number := IOList. Number - 1;
End; {FindProc}

Procedure Executer (Var Process   :PCB;    {Process
                                            control block}
                    Var Interrupt :Vector; {Interrupt
                                            vector}
```

```
                        Var Clock     :Integer;  {Clock - main-
                                                   tains "real
                                                   time" in
                                                   milliseconds}
                        Var Quan      :Integer;  {Time quantum
                                                   used for round
                                                   robin
                                                   scheduling}
                        Var Seed      :Integer;  {Input to
                                                   random number
                                                   generator}
                        Var IOList    :Overhead; {List of
                                                   processes
                                                   waiting for an
                                                   I/O operation
                                                   to be
                                                   completed}
                        Var ProcMix   :Real;     {Indicates
                                                   percentage of
                                                   I/O versus CPU
                                                   bound
                                                   processes}
                        Var Primitive :EventRec);{Used to
                                                   block and
                                                   wake up
                                                   processes
                                                   for an event}


    {*******************************************************}
    {This procedure simulates the execution of the process }
    {specified in the formal parameter list. The procedure }
    {randomly defines each field of the interrupt vector    }
    {to be TRUE or FALSE. It also increments the clock by   }
    {the local variable Clockinc.                           }
    {*******************************************************}

Var
   Done    : Boolean;     {Used to prevent certain events
                            from occurring simultaneously.}
   Temp    : Integer;     {Temporary variable}
   I       : Integer;     {Loop control variable}
```

```
Weight   : Integer;       {Proportional to Quan. As Quan
                           increases, Weight increases the
                           probability of certain events
                           occurring}
Clockinc : Integer;       {Time increment for the clock}
```

Procedure ProcInList;
```
{*******************************************************}
{Puts any process that makes an I/O request in the list }
{of such processes. It is local to Executer             }
{*******************************************************}
   Begin {ProcInList}
     Interrupt. IOReq := TRUE;
     Done := True;
     With IOList Do
       Begin
         Number:= Number +1;
         ProcId [Number]:= Process.ProcId;
       End; {With}
     Clockinc:= 50*(I-1) + Num(Seed) MOD 50;
   End; {ProcInList}


Begin {Executer}
     {*********************}
     {****Intialize data****}
     {*********************}
   Weight := Quan DIV 50;
   With Interrupt Do
     Begin
       NewProc := False;
       IOReq := False;
       ProcDone := False;
       Abort := False;
       IODone := 0;
     End; {With}
   Done := False;
   Clockinc := Quan;
   Primitive.Wait := False;
   Primitive.Signal := False;

     {**********************************}
     {**** Test for I/O completion *******}
     {**********************************}
```

```pascal
If (IOList.Number > 0) Then
  Begin {IF}
    I := 0;
    While (I < Weight) AND (Interrupt.IODone = 0) Do
      Begin {While}
        I := I + 1;
        IF Num(Seed) < Trunc(100*ProcMix) Then
          FindProc(Seed, IOList, Interrupt);
      End; { While }
  End; {IF}

    {***********************}
    {**** Test for abort ****}
    {***********************}
If Num(Seed) = 5 Then
  Begin
    Interrupt.Abort := True;
    Done := True;
  End;

    {******************************}
    {** Test for I/O request *******}
    {******************************}
If (Not Done) AND (ProcMix > 0.1) AND (IOList.Number <30)
Then
  Begin
    I := 0;
    While (I < Weight) AND (NOT Done) Do
      Begin
        I := I+1;
        If Num (Seed) <= Trunc(100* ProcMix) Then
          ProcInList;
      End; { While }
  End; {IF}

    {******************************}
    {***Check for process finishing***}
    {******************************}
If Not Done Then
  Begin
    Temp:= (Process.MaxTime - Process.CpuTime) DIV 10;
    I := 0;
    While (I < Weight) AND (Not Done) Do
```

```
      Begin
        I := I + 1;
        If Num(Seed) > Temp Then
          Begin
            Interrupt.ProcDone:= True;
            Done := True ;
            Clockinc := (Num(Seed)* Weight) MOD
            Quan;
          End; {If}
      End; {While}
  End;


  {*****************************************************}
  {Check whether process has issued a wait for an event}
  {*****************************************************}
If (Not Done) AND (Num(Seed) <= 4*Weight) Then
  Begin
    Done := True;
    Primitive.Wait := True;
    I := Num(Seed) MOD 3;
    If I = 0 Then Primitive.Event:= Event1;
    If I = 1 Then Primitive.Event:= Event2;
    If I = 2 Then Primitive.Event:= Event3;
    Clockinc := (Num(Seed)*Weight) MOD Quan;
  End;


  {*******************************************}
  {***Check for the signaling of an event ***}
  {*******************************************}
If (Num(Seed) <= 4*Weight) AND (Not Done) AND (Not
Primitive.Wait) Then
  Begin
    Primitive.Signal := True;
    I := Num(Seed) MOD 3;
    If I = 0 Then Primitive.Event:= Event1;
    If I = 1 Then Primitive.Event:= Event2;
    If I = 2 Then Primitive.Event:= Event3;
  End;


  {*********************}
  {**Increment clock******}
  {*********************}
```

```
        Clock := Clock + Clockinc;
        Weight := Clockinc DIV 50 + 1;

           {****************************}
           {***Test for a new program***}
           {****************************}
        If Num(Seed) <= 5*Weight Then
           Interrupt.NewProc:= True;

End; {Executer}

Procedure Idle( Var Clock      : Integer;
                Var Seed       : Integer;
                Var Interrupt  : Vector;
                Var IOList     : Overhead);

Var
   Pos : Integer;

Begin {Idle}
   With Interrupt Do
     Begin
       NewProc := FALSE;
       ProcDone := FALSE;
       IOReq := FALSE;
       IODone := 0;
       Abort := FALSE;
     End; {With}
   Clock := Clock + Num(Seed);
   If (IOList.Number = 0) Then
       Interrupt.NewProc := TRUE
   Else
       FindProc (Seed, IOList, Interrupt);
End; {Idle}

End. {Module}
```

≡≡≡≡≡≡ A.4 Phase IV: Future Extensions

Phases I, II, and III primarily covered memory management, scheduling, and synchronization. There are many operating system features left for a Phase IV, V, and beyond. Here are some features Executer could simulate.

a. **Data for I/O**. When the simulator models an I/O request, it could distinguish between input and output. For output, it could generate a character string. The strings could be spooled to a file and printed when the process finishes.

b. **Working sets**. There is no need for all of a process' pages to be in memory when it runs. You could determine a working set size and store only a few pages in memory. You could also add a field to the interrupt vector for page faults. It would be interesting to see if this addition reduces overall turnaround times for the processes.

c. **Different scheduling techniques**. You could experiment with other scheduling approaches such as those described in Chapter 4.

d. **Message passing**. Phase III simulated a primitive form of synchronization. You might change Executer to simulate the sending and receipt of messages. The simulator could generate messages randomly.

e. **Disk I/O**. You could define a disk with tracks and sectors. Processes could then make output requests to logical sector numbers. Your operating system would determine an actual track and sector and write a simulated output to the disk.

f. Anything else you could imagine. The author welcomes suggestions for refinements or additions to the simulator.

D. E. Boddy has described a monitor–based sample operating system written in Turbo Pascal. See his article entitled, "SOS: A Monitor-Based Operating System for Instruction." <u>SIGPLAN NOTICES</u> 23 (December 1988):115–124.

Glossary

Abort: Unexpected process termination.

Access control: A policy that determines how processes may access objects.

Access method: The algorithms used to carry out an I/O request.

Access mode: The manner in which a process accesses an object, such as reading, writing, or executing.

Access time: The time between the request for a data item and its arrival.

Ada: A high-level concurrent language that was developed for widespread portability.

Address space: The total range of addresses to which a process may refer.

Address translation: The process of converting a virtual address into a physical address.

Algorithm: A plan for solving a problem.

ALU: Arithmetic and Logic Unit. A device that does arithmetic and logic functions.

Anticipatory paging: A method whereby pages are fetched prior to their actually being needed.

Append: Add to existing data.

Applications program: A program that performs an end-user application as opposed to systems work.

Arbitration: Selection of one of several requests for a common resource.

Array: A data structure consisting of items identified by an overall name and a set of indexes or subscripts.

Arrival rate: Rate at which requests for a resource occur.

ASCII: American Standard Code for Information Interchange, a seven-bit code used in the computer industry to standardize information interchange.

Assembly language: A language using mnemonics and symbols that is logically equivalent to machine language.

Associative memory: Memory locations referenced by specifying contents instead of an address.

Asynchronous: Independent.

Attribute: Information about a variable.

Authentication: Discovering or confirming the identity of a process.

Backup: Copy of a file used in case the original is destroyed.

Banker's Algorithm: Algorithm that avoids deadlock by distinguishing safe and unsafe states.

Batch file: See command file.

Batch processing: The practice of grouping requests and commands and submitting them to the computer. Used in high-volume computer facilities to increase efficiency.

Binary tree: A tree structure in which each node has at most two child nodes.

Bit: An abbreviation for Binary Digit. A bit may be on or off, 0 or 1, yes or no.

Block: The fundamental unit for data to be stored on a disk or tape.

Block-oriented device: A device that transfers data in units of fixed size, rather than as single items.

Boot: Automatic reading of a fixed disk sector when a computer is turned on.

Boot record: The record read during a boot. It contains code to read other operating system components into memory.

Buffer: An area of storage used to hold data temporarily that is being transferred from one device to another.

Bug: An error in a program.

Bus: Parallel electrical lines connecting devices.

Busy waiting: Checking status within a short loop.

Byte: A group of bits, normally 8 bits.

C: A high-level computer language developed at Bell Laboratories for writing systems programs.

C-scan: A method for handling disk requests in which the heads always move in the same direction, returning to the request furthest away when all the requests in that direction have been satisfied.

Cache memory: High-speed memory used to store frequently used data and instructions.

Canonical mode: A mode in which a driver interprets control characters transferred to or from the computer.

Cataloged procedure: Set of JCL statements accessible through MVS' system catalog.

CAW: See Channel Address Word.

CCW: See Channel Command Word.

Central Processing Unit (CPU): The part of the computer that executes instructions, performs arithmetic and logic, and controls operations.

Channel: A secondary processor that handles I/O.

Channel Address Word (CAW): Location of a channel program.

Channel Command Word (CCW): An instruction executed by an IBM 370 channel.

Channel program: Set of CCWs.

Character-oriented device: A device that transfers data one character at a time.

Checkpoint: Point in a process where its resources are freed and can be resumed in the event of a subsequent failure.

Child: 1) Process created by a UNIX fork command. 2) Successor of a node in a tree structure.

Ciphered text: Data put into a form that makes its interpretation difficult.

Circular buffer: A buffer that is used as though its ends were connected. Also called a cyclic or ring buffer.

Circular linked list: A data structure in which each element contains a pointer to the next one and the last element contains a pointer to the first one.

Close: Execution of routines when a process is done with a file or peripheral.

Cluster: MS-DOS disk allocation unit.

Code: Description of an algorithm or data structure using semantic and syntactic rules of a programming language.

Command file: A file containing commands in the order to be executed. Also called a procedure file or batch file.

Command interpreter: See shell.

Command language: Language used to communicate with an operating system.

COMMAND.COM: MS-DOS shell.

Communication Vector Table (CVT): MVS table locating tasks, important nucleus routines, and control blocks.

Compaction: Rearrangement of code and data so all available memory is contiguous.

Compiler: A program that translates programs written in a high-level language (source code) into machine language (object code or machine code).

Compute bound: Spends most of its time doing computations, rather than I/O.

Computer network: See network.

Computer program: See program.

Computer system: A collection of components that includes a processing unit, memory, and I/O devices, as well as a power supply. Their function is to process data.

Concurrency: Operating systems topic where multiple processes exist and compete for resources at the same time.

Concurrent processes: Processes that are active at the same time and can compete for computer resources.

Condition code: Bit flag(s) indicating status of a previous operation.

Condition variable: Monitor variable used for blocking and wakeup functions.

Configuration file: A file containing a description of a resource. Also called an environment file.

Context switch: The events involved in switching a processor from one process to another.

Contiguous: Physically adjacent to one another.

Control block: Table of information.

Control Program (CP): VM operating system's component that manages computer resources.

Controller: An electronic device that manages another device such as a disk or tape drive, printer, or terminal.

CP: See Control Program.

CPU: See Central Processing Unit.

CPU-bound: See compute bound.

Critical section: A section of a process that can be executed only when other processes are guaranteed not to interfere with it.

CVT: See Communication Vector Table.

Cycle stealing: Delaying a processor from accessing a bus or module in preference of another that made a simultaneous request.

Cylinder: Collection of tracks on a disk pack lying the same distance from its center.

Data Control Block (DCB): Table describing a file's characteristics.

Data integrity: Data accuracy.

Data management: Managing a system's files or data sets.

Data set: IBM term for file.

Data structure: A pattern used to store data. Some common data structures include: queues, stacks, linked lists, trees, records, and arrays.

DCB: See Data Control Block.

DD statement: MVS JCL statement describing a file or peripheral.

Deadlock: A situation in which processes are waiting for events to occur that cannot happen because of their own current states. Also called deadly embrace.

Deadlock avoidance: Execution of resource allocation routines that avoid situations where the operating system can no longer guarantee deadlock will not occur.

Deadlock detection: Execution of routines that determine if a deadlock has occurred.

Deadlock prevention: Creation of an environment where deadlock is impossible.

Deadlock recovery: Execution of routines to remove a deadlock.

Deadly embrace: See deadlock.

Debugging: The process of finding and correcting errors (bugs) in a computer program.

Decryption: Converting from ciphered text back to plain text.

Dekker's Algorithm: Algorithm that enforces mutual exclusion between two processes.

Demand paging: A method whereby a page is fetched only when it is needed.

Demultiplexing: Receiving data from a single source, dividing it into parts, and routing each part to a different destination.

Descriptor: Data structure that describes a resource.

Device: Hardware component of a computer system.

Device controller: See controller.

Device-dependent: Classification of I/O routines that depend on a device's characteristics.

Device driver: A program that controls the detailed operations of an I/O device.

Device-independent: Classification of I/O routines that are executed regardless of the device involved in the data transfer.

Device register: Storage containing status and control information for a device.

Direct access: Getting a record quickly by specifying its location or position in a file.

Direct file: File in which a record is specified using its position in the file.

Direct Memory Access: See DMA.

Directory: Information concerning a set of files, typically including their names, sizes, types and dates and times of creation.

Dirty bit: Bit whose value indicates whether a page has been changed.

Disk: A flat circular magnetic device used to store data. Hard disks are media with large capacity (typically 20 megabytes and larger). Floppy disks are flexible pieces of plastic, usually 5 1/4 and 3 1/2 inches in diameter.

Disk drive: Device containing the read/write heads and motor that makes the disk spin.

Disk pack: Several disks mounted on a spindle.

Distributed Operating System: An operating system run by all computers in a network.

Distributed system: A network of computers, any one or group of which can be used to perform functions.

DMA: Direct Memory Access, transferring data directly between the memory and an I/O device without it passing through the CPU or being under the CPU's control.

Double buffering: The technique of using two buffers that store data being transmitted between devices. The transmitter usually stores data in one buffer at the same time the receiver is reading data from the other.

Doubly linked list: A list with both forward and backward pointers in each element.

Dynamic address translation: Replacement of a virtual address with a physical address during instruction execution.

Dynamic memory allocation: Allocating memory as processes require it.

Encryption: Converting from plain text to ciphered text.

Environment: Operating conditions.

Error correction: The detection and correction of errors in a data transmission.

Error detection: The detection of errors in a data transmission.

Exception: A condition caused by an attempt to execute an invalid operation.

EXEC statement: MVS JCL statement that causes the execution of a load module or a cataloged procedure.

Extent: MVS term for contiguous disk space.

FAT: See file allocation table.

FIFO: First In First Out. Usually used when discussing the queue data structure. Also a scheduling technique where requests are handled in the order they are submitted.

File: A named collection of data.

File allocation table (FAT): In MS-DOS, a table that determines which areas of a disk contain named files.

File descriptor: Integer that identifies an open file in UNIX.

Filter: Routine that modifies the form of input data.

Firmware: Programs stored in "Read Only Memory."

Fixed partitions: A memory management method that divides the available space into units that are fixed when the system is configured.

Flag: A single bit used as an indicator.

Floppy disk: A flexible disk storage device.

Fork: UNIX routine that creates a new process.

Fragmentation: Division into small, disconnected pieces.

Frame: An area of physical memory into which a page can be loaded.

G: 2 to the 30th power, approximately 1,000,000,000 (1 billion).

Garbage collection: The process of collecting unused segments of memory into a larger unit for later use.

Guard: Conditions that control the execution of Ada's Select commands.

Hard disk: A disk storage device that is not flexible and usually has a large capacity (20 MB or more).

Hashing: A technique for storing data using a mathematical formula to determine the location of the data.

Hardware: The physical components of a computer system, including CPU, memory, I/O devices, and interconnections.

Hexadecimal: A number system using 16 as its base.

High level language: A computer language in which the statements correspond to one or more machine-level instructions.

I/O: Input/Output.

I/O-bound: Spends most of its time doing I/O rather that computations.

I/O.SYS: MS-DOS hardware-dependent I/O routines.

Icon: Image representing an object such as a file or device.

Ilist: Collection of UNIX inodes. Also defines a UNIX directory structure.

Indefinite postponement: See starvation.

Index: Value used to identify a record uniquely in a file.

Indexed file: Method of organizing records in a file using a set of indexes and pointers to locate a record.

Initiator: MVS routine that prepares for task execution.

Inode: UNIX table that locates a file's data blocks.

Interactive: Conversational mode of computing. Users enter commands and a program responds.

Interface: A device that connects systems or components.

Interleaving: 1) Storing blocks of data in discontiguous areas on disk to allow the controller time between transfers. 2) Placing consecutive memory locations in different memory modules.

Interprocess communication: A form of information exchange between two processes.

Interrecord gap: Empty space between physical records on a tape or disk track.

Interrupt: An external signal that causes the CPU to suspend its normal operations.

Interrupt service routine: A program that responds to an interrupt.

Interrupt vector: Memory location containing address of an interrupt service routine.

JCL: See Job Control Language.

JES: See Job Entry Subsystem.

Job: Program or set of programs and data set descriptions.

Job Control Language (JCL): The language used to describe and request the resource requirements of the program to the operating system.

Job Entry Subsystem (JES): MVS scheduling component that scans JCL and stores jobs in class queues.

Job management: MVS routines concerned with job scheduling.

Job statement: MVS JCL statement that identifies a job and its limits.

Job step: The execution of a program in a job.

K: 2 to the 10th power, approximately 1000.

Kernel: See nucleus.

Key: Identifier used to identify a record uniquely.

Keyed file: File in which records are uniquely identified by a value (usually a record's field).

Label: Magnetic tape record containing descriptive information about the tape.

LAN: See Local Area Network.

Latency time (also rotational delay): Time needed for a record on a disk to rotate to the head.

Layered system: System organized as a hierarchy of levels, each constructed upon the one below it.

Leaf: The last data item on a branch in a tree data structure.

Least recently used (LRU): Policy of replacing a page not used for the longest time.

Library: Collection of files or routines.

Linked list: A list in which each element contains a pointer to its successor as well as data.

Load module: Machine language file that can be executed directly.

Local Area Network (LAN): A network implemented over a small geographical distance, such as within an office or building.

Locality: The referencing of just a few pages over a period of time by a process.

Lock: A mechanism through which access to an object may be prevented.

Logical address: The address to which a program refers.

Logical device: The device to which a program refers.

Logical record: Unit of information as seen by a program.

LRU: See least recently used.

LSI: Large Scale Integration, refers to integrated circuits with more than 100 logic gates.

M: 2 to the 20th power, approximately 1,000,000.

Machine language: Set of binary coded commands that may be executed directly by a computer.

Mailbox: Data structure used to hold messages.

Main memory: Primary storage of a computer.

Mainframe: Any of a class of large computers.

Memory: Computer component used for short-term storage of data and software.

Memory fragmentation: Division of free memory into small discontiguous pieces.

Memory protection: Restricting memory access to certain processes.

Menu: A set of selections presented to the user at one time.

Merge: The process of combining two or more data sets while preserving their original order.

Message: Unit of communications.

Microcomputer: Any of a class of small computers, usually single-user ones.

Minicomputer: Any of a class of midsized computers.

Modem: A device used to connect a computer to a telephone line.

Modular: Made up of sections which are independent of each other.

Monitor: 1) A programming language construct for mutual exclusion and synchronization. 2) A simple operating system with limited functionality.

MS-DOS: Popular single-user, single-tasking operating system used in IBM PCs and compatibles.

Multiplexing: Routing data from several devices to a single destination.

Multiprocessing: Using many processors to execute a collection of processes.

Multiprogramming: Having several programs in main memory at the same time.

Multitasking: Having several programs or tasks in main memory at the same time.

Multiuser: Able to handle many users at the same time.

Mutual exclusion: Making sure two or more processes do not access a common resource at the same time.

MVS: Operating system written for IBM mainframes.

Network: A group of computers connected by communications lines.

Node: A data item in a tree or list structure.

Nonpreemptive: Unable to remove a resource from a process until the process is finished with it.

Nucleus: Most frequently used routines and data in an operating system.

Offset: Relative position in a table or block.

Open: Execution of routines to prepare for eventual access to a file or peripheral.

Operating system: A program or set of programs that allows a user to access a computer's resources.

Overhead: Time or resources used by an operating system in providing service to its users.

OS/2: Single-user, multitasking operating system that runs on IBM PCs and compatibles: the successor to MS-DOS.

OS/360: Family of operating systems developed for IBM mainframes (System 360, System 370, and successors).

Overlay: A section of a program loaded into the memory at the exact same location as an another section.

P: One of two primitive operations on a semaphore.

Page fault: A trap generated by the hardware when a process tries to access a page not in memory.

Page replacement: Substituting one page for another when a process's memory limit is reached.

Page table: The address translation table used by a paging system.

Paging: Dividing a program into small units of fixed size (called pages) and storing them into comparably sized units of memory (called frames).

Parallel I/O: Transferring more than one data bit at a time.

Parallel processing: Using more than one CPU to perform operations on data in parallel.

Parent: 1) An item that has at least one successor in a tree. 2) UNIX process executing a system fork call.

Parity bit: An extra bit appended to a group of bits whose value establishes an even (or odd) number of 1 bits.

Partition: A fixed region of main memory assigned to a particular process.

Pascal: A high-level language developed by Niklaus Wirth for teaching structured programming techniques.

Password: A collection of letters, digits, or symbols used to gain access to a resource.

Path name: In hierarchical directories, the part of a full file name that specifies the directory containing the file.

PCB: See Process Control Block.

Peripheral: I/O device.

Personal computer: Any of a class of small computers designed for a single user.

Physical address: A collection of bits transmitted along an address bus.

Physical device: The actual identification of an I/O device.

Physical record: Group of data items stored as a single unit on an I/O device.

Pipe: An interprocess communication device between two processes. One process writes into the pipe and the other reads from it.

Plain text: Data put into a form that makes its interpretation easy.

Polling: Requesting status.

Portable: Capable of being transferred from one computer to another without changes.

Preemptive: Able to remove a resource from a process.

Primitive: A basic operation that, once started, cannot be interrupted until finished.

Privileged instruction: An instruction that can be executed only by certain users.

Procedure file: See command file.

Process: An independent entity that runs and competes for computer resources.

Process Control Block (PCB): The data structure that contains information about a process.

Process state: Classification of a process with regard to its ability to compete for resources.

Processor: A device capable of executing instructions.

Producer-Consumer Problem: Classic synchronization problem in which one process generates something and another uses it.

Program: A sequence of instructions that guides a computer in processing data.

Program counter: CPU register containing the location of the next instruction to be executed.

Programmed I/O: Input/output handled entirely by a process using the CPU.

Protection: Preventing certain processes from accessing certain resources.

Protocol: Agreed upon set of rules by which two or more processes may communicate.

Quantum: Basic time interval used in round robin scheduling indicating maximum time a process can run without interruption.

Queue: A data structure that allows items to be added only at one end, and removed only at the other.

Queuing Theory: Branch of mathematics used to study the effects of requesting and waiting for resources.

RAM: Random Access Memory. Memory for which each cell may be referenced directly by specifying its location.

RAM disk: Area of memory used as though it were a disk.

Raw mode: A mode in which a driver does not interpret control characters transferred to or from the computer.

Readers and Writers Problem: Classic synchronization problem in which many processes write to a shared resource and many others read from it.

Ready state: Process state indicating it can use the CPU.

Real-time processing: Handling of events as they occur or within specified time intervals as opposed to when it is convenient for the computer.

Record: Group of data items, manipulated as a unit.

Redirection: Obtaining input from, or directing output to, something other than the standard devices.

Reference bit: Bit whose value indicates whether a page has been referenced recently.

Register: Storage within the CPU or other device.

Rendezvous: In Ada, the point at which a caller has called a server and the server has accepted it.

Replacement strategy: Method used to decide which pages to replace in memory to make room for new ones.

Resident: Remaining in memory.

Resource: Entity supplied by a computer for the purpose of accomplishing work for a process.

Resource allocation graph: Data structure showing which processes have requested which resources and which resources have been allocated to which processes.

Response time: Time needed for an operating system to respond to a process's request.

Rollback: Reversing a partially completed transaction.

ROM: Read Only Memory. Memory from which data and instructions can be read but cannot be changed.

Rotational delay: See latency time.

Round robin: Scheduling method whereby eligible processes take turns executing and each gets a time interval in which to run without interruption.

RS-232: A standard interface for connecting serial I/O devices.

Safe state: Condition defined by Dijkstra's Banker's algorithm in which the operating system can still avoid deadlock.

Scan: A method for handling disk requests in which the heads move in one direction, reversing only when all the requests in a particular direction have been satisfied.

Scheduling: Managing a CPU or other resource by deciding when each process can use it.

Script: See command file.

Secondary storage: Media used for long-term storage of data or programs (e.g., tapes or disks).

Sector: A part of a disk track that holds one block of information.

Seek: Moving a disk head to a particular disk track.

Seek time: Time required to perform a seek.

Segment table: Data structure used to locate a page table for a particular segment.

Segmentation: Dividing processes into units of variable size (segments) and storing them separately in memory.

Semaphore: A variable that indicates if a process has access to a resource or if a specified event has occurred.

Sequential file: A data file in which the items can only be accessed in the order in which they are inserted.

Serial I/O: Data transfer one bit at a time.

Service rate: Rate at which requests for a resource and its subsequent use are satisfied.

Sharing: Two or more processes using a common resource at the same time.

Shell: A part of a program that handles user interaction, including the interpreting of requests.

Signal: An indication that an event has occurred.

Single-tasking: Capable of handling only one task at a time.

Single-user: Capable of handling only one user at a time.

Software: The set of programs used by a computer system.

Software testing: The process of checking a computer program to ensure that it performs according to specifications.

Spawning: Creating a child process.

Spooling: Simultaneous Peripheral Operations On Line. A process of using allotted memory or disk space to store data going to slow I/O devices.

Stack: A data structure that allows the entry and removal of items only from one end (the top).

Starvation (also indefinite postponement): The situation in which a process is not allowed a resource that it needs, due to low priority or some other factor for an indeterminant amount of time.

Steady state: Condition that occurs after a period of time in which a system's current responses are typical of its average responses.

Subdirectory: Directory that is a member of another directory.

Supervisor Call (SVC): An IBM machine language instruction that intentionally causes a trap.

Supervisor state: A state that allows the execution of privileged instructions and access to certain areas of memory.

Suspend: Temporarily prevent from competing for resources.

SVC: See Supervisor Call.

Swapping: The process of transferring parts of programs between main memory and secondary storage to make room for others.

Synchronize: Forced sequencing of events according to some predefined criterion.

System call: Request to use an operating system service or procedure.

System generation: Initially storing an operating system in memory.

Systems program: A program that performs an overhead function, rather than an applications or end user function.

Tape: Sequential auxiliary storage media.

Task: 1) MVS entity similar to a process. 2) Ada term for a collection of commands.

Terminal: An I/O device for interactive use.

Terminator: MVS routine that runs after completion of a job step.

Thrashing: Excessive swapping.

Throughput: Number of activities done per unit of time.

Time-sharing: A technique that allows many users to access the same computer system simultaneously.

Track: A band on a disk used for storage.

Transaction: A group of operations that together accomplish a goal and so are treated as a single unit.

Transient: Able to be swapped in and out of memory.

Trap: Automatic entry to an operating system routine caused by an unusual condition detected during an instruction's execution.

Trojan horse: A program that performs a useful function, but also has hidden functions that attempt to violate system security.

Turnaround time: Length of time between when a process enters a system and when it leaves.

UNIX: Multiuser, multitasking operating system developed at Bell Laboratories (now AT&T Bell Laboratories) for small computers.

Unsafe state: Condition defined by Dijkstra's Banker's algorithm in which a series of requests could lead to deadlock.

User: The person running software, accessing data, or otherwise using a computer's resources.

V: One of two primitive operations on a semaphore.

Variable partitions: A memory management method that divides the available space into units that vary in size, depending on the needs of requesting processes.

Vectored interrupt: An interrupt that provides an indication of its source.

Virtual address: Address that a process's instruction appears to reference.

Virtual device: See logical device.

Virtual machine: The machine that the user appears to use as opposed to the one he or she is actually using.

Virtual memory: Collection of memory locations that a process appears to be referencing.

Virus: An unauthorized set of instructions that spreads from one computer to another, either through a network or through peripheral transfers.

VMS: Operating system for DEC VAX computers.

Volume Table Of Contents (VTOC): MVS term for directory.

VTOC: See Volume Table Of Contents.

Wait state: Process state indicating a processing is waiting for something.

Wakeup: Moving process from a wait to a ready state.

Working set: The pages that a process accesses for a period of time.

Index

This book is due for return on or before the last date shown below.

14 NOV 2000

19 MAR

21 MAR 2002

3 APR 2003

17 MAR 2004

14. DEC 07.

15. MAR 18. W I T H D R A W N
                F R O M
              S T O C K

Don Gresswell Ltd., London, N21   Cat. No. 1208   DG 02242/71

DEGREE
   ONLY

23529A